# The Sequential Gospels ©

## with Solutions to Gospel Mysteries ©

### Words of Jesus in Red

Unless noted otherwise, all scriptures are from the
## King James Version of the Bible.

## Dr. Romney & Ruth Ann Ashton

ISBN 0-9679166-0-7

Eighth Edition Revised February 2000
Printed in the United States of America
Sequence Publishing
55778 Timber Lane
Elkhart, IN  46514   USA

Telephone: 574-674-5426

E-mail:  sequentialgospels@sbcglobal.net

This book is dedicated to our many wonderful friends who have strengthened our faith by living lives of uncompromising belief in the truth of every chapter and verse of the Bible.

**Take God's word and proclaim its truth. Do not be ashamed. The Bible has no fault; it does not lie or deceive. Its truth is evident to those who repent and seek God's face.**

# *Table of Contents*

## *Introductions*

## *The Sequential Gospels*

## *Appendices*

*Introduction*

*Authors' Preface*

*"Repent: for the kingdom of heaven is at hand."* (Matthew 4:17)

The Gospels are set forth **in order** and show God's plan, purpose, and expectancy for Jesus' life on earth. *The Sequential Gospels* assumes that Matthew, Mark, Luke, and John wrote sequentially according to time. The Gospel writers all start their accounts with the birth or with the baptism of Jesus and all end their accounts soon after Jesus' resurrection from the dead. This time sequencing on the macro level continues on the micro level throughout all four Gospels. A true event sequence is revealed when specific "one time" events are linked together using simple sequential time. Time sequencing of all of the different miracles and healings of Jesus reveals a progressive look at the Son of man in one complete interwoven document.

Customary study methods of the Gospel text produce areas of contradiction that do not exist when using simple sequential time as a basis for the study. Seemingly contradictory details confirm the existence of multiple similar events that are separated by hours, weeks, months, or years. By reading all four Gospels as one continuous story, gaps in time found in one Gospel are covered by another. One Biblical account adds clarity and insight to the next. Details concerning what Jesus said or did are more clearly understood when immediate past or future events are known.

Discovery of which miracles were repeated by Jesus allows a new way to study the principles of the Kingdom of God. Throughout His ministry, Jesus taught and demonstrated the principles of the Kingdom of God. The Bible requires two or three witnesses (demonstrations) to establish a principle[1].

> 2 Corinthians 13:1b    In the mouth of two or three witnesses shall
> every word be established.

Since *The Sequential Gospels* separates the events of Jesus' ministry according to time, the repeated occurrences of miracles in Jesus' ministry are very visible. Therefore, different principles of the Kingdom of God become readily apparent.

*The Sequential Gospels* is a powerful tool to study how Jesus applied His own teachings to natural situations bringing forth supernatural results. *The Sequential Gospels* showcases the progressive revelation of Jesus Christ. It emphasizes situations that prompted Jesus' words and actions. *The Sequential Gospels* will challenge the reader to consider a new look at Bible study. The result is a new confidence in the Bible, a fresh revelation of Jesus, and increased understanding of how to apply the principles that Jesus taught in our own daily lives.

The concept of *The Sequential Gospels* is not a new paradigm. However, it is one whose time has finally come. As early as 1537, Andreas Osiander, a Professor of Theology in Konigsburg, Germany suggested the sequential order of all four Gospels (*Harmonie Evangelicae libri III*). Two twentieth century writers, Ethelbert W. Bullinger[2] and A. G. Secrett[3], agree. On

---

[1] Deuteronomy 17:6, Deuteronomy 19:15, Matthew 18:16, and John 8:17
[2] Bullinger, Ethelbert W. 1911. *The Companion Bible*. London: Humphrey Milford Oxford University Press.

page 14 of *A Combined Analysis of the Four Gospels* A. G. Secrett wrote, "This book is not a 'harmony of the Gospels.' No Liberties are taken with the text. No clause, sentence or passage is transposed. Every word of each Gospel is set down in exact sequence in which it was placed by the evangelist." Large sections of Secrett's work agree with *The Sequential Gospels* and with the outlines given in Ethelbert W. Bullinger's 1911 edition of *The Companion Bible*. In Appendixes #2 and #3, Gospel pericopes of these works are compared in detail to *The Sequential Gospels*.

The use of modern high speed computers allowed the repeated changes needed to improve the alignment of the verses in *The Sequential Gospels*. Placing all verses in the Gospels into one computerized table allowed the solution of some long-standing mysteries. At the same time, however, many "new" mysteries appeared. Yet, each new mystery was solved by persistent and diligent adherence to the principle that each Gospel is written sequentially. There is complete agreement between all Gospel accounts.

# The Concept of The Sequential Gospels

*The Sequential Gospels* assumes that the books of Matthew, Mark, Luke, and John are accurate in every detail including the sequential order of events. Sequential order means that each author organized his work by placing events one after the other according to time. Therefore, all events found in the four gospels can be aligned sequentially with each other using simple sequential time. This approach preserves the sequential integrity of the scriptures and does not add or take away any words found in the Gospels.

Within *The Sequential Gospels,* all chapters and verses are in table format and always maintain their original numerical sequence. Events that occurred at the same time in Jesus' ministry are in the same horizontal row. The table includes the entire text of Matthew, Mark, Luke, and John. There are seven columns:

| Matthew | Mark | Important Events | Year of Jesus' Ministry | Key Scriptures & Footnotes | Luke | John |
|---------|------|------------------|-------------------------|----------------------------|------|------|
| The entire text of Matthew is found in this column in its original numerical order. | The entire text of Mark is found in this column in its original numerical order. | All titles found in the *Index of Important Events* and map reference numbers. | \|\|\|  The # of vertical lines indicate the year of Jesus' ministry. | All footnotes are referenced to scriptures in this column only. | The entire text of Luke is found in this column in its original numerical order. | The entire text of John is found in this column in its original numerical order. |

[3] Secrett, A. G. 1927. *A Combined Analysis of the Four Gospels.* London: Chas. J. Thynne & Jarvis LTD

No chapter or verse or parts of a verse of the King James Text has been left out. All chapters and verses remain in the original numerical sequence. Some verses have been separated into parts "a and b" or "a, b, and c." Columns maintain their original width even when blank. This format graphically displays the silence of some authors over long periods of time and is unique when compared to all other "Gospel Harmonies" and "Gospel Parallels." Verses were primarily placed into position using simple sequential time. Verses or parts of a verse were moved up or down in their respective columns until they were in the "correct" row.

Identical events found in two or more of the Gospels create a **Time Lock**. These events are placed in the same horizontal row. Any verses found before a set of *Time Lock* verses happened in sequential time prior to the *Time Lock*. Any verses following these *Time Lock* verses happened afterwards in sequential time. *Time Locks* are indicated by horizontal "Time Lock - Time Lock" lines.

**Time Clues** link verses of Matthew, Mark, Luke, and John with each other using sequential time and some speculation. *Time Clues* are sometimes the only links from Matthew and Mark to unique sections in Luke and much of John. *Time Clues* are marked by "Time Clue - Time Clue" lines.

Throughout Jesus' ministry the passage of time is counted from Passover to Passover. The number of solid lines next to the text acts as a time reference. A single solid reference line is added along side the text to mark each **Year of Jesus' Ministry**. There is no line from Jesus' birth to His baptism by John. A dashed line marks the months between Jesus' baptism and the end of His first "ministry" feast of the Passover. These lines are found in the *Index of Important Gospel Events*, the *Index of the First Verse of Every Chapter, The Sequential Gospels,* and the *Maps of Jesus' Ministry Travels*.

Twenty one maps trace the steps of Jesus as revealed by *The Sequential Gospel Text*. Solid lines with arrowheads show Jesus' travel to a known site. Dashed lines with arrowheads indicate the possible location of a destination when the exact location is not known. The maps emphasize Jesus' diligence to teach and preach repeatedly in the same places. For instance, He went three times to all the cities and villages of Galilee. On a fourth tour of Galilee, Jesus went to all of the apostles' cities. The maps show Jesus' nine trips across the sea of Galilee along with His Samaria "crusade." They also demonstrate His limited ministry in Judea and Peraea.

As you read the Gospels, it is helpful to note that Biblical words including "came to pass" and "behold" indicate passages of time. The word "And," found at the beginning of 1,850 verses in Matthew, Mark, Luke, and John, implies "then," "next," or "after that." These verses emphasize a sequential time relationship between different events.

## *The Writers of the Gospels*

The Holy Spirit chose four of Jesus' disciples to write accounts of Jesus' entire life. These were special and yet very humble men. The identity of these men is not important to the layout of this book. However, consider that Matthew, Mark, Luke, and John all knew Jesus personally and wrote about their own experiences. It is possible that they kept diaries and took notes of Jesus' sermons. Each man had to study the Old Testament scriptures to understand how Jesus fulfilled the prophesies written about Him. Faced with the task of recording Jesus' entire life, all four disciples began with His birth or His baptism by John and ended with His death and resurrection. In this macro view, all the writers wrote sequentially. Thus, there is no reason to assume that they did not write sequentially on the micro level as well.

## Matthew

Matthew was an educated man from the tribe of Levi. He had studied the Jewish law, was skilled in writing and accounting, and was a successful tax collector in Capernaum. His Gospel refers to many of the Old Testament prophecies concerning the Messiah.

Within his Gospel, Matthew does not name himself as the author. Matthew writes that "Jesus sat at meat in the house" (Matthew 9:10). Only in Luke is it recorded that Matthew made Jesus **"a great feast in his own house"** (Luke 5:29). Matthew does not list the names of the twelve apostles until they are sent forth in Matthew 10:2. He then lists himself as "Matthew the publican."

## Mark

Mark was a **young man** at the end of Jesus ministry. He followed Jesus on many great adventures and describes himself during an incident in the garden of Gethsemane on the night that Jesus was betrayed.

> Mark 14:51-52  And there followed him a certain **young man**, having a linen cloth cast about his naked body; and the young men laid hold on him: And he left the linen cloth, and fled from them naked.

Mark was present when Jesus preached. Mark was with Jesus and the disciples in the garden of Gethsemane. Mark followed Jesus after all the disciples forsook Jesus and fled (Mark 14:50-52).

Mark recounts many stories about the private lives of the disciples but speaks very respectfully of them. He takes no credit for writing his Gospel, nor does he mention his own name or tell how often he was an eye witness to the events he writes about.

## Luke

Luke undertook to write an orderly account of Jesus' life to correct error that was creeping into stories about Jesus. Luke meticulously set down what was "most surely believed among us" (Luke 1:1). As a physician, Luke understood the importance of detail and sequential relationships.

> Luke 1:1- 4  Forasmuch as many have taken in hand to set forth **in order** a declaration of those things which are **most surely believed among us**,  Even as they delivered them unto us, which from the beginning were eyewitnesses, and ministers of the word;  It seemed good to me **also**, **having had** perfect understanding of all things **from the very first**, to write unto thee **in order**[4], most excellent Theophilus,  That thou mightest know the certainty of those things, wherein thou hast been instructed.

Consider that Luke said, "...**having had** perfect understanding of **all** things **from the very first**..." (Luke 1:3). It is likely that Luke was with Jesus **from the very first**. As an

---

[4] Luke 1:3  ...to write unto thee **in order**... (The New American Standard New Testament says, "...to write it out for you **in consecutive order**...")

eyewitness Luke consistently took his own notes of Jesus' ministry. This explains how Luke kept his extensive, detailed writings **in order**. Luke alone details the prophesy concerning the birth of John the Baptist. He is also the only writer to describe Jesus' conception, birth, and presentation to the Lord in Jerusalem.

Luke keeps all personal references out of his writings in Luke and Acts until the sixteenth chapter of Acts. Only then does Luke say, "And after he [Paul] had seen the vision, immediately **we** endeavoured to go into Macedonia, assuredly gathering that the Lord had called **us** for to preach the gospel unto them" (Acts 16:10).

## *John*

John wrote an eyewitness account.

> John 19:35  And **he that saw** it bare record, and his record is true: and he knoweth that he saith true, that ye might believe.

> John 21:24-25  This is the disciple which testifieth of these things, and wrote these things: and we know that **his testimony is true**. And there are also many other things which Jesus did, the which, if they should be written every one, I suppose that even the world itself could not contain the books that should be written. Amen.

Therefore, if John was not present, he did not write concerning a particular event. This information gives tremendous insight into John's writings. When Jesus talked to the woman of Samaria, John was there. John did not go into town with the other disciples; he remained with Jesus at the well. So he alone could record the words exchanged.

John refrains from using his own name throughout his entire Gospel. John only uses somewhat vague references to himself such as "the other disciple" (John 20:2) or "that disciple" (John 21:23).

# Sequential Index of Important Gospel Events

# of lines = year of ministry

↓↓↓                                                                     page #

# Sequential Index of Important Gospel Events

# of lines = year of ministry

↓↓↓                                                     page #

| Event | Matthew | Mark | Luke | John | page # |
|---|---|---|---|---|---|
| The Hour cometh, and now is | | | | John 4:23 | 16 |
| Jesus in Galilee | | Mark 1:14b | | John 4:43 | 17 |
| Jesus came again into Cana | | | | John 4:46 | 17 |
| A certain nobleman's son was healed | | | | John 4:50 | 17 |
| 1st ministry trip to Nazareth | | | Luke 4:16 | | 17 |
| They forsook their nets, and followed him | Matt. 4:20 | Mark 1:18 | | | 18 |
| Capernaum, on the sabbath day, a man with an unclean spirit | | Mark 1:21 | Luke 4:33 | | 18 |
| 1st time Simon's wife's mother lay sick | | Mark 1:30 | Luke 4:38 | | 19 |
| 1st time Jesus went about all Galilee, preaching | Matt. 4:23 | Mark 1:39 | Luke 4:44 | | 19 |
| Blessed are the poor in spirit | Matt. 5:3 | | | | 19 |
| Jesus taught from Simon's ship | | | Luke 5:3 | | 24 |
| They forsook all, and followed him | | | Luke 5:11 | | 25 |
| There came a leper to him | Matt. 8:2 | Mark 1:40 | Luke 5:12 | | 25 |
| 1st time a centurion came to Jesus | Matt. 8:5 | | | | 25 |
| 2nd time Jesus healed Peter's wife's mother | Matt. 8:14 | | | | 26 |
| Commandment to depart unto the other side | Matt. 8:18 | | | | 26 |
| 1st great tempest in the sea, and there was a great calm | Matt. 8:24 | | | | 26 |
| Gergesenes there met him two possessed with devils | Matt. 8:28 | | | | 26 |
| One sick of the palsy & they uncovered the roof | Matt. 9:2 | Mark 2:2 | Luke 5:17 | | 27 |
| Matthew, Follow Me | Matt. 9:9 | Mark 2:14 | Luke 5:27 | | 27 |
| I will have mercy and not sacrifice | Matt. 9:13a | | | | 27 |
| Why do the disciples of John fast often? | Matt. 9:14 | Mark 2:18 | Luke 5:33 | | 27 |
| A certain ruler and the 1st woman with an issue of blood twelve years | Matt. 9:18 | | | | 28 |
| Two blind men healed | Matt. 9:29 | | | | 28 |
| The dumb spake | Matt. 9:33 | | | | 28 |
| 2nd time Jesus went about all the cities and villages, teaching in their synagogues | Matt. 9:35 | | | | 29 |
| 2nd Passover | | | | John 5:1 | 29 |
| Rise take up thy bed and walk | | | | John 5:8 | 29 |
| The Jews sought to slay Jesus, because he had done these things on the sabbath day | | | | John 5:16 | 30 |
| 1st trip through the corn field | | Mark 2:23 | Luke 6:1 | | 31 |
| 1st man healed of a withered hand | | Mark 3:1 | Luke 6:6 | | 31 |
| He ordained twelve | | Mark 3:14 | Luke 6:13 | | 32 |

# Sequential Index of Important Gospel Events

# of lines = year of ministry

↓↓↓

page #

# Sequential Index of Important Gospel Events

# of lines = year of ministry

↓↓↓                                                                                 page #

# of lines = year of ministry

↓↓↓

page #

# of lines = year of ministry

↓↓↓

# of lines = year of ministry

↓↓↓                                                                                      page #

# Index of the First Verse of Every Chapter

LUKE

MARK

MATTHEW

JOHN

| Matthew | Mark | Important Events |
|---|---|---|
| Time Lock - Time Lock | Time Lock - Time Lock | **The beginning**<br>John 1:1 |
| Time Lock - Time Lock | Time Lock - Time Lock | |
| Matt. 1:1  The book of the generation of Jesus Christ, the son of David, the son of Abraham | Mark 1:1    The beginning of the gospel of Jesus Christ, the Son of God; | **The beginning of the gospel**<br>Mark 1:1 |
| | | **Zacharias**<br>Luke 1:5 |

| The beginning. | | Time Lock - Time Lock | Time Lock - Time Lock |
|---|---|---|---|
| 1:1 In the beginning was the Word,.... | | | John 1:1  In the beginning was the Word, and the Word was with God, and the Word was God.<br>John 1:2  The same was in the beginning with God.<br>John 1:3  All things were made by him; and without him was not any thing made that was made.<br>John 1:4  In him was life; and the life was the light of men. |
| | | Time Lock - Time Lock | Time Lock - Time Lock |
| Luke 1:1 Forasmuch as many have taken in hand to set forth **in order** a declaration.... | | Luke 1:1  Forasmuch as many have taken in hand to set forth in order a declaration of those things which are most surely believed among us,<br>Luke 1:2    Even as they delivered them unto us, which from the beginning were eyewitnesses, and ministers of the word;<br>Luke 1:3  It seemed good to me also, having had perfect understanding of all things from the very first, to write unto thee in order, most excellent Theophilus,<br>Luke 1:4    That thou mightest know the certainty of those things, wherein thou hast been instructed. | John 1:5  And the light shineth in darkness; and the darkness comprehended it not. |
| 1:5...in the days of Herod...a certain priest named Zacharias,.... | | Luke 1:5  There was in the days of Herod, the king of Judaea, a certain priest named Zacharias, of the course of Abia: and his wife was of the daughters of Aaron, and her name was Elisabeth. | |
| 1:13...thou shalt call his name John. | | Luke 1:6  And they were both righteous before God, walking in all the commandments and ordinances of the Lord blameless.<br>Luke 1:7    And they had no child, because that Elisabeth was barren, and they both were now well stricken in years.<br>Luke 1:8    And it came to pass, that while he executed the priest's office before God in the order of his course,<br>Luke 1:9    According to the custom of the priest's office, his lot was to burn incense when he went into the temple of the Lord.<br>Luke 1:10  And the whole multitude of the people were praying without at the time of incense.<br>Luke 1:11  And there appeared unto him an angel of the Lord standing on the right side of the altar of incense.<br>Luke 1:12    And when Zacharias saw him, he was troubled, and fear fell upon him.<br>Luke 1:13    But the angel said unto him, Fear not, Zacharias: for thy prayer is heard; and thy wife Elisabeth shall bear thee a son, and thou shalt call his name John.<br>Luke 1:14  And thou shalt have joy and gladness; and many shall rejoice at his birth.<br>Luke 1:15    For he shall be great in the sight of the Lord, and shall drink neither wine nor strong drink; and he shall be filled with the Holy Ghost, even from his mother's womb.<br>Luke 1:16  And many of the children of Israel shall he turn to the Lord their God.<br>Luke 1:17    And he shall go before him in the spirit and power of Elias, to turn the hearts of the fathers to the children, and the disobedient to the wisdom of the just; to make ready a people prepared for the Lord.<br>Luke 1:18    And Zacharias said unto the angel, Whereby shall I know this? for I am an old man, and my wife well stricken in years.<br>Luke 1:19  And the angel answering said unto him, I am Gabriel, that stand in the presence of God; and am sent to speak unto thee, and to show thee these glad tidings.<br>Luke 1:20  And, behold, thou shalt be dumb, and not able to speak, until the day that these things shall be performed, because thou believest not my words, which shall be fulfilled in their season.<br>Luke 1:21  And the people waited for Zacharias, and marvelled that he tarried so long in the temple.<br>Luke 1:22  And when he came out, he could not | |

| Matthew | Mark | Important Events |
|---------|------|------------------|
| | | |
| | | **Elisabeth conceived** Luke 1:24 |
| | | **Gabriel sent to Mary** Luke 1:26 |
| | | |

| | | speak unto them: and they perceived that he had seen a vision in the temple: for he beckoned unto them, and remained speechless.<br>Luke 1:23   And it came to pass, that as soon as the days of his ministration were accomplished, he departed to his own house. | |
|---|---|---|---|
| | 1:24...after those days...Elisabeth conceived,.... | Luke 1:24   And after those days his wife Elisabeth conceived, and hid herself five months, saying,<br>Luke 1:25   Thus hath the Lord dealt with me in the days wherein he looked on me, to take away my reproach among men. | 1:5 |
| | 1:26...angel Gabriel was sent from God unto a city of Galilee, named Nazareth, | Luke 1:26   And in the sixth month the angel Gabriel was sent from God unto a city of Galilee, named Nazareth, | |
| | 1:27...the virgin's name was Mary. | Luke 1:27   To a virgin espoused to a man whose name was Joseph, of the house of David; and the virgin's name was Mary.<br>Luke 1:28   And the angel came in unto her, and said, Hail, thou that art highly favoured, the Lord is with thee: blessed art thou among women.<br>Luke 1:29   And when she saw him, she was troubled at his saying, and cast in her mind what manner of salutation this should be.<br>Luke 1:30   And the angel said unto her, Fear not, Mary: for thou hast found favour with God.<br>Luke 1:31   And, behold, thou shalt conceive in thy womb, and bring forth a son, and shalt call his name Jesus.<br>Luke 1:32   He shall be great, and shall be called the Son of the Highest: and the Lord God shall give unto him the throne of his father David:<br>Luke 1:33   And he shall reign over the house of Jacob for ever; and of his kingdom there shall be no end.<br>Luke 1:34   Then said Mary unto the angel, How shall this be, seeing I know not a man?<br>Luke 1:35   And the angel answered and said unto her, The Holy Ghost shall come upon thee, and the power of the Highest shall overshadow thee: therefore also that holy thing which shall be born of thee shall be called the Son of God.<br>Luke 1:36   And, behold, thy cousin Elisabeth, she hath also conceived a son in her old age: and this is the sixth month with her, who was called barren.<br>Luke 1:37   For with God nothing shall be impossible. | |
| | 1:38   And Mary said, Behold the handmaid of the Lord; be it unto me according to thy word. | Luke 1:38   And Mary said, Behold the handmaid of the Lord; be it unto me according to thy word. And the angel departed from her.<br>Luke 1:39   And Mary arose in those days, and went into the hill country with haste, into a city of Judah;<br>Luke 1:40   And entered into the house of Zacharias, and saluted Elisabeth.<br>Luke 1:41   And it came to pass, that, when Elisabeth heard the salutation of Mary, the babe leaped in her womb; and Elisabeth was filled with the Holy Ghost:<br>Luke 1:42   And she spake out with a loud voice, and said, Blessed art thou among women, and blessed is the fruit of thy womb.<br>Luke 1:43   And whence is this to me, that the mother of my Lord should come to me?<br>Luke 1:44   For, lo, as soon as the voice of thy salutation sounded in mine ears, the babe leaped in my womb for joy. | |
| | 1:45   And blessed is she that believed: for **there shall be** a performance of those things which were told her from the Lord. | Luke 1:45   And blessed is she that believed: for there shall be a performance of those things which were told her from the Lord.<br>Luke 1:46   And Mary said, My soul doth magnify the Lord,<br>Luke 1:47   And my spirit hath rejoiced in God my Saviour.<br>Luke 1:48a   For he hath regarded the low estate of | |

| Matthew | Mark | Important Events |
|---|---|---|
| | | |
| 1:1 | 1:1 | **Mary conceived**<br>Luke 1:48 |
| | | **Elisabeth brought forth a son**<br>Luke 1:57 |
| 1:1 | 1:1 | |

| | | his handmaiden: | |
|---|---|---|---|
| | Mary conceived. | Time Clue - Time Clue | |
| 1:48b **for, behold, from henceforth** all generations shall call me blessed.[1] | | Luke 1:48b    for, behold, from henceforth all generations shall call me blessed.<br>Luke 1:49   For he that is mighty hath done to me great things; and holy is his name.<br>Luke 1:50   And his mercy is on them that fear him from generation to generation.<br>Luke 1:51   He hath shown strength with his arm; he hath scattered the proud in the imagination of their hearts.<br>Luke 1:52   He hath put down the mighty from their seats, and exalted them of low degree.<br>Luke 1:53   He hath filled the hungry with good things; and the rich he hath sent empty away.<br>Luke 1:54   He hath helped his servant Israel, in remembrance of his mercy;<br>Luke 1:55   As he spake to our fathers, to Abraham, and to his seed for ever.<br>Luke 1:56   And Mary abode with her about three months, and returned to her own house. | 1:5 |
| 1:57   Now Elisabeth's full time came.... | | Luke 1:57   Now Elisabeth's full time came that she should be delivered; and she brought forth a son. | |
| 1:67   And his father Zacharias was filled with the Holy Ghost, and prophesied, saying, | | Luke 1:58   And her neighbours and her cousins heard how the Lord had shown great mercy upon her; and they rejoiced with her.<br>Luke 1:59   And it came to pass, that on the eighth day they came to circumcise the child; and they called him Zacharias, after the name of his father.<br>Luke 1:60   And his mother answered and said, Not so; but he shall be called John.<br>Luke 1:61   And they said unto her, There is none of thy kindred that is called by this name.<br>Luke 1:62   And they made signs to his father, how he would have him called.<br>Luke 1:63   And he asked for a writing table, and wrote, saying, His name is John. And they marvelled all.<br>Luke 1:64   And his mouth was opened immediately, and his tongue loosed, and he spake, and praised God.<br>Luke 1:65   And fear came on all that dwelt round about them: and all these sayings were noised abroad throughout all the hill country of Judaea.<br>Luke 1:66   And all they that heard them laid them up in their hearts, saying, What manner of child shall this be! And the hand of the Lord was with him.<br>Luke 1:67   And his father Zacharias was filled with the Holy Ghost, and prophesied, saying,<br>Luke 1:68   Blessed be the Lord God of Israel; for he hath visited and redeemed his people,<br>Luke 1:69   And hath raised up an horn of salvation for us in the house of his servant David;<br>Luke 1:70   As he spake by the mouth of his holy prophets, which have been since the world began:<br>Luke 1:71   That we should be saved from our enemies, and from the hand of all that hate us;<br>Luke 1:72   To perform the mercy promised to our fathers, and to remember his holy covenant;<br>Luke 1:73   The oath which he sware to our father Abraham,<br>Luke 1:74   That he would grant unto us, that we being delivered out of the hand of our enemies might serve him without fear,<br>Luke 1:75   In holiness and righteousness before him, all the days of our life. | 1:5 |
| 1:76   And thou, child, | | Luke 1:76   And thou, child, shalt be called the | |

---

[1] Luke 1:48b   for, behold, from henceforth all generations shall call me blessed. (*Mary is now with child of the Holy Ghost.*)

| Matthew | Mark | Important Events |
|---|---|---|
| | | |
| | | **John grew**<br>Luke 1:80 |
| Matt. 1:2  Abraham begat Isaac; and Isaac begat Jacob; and Jacob begat Judas and his brethren;<br>Matt. 1:3    And Judas begat Phares and Zara of Thamar; and Phares begat Esrom; and Esrom begat Aram;<br>Matt. 1:4      And Aram begat Aminadab; and Aminadab begat Naasson; and Naasson begat Salmon;<br>Matt. 1:5    And Salmon begat Booz of Rachab; and Booz begat Obed of Ruth; and Obed begat Jesse;<br>Matt. 1:6  And Jesse begat David the king; and David the king begat Solomon of her that had been the wife of Urias;<br>Matt. 1:7  And Solomon begat Roboam; and Roboam begat Abia; and Abia begat Asa;<br>Matt. 1:8    And Asa begat Josaphat; and Josaphat begat Joram; and Joram begat Ozias;<br>Matt. 1:9   And Ozias begat Joatham; and Joatham begat Achaz; and Achaz begat Ezekias;<br>Matt. 1:10    And Ezekias begat Manasses; and Manasses begat Amon; and Amon begat Josias;<br>Matt. 1:11    And Josias begat Jechonias and his brethren, about the time they were carried away to Babylon:<br>Matt. 1:12  And after they were brought to Babylon, Jechonias begat Salathiel; and Salathiel begat Zorobabel;<br>Matt. 1:13   And Zorobabel begat Abiud; and Abiud begat Eliakim; and Eliakim begat Azor;<br>Matt. 1:14  And Azor begat Sadoc; and Sadoc begat Achim; and Achim begat Eliud;<br>Matt. 1:15   And Eliud begat Eleazar; and Eleazar begat Matthan; and Matthan begat Jacob;<br>Matt. 1:16  And Jacob begat Joseph the husband of Mary, of whom was born Jesus, who is called Christ.<br>Matt. 1:17  So all the generations from Abraham to David are fourteen generations; and from David until the carrying away into Babylon are fourteen generations; and from the carrying away into Babylon unto Christ are fourteen generations. | 1:1 | **Joseph's lineage**<br>Matt. 1:2 |
| Matt. 1:18  Now the birth of Jesus Christ was on this wise: When as his mother Mary was espoused to Joseph, before they came together, she was found with child of the Holy Ghost.<br>Matt. 1:19   Then Joseph her husband, being a just man, and not willing to make her a public example, was minded to put her away privily.<br>Matt. 1:20    But while he thought on these things, behold, the angel of the Lord appeared unto him in a dream, saying, Joseph, thou son of David, fear not to take unto thee Mary thy wife: for that which is conceived in her is of the Holy Ghost.<br>Matt. 1:21  And she shall bring forth a son, and thou shalt call his name JESUS: for he shall save his people from their sins.<br>Matt. 1:22   Now all this was done, that it might be fulfilled which was spoken of the Lord by the prophet, saying, | 1:1 | **Now the birth of Jesus Christ was on this wise**<br>Matt. 1:18 |

| ministry year | Key Scriptures & Footnotes | Luke | John |
|---|---|---|---|
| | shalt be called the prophet of the Highest: for thou shalt go before the face of the Lord to prepare his ways; | prophet of the Highest: for thou shalt go before the face of the Lord to prepare his ways;<br>Luke 1:77  To give knowledge of salvation unto his people by the remission of their sins,<br>Luke 1:78  Through the tender mercy of our God; whereby the dayspring from on high hath visited us,<br>Luke 1:79  To give light to them that sit in darkness and in the shadow of death, to guide our feet into the way of peace. | |
| | 1:80  And the child grew, and waxed strong in spirit,.... | Luke 1:80  And the child grew, and waxed strong in spirit, and was in the deserts till the day of his showing unto Israel. | |
| | 1:2  Abraham begat Isaac; and Isaac begat Jacob; and Jacob begat Judas and his brethren;[2]<br><br>1:16  And Jacob begat Joseph the husband of Mary, of whom was born Jesus, who is called Christ. | | 1:5 |
| | 1:18  Now the birth of Jesus Christ....<br><br>1:21...thou shalt call his name JESUS: for he shall save his people from their sins. | 1:80 | 1:5 |

[2]Matthew 1:2 Abraham begat Isaac... (*This is the blood lineage of Joseph.  See Luke 3:23 for a Jesus' non-cursed lineage through Joseph.  "And Jesus...being (as was supposed) the son of Joseph."*)

| Matthew | Mark | Important Events |
|---|---|---|
| Matt. 1:23  Behold, a virgin shall be with child, and shall bring forth a son, and they shall call his name Emmanuel, which being interpreted is, God with us. Matt. 1:24  Then Joseph being raised from sleep did as the angel of the Lord had bidden him, and took unto him his wife: | | |
| Time Lock - Time Lock | | |
| | 1:1 | |
| Matt. 1:25a   And knew her not till she had brought forth her firstborn son: | | **Jesus born to Mary** Matt. 1:25a & Luke 2:7  Map 1 |
| Matt. 1:25b   and he called his name JESUS. | | **The circumcising of Jesus** Matt. 1:25b & Luke 2:21 |
| | 1:1 | Map 2 |

| ministry year | Key Scriptures & Footnotes | Luke | John |
|---|---|---|---|
| | Jesus' birth. | Time Lock - Time Lock | |
| | 2:1...decree from Caesar Augustus.... | Luke 2:1   And it came to pass in those days, that there went out a decree from Caesar Augustus, that all the world should be taxed.<br>Luke 2:2   (And this taxing was first made when Cyrenius was governor of Syria.)<br>Luke 2:3   And all went to be taxed, every one into his own city. | 1:5 |
| | 2:4...out of the city of Nazareth, into Judaea, unto the city of David, which is called Bethlehem.... | Luke 2:4   And Joseph also went up from Galilee, out of the city of Nazareth, into Judaea, unto the city of David, which is called Bethlehem; (because he was of the house and lineage of David:)<br>Luke 2:5   To be taxed with Mary his espoused wife, being great with child.<br>Luke 2:6   And so it was, that, while they were there, the days were accomplished that she should be delivered. | |
| | 2:7  And she brought forth her **firstborn** son....[3] | Luke 2:7   And she brought forth her firstborn son, and wrapped him in swaddling clothes, and laid him in a manger; because there was no room for them in the inn.<br>Luke 2:8   And there were in the same country shepherds abiding in the field, keeping watch over their flock by night.<br>Luke 2:9   And, lo, the angel of the Lord came upon them, and the glory of the Lord shone round about them: and they were sore afraid.<br>Luke 2:10   And the angel said unto them, Fear not: for, behold, I bring you good tidings of great joy, which shall be to all people.<br>Luke 2:11   For unto you is born this day in the city of David a Saviour, which is Christ the Lord.<br>Luke 2:12   And this shall be a sign unto you; Ye shall find the babe wrapped in swaddling clothes, lying in a manger.<br>Luke 2:13   And suddenly there was with the angel a multitude of the heavenly host praising God, and saying, | |
| | 2:14  Glory to God in the highest, and on earth peace, good will toward men. | Luke 2:14   Glory to God in the highest, and on earth peace, good will toward men.<br>Luke 2:15   And it came to pass, as the angels were gone away from them into heaven, the shepherds said one to another, Let us now go even unto Bethlehem, and see this thing which is come to pass, which the Lord hath made known unto us.<br>Luke 2:16   And they came with haste, and found Mary, and Joseph, and the babe lying in a manger.<br>Luke 2:17   And when they had seen it, they made known abroad the saying which was told them concerning this child.<br>Luke 2:18   And all they that heard it wondered at those things which were told them by the shepherds.<br>Luke 2:19   But Mary kept all these things, and pondered them in her heart.<br>Luke 2:20   And the shepherds returned, glorifying and praising God for all the things that they had heard and seen, as it was told unto them. | |
| | 2:21 And when eight days were accomplished for the circumcising of...JESUS.... | Luke 2:21   And when eight days were accomplished for the circumcising of the child, his name was called JESUS, which was so named of the angel before he was conceived in the womb. | |
| | 2:22...they brought him | Luke 2:22   And when the days of her purification | 1:5 |

[3] Luke 2:7  And she brought forth her **firstborn** son.... (*Jesus was born about 5 or 6 BC.  Historically Herod died in 4 BC.  From Matthew 2:16 we know Jesus was a one or two year old child when the wise men visited Him.*)

| Matthew | Mark | Important Events |
|---|---|---|
| | | |
| | 1:1 | |

| Matthew | Mark | Important Events |
|---|---|---|
| Matt. 2:1  Now when Jesus was born in Bethlehem of Judaea in the days of Herod the king, behold, there came wise men from the east to Jerusalem,<br>Matt. 2:2  Saying, Where is he that is born King of the Jews? for we have seen his star in the east, and are come to worship him.<br>Matt. 2:3  When Herod the king had heard these things, he was troubled, and all Jerusalem with him.<br>Matt. 2:4  And when he had gathered all the chief priests and scribes of the people together, he demanded of them where Christ should be born.<br>Matt. 2:5  And they said unto him, In Bethlehem of Judaea: for thus it is written by the prophet,<br>Matt. 2:6  And thou Bethlehem, in the land of Judah, art not the least among the princes of Judah: for out of thee shall come a Governor, that shall rule my people Israel.<br>Matt. 2:7  Then Herod, when he had privily called the wise men, inquired of them diligently what time the star appeared.<br>Matt. 2:8  And he sent them to Bethlehem, and said, Go and search diligently for the young child; and | | **Wise men from the east**<br>Matt. 2:1 |

| ministry year | Key Scriptures & Footnotes | Luke | John |
|---|---|---|---|
| | to Jerusalem, to present him to the Lord;.... | according to the law of Moses were accomplished, they brought him to Jerusalem, to present him to the Lord; <br> Luke 2:23   (As it is written in the law of the Lord, Every male that openeth the womb shall be called holy to the Lord;) <br> Luke 2:24   And to offer a sacrifice according to that which is said in the law of the Lord, A pair of turtledoves, or two young pigeons. | |
| | 2:25...whose name was Simeon;.... | Luke 2:25      And, behold, there was a man in Jerusalem, whose name was Simeon; and the same man was just and devout, waiting for the consolation of Israel: and the Holy Ghost was upon him. <br> Luke 2:26   And it was revealed unto him by the Holy Ghost, that he should not see death, before he had seen the Lord's Christ. <br> Luke 2:27   And he came by the Spirit into the temple: and when the parents brought in the child Jesus, to do for him after the custom of the law, <br> Luke 2:28   Then took he him up in his arms, and blessed God, and said, <br> Luke 2:29   Lord, now lettest thou thy servant depart in peace, according to thy word: <br> Luke 2:30   For mine eyes have seen thy salvation, <br> Luke 2:31   Which thou hast prepared before the face of all people; <br> Luke 2:32   A light to lighten the Gentiles, and the glory of thy people Israel. <br> Luke 2:33   And Joseph and his mother marvelled at those things which were spoken of him. <br> Luke 2:34   And Simeon blessed them, and said unto Mary his mother, Behold, this child is set for the fall and rising again of many in Israel; and for a sign which shall be spoken against; <br> Luke 2:35   (Yea, a sword shall pierce through thy own soul also,) that the thoughts of many hearts may be revealed. | |
| | 2:36  And there was one Anna,.... | Luke 2:36   And there was one Anna, a prophetess, the daughter of Phanuel, of the tribe of Aser: she was of a great age, and had lived with an husband seven years from her virginity; <br> Luke 2:37   And she was a widow of about fourscore and four years, which departed not from the temple, but served God with fastings and prayers night and day. <br> Luke 2:38      And she coming in that instant gave thanks likewise unto the Lord, and spake of him to all them that looked for redemption in Jerusalem. | |
| | | Luke 2:39a   And when they had performed all things according to the law of the Lord, | 1:5 |
| | Wise men came. | Time Lock - Time Lock | |
| | 2:1... behold, there came wise men from the east to Jerusalem, | | |
| | 2:7   Then Herod, ...**inquired** of them **diligently** what time the star appeared. <br> 2:8  And he sent them to Bethlehem.... | | |

| Matthew | Mark | Important Events |
|---|---|---|
| when ye have found him, bring me word again, that I may come and worship him also. | | |
| Matt. 2:9   When they had heard the king, they departed; and, lo, the star, which they saw in the east, went before them, till it came and stood over where the young child was.<br>Matt. 2:10   When they saw the star, they rejoiced with exceeding great joy.<br>Matt. 2:11   And when they were come into the house, they saw the young child with Mary his mother, and fell down, and worshipped him: and when they had opened their treasures, they presented unto him gifts; gold, and frankincense, and myrrh.<br>Matt. 2:12   And being warned of God in a dream that they should not return to Herod, they departed into their own country another way. | | Map 3 |
| Matt. 2:13   And when they were departed, behold, the angel of the Lord appeareth to Joseph in a dream, saying, Arise, and take the young child and his mother, and flee into Egypt, and be thou there until I bring thee word: for Herod will seek the young child to destroy him.<br>Matt. 2:14   When he arose, he took the young child and his mother by night, and departed into Egypt:<br>Matt. 2:15   And was there until the death of Herod: that it might be fulfilled which was spoken of the Lord by the prophet, saying, Out of Egypt have I called my son. | | **Joseph, Mary, And Jesus flee into Egypt**<br>Matt. 2:13<br><br>Map 4 |
| Matt. 2:16   Then Herod, when he saw that he was mocked of the wise men, was exceeding wroth, and sent forth, and slew all the children that were in Bethlehem, and in all the coasts thereof, from two years old and under, according to the time which he had diligently inquired of the wise men.<br>Matt. 2:17   Then was fulfilled that which was spoken by Jeremy the prophet, saying,<br>Matt. 2:18   In Rama was there a voice heard, lamentation, and weeping, and great mourning, Rachel weeping for her children, and would not be comforted, because they are not. | 1:1 | **Herod slew all the children**<br>Matt. 2:16 |
| Matt. 2:19   But when Herod was dead, behold, an angel of the Lord appeareth in a dream to Joseph in Egypt,<br>Matt. 2:20   Saying, Arise, and take the young child and his mother, and go into the land of Israel: for they are dead which sought the young child's life.<br>Matt. 2:21   And he arose, and took the young child and his mother, and came into the land of Israel. | | |
| Matt. 2:22   But when he heard that Archelaus did reign in Judaea in the room of his father Herod, he was afraid to go thither: notwithstanding, being warned of God in a dream, he turned aside into the parts of Galilee: | | |
| Time Lock - Time Lock | | |
| Matt. 2:23   And he came and dwelt in a city called Nazareth: that it might be fulfilled which was spoken by the prophets, He shall be called a Nazarene. | 1:1 | **Jesus moved from Egypt to Nazareth**<br>Matt. 2:23 & Luke 2:39b<br><br>Map 5 |
| | | **Jesus twelve years old**<br>Luke 2:41<br><br>Map 6<br>Map 7 |

| ministry year | Key Scriptures & Footnotes | Luke | John |
|---|---|---|---|
| | | | |
| | 2:9...the star...went before them, till it came and stood over where the young child was.<br>2: 11  And when they were come into the house, they....<br>fell down, and worshipped him:...they presented unto him gifts; gold, and frankincense, and myrrh. | | |
| | 2:13...for Herod will seek the **young child** to destroy him.<br><br>2:14  When he arose...departed into Egypt:... | | |
| | 2:16...Then Herod...slew all the children that were in Bethlehem,...from **two years old and under**, according to the time which he had **diligently** inquired of the wise men. | | 1:5 |
| | 2:19  But when Herod was dead[4], behold, an angel of the Lord appeareth in a dream to Joseph in Egypt,<br><br>2:21...came into the land of Israel. | | |
| | 2:22...Archelaus did reign in Judaea.... | | |
| | Jesus moved to Nazareth. | Time Lock - Time Lock | |
| | 2:23...they returned into Galilee, to their own city Nazareth.<br>2:40...the child grew.... | Luke 2:39b they returned into Galilee, to their own city Nazareth.<br>Luke 2:40  And the child grew, and waxed strong in spirit, filled with wisdom: and the grace of God was upon him. | 1:5 |
| | 2:41  Now his parents went to Jerusalem **every year** at the feast of the passover. | Luke 2:41  Now his parents went to Jerusalem every year at the feast of the passover.<br>Luke 2:42  And when he was twelve years old, they went up to Jerusalem after the custom of the feast.<br>Luke 2:43  And when they had fulfilled the days, as they returned, the child Jesus tarried behind in Jerusalem; and Joseph and his mother knew not of it.<br>Luke 2:44  But they, supposing him to have been in | |

[4] Matthew 2:19  But when Herod was dead.... (*Historically Herod died in 4 BC.*)

| Matthew | Mark | Important Events |
|---|---|---|
| | | |
| Time Lock - Time Lock | Time Lock - Time Lock | |
| Matt. 3:1   In those days came John the Baptist, preaching in the wilderness of Judaea,<br>Matt. 3:2   And saying, Repent ye: for the kingdom of heaven is at hand.<br>Matt. 3:3   For this is he that was spoken of by the prophet Esaias, saying, The voice of one crying in the wilderness, Prepare ye the way of the Lord, make his paths straight. | Mark 1:2   As it is written in the prophets, Behold, I send my messenger before thy face, which shall prepare thy way before thee.<br>Mark 1:3   The voice of one crying in the wilderness, Prepare ye the way of the Lord, make his paths straight. | **John the Baptist**<br>Matt. 3:1, Mark 1:2, Luke 3:2b, & John 1:6 |
| | | |
| | Mark 1:4   John did baptize in the wilderness, and preach the baptism of repentance for the remission of sins. | |
| Matt. 3:4   And the same John had his raiment of camel's hair, and a leathern girdle about his loins; | Mark 1:5   And there went out unto him all the land of Judaea, and they of Jerusalem, and were all baptized | |

| ministry year | Key Scriptures & Footnotes | Luke | John |
|---|---|---|---|
| | 2:52...Jesus increased in wisdom.... | the company, went a day's journey; and they sought him among their kinsfolk and acquaintance.<br>Luke 2:45   And when they found him not, they turned back again to Jerusalem, seeking him.<br>Luke 2:46  And it came to pass, that after three days they found him in the temple, sitting in the midst of the doctors, both hearing them, and asking them questions.<br>Luke 2:47   And all that heard him were astonished at his understanding and answers.<br>Luke 2:48    And when they saw him, they were amazed: and his mother said unto him, Son, why hast thou thus dealt with us? behold, thy father and I have sought thee sorrowing.<br>Luke 2:49   And he said unto them, How is it that ye sought me? wist ye not that I must be about my Father's business?<br>Luke 2:50   And they understood not the saying which he spake unto them.<br>Luke 2:51   And he went down with them, and came to Nazareth, and was subject unto them: but his mother kept all these sayings in her heart.<br>Luke 2:52    And Jesus increased in wisdom and stature, and in favour with God and man. | |
| | 3:1...fifteenth year...of Tiberius Caesar, Pontius Pilate...Herod...Philip... and Lysanias...<br>3:2a  Annas and Caiaphas... | Luke 3:1   Now in the fifteenth year of the reign of Tiberius Caesar, Pontius Pilate being governor of Judaea, and Herod being tetrarch of Galilee, and his brother Philip tetrarch of Ituraea and of the region of Trachonitis, and Lysanias the tetrarch of Abilene,<br>Luke 3:2a    Annas and Caiaphas being the high priests, | |
| | John the Baptist. | Time Lock - Time Lock | Time Lock - Time Lock |
| | 1:2...Behold, I send my messenger before thy face,.... | Luke 3:2b  the word of God came unto John the son of Zacharias in the wilderness. | John 1:6   There was a man sent from God, whose name was John.<br>John 1:7    The same came for a witness, to bear witness of the Light, that all men through him might believe.<br>John 1:8  He was not that Light, but was sent to bear witness of that Light. |
| | 1:9  That was the true Light.... [5]<br>1:10...and the world was made by him,....<br><br>1:14  And the Word was made flesh, and dwelt among us.... | | John 1:9    That was the true Light, which lighteth every man that cometh into the world.<br>John 1:10  He was in the world, and the world was made by him, and the world knew him not.<br>John 1:11    He came unto his own, and his own received him not.<br>John 1:12   But as many as received him, to them gave he power to become the sons of God, even to them that believe on his name:<br>John 1:13   Which were born, not of blood, nor of the will of the flesh, nor of the will of man, but of God.<br>John 1:14  And the Word was made flesh, and dwelt among us, (and we beheld his glory, the glory as of the only begotten of the Father,) full of grace and truth. |
| | 1:4  John did baptize ... and preach the baptism of repentance for the remission of sins. | Luke 3:3    And he came into all the country about Jordan, preaching the baptism of repentance for the remission of sins;<br>Luke 3:4  As it is written in the book of the words of Esaias the prophet, saying, The voice of one crying in the wilderness, Prepare ye the way of the Lord, make his paths straight.<br>Luke 3:5   Every valley shall be filled, and every mountain and hill shall be brought low; and the crooked shall be made straight, and the rough ways shall be made smooth;<br>Luke 3:6   And all flesh shall see the salvation of God. | |
| | 1:5...and were all baptized of him.... | | |

[5] John 1:9   That was the true Light.... (*Jesus*)

| Matthew | Mark | Important Events |
|---|---|---|
| and his meat was locusts and wild honey.<br>Matt. 3:5  Then went out to him Jerusalem, and all Judaea, and all the region round about Jordan,<br>Matt. 3:6   And were baptized of him in Jordan, confessing their sins. | of him in the river of Jordan, confessing their sins.<br>Mark 1:6  And John was clothed with camel's hair, and with a girdle of a skin about his loins; and he did eat locusts and wild honey; | |
| Matt. 3:7   But when he saw many of the Pharisees and Sadducees come to his baptism, he said unto them, O generation of vipers, who hath warned you to flee from the wrath to come?<br>Matt. 3:8    Bring forth therefore fruits meet for repentance:<br>Matt. 3:9  And think not to say within yourselves, We have Abraham to our father: for I say unto you, that God is able of these stones to raise up children unto Abraham.<br>Matt. 3:10  And now also the axe is laid unto the root of the trees: therefore every tree which bringeth not forth good fruit is hewn down, and cast into the fire. | | |
| Time Lock - Time Lock | Time Lock - Time Lock | |
| Matt. 3:11   I indeed baptize you with water unto repentance: but he that cometh after me is mightier than I, whose shoes I am not worthy to bear: he shall baptize you with the Holy Ghost, and with fire:<br>Matt. 3:12   Whose fan is in his hand, and he will thoroughly purge his floor, and gather his wheat into the garner; but he will burn up the chaff with unquenchable fire. | Mark 1:7  And preached, saying, There cometh one mightier than I after me, the latchet of whose shoes I am not worthy to stoop down and unloose.<br>Mark 1:8  I indeed have baptized you with water: but he shall baptize you with the Holy Ghost. | **He shall baptize you with the Holy Ghost and with fire**<br><br>Matt. 3:11, Mark 1:8, & Luke 3:16 |
| Time Lock - Time Lock | Time Lock - Time Lock | |
| Matt. 3:13   Then cometh Jesus from Galilee to Jordan unto John, to be baptized of him.<br>Matt. 3:14  But John forbad him, saying, I have need to be baptized of thee, and comest thou to me?<br>Matt. 3:15   And Jesus answering said unto him, Suffer it to be so now: for thus it becometh us to fulfil all righteousness. Then he suffered him.<br>Matt. 3:16  And Jesus, when he was baptized, went up straightway out of the water: and, lo, the heavens were opened unto him, and he saw the Spirit of God descending like a dove, and lighting upon him:<br>Matt. 3:17  And lo a voice from heaven, saying, This is my beloved Son, in whom I am well pleased. | Mark 1:9  And it came to pass in those days, that Jesus came from Nazareth of Galilee, and was baptized of John in Jordan.<br>Mark 1:10   And straightway coming up out of the water, he saw the heavens opened, and the Spirit like a dove descending upon him:<br>Mark 1:11   And there came a voice from heaven, saying, Thou art my beloved Son, in whom I am well pleased. | **Jesus baptized**<br>Matt. 3:13, Mark 1:9, & Luke 3:21<br><br>Map 8 |
| | | **Joseph's lineage** |

| ministry year | Key Scriptures & Footnotes | Luke | John |
|---|---|---|---|
| | 1:6 And John was clothed with camel's hair.... | | |
| | Matt. 3:8 Bring forth therefore fruits meet for repentance: | Luke 3:7 Then said he to the multitude that came forth to be baptized of him, O generation of vipers, who hath warned you to flee from the wrath to come? Luke 3:8 Bring forth therefore fruits worthy of repentance, and begin not to say within yourselves, We have Abraham to our father: for I say unto you, That God is able of these stones to raise up children unto Abraham. Luke 3:9 And now also the axe is laid unto the root of the trees: every tree therefore which bringeth not forth good fruit is hewn down, and cast into the fire. | 1:14 |
| | | Luke 3:10 And the people asked him, saying, What shall we do then? Luke 3:11 He answereth and saith unto them, He that hath two coats, let him impart to him that hath none; and he that hath meat, let him do likewise. Luke 3:12 Then came also publicans to be baptized, and said unto him, Master, what shall we do? Luke 3:13 And he said unto them, Exact no more than that which is appointed you. Luke 3:14 And the soldiers likewise demanded of him, saying, And what shall we do? And he said unto them, Do violence to no man, neither accuse any falsely; and be content with your wages. Luke 3:15 And as the people were in expectation, and all men mused in their hearts of John, whether he were the Christ, or not; | |
| | He cometh | Time Lock - Time Lock | |
| | 3:16 John answered...but one mightier than I cometh...**he shall baptize you with the Holy Ghost and with fire:** | Luke 3:16 John answered, saying unto them all, I indeed baptize you with water; but one mightier than I cometh, the latchet of whose shoes I am not worthy to unloose: he shall baptize you with the Holy Ghost and with fire: Luke 3:17 Whose fan is in his hand, and he will thoroughly purge his floor, and will gather the wheat into his garner; but the chaff he will burn with fire unquenchable. | 1:14 |
| | | Luke 3:18 And many other things in his exhortation preached he unto the people. | |
| | 3:20...shut up John in prison.[6] | Luke 3:19 But Herod the tetrarch, being reproved by him for Herodias his brother Philip's wife, and for all the evils which Herod had done, Luke 3:20 Added yet this above all, that he shut up John in prison. | |
| | Jesus baptized. | Time Lock - Time Lock | |
| | 1:9...Jesus came from Nazareth...and was baptized of John in Jordan. 3:16...he saw the Spirit of God descending like a dove,.... 3:17 And lo a voice from heaven, saying, **This is my beloved Son, in whom I am well pleased.** | Luke 3:21 Now when all the people were baptized, it came to pass, that Jesus also being baptized, and praying, the heaven was opened, Luke 3:22 And the Holy Ghost descended in a bodily shape like a dove upon him, and a voice came from heaven, which said, Thou art my beloved Son; in thee I am well pleased. | |
| | 3:23 And Jesus himself began to be **about thirty years of** | Luke 3:23 And Jesus himself began to be about thirty years of age, being (as was supposed) the son of Joseph, which was the son of Heli, | 1:14 |

[6] Luke 3:20 Added yet this above all, that he shut up John in prison. (*Luke 3:19 is an example of what John exhorted and preached in Luke 3:18. However, note Luke 3:20 is speaking of a future event since John is baptizing Jesus in Luke 3:21. See Luke 9:7-9 and Matthew 14:1-12 for the sequential time period of John the Baptist's imprisonment and death.*)

| Matthew | Mark | Important Events |
|---|---|---|
| | | Luke 3:23 |
| *Time Lock - Time Lock* | *Time Lock - Time Lock* | |
| Matt. 4:1   Then was Jesus led up of the Spirit into the wilderness to be tempted of the devil.<br>Matt. 4:2   And when he had fasted forty days and forty nights, he was afterward an hungered. | Mark 1:12   And immediately the Spirit driveth him into the wilderness.<br>Mark 1:13a   And he was there in the wilderness forty days, tempted of Satan; and was with the wild beasts; | **Jesus led up of the Spirit into the wilderness**<br>Matt. 4:1, Mark 1:12, & Luke 4:1<br><br>Map 9 |
| Matt. 4:3   And when the tempter came to him, he said, If thou be the Son of God, command that these stones be made bread.<br>Matt. 4:4   But he answered and said, It is written, Man shall not live by bread alone, but by every word that proceedeth out of the mouth of God. | | |

| ministry year | Key Scriptures & Footnotes | Luke | John |
|---|---|---|---|
| | **age**, being (as was supposed) the son of Joseph[7].... | Luke 3:24  Which was the son of Matthat, which was the son of Levi, which was the son of Melchi, which was the son of Janna, which was the son of Joseph, <br> Luke 3:25  Which was the son of Mattathias, which was the son of Amos, which was the son of Naum, which was the son of Esli, which was the son of Nagge, <br> Luke 3:26  Which was the son of Maath, which was the son of Mattathias, which was the son of Semei, which was the son of Joseph, which was the son of Judah, <br> Luke 3:27  Which was the son of Joanna, which was the son of Rhesa, which was the son of Zorobabel, which was the son of Salathiel, which was the son of Neri, <br> Luke 3:28  Which was the son of Melchi, which was the son of Addi, which was the son of Cosam, which was the son of Elmodam, which was the son of Er, <br> Luke 3:29  Which was the son of Jose, which was the son of Eliezer, which was the son of Jorim, which was the son of Matthat, which was the son of Levi, <br> Luke 3:30  Which was the son of Simeon, which was the son of Judah, which was the son of Joseph, which was the son of Jonan, which was the son of Eliakim, <br> Luke 3:31  Which was the son of Melea, which was the son of Menan, which was the son of Mattatha, which was the son of Nathan, which was the son of David, <br> Luke 3:32  Which was the son of Jesse, which was the son of Obed, which was the son of Booz, which was the son of Salmon, which was the son of Naasson, <br> Luke 3:33  Which was the son of Aminadab, which was the son of Aram, which was the son of Esrom, which was the son of Phares, which was the son of Judah, <br> Luke 3:34  Which was the son of Jacob, which was the son of Isaac, which was the son of Abraham, which was the son of Thara, which was the son of Nachor, <br> Luke 3:35  Which was the son of Saruch, which was the son of Ragau, which was the son of Phalec, which was the son of Heber, which was the son of Sala, <br> Luke 3:36  Which was the son of Cainan, which was the son of Arphaxad, which was the son of Sem, which was the son of Noe, which was the son of Lamech, <br> Luke 3:37  Which was the son of Mathusala, which was the son of Enoch, which was the son of Jared, which was the son of Maleleel, which was the son of Cainan, <br> Luke 3:38  Which was the son of Enos, which was the son of Seth, which was the son of Adam, which was the son of God. | |
| | | Time Lock - Time Lock | |
| | 4:1  And Jesus **being full of the Holy Ghost** returned from Jordan, and was led by the Spirit into the wilderness. | Luke 4:1  And Jesus being full of the Holy Ghost returned from Jordan, and was led by the Spirit into the wilderness, <br> Luke 4:2  Being forty days tempted of the devil. And in those days he did eat nothing: and when they were ended, he afterward hungered. | 1:14 |
| | | Luke 4:3  And the devil said unto him, If thou be the Son of God, command this stone that it be made bread. <br> Luke 4:4    And Jesus answered him, saying, It is written, That man shall not live by bread alone, but by every word of God. | |

[7] Luke 3:23  And Jesus himself began to be about thirty years of age, being (as was supposed) the son of Joseph... (*This is not Joseph's lineage by blood.  See Matthew 1:2 for the blood lineage of Joseph.*)

10

| Matthew | Mark | Important Events |
|---|---|---|
| | | |
| Matt. 4:5  Then the devil taketh him up into the holy city, and setteth him on a pinnacle of the temple, <br> Matt. 4:6  And saith unto him, If thou be the Son of God, cast thyself down: for it is written, He shall give his angels charge concerning thee: and in their hands they shall bear thee up, lest at any time thou dash thy foot against a stone. <br> Matt. 4:7  Jesus said unto him, It is written again, Thou shalt not tempt the Lord thy God. | | |
| Matt. 4:8  Again, the devil taketh him up into an exceeding high mountain, and showeth him all the kingdoms of the world, and the glory of them; <br> Matt. 4:9  And saith unto him, All these things will I give thee, if thou wilt fall down and worship me. <br> Matt. 4:10  Then saith Jesus unto him, Get thee hence, Satan: for it is written, Thou shalt worship the Lord thy God, and him only shalt thou serve. | | |
| Matt. 4:11  Then the devil leaveth him, and, behold, angels came and ministered unto him. | Mark 1:13b  and the angels ministered unto him. | |
| Time Lock - Time Lock | Time Lock - Time Lock | |
| | | |
| 4:11 | 1:13b | **1st day Jesus among them** <br> John 1:26 <br> Map 10 |

| --- | --- | --- | --- |
| 4:5 And the devil, taking him up into an high mountain, .... | Luke 4:5 And the devil, taking him up into an high mountain, showed unto him all the kingdoms of the world in a moment of time.<br>Luke 4:6 And the devil said unto him, All this power will I give thee, and the glory of them: for that is delivered unto me; and to whomsoever I will I give it.<br>Luke 4:7 If thou therefore wilt worship me, all shall be thine.<br>Luke 4:8 And Jesus answered and said unto him, Get thee behind me, Satan: for it is written, Thou shalt worship the Lord thy God, and him only shalt thou serve. | |
| | Luke 4:9 And he brought him to Jerusalem, and set him on a pinnacle of the temple, and said unto him, If thou be the Son of God, cast thyself down from hence:<br>Luke 4:10 For it is written, He shall give his angels charge over thee, to keep thee:<br>Luke 4:11 And in their hands they shall bear thee up, lest at any time thou dash thy foot against a stone.<br>Luke 4:12 And Jesus answering said unto him, It is said, Thou shalt not tempt the Lord thy God. | 1:14 |
| 4:8 **Again**, the devil taketh him up into an exceeding high mountain, and showeth him all the kingdoms of the world, and the glory of them;[8] | | |
| | Luke 4:13 And when the devil had ended all the temptation, he departed from him for a season. | |
| devil depart-angels came | Time Lock - Time Lock | Time Clue - John 1:26 |
| 1:15 John bare witness of him,.... | | John 1:15 John bare witness of him, and cried, saying, This was he of whom I spake, He that cometh after me is preferred before me: for he was before me.<br>John 1:16 And of his fulness have all we received, and grace for grace.<br>John 1:17 For the law was given by Moses, but grace and truth came by Jesus Christ.<br>John 1:18 No man hath seen God at any time; the only begotten Son, which is in the bosom of the Father, he hath declared him.<br>John 1:19 And this is the record of John, when the Jews sent priests and Levites from Jerusalem to ask him, Who art thou?<br>John 1:20 And he confessed, and denied not; but confessed, I am not the Christ.<br>John 1:21 And they asked him, What then? Art thou Elias? And he saith, I am not. Art thou that prophet? And he answered, No.<br>John 1:22 Then said they unto him, Who art thou? that we may give an answer to them that sent us. What sayest thou of thyself?<br>John 1:23 He said, I am the voice of one crying in the wilderness, Make straight the way of the Lord, as said the prophet Esaias.<br>John 1:24 And they which were sent were of the Pharisees.<br>John 1:25 And they asked him, and said unto him, Why baptizest thou then, if thou be not that Christ, nor Elias, neither that prophet? |
| 1:26 John answered...**there standeth one among you**,....<br><br>1:28...done in | 4:13 | John 1:26 John answered them, saying, I baptize with water: but there standeth one among you, whom ye know not;<br>John 1:27 He it is, who coming after me is preferred before me, whose shoe's latchet I am not worthy to unloose. |

---

[8] Matthew 4:8 Again, the devil taketh him up into an exceeding high mountain, and showeth him all the kingdoms of the world, and the glory of them; (*This is the second time the devil offered this temptation. See Luke 4:5 for the first occurrence.*)

| Matthew | Mark | Important Events |
|---------|------|------------------|
| | | |
| | | **2nd day Jesus among them, Behold the Lamb of God**<br>John 1:29 |
| | | **3rd day, Jesus among them, Behold the Lamb of God**<br>John 1:36 |
| 4:11 | 1:13b | **Jesus returned in the power of the Spirit**<br>Luke 4:14a & John 1:43a<br><br>Map 11 |
| | | |

| | Key Scriptures & Footnotes | Luke | John |
|---|---|---|---|
| | Bethabara beyond Jordan,.... | | John 1:28 These things were done in Bethabara beyond Jordan, where John was baptizing. |
| | 1:29 **The next day** John seeth Jesus...**Behold the Lamb of God**, which taketh away the sin of the world. | | John 1:29 The next day John seeth Jesus coming unto him, and saith, Behold the Lamb of God, which taketh away the sin of the world.<br>John 1:30 This is he of whom I said, After me cometh a man which is preferred before me: for he was before me.<br>John 1:31 And I knew him not: but that he should be made manifest to Israel, therefore am I come baptizing with water.<br>John 1:32 And John bare record, saying, I saw the Spirit descending from heaven like a dove, and it abode upon him.<br>John 1:33 And I knew him not: but he that sent me to baptize with water, the same said unto me, Upon whom thou shalt see the Spirit descending, and remaining on him, the same is he which baptizeth with the Holy Ghost.<br>John 1:34 And I saw, and bare record that this is the Son of God. |
| | 1:35 Again **the next day**....<br><br>1:37 And the two disciples heard him speak, and they followed Jesus.[9]<br><br><br>1:40 One of the two...was Andrew,.... | | John 1:35 Again the next day after John stood, and two of his disciples;<br>John 1:36 And looking upon Jesus as he walked, he saith, Behold the Lamb of God!<br>John 1:37 And the two disciples heard him speak, and they followed Jesus.<br>John 1:38 Then Jesus turned, and saw them following, and saith unto them, What seek ye? They said unto him, Rabbi, (which is to say, being interpreted, Master,) where dwellest thou?<br>John 1:39 He saith unto them, Come and see. They came and saw where he dwelt, and abode with him that day: for it was about the tenth hour.<br>John 1:40 One of the two which heard John speak, and followed him, was Andrew, Simon Peter's brother.<br>John 1:41 He first findeth his own brother Simon, and saith unto him, We have found the Messias, which is, being interpreted, the Christ.<br>John 1:42 And he brought him to Jesus. And when Jesus beheld him, he said, Thou art Simon the son of Jona: thou shalt be called Cephas, which is by interpretation, A stone. |
| | 1:43a The day following....<br>4:14a And Jesus **returned in the power of the Spirit** into Galilee: | Luke 4:14a And Jesus returned in the power of the Spirit into Galilee: | John 1:43a The day following Jesus would go forth into Galilee, |
| | 1:43b and findeth Philip, and saith unto him, Follow me. | | John 1:43b and findeth Philip, and saith unto him, Follow me.<br>John 1:44 Now Philip was of Bethsaida, the city of Andrew and Peter.<br>John 1:45 Philip findeth Nathanael, and saith unto him, We have found him, of whom Moses in the law, and the prophets, did write, Jesus of Nazareth, the son of Joseph.<br>John 1:46 And Nathanael said unto him, Can there any good thing come out of Nazareth? Philip saith unto him, Come and see.<br>John 1:47 Jesus saw Nathanael coming to him, and saith of him, Behold an Israelite indeed, in whom is no guile!<br>John 1:48 Nathanael saith unto him, Whence knowest thou me? Jesus answered and said unto him, Before that Philip called thee, when thou wast under the fig tree, I saw thee. |

[9] John 1:37 And the two disciples heard him speak, and they followed Jesus. (*John, the author of the book of John, was one of these two disciples.*)

| Matthew | Mark | Important Events |
|---------|------|------------------|
| | | |
| | | **Marriage in Cana of Galilee**<br>John 2:1<br><br>Map 12 |
| 4:11 | 1:13b | Map 13 |
| | | **1st Passover was at hand.**<br>John 2:13<br><br>Map 14 |

| ministry year | Key Scriptures & Footnotes | Luke | John |
|---|---|---|---|
| | | | John 1:49 Nathanael answered and saith unto him, Rabbi, thou art the Son of God; thou art the King of Israel.<br>John 1:50 Jesus answered and said unto him, Because I said unto thee, I saw thee under the fig tree, believest thou? thou shalt see greater things than these.<br>John 1:51 And he saith unto him, Verily, verily, I say unto you, Hereafter ye shall see heaven open, and the angels of God ascending and descending upon the Son of man. |
| | 2:1...marriage in Cana of Galilee;.... | | John 2:1 And the third day there was a marriage in Cana of Galilee; and the mother of Jesus was there:<br>John 2:2 And both Jesus was called, and his disciples, to the marriage.<br>John 2:3 And when they wanted wine, the mother of Jesus saith unto him, They have no wine.<br>John 2:4 Jesus saith unto her, Woman, what have I to do with thee? mine hour is not yet come.<br>John 2:5 His mother saith unto the servants, Whatsoever he saith unto you, do it.<br>John 2:6 And there were set there six waterpots of stone, after the manner of the purifying of the Jews, containing two or three firkins apiece.<br>John 2:7 Jesus saith unto them, Fill the waterpots with water. And they filled them up to the brim.<br>John 2:8 And he saith unto them, Draw out now, and bear unto the governor of the feast. And they bare it.<br>John 2:9 When the ruler of the feast had tasted the water that was made wine, and knew not whence it was: (but the servants which drew the water knew;) the governor of the feast called the bridegroom,<br>John 2:10 And saith unto him, Every man at the beginning doth set forth good wine; and when men have well drunk, then that which is worse: but thou hast kept the good wine until now.<br>John 2:11 This beginning of miracles did Jesus in Cana of Galilee, and manifested forth his glory; and his disciples believed on him. |
| | 2:12...he went down to Capernaum,...not many days. | 4:14a | John 2:12 After this he went down to Capernaum, he, and his mother, and his brethren, and his disciples: and they continued there not many days. |
| | 2:13 And the Jews' **passover** was at hand, and Jesus went up to Jerusalem,<br><br>2:15 And when he had made a scourge of small cords, he drove them all out of the temple,....[10]<br>John 2:16 And said unto them that sold doves, Take these things hence; make not my Father's house an house of merchandise. | | John 2:13 And the Jews' passover was at hand, and Jesus went up to Jerusalem,<br>John 2:14 And found in the temple those that sold oxen and sheep and doves, and the changers of money sitting:<br>John 2:15 And when he had made a scourge of small cords, he drove them all out of the temple, and the sheep, and the oxen; and poured out the changers' money, and overthrew the tables;<br>John 2:16 And said unto them that sold doves, Take these things hence; make not my Father's house an house of merchandise.<br>John 2:17 And his disciples remembered that it was written, The zeal of thine house hath eaten me up.<br>John 2:18 Then answered the Jews and said unto him, What sign showest thou unto us, seeing that thou doest these things?<br>John 2:19 Jesus answered and said unto them, Destroy this temple, and in three days I will raise it up.<br>John 2:20 Then said the Jews, Forty and six years was this temple in building, and wilt thou rear it up in three days?<br>John 2:21 But he spake of the temple of his body.<br>John 2:22 When therefore he was risen from the dead, his disciples remembered that he had said this unto them; and they believed the scripture, and the word which Jesus had said. |

---

[10] John 2:15 And when he had made a scourge of small cords, he drove them all out of the temple.... (*This is the first time Jesus cleansed temple. See Matthew 21:12, Mark 11:15, & Luke 19:45 for the second.*)

| Matthew | Mark | Important Events |
|---|---|---|
| | | **At the 1st passover, in the feast day, Jesus did miracles.** John 2:23 |
| 4:11 | 1:13b | **A Pharisee named Nicodemus** John 3:1 |
| 4:11 | 1:13b | Map 15 |

| ministry year | Key Scriptures & Footnotes | Luke | John |
|---|---|---|---|
| | 2:23...in Jerusalem at the passover, in the feast day...they saw the miracles which he did. | | John 2:23  Now when he was in Jerusalem at the passover, in the feast day, many believed in his name, when they saw the miracles which he did.<br>John 2:24  But Jesus did not commit himself unto them, because he knew all men,<br>John 2:25  And needed not that any should testify of man: for he knew what was in man. |
| | 3:1...Nicodemus.... came to Jesus by night.... | 4:14a | John 3:1  There was a man of the Pharisees, named Nicodemus, a ruler of the Jews:<br>John 3:2  The same came to Jesus by night, and said unto him, Rabbi, we know that thou art a teacher come from God: for no man can do these miracles that thou doest, except God be with him.<br>John 3:3  Jesus answered and said unto him, Verily, verily, I say unto thee, Except a man be born again, he cannot see the kingdom of God.<br>John 3:4  Nicodemus saith unto him, How can a man be born when he is old? can he enter the second time into his mother's womb, and be born?<br>John 3:5  Jesus answered, Verily, verily, I say unto thee, Except a man be born of water and of the Spirit, he cannot enter into the kingdom of God.<br>John 3:6  That which is born of the flesh is flesh; and that which is born of the Spirit is spirit.<br>John 3:7  Marvel not that I said unto thee, Ye must be born again.<br>John 3:8  The wind bloweth where it listeth, and thou hearest the sound thereof, but canst not tell whence it cometh, and whither it goeth: so is every one that is born of the Spirit.<br>John 3:9  Nicodemus answered and said unto him, How can these things be?<br>John 3:10  Jesus answered and said unto him, Art thou a master of Israel, and knowest not these things?<br>John 3:11  Verily, verily, I say unto thee, We speak that we do know, and testify that we have seen; and ye receive not our witness.<br>John 3:12  If I have told you earthly things, and ye believe not, how shall ye believe, if I tell you of heavenly things?<br>John 3:13  And no man hath ascended up to heaven, but he that came down from heaven, even the Son of man which is in heaven.<br>John 3:14  And as Moses lifted up the serpent in the wilderness, even so must the Son of man be lifted up:<br>John 3:15  That whosoever believeth in him should not perish, but have eternal life.<br>John 3:16  For God so loved the world, that he gave his only begotten Son, that whosoever believeth in him should not perish, but have everlasting life.<br>John 3:17  For God sent not his Son into the world to condemn the world; but that the world through him might be saved.<br>John 3:18  He that believeth on him is not condemned: but he that believeth not is condemned already, because he hath not believed in the name of the only begotten Son of God.<br>John 3:19  And this is the condemnation, that light is come into the world, and men loved darkness rather than light, because their deeds were evil.<br>John 3:20  For every one that doeth evil hateth the light, neither cometh to the light, lest his deeds should be reproved.<br>John 3:21  But he that doeth truth cometh to the light, that his deeds may be made manifest, that they are wrought in God. |
| | 3:22  After...came Jesus...into the land of Judaea; | 4:14a | John 3:22  After these things came Jesus and his disciples into the land of Judaea; and there he tarried with them, and baptized.<br>John 3:23  And John also was baptizing in Aenon near to Salim, because there was much water there: and they came, and were baptized. |

| Matthew | Mark | Important Events |
|---|---|---|
| | | |
| | Mark 1:14a  Now after that John was put in prison, | |
| | | |
| Matt. 4:12  Now when Jesus had heard that John was cast into prison, he departed into Galilee; | | **Jesus departed to Galilee** Matt. 4:12 & John 4:3b |
| | | **A woman of Samaria at Jacob's well** John 4:5  Map 16 |

| | Key Scriptures & Footnotes | Luke | John |
|---|---|---|---|
| | | | John 3:24  For John was not yet cast into prison.<br>John 3:25  Then there arose a question between some of John's disciples and the Jews about purifying.<br>John 3:26  And they came unto John, and said unto him, Rabbi, he that was with thee beyond Jordan, to whom thou barest witness, behold, the same baptizeth, and all men come to him.<br>John 3:27  John answered and said, A man can receive nothing, except it be given him from heaven.<br>John 3:28  Ye yourselves bear me witness, that I said, I am not the Christ, but that I am sent before him.<br>John 3:29  He that hath the bride is the bridegroom: but the friend of the bridegroom, which standeth and heareth him, rejoiceth greatly because of the bridegroom's voice: this my joy therefore is fulfilled.<br>John 3:30  He must increase, but I must decrease.<br>John 3:31  He that cometh from above is above all: he that is of the earth is earthly, and speaketh of the earth: he that cometh from heaven is above all.<br>John 3:32  And what he hath seen and heard, that he testifieth; and no man receiveth his testimony.<br>John 3:33  He that hath received his testimony hath set to his seal that God is true.<br>John 3:34  For he whom God hath sent speaketh the words of God: for God giveth not the Spirit by measure unto him.<br>John 3:35  The Father loveth the Son, and hath given all things into his hand.<br>John 3:36  He that believeth on the Son hath everlasting life: and he that believeth not the Son shall not see life; but the wrath of God abideth on him. |
| | 3:30  He must increase, but I must decrease. | | |
| | | | John 4:1  When therefore the Lord knew how the Pharisees had heard that Jesus made and baptized more disciples than John,<br>John 4:2  (Though Jesus himself baptized not, but his disciples,)<br>John 4:3a  He left Judaea, |
| | 1:14a  Now after that John was put in prison, | | |
| | John in prison | | Time Clue - Time Clue |
| | 4:12  Now when Jesus had heard that John was cast into prison, he departed into Galilee; | | John 4:3b  and departed again into Galilee. |
| | | | John 4:4  And he must needs go through Samaria. |
| | 4:5  Then cometh he to a city of Samaria.... | 4:14a | John 4:5  Then cometh he to a city of Samaria, which is called Sychar, near to the parcel of ground that Jacob gave to his son Joseph.<br>John 4:6  Now Jacob's well was there. Jesus therefore, being wearied with his journey, sat thus on the well: and it was about the sixth hour. |
| | 44:7  There cometh a woman of Samaria to draw water: Jesus saith unto her, Give me to drink.[11] | | John 4:7  There cometh a woman of Samaria to draw water: Jesus saith unto her, Give me to drink.<br>John 4:8  (For his disciples were gone away unto the city to buy meat.)<br>John 4:9  Then saith the woman of Samaria unto him, How is it that thou, being a Jew, askest drink of me, which am a woman of Samaria? for the Jews have no dealings with the Samaritans. |
| | 4:10... and he would have given thee living water. | | John 4:10  Jesus answered and said unto her, If thou knewest the gift of God, and who it is that saith to thee, Give me to drink; thou wouldest have asked of him, and he would have given thee living water.<br>John 4:11  The woman saith unto him, Sir, thou hast nothing to draw with, and the well is deep: from |

[11] John 4:7  There cometh a woman of Samaria to draw water: Jesus saith unto her, Give me to drink. (*According to John 21:24, John wrote only about the things he saw. Therefore, John must have stayed with Jesus while the other disciples went into the city to buy meat.*)

| Matthew | Mark | Important Events |
|---|---|---|
| | | |
| Time Lock - Time Lock | Time Lock - Time Lock | |
| 4:12 | 1:14a | **The Hour cometh, and now is**<br>John 4:23 |

| ministry year | Key Scriptures & Footnotes | Luke | John |
|---|---|---|---|
| | | | whence then hast thou that living water? |
| | | | John 4:12   Art thou greater than our father Jacob, which gave us the well, and drank thereof himself, and his children, and his cattle? |
| | | | John 4:13   Jesus answered and said unto her, Whosoever drinketh of this water shall thirst again: |
| | | | John 4:14   But whosoever drinketh of the water that I shall give him shall never thirst; but the water that I shall give him shall be in him a well of water springing up into everlasting life. |
| | | | John 4:15   The woman saith unto him, Sir, give me this water, that I thirst not, neither come hither to draw. |
| | | | John 4:16   Jesus saith unto her, Go, call thy husband, and come hither. |
| | | | John 4:17   The woman answered and said, I have no husband. Jesus said unto her, Thou hast well said, I have no husband: |
| | | | John 4:18   For thou hast had five husbands; and he whom thou now hast is not thy husband: in that saidst thou truly. |
| | | | John 4:19   The woman saith unto him, Sir, I perceive that thou art a prophet. |
| | | | John 4:20   Our fathers worshipped in this mountain; and ye say, that in Jerusalem is the place where men ought to worship. |
| | | | John 4:21   Jesus saith unto her, Woman, believe me, the hour cometh, when ye shall neither in this mountain, nor yet at Jerusalem, worship the Father. |
| | | | John 4:22   Ye worship ye know not what: we know what we worship: for salvation is of the Jews. |
| | The hour cometh. | Time Lock - Time Lock | Time Lock - Time Lock |
| | 4:23   But the **hour cometh, and now is**, when the true worshippers shall worship the Father **in spirit and in truth**: for the Father seeketh such to worship him. | 4:14a | John 4:23   But the hour cometh, and now is, when the true worshippers shall worship the Father in spirit and in truth: for the Father seeketh such to worship him. |
| | | | John 4:24   God is a Spirit: and they that worship him must worship him in spirit and in truth. |
| | | | John 4:25   The woman saith unto him, I know that Messias cometh, which is called Christ: when he is come, he will tell us all things. |
| | | | John 4:26   Jesus saith unto her, I that speak unto thee am he. |
| | | | John 4:27   And upon this came his disciples, and marvelled that he talked with the woman: yet no man said, What seekest thou? or, Why talkest thou with her? |
| | | | John 4:28   The woman then left her waterpot, and went her way into the city, and saith to the men, |
| | | | John 4:29   Come, see a man, which told me all things that ever I did: is not this the Christ? |
| | | | John 4:30   Then they went out of the city, and came unto him. |
| | | | John 4:31   In the mean while his disciples prayed him, saying, Master, eat. |
| | | | John 4:32   But he said unto them, I have meat to eat that ye know not of. |
| | | | John 4:33   Therefore said the disciples one to another, Hath any man brought him aught to eat? |
| | | | John 4:34   Jesus saith unto them, My meat is to do the will of him that sent me, and to finish his work. |
| | 4:35   Say not ye, There are yet four months, and then cometh harvest?... | | John 4:35   Say not ye, There are yet four months, and then cometh harvest? behold, I say unto you, Lift up your eyes, and look on the fields; for they are white already to harvest. |
| | | | John 4:36   And he that reapeth receiveth wages, and gathereth fruit unto life eternal: that both he that soweth and he that reapeth may rejoice together. |
| | | | John 4:37   And herein is that saying true, One soweth, and another reapeth. |
| | | | John 4:38   I sent you to reap that whereon ye bestowed no labour: other men laboured, and ye are entered into their labours. |
| | | | John 4:39   And many of the Samaritans of that city |

| Matthew | Mark | Important Events |
|---------|------|------------------|
| | | |
| 4:12 | Mark 1:14b   Jesus came into Galilee, | **Jesus in Galilee**<br>Mark 1:14b & John 4:43 |
| | | **Jesus came again into Cana**<br>John 4:46<br><br>**A certain nobleman's son was healed**<br>John 4:50<br><br>Map 17 |
| | | |
| | | |
| | | **1st ministry trip to Nazareth**<br>Luke 4:16<br><br>Map 18 |

| ministry year | Key Scriptures & Footnotes | Luke | John |
|---|---|---|---|
| | | | believed on him for the saying of the woman, which testified, He told me all that ever I did.<br>John 4:40  So when the Samaritans were come unto him, they besought him that he would tarry with them: and he abode there two days.<br>John 4:41  And many more believed because of his own word;<br>John 4:42  And said unto the woman, Now we believe, not because of thy saying: for we have heard him ourselves, and know that this is indeed the Christ, the Saviour of the world. |
| | 1:14b  Jesus came into Galilee, | | John 4:43  Now after two days he departed thence, and went into Galilee.<br>John 4:44  For Jesus himself testified, that a prophet hath no honour in his own country.<br>John 4:45  Then when he was come into Galilee, the Galilaeans received him, having seen all the things that he did at Jerusalem at the feast: for they also went unto the feast. |
| | 4:46  So Jesus came again into Cana of Galilee...And there was a certain nobleman, whose son was sick at Capernaum. | | John 4:46  So Jesus came again into Cana of Galilee, where he made the water wine. And there was a certain nobleman, whose son was sick at Capernaum.<br>John 4:47  When he heard that Jesus was come out of Judaea into Galilee, he went unto him, and besought him that he would come down, and heal his son: for he was at the point of death.<br>John 4:48  Then said Jesus unto him, Except ye see signs and wonders, ye will not believe.<br>John 4:49  The nobleman saith unto him, Sir, come down ere my child die.<br>John 4:50  Jesus saith unto him, Go thy way; thy son liveth. And the man believed the word that Jesus had spoken unto him, and he went his way. |
| | 4:51  And as he was now going down, his servants met him,....[12] | | John 4:51  And as he was now going down, his servants met him, and told him, saying, Thy son liveth.<br>John 4:52  Then inquired he of them the hour when he began to amend. And they said unto him, Yesterday at the seventh hour the fever left him.<br>John 4:53  So the father knew that it was at the same hour, in the which Jesus said unto him, Thy son liveth: and himself believed, and his whole house.<br>John 4:54  This is again the second miracle that Jesus did, when he was come out of Judaea into Galilee. |
| | | Luke 4:14b  and there went out a fame of him through all the region round about.<br>Luke 4:15  And he taught in their synagogues, being glorified of all. | |
| | 4:16  And he came to Nazareth....[13]<br><br><br><br>4:18  The Spirit of the Lord is upon me, because he hath anointed me.... | Luke 4:16  And he came to Nazareth, where he had been brought up: and, as his custom was, he went into the synagogue on the sabbath day, and stood up for to read.<br>Luke 4:17  And there was delivered unto him the book of the prophet Esaias. And when he had opened the book, he found the place where it was written,<br>Luke 4:18  The Spirit of the Lord is upon me, because he hath anointed me to preach the gospel to the poor; he hath sent me to heal the brokenhearted, to preach deliverance to the captives, and recovering of sight to the blind, to set at liberty them that are bruised,<br>Luke 4:19  To preach the acceptable year of the Lord.<br>Luke 4:20  And he closed the book, and he gave it again to the minister, and sat down. And the eyes of all them that were in the synagogue were fastened on him. | |

---

[12] John 4:51  And as he was now going down, his servants met him.... (*John went with the nobleman to Capernaum. We know this because John only wrote concerning what he saw personally or knew first hand. See John 21:24  This is the disciple which testifieth....*)

[13] Luke 4:16  And he came to Nazareth.... (*This is Jesus' first ministry trip to Nazareth. See Mark 6:1 for the second ministry trip to Nazareth and Matthew 13:58 for the third.*)

| Matthew | Mark | Important Events |
|---|---|---|
| | | |
| Time Lock - Time Lock | | |
| Matt. 4:13   And leaving Nazareth, he came and dwelt in Capernaum, which is upon the sea coast, in the borders of Zabulon and Nephthalim: Matt. 4:14   That it might be fulfilled which was spoken by Esaias the prophet, saying, Matt. 4:15   The land of Zabulon, and the land of Nephthalim, by the way of the sea, beyond Jordan, Galilee of the Gentiles; Matt. 4:16   The people which sat in darkness saw great light; and to them which sat in the region and shadow of death light is sprung up. | | Map 19 |
| Matt. 4:17   From that time Jesus began to preach, and to say, Repent: for the kingdom of heaven is at hand. | Mark 1:14c   preaching the gospel of the kingdom of God, Mark 1:15   And saying, The time is fulfilled, and the kingdom of God is at hand: repent ye, and believe the gospel. | |
| Time Lock - Time Lock | Time Lock - Time Lock | Time Lock |
| Matt. 4:18   And Jesus, walking by the sea of Galilee, saw two brethren, Simon called Peter, and Andrew his brother, casting a net into the sea: for they were fishers. Matt. 4:19   And he saith unto them, Follow me, and I will make you fishers of men. Matt. 4:20   And they straightway left their nets, and followed him. Matt. 4:21   And going on from thence, he saw other two brethren, James the son of Zebedee, and John his brother, in a ship with Zebedee their father, mending their nets; and he called them. Matt. 4:22   And they immediately left the ship and their father, and followed him. | Mark 1:16   Now as he walked by the sea of Galilee, he saw Simon and Andrew his brother casting a net into the sea: for they were fishers. Mark 1:17   And Jesus said unto them, Come ye after me, and I will make you to become fishers of men. Mark 1:18   And straightway they forsook their nets, and followed him. Mark 1:19   And when he had gone a little farther thence, he saw James the son of Zebedee, and John his brother, who also were in the ship mending their nets. Mark 1:20   And straightway he called them: and they left their father Zebedee in the ship with the hired servants, and went after him. | **They forsook their nets, and followed him.** Matt. 4:20 & Mark 1:18 Map 20 |
| | Mark 1:21   And they went into Capernaum; and straightway on the sabbath day he entered into the synagogue, and taught. Mark 1:22   And they were astonished at his doctrine: for he taught them as one that had authority, and not as the scribes. Mark 1:23   And there was in their synagogue a man with an unclean spirit; and he cried out, | **Capernaum, on the sabbath day, a man with an unclean spirit** Mark 1:21 & Luke 4:33 |

18

| | Key Scriptures & Footnotes | Luke | John |
|---|---|---|---|
| | | Luke 4:21   And he began to say unto them, This day is this scripture fulfilled in your ears.<br>Luke 4:22   And all bare him witness, and wondered at the gracious words which proceeded out of his mouth. And they said, Is not this Joseph's son?<br>Luke 4:23   And he said unto them, Ye will surely say unto me this proverb, Physician, heal thyself: whatsoever we have heard done in Capernaum, do also here in thy country.<br>Luke 4:24   And he said, Verily I say unto you, No prophet is accepted in his own country.<br>Luke 4:25   But I tell you of a truth, many widows were in Israel in the days of Elias, when the heaven was shut up three years and six months, when great famine was throughout all the land;<br>Luke 4:26   But unto none of them was Elias sent, save unto Sarepta, a city of Sidon, unto a woman that was a widow.<br>Luke 4:27   And many lepers were in Israel in the time of Eliseus the prophet; and none of them was cleansed, saving Naaman the Syrian.<br>Luke 4:28   And all they in the synagogue, when they heard these things, were filled with wrath,<br>Luke 4:29   And rose up, and thrust him out of the city, and led him unto the brow of the hill whereon their city was built, that they might cast him down headlong. | |
| | 4:30 But he passing through the midst.... | Luke 4:30   But he passing through the midst of them went his way, | |
| | *Jesus came to Capernaum* | *Time Lock - Time Lock* | |
| | 4:13 And leaving Nazareth, he came and dwelt in Capernaum.... | Luke 4:31a   And came down to Capernaum, a city of Galilee, | 4:54 |
| | 4:17 From that time...Repent: for the kingdom of heaven is at hand. | | |
| | *They forsook their nets.* | | |
| | 4:18 And Jesus, walking by the sea of Galilee, saw two brethren, Simon called Peter, and Andrew his brother....<br>Follow me, and I will make you **fishers of men.**<br>1:18...they **forsook their nets**, and followed him.[14]<br>4:21...James...and John his brother.... | | 4:54 |
| | 1:21 And they went into Capernaum...on the sabbath day he entered into the synagogue, and taught.<br><br>1:23...a man with an unclean spirit.... | Luke 4:31b   and taught them on the sabbath days.<br>Luke 4:32   And they were astonished at his doctrine: for his word was with power.<br>Luke 4:33   And in the synagogue there was a man, which had a spirit of an unclean devil, and cried out with a loud voice,<br>Luke 4:34   Saying, Let us alone; what have we to do with thee, thou Jesus of Nazareth? art thou come to | 4:54 |

[14] Mark 1:18   And straightway they forsook **their nets**, and followed him. (*See Luke 5:11* And when they had brought their ships to land, they forsook **all**, and followed him.)

| Matthew | Mark | Important Events |
|---|---|---|
| | Mark 1:24  Saying, Let us alone; what have we to do with thee, thou Jesus of Nazareth? art thou come to destroy us? I know thee who thou art, the Holy One of God.<br>Mark 1:25  And Jesus rebuked him, saying, Hold thy peace, and come out of him.<br>Mark 1:26  And when the unclean spirit had torn him, and cried with a loud voice, he came out of him.<br>Mark 1:27  And they were all amazed, insomuch that they questioned among themselves, saying, What thing is this? what new doctrine is this? for with authority commandeth he even the unclean spirits, and they do obey him.<br>Mark 1:28  And immediately his fame spread abroad throughout all the region round about Galilee. | Map 21 |
| | Mark 1:29  And forthwith, when they were come out of the synagogue, they entered into the house of Simon and Andrew, with James and John.<br>Mark 1:30  But Simon's wife's mother lay sick of a fever, and anon they tell him of her.<br>Mark 1:31  And he came and took her by the hand, and lifted her up; and immediately the fever left her, and she ministered unto them. | **1st time Simon's wife's mother lay sick**<br>Mark 1:30 & Luke 4:38<br><br>Map 22 |
| | Mark 1:32  And at even, when the sun did set, they brought unto him all that were diseased, and them that were possessed with devils.<br>Mark 1:33  And all the city was gathered together at the door.<br>Mark 1:34  And he healed many that were sick of divers diseases, and cast out many devils; and suffered not the devils to speak, because they knew him.<br>Mark 1:35  And in the morning, rising up a great while before day, he went out, and departed into a solitary place, and there prayed.<br>Mark 1:36  And Simon and they that were with him followed after him.<br>Mark 1:37  And when they had found him, they said unto him, All men seek for thee. | Map 23 |
| | Mark 1:38  And he said unto them, Let us go into the next towns, that I may preach there also: for therefore came I forth. | |
| Time Lock - Time Lock | Time Lock - Time Lock | |
| Matt. 4:23  And Jesus went about all Galilee, teaching in their synagogues, and preaching the gospel of the kingdom, and healing all manner of sickness and all manner of disease among the people.<br>Matt. 4:24  And his fame went throughout all Syria: and they brought unto him all sick people that were taken with divers diseases and torments, and those which were possessed with devils, and those which were lunatic, and those that had the palsy; and he healed them.<br>Matt. 4:25  And there followed him great multitudes of people from Galilee, and from Decapolis, and from Jerusalem, and from Judaea, and from beyond Jordan. | Mark 1:39  And he preached in their synagogues throughout all Galilee, and cast out devils. | **1st time Jesus went about all Galilee, preaching**<br>Matt. 4:23, Mark 1:39, & Luke 4:44<br><br>Map 24 |
| Matt. 5:1  And seeing the multitudes, he went up into a mountain: and when he was set, his disciples came unto him:<br>Matt. 5:2  And he opened his mouth, and taught them, saying,<br>Matt. 5:3  Blessed are the poor in spirit: for theirs is the kingdom of heaven. | | **Blessed are the poor in spirit**<br>Matt. 5:3<br><br>Map 25 |

| | | | |
|---|---|---|---|
| | 1:25 And Jesus rebuked him, saying, Hold thy peace, and come out of him.<br>1:26 And...he came out of him. | destroy us? I know thee who thou art; the Holy One of God.<br>Luke 4:35 And Jesus rebuked him, saying, Hold thy peace, and come out of him. And when the devil had thrown him in the midst, he came out of him, and hurt him not.<br>Luke 4:36 And they were all amazed, and spake among themselves, saying, What a word is this! for with authority and power he commandeth the unclean spirits, and they come out.<br>Luke 4:37 And the fame of him went out into every place of the country round about. | |
| | 4:38 ...And Simon's wife's mother was taken with a great fever and they besought him for her.<br>1:31 And he...took her by the hand...the fever left....[15] | Luke 4:38 And he arose out of the synagogue, and entered into Simon's house. And Simon's wife's mother was taken with a great fever; and they besought him for her.<br>Luke 4:39 And he stood over her, and rebuked the fever; and it left her: and immediately she arose and ministered unto them. | |
| | 1:32 And at even, when the sun did set, they brought unto him all that were diseased.... | Luke 4:40 Now when the sun was setting, all they that had any sick with divers diseases brought them unto him; and he laid his hands on every one of them, and healed them.<br>Luke 4:41 And devils also came out of many, crying out, and saying, Thou art Christ the Son of God. And he rebuking them suffered them not to speak: for they knew that he was Christ.<br>Luke 4:42 And when it was day, he departed and went into a desert place: and the people sought him, and came unto him, and stayed him, that he should not depart from them. | 4:54 |
| | 1:38 ...Let us go into the next towns, that I may preach there also:....[16] | Luke 4:43 And he said unto them, I must preach the kingdom of God to other cities also: for therefore am I sent. | |
| | Jesus went about Galilee | Time Lock - Time Lock | |
| | 4:23 And Jesus went about all Galilee.... | Luke 4:44 And he preached in the synagogues of Galilee. | 4:54 |
| | 5:1 And seeing the multitudes, he went up into a mountain....<br>5:2...and taught them, saying...<br>5:3 Blessed are the poor in spirit: for theirs | | |

[15] Mark 1:31 And he came and took her by the hand, and lifted her up; and immediately the fever left her.... (*This is the first time Jesus healed her. See Matthew 8:14 for the second time.*)
[16] Mark 1:38 And he said unto them, Let us go into the next towns, that I may preach there also:.... (*We do not know if Peter went with Jesus on this tour; however, by Luke 5:1 Peter had returned to fishing all night.*)

| Matthew | Mark | Important Events |
|---|---|---|
| Matt. 5:4 Blessed are they that mourn: for they shall be comforted.<br>Matt. 5:5 Blessed are the meek: for they shall inherit the earth.<br>Matt. 5:6 Blessed are they which do hunger and thirst after righteousness: for they shall be filled.<br>Matt. 5:7 Blessed are the merciful: for they shall obtain mercy.<br>Matt. 5:8 Blessed are the pure in heart: for they shall see God.<br>Matt. 5:9 Blessed are the peacemakers: for they shall be called the children of God.<br>Matt. 5:10 Blessed are they which are persecuted for righteousness' sake: for theirs is the kingdom of heaven.<br>Matt. 5:11 Blessed are ye, when men shall revile you, and persecute you, and shall say all manner of evil against you falsely, for my sake. | | |
| Matt. 5:12 Rejoice, and be exceeding glad: for great is your reward in heaven: for so persecuted they the prophets which were before you.<br>Matt. 5:13 Ye are the salt of the earth: but if the salt have lost his savour, wherewith shall it be salted? it is thenceforth good for nothing, but to be cast out, and to be trodden under foot of men.<br>Matt. 5:14 Ye are the light of the world. A city that is set on an hill cannot be hid.<br>Matt. 5:15 Neither do men light a candle, and put it under a bushel, but on a candlestick; and it giveth light unto all that are in the house.<br>Matt. 5:16 Let your light so shine before men, that they may see your good works, and glorify your Father which is in heaven.<br>Matt. 5:17 Think not that I am come to destroy the law, or the prophets: I am not come to destroy, but to fulfil.<br>Matt. 5:18 For verily I say unto you, Till heaven and earth pass, one jot or one tittle shall in no wise pass from the law, till all be fulfilled.<br>Matt. 5:19 Whosoever therefore shall break one of these least commandments, and shall teach men so, he shall be called the least in the kingdom of heaven: but whosoever shall do and teach them, the same shall be called great in the kingdom of heaven.<br>Matt. 5:20 For I say unto you, That except your righteousness shall exceed the righteousness of the scribes and Pharisees, ye shall in no case enter into the kingdom of heaven.<br>Matt. 5:21 Ye have heard that it was said by them of old time, Thou shalt not kill; and whosoever shall kill shall be in danger of the judgment:<br>Matt. 5:22 But I say unto you, That whosoever is angry with his brother without a cause shall be in danger of the judgment: and whosoever shall say to his brother, Raca, shall be in danger of the council: but whosoever shall say, Thou fool, shall be in danger of hell fire.<br>Matt. 5:23 Therefore if thou bring thy gift to the altar, and there rememberest that thy brother hath aught against thee;<br>Matt. 5:24 Leave there thy gift before the altar, and go thy way; first be reconciled to thy brother, and then come and offer thy gift.<br>Matt. 5:25 Agree with thine adversary quickly, whiles thou art in the way with him; lest at any time the adversary deliver thee to the judge, and the judge deliver thee to the officer, and thou be cast into prison.<br>Matt. 5:26 Verily I say unto thee, Thou shalt by no means come out thence, till thou hast paid the uttermost farthing. | 1:39 | |

| ministry year | Key Scriptures & Footnotes | Luke | John |
|---|---|---|---|
| | is the kingdom of heaven.[17] | | |
| | 5:12  Rejoice.... | 4:44 | 4:54 |
| | 55:13  Ye are the salt of the earth.... | | |
| | 5:14  Ye are the light of the world. | | |
| | 5:18 ...one jot or one tittle shall in no wise pass from the law, till all be fulfilled. | | |
| | 5:24 ...first be reconciled to thy brother, and then come and offer thy gift. | | |

[17] Matthew 5:3   Blessed are the poor in spirit: for theirs is the kingdom of heaven. (*See Luke 6:20* ...Blessed be ye poor....)

Matt. 5:27  Ye have heard that it was said by them of old time, Thou shalt not commit adultery:

Matt. 5:28  But I say unto you, That whosoever looketh on a woman to lust after her hath committed adultery with her already in his heart.

Matt. 5:29  And if thy right eye offend thee, pluck it out, and cast it from thee: for it is profitable for thee that one of thy members should perish, and not that thy whole body should be cast into hell.

Matt. 5:30  And if thy right hand offend thee, cut it off, and cast it from thee: for it is profitable for thee that one of thy members should perish, and not that thy whole body should be cast into hell.

Matt. 5:31  It hath been said, Whosoever shall put away his wife, let him give her a writing of divorcement:

Matt. 5:32  But I say unto you, That whosoever shall put away his wife, saving for the cause of fornication, causeth her to commit adultery: and whosoever shall marry her that is divorced committeth adultery.

Matt. 5:33  Again, ye have heard that it hath been said by them of old time, Thou shalt not forswear thyself, but shalt perform unto the Lord thine oaths:

Matt. 5:34  But I say unto you, Swear not at all; neither by heaven; for it is God's throne:

Matt. 5:35  Nor by the earth; for it is his footstool: neither by Jerusalem; for it is the city of the great King.

Matt. 5:36  Neither shalt thou swear by thy head, because thou canst not make one hair white or black.

Matt. 5:37  But let your communication be, Yea, yea; Nay, nay: for whatsoever is more than these cometh of evil.

Matt. 5:38  Ye have heard that it hath been said, An eye for an eye, and a tooth for a tooth:

Matt. 5:39  But I say unto you, That ye resist not evil: but whosoever shall smite thee on thy right cheek, turn to him the other also.

Matt. 5:40  And if any man will sue thee at the law, and take away thy coat, let him have thy cloak also.

Matt. 5:41  And whosoever shall compel thee to go a mile, go with him twain.

Matt. 5:42  Give to him that asketh thee, and from him that would borrow of thee turn not thou away.

Matt. 5:43  Ye have heard that it hath been said, Thou shalt love thy neighbour, and hate thine enemy.

Matt. 5:44  But I say unto you, Love your enemies, bless them that curse you, do good to them that hate you, and pray for them which despitefully use you, and persecute you;

Matt. 5:45  That ye may be the children of your Father which is in heaven: for he maketh his sun to rise on the evil and on the good, and sendeth rain on the just and on the unjust.

Matt. 5:46  For if ye love them which love you, what reward have ye? do not even the publicans the same?

Matt. 5:47  And if ye salute your brethren only, what do ye more than others? do not even the publicans so?

Matt. 5:48  Be ye therefore perfect, even as your Father which is in heaven is perfect.

Matt. 6:1  Take heed that ye do not your alms before men, to be seen of them: otherwise ye have no reward of your Father which is in heaven.

Matt. 6:2  Therefore when thou doest thine alms, do not sound a trumpet before thee, as the hypocrites do in the synagogues and in the streets, that they may have glory of men. Verily I say unto you, They have their reward.

Matt. 6:3  But when thou doest alms, let not thy left hand know what thy right hand doeth:

Matt. 6:4  That thine alms may be in secret: and thy

5:28...whosoever looketh on a woman to lust after her hath committed adultery with her already in his heart.

5:30  And if thy right hand offend thee, cut it off, and cast it from thee....

5:32...whosoever shall marry her that is divorced committeth adultery.

5:39...but whosoever shall smite thee on thy right cheek, turn to him the other also.

5:44...Love your enemies, bless them that curse you, do good to them that hate you,....

6:3  But when thou doest alms, let not thy left hand know what

| Matthew | Mark | Important Events |
|---|---|---|
| Father which seeth in secret himself shall reward thee openly.<br>Matt. 6:5  And when thou prayest, thou shalt not be as the hypocrites are: for they love to pray standing in the synagogues and in the corners of the streets, that they may be seen of men. Verily I say unto you, They have their reward.<br>Matt. 6:6  But thou, when thou prayest, enter into thy closet, and when thou hast shut thy door, pray to thy Father which is in secret; and thy Father which seeth in secret shall reward thee openly.<br>Matt. 6:7  But when ye pray, use not vain repetitions, as the heathen do: for they think that they shall be heard for their much speaking.<br>Matt. 6:8  Be not ye therefore like unto them: for your Father knoweth what things ye have need of, before ye ask him. | | |
| Matt. 6:9  After this manner therefore pray ye: Our Father which art in heaven, Hallowed be thy name.<br>Matt. 6:10  Thy kingdom come. Thy will be done in earth, as it is in heaven.<br>Matt. 6:11  Give us this day our daily bread.<br>Matt. 6:12  And forgive us our debts, as we forgive our debtors.<br>Matt. 6:13  And lead us not into temptation, but deliver us from evil: For thine is the kingdom, and the power, and the glory, for ever. Amen.<br>Matt. 6:14  For if ye forgive men their trespasses, your heavenly Father will also forgive you:<br>Matt. 6:15  But if ye forgive not men their trespasses, neither will your Father forgive your trespasses.<br>Matt. 6:16  Moreover when ye fast, be not, as the hypocrites, of a sad countenance: for they disfigure their faces, that they may appear unto men to fast. Verily I say unto you, They have their reward.<br>Matt. 6:17  But thou, when thou fastest, anoint thine head, and wash thy face;<br>Matt. 6:18  That thou appear not unto men to fast, but unto thy Father which is in secret: and thy Father, which seeth in secret, shall reward thee openly.<br>Matt. 6:19  Lay not up for yourselves treasures upon earth, where moth and rust doth corrupt, and where thieves break through and steal:<br>Matt. 6:20  But lay up for yourselves treasures in heaven, where neither moth nor rust doth corrupt, and where thieves do not break through nor steal:<br>Matt. 6:21  For where your treasure is, there will your heart be also.<br>Matt. 6:22  The light of the body is the eye: if therefore thine eye be single, thy whole body shall be full of light.<br>Matt. 6:23  But if thine eye be evil, thy whole body shall be full of darkness. If therefore the light that is in thee be darkness, how great is that darkness!<br>Matt. 6:24  No man can serve two masters: for either he will hate the one, and love the other; or else he will hold to the one, and despise the other. Ye cannot serve God and mammon.<br>Matt. 6:25  Therefore I say unto you, Take no thought for your life, what ye shall eat, or what ye shall drink; nor yet for your body, what ye shall put on. Is not the life more than meat, and the body than raiment?<br>Matt. 6:26  Behold the fowls of the air: for they sow not, neither do they reap, nor gather into barns; yet your heavenly Father feedeth them. Are ye not much better than they?<br>Matt. 6:27  Which of you by taking thought can add one cubit unto his stature?<br>Matt. 6:28  And why take ye thought for raiment? | 1:39 | |

| | thy right hand doeth:.... | | |
| | 6:6 But thou, when thou prayest, enter into thy closet.... | | |
| | 6:9 ...Our Father which art in heaven, Hallowed be thy name.[18] | 4:44 | 4:54 |
| | 6:16 Moreover when ye fast.... | | |
| | 6:20 But lay up for yourselves treasures in heaven.... | | |
| | 6:24 No man can serve two masters.... | | |

[18] Matthew 6:9   After this manner therefore pray ye: Our Father which art in heaven, Hallowed be thy name. (*See Luke 11:2 for the second time Jesus taught the same prayer.*)

| Matthew | Mark | Important Events |
|---|---|---|
| Consider the lilies of the field, how they grow; they toil not, neither do they spin:<br>Matt. 6:29    And yet I say unto you, That even Solomon in all his glory was not arrayed like one of these.<br>Matt. 6:30   Wherefore, if God so clothe the grass of the field, which today is, and tomorrow is cast into the oven, shall he not much more clothe you, O ye of little faith?<br>Matt. 6:31   Therefore take no thought, saying, What shall we eat? or, What shall we drink? or, Wherewithal shall we be clothed?<br>Matt. 6:32   (For after all these things do the Gentiles seek:) for your heavenly Father knoweth that ye have need of all these things. | | |
| Matt. 6:33   But seek ye first the kingdom of God, and his righteousness; and all these things shall be added unto you.<br>Matt. 6:34    Take therefore no thought for the morrow: for the morrow shall take thought for the things of itself. Sufficient unto the day is the evil thereof. | | |
| Matt. 7:1   Judge not, that ye be not judged.<br>Matt. 7:2   For with what judgment ye judge, ye shall be judged: and with what measure ye mete, it shall be measured to you again.<br>Matt. 7:3   And why beholdest thou the mote that is in thy brother's eye, but considerest not the beam that is in thine own eye?<br>Matt. 7:4   Or how wilt thou say to thy brother, Let me pull out the mote out of thine eye; and, behold, a beam is in thine own eye?<br>Matt. 7:5   Thou hypocrite, first cast out the beam out of thine own eye; and then shalt thou see clearly to cast out the mote out of thy brother's eye.<br>Matt. 7:6   Give not that which is holy unto the dogs, neither cast ye your pearls before swine, lest they trample them under their feet, and turn again and rend you.<br>Matt. 7:7   Ask, and it shall be given you; seek, and ye shall find; knock, and it shall be opened unto you:<br>Matt. 7:8    For every one that asketh receiveth; and he that seeketh findeth; and to him that knocketh it shall be opened.<br>Matt. 7:9   Or what man is there of you, whom if his son ask bread, will he give him a stone?<br>Matt. 7:10    Or if he ask a fish, will he give him a serpent?<br>Matt. 7:11   If ye then, being evil, know how to give good gifts unto your children, how much more shall your Father which is in heaven give good things to them that ask him?<br>Matt. 7:12   Therefore all things whatsoever ye would that men should do to you, do ye even so to them: for this is the law and the prophets.<br>Matt. 7:13   Enter ye in at the strait gate: for wide is the gate, and broad is the way, that leadeth to destruction, and many there be which go in thereat:<br>Matt. 7:14   Because strait is the gate, and narrow is the way, which leadeth unto life, and few there be that find it.<br>Matt. 7:15   Beware of false prophets, which come to you in sheep's clothing, but inwardly they are ravening wolves.<br>Matt. 7:16   Ye shall know them by their fruits. Do men gather grapes of thorns, or figs of thistles? | 1:39 | |

| ministry year | Key Scriptures & Footnotes | Luke | John |
|---|---|---|---|
| | 6:33 But seek ye first the kingdom of God, and his righteousness; and all these things shall be added unto you.[19] | | |
| | | 4:44 | 4:54 |
| | 7:6...neither cast ye your pearls before swine.... | | |
| | 7:7 Ask, and it shall be given you; seek, and ye shall find; knock, and it shall be opened unto you: [20] | | |
| | 7:11...how much more shall your Father which is in heaven give good things to them that ask him? | | |
| | 7:13 Enter ye in at the strait gate.... | | |

[19] Matthew 6:33 But seek ye first the kingdom of God, and his righteousness; and all these things shall be added unto you. (*See Luke 12:31* But rather seek ye the kingdom of God; and all these things shall be added unto you.)
[20] Matthew 7:7 Ask, and it shall be given you; seek, and ye shall find; knock, and it shall be opened unto you: (*See Luke 11:9 for the second time that Jesus taught this*.)
[21] Matthew 7:24 ...I will liken him unto a wise man, which built his house upon a rock: (*See Luke 6:47-49 when Jesus teaches this again*.)

| Matthew | Mark | Important Events |
|---|---|---|
| Matt. 7:17   Even so every good tree bringeth forth good fruit; but a corrupt tree bringeth forth evil fruit.<br>Matt. 7:18   A good tree cannot bring forth evil fruit, neither can a corrupt tree bring forth good fruit.<br>Matt. 7:19   Every tree that bringeth not forth good fruit is hewn down, and cast into the fire.<br>Matt. 7:20   Wherefore by their fruits ye shall know them.<br>Matt. 7:21   Not every one that saith unto me, Lord, Lord, shall enter into the kingdom of heaven; but he that doeth the will of my Father which is in heaven.<br>Matt. 7:22   Many will say to me in that day, Lord, Lord, have we not prophesied in thy name? and in thy name have cast out devils? and in thy name done many wonderful works?<br>Matt. 7:23   And then will I profess unto them, I never knew you: depart from me, ye that work iniquity.<br>Matt. 7:24   Therefore whosoever heareth these sayings of mine, and doeth them, I will liken him unto a wise man, which built his house upon a rock:<br>Matt. 7:25   And the rain descended, and the floods came, and the winds blew, and beat upon that house; and it fell not: for it was founded upon a rock.<br>Matt. 7:26   And every one that heareth these sayings of mine, and doeth them not, shall be likened unto a foolish man, which built his house upon the sand:<br>Matt. 7:27   And the rain descended, and the floods came, and the winds blew, and beat upon that house; and it fell: and great was the fall of it.<br>Matt. 7:28   And it came to pass, when Jesus had ended these sayings, the people were astonished at his doctrine:<br>Matt. 7:29   For he taught them as one having authority, and not as the scribes. | | |
| Matt. 8:1   When he was come down from the mountain, great multitudes followed him. | 1:39 | |
| | | **Jesus taught from Simon's ship**<br>Luke 5:3<br><br>Map 26 |

| ministry year | Key Scriptures & Footnotes | Luke | John |
|---|---|---|---|
| | 7:17 Even so every good tree bringeth forth good fruit.... | | |
| | 7:23 And then will I profess unto them, I never knew you: depart from me, ye that work iniquity. 7:24...a wise man, [21] which built his house upon a rock.... | | |
| | 7:29...he taught them as one having authority.... | | |
| | 8:1 When he...down from the mountain,.... | | 4:54 |
| | 5:3 And he entered into one of the ships, which was Simon's.... 5:4...let down your nets for a draught. | Luke 5:1 And it came to pass, that, as the people pressed upon him to hear the word of God, he stood by the lake of Gennesaret, Luke 5:2 And saw two ships standing by the lake: but the fishermen were gone out of them, and were washing their nets. Luke 5:3 And he entered into one of the ships, which was Simon's, and prayed him that he would thrust out a little from the land. And he sat down, and taught the people out of the ship. Luke 5:4 Now when he had left speaking, he said unto Simon, Launch out into the deep, and let down your nets for a draught. Luke 5:5 And Simon answering said unto him, Master, we have toiled all the night, and have taken nothing: nevertheless at thy word I will let down the net. Luke 5:6 And when they had this done, they inclosed a great multitude of fishes: and their net brake. Luke 5:7 And they beckoned unto their partners, which were in the other ship, that they should come and help them. And they came, and filled both the ships, so that they began to sink. Luke 5:8 When Simon Peter saw it, he fell down at Jesus' knees, saying, Depart from me; for I am a sinful man, O Lord. Luke 5:9 For he was astonished, and all that were with him, at the draught of the fishes which they had taken: Luke 5:10a And so was also James, and John, the sons of Zebedee, which were partners with Simon. | |

| Matthew | Mark | Important Events |
|---|---|---|
| | | **They forsook all, and followed him.** Luke 5:11 Map 27 |
| Time Lock - Time Lock | Time Lock - Time Lock | |
| Matt. 8:2   And, behold, there came a leper and worshipped him, saying, Lord, if thou wilt, thou canst make me clean. Matt. 8:3  And Jesus put forth his hand, and touched him, saying, I will; be thou clean. And immediately his leprosy was cleansed. Matt. 8:4  And Jesus saith unto him, See thou tell no man; but go thy way, show thyself to the priest, and offer the gift that Moses commanded, for a testimony unto them. | Mark 1:40     And there came a leper to him, beseeching him, and kneeling down to him, and saying unto him, If thou wilt, thou canst make me clean. Mark 1:41    And Jesus, moved with compassion, put forth his hand, and touched him, and saith unto him, I will; be thou clean. Mark 1:42     And as soon as he had spoken, immediately the leprosy departed from him, and he was cleansed. Mark 1:43     And he straitly charged him, and forthwith sent him away; Mark 1:44  And saith unto him, See thou say nothing to any man: but go thy way, show thyself to the priest, and offer for thy cleansing those things which Moses commanded, for a testimony unto them. | **There came a leper to him** Matt. 8:2, Mark 1:40, & Luke 5:12 Map 28 |
| | Mark 1:45  But he went out, and began to publish it much, and to blaze abroad the matter, insomuch that Jesus could no more openly enter into the city, but was without in desert places: and they came to him from every quarter. | Map 29 |
| | | |
| Matt. 8:5     And when Jesus was entered into Capernaum, there came unto him a centurion, beseeching him, Matt. 8:6  And saying, Lord, my servant lieth at home sick of the palsy, grievously tormented. Matt. 8:7  And Jesus saith unto him, I will come and heal him. Matt. 8:8  The centurion answered and said, Lord, I am not worthy that thou shouldest come under my roof: but speak the word only, and my servant shall be healed. Matt. 8:9   For I am a man under authority, having soldiers under me: and I say to this man, Go, and he goeth; and to another, Come, and he cometh; and to my servant, Do this, and he doeth it. Matt. 8:10   When Jesus heard it, he marvelled, and said to them that followed, Verily I say unto you, I have not found so great faith, no, not in Israel. Matt. 8:11    And I say unto you, That many shall come from the east and west, and shall sit down with Abraham, and Isaac, and Jacob, in the kingdom of heaven. Matt. 8:12  But the children of the kingdom shall be cast out into outer darkness: there shall be weeping and gnashing of teeth. Matt. 8:13  And Jesus said unto the centurion, Go thy way; and as thou hast believed, so be it done unto thee. And his servant was healed in the selfsame hour. | | **1st time a centurion came to Jesus** Matt. 8:5 Map 30 |

| ministry year | Key Scriptures & Footnotes | Luke | John |
|---|---|---|---|
| | 5:10b...Fear not; from henceforth **thou shalt catch men.**[22] 5:11...they **forsook all**, and followed him.[23] | Luke 5:10b  And Jesus said unto Simon, Fear not; from henceforth thou shalt catch men. Luke 5:11  And when they had brought their ships to land, they forsook all, and followed him. | |
| | There came a leper to him | Time Lock - Time Lock | |
| | 5:12 ...when he was in a certain city,.... 8:2...there came a leper.... 8:3...I will: be thou clean.... | Luke 5:12  And it came to pass, when he was in a certain city, behold a man full of leprosy: who seeing Jesus fell on his face, and besought him, saying, Lord, if thou wilt, thou canst make me clean. Luke 5:13  And he put forth his hand, and touched him, saying, I will: be thou clean. And immediately the leprosy departed from him. Luke 5:14  And he charged him to tell no man: but go, and show thyself to the priest, and offer for thy cleansing, according as Moses commanded, for a testimony unto them. | 4:54 |
| | 1:45 ...but was without in desert places:.... | Luke 5:15  But so much the more went there a fame abroad of him: and great multitudes came together to hear, and to be healed by him of their infirmities. | |
| | 5:16... [24]withdrew...into the wilderness, and prayed | Luke 5:16  And he withdrew himself into the wilderness, and prayed | |
| | 8:5  And when Jesus was entered into Capernaum, there came unto him a centurion.... 8:6  And saying, Lord, my servant....[25] 8:8...but speak the word only.... 8:10  When Jesus heard it, he marvelled ...I have not found so great faith, no, not in Israel. | | |

---

[22] Luke 5:10b  And Jesus said unto Simon, Fear not; from henceforth thou shalt catch men. (*See Mark 1:17* ...I will make you to become fishers of men.)

[23] Luke 5:11  And when they had brought their ships to land, they forsook **all**, and followed him. (*See Mark 1:18* And straightway forsook **their nets**....)

[24] Luke 5:16  And he withdrew himself into the wilderness, and prayed. (And he *often* withdrew himself....  *"Often" is implied by the Greek.*)

[25] Matthew 8:6  And saying, Lord, my servant.... (*Some translations say* "**the child of me**" *and not* "my servant." *The Greek word translated* servant *in Matthew 8:6 is different from the Greek word translated* servant *in Luke 7:2.  For a second healing account see Luke 7:2* And a certain centurion's **servant**....)

| Matthew | Mark | Important Events |
|---|---|---|
| Matt. 8:14   And when Jesus was come into Peter's house, he saw his wife's mother laid, and sick of a fever.<br>Matt. 8:15   And he touched her hand, and the fever left her: and she arose, and ministered unto them. | | **2nd time Jesus healed Peter's wife's mother.**<br>Matt. 8:14 |
| Matt. 8:16   When the even was come, they brought unto him many that were possessed with devils: and he cast out the spirits with his word, and healed all that were sick:<br>Matt. 8:17   That it might be fulfilled which was spoken by Esaias the prophet, saying, Himself took our infirmities, and bare our sicknesses. | 1:45 | |
| Matt. 8:18   Now when Jesus saw great multitudes about him, he gave commandment to depart unto the other side. | | **Commandment to depart unto the other side**<br>Matt. 8:18 |
| Matt. 8:19   And a certain scribe came, and said unto him, Master, I will follow thee whithersoever thou goest.<br>Matt. 8:20   And Jesus saith unto him, The foxes have holes, and the birds of the air have nests; but the Son of man hath not where to lay his head.<br>Matt. 8:21   And another of his disciples said unto him, Lord, suffer me first to go and bury my father.<br>Matt. 8:22   But Jesus said unto him, Follow me; and let the dead bury their dead. | | |
| Matt. 8:23   And when he was entered into a ship, his disciples followed him.<br>Matt. 8:24   And, behold, there arose a great tempest in the sea, insomuch that the ship was covered with the waves: but he was asleep.<br>Matt. 8:25   And his disciples came to him, and awoke him, saying, Lord, save us: we perish.<br>Matt. 8:26   And he saith unto them, Why are ye fearful, O ye of little faith? Then he arose, and rebuked the winds and the sea; and there was a great calm.<br>Matt. 8:27   But the men marvelled, saying, What manner of man is this, that even the winds and the sea obey him! | 1:45 | **1st great tempest in the sea, and there was a great calm.**<br>Matt. 8:24<br><br>Map 31 |
| Matt. 8:28   And when he was come to the other side into the country of the Gergesenes, there met him two possessed with devils, coming out of the tombs, exceeding fierce, so that no man might pass by that way.<br>Matt. 8:29   And, behold, they cried out, saying, What have we to do with thee, Jesus, thou Son of God? art thou come hither to torment us before the time?<br>Matt. 8:30   And there was a good way off from them an herd of many swine feeding.<br>Matt. 8:31   So the devils besought him, saying, If thou cast us out, suffer us to go away into the herd of swine.<br>Matt. 8:32   And he said unto them, Go. And when they were come out, they went into the herd of swine: and, behold, the whole herd of swine ran violently down a steep place into the sea, and perished in the waters.<br>Matt. 8:33   And they that kept them fled, and went their ways into the city, and told every thing, and | | **Gergesenes there met him two possessed with devils.**<br>Matt. 8:28<br><br>Map 32 |

| ministry year | Key Scriptures & Footnotes | Luke | John |
|---|---|---|---|
| | 8:14... Jesus was come into Peter's house, he saw.... <br> 8:15 And he touched her hand, and the fever left her:....[26] | | |
| | 8:16...they brought unto him many that were possessed with devils...and healed all that were sick: | 5:16 | 4:54 |
| | 8:18...gave commandment to depart unto the other side. | | |
| | 8:19 And a certain scribe came.... <br> 8:20 And Jesus saith ... The foxes have holes ... but the Son of man hath not where to lay his head.[27] <br> 8:22...Follow me; and let the dead bury their dead. | | |
| | 8:23 And when he was entered into a ship,.... <br> Matt. 8:24 And, behold, there arose a great tempest in the sea,....[28] <br> 8:25 ...saying, Lord, save us: we perish. <br> 8:26...Why are ye fearful, O ye of **little faith**?.... | 5:16 | 4:54 |
| | 8:28...the country of the Gergesenes.... there met him two possessed with devils,.... <br><br> 8:30 And there was a good way off from them an herd of many swine....[29] <br><br> 8:32 And he said unto them, Go..... | | |

---

[26] Matthew 8:15 And he touched her hand, and the fever left her: and she arose, and ministered unto them. (*This is the second time Jesus healed her. See Mark 1:31 and Luke 4:39 for the first time.*)

[27] Matthew 8:20 And Jesus saith unto him, The foxes have holes, and the birds of the air have nests; but the Son of man hath not where to lay his head. (*Two years later in Luke 9:58 Jesus said "Foxes have holes, and the birds of the air have nests; but the Son of man hath not where to lay his head."*)

[28] Matthew 8:24 And, behold, there arose a great tempest in the sea.... (*This is the first storm at sea. See Mark 4:35 & Luke 8:22 for the second storm at sea.*)

[29] Matthew 8:30 And there was a good way off from them an herd of many swine feeding. (*Compare with Luke 8:32 and Mark 5:11 Now there was there nigh unto the mountains a great herd of swine feeding.*)

| Matthew | Mark | Important Events |
|---|---|---|
| what was befallen to the possessed of the devils.<br>Matt. 8:34 And, behold, the whole city came out to meet Jesus: and when they saw him, they besought him that he would depart out of their coasts. | | |
| Matt. 9:1 And he entered into a ship, and passed over, and came into his own city | Mark 2:1 And again he entered into Capernaum after some days; and it was noised that he was in the house. | Map 33 |
| *Time Lock - Time Lock* | *Time Lock - Time Lock* | |
| Matt. 9:2 And, behold, they brought to him a man sick of the palsy, lying on a bed: and Jesus seeing their faith said unto the sick of the palsy; Son, be of good cheer; thy sins be forgiven thee.<br>Matt. 9:3 And, behold, certain of the scribes said within themselves, This man blasphemeth.<br>Matt. 9:4 And Jesus knowing their thoughts said, Wherefore think ye evil in your hearts?<br>Matt. 9:5 For whether is easier, to say, Thy sins be forgiven thee; or to say, Arise, and walk?<br>Matt. 9:6 But that ye may know that the Son of man hath power on earth to forgive sins, (then saith he to the sick of the palsy,) Arise, take up thy bed, and go unto thine house.<br>Matt. 9:7 And he arose, and departed to his house.<br>Matt. 9:8 But when the multitudes saw it, they marvelled, and glorified God, which had given such power unto men. | Mark 2:2 And straightway many were gathered together, insomuch that there was no room to receive them, no, not so much as about the door: and he preached the word unto them.<br>Mark 2:3 And they come unto him, bringing one sick of the palsy, which was borne of four.<br>Mark 2:4 And when they could not come nigh unto him for the press, they uncovered the roof where he was: and when they had broken it up, they let down the bed wherein the sick of the palsy lay.<br>Mark 2:5 When Jesus saw their faith, he said unto the sick of the palsy, Son, thy sins be forgiven thee.<br>Mark 2:6 But there were certain of the scribes sitting there, and reasoning in their hearts,<br>Mark 2:7 Why doth this man thus speak blasphemies? who can forgive sins but God only?<br>Mark 2:8 And immediately when Jesus perceived in his spirit that they so reasoned within themselves, he said unto them, Why reason ye these things in your hearts?<br>Mark 2:9 Whether is it easier to say to the sick of the palsy, Thy sins be forgiven thee; or to say, Arise, and take up thy bed, and walk?<br>Mark 2:10 But that ye may know that the Son of man hath power on earth to forgive sins, (he saith to the sick of the palsy,)<br>Mark 2:11 I say unto thee, Arise, and take up thy bed, and go thy way into thine house.<br>Mark 2:12 And immediately he arose, took up the bed, and went forth before them all; insomuch that they were all amazed, and glorified God, saying, We never saw it on this fashion. | **One sick of the palsy & they uncovered the roof**<br>Matt. 9:2, Mark 2:2, & Luke 5:17 |
| | Mark 2:13 And he went forth again by the sea side; and all the multitude resorted unto him, and he taught them. | |
| *Time Lock - Time Lock* | *Time Lock - Time Lock* | |
| Matt. 9:9 And as Jesus passed forth from thence, he saw a man, named Matthew, sitting at the receipt of custom: and he saith unto him, Follow me. And he arose, and followed him. | Mark 2:14 And as he passed by, he saw Levi the son of Alphaeus sitting at the receipt of custom, and said unto him, Follow me. And he arose and followed him. | **Matthew, Follow Me**<br>Matt. 9:9, Mark 2:14, & Luke 5:27<br><br>Map 34 |
| Matt. 9:10 And it came to pass, as Jesus sat at meat in the house, behold, many publicans and sinners came and sat down with him and his disciples.<br>Matt. 9:11 And when the Pharisees saw it, they said unto his disciples, Why eateth your Master with publicans and sinners?<br>Matt. 9:12 But when Jesus heard that, he said unto them, They that be whole need not a physician, but they that are sick. | Mark 2:15 And it came to pass, that, as Jesus sat at meat in his house, many publicans and sinners sat also together with Jesus and his disciples: for there were many, and they followed him.<br>Mark 2:16 And when the scribes and Pharisees saw him eat with publicans and sinners, they said unto his disciples, How is it that he eateth and drinketh with publicans and sinners?<br>Mark 2:17a When Jesus heard it, he saith unto them, They that are whole have no need of the physician, but they that are sick: | |
| Matt. 9:13a But go ye and learn what that meaneth, I will have mercy, and not sacrifice:. | | **I will have mercy and not sacrifice**<br>Matt. 9:13a |
| Matt. 9:13b for I am not come to call the righteous, but sinners to repentance | Mark 2:17b I came not to call the righteous, but sinners to repentance. | |
| Matt. 9:14 Then came to him the disciples of John, saying, Why do we and the Pharisees fast oft, but thy | Mark 2:18 And the disciples of John and of the Pharisees used to fast: and they come and say unto | **Why do the disciples of** |

| ministry year | Key Scriptures & Footnotes | Luke | John |
|---|---|---|---|
| | 8:34...they besought him that he would depart out of their coasts. | | |
| | 9:1...his own city. 2:1...Capernaum... in the house.... | | |
| | One sick of palsy. | Time Lock - Time Lock | |
| | 2:4...they uncovered the roof where he was....<br><br><br><br><br><br><br><br><br><br><br><br><br><br><br><br><br>2:12...And immediately he rose up before them.... | Luke 5:17  And it came to pass on a certain day, as he was teaching, that there were Pharisees and doctors of the law sitting by, which were come out of every town of Galilee, and Judaea, and Jerusalem: and the power of the Lord was present to heal them.<br>Luke 5:18  And, behold, men brought in a bed a man which was taken with a palsy: and they sought means to bring him in, and to lay him before him.<br>Luke 5:19  And when they could not find by what way they might bring him in because of the multitude, they went upon the housetop, and let him down through the tiling with his couch into the midst before Jesus.<br>Luke 5:20  And when he saw their faith, he said unto him, Man, thy sins are forgiven thee.<br>Luke 5:21  And the scribes and the Pharisees began to reason, saying, Who is this which speaketh blasphemies? Who can forgive sins, but God alone?<br>Luke 5:22  But when Jesus perceived their thoughts, he answering said unto them, What reason ye in your hearts?<br>Luke 5:23  Whether is easier, to say, Thy sins be forgiven thee; or to say, Rise up and walk?<br>Luke 5:24  But that ye may know that the Son of man hath power upon earth to forgive sins (he said unto the sick of the palsy,) I say unto thee, Arise, and take up thy couch, and go into thine house.<br>Luke 5:25  And immediately he rose up before them, and took up that whereon he lay, and departed to his own house, glorifying God.<br>Luke 5:26  And they were all amazed, and they glorified God, and were filled with fear, saying, We have seen strange things today. | 4:54 |
| | 12:13  And he went forth again by the sea side.... | | |
| | Matthew called | Time Lock - Time Lock | |
| | 9:9...Matthew, sitting at the receipt of custom: and he saith unto him, Follow me. | Luke 5:27  And after these things he went forth, and saw a publican, named Levi, sitting at the receipt of custom: and he said unto him, Follow me.<br>Luke 5:28  And he left all, rose up, and followed him. | 4:54 |
| | Luke 5:29  And Levi made him a great feast in his own house....<br><br><br>5:31...They that are whole need not a physician;.... | Luke 5:29  And Levi made him a great feast in his own house: and there was a great company of publicans and of others that sat down with them.<br>Luke 5:30  But their scribes and Pharisees murmured against his disciples, saying, Why do ye eat and drink with publicans and sinners?<br>Luke 5:31  And Jesus answering said unto them, They that are whole need not a physician; but they that are sick. | |
| | | Luke 5:32  I came not to call the righteous, but sinners to repentance. | |
| | 5:33... Why do the disciples of John fast | Luke 5:33  And they said unto him, Why do the disciples of John fast often, and make prayers, and | 4:54 |

| Matthew | Mark | Important Events |
|---|---|---|
| disciples fast not?<br>Matt. 9:15 And Jesus said unto them, Can the children of the bridechamber mourn, as long as the bridegroom is with them? but the days will come, when the bridegroom shall be taken from them, and then shall they fast.<br>Matt. 9:16 No man putteth a piece of new cloth unto an old garment, for that which is put in to fill it up taketh from the garment, and the rent is made worse.<br>Matt. 9:17 Neither do men put new wine into old bottles: else the bottles break, and the wine runneth out, and the bottles perish: but they put new wine into new bottles, and both are preserved. | him, Why do the disciples of John and of the Pharisees fast, but thy disciples fast not?<br>Mark 2:19 And Jesus said unto them, Can the children of the bridechamber fast, while the bridegroom is with them? as long as they have the bridegroom with them, they cannot fast.<br>Mark 2:20 But the days will come, when the bridegroom shall be taken away from them, and then shall they fast in those days.<br>Mark 2:21 No man also seweth a piece of new cloth on an old garment: else the new piece that filled it up taketh away from the old, and the rent is made worse.<br>Mark 2:22 And no man putteth new wine into old bottles: else the new wine doth burst the bottles, and the wine is spilled, and the bottles will be marred: but new wine must be put into new bottles. | **John fast often?**<br>Matt. 9:14, Mark 2:18, & Luke 5:33 |
| Time Lock & Time Clue | Time Lock - Time Lock | Clue - While he spake |
| Matt. 9:18 While he spake these things unto them, behold, there came a certain ruler, and worshipped him, saying, My daughter is even now dead: but come and lay thy hand upon her, and she shall live.<br>Matt. 9:19 And Jesus arose, and followed him, and so did his disciples.<br>Matt. 9:20 And, behold, a woman, which was diseased with an issue of blood twelve years, came behind him, and touched the hem of his garment:<br>Matt. 9:21 For she said within herself, If I may but touch his garment, I shall be whole.<br>Matt. 9:22 But Jesus turned him about, and when he saw her, he said, Daughter, be of good comfort; thy faith hath made thee whole. And the woman was made whole from that hour. | | **A certain ruler and the 1st woman with an issue of blood twelve years**<br>Matt. 9:18<br><br>Map 35 |
| Matt. 9:23 And when Jesus came into the ruler's house, and saw the minstrels and the people making a noise,<br>Matt. 9:24 He said unto them, Give place: for the maid is not dead, but sleepeth. And they laughed him to scorn.<br>Matt. 9:25 But when the people were put forth, he went in, and took her by the hand, and the maid arose.<br>Matt. 9:26 And the fame hereof went abroad into all that land. | | |
| Matt. 9:27 And when Jesus departed thence, two blind men followed him, crying, and saying, Thou Son of David, have mercy on us.<br>Matt. 9:28 And when he was come into the house, the blind men came to him: and Jesus saith unto them, Believe ye that I am able to do this? They said unto him, Yea, Lord.<br>Matt. 9:29 Then touched he their eyes, saying, According to your faith be it unto you.<br>Matt. 9:30 And their eyes were opened; and Jesus straitly charged them, saying, See that no man know it.<br>Matt. 9:31 But they, when they were departed, spread abroad his fame in all that country. | | **Two blind men healed**<br>Matt. 9:29 |
| Matt. 9:32 As they went out, behold, they brought to him a dumb man possessed with a devil. | | **The dumb spake**<br>Matt. 9:33 |

| ministry year | Key Scriptures & Footnotes | Luke | John |
|---|---|---|---|

| | often,.... | likewise the disciples of the Pharisees; but thine eat and drink? | |

Luke 5:34  And he said unto them, Can ye make the children of the bridechamber fast, while the bridegroom is with them?

Luke 5:35  But the days will come, when the bridegroom shall be taken away from them, and then shall they fast in those days.

Luke 5:36  And he spake also a parable unto them; No man putteth a piece of a new garment upon an old; if otherwise, then both the new maketh a rent, and the piece that was taken out of the new agreeth not with the old.

Luke 5:37  And no man putteth new wine into old bottles; else the new wine will burst the bottles, and be spilled, and the bottles shall perish.

Luke 5:38  But new wine must be put into new bottles; and both are preserved.

Luke 5:39  No man also having drunk old wine straightway desireth new: for he saith, The old is better.

New wine in new bottles.

Time Lock - Time Lock

9:18  While he spake these things unto them, behold, there came a certain ruler[30], and worshipped him, saying, My daughter is even now dead....

9:20  And, behold, a woman, which was diseased with an issue of blood twelve years[31], came behind him, and touched the hem of his garment:

9:27...**two blind men** followed him....

9:28  And when he was come into **the house**, the blind men came to him....

9:29...According to your faith be it unto you.

9:30  And their eyes were opened....

9:32  As they went out, behold, they brought to

---

[30] Matthew 9:18  While he spake these things unto them, behold, there came a certain ruler, and worshipped him, saying, My daughter **is even now dead**.... (*This is not the same event found in Mark 5:23 and Luke 8:42. In that event, Jairus' daughter was* **"at the point of death"** *but she was not dead when Jairus first came to Jesus for help.*)

[31] Matthew 9:20  And, behold, a woman, which was diseased with an issue of blood twelve years.... (*By time sequence, this woman is not the same as the woman found in Mark 5:25 and Luke 8:43.*)

28

| Matthew | Mark | Important Events |
|---|---|---|
| Matt. 9:33   And when the devil was cast out, the dumb spake: and the multitudes marvelled, saying, It was never so seen in Israel.<br>Matt. 9:34   But the Pharisees said, He casteth out devils through the prince of the devils. | | |
| Matt. 9:35   And Jesus went about all the cities and villages, teaching in their synagogues, and preaching the gospel of the kingdom, and healing every sickness and every disease among the people.<br>Matt. 9:36  But when he saw the multitudes, he was moved with compassion on them, because they fainted, and were scattered abroad, as sheep having no shepherd.<br>Matt. 9:37    Then saith he unto his disciples, The harvest truly is plenteous, but the labourers are few;<br>Matt. 9:38  Pray ye therefore the Lord of the harvest, that he will send forth labourers into his harvest. | | **2nd time Jesus went about all the cities and villages, teaching in their synagogues**<br>Matt. 9:35<br><br>Map 36 |
| | | **2nd Passover**<br>John 5:1<br><br>Map 37 |
| 9:38 | 2:22 | **Rise take up thy bed and walk**<br>John 5:8 |

| ministry year | Key Scriptures & Footnotes | Luke | John |
|---|---|---|---|
| | him a dumb man.... 9:33 ... It was never so seen in Israel.[32] 9:34 But the Pharisees said,....[33] | | |
| | 9:35 And Jesus went about **all** the cities and villages, teaching in their synagogues, and preaching...and healing.... 9:38 Pray ye therefore the Lord of the harvest, that he will send forth labourers into his harvest. | | |
| | Time Clue | | Time Clue - See the 3rd footnote for John 5:1 |
| | 5:1 After this[34] there was a feast[35] of the Jews; and Jesus went up to Jerusalem.[36] | | John 5:1 After this there was a feast of the Jews; and Jesus went up to Jerusalem. John 5:2 Now there is at Jerusalem by the sheep market a pool, which is called in the Hebrew tongue Bethesda, having five porches. John 5:3 In these lay a great multitude of impotent folk, of blind, halt, withered, waiting for the moving of the water. |
| | 5:4 For an angel went down at a certain season into the pool.... 5:5 And a certain man.... | | John 5:4 For an angel went down at a certain season into the pool, and troubled the water: whosoever then first after the troubling of the water stepped in was made whole of whatsoever disease he had. John 5:5 And a certain man was there, which had an infirmity thirty and eight years. John 5:6 When Jesus saw him lie, and knew that he had been now a long time in that case, he saith unto him, Wilt thou be made whole? John 5:7 The impotent man answered him, Sir, I have no man, when the water is troubled, to put me into the pool: but while I am coming, another steppeth down before me. |
| | 5:8...Rise, take up thy bed, and walk. | 5:39 | John 5:8 Jesus saith unto him, Rise, take up thy bed, and walk. John 5:9 And immediately the man was made whole, and took up his bed, and walked: and on the same day was the sabbath. John 5:10 The Jews therefore said unto him that was cured, It is the sabbath day: it is not lawful for thee to carry thy bed. John 5:11 He answered them, He that made me whole, the same said unto me, Take up thy bed, and walk. John 5:12 Then asked they him, What man is that which said unto thee, Take up thy bed, and walk? John 5:13 And he that was healed wist not who it was: for Jesus had conveyed himself away, a multitude being in that place. John 5:14 Afterward Jesus findeth him in the temple, and said unto him, Behold, thou art made whole: sin no more, lest a worse thing come unto thee. |

[32] Matthew 9:33 ...and the multitudes marvelled, saying, **It was never so seen in Israel.** (*This statement was made during Jesus' first year of ministry.*)

[33] Matthew 9:34 But the Pharisees said, He casteth out devils through the prince of the devils. (*See Matthew 12:24 and John 8:48 for similar events.*)

[34] John 5:1 **After this** there was a feast of the Jews.... (*John left Jesus in Cana and returned to Capernaum with the nobleman. This explains how John knew what happened to the nobleman's family recorded in John 4:51-54. Jesus went to Nazareth before going to Capernaum in Luke 4:16-31a. John rejoined Jesus, for a time, when he "left his father Zebedee in the ship" in Mark 1:20. John permanently joined Jesus when he "forsook* **all***, and followed him" in* Luke 5:11.)

[35] John 5:1 After this there was a **feast of the Jews**.... (*This is the first account from John after he "forsook* **all***, and followed him" in Luke 5:11. This was probably ministry Passover #2; however, the "feast of the Jews" could have been the feast of Trumpets in the fall or the feast of Dedication in the winter before ministry Passover #2. The first ministry Passover is found in John 2:13, the third in John 6:4, and the fourth in John 11:55.*)

[36] John 5:1 After this there was a feast of the Jews; and Jesus went **up to Jerusalem.** (***Time Clue** - The time of Luke 6:1 and Mark 2:23 is "the second sabbath after the first...." Therefore, Luke 6:1 and Mark 2:23 are found following the Passover of John 5:1.*)

| Matthew | Mark | Important Events |
|---|---|---|
| | | |
| | | **The Jews sought to slay Jesus, because he had done these things on the sabbath day.** John 5:16 |
| 9:38 | 2:22 | |

| ministry year | Key Scriptures & Footnotes | Luke | John |
|---|---|---|---|
| | | | John 5:15  The man departed, and told the Jews that it was Jesus, which had made him whole. |
| | 5:16...he had done these things on the sabbath day. | | John 5:16    And therefore did the Jews persecute Jesus, and sought to slay him, because he had done these things on the sabbath day.<br>John 5:17    But Jesus answered them, My Father worketh hitherto, and I work.<br>John 5:18  Therefore the Jews sought the more to kill him, because he not only had broken the sabbath, but said also that God was his Father, making himself equal with God. |
| | 5:19  Then answered Jesus and said unto them, Verily, verily, I say unto you, The Son can do nothing of himself, but what he seeth the Father do:.... | 5:39 | John 5:19  Then answered Jesus and said unto them, Verily, verily, I say unto you, The Son can do nothing of himself, but what he seeth the Father do: for what things soever he doeth, these also doeth the Son likewise.<br>John 5:20  For the Father loveth the Son, and showeth him all things that himself doeth: and he will show him greater works than these, that ye may marvel.<br>John 5:21  For as the Father raiseth up the dead, and quickeneth them; even so the Son quickeneth whom he will.<br>John 5:22   For the Father judgeth no man, but hath committed all judgment unto the Son:<br>John 5:23  That all men should honour the Son, even as they honour the Father. He that honoureth not the Son honoureth not the Father which hath sent him. |
| | 5:24  He that heareth my word, and believeth on him that sent me, hath everlasting life....<br>5:25...The hour is coming, and now is, when the dead shall hear the voice of the Son of God:.... | | John 5:24   Verily, verily, I say unto you, He that heareth my word, and believeth on him that sent me, hath everlasting life, and shall not come into condemnation; but is passed from death unto life.<br>John 5:25  Verily, verily, I say unto you, The hour is coming, and now is, when the dead shall hear the voice of the Son of God: and they that hear shall live.<br>John 5:26  For as the Father hath life in himself; so hath he given to the Son to have life in himself;<br>John 5:27   And hath given him authority to execute judgment also, because he is the Son of man.<br>John 5:28  Marvel not at this: for the hour is coming, in the which all that are in the graves shall hear his voice,<br>John 5:29  And shall come forth; they that have done good, unto the resurrection of life; and they that have done evil, unto the resurrection of damnation.<br>John 5:30   I can of mine own self do nothing: as I hear, I judge: and my judgment is just; because I seek not mine own will, but the will of the Father which hath sent me.<br>John 5:31  If I bear witness of myself, my witness is not true.<br>John 5:32    There is another that beareth witness of me; and I know that the witness which he witnesseth of me is true.<br>John 5:33  Ye sent unto John, and he bare witness unto the truth.<br>John 5:34  But I receive not testimony from man: but these things I say, that ye might be saved.<br>John 5:35  He was a burning and a shining light: and ye were willing for a season to rejoice in his light.<br>John 5:36   But I have greater witness than that of John: for the works which the Father hath given me to finish, the same works that I do, bear witness of me, that the Father hath sent me.<br>John 5:37   And the Father himself, which hath sent me, hath borne witness of me. Ye have neither heard his voice at any time, nor seen his shape.<br>John 5:38  And ye have not his word abiding in you: for whom he hath sent, him ye believe not.<br>John 5:39  Search the scriptures; for in them ye think ye have eternal life: and they are they which testify of me. |

| Matthew | Mark | Important Events |
|---------|------|------------------|
| | | |
| | Time Lock - Time Lock | |
| 9:38 | Mark 2:23 And it came to pass, that he went through the corn fields on the sabbath day; and his disciples began, as they went, to pluck the ears of corn.<br>Mark 2:24 And the Pharisees said unto him, Behold, why do they on the sabbath day that which is not lawful?<br>Mark 2:25 And he said unto them, Have ye never read what David did, when he had need, and was an hungered, he, and they that were with him?<br>Mark 2:26 How he went into the house of God in the days of Abiathar the high priest, and did eat the showbread, which is not lawful to eat but for the priests, and gave also to them which were with him?<br>Mark 2:27 And he said unto them, The sabbath was made for man, and not man for the sabbath:<br>Mark 2:28 Therefore the Son of man is Lord also of the sabbath. | **1st trip through the corn field**<br>Mark 2:23 & Luke 6:1<br><br>Map 38 |
| | Mark 3:1 And he entered again into the synagogue; and there was a man there which had a withered hand.<br>Mark 3:2 And they watched him, whether he would heal him on the sabbath day; that they might accuse him.<br>Mark 3:3 And he saith unto the man which had the withered hand, Stand forth.<br>Mark 3:4 And he saith unto them, Is it lawful to do good on the sabbath days, or to do evil? to save life, or to kill? But they held their peace.<br>Mark 3:5 And when he had looked round about on them with anger, being grieved for the hardness of their hearts, he saith unto the man, Stretch forth thine hand. And he stretched it out: and his hand was restored whole as the other.<br>Mark 3:6 And the Pharisees went forth, and straightway took counsel with the Herodians against him, how they might destroy him. | **1st man healed of a withered hand.**<br>Mark 3:1 & Luke 6:6<br><br>Map 39 |
| | Mark 3:7 But Jesus withdrew himself with his disciples to the sea: and a great multitude from Galilee followed him, and from Judaea,<br>Mark 3:8 And from Jerusalem, and from Idumaea, and from beyond Jordan; and they about Tyre and Sidon, a great multitude, when they had heard what great things he did, came unto him.<br>Mark 3:9 And he spake to his disciples, that a small ship should wait on him because of the multitude, lest they should throng him.<br>Mark 3:10 For he had healed many; insomuch that | Map 40 |

31

| | | | |
|---|---|---|---|
| | | | John 5:40  And ye will not come to me, that ye might have life.<br>John 5:41  I receive not honour from men.<br>John 5:42  But I know you, that ye have not the love of God in you.<br>John 5:43  I am come in my Father's name, and ye receive me not: if another shall come in his own name, him ye will receive.<br>John 5:44   How can ye believe, which receive honour one of another, and seek not the honour that cometh from God only?<br>John 5:45  Do not think that I will accuse you to the Father: there is one that accuseth you, even Moses, in whom ye trust.<br>John 5:46   For had ye believed Moses, ye would have believed me: for he wrote of me.<br>John 5:47   But if ye believe not his writings, how shall ye believe my words? |
| | Through corn fields | Time Lock - Time Lock | Time Clue - The first harvest after the passover. |
| | 6:1...on the second sabbath after the first, that he went through the corn fields;....[37]<br><br>2:25  And he said unto them, Have ye never read what David did,.... | Luke 6:1   And it came to pass on the second sabbath after the first, that he went through the corn fields; and his disciples plucked the ears of corn, and did eat, rubbing them in their hands.<br>Luke 6:2   And certain of the Pharisees said unto them, Why do ye that which is not lawful to do on the sabbath days?<br>Luke 6:3  And Jesus answering them said, Have ye not read so much as this, what David did, when himself was an hungered, and they which were with him.<br>Luke 6:4  How he went into the house of God, and did take and eat the showbread, and gave also to them that were with him; which it is not lawful to eat but for the priests alone?<br>Luke 6:5   And he said unto them, That the Son of man is Lord also of the sabbath. | |
| | 3:1  And he entered again into the synagogue....[38]<br>6:6...another sabbath... and there was a man whose right hand was withered.<br><br>3:4  And he saith unto them, Is it lawful to do good on the sabbath days....<br><br>6:10...he said unto the man, Stretch forth thy hand..... | Luke 6:6   And it came to pass also on another sabbath, that he entered into the synagogue and taught: and there was a man whose right hand was withered.<br>Luke 6:7   And the scribes and Pharisees watched him, whether he would heal on the sabbath day; that they might find an accusation against him.<br>Luke 6:8  But he knew their thoughts, and said to the man which had the withered hand, Rise up, and stand forth in the midst. And he arose and stood forth.<br>Luke 6:9   Then said Jesus unto them, I will ask you one thing; Is it lawful on the sabbath days to do good, or to do evil? to save life, or to destroy it?<br>Luke 6:10   And looking round about upon them all, he said unto the man, Stretch forth thy hand. And he did so: and his hand was restored whole as the other.<br>Luke 6:11   And they were filled with madness; and communed one with another what they might do to Jesus. | |
| | 3:7  But Jesus withdrew himself with his disciples to the sea....<br><br><br>3:9  And he spake to his disciples, that a small ship should wait on him.... | | |

[37]Luke 6:1   And it came to pass on the second sabbath after the first, that he went through the corn fields; and his disciples plucked the ears of corn, and did eat, rubbing them in their hands. (*This is the first time the disciples "plucked the ears of corn." This early harvest could have been a barley harvest just after the second Passover found in John 5:1.  See Matthew 12:1-8 for the second time the disciples "plucked the ears of corn."*)

[38] Mark 3:1   And he entered again into the synagogue; and there was a man there which had a withered hand. (*This was the first man with a withered hand.  See Matthew 12:9 for the second man with a withered hand.*)

| Matthew | Mark | Important Events |
|---|---|---|
| | they pressed upon him for to touch him, as many as had plagues.<br>Mark 3:11  And unclean spirits, when they saw him, fell down before him, and cried, saying, Thou art the Son of God.<br>Mark 3:12   And he straitly charged them that they should not make him known. | |
| 9:38 | Mark 3:13a  And he goeth up into a mountain, | |
| | Time Lock - Time Lock | |
| | Mark 3:13b   and calleth unto him whom he would: and they came unto him.<br>Mark 3:14   And he ordained twelve, that they should be with him, and that he might send them forth to preach,<br>Mark 3:15   And to have power to heal sicknesses, and to cast out devils:<br>Mark 3:16  And Simon he surnamed Peter;<br>Mark 3:17  And James the son of Zebedee, and John the brother of James; and he surnamed them Boanerges, which is, The sons of thunder:<br>Mark 3:18        And Andrew, and Philip, and Bartholomew, and Matthew, and Thomas, and James the son of Alphaeus, and Thaddaeus, and Simon the Canaanite,<br>Mark 3:19  And Judas Iscariot, which also betrayed him: and they went into an house. | **He ordained twelve**<br>Mark 3:14 & Luke 6:13<br><br>Map 41 |
| | Time Lock - Time Lock | |
| | | Map 42 |
| 9:38 | | **Blessed be the poor for yours is the kingdom of heaven**<br>Luke 6:20 |

| ministry year | Key Scriptures & Footnotes | Luke | John |
|---|---|---|---|
| | 6:12...into a mountain to pray, and continued all night in prayer to God. | Luke 6:12  And it came to pass in those days, that he went out into a mountain to pray, and continued all night in prayer to God. | 5:47 |
| | He chose twelve. | Time Lock - Time Lock | |
| | 6:13...and of them he chose twelve.... | Luke 6:13  And when it was day, he called unto him his disciples: and of them he chose twelve, whom also he named apostles;<br>Luke 6:14  Simon, (whom he also named Peter,) and Andrew his brother, James and John, Philip and Bartholomew,<br>Luke 6:15  Matthew and Thomas, James the son of Alphaeus, and Simon called Zelotes,<br>Luke 6:16  And Judas the brother of James, and Judas Iscariot, which also was the traitor. | |
| | He chose twelve. | Time Lock - Time Lock | |
| | 6:17...and stood in the plain,.... | Luke 6:17  And he came down with them, and stood in the plain, and the company of his disciples, and a great multitude of people out of all Judaea and Jerusalem, and from the sea coast of Tyre and Sidon, which came to hear him, and to be healed of their diseases;<br>Luke 6:18  And they that were vexed with unclean spirits: and they were healed. | |
| | 6:19... there went virtue out of him, and healed them all. | Luke 6:19  And the whole multitude sought to touch him: for there went virtue out of him, and healed them all. | |
| | 6:20  And he lifted up his eyes on his disciples, and said, Blessed be ye poor: for yours is the kingdom of God.[39] | Luke 6:20  And he lifted up his eyes on his disciples, and said, Blessed be ye poor: for yours is the kingdom of God.<br>Luke 6:21  Blessed are ye that hunger now: for ye shall be filled. Blessed are ye that weep now: for ye shall laugh.<br>Luke 6:22  Blessed are ye, when men shall hate you, and when they shall separate you from their company, and shall reproach you, and cast out your name as evil, for the Son of man's sake.<br>Luke 6:23  Rejoice ye in that day, and leap for joy: for, behold, your reward is great in heaven: for in the like manner did their fathers unto the prophets.<br>Luke 6:24  But woe unto you that are rich! for ye have received your consolation.<br>Luke 6:25  Woe unto you that are full! for ye shall hunger. Woe unto you that laugh now! for ye shall mourn and weep.<br>Luke 6:26  Woe unto you, when all men shall speak well of you! for so did their fathers to the false prophets.<br>Luke 6:27  But I say unto you which hear, Love your enemies, do good to them which hate you,<br>Luke 6:28  Bless them that curse you, and pray for them which despitefully use you.<br>Luke 6:29  And unto him that smiteth thee on the one cheek offer also the other; and him that taketh away thy cloak forbid not to take thy coat also.<br>Luke 6:30  Give to every man that asketh of thee; | 5:47 |

[39] Luke 6:20  ...Blessed be ye poor: for yours is the kingdom of God. (*See Matthew 5:3*  Blessed are the poor in spirit....)

| Matthew | Mark | Important Events |
|---------|------|------------------|
| | | |

Time Clue - Time Clue

| Matthew | Mark | Important Events |
|---------|------|------------------|
| 9:38 | Mark 3:20   And the multitude cometh together again, so that they could not so much as eat bread.<br>Mark 3:21   And when his friends heard of it, they went out to lay hold on him: for they said, He is | **How can Satan cast out Satan?**<br>Mark 3:23 |

and of him that taketh away thy goods ask them not again.

Luke 6:31   And as ye would that men should do to you, do ye also to them likewise.

Luke 6:32   For if ye love them which love you, what thank have ye? for sinners also love those that love them.

Luke 6:33   And if ye do good to them which do good to you, what thank have ye? for sinners also do even the same.

Luke 6:34   And if ye lend to them of whom ye hope to receive, what thank have ye? for sinners also lend to sinners, to receive as much again.

Luke 6:35   But love ye your enemies, and do good, and lend, hoping for nothing again; and your reward shall be great, and ye shall be the children of the Highest: for he is kind unto the unthankful and to the evil.

Luke 6:36   Be ye therefore merciful, as your Father also is merciful.

Luke 6:37   Judge not, and ye shall not be judged: condemn not, and ye shall not be condemned: forgive, and ye shall be forgiven:

Luke 6:38   Give, and it shall be given unto you; good measure, pressed down, and shaken together, and running over, shall men give into your bosom. For with the same measure that ye mete withal it shall be measured to you again.

Luke 6:39   And he spake a parable unto them, Can the blind lead the blind? shall they not both fall into the ditch?

Luke 6:40   The disciple is not above his master: but every one that is perfect shall be as his master.

Luke 6:41   And why beholdest thou the mote that is in thy brother's eye, but perceivest not the beam that is in thine own eye?

Luke 6:42   Either how canst thou say to thy brother, Brother, let me pull out the mote that is in thine eye, when thou thyself beholdest not the beam that is in thine own eye? Thou hypocrite, cast out first the beam out of thine own eye, and then shalt thou see clearly to pull out the mote that is in thy brother's eye.

Luke 6:43   For a good tree bringeth not forth corrupt fruit; neither doth a corrupt tree bring forth good fruit.

Luke 6:44   For every tree is known by his own fruit. For of thorns men do not gather figs, nor of a bramble bush gather they grapes.

Luke 6:45   A good man out of the good treasure of his heart bringeth forth that which is good; and an evil man out of the evil treasure of his heart bringeth forth that which is evil: for of the abundance of the heart his mouth speaketh.

Luke 6:46   And why call ye me, Lord, Lord, and do not the things which I say?

Luke 6:47   Whosoever cometh to me, and heareth my sayings, and doeth them, I will show you to whom he is like:

Luke 6:48   He is like a man which built an house, and digged deep, and laid the foundation on a rock: and when the flood arose, the stream beat vehemently upon that house, and could not shake it: for it was founded upon a rock.

Luke 6:49   But he that heareth, and doeth not, is like a man that without a foundation built an house upon the earth; against which the stream did beat vehemently, and immediately it fell; and the ruin of that house was great.

| Together again. | Time Clue - Time Clue | |
|---|---|---|
| 3:20  And the multitude cometh **together again**, so that they could not so much | | 5:47 |

| Matthew | Mark | Important Events |
|---|---|---|
|  | beside himself. Mark 3:22 And the scribes which came down from Jerusalem said, He hath Beelzebub, and by the prince of the devils casteth he out devils. Mark 3:23 And he called them unto him, and said unto them in parables, How can Satan cast out Satan? Mark 3:24 And if a kingdom be divided against itself, that kingdom cannot stand. Mark 3:25 And if a house be divided against itself, that house cannot stand. Mark 3:26 And if Satan rise up against himself, and be divided, he cannot stand, but hath an end. Mark 3:27 No man can enter into a strong man's house, and spoil his goods, except he will first bind the strong man; and then he will spoil his house. Mark 3:28 Verily I say unto you, All sins shall be forgiven unto the sons of men, and blasphemies wherewith soever they shall blaspheme: Mark 3:29 But he that shall blaspheme against the Holy Ghost hath never forgiveness, but is in danger of eternal damnation: Mark 3:30 Because they said, He hath an unclean spirit. |  |
|  | Mark 3:31 There came then his brethren and his mother, and, standing without, sent unto him, calling him. Mark 3:32 And the multitude sat about him, and they said unto him, Behold, thy mother and thy brethren without seek for thee. Mark 3:33 And he answered them, saying, Who is my mother, or my brethren? Mark 3:34 And he looked round about on them which sat about him, and said, Behold my mother and my brethren! Mark 3:35 For whosoever shall do the will of God, the same is my brother, and my sister, and mother. | **1st time Jesus' mother tried to call Him out of a meeting** Mark 3:31 |
|  | Time Clue - Time Clue |  |
| 9:38 |  | Map 43 |
|  |  | **2nd time the centurion had someone sick and ready to die at his house** Luke 7:2 |

34

| ministry year | Key Scriptures & Footnotes | Luke | John |
|---|---|---|---|
| | as eat bread. | | |
| | 3:31 There came then his brethren and his mother,....[40] | | |
| | He entered Capernaum. | Time Clue - Time Clue | |
| | 7:1...entered into Capernaum | Luke 7:1 Now when he had ended all his sayings in the audience of the people, he entered into Capernaum. | 5:47 |
| | 7:2 And a certain centurion's **servant**....[41] | Luke 7:2 And a certain centurion's servant, who was dear unto him, was sick, and ready to die.<br>Luke 7:3 And when he heard of Jesus, he sent unto him the elders of the Jews, beseeching him that he would come and heal his servant.<br>Luke 7:4 And when they came to Jesus, they besought him instantly, saying, That he was worthy for whom he should do this:<br>Luke 7:5 For he loveth our nation, and he hath built us a synagogue.<br>Luke 7:6 Then Jesus went with them. And when he was now not far from the house, the centurion sent friends to him, saying unto him, Lord, trouble not thyself: for I am not worthy that thou shouldest enter under my roof: | |
| | 7:7...but say in a word, and my servant shall be healed. | Luke 7:7 Wherefore neither thought I myself worthy to come unto thee: but say in a word, and my servant shall be healed.<br>Luke 7:8 For I also am a man set under authority, having under me soldiers, and I say unto one, Go, and he goeth; and to another, Come, and he cometh; and to my servant, Do this, and he doeth it. | |
| | 7:9...he marvelled at him...I have not found | Luke 7:9 When Jesus heard these things, he marvelled at him, and turned him about, and said unto | |

[40] Mark 3:31 There came then his brethren and his mother.... (*This is the first time His brethren and His mother come to see Jesus. See Luke 8:19 for the second time and Matthew 12:46 for the third time they came.*)
[41] Luke 7:2 And a certain centurion's **servant**.... (*This is the second person that Jesus healed in the centurion's house. See the Matthew 8:6 footnote which discusses the healing of the centurion's "child."*)

| Matthew | Mark | Important Events |
|---------|------|------------------|
| | | |
| 9:38 | | **In Nain, Jesus raised the widow's son from the dead** Luke 7:11<br><br>Map 44 |
| | | **1st time John the Baptist sent two of his disciples to ask Jesus questions** Luke 7:20 |
| 9:38 | 3:35 | |
| | | |

| | | | |
|---|---|---|---|
| | so great faith, no, not in Israel.[42] | the people that followed him, I say unto you, I have not found so great faith, no, not in Israel.<br>Luke 7:10  And they that were sent, returning to the house, found the servant whole that had been sick. | |
| | 7:11...the day after,...he went into a city called Nain;.... | Luke 7:11  And it came to pass the day after, that he went into a city called Nain; and many of his disciples went with him, and much people.<br>Luke 7:12  Now when he came nigh to the gate of the city, behold, there was a dead man carried out, the only son of his mother, and she was a widow: and much people of the city was with her. | 5:47 |
| | 7:13...the Lord saw her, he had compassion on her....<br>7:14  And he came and touched the bier...Young man, I say unto thee, Arise. | Luke 7:13  And when the Lord saw her, he had compassion on her, and said unto her, Weep not.<br>Luke 7:14  And he came and touched the bier: and they that bare him stood still. And he said, Young man, I say unto thee, Arise.<br>Luke 7:15  And he that was dead sat up, and began to speak. And he delivered him to his mother.<br>Luke 7:16  And there came a fear on all: and they glorified God, saying, That a great prophet is risen up among us; and, That God hath visited his people.<br>Luke 7:17  And this rumour of him went forth throughout all Judaea, and throughout all the region round about. | |
| | | Luke 7:18  And the disciples of John showed him of all these things.<br>Luke 7:19  And John calling unto him two of his disciples sent them to Jesus, saying, Art thou he that should come? or look we for another? | |
| | 7:20...John Baptist hath sent us unto thee, saying, Art thou he that should come?[43] | Luke 7:20  When the men were come unto him, they said, John Baptist hath sent us unto thee, saying, Art thou he that should come? or look we for another?<br>Luke 7:21  And in that same hour he cured many of their infirmities and plagues, and of evil spirits; and unto many that were blind he gave sight. | |
| | 7:22 ...tell John what things ye have seen and heard....<br>7:23  And blessed is he, whosoever shall not be offended in me. | Luke 7:22  Then Jesus answering said unto them, Go your way, and tell John what things ye have seen and heard; how that the blind see, the lame walk, the lepers are cleansed, the deaf hear, the dead are raised, to the poor the gospel is preached.<br>Luke 7:23  And blessed is he, whosoever shall not be offended in me. | |
| | | Luke 7:24  And when the messengers of John were departed, he began to speak unto the people concerning John, What went ye out into the wilderness for to see? A reed shaken with the wind?<br>Luke 7:25  But what went ye out for to see? A man clothed in soft raiment? Behold, they which are gorgeously apparelled, and live delicately, are in kings' courts.<br>Luke 7:26  But what went ye out for to see? A prophet? Yea, I say unto you, and much more than a prophet.<br>Luke 7:27  This is he, of whom it is written, Behold, I send my messenger before thy face, which shall prepare thy way before thee.<br>Luke 7:28  For I say unto you, Among those that are born of women there is not a greater prophet than John the Baptist: but he that is least in the kingdom of God is greater than he. | 5:47 |
| | 7:30  But the Pharisees and lawyers rejected the counsel of God.... | Luke 7:29  And all the people that heard him, and the publicans, justified God, being baptized with the baptism of John.<br>Luke 7:30  But the Pharisees and lawyers rejected the counsel of God against themselves, being not baptized of him. | |

[42] Luke 7:9  ...I say unto you, I have not found so great faith, no, not in Israel. (*For this second healing, the centurion showed even greater faith by **sending friends** to ask Jesus to "say in a word, and my servant shall be healed." The first time the centurion **personally came** to Jesus for help. The first account is found in Matthew 8:5.*)

[43] Luke 7:20  When the men were come unto him, they said, John Baptist hath sent us unto thee, saying, Art thou he that should come? or look we for another? (*See Matthew 11:2 for the second time that John sent two of his disciples to Jesus.*)

| Matthew | Mark | Important Events |
|---|---|---|
| 9:38 | | |
| 9:38 | | **Jesus' feet anointed with alabaster box of ointment**<br>Luke 7:37<br><br>Map 45 |
| 9:38 | | **3rd time Jesus went throughout every city and village of** |

| ministry year | Key Scriptures & Footnotes | Luke | | John |
|---|---|---|---|---|

| ministry year | Key Scriptures & Footnotes | Luke | John |
|---|---|---|---|
| | | Luke 7:31   And the Lord said, Whereunto then shall I liken the men of this generation? and to what are they like? Luke 7:32   They are like unto children sitting in the marketplace, and calling one to another, and saying, We have piped unto you, and ye have not danced; we have mourned to you, and ye have not wept. Luke 7:33   For John the Baptist came neither eating bread nor drinking wine; and ye say, He hath a devil. Luke 7:34    The Son of man is come eating and drinking; and ye say, Behold a gluttonous man, and a winebibber, a friend of publicans and sinners! Luke 7:35   But wisdom is justified of all her children.  — 5:47 | |
| | 7:36  And one of the Pharisees desired him that he would eat with him..... 7:37  And, behold, a woman in the city, which was a sinner...brought an alabaster box of ointment,....[44] | Luke 7:36   And one of the Pharisees desired him that he would eat with him. And he went into the Pharisee's house, and sat down to meat. Luke 7:37   And, behold, a woman in the city, which was a sinner, when she knew that Jesus sat at meat in the Pharisee's house, brought an alabaster box of ointment, Luke 7:38   And stood at his feet behind him weeping, and began to wash his feet with tears, and did wipe them with the hairs of her head, and kissed his feet, and anointed them with the ointment. Luke 7:39    Now when the Pharisee which had bidden him saw it, he spake within himself, saying, This man, if he were a prophet, would have known who and what manner of woman this is that toucheth him: for she is a sinner. Luke 7:40    And Jesus answering said unto him, Simon, I have somewhat to say unto thee. And he saith, Master, say on. Luke 7:41   There was a certain creditor which had two debtors: the one owed five hundred pence, and the other fifty. Luke 7:42    And when they had nothing to pay, he frankly forgave them both. Tell me therefore, which of them will love him most? Luke 7:43   Simon answered and said, I suppose that he, to whom he forgave most. And he said unto him, Thou hast rightly judged. Luke 7:44   And he turned to the woman, and said unto Simon, Seest thou this woman? I entered into thine house, thou gavest me no water for my feet: but she hath washed my feet with tears, and wiped them with the hairs of her head. Luke 7:45   Thou gavest me no kiss: but this woman since the time I came in hath not ceased to kiss my feet. Luke 7:46   My head with oil thou didst not anoint: but this woman hath anointed my feet with ointment. Luke 7:47    Wherefore I say unto thee, Her sins, which are many, are forgiven; for she loved much: but to whom little is forgiven, the same loveth little. Luke 7:48    And he said unto her, Thy sins are forgiven. Luke 7:49   And they that sat at meat with him began to say within themselves, Who is this that forgiveth sins also? Luke 7:50   And he said to the woman, Thy faith hath saved thee; go in peace.  — 5:47 | |
| | 7:50...Thy faith hath saved thee; go in peace. | | |
| | He went to every city. | Time Clue - Time Clue | |
| | 8:1 And it came to pass **afterward**, that he went throughout every city and village.... | Luke 8:1    And it came to pass afterward, that he went throughout every city and village, preaching and showing the glad tidings of the kingdom of God: and the twelve were with him, Luke 8:2    And certain women, which had been healed of evil spirits and infirmities, Mary called Magdalene, out of whom went seven devils,  — 5:47 | |

[44] Luke 7:37   And, behold, a woman in the city, which was a sinner, when she knew that Jesus sat at meat in the Pharisee's house, brought an alabaster box of ointment, (See John 12:3 for the second time and Matthew 26:7 & Mark 14:3 for the third time that Jesus was anointed.)

| Matthew | Mark | Important Events |
|---|---|---|
| | | **Galilee, preaching**<br>Luke 8:1<br><br>Map 46 |
| | *Time Clue - Time Clue* | |
| | Mark 4:1　And he began again to teach by the sea side: and there was gathered unto him a great multitude, so that he entered into a ship, and sat in the sea; and the whole multitude was by the sea on the land. | **2nd time Jesus entered into a ship to teach**<br>Mark 4:1<br><br>Map 47 |
| | *Time Lock - Time Lock* | |
| | Mark 4:2　And he taught them many things by parables, and said unto them in his doctrine,<br>Mark 4:3　Hearken; Behold, there went out a sower to sow:<br>Mark 4:4　And it came to pass, as he sowed, some fell by the way side, and the fowls of the air came and devoured it up.<br>Mark 4:5　And some fell on stony ground, where it had not much earth; and immediately it sprang up, because it had no depth of earth:<br>Mark 4:6　But when the sun was up, it was scorched; and because it had no root, it withered away.<br>Mark 4:7　And some fell among thorns, and the thorns grew up, and choked it, and it yielded no fruit.<br>Mark 4:8　And other fell on good ground, and did yield fruit that sprang up and increased; and brought forth, some thirty, and some sixty, and some an hundred.<br>Mark 4:9　And he said unto them, He that hath ears to hear, let him hear. | **Parable of the sower**<br>Mark 4:2, & Luke 8:4 |
| | *Time Lock - Time Lock* | |
| 9:38 | Mark 4:10　And when he was alone, they that were about him with the twelve asked of him the parable.<br>Mark 4:11　And he said unto them, Unto you it is given to know the mystery of the kingdom of God: but unto them that are without, all these things are done in parables:<br>Mark 4:12　That seeing they may see, and not perceive; and hearing they may hear, and not understand; lest at any time they should be converted, and their sins should be forgiven them.<br>Mark 4:13　And he said unto them, Know ye not this parable? and how then will ye know all parables? | |
| | Mark 4:14　The sower soweth the word.<br>Mark 4:15　And these are they by the way side, where the word is sown; but when they have heard, Satan cometh immediately, and taketh away the word that was sown in their hearts.<br>Mark 4:16　And these are they likewise which are sown on stony ground; who, when they have heard the word, immediately receive it with gladness;<br>Mark 4:17　And have no root in themselves, and so endure but for a time: afterward, when affliction or persecution ariseth for the word's sake, immediately they are offended.<br>Mark 4:18　And these are they which are sown among thorns; such as hear the word,<br>Mark 4:19　And the cares of this world, and the deceitfulness of riches, and the lusts of other things entering in, choke the word, and it becometh unfruitful.<br>Mark 4:20　And these are they which are sown on good ground; such as hear the word, and receive it, | |

| ministry year | Key Scriptures & Footnotes | Luke | John |
|---|---|---|---|
| | | Luke 8:3   And Joanna the wife of Chuza Herod's steward, and Susanna, and many others, which ministered unto him of their substance. | |
| | He taught by the sea. | Time Clue - Time Clue | |
| | 4:1  And he began again to teach by the sea side:...a great multitude, so...he entered into a ship,.... | | |
| | A sower went out. | Time Lock - Time Lock | |
| | 8:5  A sower went out....[45] | Luke 8:4   And when much people were gathered together, and were come to him out of every city, he spake by a parable:<br>Luke 8:5   A sower went out to sow his seed: and as he sowed, some fell by the way side; and it was trodden down, and the fowls of the air devoured it.<br>Luke 8:6  And some fell upon a rock; and as soon as it was sprung up, it withered away, because it lacked moisture.<br>Luke 8:7   And some fell among thorns; and the thorns sprang up with it, and choked it.<br>Luke 8:8  And other fell on good ground, and sprang up, and bare fruit an hundredfold. And when he had said these things, he cried, He that hath ears to hear, let him hear.<br>. | |
| | The twelve asked Him. | Time Lock - Time Lock | |
| | 4:10  And when he was alone....[46] | Luke 8:9  And his disciples asked him, saying, What might this parable be?<br>Luke 8:10  And he said, Unto you it is given to know the mysteries of the kingdom of God: but to others in parables; that seeing they might not see, and hearing they might not understand. | 5:47 |
| | 4:13...Know ye not this parable?.... | | |
| | 8:11  Now the parable is this: The seed is the word of God. | Luke 8:11   Now the parable is this: The seed is the word of God.<br>Luke 8:12  Those by the way side are they that hear; then cometh the devil, and taketh away the word out of their hearts, lest they should believe and be saved.<br>Luke 8:13  They on the rock are they, which, when they hear, receive the word with joy; and these have no root, which for a while believe, and in time of temptation fall away.<br>Luke 8:14   And that which fell among thorns are they, which, when they have heard, go forth, and are choked with cares and riches and pleasures of this life, and bring no fruit to perfection.<br>Luke 8:15   But that on the good ground are they, which in an honest and good heart, having heard the word, keep it, and bring forth fruit with patience. | |

---

[45] Luke 8:5  A sower went out to sow his seed: and as he sowed, some fell by the way side; and it was trodden down, and the fowls of the air devoured it. (*See Matthew 13:3* ...Behold, a sower went forth to sow;)
[46] Mark 4:10  And when he was alone, they that were about him with the twelve asked of him the parable. (*Jesus was no longer teaching the multitude in the ship of Mark 4:1.*)

37

| Matthew | Mark | Important Events |
|---|---|---|
| | and bring forth fruit, some thirtyfold, some sixty, and some an hundred. | |
| | Time Lock - Time Lock | |
| 9:38 | Mark 4:21　And he said unto them, Is a candle brought to be put under a bushel, or under a bed? and not to be set on a candlestick?<br>Mark 4:22　For there is nothing hid, which shall not be manifested; neither was any thing kept secret, but that it should come abroad.<br>Mark 4:23　If any man have ears to hear, let him hear. | |
| | Mark 4:24　And he said unto them, Take heed what ye hear: with what measure ye mete, it shall be measured to you: and unto you that hear shall more be given.<br>Mark 4:25　For he that hath, to him shall be given: and he that hath not, from him shall be taken even that which he hath. | |
| | Time Clue - Time Clue | |
| | Mark 4:26　And he said, So is the kingdom of God, as if a man should cast seed into the ground;<br>Mark 4:27　And should sleep, and rise night and day, and the seed should spring and grow up, he knoweth not how.<br>Mark 4:28　For the earth bringeth forth fruit of herself; first the blade, then the ear, after that the full corn in the ear.<br>Mark 4:29　But when the fruit is brought forth, immediately he putteth in the sickle, because the harvest is come. | |
| | | **2nd time Jesus' mother and brothers came calling for Him**<br>Luke 8:19<br>Map 48 |
| | Mark 4:30　And he said, Whereunto shall we liken the kingdom of God? or with what comparison shall we compare it?<br>Mark 4:31　It is like a grain of mustard seed, which, when it is sown in the earth, is less than all the seeds that be in the earth:<br>Mark 4:32　But when it is sown, it groweth up, and becometh greater than all herbs, and shooteth out great branches; so that the fowls of the air may lodge under the shadow of it. | |
| | Mark 4:33　And with many such parables spake he the word unto them, as they were able to hear it.<br>Mark 4:34　But without a parable spake he not unto them: and when they were alone, he expounded all things to his disciples. | |
| | Time Lock - Time Lock | |
| 9:38 | Mark 4:35　And the same day, when the even was come, he saith unto them, Let us pass over unto the other side.<br>Mark 4:36　And when they had sent away the multitude, they took him even as he was in the ship. And there were also with him other little ships.<br>Mark 4:37　And there arose a great storm of wind, and the waves beat into the ship, so that it was now full.<br>Mark 4:38　And he was in the hinder part of the ship, | **2nd storm of wind on the lake**<br>Mark 4:37 & Luke 8:23<br>Map 49 |

| ministry year | Key Scriptures & Footnotes | Luke | John |
|---|---|---|---|
| | | | |
| | Candle on candlestick. | Time Lock - Time Lock | |
| | 8:16 No man, when he hath lighted a candle.... | Luke 8:16 No man, when he hath lighted a candle, covereth it with a vessel, or putteth it under a bed; but setteth it on a candlestick, that they which enter in may see the light. | 5:47 |
| | 8:17 For nothing is secret, that shall not be made manifest.... | Luke 8:17 For nothing is secret, that shall not be made manifest; neither any thing hid, that shall not be known and come abroad. | |
| | | Luke 8:18 Take heed therefore how ye hear: for whosoever hath, to him shall be given; and whosoever hath not, from him shall be taken even that which he seemeth to have. | |
| | Then came His mother. | Time Clue - Time Clue | |
| | 4:26 And he said, So is the kingdom of God, as if...[47] | | |
| | 8:19 **Then came** to him his mother and his brethren....[48] | Luke 8:19 Then came to him his mother and his brethren, and could not come at him for the press. Luke 8:20 And it was told him by certain which said, Thy mother and thy brethren stand without, desiring to see thee. | |
| | 8:21...My mother and my brethren are these which **hear** the word of God, **and do it.** | Luke 8:21 And he answered and said unto them, My mother and my brethren are these which hear the word of God, and do it. | |
| | 7:34 But without a parable spake he not unto them:.... | | |
| | Go over to other side. | Time Lock - Time Lock | |
| | 4:35 And the same day, when the even was come.... 8:22... he went into a ship.... 4:36... And there were also with him **other** little **ships**.... 8:23...and there came down a storm....[49] | Luke 8:22 Now it came to pass on a certain day, that he went into a ship with his disciples: and he said unto them, Let us go over unto the other side of the lake. And they launched forth. Luke 8:23 But as they sailed he fell asleep: and there came down a storm of wind on the lake; and they were filled with water, and were in jeopardy. Luke 8:24 And they came to him, and awoke him, saying, Master, master, we perish. Then he arose, and rebuked the wind and the raging of the water: | 5:47 |

[47] Mark 4:26 And he said, So is the kingdom of God, as if... (*Jesus is now telling another parable. So, according to Mark 4:33-34, He was again speaking to a crowd. This may be the crowd which causes the press of Luke 8:19.*)

[48] Luke 8:19 Then came to him his mother and his brethren.... (*Jesus is again teaching to a large group of people. This is the second time His mother and His brethren came to see Jesus while He taught. See Mark 3:31 for first time and Matthew 12:46 for the third time.*)

[49] Luke 8:23 & Mark 4:37 ...there came down a storm of wind on the lake.... (*This is the second storm at sea. See Matthew 8:23 for the first storm at sea.*)

| Matthew | Mark | Important Events |
|---|---|---|
|  | asleep on a pillow: and they awake him, and say unto him, Master, carest thou not that we perish? Mark 4:39 And he arose, and rebuked the wind, and said unto the sea, Peace, be still. And the wind ceased, and there was a great calm. |  |
|  | Mark 4:40 And he said unto them, Why are ye so fearful? how is it that ye have no faith? Mark 4:41 And they feared exceedingly, and said one to another, What manner of man is this, that even the wind and the sea obey him? | **How is it that you have no faith?** Mark 4:40 |
|  | Time Lock - Time Lock |  |
| 9:38 | Mark 5:1 And they came over unto the other side of the sea, into the country of the Gadarenes. Mark 5:2 And when he was come out of the ship, immediately there met him out of the tombs a man with an unclean spirit, Mark 5:3 Who had his dwelling among the tombs; and no man could bind him, no, not with chains: Mark 5:4 Because that he had been often bound with fetters and chains, and the chains had been plucked asunder by him, and the fetters broken in pieces: neither could any man tame him. Mark 5:5 And always, night and day, he was in the mountains, and in the tombs, crying, and cutting himself with stones. Mark 5:6 But when he saw Jesus afar off, he ran and worshipped him, Mark 5:7 And cried with a loud voice, and said, What have I to do with thee, Jesus, thou Son of the most high God? I adjure thee by God, that thou torment me not. Mark 5:8 For he said unto him, Come out of the man, thou unclean spirit. Mark 5:9 And he asked him, What is thy name? And he answered, saying, My name is Legion: for we are many. Mark 5:10 And he besought him much that he would not send them away out of the country. | **Jesus set the man of the Gadarenes free from an unclean spirit and free from Legion** Mark 5:1 & Luke 8:26  Map 50 |
| 9:38 | Mark 5:11 Now there was there nigh unto the mountains a great herd of swine feeding. Mark 5:12 And all the devils besought him, saying, Send us into the swine, that we may enter into them. Mark 5:13 And forthwith Jesus gave them leave. And the unclean spirits went out, and entered into the swine: and the herd ran violently down a steep place into the sea, (they were about two thousand;) and were choked in the sea. Mark 5:14 And they that fed the swine fled, and told it in the city, and in the country. And they went out to see what it was that was done. Mark 5:15 And they come to Jesus, and see him that was possessed with the devil, and had the legion, sitting, and clothed, and in his right mind: and they were afraid. Mark 5:16 And they that saw it told them how it befell to him that was possessed with the devil, and also concerning the swine. Mark 5:17 And they began to pray him to depart out of their coasts. Mark 5:18 And when he was come into the ship, he | **2nd group of devils to enter into swine** Mark 5:13, & Luke 8:33 |

| ministry year | Key Scriptures & Footnotes | Luke | John |
|---|---|---|---|
| | **4:38**...Master, **carest thou not** that we perish? **4:39** And he arose, and rebuked the wind...Peace, be still. And the wind ceased, and there was a great calm. | and they ceased, and there was a calm. | |
| | **4:40**...how is it that ye have **no faith**? | Luke 8:25 And he said unto them, Where is your faith? And they being afraid wondered, saying one to another, What manner of man is this! for he commandeth even the winds and water, and they obey him. | |
| | The Gadarenes. | Time Lock - Time Lock | |
| | **5:1**...**Gadarenes**.... | Luke 8:26 And they arrived at the country of the Gadarenes, which is over against Galilee. | 5:47 |
| | **5:2**...a man with **an unclean spirit**,....[50] | Luke 8:27 And when he went forth to land, there met him out of the city a certain man, which had devils long time, and ware no clothes, neither abode in any house, but in the tombs. Luke 8:28 When he saw Jesus, he cried out, and fell down before him, and with a loud voice said, What have I to do with thee, Jesus, thou Son of God most high? I beseech thee, torment me not. | |
| | **8:29** (For he had commanded the unclean spirit to come out of the man..... | Luke 8:29 (For he had commanded the unclean spirit to come out of the man. For oftentimes it had caught him: and he was kept bound with chains and in fetters; and he brake the bands, and was driven of the devil into the wilderness.) | |
| | **8:30**...And he said, **Legion**:.... | Luke 8:30 And Jesus asked him, saying, What is thy name? And he said, Legion: because many devils were entered into him. Luke 8:31 And they besought him that he would not command them to go out into the deep. | |
| | **8:32** And there was there an herd of many swine feeding on the mountain....[51] **5:11** Now there was there nigh unto the mountains a great herd of swine feeding.[52] **8:33** Then went the devils out of the man, and entered into the swine:.... | Luke 8:32 And there was there an herd of many swine feeding on the mountain: and they besought him that he would suffer them to enter into them. And he suffered them. Luke 8:33 Then went the devils out of the man, and entered into the swine: and the herd ran violently down a steep place into the lake, and were choked. Luke 8:34 When they that fed them saw what was done, they fled, and went and told it in the city and in the country. Luke 8:35 Then they went out to see what was done; and came to Jesus, and found the man, out of whom the devils were departed, sitting at the feet of Jesus, clothed, and in his right mind: and they were afraid. Luke 8:36 They also which saw it told them by what means he that was possessed of the devils was healed. Luke 8:37 Then the whole multitude of the country of the Gadarenes round about besought him to depart from them; for they were taken with great fear: and he went up into the ship, and returned back again. Luke 8:38 Now the man out of whom the devils | 5:47 |

[50] Mark 5:2 And when he was come out of the ship, immediately there met him out of the tombs a man with an unclean spirit, (*After arriving on shore following the second storm at sea, Jesus met* **one** *man was possessed with Legion. According to Matthew 8:28, after the first storm at sea* "there met him **two** possessed with devils.")

[51] Luke 8:32 And there was there an herd of **many swine feeding on the mountain**.... (*Compare with Matthew 8:30* And there was a good way off from them an herd *of many swine feeding.*)

[52] Mark 5:11 Now there was there **nigh unto the mountains a great herd of swine feeding**. (*Compare with Matthew 8:30* And there was a good way off from them an herd *of many swine feeding.*)

| Matthew | Mark | Important Events |
|---|---|---|
| | that had been possessed with the devil prayed him that he might be with him.<br>Mark 5:19　Howbeit Jesus suffered him not, but saith unto him, Go home to thy friends, and tell them how great things the Lord hath done for thee, and hath had compassion on thee.<br>Mark 5:20　And he departed, and began to publish in Decapolis how great things Jesus had done for him: and all men did marvel. | |
| | Mark 5:21　And when Jesus was passed over again by ship unto the other side, much people gathered unto him: and he was nigh unto the sea. | Map 51 |
| | Time Lock - Time Lock | |
| | Mark 5:22　And, behold, there cometh one of the rulers of the synagogue, Jairus by name; and when he saw him, he fell at his feet,<br>Mark 5:23　And besought him greatly, saying, My little daughter lieth at the point of death: I pray thee, come and lay thy hands on her, that she may be healed; and she shall live.<br>Mark 5:24　And Jesus went with him; and much people followed him, and thronged him. | **Jairus' daughter & the 2nd woman with an issue of blood twelve years**<br>Mark 5:22, & Luke 8:41<br><br>Map 52 |
| | Mark 5:25　And a certain woman, which had an issue of blood twelve years,<br>Mark 5:26　And had suffered many things of many physicians, and had spent all that she had, and was nothing bettered, but rather grew worse,<br>Mark 5:27　When she had heard of Jesus, came in the press behind, and touched his garment.<br>Mark 5:28　For she said, If I may touch but his clothes, I shall be whole.<br>Mark 5:29　And straightway the fountain of her blood was dried up; and she felt in her body that she was healed of that plague.<br>Mark 5:30　And Jesus, immediately knowing in himself that virtue had gone out of him, turned him about in the press, and said, Who touched my clothes?<br>Mark 5:31　And his disciples said unto him, Thou seest the multitude thronging thee, and sayest thou, Who touched me?<br>Mark 5:32　And he looked round about to see her that had done this thing.<br>Mark 5:33　But the woman fearing and trembling, knowing what was done in her, came and fell down before him, and told him all the truth.<br>Mark 5:34　And he said unto her, Daughter, thy faith hath made thee whole; go in peace, and be whole of thy plague. | |
| | Mark 5:35　While he yet spake, there came from the ruler of the synagogue's house certain which said, Thy daughter is dead: why troublest thou the Master any further?<br>Mark 5:36　As soon as Jesus heard the word that was spoken, he saith unto the ruler of the synagogue, Be not afraid, only believe. | |
| 9:38 | Mark 5:37　And he suffered no man to follow him, save Peter, and James, and John the brother of James.<br>Mark 5:38　And he cometh to the house of the ruler of the synagogue, and seeth the tumult, and them that wept and wailed greatly.<br>Mark 5:39　And when he was come in, he saith unto them, Why make ye this ado, and weep? the damsel | |

| ministry year | Key Scriptures & Footnotes | Luke | John |
|---|---|---|---|
| | | were departed besought him that he might be with him: but Jesus sent him away, saying, Luke 8:39   Return to thine own house, and show how great things God hath done unto thee. And he went his way, and published throughout the whole city how great things Jesus had done unto him. | |
| | 5:21 And when Jesus was passed over...and **he was nigh unto the sea**. | Luke 8:40   And it came to pass, that, when Jesus was returned, the people gladly received him: for they were all waiting for him. | |
| | Jairus' daughter dying | Time Lock - Time Lock | |
| | 8:41...there came a man named Jairus[53].... | Luke 8:41    And, behold, there came a man named Jairus, and he was a ruler of the synagogue: and he fell down at Jesus' feet, and besought him that he would come into his house: Luke 8:42    For he had one only daughter, about twelve years of age, and she lay a dying. But as he went the people thronged him. | 5:47 |
| | 5:25 And a certain woman, which had an issue of blood twelve years[54], | Luke 8:43   And a woman having an issue of blood twelve years, which had spent all her living upon physicians, neither could be healed of any, Luke 8:44   Came behind him, and touched the border of his garment: and immediately her issue of blood stanched. Luke 8:45   And Jesus said, Who touched me? When all denied, Peter and they that were with him said, Master, the multitude throng thee and press thee, and sayest thou, Who touched me? Luke 8:46   And Jesus said, Somebody hath touched me: for I perceive that virtue is gone out of me. Luke 8:47   And when the woman saw that she was not hid, she came trembling, and falling down before him, she declared unto him before all the people for what cause she had touched him, and how she was healed immediately. Luke 8:48   And he said unto her, Daughter, be of good comfort: thy faith hath made thee whole; go in peace. | |
| | 8:50...Fear not: believe only, and she shall be made whole. | Luke 8:49   While he yet spake, there cometh one from the ruler of the synagogue's house, saying to him, Thy daughter is dead; trouble not the Master. Luke 8:50   But when Jesus heard it, he answered him, saying, Fear not: believe only, and she shall be made whole. | 5:47 |
| | | Luke 8:51   And when he came into the house, he suffered no man to go in, save Peter, and James, and John, and the father and the mother of the maiden. Luke 8:52   And all wept, and bewailed her: but he said, Weep not; she is not dead, but sleepeth. Luke 8:53   And they laughed him to scorn, knowing that she was dead. | |

[53] Mark 5:22   And, behold, there cometh one of the rulers of the synagogue, Jairus by name.... (*This is not the same event found in Matthew 9:18. In that event, the rulers' daughter was* **"even now dead."** *However, in this event, Jairus' daughter was not dead when he first came to Jesus for help. Ethelbert W. Bullinger and A. G. Secrett agree. To investigate Bullinger and Secrett's order of events see Appendices #2 and #3.*)
[54] Mark 5:25   And a certain woman, which had an issue of blood twelve years, (*By time sequence, this woman is not the same as the woman found in Matthew 9:20.*)

| Matthew | Mark | Important Events |
|---|---|---|
| | is not dead, but sleepeth.<br>Mark 5:40  And they laughed him to scorn. But when he had put them all out, he taketh the father and the mother of the damsel, and them that were with him, and entereth in where the damsel was lying.<br>Mark 5:41  And he took the damsel by the hand, and said unto her, Talitha cumi; which is, being interpreted, Damsel, I say unto thee, arise.<br>Mark 5:42  And straightway the damsel arose, and walked; for she was of the age of twelve years. And they were astonished with a great astonishment.<br>Mark 5:43  And he charged them straitly that no man should know it; and commanded that something should be given her to eat. | |
| | Time Lock - Time Lock | |
| | Mark 6:1  And he went out from thence, and came into his own country; and his disciples follow him.<br>Mark 6:2  And when the sabbath day was come, he began to teach in the synagogue: and many hearing him were astonished, saying, From whence hath this man these things? and what wisdom is this which is given unto him, that even such mighty works are wrought by his hands?<br>Mark 6:3  Is not this the carpenter, the son of Mary, the brother of James, and Joses, and of Judah, and Simon? and are not his sisters here with us? And they were offended at him.<br>Mark 6:4  But Jesus said unto them, A prophet is not without honour, but in his own country, and among his own kin, and in his own house.<br>Mark 6:5  And he could there do no mighty work, save that he laid his hands upon a few sick folk, and healed them.<br>Mark 6:6a  And he marvelled because of their unbelief. | **2nd ministry trip to Nazareth**<br>Mark 6:1<br><br>Map 53 |
| | Mark 6:6b  And he went round about the villages, teaching. | **Jesus went about the villages teaching**<br>Mark 6:6b<br><br>Map 54 |
| Time Lock - Time Lock | Time Lock - Time Lock | |
| Matt. 10:1  And when he had called unto him his twelve disciples, he gave them power against unclean spirits, to cast them out, and to heal all manner of sickness and all manner of disease. | Mark 6:7  And he called unto him the twelve, and began to send them forth by two and two; and gave them power over unclean spirits; | **The twelve, sent forth by two and two**<br>Matt. 10:1, Mark 6:7, & Luke 9:1 |
| Matt. 10:2  Now the names of the twelve apostles are these; The first, Simon, who is called Peter, and Andrew his brother; James the son of Zebedee, and John his brother;<br>Matt. 10:3  Philip, and Bartholomew; Thomas, and Matthew the publican; James the son of Alphaeus, and Lebbaeus, whose surname was Thaddaeus;<br>Matt. 10:4 Simon the Canaanite, and Judas Iscariot, who also betrayed him.<br>Matt. 10:5  These twelve Jesus sent forth, and commanded them, saying, Go not into the way of the Gentiles, and into any city of the Samaritans enter ye not:<br>Matt. 10:6  But go rather to the lost sheep of the house of Israel.<br>Matt. 10:7  And as ye go, preach, saying, The | | |

| ministry year | Key Scriptures & Footnotes | Luke | John |
|---|---|---|---|
| | 5:41 And he took the damsel by the hand, and said unto her, Talitha cumi; which is, being interpreted, Damsel, I say unto thee, arise. | Luke 8:54 And he put them all out, and took her by the hand, and called, saying, Maid, arise. Luke 8:55 And her spirit came again, and she arose straightway: and he commanded to give her meat. Luke 8:56 And her parents were astonished: but he charged them that they should tell no man what was done. | |
| | Departed Jairus' house. | Time Lock - Time Lock | |
| | 6:1 ...and came into his own country;....[55] | | 5:47 |
| | The twelve sent forth. | Time Lock - Time Lock | |
| | 6:7 And he called his twelve.... 9:2 And **he sent them to preach** the kingdom of God, and to heal the sick.[56] | Luke 9:1 Then he called his twelve disciples together, and gave them power and authority over all devils, and to cure diseases. Luke 9:2 And he sent them to preach the kingdom of God, and to heal the sick. | 5:47 |
| | 10:5 These twelve Jesus sent forth,.... | | |

---

[55] Mark 6:1b and came into his own country.... (This was *Jesus' second ministry trip to Nazareth. See Luke 4:16 for the first ministry trip to Nazareth and Matthew 13:58 for the third.*)
[56] Luke 9:2 And he sent them to preach the kingdom of God, and to heal the sick. (*See Luke 10:1 After these things the Lord appointed other seventy also, and sent them two and two before his face into every city and place, whither he himself would come.*)

| Matthew | Mark | Important Events |
|---|---|---|
| kingdom of heaven is at hand.<br>Matt. 10:8 Heal the sick, cleanse the lepers, raise the dead, cast out devils: freely ye have received, freely give. | | |
| Matt. 10:9 Provide neither gold, nor silver, nor brass in your purses,<br>Matt. 10:10 Nor scrip for your journey, neither two coats, neither shoes, nor yet staves: for the workman is worthy of his meat.<br>Matt. 10:11 And into whatsoever city or town ye shall enter, inquire who in it is worthy; and there abide till ye go thence. | Mark 6:8 And commanded them that they should take nothing for their journey, save a staff only; no scrip, no bread, no money in their purse:<br>Mark 6:9 But be shod with sandals; and not put on two coats. | |
| Matt. 10:12 And when ye come into an house, salute it.<br>Matt. 10:13 And if the house be worthy, let your peace come upon it: but if it be not worthy, let your peace return to you. | Mark 6:10 And he said unto them, In what place soever ye enter into an house, there abide till ye depart from that place. | |
| Matt. 10:14 And whosoever shall not receive you, nor hear your words, when ye depart out of that house or city, shake off the dust of your feet.<br>Matt. 10:15 Verily I say unto you, It shall be more tolerable for the land of Sodom and Gomorrha in the day of judgment, than for that city. | Mark 6:11 And whosoever shall not receive you, nor hear you, when ye depart thence, shake off the dust under your feet for a testimony against them. Verily I say unto you, It shall be more tolerable for Sodom and Gomorrha in the day of judgment, than for that city. | |
| Matt. 10:16 Behold, I send you forth as sheep in the midst of wolves: be ye therefore wise as serpents, and harmless as doves.<br>Matt. 10:17 But beware of men: for they will deliver you up to the councils, and they will scourge you in their synagogues;<br>Matt. 10:18 And ye shall be brought before governors and kings for my sake, for a testimony against them and the Gentiles.<br>Matt. 10:19 But when they deliver you up, take no thought how or what ye shall speak: for it shall be given you in that same hour what ye shall speak.<br>Matt. 10:20 For it is not ye that speak, but the Spirit of your Father which speaketh in you.<br>Matt. 10:21 And the brother shall deliver up the brother to death, and the father the child: and the children shall rise up against their parents, and cause them to be put to death.<br>Matt. 10:22 And ye shall be hated of all men for my name's sake: but he that endureth to the end shall be saved.<br>Matt. 10:23 But when they persecute you in this city, flee ye into another: for verily I say unto you, Ye shall not have gone over the cities of Israel, till the Son of man be come.<br>Matt. 10:24 The disciple is not above his master, nor the servant above his lord.<br>Matt. 10:25 It is enough for the disciple that he be as his master, and the servant as his lord. If they have called the master of the house Beelzebub, how much more shall they call them of his household?<br>Matt. 10:26 Fear them not therefore: for there is nothing covered, that shall not be revealed; and hid, that shall not be known.<br>Matt. 10:27 What I tell you in darkness, that speak ye in light: and what ye hear in the ear, that preach ye upon the housetops.<br>Matt. 10:28 And fear not them which kill the body, but are not able to kill the soul: but rather fear him which is able to destroy both soul and body in hell.<br>Matt. 10:29 Are not two sparrows sold for a farthing? and one of them shall not fall on the ground without your Father.<br>Matt. 10:30 But the very hairs of your head are all numbered.<br>Matt. 10:31 Fear ye not therefore, ye are of more value than many sparrows.<br>Matt. 10:32 Whosoever therefore shall confess me before men, him will I confess also before my Father | | |

| ministry year | Key Scriptures & Footnotes | Luke | John |
|---|---|---|---|
| | 9:3... Take nothing for your journey, neither staves, nor scrip, neither bread, neither money; neither have two coats apiece. | Luke 9:3   And he said unto them, Take nothing for your journey, neither staves, nor scrip, neither bread, neither money; neither have two coats apiece. | |
| | | Luke 9:4    And whatsoever house ye enter into, there abide, and thence depart. | |
| | | Luke 9:5    And whosoever will not receive you, when ye go out of that city, shake off the very dust from your feet for a testimony against them. | |
| | | 9:5 | 5:47 |
| | 10:22  ... but he that endureth to the end shall be saved. | | |

| Matthew | Mark | Important Events |
|---|---|---|
| which is in heaven. | | |
| Matt. 10:33 But whosoever shall deny me before men, him will I also deny before my Father which is in heaven. | | |
| Matt. 10:34 Think not that I am come to send peace on earth: I came not to send peace, but a sword. | | |
| Matt. 10:35 For I am come to set a man at variance against his father, and the daughter against her mother, and the daughter-in-law against her mother-in-law. | | |
| Matt. 10:36 And a man's foes shall be they of his own household. | | |
| Matt. 10:37 He that loveth father or mother more than me is not worthy of me: and he that loveth son or daughter more than me is not worthy of me. | | |
| Matt. 10:38 And he that taketh not his cross, and followeth after me, is not worthy of me. | | |
| Matt. 10:39 He that findeth his life shall lose it: and he that loseth his life for my sake shall find it. | | |
| Matt. 10:40 He that receiveth you receiveth me, and he that receiveth me receiveth him that sent me. | | |
| Matt. 10:41 He that receiveth a prophet in the name of a prophet shall receive a prophet's reward; and he that receiveth a righteous man in the name of a righteous man shall receive a righteous man's reward. | | |
| Matt. 10:42 And whosoever shall give to drink unto one of these little ones a cup of cold water only in the name of a disciple, verily I say unto you, he shall in no wise lose his reward. | | |
| Time Lock - Time Lock | Time Lock - Time Lock | |
| Matt. 11:1 And it came to pass, when Jesus had made an end of commanding his twelve disciples, he departed thence to teach and to preach in their cities. | Mark 6:12 And they went out, and preached that men should repent. Mark 6:13 And they cast out many devils, and anointed with oil many that were sick, and healed them. | **Jesus departed to preach in their cities.** Matt. 11:1, Mark 6:12, & Luke 9:6 Map 55 |
| Matt. 11:2 Now when John had heard in the prison the works of Christ, he sent two of his disciples, Matt. 11:3 And said unto him, Art thou he that should come, or do we look for another? Matt. 11:4 Jesus answered and said unto them, Go and show John again those things which ye do hear and see: Matt. 11:5 The blind receive their sight, and the lame walk, the lepers are cleansed, and the deaf hear, the dead are raised up, and the poor have the gospel preached to them. Matt. 11:6 And blessed is he, whosoever shall not be offended in me. Matt. 11:7 And as they departed, Jesus began to say unto the multitudes concerning John, What went ye out into the wilderness to see? A reed shaken with the wind? Matt. 11:8 But what went ye out for to see? A man clothed in soft raiment? behold, they that wear soft clothing are in kings' houses. Matt. 11:9 But what went ye out for to see? A prophet? yea, I say unto you, and more than a prophet. Matt. 11:10 For this is he, of whom it is written, Behold, I send my messenger before thy face, which shall prepare thy way before thee. Matt. 11:11 Verily I say unto you, Among them that are born of women there hath not risen a greater than John the Baptist: notwithstanding he that is least in the kingdom of heaven is greater than he. Matt. 11:12 And from the days of John the Baptist | | **2nd time John sent two of his disciples to Jesus.** Matt. 11:2 |

| ministry year | Key Scriptures & Footnotes | Luke | John |
|---|---|---|---|
| | Jesus went out to preach. | Time Lock - Time Lock | |
| | 11:1...he departed thence to teach and to preach in their cities. | Luke 9:6  And they departed, and went through the towns, preaching the gospel, and healing every where. | 5:47 |
| | 11:2  Now when John had heard in the prison the works of Christ, , he sent two of his disciples,[57]<br>11:4 ...Go and show John **again**....<br>11:5  The blind receive their sight, and the lame walk....<br><br>11:6  And blessed is he, whosoever shall not be offended in me. | | |

---

[57] Matthew 11:2  Now when John had heard in the prison the works of Christ, he sent two of his disciples, (*This was the second time that John sent two of his disciples to Jesus.  See Luke 7:19 for the first  time.*)

| Matthew | Mark | Important Events |
|---|---|---|
| until now the kingdom of heaven suffereth violence, and the violent take it by force.<br>Matt. 11:13    For all the prophets and the law prophesied until John.<br>Matt. 11:14    And if ye will receive it, this is Elias, which was for to come.<br>Matt. 11:15    He that hath ears to hear, let him hear.<br>Matt. 11:16    But whereunto shall I liken this generation? It is like unto children sitting in the markets, and calling unto their fellows,<br>Matt. 11:17    And saying, We have piped unto you, and ye have not danced; we have mourned unto you, and ye have not lamented.<br>Matt. 11:18    For John came neither eating nor drinking, and they say, He hath a devil.<br>Matt. 11:19    The Son of man came eating and drinking, and they say, Behold a man gluttonous, and a winebibber, a friend of publicans and sinners. But wisdom is justified of her children. | | |
| Matt. 11:20    Then began he to upbraid the cities wherein most of his mighty works were done, because they repented not:<br>Matt. 11:21    Woe unto thee, Chorazin! woe unto thee, Bethsaida! for if the mighty works, which were done in you, had been done in Tyre and Sidon, they would have repented long ago in sackcloth and ashes.<br>Matt. 11:22    But I say unto you, It shall be more tolerable for Tyre and Sidon at the day of judgment, than for you.<br>Matt. 11:23    And thou, Capernaum, which art exalted unto heaven, shalt be brought down to hell: for if the mighty works, which have been done in thee, had been done in Sodom, it would have remained until this day.<br>Matt. 11:24    But I say unto you, That it shall be more tolerable for the land of Sodom in the day of judgment, than for thee.<br>Matt. 11:25    At that time Jesus answered and said, I thank thee, O Father, Lord of heaven and earth, because thou hast hid these things from the wise and prudent, and hast revealed them unto babes.<br>Matt. 11:26    Even so, Father: for so it seemed good in thy sight.<br>Matt. 11:27    All things are delivered unto me of my Father: and no man knoweth the Son, but the Father; neither knoweth any man the Father, save the Son, and he to whomsoever the Son will reveal him.<br>Matt. 11:28    Come unto me, all ye that labour and are heavy laden, and I will give you rest.<br>Matt. 11:29    Take my yoke upon you, and learn of me; for I am meek and lowly in heart: and ye shall find rest unto your souls.<br>Matt. 11:30    For my yoke is easy, and my burden is light. | 6:13 | |
| Matt. 12:1    At that time Jesus went on the sabbath day through the corn; and his disciples were an hungered, and began to pluck the ears of corn, and to eat.<br>Matt. 12:2    But when the Pharisees saw it, they said unto him, Behold, thy disciples do that which is not lawful to do upon the sabbath day.<br>Matt. 12:3    But he said unto them, Have ye not read what David did, when he was an hungered, and they that were with him;<br>Matt. 12:4    How he entered into the house of God, | 6:13 | **2nd trip through the corn field**<br>Matt. 12:1<br><br>Map 56 |

| ministry year | Key Scriptures & Footnotes | Luke | John |
|---|---|---|---|
| | | 9:6 | 5:47 |
| | 11:21   Woe unto thee, Chorazin! woe unto thee, Bethsaida!....[58] | | |
| | 12:1  At that time Jesus went on the sabbath day through the corn....[59] | 9:6 | 5:47 |
| | 12:3 ...Have ye not read what David did.... | | |

---

[58] Matthew 11:21   Woe unto thee, Chorazin! woe unto thee, Bethsaida!....(*See Luke 10:13 for the second time Jesus said, "* Woe unto thee, Chorazin! woe unto thee, Bethsaida!....")

[59] Matthew 12:1   At that time Jesus went on the sabbath day through the corn; and his disciples were an hungered, and began to pluck the ears of corn, and to eat. (*This is the second time the disciples plucked* "the ears of corn." *Since it was now summer, it was the time of the wheat harvest. See Mark 2:23-28 & Luke 6:1-5 for the first time the disciples plucked* "the ears of corn.")

[60] Matthew 12:7   But if ye had known what this meaneth, I will have mercy, and not sacrifice.... (*See Matthew 9:13*   But go ye and learn what that meaneth, I will have mercy, and not sacrifice...)

| Matthew | Mark | Important Events |
|---|---|---|
| and did eat the showbread, which was not lawful for him to eat, neither for them which were with him, but only for the priests? Matt. 12:5 Or have ye not read in the law, how that on the sabbath days the priests in the temple profane the sabbath, and are blameless? Matt. 12:6 But I say unto you, That in this place is one greater than the temple. Matt. 12:7 But if ye had known what this meaneth, I will have mercy, and not sacrifice, ye would not have condemned the guiltless. Matt. 12:8 For the Son of man is Lord even of the sabbath day. | | |
| Matt. 12:9 And when he was departed thence, he went into their synagogue: Matt. 12:10 And, behold, there was a man which had his hand withered. And they asked him, saying, Is it lawful to heal on the sabbath days? that they might accuse him. Matt. 12:11 And he said unto them, What man shall there be among you, that shall have one sheep, and if it fall into a pit on the sabbath day, will he not lay hold on it, and lift it out? Matt. 12:12 How much then is a man better than a sheep? Wherefore it is lawful to do well on the sabbath days. Matt. 12:13 Then saith he to the man, Stretch forth thine hand. And he stretched it forth; and it was restored whole, like as the other. Matt. 12:14 Then the Pharisees went out, and held a council against him, how they might destroy him. | | **2nd man healed of a withered hand.** Matt. 12:10 Map 57 |
| Matt. 12:15 But when Jesus knew it, he withdrew himself from thence: and great multitudes followed him, and he healed them all; Matt. 12:16 And charged them that they should not make him known: Matt. 12:17 That it might be fulfilled which was spoken by Esaias the prophet, saying, Matt. 12:18 Behold my servant, whom I have chosen; my beloved, in whom my soul is well pleased: I will put my spirit upon him, and he shall show judgment to the Gentiles. Matt. 12:19 He shall not strive, nor cry; neither shall any man hear his voice in the streets. Matt. 12:20 A bruised reed shall he not break, and smoking flax shall he not quench, till he send forth judgment unto victory. Matt. 12:21 And in his name shall the Gentiles trust. | 6:13 | Map 58 |
| Matt. 12:22 Then was brought unto him one possessed with a devil, blind, and dumb: and he healed him, insomuch that the blind and dumb both spake and saw. Matt. 12:23 And all the people were amazed, and said, Is not this the son of David? Matt. 12:24 But when the Pharisees heard it, they said, This fellow doth not cast out devils, but by Beelzebub the prince of the devils. Matt. 12:25 And Jesus knew their thoughts, and said unto them, Every kingdom divided against itself is brought to desolation; and every city or house divided against itself shall not stand: Matt. 12:26 And if Satan cast out Satan, he is divided against himself; how shall then his kingdom stand? Matt. 12:27 And if I by Beelzebub cast out devils, by whom do your children cast them out? therefore they shall be your judges. Matt. 12:28 But if I cast out devils by the Spirit of God, then the kingdom of God is come unto you. | 6:13 | **Jesus healed one possessed with a devil, blind, and dumb** Matt. 12:22 |

| ministry year | Key Scriptures & Footnotes | Luke | John |
|---|---|---|---|
| | 12:7 But if ye had known what this meaneth, I will have mercy, and not sacrifice, [60] ye would not have condemned the guiltless. | | |
| | 12:10 And, behold, there was a man which had his hand withered.[61] And they asked him, saying, Is it lawful to heal on the sabbath days?....<br><br>12:13...Stretch forth thine hand..... | | |
| | | 9:6 | 5:47 |
| | 12:22 Then was brought unto him one possessed with a devil, blind, and dumb: and he healed him...both spake and saw.<br>12:24 But when the Pharisees heard it, they said, This fellow doth not cast out devils, but by Beelzebub....[62]<br><br>12:28 But if I cast out devils by the Spirit of | 9:6 | 5:47 |

---

[61] Matthew 12:10 And, behold, there was a man which had his hand withered.... (*This is the second man with a withered hand. See Mark 3:1 & Luke 6:6 for the first man with a withered hand.*)
[62] Matthew 12:24 This fellow doth not cast out devils, but by Beelzebub.... (*See Matthew 9:32-34 and John 8:49 for similar accounts.*)

| Matthew | Mark | Important Events |
|---|---|---|
| Matt. 12:29 Or else how can one enter into a strong man's house, and spoil his goods, except he first bind the strong man? and then he will spoil his house.<br>Matt. 12:30 He that is not with me is against me; and he that gathereth not with me scattereth abroad.<br>Matt. 12:31 Wherefore I say unto you, All manner of sin and blasphemy shall be forgiven unto men: but the blasphemy against the Holy Ghost shall not be forgiven unto men.<br>Matt. 12:32 And whosoever speaketh a word against the Son of man, it shall be forgiven him: but whosoever speaketh against the Holy Ghost, it shall not be forgiven him, neither in this world, neither in the world to come.<br>Matt. 12:33 Either make the tree good, and his fruit good; or else make the tree corrupt, and his fruit corrupt: for the tree is known by his fruit.<br>Matt. 12:34 O generation of vipers, how can ye, being evil, speak good things? for out of the abundance of the heart the mouth speaketh.<br>Matt. 12:35 A good man out of the good treasure of the heart bringeth forth good things: and an evil man out of the evil treasure bringeth forth evil things.<br>Matt. 12:36 But I say unto you, That every idle word that men shall speak, they shall give account thereof in the day of judgment.<br>Matt. 12:37 For by thy words thou shalt be justified, and by thy words thou shalt be condemned. | | |
| Matt. 12:38 Then certain of the scribes and of the Pharisees answered, saying, Master, we would see a sign from thee.<br>Matt. 12:39 But he answered and said unto them, An evil and adulterous generation seeketh after a sign; and there shall no sign be given to it, but the sign of the prophet Jonas:<br>Matt. 12:40 For as Jonas was three days and three nights in the whale's belly; so shall the Son of man be three days and three nights in the heart of the earth.<br>Matt. 12:41 The men of Nineveh shall rise in judgment with this generation, and shall condemn it: because they repented at the preaching of Jonas; and, behold, a greater than Jonas is here.<br>Matt. 12:42 The queen of the south shall rise up in the judgment with this generation, and shall condemn it: for she came from the uttermost parts of the earth to hear the wisdom of Solomon; and, behold, a greater than Solomon is here.<br>Matt. 12:43 When the unclean spirit is gone out of a man, he walketh through dry places, seeking rest, and findeth none.<br>Matt. 12:44 Then he saith, I will return into my house from whence I came out; and when he is come, he findeth it empty, swept, and garnished.<br>Matt. 12:45 Then goeth he, and taketh with himself seven other spirits more wicked than himself, and they enter in and dwell there: and the last state of that man is worse than the first. Even so shall it be also unto this wicked generation. | 6:13 | **We would see a sign from thee**<br>Matt. 12:38 |
| Matt. 12:46 While he yet talked to the people, behold, his mother and his brethren stood without, desiring to speak with him.<br>Matt. 12:47 Then one said unto him, Behold, thy mother and thy brethren stand without, desiring to | | **3rd time Jesus' mother tried to call Him out of** |

| ministry year | Key Scriptures & Footnotes | Luke | John |
|---|---|---|---|
| | God, then the kingdom of God is come unto you.<br><br>12:31...but the blasphemy against the Holy Ghost shall not be forgiven unto men. | | |
| | 12:38...we would see a sign from thee.<br><br>12:39... and there shall no sign be given to it, but the sign of the prophet Jonas:<br>12:40 For as Jonas was three days and three nights in the whale's belly; so shall the Son of man be three days and three nights in the heart of the earth.[63] | 9:6 | 5:47 |
| | 12:45...seven other spirits more wicked....[64] Even so shall it be also unto this wicked generation. | | |
| | 12:46...his mother and his brethren stood without, desiring to speak with him.[65] | | |

---

[63] Matthew 12:39-40 But he answered and said unto them, An evil and adulterous generation seeketh after a sign; and there shall no sign be given to it, **but the sign of the prophet Jonas**: For as Jonas was **three days** and **three nights** in the whale's belly; so shall the Son of man be **three days** and **three nights in the heart of the earth**. (*See Matthew 16:4a* A wicked and adulterous generation seeketh after a sign; and there shall no sign be given unto it, **but the sign of the prophet Jonas**. *Also see Luke 11:29* ...This is an evil generation: they seek a sign; and there shall no sign be given it, **but the sign of Jonas the prophet**.)
[64] Matthew 12:45 Then goeth he, and taketh with himself seven other spirits more wicked than himself.... (*See Luke 11:26 for another time that Jesus taught about this.*)
[65] Matthew 12:46 ...his mother and his brethren stood without, desiring to speak with him. (*This is the third time they desired to see Jesus during a meeting. See Mark 3:31 for first time and Luke 8:19 for the second time they desired to see Jesus.*)

| Matthew | Mark | Important Events |
|---|---|---|
| speak with thee.<br>Matt. 12:48 But he answered and said unto him that told him, Who is my mother? and who are my brethren?<br>Matt. 12:49 And he stretched forth his hand toward his disciples, and said, Behold my mother and my brethren!<br>Matt. 12:50 For whosoever shall do the will of my Father which is in heaven, the same is my brother, and sister, and mother. | | **a meeting**<br>Matt. 12:46<br><br>Map 59 |
| Matt. 13:1 The same day went Jesus out of the house, and sat by the sea side.<br>Matt. 13:2 And great multitudes were gathered together unto him, so that he went into a ship, and sat; and the whole multitude stood on the shore.<br>Matt. 13:3 And he spake many things unto them in parables, saying, Behold, a sower went forth to sow;<br>Matt. 13:4 And when he sowed, some seeds fell by the way side, and the fowls came and devoured them up:<br>Matt. 13:5 Some fell upon stony places, where they had not much earth: and forthwith they sprung up, because they had no deepness of earth:<br>Matt. 13:6 And when the sun was up, they were scorched; and because they had no root, they withered away.<br>Matt. 13:7 And some fell among thorns; and the thorns sprung up, and choked them:<br>Matt. 13:8 But other fell into good ground, and brought forth fruit, some an hundredfold, some sixtyfold, some thirtyfold.<br>Matt. 13:9 Who hath ears to hear, let him hear. | 6:13 | **Parable of the sower, taught at sea side**<br>Matt. 13:1<br><br>Map 60<br>Map 61 |
| Matt. 13:10 And the disciples came, and said unto him, Why speakest thou unto them in parables?<br>Matt. 13:11 He answered and said unto them, Because it is given unto you to know the mysteries of the kingdom of heaven, but to them it is not given.<br>Matt. 13:12 For whosoever hath, to him shall be given, and he shall have more abundance: but whosoever hath not, from him shall be taken away even that he hath.<br>Matt. 13:13 Therefore speak I to them in parables: because they seeing see not; and hearing they hear not, neither do they understand.<br>Matt. 13:14 And in them is fulfilled the prophecy of Esaias, which saith, By hearing ye shall hear, and shall not understand; and seeing ye shall see, and shall not perceive:<br>Matt. 13:15 For this people's heart is waxed gross, and their ears are dull of hearing, and their eyes they have closed; lest at any time they should see with their eyes, and hear with their ears, and should understand with their heart, and should be converted, and I should heal them.<br>Matt. 13:16 But blessed are your eyes, for they see: and your ears, for they hear.<br>Matt. 13:17 For verily I say unto you, That many prophets and righteous men have desired to see those things which ye see, and have not seen them; and to hear those things which ye hear, and have not heard them.<br>Matt. 13:18 Hear ye therefore the parable of the sower.<br>Matt. 13:19 When any one heareth the word of the kingdom, and understandeth it not, then cometh the wicked one, and catcheth away that which was sown in his heart. This is he which received seed by the way side.<br>Matt. 13:20 But he that received the seed into stony places, the same is he that heareth the word, and | | |

| ministry year | Key Scriptures & Footnotes | Luke | John |
|---|---|---|---|
| | 12:49...Behold my mother and my brethren! | | |
| | 13:1 The same day went Jesus out of the house, and sat by the sea side.<br>13:2 ...he went into a ship, and sat....<br>13:3...Behold, a sower went forth to sow;[66] | 9:6 | 5:47 |

---

[66] Matthew 13:3 ...saying, Behold, a sower went forth to sow; (*See Mark 4:3 & Luke 8:5 for another time that Jesus taught this parable.*)

| Matthew | Mark | Important Events |
|---|---|---|
| anon with joy receiveth it;<br>Matt. 13:21 Yet hath he not root in himself, but dureth for a while: for when tribulation or persecution ariseth because of the word, by and by he is offended.<br>Matt. 13:22 He also that received seed among the thorns is he that heareth the word; and the care of this world, and the deceitfulness of riches, choke the word, and he becometh unfruitful.<br>Matt. 13:23 But he that received seed into the good ground is he that heareth the word, and understandeth it; which also beareth fruit, and bringeth forth, some an hundredfold, some sixty, some thirty.<br>Matt. 13:24 Another parable put he forth unto them, saying, The kingdom of heaven is likened unto a man which sowed good seed in his field:<br>Matt. 13:25 But while men slept, his enemy came and sowed tares among the wheat, and went his way.<br>Matt. 13:26 But when the blade was sprung up, and brought forth fruit, then appeared the tares also.<br>Matt. 13:27 So the servants of the householder came and said unto him, Sir, didst not thou sow good seed in thy field? from whence then hath it tares?<br>Matt. 13:28 He said unto them, An enemy hath done this. The servants said unto him, Wilt thou then that we go and gather them up?<br>Matt. 13:29 But he said, Nay; lest while ye gather up the tares, ye root up also the wheat with them.<br>Matt. 13:30 Let both grow together until the harvest: and in the time of harvest I will say to the reapers, Gather ye together first the tares, and bind them in bundles to burn them: but gather the wheat into my barn. | | |
| Matt. 13:31 Another parable put he forth unto them, saying, The kingdom of heaven is like to a grain of mustard seed, which a man took, and sowed in his field:<br>Matt. 13:32 Which indeed is the least of all seeds: but when it is grown, it is the greatest among herbs, and becometh a tree, so that the birds of the air come and lodge in the branches thereof.<br>Matt. 13:33 Another parable spake he unto them; The kingdom of heaven is like unto leaven, which a woman took, and hid in three measures of meal, till the whole was leavened.<br>Matt. 13:34 All these things spake Jesus unto the multitude in parables; and without a parable spake he not unto them:<br>Matt. 13:35 That it might be fulfilled which was spoken by the prophet, saying, I will open my mouth in parables; I will utter things which have been kept secret from the foundation of the world. | 6:13 | |
| Matt. 13:36 Then Jesus sent the multitude away, and went into the house: and his disciples came unto him, saying, Declare unto us the parable of the tares of the field.<br>Matt. 13:37 He answered and said unto them, He that soweth the good seed is the Son of man;<br>Matt. 13:38 The field is the world; the good seed are the children of the kingdom; but the tares are the children of the wicked one;<br>Matt. 13:39 The enemy that sowed them is the devil; the harvest is the end of the world; and the reapers are the angels.<br>Matt. 13:40 As therefore the tares are gathered and burned in the fire; so shall it be in the end of this world. | 6:13 | **Jesus explained parable of the tares**<br>Matt. 13:36 |

| ministry year | Key Scriptures & Footnotes | Luke | John |
|---|---|---|---|
| | 13:30 Let both grow together until the harvest: and in the time of harvest I will say to the reapers, Gather ye together first the tares, and bind them in bundles to burn them: but gather the wheat into my barn. | | |
| | 13:31...The kingdom of heaven is like to a grain of mustard seed.... | 9:6 | 5:47 |
| | 13:36 Then Jesus sent the multitude away[67], and went into the house:.... 13:37...He that soweth the good seed is the Son of man; | 9:6 | 5:47 |

[67] Matthew 13:36   Then Jesus sent the multitude away, and went into the house: and his disciples came unto him, saying,   Declare unto us the parable of the tares of the field.  (*Previously Jesus had explained, in Mark 4:10-20, the parable **of the sower of** the* **word** *to* "they that were about him with the twelve." *In Matthew 13:18-23, Jesus again explained the parable **of the sower of** the* **word** *to the disciples.  In Matthew 13:36-43, Jesus explained the parable **of the tares of the field** also known as the parable **of the sower of the children of the kingdom**.*)

| Matthew | Mark | Important Events |
|---|---|---|
| Matt. 13:41 The Son of man shall send forth his angels, and they shall gather out of his kingdom all things that offend, and them which do iniquity; Matt. 13:42 And shall cast them into a furnace of fire: there shall be wailing and gnashing of teeth. Matt. 13:43 Then shall the righteous shine forth as the sun in the kingdom of their Father. Who hath ears to hear, let him hear. Matt. 13:44 Again, the kingdom of heaven is like unto treasure hid in a field; the which when a man hath found, he hideth, and for joy thereof goeth and selleth all that he hath, and buyeth that field. Matt. 13:45 Again, the kingdom of heaven is like unto a merchant man, seeking goodly pearls: Matt. 13:46 Who, when he had found one pearl of great price, went and sold all that he had, and bought it. Matt. 13:47 Again, the kingdom of heaven is like unto a net, that was cast into the sea, and gathered of every kind: Matt. 13:48 Which, when it was full, they drew to shore, and sat down, and gathered the good into vessels, but cast the bad away. Matt. 13:49 So shall it be at the end of the world: the angels shall come forth, and sever the wicked from among the just, Matt. 13:50 And shall cast them into the furnace of fire: there shall be wailing and gnashing of teeth. Matt. 13:51 Jesus saith unto them, Have ye understood all these things? They say unto him, Yea, Lord. Matt. 13:52 Then said he unto them, Therefore every scribe which is instructed unto the kingdom of heaven is like unto a man that is an householder, which bringeth forth out of his treasure things new and old. | | |
| Matt. 13:53 And it came to pass, that when Jesus had finished these parables, he departed thence. Matt. 13:54 And when he was come into his own country, he taught them in their synagogue, insomuch that they were astonished, and said, Whence hath this man this wisdom, and these mighty works? Matt. 13:55 Is not this the carpenter's son? is not his mother called Mary? and his brethren, James, and Joses, and Simon, and Judas? Matt. 13:56 And his sisters, are they not all with us? Whence then hath this man all these things? Matt. 13:57 And they were offended in him. But Jesus said unto them, A prophet is not without honour, save in his own country, and in his own house. Matt. 13:58 And he did not many mighty works there because of their unbelief. | | **3rd ministry trip to Nazareth** Matt. 13:54  Map 62 |
| Time Lock - Time Lock | Time Lock - Time Lock | |
| Matt. 14:1 At that time Herod the tetrarch heard of the fame of Jesus, Matt. 14:2 And said unto his servants, This is John the Baptist; he is risen from the dead; and therefore mighty works do show forth themselves in him. Matt. 14:3 For Herod had laid hold on John, and bound him, and put him in prison for Herodias' sake, his brother Philip's wife. Matt. 14:4 For John said unto him, It is not lawful for thee to have her. Matt. 14:5 And when he would have put him to death, he feared the multitude, because they counted him as a prophet. Matt. 14:6 But when Herod's birthday was kept, the daughter of Herodias danced before them, and pleased Herod. Matt. 14:7 Whereupon he promised with an oath to | Mark 6:14 And king Herod heard of him; (for his name was spread abroad:) and he said, That John the Baptist was risen from the dead, and therefore mighty works do show forth themselves in him. Mark 6:15 Others said, That it is Elias. And others said, That it is a prophet, or as one of the prophets. Mark 6:16 But when Herod heard thereof, he said, It is John, whom I beheaded: he is risen from the dead. Mark 6:17 For Herod himself had sent forth and laid hold upon John, and bound him in prison for Herodias' sake, his brother Philip's wife: for he had married her. Mark 6:18 For John had said unto Herod, It is not lawful for thee to have thy brother's wife. Mark 6:19 Therefore Herodias had a quarrel against him, and would have killed him; but she could | **King Herod heard of Jesus** Matt. 14:1, Mark 6:14, & Luke 9:7  Map 63 |

| | Key Scriptures & Footnotes | Luke | John |
|---|---|---|---|
| | 13:53...he departed thence.<br>13:54 And when he was come into his own country,....[68] | 9:6 | 5:47 |
| | 13:57 And they were offended in him.....<br>13:58...And he did not many mighty works there because of their unbelief. | | |
| | John the Baptist's death. | Time Lock - Time Lock | |
| | 9:9 And Herod said, John have I beheaded: but who is this,.... | Luke 9:7  Now Herod the tetrarch heard of all that was done by him: and he was perplexed, because that it was said of some, that John was risen from the dead;<br>Luke 9:8  And of some, that Elias had appeared; and of others, that one of the old prophets was risen again.<br>Luke 9:9   And Herod said, John have I beheaded: but who is this, of whom I hear such things? And he desired to see him. | 5:47 |

[68] Matthew 13:54   And when he was come into his own country...? (*This is Jesus' third ministry trip to Nazareth.  See Luke 4:16 for the first trip and Mark 6:1 for the second trip.*)

| Matthew | Mark | Important Events |
|---|---|---|
| give her whatsoever she would ask. | not:<br>Mark 6:20  For Herod feared John, knowing that he was a just man and an holy, and observed him; and when he heard him, he did many things, and heard him gladly.<br>Mark 6:21  And when a convenient day was come, that Herod on his birthday made a supper to his lords, high captains, and chief estates of Galilee;<br>Mark 6:22  And when the daughter of the said Herodias came in, and danced, and pleased Herod and them that sat with him, the king said unto the damsel, Ask of me whatsoever thou wilt, and I will give it thee.<br>Mark 6:23  And he sware unto her, Whatsoever thou shalt ask of me, I will give it thee, unto the half of my kingdom. | |
| Matt. 14:8  And she, being before instructed of her mother, said, Give me here John Baptist's head in a charger.<br>Matt. 14:9  And the king was sorry: nevertheless for the oath's sake, and them which sat with him at meat, he commanded it to be given her.<br>Matt. 14:10  And he sent, and beheaded John in the prison.<br>Matt. 14:11  And his head was brought in a charger, and given to the damsel: and she brought it to her mother.<br>Matt. 14:12  And his disciples came, and took up the body, and buried it, and went and told Jesus. | Mark 6:24  And she went forth, and said unto her mother, What shall I ask? And she said, The head of John the Baptist.<br>Mark 6:25  And she came in straightway with haste unto the king, and asked, saying, I will that thou give me by and by in a charger the head of John the Baptist.<br>Mark 6:26  And the king was exceeding sorry; yet for his oath's sake, and for their sakes which sat with him, he would not reject her.<br>Mark 6:27  And immediately the king sent an executioner, and commanded his head to be brought: and he went and beheaded him in the prison,<br>Mark 6:28  And brought his head in a charger, and gave it to the damsel: and the damsel gave it to her mother.<br>Mark 6:29  And when his disciples heard of it, they came and took up his corpse, and laid it in a tomb. | |
| Time Lock - Time Lock | Time Lock - Time Lock | |
| Matt. 14:13a  When Jesus heard of it, he departed thence by ship into a desert place apart: | Mark 6:30  And the apostles gathered themselves together unto Jesus, and told him all things, both what they had done, and what they had taught.<br>Mark 6:31  And he said unto them, Come ye yourselves apart into a desert place, and rest a while: for there were many coming and going, and they had no leisure so much as to eat.<br>Mark 6:32  And they departed into a desert place by ship privately. | **Jesus heard of John's death and departed by ship**<br>Matt. 14:13a, Mark 6:32, Luke 9:10, & John 6:1<br><br>Map 64 |
| Matt. 14:13b  and when the people had heard thereof, they followed him on foot out of the cities.<br>Matt. 14:14  And Jesus went forth, and saw a great multitude, and was moved with compassion toward them, and he healed their sick. | Mark 6:33  And the people saw them departing, and many knew him, and ran afoot thither out of all cities, and outwent them, and came together unto him.<br>Mark 6:34  And Jesus, when he came out, saw much people, and was moved with compassion toward them, because they were as sheep not having a shepherd: and he began to teach them many things. | |
| | | **3rd Passover was nigh.**<br>John 6:4 |
| Time Lock - Time Lock | Time Lock - Time Lock | |
| Matt. 14:15  And when it was evening, his disciples came to him, saying, This is a desert place, and the time is now past; send the multitude away, that they may go into the villages, and buy themselves victuals.<br>Matt. 14:16  But Jesus said unto them, They need not | Mark 6:35  And when the day was now far spent, his disciples came unto him, and said, This is a desert place, and now the time is far passed:<br>Mark 6:36  Send them away, that they may go into the country round about, and into the villages, and | **Jesus feeds the 5000**<br>Matt. 14:15, Mark 6:35, Luke 9:12, & |

| ministry year | Key Scriptures & Footnotes | Luke | John |
|---|---|---|---|
| | 14:8 And she, being before instructed of her mother, said, Give me here John Baptist's head in a charger. [69] 6:24 And she went forth, and said unto her mother, What shall I ask? And she said, The head of John the Baptist. | | |
| | Jesus departed to desert. | Time Lock - Time Lock | Time Lock - Time Lock |
| | 14:13a Jesus heard of it, he departed thence by ship into a desert place apart:.... | Luke 9:10 And the apostles, when they were returned, told him all that they had done. And he took them, and went aside privately into a desert place belonging to the city called Bethsaida. | John 6:1 After these things Jesus went over the sea of Galilee, which is the sea of Tiberias. |
| | 6:33 And the people saw... and ran afoot thither out of all cities, and **outwent them**, and came together unto him. | Luke 9:11 And the people, when they knew it, followed him: and he received them, and spake unto them of the kingdom of God, and healed them that had need of healing. | John 6:2 And a great multitude followed him, because they saw his miracles which he did on them that were diseased. John 6:3 And Jesus went up into a mountain, and there he sat with his disciples. |
| | 6:4...passover,[70] a feast of the Jews, was nigh. | | John 6:4 And the passover, a feast of the Jews, was nigh. |
| | Feeding they 5000. | Time Lock - Time Lock | Time Lock - Time Lock |
| | 6:35...a desert place.... | Luke 9:12 And when the day began to wear away, then came the twelve, and said unto him, Send the multitude away, that they may go into the towns and country round about, and lodge, and get victuals: for we are here in a desert place. | John 6:5 When Jesus then lifted up his eyes, and saw a great company come unto him, he saith unto Philip, Whence shall we buy bread, that these may eat? John 6:6 And this he said to prove him: for he himself knew what he would do. |

[69] Matthew 14:8 And she, being **before instructed** of her mother.... (*Some translations of Matthew 14:8 say that Herodias' daughter, was "prompted" or "urged on" by her mother to ask for John Baptist's head in a charger.*)
[70] John 6:4 And the passover, a feast of the Jews, was nigh. (*This is the third Passover since Jesus' baptism by John the Baptist. This Passover took place after John 6:71 and before John 7:1. The first Passover is found in John 2:13, the second in John 5:1, and the fourth in John 11:55.*)
[71] Matthew 14:21 And they that had eaten were about five thousand men, beside women and children. (*See the feeding of the 4000 in Matthew 15:32 & Mark 8:1*)

| Matthew | Mark | Important Events |
|---|---|---|
| depart; give ye them to eat.<br>Matt. 14:17   And they say unto him, We have here but five loaves, and two fishes.<br>Matt. 14:18  He said, Bring them hither to me.<br>Matt. 14:19  And he commanded the multitude to sit down on the grass, and took the five loaves, and the two fishes, and looking up to heaven, he blessed, and brake, and gave the loaves to his disciples, and the disciples to the multitude.<br>Matt. 14:20   And they did all eat, and were filled: and they took up of the fragments that remained twelve baskets full.<br>Matt. 14:21   And they that had eaten were about five thousand men, beside women and children.<br>Matt. 14:22   And straightway Jesus constrained his disciples to get into a ship, and to go before him unto the other side, while he sent the multitudes away. | buy themselves bread: for they have nothing to eat.<br>Mark 6:37   He answered and said unto them, Give ye them to eat. And they say unto him, Shall we go and buy two hundred pennyworth of bread, and give them to eat?<br>Mark 6:38   He saith unto them, How many loaves have ye? go and see. And when they knew, they say, Five, and two fishes.<br>Mark 6:39  And he commanded them to make all sit down by companies upon the green grass.<br>Mark 6:40  And they sat down in ranks, by hundreds, and by fifties.<br>Mark 6:41   And when he had taken the five loaves and the two fishes, he looked up to heaven, and blessed, and brake the loaves, and gave them to his disciples to set before them; and the two fishes divided he among them all.<br>Mark 6:42  And they did all eat, and were filled.<br>Mark 6:43   And they took up twelve baskets full of the fragments, and of the fishes.<br>Mark 6:44  And they that did eat of the loaves were about five thousand men.<br>Mark 6:45   And straightway he constrained his disciples to get into the ship, and to go to the other side before unto Bethsaida, while he sent away the people. | John 6:5 |
| _Time Lock - Time Lock_ | _Time Lock - Time Lock_ | |
| Matt. 14:23a   And when he had sent the multitudes away, | Mark 6:46a   And when he had sent them away, | **Jesus sent the 5000 away**<br>Matt. 14:23a & Mark 6:46a |
| Matt. 14:23b   he went up into a mountain apart to pray: and when the evening was come, he was there alone.<br>Matt. 14:24  But the ship was now in the midst of the sea, tossed with waves: for the wind was contrary.<br>Matt. 14:25   And in the fourth watch of the night Jesus went unto them, walking on the sea.<br>Matt. 14:26  And when the disciples saw him walking on the sea, they were troubled, saying, It is a spirit; and they cried out for fear.<br>Matt. 14:27  But straightway Jesus spake unto them, saying, Be of good cheer; it is I; be not afraid.<br>Matt. 14:28  And Peter answered him and said, Lord, if it be thou, bid me come unto thee on the water.<br>Matt. 14:29   And he said, Come. And when Peter was come down out of the ship, he walked on the water, to go to Jesus.<br>Matt. 14:30  But when he saw the wind boisterous, he was afraid; and beginning to sink, he cried, saying, Lord, save me.<br>Matt. 14:31   And immediately Jesus stretched forth his hand, and caught him, and said unto him, O thou of little faith, wherefore didst thou doubt? | Mark 6:46b   he departed into a mountain to pray.<br>Mark 6:47  And when even was come, the ship was in the midst of the sea, and he alone on the land.<br>Mark 6:48   And he saw them toiling in rowing; for the wind was contrary unto them: and about the fourth watch of the night he cometh unto them, walking upon the sea, and would have passed by them.<br>Mark 6:49  But when they saw him walking upon the sea, they supposed it had been a spirit, and cried out:<br>Mark 6:50  For they all saw him, and were troubled. And immediately he talked with them, and saith unto them, Be of good cheer: it is I; be not afraid. | Map 65<br>**1st night that Jesus walks on the water**<br>Matt. 14:25 & Mark 6:48<br><br>Map 66 |
| Matt. 14:32  And when they were come into the ship, the wind ceased.<br>Matt. 14:33   Then they that were in the ship came and worshipped him, saying, Of a truth thou art the Son of God. | Mark 6:51  And he went up unto them into the ship; and the wind ceased: and they were sore amazed in themselves beyond measure, and wondered.<br>Mark 6:52   For they considered not the miracle of the loaves: for their heart was hardened. | Map 67 |
| Matt. 14:34   And when they were gone over, they came into the land of Gennesaret. | Mark 6:53   And when they had passed over, they came into the land of Gennesaret, and drew to the shore. | Map 68 |

| ministry year | Key Scriptures & Footnotes | Luke | John |
|---|---|---|---|
| | 14:17 And they say unto him, We have here but five loaves, and two fishes. | Luke 9:13 But he said unto them, Give ye them to eat. And they said, We have no more but five loaves and two fishes; except we should go and buy meat for all this people.<br>Luke 9:14 For they were about five thousand men. And he said to his disciples, Make them sit down by fifties in a company.<br>Luke 9:15 And they did so, and made them all sit down.<br>Luke 9:16 Then he took the five loaves and the two fishes, and looking up to heaven, he blessed them, and brake, and gave to the disciples to set before the multitude.<br>Luke 9:17 And they did eat, and were all filled: and there was taken up of fragments that remained to them twelve baskets. | John 6:7 Philip answered him, Two hundred pennyworth of bread is not sufficient for them, that every one of them may take a little.<br>John 6:8 One of his disciples, Andrew, Simon Peter's brother, saith unto him,<br>John 6:9 There is a lad here, which hath five barley loaves, and two small fishes: but what are they among so many?<br>John 6:10 And Jesus said, Make the men sit down. Now there was much grass in the place. So the men sat down, in number about five thousand.<br>John 6:11 And Jesus took the loaves; and when he had given thanks, he distributed to the disciples, and the disciples to them that were set down; and likewise of the fishes as much as they would.<br>John 6:12 When they were filled, he said unto his disciples, Gather up the fragments that remain, that nothing be lost.<br>John 6:13 Therefore they gathered them together, and filled twelve baskets with the fragments of the five barley loaves, which remained over and above unto them that had eaten. |
| | 14:21 And they that had eaten were about **five thousand** men....[71] | | |
| | 6:45 And straightway he constrained his disciples... to go...unto Bethsaida[72], while he sent away the people. | | |
| | Jesus sent thyem away. | Time Lock - Time Lock | Time Clue - See John 6:15 |
| | 14:23a And when **he** had **sent** the multitudes away, | | |
| | 6:46...**he departed** into a mountain **to pray.**<br>14:24 But the ship was now in the midst of the sea, **tossed with waves**:<br>14:25 And in the fourth watch of the night Jesus went unto them, walking on the sea.[73] | | |
| | 6:51 And he went up unto them into the ship; and the **wind ceased**:....<br>6:52 For they **considered not the miracle** of the loaves:... | 9:17 | 6:13 |
| | 6:53 And...they came into the **land of Gennesaret**,.... | | |

---

[72] Mark 6:45 And straightway he constrained his disciples to...go...unto Bethsaida, while he sent away the people. (*The disciples were sent to Bethsaida. It is possible that they were returning from Bethsaida when Jesus saw them "toiling in rowing" in Mark 6:48. Then "they came into the land of Gennesaret" in Mark 6:53.*)
[73] Matthew 14:25 And in the fourth watch of the night Jesus went unto them, walking on the sea. (*See John 6:19 for the next time that Jesus walked on the sea.*)

| Matthew | Mark | Important Events |
|---|---|---|
| | Mark 6:54   And when they were come out of the ship, straightway they knew him, | |
| Matt. 14:35   And when the men of that place had knowledge of him, they sent out into all that country round about, and brought unto him all that were diseased;<br>Matt. 14:36   And besought him that they might only touch the hem of his garment: and as many as touched were made perfectly whole. | Mark 6:55   And ran through that whole region round about, and began to carry about in beds those that were sick, where they heard he was.<br>Mark 6:56     And whithersoever he entered, into villages, or cities, or country, they laid the sick in the streets, and besought him that they might touch if it were but the border of his garment: and as many as touched him were made whole. | Map 69 |
| *Time Lock - Time Lock* | *Time Lock - Time Lock* | |
| | | **Jesus leaves without first sending the people away**<br>John 6:15<br><br>Map 70 |
| | | **2nd night that Jesus walks on the water**<br>John 6:19<br><br>Map 71 |
| | | Map 72 |
| | | |
| 14:36 | 6:56 | |

| ministry year | Key Scriptures & Footnotes | Luke | John |
|---|---|---|---|
| | 6:54 And when they were come out of the ship, straightway they knew him, | | |
| | 14:36...and as many as touched were made perfectly whole. | | |
| | Jesus departed alone. | | Time Clue - Time Clue |
| | 6:14 Then those men, when they had seen the miracle that Jesus did,.... 6:15 When Jesus therefore perceived that they would come and take him by force, to make him a king, he **departed again** into a mountain himself alone. 6:17 And entered into a ship, and went over the sea **toward Capernaum**. 6:18 And **the sea arose** by reason of a great wind that blew. | 9:17 | John 6:14 Then those men, when they had seen the miracle that Jesus did, said, This is of a truth that prophet that should come into the world. John 6:15 When Jesus therefore perceived that they would come and take him by force, to make him a king, he departed again into a mountain himself alone. John 6:16 And when even was now come, his disciples went down unto the sea, John 6:17 And entered into a ship, and went over the sea toward Capernaum. And it was now dark, and Jesus was not come to them. John 6:18 And the sea arose by reason of a great wind that blew. |
| | 6:19 ...they see Jesus walking on the sea[74], and drawing nigh unto the ship:.... 6:20 ...It is I; be not afraid. | | John 6:19 So when they had rowed about five and twenty or thirty furlongs, they see Jesus walking on the sea, and drawing nigh unto the ship: and they were afraid. John 6:20 But he saith unto them, It is I; be not afraid. |
| | 6:21 ...and **immediately** the ship was at the land whither they went. | | John 6:21 Then they willingly received him into the ship: and immediately the ship was at the land whither they went. |
| | Jesus in Capernaum | | Time Clue - John 6:17 & 6:59. |
| | 6:22 The day following, 6:24 When the people therefore saw that Jesus was not there, neither his disciples, they also took shipping, and came to **Capernaum**, seeking for Jesus. | 9:17 | John 6:22 The day following, when the people which stood on the other side of the sea saw that there was none other boat there, save that one whereinto his disciples were entered, and that Jesus went not with his disciples into the boat, but that his disciples were gone away alone; John 6:23 (Howbeit there came other boats from Tiberias nigh unto the place where they did eat bread, after that the Lord had given thanks:) John 6:24 When the people therefore saw that Jesus was not there, neither his disciples, they also took shipping, and came to Capernaum, seeking for Jesus. John 6:25 And when they had found him on the other side of the sea, they said unto him, Rabbi, when camest thou hither? John 6:26 Jesus answered them and said, Verily, verily, I say unto you, Ye seek me, not because ye saw the miracles, but because ye did eat of the loaves, and were filled. John 6:27 Labour not for the meat which perisheth, but for that meat which endureth unto everlasting life, which the Son of man shall give unto you: for him hath God the Father sealed. John 6:28 Then said they unto him, What shall we do, that we might work the works of God? John 6:29 Jesus answered and said unto them, This is the work of God, that ye believe on him whom he |

[74] John 6:19 ...they see Jesus walking on the sea, (*See Matthew 14:25 & Mark 6:48 for the first time that Jesus walked on the sea.*)

| Matthew | Mark | Important Events |
|---|---|---|
| | | |
| 14:36 | 6:56 | |

| | | | hath sent. |

**John** (continued)

John 6:30  They said therefore unto him, What sign showest thou then, that we may see, and believe thee? what dost thou work?

John 6:31  Our fathers did eat manna in the desert; as it is written, He gave them bread from heaven to eat.

John 6:32  Then Jesus said unto them, Verily, verily, I say unto you, Moses gave you not that bread from heaven; but my Father giveth you the true bread from heaven.

John 6:33  For the bread of God is he which cometh down from heaven, and giveth life unto the world.

John 6:34  Then said they unto him, Lord, evermore give us this bread.

John 6:35  And Jesus said unto them, I am the bread of life: he that cometh to me shall never hunger; and he that believeth on me shall never thirst.

John 6:36  But I said unto you, That ye also have seen me, and believe not.

John 6:37  All that the Father giveth me shall come to me; and him that cometh to me I will in no wise cast out.

John 6:38  For I came down from heaven, not to do mine own will, but the will of him that sent me.

John 6:39  And this is the Father's will which hath sent me, that of all which he hath given me I should lose nothing, but should raise it up again at the last day.

John 6:40  And this is the will of him that sent me, that every one which seeth the Son, and believeth on him, may have everlasting life: and I will raise him up at the last day.

**9:17**

John 6:41  The Jews then murmured at him, because he said, I am the bread which came down from heaven.

**6:42  And they said, Is not this Jesus, the son of Joseph, whose father and mother we know?** how is it then that he saith, I came down from heaven?

John 6:42  And they said, Is not this Jesus, the son of Joseph, whose father and mother we know? how is it then that he saith, I came down from heaven?

John 6:43  Jesus therefore answered and said unto them, Murmur not among yourselves.

John 6:44  No man can come to me, except the Father which hath sent me draw him: and I will raise him up at the last day.

John 6:45  It is written in the prophets, And they shall be all taught of God. Every man therefore that hath heard, and hath learned of the Father, cometh unto me.

John 6:46  Not that any man hath seen the Father, save he which is of God, he hath seen the Father.

John 6:47  Verily, verily, I say unto you, He that believeth on me hath everlasting life.

John 6:48  I am that bread of life.

John 6:49  Your fathers did eat manna in the wilderness, and are dead.

John 6:50  This is the bread which cometh down from heaven, that a man may eat thereof, and not die.

**6:51  I am the living bread which came down from heaven: if any man eat of this bread, he shall live for ever: and the bread that I will give is my flesh, which I will give for the life of the world.**

John 6:51  I am the living bread which came down from heaven: if any man eat of this bread, he shall live for ever: and the bread that I will give is my flesh, which I will give for the life of the world.

John 6:52  The Jews therefore strove among themselves, saying, How can this man give us his flesh to eat?

John 6:53  Then Jesus said unto them, Verily, verily, I say unto you, Except ye eat the flesh of the Son of man, and drink his blood, ye have no life in you.

John 6:54  Whoso eateth my flesh, and drinketh my blood, hath eternal life; and I will raise him up at the last day.

**6:55  For my flesh is meat indeed, and my blood is drink indeed**

John 6:55  For my flesh is meat indeed, and my blood is drink indeed.

John 6:56  He that eateth my flesh, and drinketh my blood, dwelleth in me, and I in him.

53

| Matthew | Mark | Important Events |
|---|---|---|
| 14:36 | 6:56 | |

| Time Lock - Time Lock | Time Lock - Time Lock | |

Matt. 15:1   Then came to Jesus scribes and Pharisees, which were of Jerusalem, saying,

Matt. 15:2   Why do thy disciples transgress the tradition of the elders? for they wash not their hands when they eat bread.

Matt. 15:3   But he answered and said unto them, Why do ye also transgress the commandment of God by your tradition?

Matt. 15:4  For God commanded, saying, Honour thy father and mother: and, He that curseth father or mother, let him die the death.

Matt. 15:5   But ye say, Whosoever shall say to his father or his mother, It is a gift, by whatsoever thou mightest be profited by me;

Matt. 15:6  And honour not his father or his mother, he shall be free. Thus have ye made the commandment of God of none effect by your tradition.

Mark 7:1   Then came together unto him the Pharisees, and certain of the scribes, which came from Jerusalem.

Mark 7:2  And when they saw some of his disciples eat bread with defiled, that is to say, with unwashen, hands, they found fault.

Mark 7:3  For the Pharisees, and all the Jews, except they wash their hands oft, eat not, holding the tradition of the elders.

Mark 7:4   And when they come from the market, except they wash, they eat not. And many other things there be, which they have received to hold, as the washing of cups, and pots, brasen vessels, and of tables.

Mark 7:5   Then the Pharisees and scribes asked him, Why walk not thy disciples according to the tradition of the elders, but eat bread with unwashen hands?

Mark 7:6   He answered and said unto them, Well

| ministry year | Key Scriptures & Footnotes | Luke | John |
|---|---|---|---|
| | **6:59** These things **said he in the synagogue**, as he taught in **Capernaum.** | | John 6:57 As the living Father hath sent me, and I live by the Father: so he that eateth me, even he shall live by me.<br>John 6:58 This is that bread which came down from heaven: not as your fathers did eat manna, and are dead: he that eateth of this bread shall live for ever.<br>John 6:59 These things said he in the synagogue, as he taught in Capernaum. |
| | **6:67**...Will ye also go away?<br>**6:68**...Then Simon Peter answered him, Lord, to whom shall we go? thou hast the words of eternal life. | 9:17 | John 6:60 Many therefore of his disciples, when they had heard this, said, This is an hard saying; who can hear it?<br>John 6:61 When Jesus knew in himself that his disciples murmured at it, he said unto them, Doth this offend you?<br>John 6:62 What and if ye shall see the Son of man ascend up where he was before?<br>John 6:63 It is the spirit that quickeneth; the flesh profiteth nothing: the words that I speak unto you, they are spirit, and they are life.<br>John 6:64 But there are some of you that believe not. For Jesus knew from the beginning who they were that believed not, and who should betray him.<br>John 6:65 And he said, Therefore said I unto you, that no man can come unto me, except it were given unto him of my Father.<br>John 6:66 From that time many of his disciples went back, and walked no more with him.<br>John 6:67 Then said Jesus unto the twelve, Will ye also go away?<br>John 6:68 Then Simon Peter answered him, Lord, to whom shall we go? thou hast the words of eternal life.<br>John 6:69 And we believe and are sure that thou art that Christ, the Son of the living God.<br>John 6:70 Jesus answered them, Have not I chosen you twelve, and one of you is a devil?<br>John 6:71 He spake of Judas Iscariot the son of Simon: for he it was that should betray him, being one of the twelve. |
| | John 6:4 And the passover, a feast of the Jews, was nigh..<br>John 7:1 After these things Jesus walked in Galilee: for he would not walk in Jewry, because the Jews sought to kill him.[75]<br>Pharisees from. Jerusalem | 9:17 | Time Clue - Time Clue |
| | **15:1** Then came to Jesus scribes and Pharisees, which were **of Jerusalem**, saying,....<br>**7:1** Then came together unto him the Pharisees, and certain of the scribes, which came **from Jerusalem**. | | |

---

[75] John 7:1 **After these things** Jesus walked in Galilee: for he would not walk in Jewry, because the Jews sought to kill him. (*The third Passover feast mentioned in John 6:4 happened after John 6:71 and before John 7:1. Some of the events of this Passover time are recorded in Matthew and Mark. Matthew 15:1 & Mark 7:1 say that Pharisees and scribes came from Jerusalem and questioned Jesus. When Jesus' answered them, Matthew 15:12 says that* "the Pharisees were offended." "**After these things**...*the Jews sought to kill him.*")

| Matthew | Mark | Important Events |
|---|---|---|
| Matt. 15:7　Ye hypocrites, well did Esaias prophesy of you, saying,<br>Matt. 15:8　This people draweth nigh unto me with their mouth, and honoureth me with their lips; but their heart is far from me.<br>Matt. 15:9　But in vain they do worship me, teaching for doctrines the commandments of men. | hath Esaias prophesied of you hypocrites, as it is written, This people honoureth me with their lips, but their heart is far from me.<br>Mark 7:7　Howbeit in vain do they worship me, teaching for doctrines the commandments of men.<br>Mark 7:8　For laying aside the commandment of God, ye hold the tradition of men, as the washing of pots and cups: and many other such like things ye do.<br>Mark 7:9　And he said unto them, Full well ye reject the commandment of God, that ye may keep your own tradition.<br>Mark 7:10　For Moses said, Honour thy father and thy mother; and, Whoso curseth father or mother, let him die the death:<br>Mark 7:11　But ye say, If a man shall say to his father or mother, It is Corban, that is to say, a gift, by whatsoever thou mightest be profited by me; he shall be free.<br>Mark 7:12　And ye suffer him no more to do aught for his father or his mother;<br>Mark 7:13　Making the word of God of none effect through your tradition, which ye have delivered: and many such like things do ye. | |
| Matt. 15:10　And he called the multitude, and said unto them, Hear, and understand:<br>Matt. 15:11　Not that which goeth into the mouth defileth a man; but that which cometh out of the mouth, this defileth a man. | Mark 7:14　And when he had called all the people unto him, he said unto them, Hearken unto me every one of you, and understand:<br>Mark 7:15　There is nothing from without a man, that entering into him can defile him: but the things which come out of him, those are they that defile the man.<br>Mark 7:16　If any man have ears to hear, let him hear. | |
| Matt. 15:12　Then came his disciples, and said unto him, Knowest thou that the Pharisees were offended, after they heard this saying?<br>Matt. 15:13　But he answered and said, Every plant, which my heavenly Father hath not planted, shall be rooted up.<br>Matt. 15:14　Let them alone: they be blind leaders of the blind. And if the blind lead the blind, both shall fall into the ditch. | | |
| Time Lock - Time Lock | Time Lock - Time Lock | |
| Matt. 15:15　Then answered Peter and said unto him, Declare unto us this parable.<br>Matt. 15:16　And Jesus said, Are ye also yet without understanding?<br>Matt. 15:17　Do not ye yet understand, that whatsoever entereth in at the mouth goeth into the belly, and is cast out into the draught?<br>Matt. 15:18　But those things which proceed out of the mouth come forth from the heart; and they defile the man.<br>Matt. 15:19　For out of the heart proceed evil thoughts, murders, adulteries, fornications, thefts, false witness, blasphemies:<br>Matt. 15:20　These are the things which defile a man: but to eat with unwashen hands defileth not a man. | Mark 7:17　And when he was entered into the house from the people, his disciples asked him concerning the parable.<br>Mark 7:18　And he saith unto them, Are ye so without understanding also? Do ye not perceive, that whatsoever thing from without entereth into the man, it cannot defile him;<br>Mark 7:19　Because it entereth not into his heart, but into the belly, and goeth out into the draught, purging all meats?<br>Mark 7:20　And he said, That which cometh out of the man, that defileth the man.<br>Mark 7:21　For from within, out of the heart of men, proceed evil thoughts, adulteries, fornications, murders,<br>Mark 7:22　Thefts, covetousness, wickedness, deceit, lasciviousness, an evil eye, blasphemy, pride, foolishness:<br>Mark 7:23　All these evil things come from within, and defile the man. | |
| | | **Jesus walked in Galilee**<br>John 7:1<br><br>Map 74 |

| ministry year | Key Scriptures & Footnotes | Luke | John |
|---|---|---|---|
| | 15:10 And he called the multitude,.... | 9:17 | 6:71 |
| | Entered the house. | | |
| | 7:17 And when he was entered into the house... | 9:17 | 6:71 |
| | Jesus walked in Galilee. | | Time Clue - Time Clue |
| | 7:1...After these things Jesus walked in Galilee: for he would not walk in Jewry, because the Jews sought to kill him. [76] | 9:17 | John 7:1 After these things Jesus walked in Galilee: for he would not walk in Jewry, because the Jews sought to kill him. |

[76] John 7:1 **After these things** Jesus walked in Galilee.... (*The third Passover mentioned in John 6:4 did not happen before John 6:71. When John says, "After these things," he is referring to the previous events that he recorded and also the Passover events that he did not record.*)

| Matthew | Mark | Important Events |
|---|---|---|
| Time Lock - Time Lock | Time Lock - Time Lock | |
| Matt. 15:21 Then Jesus went thence, and departed into the coasts of Tyre and Sidon. Matt. 15:22 And, behold, a woman of Canaan came out of the same coasts, and cried unto him, saying, Have mercy on me, O Lord, thou Son of David; my daughter is grievously vexed with a devil. Matt. 15:23 But he answered her not a word. And his disciples came and besought him, saying, Send her away; for she crieth after us. Matt. 15:24 But he answered and said, I am not sent but unto the lost sheep of the house of Israel. Matt. 15:25 Then came she and worshipped him, saying, Lord, help me. Matt. 15:26 But he answered and said, It is not meet to take the children's bread, and to cast it to dogs. Matt. 15:27 And she said, Truth, Lord: yet the dogs eat of the crumbs which fall from their masters' table. Matt. 15:28 Then Jesus answered and said unto her, O woman, great is thy faith: be it unto thee even as thou wilt. And her daughter was made whole from that very hour. | Mark 7:24 And from thence he arose, and went into the borders of Tyre and Sidon, and entered into an house, and would have no man know it: but he could not be hid. Mark 7:25 For a certain woman, whose young daughter had an unclean spirit, heard of him, and came and fell at his feet: Mark 7:26 The woman was a Greek, a Syrophenician by nation; and she besought him that he would cast forth the devil out of her daughter. Mark 7:27 But Jesus said unto her, Let the children first be filled: for it is not meet to take the children's bread, and to cast it unto the dogs. Mark 7:28 And she answered and said unto him, Yes, Lord: yet the dogs under the table eat of the children's crumbs. Mark 7:29 And he said unto her, For this saying go thy way; the devil is gone out of thy daughter. Mark 7:30 And when she was come to her house, she found the devil gone out, and her daughter laid upon the bed. | **Jesus heals the daughter of a woman of Canaan** Matt. 15:22 & Mark 7:25 Map 75 |
| Time Lock - Time Lock | Time Lock - Time Lock | |
| Matt. 15:29 And Jesus departed from thence, and came nigh unto the sea of Galilee; and went up into a mountain, and sat down there. Matt. 15:30 And great multitudes came unto him, having with them those that were lame, blind, dumb, maimed, and many others, and cast them down at Jesus' feet; and he healed them: Matt. 15:31 Insomuch that the multitude wondered, when they saw the dumb to speak, the maimed to be whole, the lame to walk, and the blind to see: and they glorified the God of Israel. | Mark 7:31 And again, departing from the coasts of Tyre and Sidon, he came unto the sea of Galilee, through the midst of the coasts of Decapolis. Mark 7:32 And they bring unto him one that was deaf, and had an impediment in his speech; and they beseech him to put his hand upon him. Mark 7:33 And he took him aside from the multitude, and put his fingers into his ears, and he spit, and touched his tongue; Mark 7:34 And looking up to heaven, he sighed, and saith unto him, Ephphatha, that is, Be opened. Mark 7:35 And straightway his ears were opened, and the string of his tongue was loosed, and he spake plain. Mark 7:36 And he charged them that they should tell no man: but the more he charged them, so much the more a great deal they published it; Mark 7:37 And were beyond measure astonished, saying, He hath done all things well: he maketh both the deaf to hear, and the dumb to speak. | Map 76 |
| Time Lock - Time Lock | Time Lock - Time Lock | |
| Matt. 15:32 Then Jesus called his disciples unto him, and said, I have compassion on the multitude, because they continue with me now three days, and have nothing to eat: and I will not send them away fasting, lest they faint in the way. Matt. 15:33 And his disciples say unto him, Whence should we have so much bread in the wilderness, as to fill so great a multitude? Matt. 15:34 And Jesus saith unto them, How many loaves have ye? And they said, Seven, and a few little fishes. Matt. 15:35 And he commanded the multitude to sit down on the ground. Matt. 15:36 And he took the seven loaves and the fishes, and gave thanks, and brake them, and gave to his disciples, and the disciples to the multitude. Matt. 15:37 And they did all eat, and were filled: and they took up of the broken meat that was left seven baskets full. Matt. 15:38 And they that did eat were four thousand men, beside women and children. | Mark 8:1 In those days the multitude being very great, and having nothing to eat, Jesus called his disciples unto him, and saith unto them, Mark 8:2 I have compassion on the multitude, because they have now been with me three days, and have nothing to eat: Mark 8:3 And if I send them away fasting to their own houses, they will faint by the way: for divers of them came from far. Mark 8:4 And his disciples answered him, From whence can a man satisfy these men with bread here in the wilderness? Mark 8:5 And he asked them, How many loaves have ye? And they said, Seven. Mark 8:6 And he commanded the people to sit down on the ground: and he took the seven loaves, and gave thanks, and brake, and gave to his disciples to set before them; and they did set them before the people. Mark 8:7 And they had a few small fishes: and he blessed, and commanded to set them also before them. Mark 8:8 So they did eat, and were filled: and they | **Jesus feeds the 4 0 0 0** Matt. 15:32 & Mark 8:1 Map 77 |

| ministry year | Key Scriptures & Footnotes | Luke | John |
|---|---|---|---|
| | **Jesus went to Tyre.** | | |
| | 7:24 And from thence he arose, and went into the borders of Tyre and Sidon,.... | | |
| | **Jesus came to Decapolis.** | | |
| | 7:31...he came unto the sea of Galilee, through the midst of the coasts of Decapolis.<br>7:32 And they bring unto him one that was deaf, and had an impediment in his speech;....<br>7:34...he sighed, and saith unto him, Ephphatha, that is, Be opened.<br>7:35 And...his ears were opened,...and he spake plain. | 9:17 | 7:1 |
| | **Jesus feeds the 4000.** | | |
| | 8:2 I have compassion on the multitude, because they have now **been with me three days**, and have nothing to eat:<br>15:34...Seven, and a few little fishes.<br><br>15:36 And he took the seven loaves and the fishes, and gave thanks, and brake them,.... | 9:17 | 7:1 |

| Matthew | Mark | Important Events |
|---|---|---|
| | took up of the broken meat that was left seven baskets.<br>Mark 8:9a   And they that had eaten were about four thousand: | |
| Time Lock - Time Lock | Time Lock - Time Lock | |
| Matt. 15:39   And he sent away the multitude, and took ship, and came into the coasts of Magdala.<br>Matt. 16:1   The Pharisees also with the Sadducees came, and tempting desired him that he would show them a sign from heaven.<br>Matt. 16:2   He answered and said unto them, When it is evening, ye say, It will be fair weather: for the sky is red.<br>Matt. 16:3   And in the morning, It will be foul weather today: for the sky is red and lowering. O ye hypocrites, ye can discern the face of the sky; but can ye not discern the signs of the times?<br>Matt. 16:4a   A wicked and adulterous generation seeketh after a sign; and there shall no sign be given unto it, but the sign of the prophet Jonas. | Mark 8:9b   and he sent them away.<br>Mark 8:10   And straightway he entered into a ship with his disciples, and came into the parts of Dalmanutha.<br>Mark 8:11   And the Pharisees came forth, and began to question with him, seeking of him a sign from heaven, tempting him.<br>Mark 8:12   And he sighed deeply in his spirit, and saith, Why doth this generation seek after a sign? verily I say unto you, There shall no sign be given unto this generation. | **Jesus sent away the 4000**<br>Matt. 15:39 & Mark 8:9b<br><br>Map 78 |
| Matt. 16:4b   And he left them, and departed.<br>Matt. 16:5   And when his disciples were come to the other side, they had forgotten to take bread.<br>Matt. 16:6   Then Jesus said unto them, Take heed and beware of the leaven of the Pharisees and of the Sadducees.<br>Matt. 16:7   And they reasoned among themselves, saying, It is because we have taken no bread.<br>Matt. 16:8   Which when Jesus perceived, he said unto them, O ye of little faith, why reason ye among yourselves, because ye have brought no bread?<br>Matt. 16:9   Do ye not yet understand, neither remember the five loaves of the five thousand, and how many baskets ye took up?<br>Matt. 16:10   Neither the seven loaves of the four thousand, and how many baskets ye took up?<br>Matt. 16:11   How is it that ye do not understand that I spake it not to you concerning bread, that ye should beware of the leaven of the Pharisees and of the Sadducees?<br>Matt. 16:12   Then understood they how that he bade them not beware of the leaven of bread, but of the doctrine of the Pharisees and of the Sadducees. | Mark 8:13   And he left them, and entering into the ship again departed to the other side.<br>Mark 8:14   Now the disciples had forgotten to take bread, neither had they in the ship with them more than one loaf.<br>Mark 8:15   And he charged them, saying, Take heed, beware of the leaven of the Pharisees, and of the leaven of Herod.<br>Mark 8:16   And they reasoned among themselves, saying, It is because we have no bread.<br>Mark 8:17   And when Jesus knew it, he saith unto them, Why reason ye, because ye have no bread? perceive ye not yet, neither understand? have ye your heart yet hardened?<br>Mark 8:18   Having eyes, see ye not? and having ears, hear ye not? and do ye not remember?<br>Mark 8:19   When I brake the five loaves among five thousand, how many baskets full of fragments took ye up? They say unto him, Twelve.<br>Mark 8:20   And when the seven among four thousand, how many baskets full of fragments took ye up? And they said, Seven.<br>Mark 8:21   And he said unto them, How is it that ye do not understand? | Map 79 |
| Time Lock - Time Lock | Time Lock - Time Lock | |

| ministry year | Key Scriptures & Footnotes | Luke | John |
|---|---|---|---|
| | 8:9a And they that had eaten were about **four thousand**....[77] | | |
| | Jesus sent them away. | | |
| | 15:39 And **he sent** away the multitude, and took ship, and came into the coasts of Magdala.<br>8:10...came into the parts of Dalmanutha. | 9:17 | 7:1 |
| | 8:13 And he left them, and entering into the ship **again** departed to the other side....[78] | | |
| | Feast of Tabernacles | | Time Clue - See footnote for John 7:2 |
| | 7:2 Now the Jews' **feast of tabernacles** was at hand. [79]<br>7:3 His brethren therefore said....[80]<br><br>7:6...My time is not yet come:.... | 9:17 | John 7:2 Now the Jews' feast of tabernacles was at hand.<br>John 7:3 His brethren therefore said unto him, Depart hence, and go into Judaea, that thy disciples also may see the works that thou doest.<br>John 7:4 For there is no man that doeth any thing in secret, and he himself seeketh to be known openly. If thou do these things, show thyself to the world.<br>John 7:5 For neither did his brethren believe in him.<br>John 7:6 Then Jesus said unto them, My time is not yet come: but your time is always ready.<br>John 7:7 The world cannot hate you; but me it hateth, because I testify of it, that the works thereof are evil. |

[77] Mark 8:9a And they that had eaten were about four thousand: (*See the feeding of the 5000 in Matthew 14:15, Mark 6:35, Luke 9:12, and John 6:5.*)

[78] Mark 8:13 And he left them, and entering into the ship again departed to the other side. (*Jesus may have been taking the ship back to the place where He feed the 4000. That was a wilderness area according to Matthew 15:33. If they were going directly to the city of Bethsaida, Mark 8:22, then the disciples may not have been concerned about the amount of bread they had with them found in Matthew 16:5 & Mark 8:14. The time space between Mark 8:21 and Mark 8:22 allows Jesus and the disciples time to attend the feast of tabernacles of John 7:2-53. This correlates with the footnote for John 7:2.*)

[79] John 7:2 Now the Jews' feast of tabernacles was at hand. (*This is in the fall after the third Passover. We cannot be certain that Jesus went to the Feast of Tabernacles before He went to Bethsaida and to the towns of Caesarea Philippi. However, the feast gave the disciples time with their families and friends. This would have given them a knowledgeable basis to answer Jesus' question when he inquires of them in Matthew 16:13 saying,* "Whom do men say that I the Son of man am?")

[80] John 7:3 His brethren therefore said unto him, Depart hence, and go into Judaea.... (*Jesus may have been in Nazareth visiting His family.*)

| Matthew | Mark | Important Events |
|---------|------|------------------|
|         |      |                  |
|         |      | Map 80           |
| 16:12   | 8:21 | **Jesus went up to the feast of tabernacles** John 7:10 |
|         |      | Map 81           |
| 16:12   | 8:21 |                  |

| ministry year | Key Scriptures & Footnotes | Luke | John |
|---|---|---|---|
| | 7:8...I go not up yet unto this feast;.... | | John 7:8  Go ye up unto this feast: I go not up yet unto this feast; for my time is not yet full come. |
| | 7:9...he abode still in Galilee. | | John 7:9  When he had said these words unto them, he abode still in Galilee. |
| | Departed from Galilee. | | Time Clue - Time Clue |
| | 7:10...then went he also up unto the feast,....[81] | 9:17 | John 7:10  But when his brethren were gone up, then went he also up unto the feast, not openly, but as it were in secret. |
| | 7:11  Then the Jews sought him at the feast,.... | 9:17 | John 7:11  Then the Jews sought him at the feast, and said, Where is he?
John 7:12  And there was much murmuring among the people concerning him: for some said, He is a good man: others said, Nay; but he deceiveth the people.
John 7:13  Howbeit no man spake openly of him for fear of the Jews. |
| | John 7:14  Now about the midst of the feast Jesus went up into the temple, and taught. | | John 7:14  Now about the midst of the feast Jesus went up into the temple, and taught.
John 7:15  And the Jews marvelled, saying, How knoweth this man letters, having never learned?
John 7:16  Jesus answered them, and said, My doctrine is not mine, but his that sent me.
John 7:17  If any man will do his will, he shall know of the doctrine, whether it be of God, or whether I speak of myself.
John 7:18  He that speaketh of himself seeketh his own glory: but he that seeketh his glory that sent him, the same is true, and no unrighteousness is in him.
John 7:19  Did not Moses give you the law, and yet none of you keepeth the law? Why go ye about to kill me?
John 7:20  The people answered and said, Thou hast a devil: who goeth about to kill thee?
John 7:21  Jesus answered and said unto them, I have done one work, and ye all marvel.
John 7:22  Moses therefore gave unto you circumcision; (not because it is of Moses, but of the fathers;) and ye on the sabbath day circumcise a man.
John 7:23  If a man on the sabbath day receive circumcision, that the law of Moses should not be broken; are ye angry at me, because I have made a man every whit whole on the sabbath day?
John 7:24  Judge not according to the appearance, but judge righteous judgment.
John 7:25  Then said some of them of Jerusalem, Is not this he, whom they seek to kill?
John 7:26  But, lo, he speaketh boldly, and they say nothing unto him. Do the rulers know indeed that this is the very Christ?
John 7:27  Howbeit we know this man whence he is: but when Christ cometh, no man knoweth whence he is.
John 7:28  Then cried Jesus in the temple as he taught, saying, Ye both know me, and ye know whence I am: and I am not come of myself, but he that sent me is true, whom ye know not.
John 7:29  But I know him: for I am from him, and he hath sent me. |
| | 7:30  Then they sought to take him: but no man laid hands on him, because his hour was not yet come. | | John 7:30  Then they sought to take him: but no man laid hands on him, because his hour was not yet come.
John 7:31  And many of the people believed on him, and said, When Christ cometh, will he do more miracles than these which this man hath done?
John 7:32  The Pharisees heard that the people |

[81] John 7:10  But when his brethren were gone up, then went he also up unto the feast, not openly, but as it were in secret. (This is the *Feast of Tabernacles held in Jerusalem in the fall after the third Passover.*)

| Matthew | Mark | Important Events |
|---------|------|------------------|
| | | |
| 16:12 | 8:21 | |
| | | Map 82 |
| | Time Clue - Time Clue | |
| | Mark 8:22   And he cometh to Bethsaida; and they bring a blind man unto him, and besought him to touch him.<br>Mark 8:23   And he took the blind man by the hand, and led him out of the town; and when he had spit on his eyes, and put his hands upon him, he asked him if he saw aught.<br>Mark 8:24   And he looked up, and said, I see men as trees, walking. | Map 83 |

| ministry year | Key Scriptures & Footnotes | Luke | John |
| --- | --- | --- | --- |
| | | | murmured such things concerning him; and the Pharisees and the chief priests sent officers to take him. |
| | | | John 7:33   Then said Jesus unto them, Yet a little while am I with you, and then I go unto him that sent me. |
| | | | John 7:34   Ye shall seek me, and shall not find me: and where I am, thither ye cannot come. |
| | | | John 7:35   Then said the Jews among themselves, Whither will he go, that we shall not find him? will he go unto the dispersed among the Gentiles, and teach the Gentiles? |
| | | | John 7:36   What manner of saying is this that he said, Ye shall seek me, and shall not find me: and where I am, thither ye cannot come? |
| | Last day of feast. | | Time Clue - Time Clue |
| | 7:37 In **the last day**, that great day of the feast,[82] Jesus stood and cried, saying, If any man thirst, let him come unto me, and drink.  7:38  He that believeth on me, as the scripture hath said, out of his belly shall flow rivers of living water. | 9:17 | John 7:37   In the last day, that great day of the feast, Jesus stood and cried, saying, If any man thirst, let him come unto me, and drink. |
| | | | John 7:38   He that believeth on me, as the scripture hath said, out of his belly shall flow rivers of living water. |
| | | | John 7:39   (But this spake he of the Spirit, which they that believe on him should receive: for the Holy Ghost was not yet given; because that Jesus was not yet glorified.) |
| | | | John 7:40   Many of the people therefore, when they heard this saying, said, Of a truth this is the Prophet. |
| | | | John 7:41   Others said, This is the Christ. But some said, Shall Christ come out of Galilee? |
| | | | John 7:42   Hath not the scripture said, That Christ cometh of the seed of David, and out of the town of Bethlehem, where David was? |
| | | | John 7:43   So there was a division among the people because of him. |
| | | | John 7:44   And some of them would have taken him; but no man laid hands on him. |
| | | | John 7:45   Then came the officers to the chief priests and Pharisees; and they said unto them, Why have ye not brought him? |
| | 7:46  The officers answered, Never man spake like this man. | | John 7:46   The officers answered, Never man spake like this man. |
| | | | John 7:47   Then answered them the Pharisees, Are ye also deceived? |
| | | | John 7:48   Have any of the rulers or of the Pharisees believed on him? |
| | | | John 7:49   But this people who knoweth not the law are cursed. |
| | | | John 7:50   Nicodemus saith unto them, (he that came to Jesus by night, being one of them,) |
| | | | John 7:51   Doth our law judge any man, before it hear him, and know what he doeth? |
| | | | John 7:52   They answered and said unto him, Art thou also of Galilee? Search, and look: for out of Galilee ariseth no prophet. |
| | 7:53  And **every man** went unto his own house[83] | | John 7:53   And every man went unto his own house. |
| | Jesus came to Bethsaida. | | Time Clue - See footnote for John 7:53 |
| | 8:22...he **cometh to Bethsaida**....  8:23...spit on his eyes.... | | |

---

[82] John 7:37   In the last day, that great day of the feast.... (*This is the last day Feast of Tabernacles mentioned in John 7:10.  See Leviticus 23:36 ...on the eight day shall be an holy convocation unto you....*)

[83] John 7:53    And every man went unto his **own house**. (*Jesus departed from Jerusalem after the Feast of Tabernacles.  He probably returned to His "own house" in Galilee.*)

| Matthew | Mark | Important Events |
|---|---|---|
| | Mark 8:25   After that he put his hands again upon his eyes, and made him look up: and he was restored, and saw every man clearly.<br>Mark 8:26    And he sent him away to his house, saying, Neither go into the town, nor tell it to any in the town. | |
| <center>Time Lock - Time Lock</center> | <center>Time Lock - Time Lock</center> | |
| Matt. 16:13   When Jesus came into the coasts of Caesarea Philippi, he asked his disciples, saying, Whom do men say that I the Son of man am?<br>Matt. 16:14   And they said, Some say that thou art John the Baptist: some, Elias; and others, Jeremias, or one of the prophets.<br>Matt. 16:15   He saith unto them, But whom say ye that I am?<br>Matt. 16:16   And Simon Peter answered and said, Thou art the Christ, the Son of the living God.<br>Matt. 16:17   And Jesus answered and said unto him, Blessed art thou, Simon Bar-jona: for flesh and blood hath not revealed it unto thee, but my Father which is in heaven.<br>Matt. 16:18   And I say also unto thee, That thou art Peter, and upon this rock I will build my church; and the gates of hell shall not prevail against it.<br>Matt. 16:19   And I will give unto thee the keys of the kingdom of heaven: and whatsoever thou shalt bind on earth shall be bound in heaven: and whatsoever thou shalt loose on earth shall be loosed in heaven.<br>Matt. 16:20   Then charged he his disciples that they should tell no man that he was Jesus the Christ. | Mark 8:27   And Jesus went out, and his disciples, into the towns of Caesarea Philippi: and by the way he asked his disciples, saying unto them, Whom do men say that I am?<br>Mark 8:28   And they answered, John the Baptist: but some say, Elias; and others, One of the prophets.<br>Mark 8:29   And he saith unto them, But whom say ye that I am? And Peter answereth and saith unto him, Thou art the Christ.<br>Mark 8:30   And he charged them that they should tell no man of him. | **Trip to the towns of Caesarea Philippi**<br>Matt. 16:13, Mark 8:27, & Luke 9:18<br><br>Map 84 |
| Matt. 16:21   From that time forth began Jesus to show unto his disciples, how that he must go unto Jerusalem, and suffer many things of the elders and chief priests and scribes, and be killed, and be raised again the third day.<br>Matt. 16:22    Then Peter took him, and began to rebuke him, saying, Be it far from thee, Lord: this shall not be unto thee.<br>Matt. 16:23  But he turned, and said unto Peter, Get thee behind me, Satan: thou art an offence unto me: for thou savourest not the things that be of God, but those that be of men. | Mark 8:31   And he began to teach them, that the Son of man must suffer many things, and be rejected of the elders, and of the chief priests, and scribes, and be killed, and after three days rise again.<br>Mark 8:32    And he spake that saying openly. And Peter took him, and began to rebuke him.<br>Mark 8:33   But when he had turned about and looked on his disciples, he rebuked Peter, saying, Get thee behind me, Satan: for thou savourest not the things that be of God, but the things that be of men. | |
| <center>Time Lock - Time Lock</center> | <center>Time Lock - Time Lock</center> | |
| Matt. 16:24   Then said Jesus unto his disciples, If any man will come after me, let him deny himself, and take up his cross, and follow me.<br>Matt. 16:25   For whosoever will save his life shall lose it: and whosoever will lose his life for my sake shall find it.<br>Matt. 16:26   For what is a man profited, if he shall gain the whole world, and lose his own soul? or what shall a man give in exchange for his soul?<br>Matt. 16:27   For the Son of man shall come in the glory of his Father with his angels; and then he shall reward every man according to his works. | Mark 8:34   And when he had called the people unto him with his disciples also, he said unto them, Whosoever will come after me, let him deny himself, and take up his cross, and follow me.<br>Mark 8:35   For whosoever will save his life shall lose it; but whosoever shall lose his life for my sake and the gospel's, the same shall save it.<br>Mark 8:36   For what shall it profit a man, if he shall gain the whole world, and lose his own soul?<br>Mark 8:37   Or what shall a man give in exchange for his soul?<br>Mark 8:38   Whosoever therefore shall be ashamed of me and of my words in this adulterous and sinful generation; of him also shall the Son of man be ashamed, when he cometh in the glory of his Father with the holy angels. | |
| Matt. 16:28   Verily I say unto you, There be some standing here, which shall not taste of death, till they see the Son of man coming in his kingdom | Mark 9:1   And he said unto them, Verily I say unto you, That there be some of them that stand here, which shall not taste of death, till they have seen the kingdom of God come with power. | |
| <center>Time Lock - Time Lock</center> | <center>Time Lock - Time Lock</center> | |
| Matt. 17:1   And after six days Jesus taketh Peter, James, and John his brother, and bringeth them up into an high mountain apart,<br>Matt. 17:2   And was transfigured before them: and his face did shine as the sun, and his raiment was white as the light.<br>Matt. 17:3   And, behold, there appeared unto them Moses and Elias talking with him. | Mark 9:2   And after six days Jesus taketh with him Peter, and James, and John, and leadeth them up into an high mountain apart by themselves: and he was transfigured before them.<br>Mark 9:3    And his raiment became shining, exceeding white as snow; so as no fuller on earth can white them.<br>Mark 9:4   And there appeared unto them Elias with | **Jesus was transfigured**<br>Matt. 17:2, Mark 9:2, & Luke 9:29<br><br>Map 85 |

| ministry year | Key Scriptures & Footnotes | Luke | John |
|---|---|---|---|
| | 8:25...and made him look up: and he was restored,.... | | |
| | Thou art the Christ. | Time Lock - Time Lock | |
| | 16:13 When Jesus came into the coasts of Caesarea Philippi, he asked his disciples, saying, Whom do men say that I the Son of man am?<br><br>16:16 And Simon Peter answered and said, **Thou art the Christ, the Son of the living God.** | Luke 9:18 And it came to pass, as he was alone praying, his disciples were with him: and he asked them, saying, Whom say the people that I am?<br>Luke 9:19 They answering said, John the Baptist; but some say, Elias; and others say, that one of the old prophets is risen again.<br>Luke 9:20 He said unto them, But whom say ye that I am? Peter answering said, The Christ of God.<br>Luke 9:21 And he straitly charged them, and commanded them to tell no man that thing; | 7:53 |
| | 16:21 **From that time forth** began Jesus to show unto his disciples, how that he must go unto Jerusalem, and suffer many things | Luke 9:22 Saying, The Son of man must suffer many things, and be rejected of the elders and chief priests and scribes, and be slain, and be raised the third day. | |
| | Take up your cross. | Time Lock - Time Lock | |
| | 8:34 And when he had called the people unto him...let him deny himself, and take up his cross, and follow me. | Luke 9:23 And he said to them all, If any man will come after me, let him deny himself, and take up his cross daily, and follow me.<br>Luke 9:24 For whosoever will save his life shall lose it: but whosoever will lose his life for my sake, the same shall save it.<br>Luke 9:25 For what is a man advantaged, if he gain the whole world, and lose himself, or be cast away?<br>Luke 9:26 For whosoever shall be ashamed of me and of my words, of him shall the Son of man be ashamed, when he shall come in his own glory, and in his Father's, and of the holy angels. | 7:53 |
| | | Luke 9:27 But I tell you of a truth, there be some standing here, which shall not taste of death, till they see the kingdom of God. | |
| | Jesus, Peter, James, John | Time Lock - Time Lock | |
| | 9:2 And after **six** days Jesus taketh....<br>9:28 And it came to pass **about an eight** days **after these sayings**....<br>17:2 And was transfigured before | Luke 9:28 And it came to pass about an eight days after these sayings, he took Peter and John and James, and went up into a mountain to pray.<br>Luke 9:29 And as he prayed, the fashion of his countenance was altered, and his raiment was white and glistering.<br>Luke 9:30 And, behold, there talked with him two men, which were Moses and Elias: | |

| Matthew | Mark | Important Events |
|---|---|---|
| | Moses: and they were talking with Jesus. | |
| Matt. 17:4    Then answered Peter, and said unto Jesus, Lord, it is good for us to be here: if thou wilt, let us make here three tabernacles; one for thee, and one for Moses, and one for Elias.<br>Matt. 17:5    While he yet spake, behold, a bright cloud overshadowed them: and behold a voice out of the cloud, which said, This is my beloved Son, in whom I am well pleased; hear ye him.<br> Matt. 17:6  And when the disciples heard it, they fell on their face, and were sore afraid.<br>Matt. 17:7  And Jesus came and touched them, and said, Arise, and be not afraid.<br>Matt. 17:8   And when they had lifted up their eyes, they saw no man, save Jesus only. | Mark 9:5    And Peter answered and said to Jesus, Master, it is good for us to be here: and let us make three tabernacles; one for thee, and one for Moses, and one for Elias.<br>Mark 9:6  For he wist not what to say; for they were sore afraid.<br>Mark 9:7  And there was a cloud that overshadowed them: and a voice came out of the cloud, saying, This is my beloved Son: hear him.<br>Mark 9:8    And suddenly, when they had looked round about, they saw no man any more, save Jesus only with themselves. | |
| Matt. 17:9    And as they came down from the mountain, Jesus charged them, saying, Tell the vision to no man, until the Son of man be risen again from the dead. | Mark 9:9    And as they came down from the mountain, he charged them that they should tell no man what things they had seen, till the Son of man were risen from the dead.<br>Mark 9:10    And they kept that saying with themselves, questioning one with another what the rising from the dead should mean. | Map 86 |
| Matt. 17:10    And his disciples asked him, saying, Why then say the scribes that Elias must first come?<br>Matt. 17:11  And Jesus answered and said unto them, Elias truly shall first come, and restore all things.<br>Matt. 17:12   But I say unto you, That Elias is come already, and they knew him not, but have done unto him whatsoever they listed. Likewise shall also the Son of man suffer of them.<br>Matt. 17:13    Then the disciples understood that he spake unto them of John the Baptist. | Mark 9:11  And they asked him, saying, Why say the scribes that Elias must first come?<br>Mark 9:12    And he answered and told them, Elias verily cometh first, and restoreth all things; and how it is written of the Son of man, that he must suffer many things, and be set at nought.<br>Mark 9:13  But I say unto you, That Elias is indeed come, and they have done unto him whatsoever they listed, as it is written of him.. | |
| Matt. 17:14    And when they were come to the multitude, there came to him a certain man, kneeling down to him, and saying,<br>Matt. 17:15  Lord, have mercy on my son: for he is lunatic, and sore vexed: for ofttimes he falleth into the fire, and oft into the water.<br>Matt. 17:16  And I brought him to thy disciples, and they could not cure him.<br>Matt. 17:17   Then Jesus answered and said, O faithless and perverse generation, how long shall I be with you? how long shall I suffer you? bring him hither to me. | Mark 9:14    And when he came to his disciples, he saw a great multitude about them, and the scribes questioning with them.<br>Mark 9:15    And straightway all the people, when they beheld him, were greatly amazed, and running to him saluted him.<br>Mark 9:16  And he asked the scribes, What question ye with them?<br>Mark 9:17  And one of the multitude answered and said, Master, I have brought unto thee my son, which hath a dumb spirit;<br>Mark 9:18    And wheresoever he taketh him, he teareth him: and he foameth, and gnasheth with his teeth, and pineth away: and I spake to thy disciples that they should cast him out; and they could not.<br>Mark 9:19  He answereth him, and saith, O faithless generation, how long shall I be with you? how long shall I suffer you? bring him unto me. | |
| | Mark 9:20    And they brought him unto him: and when he saw him, straightway the spirit tare him; and he fell on the ground, and wallowed foaming.<br>Mark 9:21  And he asked his father, How long is it ago since this came unto him? And he said, Of a child.<br>Mark 9:22  And ofttimes it hath cast him into the fire, and into the waters, to destroy him: but if thou canst do any thing, have compassion on us, and help us.<br>Mark 9:23  Jesus said unto him, If thou canst believe, all things are possible to him that believeth.<br>Mark 9:24    And straightway the father of the child cried out, and said with tears, Lord, I believe; help thou mine unbelief. | |
| Matt. 17:18    And Jesus rebuked the devil; and he departed out of him: and the child was cured from that very hour. | Mark 9:25    When Jesus saw that the people came running together, he rebuked the foul spirit, saying unto him, Thou dumb and deaf spirit, I charge thee, | |

| ministry year | Key Scriptures & Footnotes | Luke | John |
|---|---|---|---|
| them:.... | | Luke 9:31 Who appeared in glory, and spake of his decease which he should accomplish at Jerusalem.<br>Luke 9:32 But Peter and they that were with him were heavy with sleep: and when they were awake, they saw his glory, and the two men that stood with him. | |
| | 9:7...a voice came out of the cloud, saying, This is my beloved Son: hear him. | Luke 9:33 And it came to pass, as they departed from him, Peter said unto Jesus, Master, it is good for us to be here: and let us make three tabernacles; one for thee, and one for Moses, and one for Elias: not knowing what he said.<br>Luke 9:34 While he thus spake, there came a cloud, and overshadowed them: and they feared as they entered into the cloud.<br>Luke 9:35 And there came a voice out of the cloud, saying, This is my beloved Son: hear him.<br>Luke 9:36a And when the voice was past, Jesus was found alone. | 7:53 |
| | 9:37...on the next day....<br>17:9...as they came down from the mountain... | Luke 9:36b And they kept it close, and told no man in those days any of those things which they had seen.<br>Luke 9:37a And it came to pass, that on the next day, | 7:53 |
| | | | |
| | 17:15 Lord, have mercy on my son:.... | Luke 9:37b when they were come down from the hill, much people met him.<br>Luke 9:38 And, behold, a man of the company cried out, saying, Master, I beseech thee, look upon my son: for he is mine only child.<br>Luke 9:39 And, lo, a spirit taketh him, and he suddenly crieth out; and it teareth him that he foameth again, and bruising him hardly departeth from him.<br>Luke 9:40 And I besought thy disciples to cast him out; and they could not.<br>Luke 9:41 And Jesus answering said, O faithless and perverse generation, how long shall I be with you, and suffer you? Bring thy son hither. | |
| | | Luke 9:42a And as he was yet a-coming, the devil threw him down, and tare him. | |
| | | Luke 9:42b And Jesus rebuked the unclean spirit, and healed the child, and delivered him again to his father. | 7:53 |

| Matthew | Mark | Important Events |
|---|---|---|
| | come out of him, and enter no more into him.<br>Mark 9:26   And the spirit cried, and rent him sore, and came out of him: and he was as one dead; insomuch that many said, He is dead.<br>Mark 9:27  But Jesus took him by the hand, and lifted him up; and he arose. | |
| Matt. 17:19  Then came the disciples to Jesus apart, and said, Why could not we cast him out?<br>Matt. 17:20   And Jesus said unto them, Because of your unbelief: for verily I say unto you, If ye have faith as a grain of mustard seed, ye shall say unto this mountain, Remove hence to yonder place; and it shall remove; and nothing shall be impossible unto you.<br>Matt. 17:21   Howbeit this kind goeth not out but by prayer and fasting. | Mark 9:28   And when he was come into the house, his disciples asked him privately, Why could not we cast him out?<br>Mark 9:29   And he said unto them, This kind can come forth by nothing, but by prayer and fasting. | |
| Time Lock - Time Lock | Time Lock - Time Lock | |
| Matt. 17:22  And while they abode in Galilee, Jesus said unto them, The Son of man shall be betrayed into the hands of men:<br>Matt. 17:23   And they shall kill him, and the third day he shall be raised again. And they were exceeding sorry. | Mark 9:30   And they departed thence, and passed through Galilee; and he would not that any man should know it.<br>Mark 9:31  For he taught his disciples, and said unto them, The Son of man is delivered into the hands of men, and they shall kill him; and after that he is killed, he shall rise the third day.<br>Mark 9:32  But they understood not that saying, and were afraid to ask him. | Map 87 |
| | | |
| | | |
| Time Lock - Time Lock | Time Lock - Time Lock | |
| Matt. 17:24       And when they were come to Capernaum, they that received tribute money came to Peter, and said, Doth not your master pay tribute?<br>Matt. 17:25  He saith, Yes. And when he was come into the house, Jesus prevented him, saying, What thinkest thou, Simon? of whom do the kings of the earth take custom or tribute? of their own children, or of strangers?<br>Matt. 17:26  Peter saith unto him, Of strangers. Jesus saith unto him, Then are the children free.<br>Matt. 17:27   Notwithstanding, lest we should offend them, go thou to the sea, and cast an hook, and take up the fish that first cometh up; and when thou hast opened his mouth, thou shalt find a piece of money: that take, and give unto them for me and thee. | Mark 9:33a   And he came to Capernaum | Map 88 |
| | Time Clue - Time Clue - Time Clue | |
| | Mark 9:33b: and being in the house he asked them, What was it that ye disputed among yourselves by the way?<br>Mark 9:34  But they held their peace: for by the way they had disputed among themselves, who should be the greatest. | |
| Matt. 18:1  At the same time came the disciples unto Jesus, saying, Who is the greatest in the kingdom of heaven?<br>Matt. 18:2    And Jesus called a little child unto him, and set him in the midst of them, | Mark 9:35  And he sat down, and called the twelve, and saith unto them, If any man desire to be first, the same shall be last of all, and servant of all.<br>Mark 9:36   And he took a child, and set him in the midst of them: and when he had taken him in his arms, he said unto them, | |

| ministry year | Key Scriptures & Footnotes | Luke | John |
|---|---|---|---|
| | | | |
| | 17:20 And Jesus said unto them, Because of your unbelief:.... <br><br> 17:21 Howbeit this kind goeth not out but by prayer and fasting. | | |
| | They abode in Galilee. | Time Lock - Time Lock | |
| | 17:22 And while they abode in Galilee, Jesus said unto them, The Son of man shall be betrayed into the hands of men: | Luke 9:43 And they were all amazed at the mighty power of God. But while they wondered every one at all things which Jesus did, he said unto his disciples, <br> Luke 9:44 Let these sayings sink down into your ears: for the Son of man shall be delivered into the hands of men. <br> Luke 9:45 But they understood not this saying, and it was hid from them, that they perceived it not: and they feared to ask him of that saying. | 7:53 |
| | Who is the greatest?. | Time Clue - Time Clue | |
| | 9:46 ...**which** of them should be **greatest**. | Luke 9:46 Then there arose a reasoning among them, which of them should be greatest. | |
| | 9:47 And Jesus,...took a child, and set him by him,[84] | Luke 9:47 And Jesus, perceiving the thought of their heart, took a child, and set him by him, | |
| | | Luke 9:48 And said unto them, Whosoever shall receive this child in my name receiveth me: and whosoever shall receive me receiveth him that sent me: for he that is least among you all, the same shall be great. | |
| | Came to Capernaum. | Time Clue - See footnote for Mark 9:34 | |
| | 9:33a And he came to Capernaum.... <br><br><br><br> 17:27...cast an hook...find a piece of money;.... | | 7:53 |
| | Who is the greatest? | | |
| | 9:34 But they held their peace: **for by the way** they had disputed...**who** should be the **greatest**.[85] | 9:48 | 7:53 |
| | 18:1...**Who is the greatest** in the kingdom of heaven? | | |

---

[84] Luke 9:47 And Jesus, perceiving the thought of their heart, took a child, and set him by him, (*At first it seems that the discussion with the child of Luke 9:47 is the same as the discussion found in Matthew 18:2 & Mark 9:36. On the contrary, by time sequence, the Luke account occurs on the way to Capernaum and the Matthew and Mark accounts occur in the house in Capernaum.*)
[85] Mark 9:34 But they held their peace: for **by the way** they had disputed among themselves, who should be the greatest. (*This disputing happened before they came to Capernaum. See Luke 9:46 Then there arose a reasoning among them, which of them should be greatest.*)

| Matthew | Mark | Important Events |
|---|---|---|
| Matt. 18:3  And said, Verily I say unto you, Except ye be converted, and become as little children, ye shall not enter into the kingdom of heaven.<br>Matt. 18:4  Whosoever therefore shall humble himself as this little child, the same is greatest in the kingdom of heaven. | | |
| Time Lock - Time Lock | Time Lock - Time Lock | |
| Matt. 18:5  And whoso shall receive one such little child in my name receiveth me.<br>Matt. 18:6  But whoso shall offend one of these little ones which believe in me, it were better for him that a millstone were hanged about his neck, and that he were drowned in the depth of the sea.<br>Matt. 18:7  Woe unto the world because of offences! for it must needs be that offences come; but woe to that man by whom the offence cometh!<br>Matt. 18:8  Wherefore if thy hand or thy foot offend thee, cut them off, and cast them from thee: it is better for thee to enter into life halt or maimed, rather than having two hands or two feet to be cast into everlasting fire.<br>Matt. 18:9  And if thine eye offend thee, pluck it out, and cast it from thee: it is better for thee to enter into life with one eye, rather than having two eyes to be cast into hell fire.<br>Matt. 18:10  Take heed that ye despise not one of these little ones; for I say unto you, That in heaven their angels do always behold the face of my Father which is in heaven.<br>Matt. 18:11  For the Son of man is come to save that which was lost. | Mark 9:37  Whosoever shall receive one of such children in my name, receiveth me: and whosoever shall receive me, receiveth not me, but him that sent me. | **Receive one of such children in my name**<br><br>Matt. 18:5 & Mark 9:37 |
| Matt. 18:12  How think ye? if a man have an hundred sheep, and one of them be gone astray, doth he not leave the ninety and nine, and goeth into the mountains, and seeketh that which is gone astray?<br>Matt. 18:13  And if so be that he find it, verily I say unto you, he rejoiceth more of that sheep, than of the ninety and nine which went not astray.<br>Matt. 18:14  Even so it is not the will of your Father which is in heaven, that one of these little ones should perish.<br>Matt. 18:15  Moreover if thy brother shall trespass against thee, go and tell him his fault between thee and him alone: if he shall hear thee, thou hast gained thy brother.<br>Matt. 18:16  But if he will not hear thee, then take with thee one or two more, that in the mouth of two or three witnesses every word may be established.<br>Matt. 18:17  And if he shall neglect to hear them, tell it unto the church: but if he neglect to hear the church, let him be unto thee as an heathen man and a publican.<br>Matt. 18:18  Verily I say unto you, Whatsoever ye shall bind on earth shall be bound in heaven: and whatsoever ye shall loose on earth shall be loosed in heaven.<br>Matt. 18:19  Again I say unto you, That if two of you shall agree on earth as touching any thing that they shall ask, it shall be done for them of my Father which is in heaven.<br>Matt. 18:20  For where two or three are gathered together in my name, there am I in the midst of them. | | |
| Matt. 18:21  Then came Peter to him, and said, Lord, how oft shall my brother sin against me, and I forgive him? till seven times?<br>Matt. 18:22  Jesus saith unto him, I say not unto thee, Until seven times: but, Until seventy times seven. | | **Forgive seventy times seven**<br><br>Matt. 18:22 |

| ministry year | Key Scriptures & Footnotes | Luke | John |
|---|---|---|---|
| | Receive one such | | |
| | | 9:48 | 7:53 |
| | | 9:48 | 7:53 |
| | 18:20  For where two or three are gathered together in my name, there am I in the midst of them. | | |
| | 18:21... how oft shall my brother **sin** against me, and I forgive him? .... 18:22...seventy times seven.[86] | | |

---

[86] Matthew 18:22   Jesus saith unto him, I say not unto thee, Until seven times: but, Until seventy times seven. (*So if your brother* **sin** *against you, forgive* seventy times seven.   *But if your brother* **trespass** *against thee, as in Luke 17:4,* seven times in a day, and seven times in a day turn again to thee, saying, I repent; thou shalt forgive him.)

| Matthew | Mark | Important Events |
|---|---|---|
| Matt. 18:23 Therefore is the kingdom of heaven likened unto a certain king, which would take account of his servants.<br>Matt. 18:24 And when he had begun to reckon, one was brought unto him, which owed him ten thousand talents.<br>Matt. 18:25 But forasmuch as he had not to pay, his lord commanded him to be sold, and his wife, and children, and all that he had, and payment to be made.<br>Matt. 18:26 The servant therefore fell down, and worshipped him, saying, Lord, have patience with me, and I will pay thee all.<br>Matt. 18:27 Then the lord of that servant was moved with compassion, and loosed him, and forgave him the debt.<br>Matt. 18:28 But the same servant went out, and found one of his fellow-servants, which owed him an hundred pence: and he laid hands on him, and took him by the throat, saying, Pay me that thou owest.<br>Matt. 18:29 And his fellow-servant fell down at his feet, and besought him, saying, Have patience with me, and I will pay thee all.<br>Matt. 18:30 And he would not: but went and cast him into prison, till he should pay the debt.<br>Matt. 18:31 So when his fellow-servants saw what was done, they were very sorry, and came and told unto their lord all that was done.<br>Matt. 18:32 Then his lord, after that he had called him, said unto him, O thou wicked servant, I forgave thee all that debt, because thou desiredst me:<br>Matt. 18:33 Shouldest not thou also have had compassion on thy fellow-servant, even as I had pity on thee?<br>Matt. 18:34 And his lord was wroth, and delivered him to the tormentors, till he should pay all that was due unto him.<br>Matt. 18:35 So likewise shall my heavenly Father do also unto you, if ye from your hearts forgive not every one his brother their trespasses. | | |
| | Mark 9:38 And John answered him, saying, Master, we saw one casting out devils in thy name, and he followeth not us: and we forbad him, because he followeth not us.<br>Mark 9:39 But Jesus said, Forbid him not: for there is no man which shall do a miracle in my name, that can lightly speak evil of me.<br>Mark 9:40 For he that is not against us is on our part.<br>Mark 9:41 For whosoever shall give you a cup of water to drink in my name, because ye belong to Christ, verily I say unto you, he shall not lose his reward.<br>Mark 9:42 And whosoever shall offend one of these little ones that believe in me, it is better for him that a millstone were hanged about his neck, and he were cast into the sea.<br>Mark 9:43 And if thy hand offend thee, cut it off: it is better for thee to enter into life maimed, than having two hands to go into hell, into the fire that never shall be quenched:<br>Mark 9:44 Where their worm dieth not, and the fire is not quenched.<br>Mark 9:45 And if thy foot offend thee, cut it off: it is better for thee to enter halt into life, than having two feet to be cast into hell, into the fire that never shall be quenched:<br>Mark 9:46 Where their worm dieth not, and the fire is not quenched.<br>Mark 9:47 And if thine eye offend thee, pluck it out: it is better for thee to enter into the kingdom of God with one eye, than having two eyes to be cast into hell fire:<br>Mark 9:48 Where their worm dieth not, and the fire | |

| | | 9:48 | 7:53 |
|---|---|---|---|
| | 18:35  So likewise shall my heavenly Father do also unto you, if ye from your hearts forgive not every one his brother their trespasses. | | |
| | 9:50..Forbid him not: for he that is not against us is for us. | Luke 9:49   And John answered and said, Master, we saw one casting out devils in thy name; and we forbad him, because he followeth not with us.<br>Luke 9:50   And Jesus said unto him, Forbid him not: for he that is not against us is for us. | 7:53 |

| Matthew | Mark | Important Events |
|---|---|---|
| | is not quenched.<br>Mark 9:49   For every one shall be salted with fire, and every sacrifice shall be salted with salt.<br>Mark 9:50   Salt is good: but if the salt have lost his saltness, wherewith will ye season it? Have salt in yourselves, and have peace one with another. | . |
| <div align="center">Time Lock - Time Lock</div> | <div align="center">Time Lock - Time Lock</div> | |
| Matt. 19:1a   And it came to pass, that when Jesus had finished these sayings, he departed from Galilee, | Mark 10:1a   And he arose from thence, | **The time that He should be received up**<br>Matt. 19:1a, Mark 10:1a, & Luke 9:51<br><br>Map 89<br>Map 90 |
| | | **The Lord appointed other seventy**<br>Luke 10:1<br><br>Map 91 |
| 19:1a | 10:1a | |

| | | | |
|---|---|---|---|
| | Mark 9:50...and have peace one with another | | |
| | He departed from Galilee | Time Clue - Time Clue | |
| | 19:1a...he departed from Galilee, 9:51...when the time was come that he **should be received up**, he stedfastly set his face to go to Jerusalem,[87] 9:53 And they did not receive him,.... | Luke 9:51 And it came to pass, when the time was come that he should be received up, he stedfastly set his face to go to Jerusalem, Luke 9:52 And sent messengers before his face: and they went, and entered into a village of the Samaritans, to make ready for him. Luke 9:53 And they did not receive him, because his face was as though he would go to Jerusalem. Luke 9:54 And when his disciples James and John saw this, they said, Lord, wilt thou that we command fire to come down from heaven, and consume them, even as Elias did? Luke 9:55 But he turned, and rebuked them, and said, Ye know not what manner of spirit ye are of. Luke 9:56 For the Son of man is not come to destroy men's lives, but to save them. And they went to another village. | 7:53 |
| | 9:57 And it came to pass, that, as they went in the way,.... 9:58...Foxes have holes, and birds of the air have nests; but the Son of man hath not where to lay his head.[88] 9:60...Let the dead bury their dead:.... 9:62...No man, having put his hand to the plough, and looking back, is fit for the kingdom of God. | Luke 9:57 And it came to pass, that, as they went in the way, a certain man said unto him, Lord, I will follow thee whithersoever thou goest. Luke 9:58 And Jesus said unto him, Foxes have holes, and birds of the air have nests; but the Son of man hath not where to lay his head. Luke 9:59 And he said unto another, Follow me. But he said, Lord, suffer me first to go and bury my father. Luke 9:60 Jesus said unto him, Let the dead bury their dead: but go thou and preach the kingdom of God. Luke 9:61 And another also said, Lord, I will follow thee; but let me first go bid them farewell, which are at home at my house. Luke 9:62 And Jesus said unto him, No man, having put his hand to the plough, and looking back, is fit for the kingdom of God. | |
| | Jesus appointed seventy. | Time Clue - Time Clue | |
| | 10:1...Lord appointed other seventy also, and sent them two and two before his face into every city and place, whither he himself would come.[89] | Luke 10:1 After these things the Lord appointed other seventy also, and sent them two and two before his face into every city and place, whither he himself would come. | |
| | 10:3 Go your ways: behold, I send you forth as lambs among wolves. | Luke 10:2 Therefore said he unto them, The harvest truly is great, but the labourers are few: pray ye therefore the Lord of the harvest, that he would send forth labourers into his harvest. Luke 10:3 Go your ways: behold, I send you forth as lambs among wolves. Luke 10:4 Carry neither purse, nor scrip, nor shoes: and salute no man by the way. Luke 10:5 And into whatsoever house ye enter, first say, Peace be to this house. Luke 10:6 And if the son of peace be there, your | 7:53 |

---

[87] Luke 9:51 And it came to pass, when the time was come that he should be received up, he stedfastly set his face to go to Jerusalem, (*Jesus was going to the feast of the dedication. See John 10:22* And it was at Jerusalem the feast of the dedication, *and it was winter.*)

[88] Luke 9:58 And Jesus said unto him, Foxes have holes, and birds of the air have nests; but the Son of man hath not where to lay his head. (*Two years earlier, in Matthew 8:20, Jesus said,* "The foxes have holes, and the birds of the air have nests; but the Son of man hath not where to lay his head. ")

[89] Luke 10:1 After these things the Lord appointed other seventy also, and sent them.... (*This is one and one half years after Jesus first sent out the twelve two by two. See Luke 9:1* Then he called his twelve disciples together, and gave them power and authority over all devils, and to cure diseases.)

[90] Luke 10:13 Woe unto thee, Chorazin! woe unto thee, Bethsaida!... (*See Matthew 11:21 for the first time that Jesus said,* "Woe unto thee, Chorazin! woe unto thee, Bethsaida!....")

| Matthew | Mark | Important Events |
|---------|------|------------------|
|  |  |  |
| 19:1a | 10:1a |  |
|  |  |  |
| 19:1a | 10:1a |  |

| ministry year | Key Scriptures & Footnotes | Luke | John |
|---|---|---|---|
| | | peace shall rest upon it: if not, it shall turn to you again.<br>Luke 10:7   And in the same house remain, eating and drinking such things as they give: for the labourer is worthy of his hire. Go not from house to house.<br>Luke 10:8   And into whatsoever city ye enter, and they receive you, eat such things as are set before you:<br>Luke 10:9   And heal the sick that are therein, and say unto them, The kingdom of God is come nigh unto you.<br>Luke 10:10   But into whatsoever city ye enter, and they receive you not, go your ways out into the streets of the same, and say,<br>Luke 10:11   Even the very dust of your city, which cleaveth on us, we do wipe off against you: notwithstanding be ye sure of this, that the kingdom of God is come nigh unto you.<br>Luke 10:12   But I say unto you, that it shall be more tolerable in that day for Sodom, than for that city. | |
| | 10:13 Woe unto thee, Chorazin! woe unto thee, Bethsaida!.... [90] | Luke 10:13   Woe unto thee, Chorazin! woe unto thee, Bethsaida! for if the mighty works had been done in Tyre and Sidon, which have been done in you, they had a great while ago repented, sitting in sackcloth and ashes.<br>Luke 10:14   But it shall be more tolerable for Tyre and Sidon at the judgment, than for you.<br>Luke 10:15   And thou, Capernaum, which art exalted to heaven, shalt be thrust down to hell.<br>Luke 10:16   He that heareth you heareth me; and he that despiseth you despiseth me; and he that despiseth me despiseth him that sent me. | |
| | 10:17 And the seventy returned again with joy,....<br>10:18...I beheld Satan as lightning fall from heaven. | Luke 10:17   And the seventy returned again with joy, saying, Lord, even the devils are subject unto us through thy name.<br>Luke 10:18   And he said unto them, I beheld Satan as lightning fall from heaven.<br>Luke 10:19   Behold, I give unto you power to tread on serpents and scorpions, and over all the power of the enemy: and nothing shall by any means hurt you.<br>Luke 10:20   Notwithstanding in this rejoice not, that the spirits are subject unto you; but rather rejoice, because your names are written in heaven. | 7:53 |
| | 10:23...Blessed are the eyes which see the things that ye see: | Luke 10:21   In that hour Jesus rejoiced in spirit, and said, I thank thee, O Father, Lord of heaven and earth, that thou hast hid these things from the wise and prudent, and hast revealed them unto babes: even so, Father; for so it seemed good in thy sight.<br>Luke 10:22   All things are delivered to me of my Father: and no man knoweth who the Son is, but the Father; and who the Father is, but the Son, and he to whom the Son will reveal him.<br>Luke 10:23   And he turned him unto his disciples, and said privately, Blessed are the eyes which see the things that ye see:<br>Luke 10:24   For I tell you, that many prophets and kings have desired to see those things which ye see, and have not seen them; and to hear those things which ye hear, and have not heard them. | |
| | 10:25 And, behold, a certain lawyer stood up, and tempted him,[91]...saying, Master, what shall I do to inherit eternal life?[92] | Luke 10:25   And, behold, a certain lawyer stood up, and tempted him, saying, Master, what shall I do to inherit eternal life?<br>Luke 10:26   He said unto him, What is written in the law? how readest thou?<br>Luke 10:27   And he answering said, Thou shalt love the Lord thy God with all thy heart, and with all thy soul, and with all thy strength, and with all thy mind; and thy neighbour as thyself. | 7:53 |

[91] Luke 10:25a   And, behold, a certain lawyer stood up, and tempted him,.... (*This may have been a Samaritan lawyer since they are in Samaria.*  Next, Jesus tells the story of "a certain Samaritan" in Luke 10:33.)

[92] Luke 10:25b   ...saying, Master, what shall I do to inherit eternal life? (*To inherit eternal life you must do Luke 10:27, which is* "the first commandment of all" *as seen in Mark 12:28-31.*)

| Matthew | Mark | Important Events |
|---------|------|------------------|
| | | |
| 19:1a | 10:1a | **Mary hath chosen that good part** Luke 10:42<br><br>Map 92 |
| 19:1a | 10:1a | **When ye pray, say, Our Father which art in heaven** Luke 11:2 |

| ministry year | Key Scriptures & Footnotes | Luke | John |
|---|---|---|---|
| | 10:30..A certain man went down from Jerusalem to Jericho,.... | Luke 10:28    And he said unto him, Thou hast answered right: this do, and thou shalt live.<br>Luke 10:29    But he, willing to justify himself, said unto Jesus, And who is my neighbour?<br>Luke 10:30    And Jesus answering said, A certain man went down from Jerusalem to Jericho, and fell among thieves, which stripped him of his raiment, and wounded him, and departed, leaving him half dead.<br>Luke 10:31    And by chance there came down a certain priest that way: and when he saw him, he passed by on the other side.<br>Luke 10:32    And likewise a Levite, when he was at the place, came and looked on him, and passed by on the other side. | |
| | 10:33 But a certain Samaritan,.... | Luke 10:33    But a certain Samaritan, as he journeyed, came where he was: and when he saw him, he had compassion on him,<br>Luke 10:34    And went to him, and bound up his wounds, pouring in oil and wine, and set him on his own beast, and brought him to an inn, and took care of him.<br>Luke 10:35  And on the morrow when he departed, he took out two pence, and gave them to the host, and said unto him, Take care of him; and whatsoever thou spendest more, when I come again, I will repay thee.<br>Luke 10:36  Which now of these three, thinkest thou, was neighbour unto him that fell among the thieves?<br>Luke 10:37  And he said, He that showed mercy on him. Then said Jesus unto him, Go, and do thou likewise. | |

| | Jesus in Bethany. | Time Clue - Time Clue | |
|---|---|---|---|
| | 10:38...he entered into a certain village : and a certain woman named Martha received him into her house.[93] | Luke 10:38  Now it came to pass, as they went, that he entered into a certain village: and a certain woman named Martha received him into her house.<br>Luke 10:39  And she had a sister called Mary, which also sat at Jesus' feet, and heard his word.<br>Luke 10:40  But Martha was cumbered about much serving, and came to him, and said, Lord, dost thou not care that my sister hath left me to serve alone? bid her therefore that she help me.<br>Luke 10:41  And Jesus answered and said unto her, Martha, Martha, thou art careful and troubled about many things:<br>Luke 10:42  But one thing is needful: and Mary hath chosen that good part, which shall not be taken away from her. | 7:53 |
| | 11:1...as he was praying in a certain place,....<br><br>11:2  And he said unto them, When ye pray, say, Our Father which art in heaven,....[94] | Luke 11:1    And it came to pass, that, as he was praying in a certain place, when he ceased, one of his disciples said unto him, Lord, teach us to pray, as John also taught his disciples.<br>Luke 11:2    And he said unto them, When ye pray, say, Our Father which art in heaven, Hallowed be thy name. Thy kingdom come. Thy will be done, as in heaven, so in earth.<br>Luke 11:3  Give us day by day our daily bread.<br>Luke 11:4    And forgive us our sins; for we also forgive every one that is indebted to us. And lead us not into temptation; but deliver us from evil.<br>Luke 11:5    And he said unto them, Which of you shall have a friend, and shall go unto him at midnight, and say unto him, Friend, lend me three loaves;<br>Luke 11:6  For a friend of mine in his journey is come to me, and I have nothing to set before him?<br>Luke 11:7  And he from within shall answer and say, Trouble me not: the door is now shut, and my children are with me in bed; I cannot rise and give thee.<br>Luke 11:8  I say unto you, Though he will not rise and give him, because he is his friend, yet because of his importunity he will rise and give him as many as | 7:53 |

[93] Luke 10:38...a certain woman named Martha received him into her house. (*Martha's house was in Bethany, near Jerusalem.*)
[94] Luke 11:2  And he said unto them, When ye pray, say, Our Father which art in heaven.... (*See Matthew 6:9 for the first time Jesus taught the same prayer.*)

| Matthew | Mark | Important Events |
|---|---|---|
|  |  |  |
| 19:1a | 10:1a |  |
| 19:1a | 10:1a |  |
|  |  |  |

| ministry year | Key Scriptures & Footnotes | Luke | John |
|---|---|---|---|
| | | he needeth. | |
| | 11:9 And I say unto you, Ask, and it shall be given you; seek, and ye shall find; knock, and it shall be opened unto you.[95]<br><br>11:13 how much more shall your heavenly Father **give the Holy Spirit** to them that ask him? | Luke 11:9 And I say unto you, Ask, and it shall be given you; seek, and ye shall find; knock, and it shall be opened unto you.<br>Luke 11:10 For every one that asketh receiveth; and he that seeketh findeth; and to him that knocketh it shall be opened.<br>Luke 11:11 If a son shall ask bread of any of you that is a father, will he give him a stone? or if he ask a fish, will he for a fish give him a serpent?<br>Luke 11:12 Or if he shall ask an egg, will he offer him a scorpion?<br>Luke 11:13 If ye then, being evil, know how to give good gifts unto your children: how much more shall your heavenly Father give the Holy Spirit to them that ask him? | |
| | 11:14 And he was casting out a devil,....<br><br>11:15 But some of them said, He casteth out devils through Beelzebub[96]....<br>11:17 But he, knowing their thoughts,....<br><br><br><br><br><br><br><br><br><br><br><br><br><br><br><br><br><br>11:26 Then goeth he, and taketh to him seven other spirits....[97] | Luke 11:14 And he was casting out a devil, and it was dumb. And it came to pass, when the devil was gone out, the dumb spake; and the people wondered.<br>Luke 11:15 But some of them said, He casteth out devils through Beelzebub the chief of the devils.<br>Luke 11:16 And others, tempting him, sought of him a sign from heaven.<br>Luke 11:17 But he, knowing their thoughts, said unto them, Every kingdom divided against itself is brought to desolation; and a house divided against a house falleth.<br>Luke 11:18 If Satan also be divided against himself, how shall his kingdom stand? because ye say that I cast out devils through Beelzebub.<br>Luke 11:19 And if I by Beelzebub cast out devils, by whom do your sons cast them out? therefore shall they be your judges.<br>Luke 11:20 But if I with the finger of God cast out devils, no doubt the kingdom of God is come upon you.<br>Luke 11:21 When a strong man armed keepeth his palace, his goods are in peace:<br>Luke 11:22 But when a stronger than he shall come upon him, and overcome him, he taketh from him all his armour wherein he trusted, and divideth his spoils.<br>Luke 11:23 He that is not with me is against me: and he that gathereth not with me scattereth.<br>Luke 11:24 When the unclean spirit is gone out of a man, he walketh through dry places, seeking rest; and finding none, he saith, I will return unto my house whence I came out.<br>Luke 11:25 And when he cometh, he findeth it swept and garnished.<br>Luke 11:26 Then goeth he, and taketh to him seven other spirits more wicked than himself; and they enter in, and dwell there: and the last state of that man is worse than the first. | 7:53 |
| | | Luke 11:27 And it came to pass, as he spake these things, a certain woman of the company lifted up her voice, and said unto him, Blessed is the womb that bare thee, and the paps which thou hast sucked.<br>Luke 11:28 But he said, Yea rather, blessed are they that hear the word of God, and keep it. | 7:53 |
| | 11:29 And when the people were gathered thick together,.... | Luke 11:29 And when the people were gathered thick together, he began to say, This is an evil generation: they seek a sign; and there shall no sign be given it, but the sign of Jonas the prophet.<br>Luke 11:30 For as Jonas was a sign unto the Ninevites, so shall also the Son of man be to this | |

[95] Luke 11:9 And I say unto you, Ask, and it shall be given you; seek, and ye shall find; knock, and it shall be opened unto you. (*See Matthew 7:7 when Jesus taught this to the multitudes.*)

[96] Luke 11:15 But some of them said, He casteth out devils through Beelzebub.... (*See Matthew 9:34 when the Pharisees said,* "He casteth out devils through the prince of the devils.")

[97] Luke 11:26 Then goeth he, and taketh to him seven other spirits more wicked than himself....(*See Matthew 12:45 for another time that Jesus said,* "Then goeth he, and taketh with himself seven other spirits more wicked than himself....")

| Matthew | Mark | Important Events |
|---------|------|------------------|
|         |      |                  |
| 19:1a   | 10:1a |                 |
| 19:1a   | 10:1a |                 |

| ministry<br>year | Key Scriptures<br>& Footnotes | Luke | John |
|---|---|---|---|
| | | generation.<br>Luke 11:31  The queen of the south shall rise up in the judgment with the men of this generation, and condemn them: for she came from the utmost parts of the earth to hear the wisdom of Solomon; and, behold, a greater than Solomon is here.<br>Luke 11:32  The men of Nineve shall rise up in the judgment with this generation, and shall condemn it: for they repented at the preaching of Jonas; and, behold, a greater than Jonas is here. | |
| | 11:34 The light of the body is the eye:... | Luke 11:33  No man, when he hath lighted a candle, putteth it in a secret place, neither under a bushel, but on a candlestick, that they which come in may see the light.<br>Luke 11:34    The light of the body is the eye: therefore when thine eye is single, thy whole body also is full of light; but when thine eye is evil, thy body also is full of darkness.<br>Luke 11:35  Take heed therefore that the light which is in thee be not darkness.<br>Luke 11:36  If thy whole body therefore be full of light, having no part dark, the whole shall be full of light, as when the bright shining of a candle doth give thee light. | 7:53 |
| | 11:37...a certain Pharisee besought him to dine....<br><br><br><br><br><br><br>11:41  But rather **give alms** of such things as ye have; **and**, behold, **all things are clean unto you**. | Luke 11:37  And as he spake, a certain Pharisee besought him to dine with him: and he went in, and sat down to meat.<br>Luke 11:38    And when the Pharisee saw it, he marvelled that he had not first washed before dinner.<br>Luke 11:39  And the Lord said unto him, Now do ye Pharisees make clean the outside of the cup and the platter; but your inward part is full of ravening and wickedness.<br>Luke 11:40    Ye fools, did not he that made that which is without make that which is within also?<br>Luke 11:41  But rather give alms of such things as ye have; and, behold, all things are clean unto you.<br>Luke 11:42  But woe unto you, Pharisees! for ye tithe mint and rue and all manner of herbs, and pass over judgment and the love of God: these ought ye to have done, and not to leave the other undone.<br>Luke 11:43  Woe unto you, Pharisees! for ye love the uppermost seats in the synagogues, and greetings in the markets.<br>Luke 11:44  Woe unto you, scribes and Pharisees, hypocrites! for ye are as graves which appear not, and the men that walk over them are not aware of them.<br>Luke 11:45    Then answered one of the lawyers, and said unto him, Master, thus saying thou reproachest us also.<br>Luke 11:46    And he said, Woe unto you also, ye lawyers! for ye lade men with burdens grievous to be borne, and ye yourselves touch not the burdens with one of your fingers.<br>Luke 11:47    Woe unto you! for ye build the sepulchres of the prophets, and your fathers killed them.<br>Luke 11:48  Truly ye bear witness that ye allow the deeds of your fathers: for they indeed killed them, and ye build their sepulchres.<br>Luke 11:49  Therefore also said the wisdom of God, I will send them prophets and apostles, and some of them they shall slay and persecute:<br>Luke 11:50  That the blood of all the prophets, which was shed from the foundation of the world, may be required of this generation;<br>Luke 11:51  From the blood of Abel unto the blood of Zacharias, which perished between the altar and the temple: verily I say unto you, It shall be required of this generation.<br>Luke 11:52  Woe unto you, lawyers! for ye have taken away the key of knowledge: ye entered not in | 7:53 |

| Matthew | Mark | Important Events |
|---|---|---|
| | | |
| 19:1a | 10:1a | |
| | | |
| 19:1a | 10:1a | |

| | | | |
|---|---|---|---|
| | | yourselves, and them that were entering in ye hindered. | |
| | 11:54  Laying wait...that they might accuse him,....[98] | Luke 11:53   And as he said these things unto them, the scribes   and the Pharisees began to urge him vehemently, and to provoke him to speak of many things: <br> Luke 11:54   Laying wait for him, and seeking to catch something out of his mouth, that they might accuse him. | 7:53 |
| | Time Clue - Time Clue | Time Clue - - See footnote for Luke 11:54 | Time Clue - Time Clue |
| | 12:1   In the mean time, when there were gathered together an **innumerable multitude** of people, insomuch that they trode one upon another,.... | Luke 12:1    In the mean time, when there were gathered together an innumerable multitude of people, insomuch that they trode one upon another, he began to say unto his disciples first of all, Beware ye of the leaven of the Pharisees, which is hypocrisy. <br> Luke 12:2   For there is nothing covered, that shall not be revealed; neither hid, that shall not be known. <br> Luke 12:3   Therefore whatsoever ye have spoken in darkness shall be heard in the light; and that which ye have spoken in the ear in closets shall be proclaimed upon the housetops. <br> Luke 12:4   And I say unto you my friends, Be not afraid of them that kill the body, and after that have no more that they can do. <br> Luke 12:5   But I will forewarn you whom ye shall fear: Fear him, which after he hath killed hath power to cast into hell; yea, I say unto you, Fear him. <br> Luke 12:6   Are not five sparrows sold for two farthings, and not one of them is forgotten before God? <br> Luke 12:7  But even the very hairs of your head are all numbered. Fear not therefore: ye are of more value than many sparrows. <br> Luke 12:8   Also I say unto you, Whosoever shall confess me before men, him shall the Son of man also confess before the angels of God: <br> Luke 12:9  But he that denieth me before men shall be denied before the angels of God. <br> Luke 12:10    And whosoever shall speak a word against the Son of man, it shall be forgiven him: but unto him that blasphemeth against the Holy Ghost it shall not be forgiven. <br> Luke 12:11    And when they bring you unto the synagogues, and unto magistrates, and powers, take ye no thought how or what thing ye shall answer, or what ye shall say: <br> Luke 12:12  For the Holy Ghost shall teach you in the same hour what ye ought to say. <br> Luke 12:13  And one of the company said unto him, Master, speak to my brother, that he divide the inheritance with me. <br> Luke 12:14  And he said unto him, Man, who made me a judge or a divider over you? <br> Luke 12:15  And he said unto them, Take heed, and beware of covetousness: for a man's life consisteth not in the abundance of the things which he possesseth. | |
| | | Luke 12:16    And he spake a parable unto them, saying, The ground of a certain rich man brought forth plentifully: <br> Luke 12:17    And he thought within himself, saying, What shall I do, because I have no room where to bestow my fruits? <br> Luke 12:18    And he said, This will I do: I will pull down my barns, and build greater; and there will I bestow all my fruits and my goods. <br> Luke 12:19   And I will say to my soul, Soul, thou hast | 7:53 |

[98] Luke 11:53b-54...and the Pharisees **began** to urge him vehemently, and to provoke him to speak of many things:  Laying wait for him, and seeking to catch something out of his mouth, that they might accuse him. (*Jesus recently arrived in Bethany in Luke 10:38 to attend the Feast of Dedication found in John 10:22.  John 8:1-10:39 illustrates the Pharisees' continued quest to accuse Jesus and even take up stones to stone Him in John 8:59 and 10:31.  Luke 11:53-54 provides a Time Clue that John 8:1-10:39 follows Luke 10:38-13:9.*)

| Matthew | Mark | Important Events |
|---------|------|------------------|
| | | |
| 19:1a | 10:1a | |

| | | much goods laid up for many years; take thine ease, eat, drink, and be merry. | |
| | | Luke 12:20  But God said unto him, Thou fool, this night thy soul shall be required of thee: then whose shall those things be, which thou hast provided? | |
| | | Luke 12:21  So is he that layeth up treasure for himself, and is not rich toward God. | |
| | | Luke 12:22  And he said unto his disciples, Therefore I say unto you, Take no thought for your life, what ye shall eat; neither for the body, what ye shall put on. | |
| | | Luke 12:23  The life is more than meat, and the body is more than raiment. | |
| | | Luke 12:24  Consider the ravens: for they neither sow nor reap; which neither have storehouse nor barn; and God feedeth them: how much more are ye better than the fowls? | |
| | | Luke 12:25  And which of you with taking thought can add to his stature one cubit? | |
| | | Luke 12:26  If ye then be not able to do that thing which is least, why take ye thought for the rest? | |
| | | Luke 12:27  Consider the lilies how they grow: they toil not, they spin not; and yet I say unto you, that Solomon in all his glory was not arrayed like one of these. | |
| | | Luke 12:28  If then God so clothe the grass, which is today in the field, and tomorrow is cast into the oven; how much more will he clothe you, O ye of little faith? | |
| | | Luke 12:29  And seek not ye what ye shall eat, or what ye shall drink, neither be ye of doubtful mind. | |
| | | Luke 12:30  For all these things do the nations of the world seek after: and your Father knoweth that ye have need of these things. | |
| 12:31  But rather seek ye the kingdom of God; and all these things shall be added unto you. [99] | Luke 12:31  But rather seek ye the kingdom of God; and all these things shall be added unto you. | 7:53 |
| | | Luke 12:32  Fear not, little flock; for it is your Father's good pleasure to give you the kingdom. | |
| | | Luke 12:33  Sell that ye have, and give alms; provide yourselves bags which wax not old, a treasure in the heavens that faileth not, where no thief approacheth, neither moth corrupteth. | |
| | | Luke 12:34  For where your treasure is, there will your heart be also. | |
| | | Luke 12:35  Let your loins be girded about, and your lights burning; | |
| | | Luke 12:36  And ye yourselves like unto men that wait for their lord, when he will return from the wedding; that when he cometh and knocketh, they may open unto him immediately. | |
| | | Luke 12:37  Blessed are those servants, whom the lord when he cometh shall find watching: verily I say unto you, that he shall gird himself, and make them to sit down to meat, and will come forth and serve them. | |
| | | Luke 12:38  And if he shall come in the second watch, or come in the third watch, and find them so, blessed are those servants. | |
| | | Luke 12:39  And this know, that if the goodman of the house had known what hour the thief would come, he would have watched, and not have suffered his house to be broken through. | |
| | | Luke 12:40  Be ye therefore ready also: for the Son of man cometh at an hour when ye think not. | |
| | | Luke 12:41  Then Peter said unto him, Lord, speakest thou this parable unto us, or even to all? | |
| | | Luke 12:42  And the Lord said, Who then is that faithful and wise steward, whom his lord shall make ruler over his household, to give them their portion of meat in due season? | |
| | | Luke 12:43  Blessed is that servant, whom his lord | |

[99] Luke 12:31  But rather seek ye the kingdom of God; and all these things shall be added unto you. (*See Matthew 6:33*  But seek ye first the kingdom of God, and his righteousness; and all these things shall be added unto you.)

| Matthew | Mark | Important Events |
|---------|------|------------------|
| | | |
| 19:1a | 10:1a | **I am come to send fire on the earth;** Luke 12:49 |
| 19:1a | 10:1a | |

72

when he cometh shall find so doing.

Luke 12:44  Of a truth I say unto you, that he will make him ruler over all that he hath.

Luke 12:45  But and if that servant say in his heart, My lord delayeth his coming; and shall begin to beat the menservants and maidens, and to eat and drink, and to be drunken;

Luke 12:46  The lord of that servant will come in a day when he looketh not for him, and at an hour when he is not aware, and will cut him in sunder, and will appoint him his portion with the unbelievers.

Luke 12:47  And that servant, which knew his lord's will, and prepared not himself, neither did according to his will, shall be beaten with many stripes.

Luke 12:48  But he that knew not, and did commit things worthy of stripes, shall be beaten with few stripes. For unto whomsoever much is given, of him shall be much required: and to whom men have committed much, of him they will ask the more.

---

**12:49 I am come to send fire on the earth;....**

**12:50 But I have a baptism to be baptized with; and how am I straitened till it be accomplished!**

Luke 12:49  I am come to send fire on the earth; and what will I, if it be already kindled?

Luke 12:50  But I have a baptism to be baptized with; and how am I straitened till it be accomplished!

Luke 12:51  Suppose ye that I am come to give peace on earth? I tell you, Nay; but rather division:

Luke 12:52  For from henceforth there shall be five in one house divided, three against two, and two against three.

Luke 12:53  The father shall be divided against the son, and the son against the father; the mother against the daughter, and the daughter against the mother; the mother-in-law against her daughter-in-law, and the daughter-in-law against her mother-in-law.

Luke 12:54  And he said also to the people, When ye see a cloud rise out of the west, straightway ye say, There cometh a shower; and so it is.

Luke 12:55  And when ye see the south wind blow, ye say, There will be heat; and it cometh to pass.

Luke 12:56  Ye hypocrites, ye can discern the face of the sky and of the earth; but how is it that ye do not discern this time?

Luke 12:57  Yea, and why even of yourselves judge ye not what is right?

Luke 12:58  When thou goest with thine adversary to the magistrate, as thou art in the way, give diligence that thou mayest be delivered from him; lest he hale thee to the judge, and the judge deliver thee to the officer, and the officer cast thee into prison.

Luke 12:59  I tell thee, thou shalt not depart thence, till thou hast paid the very last mite.

*John: 7:53*

---

Luke 13:1  There were present at that season some that told him of the Galilaeans, whose blood Pilate had mingled with their sacrifices.

Luke 13:2  And Jesus answering said unto them, Suppose ye that these Galilaeans were sinners above all the Galilaeans, because they suffered such things?

Luke 13:3  I tell you, Nay: but, except ye repent, ye shall all likewise perish.

Luke 13:4  Or those eighteen, upon whom the tower in Siloam fell, and slew them, think ye that they were sinners above all men that dwelt in Jerusalem?

Luke 13:5  I tell you, Nay: but, except ye repent, ye shall all likewise perish.

Luke 13:6  He spake also this parable; A certain man had a fig tree planted in his vineyard; and he came and sought fruit thereon, and found none.

Luke 13:7  Then said he unto the dresser of his vineyard, Behold, these three years I come seeking fruit on this fig tree, and find none: cut it down; why cumbereth it the ground?

Luke 13:8  And he answering said unto him, Lord, let it alone this year also, till I shall dig about it, and dung it:

*John: 7:53*

| Matthew | Mark | Important Events |
|---------|------|------------------|
|  |  |  |
|  |  |  |
|  |  | **Woman was taken in adultery** John 8:3 Map 93 |
| 19:1a | 10:1a |  |

| ministry year | Key Scriptures & Footnotes | Luke | John |
|---|---|---|---|
| | | Luke 13:9 And if it bear fruit, well: and if not, then after that thou shalt cut it down. | |
| | Jesus continued in Jerusalem. | Time Clue - Luke 13:10 & Luke 13:22 | Time Clue - Time Clue |
| | 8:1 Jesus went unto the mount of Olives.[100] 8:2...in the morning he came **again** into the temple,....[101] 8:3...woman was taken in adultery;.... | | John 8:1 Jesus went unto the mount of Olives. John 8:2 And early in the morning he came again into the temple, and all the people came unto him; and he sat down, and taught them. John 8:3 And the scribes and Pharisees brought unto him a woman taken in adultery; and when they had set her in the midst, John 8:4 They say unto him, Master, this woman was taken in adultery, in the very act. John 8:5 Now Moses in the law commanded us, that such should be stoned: but what sayest thou? John 8:6 This they said, tempting him, that they might have to accuse him. But Jesus stooped down, and with his finger wrote on the ground, as though he heard them not. John 8:7 So when they continued asking him, he lifted up himself, and said unto them, He that is without sin among you, let him first cast a stone at her. John 8:8 And again he stooped down, and wrote on the ground. John 8:9 And they which heard it, being convicted by their own conscience, went out one by one, beginning at the eldest, even unto the last: and Jesus was left alone, and the woman standing in the midst. John 8:10 When Jesus had lifted up himself, and saw none but the woman, he said unto her, Woman, where are those thine accusers? hath no man condemned thee? |
| | 8:11...Neither do I condemn thee: go, and sin no more. | | John 8:11 She said, No man, Lord. And Jesus said unto her, Neither do I condemn thee: go, and sin no more. |
| | 8:12 Then spake Jesus again.... | 13:9 | John 8:12 Then spake Jesus again unto them, saying, I am the light of the world: he that followeth me shall not walk in darkness, but shall have the light of life. John 8:13 The Pharisees therefore said unto him, Thou bearest record of thyself; thy record is not true. John 8:14 Jesus answered and said unto them, Though I bear record of myself, yet my record is true: for I know whence I came, and whither I go; but ye cannot tell whence I come, and whither I go. John 8:15 Ye judge after the flesh; I judge no man. John 8:16 And yet if I judge, my judgment is true: for I am not alone, but I and the Father that sent me. John 8:17 It is also written in your law, that the testimony of two men is true. John 8:18 I am one that bear witness of myself, and the Father that sent me beareth witness of me. John 8:19 Then said they unto him, Where is thy Father? Jesus answered, Ye neither know me, nor my Father: if ye had known me, ye should have known my Father also. John 8:20 These words spake Jesus in the treasury, as he taught in the temple: and no man laid hands on him; for his hour was not yet come. John 8:21 Then said Jesus again unto them, I go my way, and ye shall seek me, and shall die in your sins: whither I go, ye cannot come. |
| | 8:20 These words spake Jesus in the treasury,.... | | John 8:22 Then said the Jews, Will he kill himself? |

---

[100] John 8:1 Jesus went unto the mount of Olives. (*Jesus continued in the area of Jerusalem. Jesus was in Bethany in Luke 10:38-13:9. In John 8:1-10:39 we find that Jesus remained in the area of Bethany and Jerusalem. Next, Jesus "went beyond the Jordan" in John 10:40. He returned to Bethany to call Lazarus forth from the grave in John 11:43. Then, Jesus went to Ephraim and there continued with His disciples as seen in John 11:54. After that, Luke 13:10 says, "And he was teaching in one of the synagogues on the sabbath." In Luke 13:22 Jesus is again "journeying toward Jerusalem." To head again "toward Jerusalem," requires Jesus to leave the Jerusalem area between Luke 13:9 and Luke 13:10. John 8:1-11:54 explains the time gap in events between Luke 13:9 and Luke 13:10.*)

[101] John 8:2 ...he came again into the temple.... (*The temple in Jerusalem.*)

| Matthew | Mark | Important Events |
|---------|------|------------------|
|         |      |                  |

| | | | because he saith, Whither I go, ye cannot come. |

**John 8:23** And he said unto them, Ye are from beneath; I am from above: ye are of this world; I am not of this world.

**John 8:24** I said therefore unto you, that ye shall die in your sins: for if ye believe not that I am he, ye shall die in your sins.

**John 8:25** Then said they unto him, Who art thou? And Jesus saith unto them, Even the same that I said unto you from the beginning.

**John 8:26** I have many things to say and to judge of you: but he that sent me is true; and I speak to the world those things which I have heard of him.

**John 8:27** They understood not that he spake to them of the Father.

**John 8:28** Then said Jesus unto them, When ye have lifted up the Son of man, then shall ye know that I am he, and that I do nothing of myself; but as my Father hath taught me, I speak these things.

**John 8:29** And he that sent me is with me: the Father hath not left me alone; for I do always those things that please him.

**John 8:30** As he spake these words, many believed on him.

**John 8:31** Then said Jesus to those Jews which believed on him, If ye continue in my word, then are ye my disciples indeed;

**John 8:32** And ye shall know the truth, and the truth shall make you free.

**John 8:33** They answered him, We be Abraham's seed, and were never in bondage to any man: how sayest thou, Ye shall be made free?

**John 8:34** Jesus answered them, Verily, verily, I say unto you, Whosoever committeth sin is the servant of sin.

**John 8:35** And the servant abideth not in the house for ever: but the Son abideth ever.

**John 8:36** If the Son therefore shall make you free, ye shall be free indeed.

**John 8:37** I know that ye are Abraham's seed; but ye seek to kill me, because my word hath no place in you.

**John 8:38** I speak that which I have seen with my Father: and ye do that which ye have seen with your father.

**John 8:39** They answered and said unto him, Abraham is our father. Jesus saith unto them, If ye were Abraham's children, ye would do the works of Abraham.

**John 8:40** But now ye seek to kill me, a man that hath told you the truth, which I have heard of God: this did not Abraham.

**John 8:41** Ye do the deeds of your father. Then said they to him, We be not born of fornication; we have one Father, even God.

**John 8:42** Jesus said unto them, If God were your Father, ye would love me: for I proceeded forth and came from God; neither came I of myself, but he sent me.

**John 8:43** Why do ye not understand my speech? even because ye cannot hear my word.

**John 8:44** Ye are of your father the devil, and the lusts of your father ye will do. He was a murderer from the beginning, and abode not in the truth, because there is no truth in him. When he speaketh a lie, he speaketh of his own: for he is a liar, and the father of it.

**John 8:45** And because I tell you the truth, ye believe me not.

**John 8:46** Which of you convinceth me of sin? And if I say the truth, why do ye not believe me?

**John 8:47** He that is of God heareth God's words: ye therefore hear them not, because ye are not of God.

Key Scriptures & Footnotes column:

**8:30** As he spake these words, many believed on him.

| Matthew | Mark | Important Events |
|---|---|---|
| 19:1a | 10:1a | |
| 19:1a | 10:1a | **1st time in Jerusalem they took up stones to cast at Jesus** John 8:59 |
| | | **Go, wash in the pool of Siloam** John 9:7 |
| 19:1a | 10:1a | |

| ministry year | Key Scriptures & Footnotes | Luke | John |
|---|---|---|---|
| | | 13:9 | John 8:48   Then answered the Jews, and said unto him, Say we not well that thou art a Samaritan, and hast a devil? |
| | 8:49   Jesus answered, I have not a devil....[102] | | John 8:49   Jesus answered, I have not a devil; but I honour my Father, and ye do dishonour me. |
| | | | John 8:50   And I seek not mine own glory: there is one that seeketh and judgeth. |
| | | | John 8:51   Verily, verily, I say unto you, If a man keep my saying, he shall never see death. |
| | | | John 8:52   Then said the Jews unto him, Now we know that thou hast a devil. Abraham is dead, and the prophets; and thou sayest, If a man keep my saying, he shall never taste of death. |
| | | | John 8:53   Art thou greater than our father Abraham, which is dead? and the prophets are dead: whom makest thou thyself? |
| | | | John 8:54   Jesus answered, If I honour myself, my honour is nothing: it is my Father that honoureth me; of whom ye say, that he is your God: |
| | | | John 8:55   Yet ye have not known him; but I know him: and if I should say, I know him not, I shall be a liar like unto you: but I know him, and keep his saying. |
| | | | John 8:56   Your father Abraham rejoiced to see my day: and he saw it, and was glad. |
| | | | John 8:57   Then said the Jews unto him, Thou art not yet fifty years old, and hast thou seen Abraham? |
| | Took they up stones | | Time Clue - Laying wait for him.... Luke 11:53-54 |
| | 8:58...Before Abraham was, I am.<br><br>8:59   Then took **they up stones to cast at him:**....[103] | 13:9 | John 8:58   Jesus said unto them, Verily, verily, I say unto you, Before Abraham was, I am.<br>John 8:59   Then took they up stones to cast at him: but Jesus hid himself, and went out of the temple, going through the midst of them, and so passed by. |
| | 9:1   And as Jesus passed by, he saw a man which was blind from his birth.<br><br>9:3...Neither hath this man sinned, nor his parents: but that the works of God should be made manifest in him. | | John 9:1   And as Jesus passed by, he saw a man which was blind from his birth.<br>John 9:2   And his disciples asked him, saying, Master, who did sin, this man, or his parents, that he was born blind?<br>John 9:3   Jesus answered, Neither hath this man sinned, nor his parents: but that the works of God should be made manifest in him.<br>John 9:4   I must work the works of him that sent me, while it is day: the night cometh, when no man can work.<br>John 9:5   As long as I am in the world, I am the light of the world.<br>John 9:6   When he had thus spoken, he spat on the ground, and made clay of the spittle, and he anointed the eyes of the blind man with the clay, |
| | 9:7   And said unto him, Go, wash in the pool of Siloam,.... | | John 9:7   And said unto him, Go, wash in the pool of Siloam, (which is by interpretation, Sent.) He went his way therefore, and washed, and came seeing. |
| | | 13:9 | John 9:8   The neighbours therefore, and they which before had seen him that he was blind, said, Is not this he that sat and begged?<br>John 9:9   Some said, This is he: others said, He is like him: but he said, I am he.<br>John 9:10   Therefore said they unto him, How were thine eyes opened?<br>John 9:11   He answered and said, A man that is called Jesus made clay, and anointed mine eyes, and said unto me, Go to the pool of Siloam, and wash: and I went and washed, and I received sight.<br>John 9:12   Then said they unto him, Where is he? He said, I know not.<br>John 9:13   They brought to the Pharisees him that |

---

[102] John 8:49   I have not a devil.... (*See Matthew 9:32-34 and Matthew 12:24 for similar events.*)
[103] John 8:59   Then took they up stones...(*This was the first time in Jerusalem that the Jews took up stones to stone Jesus.  See John 10:31 for the second time.  The Jews were fulfilling their desire of Luke 11:53-54.*)

| Matthew | Mark | Important Events |
|---------|------|------------------|
|         |      |                  |

19:1a

10:1a

aforetime was blind.

John 9:14   And it was the sabbath day when Jesus made the clay, and opened his eyes.

John 9:15   Then again the Pharisees also asked him how he had received his sight. He said unto them, He put clay upon mine eyes, and I washed, and do see.

John 9:16   Therefore said some of the Pharisees, This man is not of God, because he keepeth not the sabbath day. Others said, How can a man that is a sinner do such miracles? And there was a division among them.

John 9:17   They say unto the blind man again, What sayest thou of him, that he hath opened thine eyes? He said, He is a prophet.

John 9:18   But the Jews did not believe concerning him, that he had been blind, and received his sight, until they called the parents of him that had received his sight.

John 9:19   And they asked them, saying, Is this your son, who ye say was born blind? how then doth he now see?

John 9:20   His parents answered them and said, We know that this is our son, and that he was born blind:

John 9:21   But by what means he now seeth, we know not; or who hath opened his eyes, we know not: he is of age; ask him: he shall speak for himself.

John 9:22   These words spake his parents, because they feared the Jews: for the Jews had agreed already, that if any man did confess that he was Christ, he should be put out of the synagogue.

John 9:23   Therefore said his parents, He is of age; ask him.

John 9:24   Then again called they the man that was blind, and said unto him, Give God the praise: we know that this man is a sinner.

**9:25...one thing I know, that, whereas I was blind, now I see.**

John 9:25   He answered and said, Whether he be a sinner or no, I know not: one thing I know, that, whereas I was blind, now I see.

John 9:26   Then said they to him again, What did he to thee? how opened he thine eyes?

John 9:27   He answered them, I have told you already, and ye did not hear: wherefore would ye hear it again? will ye also be his disciples?

John 9:28   Then they reviled him, and said, Thou art his disciple; but we are Moses' disciples.

John 9:29   We know that God spake unto Moses: as for this fellow, we know not from whence he is.

John 9:30   The man answered and said unto them, Why herein is a marvellous thing, that ye know not from whence he is, and yet he hath opened mine eyes.

John 9:31   Now we know that God heareth not sinners: but if any man be a worshipper of God, and doeth his will, him he heareth.

John 9:32   Since the world began was it not heard that any man opened the eyes of one that was born blind.

John 9:33   If this man were not of God, he could do nothing.

John 9:34   They answered and said unto him, Thou wast altogether born in sins, and dost thou teach us? And they cast him out.

John 9:35   Jesus heard that they had cast him out; and when he had found him, he said unto him, Dost thou believe on the Son of God?

John 9:36   He answered and said, Who is he, Lord, that I might believe on him?

John 9:37   And Jesus said unto him, Thou hast both seen him, and it is he that talketh with thee.

John 9:38   And he said, Lord, I believe. And he worshipped him.

**9:39  And Jesus said, For judgment I am** | 13:9 | John 9:39  And Jesus said, For judgment I am come into this world, that they which see not might see; and

| Matthew | Mark | Important Events |
|---------|------|------------------|
| | | |
| 19:1a | 10:1a | **Jerusalem the feast of the dedication, and it was winter** |

| ministry year | Key Scriptures & Footnotes | Luke | John |
| --- | --- | --- | --- |
| | come into this world, that they which see not might see; and that they which see might be made blind. | | that they which see might be made blind. John 9:40  And some of the Pharisees which were with him heard these words, and said unto him, Are we blind also? John 9:41  Jesus said unto them, If ye were blind, ye should have no sin: but now ye say, We see; therefore your sin remaineth. John 10:1  Verily, verily, I say unto you, He that entereth not by the door into the sheepfold, but climbeth up some other way, the same is a thief and a robber. John 10:2  But he that entereth in by the door is the shepherd of the sheep. John 10:3  To him the porter openeth; and the sheep hear his voice: and he calleth his own sheep by name, and leadeth them out. John 10:4  And when he putteth forth his own sheep, he goeth before them, and the sheep follow him: for they know his voice. John 10:5  And a stranger will they not follow, but will flee from him: for they know not the voice of strangers. John 10:6  This parable spake Jesus unto them: but they understood not what things they were which he spake unto them. John 10:7  Then said Jesus unto them again, Verily, verily, I say unto you, I am the door of the sheep. John 10:8  All that ever came before me are thieves and robbers: but the sheep did not hear them. John 10:9  I am the door: by me if any man enter in, he shall be saved, and shall go in and out, and find pasture. John 10:10  The thief cometh not, but for to steal, and to kill, and to destroy: I am come that they might have life, and that they might have it more abundantly. John 10:11  I am the good shepherd: the good shepherd giveth his life for the sheep. John 10:12  But he that is an hireling, and not the shepherd, whose own the sheep are not, seeth the wolf coming, and leaveth the sheep, and fleeth: and the wolf catcheth them, and scattereth the sheep. John 10:13  The hireling fleeth, because he is an hireling, and careth not for the sheep. John 10:14  I am the good shepherd, and know my sheep, and am known of mine. John 10:15  As the Father knoweth me, even so know I the Father: and I lay down my life for the sheep. John 10:16  And other sheep I have, which are not of this fold: them also I must bring, and they shall hear my voice; and there shall be one fold, and one shepherd. John 10:17  Therefore doth my Father love me, because I lay down my life, that I might take it again. John 10:18  No man taketh it from me, but I lay it down of myself. I have power to lay it down, and I have power to take it again. This commandment have I received of my Father. John 10:19  There was a division therefore again among the Jews for these sayings. John 10:20  And many of them said, He hath a devil, and is mad; why hear ye him? John 10:21  Others said, These are not the words of him that hath a devil. Can a devil open the eyes of the blind? |
| | 10:9 I am the door:.... | | |
| | Jesus feast of dedication | | Time Clue - Time Clue |
| | 10:22 **And it was** at Jerusalem the **feast of the dedication**, and it was **winter**.[104] | 13:9 | John 10:22  And it was at Jerusalem the feast of the dedication, and it was winter. John 10:23  And Jesus walked in the temple in Solomon's porch. John 10:24  Then came the Jews round about him, |

[104] John 10:22  And it was at Jerusalem the feast of the dedication, and it was winter. (*December after the Feast of Tabernacles found in John 7:2-53.*)

| Matthew | Mark | Important Events |
|---------|------|------------------|
| | | John 10:22<br>Map 94 |
| | | **2nd time they took up stones to cast at Jesus**<br>John 10:31 |
| Time Clue - Time Clue | Time Clue - Time Clue | |
| 19:1a | 10:1a | Map 95 |
| | | **Now a certain man was sick, named Lazarus**<br>John 11:1 |
| 19:1a | 10:1a | |

| ministry year | Key Scriptures & Footnotes | Luke | John |
|---|---|---|---|
| | | | and said unto him, How long dost thou make us to doubt? If thou be the Christ, tell us plainly. |
| | | | John 10:25   Jesus answered them, I told you, and ye believed not: the works that I do in my Father's name, they bear witness of me. |
| | | | John 10:26   But ye believe not, because ye are not of my sheep, as I said unto you. |
| | | | John 10:27   My sheep hear my voice, and I know them, and they follow me: |
| | | | John 10:28   And I give unto them eternal life; and they shall never perish, neither shall any man pluck them out of my hand. |
| | | | John 10:29   My Father, which gave them me, is greater than all; and no man is able to pluck them out of my Father's hand. |
| | | | John 10:30  I and my Father are one. |
| | Took they up stones | | Time Clue - Laying wait for him.... Luke 11:53-54 |
| | 10:31   Then the Jews took up stones **again** to stone him.[105] | | John 10:31   Then the Jews took up stones again to stone him. |
| | | | John 10:32  Jesus answered them, Many good works have I shown you from my Father; for which of those works do ye stone me? |
| | | | John 10:33   The Jews answered him, saying, For a good work we stone thee not; but for blasphemy; and because that thou, being a man, makest thyself God. |
| | | | John 10:34  Jesus answered them, Is it not written in your law, I said, Ye are gods? |
| | | | John 10:35   If he called them gods, unto whom the word of God came, and the scripture cannot be broken; |
| | | | John 10:36   Say ye of him, whom the Father hath sanctified, and sent into the world, Thou blasphemest; because I said, I am the Son of God? |
| | | | John 10:37   If I do not the works of my Father, believe me not. |
| | | | John 10:38   But if I do, though ye believe not me, believe the works: that ye may know, and believe, that the Father is in me, and I in him. |
| | Went beyond the Jordan | Time Clue - Time Clue | Time Clue - Time Clue |
| | 10:39   Therefore they sought again to take him: but **he escaped** out of their hand, 10:40  And **went away again beyond Jordan** into the place where John at first baptized; and there he abode. | 13:9 | John 10:39   Therefore they sought again to take him: but he escaped out of their hand, John 10:40   And went away again beyond Jordan into the place where John at first baptized; and there he abode. John 10:41   And many resorted unto him, and said, John did no miracle: but all things that John spake of this man were true. John 10:42   And many believed on him there. |
| | 11:1  Now a certain man was sick, named Lazarus, of Bethany,.... | | John 11:1   Now a certain man was sick, named Lazarus, of Bethany, the town of Mary and her sister Martha. John 11:2  (It was that Mary which anointed the Lord with ointment, and wiped his feet with her hair, whose brother Lazarus was sick.) John 11:3  Therefore his sisters sent unto him, saying, Lord, behold, he whom thou lovest is sick. |
| | 11:6...he abode two days still in the same place where he was. 11:7..Let us go into Judaea again. | 13:9 | John 11:4   When Jesus heard that, he said, This sickness is not unto death, but for the glory of God, that the Son of God might be glorified thereby. John 11:5   Now Jesus loved Martha, and her sister, and Lazarus. John 11:6  When he had heard therefore that he was sick, he abode two days still in the same place where he was. John 11:7   Then after that saith he to his disciples, Let us go into Judaea again. John 11:8   His disciples say unto him, Master, the Jews of late sought to stone thee; and goest thou thither again? |

[105] John 10:31   Then the Jews took up stones again to stone him. (*See John 8:59 for the first time that the Jews took up stones to stone Jesus.*)

| | | |
|---|---|---|
| 19:1a | 10:1a | Map 96 |

| ministry year | Key Scriptures & Footnotes | Luke | John |
|---|---|---|---|
| | | | John 11:9  Jesus answered, Are there not twelve hours in the day? If any man walk in the day, he stumbleth not, because he seeth the light of this world. John 11:10  But if a man walk in the night, he stumbleth, because there is no light in him. John 11:11  These things said he: and after that he saith unto them, Our friend Lazarus sleepeth; but I go, that I may awake him out of sleep. John 11:12  Then said his disciples, Lord, if he sleep, he shall do well. John 11:13  Howbeit Jesus spake of his death: but they thought that he had spoken of taking of rest in sleep. John 11:14  Then said Jesus unto them plainly, Lazarus is dead. John 11:15  And I am glad for your sakes that I was not there, to the intent ye may believe; nevertheless let us go unto him. John 11:16  Then said Thomas, which is called Didymus, unto his fellowdisciples, Let us also go, that we may die with him. |
| | Jesus returns to Bethany. | | Time Clue - Time Clue |
| 11:17 Then when Jesus came, he found that he had lain in the grave four days already. 11:18 Now Bethany was nigh unto Jerusalem,.... | 13:9 | | John 11:17  Then when Jesus came, he found that he had lain in the grave four days already. John 11:18  Now Bethany was nigh unto Jerusalem, about fifteen furlongs off: John 11:19  And many of the Jews came to Martha and Mary, to comfort them concerning their brother. John 11:20  Then Martha, as soon as she heard that Jesus was coming, went and met him: but Mary sat still in the house. John 11:21  Then said Martha unto Jesus, Lord, if thou hadst been here, my brother had not died. John 11:22  But I know, that even now, whatsoever thou wilt ask of God, God will give it thee. John 11:23  Jesus saith unto her, Thy brother shall rise again. John 11:24  Martha saith unto him, I know that he shall rise again in the resurrection at the last day. John 11:25  Jesus said unto her, I am the resurrection, and the life: he that believeth in me, though he were dead, yet shall he live: John 11:26  And whosoever liveth and believeth in me shall never die. Believest thou this? John 11:27  She saith unto him, Yea, Lord: I believe that thou art the Christ, the Son of God, which should come into the world. John 11:28  And when she had so said, she went her way, and called Mary her sister secretly, saying, The Master is come, and calleth for thee. John 11:29  As soon as she heard that, she arose quickly, and came unto him. John 11:30  Now Jesus was not yet come into the town, but was in that place where Martha met him. John 11:31  The Jews then which were with her in the house, and comforted her, when they saw Mary, that she rose up hastily and went out, followed her, saying, She goeth unto the grave to weep there. John 11:32  Then when Mary was come where Jesus was, and saw him, she fell down at his feet, saying unto him, Lord, if thou hadst been here, my brother had not died. John 11:33  When Jesus therefore saw her weeping, and the Jews also weeping which came with her, he groaned in the spirit, and was troubled, John 11:34  And said, Where have ye laid him? They said unto him, Lord, come and see. John 11:35  Jesus wept. John 11:36  Then said the Jews, Behold how he loved him! John 11:37  And some of them said, Could not this man, which opened the eyes of the blind, have caused that even this man should not have died? |

| Matthew | Mark | Important Events |
|---------|------|------------------|
| | | |
| 19:1a | 10:1a | |
| | | |
| | | **Jesus went into a city called Ephraim** John 11:54 Map 97 |
| 19:1a | 10:1a | **Jesus healed a woman who had a spirit of infirmity eighteen years** Luke 13:11 |

| | | | John 11:38  Jesus therefore again groaning in himself cometh to the grave. It was a cave, and a stone lay upon it.<br>John 11:39  Jesus said, Take ye away the stone. Martha, the sister of him that was dead, saith unto him, Lord, by this time he stinketh: for he hath been dead four days.<br>John 11:40  Jesus saith unto her, Said I not unto thee, that, if thou wouldest believe, thou shouldest see the glory of God?<br>John 11:41  Then they took away the stone from the place where the dead was laid. And Jesus lifted up his eyes, and said, Father, I thank thee that thou hast heard me.<br>John 11:42  And I knew that thou hearest me always: but because of the people which stand by I said it, that they may believe that thou hast sent me. |
| | 11:43  And when he thus had spoken, he cried with a loud voice, **Lazarus, come forth.** | | John 11:43  And when he thus had spoken, he cried with a loud voice, Lazarus, come forth.<br>John 11:44  And he that was dead came forth, bound hand and foot with graveclothes: and his face was bound about with a napkin. Jesus saith unto them, Loose him, and let him go.<br>John 11:45  Then many of the Jews which came to Mary, and had seen the things which Jesus did, believed on him. |
| | 11:46  But some of them went their ways to the Pharisees,.... | 13:9 | John 11:46  But some of them went their ways to the Pharisees, and told them what things Jesus had done.<br>John 11:47  Then gathered the chief priests and the Pharisees a council, and said, What do we? for this man doeth many miracles.<br>John 11:48  If we let him thus alone, all men will believe on him: and the Romans shall come and take away both our place and nation.<br>John 11:49  And one of them, named Caiaphas, being the high priest that same year, said unto them, Ye know nothing at all, |
| | 11:50  Nor consider that it is expedient for us, that **one man should die** for the people, and that the whole nation perish not. [106]<br>11:53  Then from that day forth they took counsel together for to put him to death. | | John 11:50  Nor consider that it is expedient for us, that one man should die for the people, and that the whole nation perish not.<br>John 11:51  And this spake he not of himself: but being high priest that year, he prophesied that Jesus should die for that nation;<br>John 11:52  And not for that nation only, but that also he should gather together in one the children of God that were scattered abroad.<br>John 11:53  Then from that day forth they took counsel together for to put him to death. |
| | Jesus to Ephraim. | | Time Clue - Time Clue |
| | 11:54  Jesus...**went** thence...**into a city called Ephraim**, and there continued with his disciples. | | John 11:54  Jesus therefore walked no more openly among the Jews; but went thence unto a country near to the wilderness, into a city called Ephraim, and there continued with his disciples. |
| | One of the synagogues | Time Clue - Luke 13:10 & 13:22 | Time Clue - Time Clue |
| | 13:10  And **he was teaching in one of the synagogues** on the sabbath.<br><br>13:12  And when Jesus saw her, he called her to him, and said unto her, Woman, thou art loosed from thine infirmity. | Luke 13:10  And he was teaching in one of the synagogues on the sabbath.<br>Luke 13:11  And, behold, there was a woman which had a spirit of infirmity eighteen years, and was bowed together, and could in no wise lift up herself.<br>Luke 13:12  And when Jesus saw her, he called her to him, and said unto her, Woman, thou art loosed from thine infirmity.<br>Luke 13:13  And he laid his hands on her: and immediately she was made straight, and glorified God.<br>Luke 13:14  And the ruler of the synagogue | |

[106] John 11:50  Nor consider that it is expedient for us, that one man should die for the people.... (*John probably heard this speech in person since he only testified of those things that he witnessed according to John 19:35 and John 21:24. John could have then returned to tell Jesus. This would explain why Jesus knew to walk* "no more openly among the Jews" *as seen in John 11:54.)*

| Matthew | Mark | Important Events |
|---------|------|------------------|
|  |  |  |
| 19:1a | 10:1a |  |
| 19:1a | 10:1a | **Map 98** |
| 19:1a | 10:1a | **Map 99** |

| | | Luke | John |
|---|---|---|---|
| | | answered with indignation, because that Jesus had healed on the sabbath day, and said unto the people, There are six days in which men ought to work: in them therefore come and be healed, and not on the sabbath day.<br>Luke 13:15  The Lord then answered him, and said, Thou hypocrite, doth not each one of you on the sabbath loose his ox or his ass from the stall, and lead him away to watering?<br>Luke 13:16    And ought not this woman, being a daughter of Abraham, whom Satan hath bound, lo, these eighteen years, be loosed from this bond on the sabbath day?<br>Luke 13:17  And when he had said these things, all his adversaries were ashamed: and all the people rejoiced for all the glorious things that were done by him. | |
| | | Luke 13:18  Then said he, Unto what is the kingdom of God like? and whereunto shall I resemble it?<br>Luke 13:19  It is like a grain of mustard seed, which a man took, and cast into his garden; and it grew, and waxed a great tree; and the fowls of the air lodged in the branches of it.<br>Luke 13:20    And again he said, Whereunto shall I liken the kingdom of God?<br>Luke 13:21    It is like leaven, which a woman took and hid in three measures of meal, till the whole was leavened. | 11:54 |
| | Teaching toward Jerusalem | Time Clue - Time Clue | |
| | **13:22 And he went through the cities and villages,[107] teaching, and journeying toward Jerusalem.** | Luke 13:22    And he went through the cities and villages, teaching, and journeying toward Jerusalem.<br>Luke 13:23  Then said one unto him, Lord, are there few that be saved? And he said unto them,<br>Luke 13:24    Strive to enter in at the strait gate: for many, I say unto you, will seek to enter in, and shall not be able.<br>Luke 13:25    When once the master of the house is risen up, and hath shut to the door, and ye begin to stand without, and to knock at the door, saying, Lord, Lord, open unto us; and he shall answer and say unto you, I know you not whence ye are:<br>Luke 13:26    Then shall ye begin to say, We have eaten and drunk in thy presence, and thou hast taught in our streets.<br>Luke 13:27  But he shall say, I tell you, I know you not whence ye are; depart from me, all ye workers of iniquity.<br>Luke 13:28    There shall be weeping and gnashing of teeth, when ye shall see Abraham, and Isaac, and Jacob, and all the prophets, in the kingdom of God, and you yourselves thrust out. | 11:54 |
| | 13:30 And, behold, there are last which shall be first, and there are first which shall be last.[108] | Luke 13:29    And they shall come from the east, and from the west, and from the north, and from the south, and shall sit down in the kingdom of God.<br>Luke 13:30    And, behold, there are last which shall be first, and there are first which shall be last. | |
| | 13:31...Pharisees, saying...depart hence: for Herod will kill thee<br>13:32...Go ye, and tell that fox,.... | Luke 13:31    The same day there came certain of the Pharisees, saying unto him, Get thee out, and depart hence: for Herod will kill thee.<br>Luke 13:32    And he said unto them, Go ye, and tell that fox, Behold, I cast out devils, and I do cures today and tomorrow, and the third day I shall be perfected.<br>Luke 13:33    Nevertheless I must walk today, and tomorrow, and the day following: for it cannot be that | 11:54 |
| | Luke 13:34  O | | |

[107] Luke 13:22  And he went through the cities and villages, teaching, and journeying toward Jerusalem. (*Luke 17:11 says He passed through the midst of Samaria and Galilee on His way to Jerusalem. This indicates a north and easterly route on His way to the coasts of Judeae beyond the Jordan found in Matthew 19:1b.*)

[108] Luke 13:30  And, behold, there are last which shall be first, and there are first which shall be last. (*First, see Matthew 19:30* But many that are first shall be last; and the last shall be first. *Secondly, see Mark 10:31* But many that are first shall be last; and the last first. *Lastly, see Matthew 20:16* So the last shall be first, and the first last:...)

| Matthew | Mark | Important Events |
|---------|------|------------------|
|  |  |  |
|  |  | **Jesus healed a man with dropsy** Luke 14:2 |
| 19:1a | 10:1a |  |
| 19:1a | 10:1a |  |

| ministry year | Key Scriptures & Footnotes | Luke | John |
|---|---|---|---|
| | Jerusalem, Jerusalem, which killest the prophets, and stonest them....[109]<br>13:35...Ye shall not see me, until the time come when ye shall say, Blessed is he that cometh in the name of the Lord.[110] | a prophet perish out of Jerusalem.<br>Luke 13:34  O Jerusalem, Jerusalem, which killest the prophets, and stonest them that are sent unto thee; how often would I have gathered thy children together, as a hen doth gather her brood under her wings, and ye would not!<br>Luke 13:35  Behold, your house is left unto you desolate: and verily I say unto you, Ye shall not see me, until the time come when ye shall say, Blessed is he that cometh in the name of the Lord. | |
| | 14:1...he went into the house of one of the chief Pharisees to eat bread on the sabbath day,....<br>14:2...a certain man before him which had the dropsy. | Luke 14:1  And it came to pass, as he went into the house of one of the chief Pharisees to eat bread on the sabbath day, that they watched him.<br>Luke 14:2  And, behold, there was a certain man before him which had the dropsy.<br>Luke 14:3  And Jesus answering spake unto the lawyers and Pharisees, saying, Is it lawful to heal on the sabbath day?<br>Luke 14:4  And they held their peace. And he took him, and healed him, and let him go; | |
| | | Luke 14:5  And answered them, saying, Which of you shall have an ass or an ox fallen into a pit, and will not straightway pull him out on the sabbath day?<br>Luke 14:6  And they could not answer him again to these things.<br>Luke 14:7  And he put forth a parable to those which were bidden, when he marked how they chose out the chief rooms; saying unto them,<br>Luke 14:8  When thou art bidden of any man to a wedding, sit not down in the highest room; lest a more honourable man than thou be bidden of him;<br>Luke 14:9  And he that bade thee and him come and say to thee, Give this man place; and thou begin with shame to take the lowest room.<br>Luke 14:10  But when thou art bidden, go and sit down in the lowest room; that when he that bade thee cometh, he may say unto thee, Friend, go up higher: then shalt thou have worship in the presence of them that sit at meat with thee.<br>Luke 14:11  For whosoever exalteth himself shall be abased; and he that humbleth himself shall be exalted.<br>Luke 14:12  Then said he also to him that bade him, When thou makest a dinner or a supper, call not thy friends, nor thy brethren, neither thy kinsmen, nor thy rich neighbours; lest they also bid thee again, and a recompence be made thee.<br>Luke 14:13  But when thou makest a feast, call the poor, the maimed, the lame, the blind:<br>Luke 14:14  And thou shalt be blessed; for they cannot recompense thee: for thou shalt be recompensed at the resurrection of the just.<br>Luke 14:15  And when one of them that sat at meat with him heard these things, he said unto him, Blessed is he that shall eat bread in the kingdom of God. | 11:54 |
| | 14:16...A certain man made a great supper, and bade many: | Luke 14:16  Then said he unto him, A certain man made a great supper, and bade many:<br>Luke 14:17  And sent his servant at supper time to say to them that were bidden, Come; for all things are now ready.<br>Luke 14:18  And they all with one consent began to make excuse. The first said unto him, I have bought a piece of ground, and I must needs go and see it: I pray thee have me excused.<br>Luke 14:19  And another said, I have bought five | 11:54 |

---

[109] Luke 13:34  O Jerusalem, Jerusalem, which killest the prophets, and stonest them that are sent unto thee; how often would I have gathered thy children together, as a hen doth gather her brood under her wings, and ye would not! (*See Luke 19:41*  And when he was come near, he beheld the city, and wept over it, *Also see Matthew 23:37*  O Jerusalem, Jerusalem, thou that killest the prophets, and stonest them...!)

[110] Luke 13:35  Behold, your house is left unto you desolate: and verily I say unto you, Ye shall not see me, until the time come when ye shall say, **Blessed is he that cometh in the name of the Lord**. (*The people could see Jesus on "Palm Sunday" because their words fulfilled this prophesy. See John 12:12-13* ...when they heard that Jesus was coming to Jerusalem,  Took branches of palm trees, and went forth to meet him, and cried, Hosanna: **Blessed is the King of Israel that cometh in the name of the Lord.**)

| Matthew | Mark | Important Events |
|---------|------|------------------|
|  |  |  |
| 19:1a | 10:1a |  |
| 19:1a | 10:1a |  |

| ministry year | Key Scriptures & Footnotes | Luke | John |
|---|---|---|---|
| | | yoke of oxen, and I go to prove them: I pray thee have me excused.<br>Luke 14:20   And another said, I have married a wife, and therefore I cannot come.<br>Luke 14:21   So that servant came, and showed his lord these things. Then the master of the house being angry said to his servant, Go out quickly into the streets and lanes of the city, and bring in hither the poor, and the maimed, and the halt, and the blind.<br>Luke 14:22   And the servant said, Lord, it is done as thou hast commanded, and yet there is room.<br>Luke 14:23   And the lord said unto the servant, Go out unto the highways and hedges, and compel them to come in, that my house may be filled.<br>Luke 14:24   For I say unto you, That none of those men which were bidden shall taste of my supper. | |
| | 14:25   And there went **great multitudes** with him:.... | Luke 14:25   And there went great multitudes with him: and he turned, and said unto them,<br>Luke 14:26   If any man come to me, and hate not his father, and mother, and wife, and children, and brethren, and sisters, yea, and his own life also, he cannot be my disciple.<br>Luke 14:27   And whosoever doth not bear his cross, and come after me, cannot be my disciple.<br>Luke 14:28   For which of you, intending to build a tower, sitteth not down first, and counteth the cost, whether he have sufficient to finish it?<br>Luke 14:29   Lest haply, after he hath laid the foundation, and is not able to finish it, all that behold it begin to mock him,<br>Luke 14:30   Saying, This man began to build, and was not able to finish.<br>Luke 14:31   Or what king, going to make war against another king, sitteth not down first, and consulteth whether he be able with ten thousand to meet him that cometh against him with twenty thousand?<br>Luke 14:32   Or else, while the other is yet a great way off, he sendeth an ambassage, and desireth conditions of peace.<br>Luke 14:33   So likewise, whosoever he be of you that forsaketh not all that he hath, he cannot be my disciple.<br>Luke 14:34   Salt is good: but if the salt have lost his savour, wherewith shall it be seasoned?<br>Luke 14:35   It is neither fit for the land, nor yet for the dunghill; but men cast it out. He that hath ears to hear, let him hear. | 11:54 |
| | 15:1   Then drew near unto him all the publicans and sinners.... | Luke 15:1   Then drew near unto him all the publicans and sinners for to hear him.<br>Luke 15:2   And the Pharisees and scribes murmured, saying, This man receiveth sinners, and eateth with them.<br>Luke 15:3   And he spake this parable unto them, saying,<br>Luke 15:4   What man of you, having an hundred sheep, if he lose one of them, doth not leave the ninety and nine in the wilderness, and go after that which is lost, until he find it?<br>Luke 15:5   And when he hath found it, he layeth it on his shoulders, rejoicing.<br>Luke 15:6   And when he cometh home, he calleth together his friends and neighbours, saying unto them, Rejoice with me; for I have found my sheep which was lost.<br>Luke 15:7   I say unto you, that likewise joy shall be in heaven over one sinner that repenteth, more than over ninety and nine just persons, which need no repentance.<br>Luke 15:8   Either what woman having ten pieces of silver, if she lose one piece, doth not light a candle, and sweep the house, and seek diligently till she find it?<br>Luke 15:9   And when she hath found it, she calleth | 11:54 |

| Matthew | Mark | Important Events |
|---------|------|------------------|
| 19:1a | 10:1a | **A certain man had two sons**<br>Luke 15:11 |
| 19:1a | 10:1a | **Give an account of thy stewardship** |

| | | her friends and her neighbours together, saying, Rejoice with me; for I have found the piece which I had lost.<br>Luke 15:10  Likewise, I say unto you, there is joy in the presence of the angels of God over one sinner that repenteth. | |
|---|---|---|---|
| 15:11  And he said, A certain man had two sons: | | Luke 15:11    And he said, A certain man had two sons:<br>Luke 15:12   And the younger of them said to his father, Father, give me the portion of goods that falleth to me. And he divided unto them his living.<br>Luke 15:13   And not many days after the younger son gathered all together, and took his journey into a far country, and there wasted his substance with riotous living.<br>Luke 15:14   And when he had spent all, there arose a mighty famine in that land; and he began to be in want.<br>Luke 15:15   And he went and joined himself to a citizen of that country; and he sent him into his fields to feed swine.<br>Luke 15:16  And he would fain have filled his belly with the husks that the swine did eat: and no man gave unto him.<br>Luke 15:17  And when he came to himself, he said, How many hired servants of my father's have bread enough and to spare, and I perish with hunger!<br>Luke 15:18  I will arise and go to my father, and will say unto him, Father, I have sinned against heaven, and before thee,<br>Luke 15:19  And am no more worthy to be called thy son: make me as one of thy hired servants.<br>Luke 15:20   And he arose, and came to his father. But when he was yet a great way off, his father saw him, and had compassion, and ran, and fell on his neck, and kissed him.<br>Luke 15:21    And the son said unto him, Father, I have sinned against heaven, and in thy sight, and am no more worthy to be called thy son.<br>Luke 15:22   But the father said to his servants, Bring forth the best robe, and put it on him; and put a ring on his hand, and shoes on his feet:<br>Luke 15:23   And bring hither the fatted calf, and kill it; and let us eat, and be merry:<br>Luke 15:24   For this my son was dead, and is alive again; he was lost, and is found. And they began to be merry.<br>Luke 15:25   Now his elder son was in the field: and as he came and drew nigh to the house, he heard music and dancing.<br>Luke 15:26  And he called one of the servants, and asked what these things meant.<br>Luke 15:27   And he said unto him, Thy brother is come; and thy father hath killed the fatted calf, because he hath received him safe and sound.<br>Luke 15:28   And he was angry, and would not go in: therefore came his father out, and entreated him.<br>Luke 15:29  And he answering said to his father, Lo, these many years do I serve thee, neither transgressed I at any time thy commandment: and yet thou never gavest me a kid, that I might make merry with my friends:<br>Luke 15:30   But as soon as this thy son was come, which hath devoured thy living with harlots, thou hast killed for him the fatted calf.<br>Luke 15:31  And he said unto him, Son, thou art ever with me, and all that I have is thine.<br>Luke 15:32   It was meet that we should make merry, and be glad: for this thy brother was dead, and is alive again; and was lost, and is found. | 11:54 |
| 16:1  And he said also unto his disciples,.... | | Luke 16:1  And he said also unto his disciples, There was a certain rich man, which had a steward; and the same was accused unto him that he had wasted his | 11:54 |

84

| Matthew | Mark | Important Events |
|---------|------|------------------|
|  |  | Luke 16:2 |
| 19:1a | 10:1a | **A certain beggar named Lazarus**<br>Luke 16:20 |

goods.

Luke 16:2   And he called him, and said unto him, How is it that I hear this of thee? give an account of thy stewardship; for thou mayest be no longer steward.

Luke 16:3   Then the steward said within himself, What shall I do? for my lord taketh away from me the stewardship: I cannot dig; to beg I am ashamed.

Luke 16:4   I am resolved what to do, that, when I am put out of the stewardship, they may receive me into their houses.

Luke 16:5   So he called every one of his lord's debtors unto him, and said unto the first, How much owest thou unto my lord?

Luke 16:6   And he said, An hundred measures of oil. And he said unto him, Take thy bill, and sit down quickly, and write fifty.

Luke 16:7   Then said he to another, And how much owest thou? And he said, An hundred measures of wheat. And he said unto him, Take thy bill, and write fourscore.

Luke 16:8   And the lord commended the unjust steward, because he had done wisely: for the children of this world are in their generation wiser than the children of light.

Luke 16:9   And I say unto you, Make to yourselves friends of the mammon of unrighteousness; that, when ye fail, they may receive you into everlasting habitations.

Luke 16:10   He that is faithful in that which is least is faithful also in much: and he that is unjust in the least is unjust also in much.

Luke 16:11   If therefore ye have not been faithful in the unrighteous mammon, who will commit to your trust the true riches?

Luke 16:12   And if ye have not been faithful in that which is another man's, who shall give you that which is your own?

Luke 16:13   No servant can serve two masters: for either he will hate the one, and love the other; or else he will hold to the one, and despise the other. Ye cannot serve God and mammon.

Luke 16:14   And the Pharisees also, who were covetous, heard all these things: and they derided him.

Luke 16:15   And he said unto them, Ye are they which justify yourselves before men; but God knoweth your hearts: for that which is highly esteemed among men is abomination in the sight of God.

Luke 16:16   The law and the prophets were until John: since that time the kingdom of God is preached, and every man presseth into it.

Luke 16:17   And it is easier for heaven and earth to pass, than one tittle of the law to fail.

Luke 16:18   Whosoever putteth away his wife, and marrieth another, committeth adultery: and whosoever marrieth her that is put away from her husband committeth adultery.

Luke 16:19   There was a certain rich man, which was clothed in purple and fine linen, and fared sumptuously every day:

Luke 16:20   And there was a certain beggar named Lazarus, which was laid at his gate, full of sores,

Luke 16:21   And desiring to be fed with the crumbs which fell from the rich man's table: moreover the dogs came and licked his sores.

Luke 16:22   And it came to pass, that the beggar died, and was carried by the angels into Abraham's bosom: the rich man also died, and was buried;

Luke 16:23   And in hell he lift up his eyes, being in torments, and seeth Abraham afar off, and Lazarus in his bosom.

**Footnotes (left column):**

16:2...give an account of thy stewardship;....

16:20...a certain beggar named Lazarus,....

**John column:**

11:54

| Matthew | Mark | Important Events |
|---------|------|------------------|
| 19:1a | 10:1a | |
| 19:1a | 10:1a | **Ten lepers cleansed** Luke 17:12 Map 100 |

| | | Luke | John |
|---|---|---|---|
| | | Luke 16:24 And he cried and said, Father Abraham, have mercy on me, and send Lazarus, that he may dip the tip of his finger in water, and cool my tongue; for I am tormented in this flame.<br>Luke 16:25 But Abraham said, Son, remember that thou in thy lifetime receivedst thy good things, and likewise Lazarus evil things: but now he is comforted, and thou art tormented.<br>Luke 16:26 And beside all this, between us and you there is a great gulf fixed: so that they which would pass from hence to you cannot; neither can they pass to us, that would come from thence.<br>Luke 16:27 Then he said, I pray thee therefore, father, that thou wouldest send him to my father's house:<br>Luke 16:28 For I have five brethren; that he may testify unto them, lest they also come into this place of torment.<br>Luke 16:29 Abraham saith unto him, They have Moses and the prophets; let them hear them.<br>Luke 16:30 And he said, Nay, father Abraham: but if one went unto them from the dead, they will repent.<br>Luke 16:31 And he said unto him, If they hear not Moses and the prophets, neither will they be persuaded, though one rose from the dead. | |
| | 17:3 ...If **thy brother** trespass against thee...<br><br>17:4 And if he **trespass** against thee seven times in a day, and seven times in a day turn again to thee, saying, I repent; thou shalt forgive him.[111] | Luke 17:1 Then said he unto the disciples, It is impossible but that offences will come: but woe unto him, through whom they come!<br>Luke 17:2 It were better for him that a millstone were hanged about his neck, and he cast into the sea, than that he should offend one of these little ones.<br>Luke 17:3 Take heed to yourselves: If thy brother trespass against thee, rebuke him; and if he repent, forgive him.<br>Luke 17:4 And if he trespass against thee seven times in a day, and seven times in a day turn again to thee, saying, I repent; thou shalt forgive him.<br>Luke 17:5 And the apostles said unto the Lord, Increase our faith.<br>Luke 17:6 And the Lord said, If ye had faith as a grain of mustard seed, ye might say unto this sycamine tree, Be thou plucked up by the root, and be thou planted in the sea; and it should obey you.<br>Luke 17:7 But which of you, having a servant plowing or feeding cattle, will say unto him by and by, when he is come from the field, Go and sit down to meat?<br>Luke 17:8 And will not rather say unto him, Make ready wherewith I may sup, and gird thyself, and serve me, till I have eaten and drunken; and afterward thou shalt eat and drink?<br>Luke 17:9 Doth he thank that servant because he did the things that were commanded him? I trow not.<br>Luke 17:10 So likewise ye, when ye shall have done all those things which are commanded you, say, We are unprofitable servants: we have done that which was our duty to do. | 11:54 |
| | Passed through Samaria. | Time Clue - Time Clue | |
| | 17:11 And it came to pass, **as he went to Jerusalem, that he passed through the midst of Samaria and Galilee.**[112]<br>17:12...there met him ten men that were lepers,.... | Luke 17:11 And it came to pass, as he went to Jerusalem, that he passed through the midst of Samaria and Galilee.<br>Luke 17:12 And as he entered into a certain village, there met him ten men that were lepers, which stood afar off:<br>Luke 17:13 And they lifted up their voices, and said, Jesus, Master, have mercy on us.<br>Luke 17:14 And when he saw them, he said unto | 11:54 |

[111] Luke 17:4 And if he **trespass** against thee seven times in a day, and seven times in a day turn again to thee, saying, I repent; thou shalt forgive him. (*Matthew 18:21-22* Then came Peter to him, and said, Lord, how oft shall my brother **sin** against me, and I forgive him? till seven times? Jesus saith unto him, I say not unto thee, Until seven times: but, Until seventy times seven.)

[112] Luke 17:11 And it came to pass, as he went to Jerusalem, that he passed through the midst of Samaria and Galilee. (*Jesus was on a north and easterly route on His way to the coasts of Judeae beyond the Jordan found in Matthew 19:1b.*)

| Matthew | Mark | Important Events |
|---------|------|------------------|
| 19:1a | 10:1a | |
| 19:1a | 10:1a | **A judge, which feared not God**<br>Luke 18:1 |

| ministry year | Key Scriptures & Footnotes | Luke | John |
|---|---|---|---|
| | 17:13 And they...said, Jesus, **Master**, have mercy on us. | them, Go show yourselves unto the priests. And it came to pass, that, as they went, they were cleansed. Luke 17:15 And one of them, when he saw that he was healed, turned back, and with a loud voice glorified God, Luke 17:16 And fell down on his face at his feet, giving him thanks: and he was a Samaritan. Luke 17:17 And Jesus answering said, Were there not ten cleansed? but where are the nine? | |
| | 17:19 And he said unto him, Arise, go thy way: thy faith hath made thee **whole**. | Luke 17:18 There are not found that returned to give glory to God, save this stranger. Luke 17:19 And he said unto him, Arise, go thy way: thy faith hath made thee whole. | |
| | 17:20...The kingdom of God cometh not with observation: | Luke 17:20 And when he was demanded of the Pharisees, when the kingdom of God should come, he answered them and said, The kingdom of God cometh not with observation: Luke 17:21 Neither shall they say, Lo here! or, lo there! for, behold, the kingdom of God is within you. Luke 17:22 And he said unto the disciples, The days will come, when ye shall desire to see one of the days of the Son of man, and ye shall not see it. Luke 17:23 And they shall say to you, See here; or, see there: go not after them, nor follow them. Luke 17:24 For as the lightning, that lighteneth out of the one part under heaven, shineth unto the other part under heaven; so shall also the Son of man be in his day. Luke 17:25 But first must he suffer many things, and be rejected of this generation. Luke 17:26 And as it was in the days of Noe, so shall it be also in the days of the Son of man. Luke 17:27 They did eat, they drank, they married wives, they were given in marriage, until the day that Noe entered into the ark, and the flood came, and destroyed them all. Luke 17:28 Likewise also as it was in the days of Lot; they did eat, they drank, they bought, they sold, they planted, they builded; Luke 17:29 But the same day that Lot went out of Sodom it rained fire and brimstone from heaven, and destroyed them all. Luke 17:30 Even thus shall it be in the day when the Son of man is revealed. Luke 17:31 In that day, he which shall be upon the housetop, and his stuff in the house, let him not come down to take it away: and he that is in the field, let him likewise not return back. Luke 17:32 Remember Lot's wife. Luke 17:33 Whosoever shall seek to save his life shall lose it; and whosoever shall lose his life shall preserve it. Luke 17:34 I tell you, in that night there shall be two men in one bed; the one shall be taken, and the other shall be left. Luke 17:35 Two women shall be grinding together; the one shall be taken, and the other left. Luke 17:36 Two men shall be in the field; the one shall be taken, and the other left. Luke 17:37 And they answered and said unto him, Where, Lord? And he said unto them, Wheresoever the body is, thither will the eagles be gathered together. | 11:54 |
| | | Luke 18:1 And he spake a parable unto them to this end, that men ought always to pray, and not to faint; Luke 18:2 Saying, There was in a city a judge, which feared not God, neither regarded man: Luke 18:3 And there was a widow in that city; and she came unto him, saying, Avenge me of mine adversary. Luke 18:4 And he would not for a while: but afterward he said within himself, Though I fear not God, nor regard man; | 11:54 |

| Matthew | Mark | Important Events |
|---|---|---|
| | | |
| | | |
| Time Clue - Time Clue | Time Clue - Time Clue | |
| Matt. 19:1b and came into the coasts of Judaea beyond Jordan;<br>Matt. 19:2 And great multitudes followed him; and he healed them there. | Mark 10:1b and cometh into the coasts of Judaea by the farther side of Jordan: and the people resort unto him again; and, as he was wont, he taught them again. | **Coasts of Judaea beyond Jordan**<br>Matt. 19:1b & Mark 10:1b<br>Map 101 |
| Matt. 19:3 The Pharisees also came unto him, tempting him, and saying unto him, Is it lawful for a man to put away his wife for every cause? | Mark 10:2 And the Pharisees came to him, and asked him, Is it lawful for a man to put away his wife? tempting him. | |
| | Mark 10:3 And he answered and said unto them, What did Moses command you?<br>Mark 10:4 And they said, Moses suffered to write a bill of divorcement, and to put her away.<br>Mark 10:5 And Jesus answered and said unto them, For the hardness of your heart he wrote you this precept. | |
| Matt. 19:4 And he answered and said unto them, Have ye not read, that he which made them at the beginning made them male and female,<br>Matt. 19:5 And said, For this cause shall a man leave father and mother, and shall cleave to his wife: and they twain shall be one flesh?<br>Matt. 19:6 Wherefore they are no more twain, but one flesh. What therefore God hath joined together, let not man put asunder. | Mark 10:6 But from the beginning of the creation God made them male and female.<br>Mark 10:7 For this cause shall a man leave his father and mother, and cleave to his wife;<br>Mark 10:8 And they twain shall be one flesh: so then they are no more twain, but one flesh.<br>Mark 10:9 What therefore God hath joined together, let not man put asunder. | |
| Matt. 19:7 They say unto him, Why did Moses then command to give a writing of divorcement, and to put her away?<br>Matt. 19:8 He saith unto them, Moses because of the hardness of your hearts suffered you to put away your wives: but from the beginning it was not so.<br>Matt. 19:9 And I say unto you, Whosoever shall put away his wife, except it be for fornication, and shall marry another, committeth adultery: and whoso marrieth her which is put away doth commit adultery.<br>Matt. 19:10 His disciples say unto him, If the case of the man be so with his wife, it is not good to marry. | | |

| ministry year | Key Scriptures & Footnotes | Luke | John |
|---|---|---|---|
| | | Luke 18:5  Yet because this widow troubleth me, I will avenge her, lest by her continual coming she weary me.<br>Luke 18:6  And the Lord said, Hear what the unjust judge saith.<br>Luke 18:7  And shall not God avenge his own elect, which cry day and night unto him, though he bear long with them?<br>Luke 18:8  I tell you that he will avenge them speedily. Nevertheless when the Son of man cometh, shall he find faith on the earth? | |
| | | Luke 18:9  And he spake this parable unto certain which trusted in themselves that they were righteous, and despised others:<br>Luke 18:10  Two men went up into the temple to pray; the one a Pharisee, and the other a publican.<br>Luke 18:11  The Pharisee stood and prayed thus with himself, God, I thank thee, that I am not as other men are, extortioners, unjust, adulterers, or even as this publican.<br>Luke 18:12  I fast twice in the week, I give tithes of all that I possess.<br>Luke 18:13  And the publican, standing afar off, would not lift up so much as his eyes unto heaven, but smote upon his breast, saying, God be merciful to me a sinner.<br>Luke 18:14  I tell you, this man went down to his house justified rather than the other: for every one that exalteth himself shall be abased; and he that humbleth himself shall be exalted. | |
| | Came to coasts of Judaea | Time Clue - Time Clue | |
| | 19:1b and came into the coasts of Judaea beyond Jordan;[113] | | 11:54 |
| | 10:2...Is it lawful for a man to put away his wife?.... | | |
| | | | |
| | | | |
| | | 18:14 | 11:54 |

[113] Matthew 19:1b and came into the coasts of Judaea beyond Jordan; (*There is a substantial time lock at Matthew 19:14, Mark 10:14, & Luke 18:16.  This helps provide a strong time clue linking Luke 18:14 to Matthew 19:1b & Mark 10:1b.*)

| Matthew | Mark | Important Events |
|---|---|---|
| Matt. 19:11 But he said unto them, All men cannot receive this saying, save they to whom it is given. Matt. 19:12 For there are some eunuchs, which were so born from their mother's womb: and there are some eunuchs, which were made eunuchs of men: and there be eunuchs, which have made themselves eunuchs for the kingdom of heaven's sake. He that is able to receive it, let him receive it. | | |
| | Mark 10:10 And in the house his disciples asked him again of the same matter. Mark 10:11 And he saith unto them, Whosoever shall put away his wife, and marry another, committeth adultery against her. Mark 10:12 And if a woman shall put away her husband, and be married to another, she committeth adultery. | |
| Time Lock - Time Lock | Time Lock - Time Lock | |
| Matt. 19:13 Then were there brought unto him little children, that he should put his hands on them, and pray: and the disciples rebuked them. Matt. 19:14 But Jesus said, Suffer little children, and forbid them not, to come unto me: for of such is the kingdom of heaven. Matt. 19:15 And he laid his hands on them, and departed thence. | Mark 10:13 And they brought young children to him, that he should touch them: and his disciples rebuked those that brought them. Mark 10:14 But when Jesus saw it, he was much displeased, and said unto them, Suffer the little children to come unto me, and forbid them not: for of such is the kingdom of God. Mark 10:15 Verily I say unto you, Whosoever shall not receive the kingdom of God as a little child, he shall not enter therein. Mark 10:16 And he took them up in his arms, put his hands upon them, and blessed them. | **Suffer the little children to come unto me** Matt. 19:14, Mark 10:14, & Luke 18:16 |
| Time Lock - Time Lock | Time Lock - Time Lock | Time Lock |
| Matt. 19:16 And, behold, one came and said unto him, Good Master, what good thing shall I do, that I may have eternal life? Matt. 19:17 And he said unto him, Why callest thou me good? there is none good but one, that is, God: but if thou wilt enter into life, keep the commandments. Matt. 19:18 He saith unto him, Which? Jesus said, Thou shalt do no murder, Thou shalt not commit adultery, Thou shalt not steal, Thou shalt not bear false witness, Matt. 19:19 Honour thy father and thy mother: and, Thou shalt love thy neighbour as thyself. Matt. 19:20 The young man saith unto him, All these things have I kept from my youth up: what lack I yet? Matt. 19:21 Jesus said unto him, If thou wilt be perfect, go and sell that thou hast, and give to the poor, and thou shalt have treasure in heaven: and come and follow me. Matt. 19:22 But when the young man heard that saying, he went away sorrowful: for he had great possessions. Matt. 19:23 Then said Jesus unto his disciples, Verily I say unto you, That a rich man shall hardly enter into the kingdom of heaven. | Mark 10:17 And when he was gone forth into the way, there came one running, and kneeled to him, and asked him, Good Master, what shall I do that I may inherit eternal life? Mark 10:18 And Jesus said unto him, Why callest thou me good? there is none good but one, that is, God. Mark 10:19 Thou knowest the commandments, Do not commit adultery, Do not kill, Do not steal, Do not bear false witness, Defraud not, Honour thy father and mother. Mark 10:20 And he answered and said unto him, Master, all these have I observed from my youth. Mark 10:21 Then Jesus beholding him loved him, and said unto him, One thing thou lackest: go thy way, sell whatsoever thou hast, and give to the poor, and thou shalt have treasure in heaven: and come, take up the cross, and follow me. Mark 10:22 And he was sad at that saying, and went away grieved: for he had great possessions. Mark 10:23 And Jesus looked round about, and saith unto his disciples, How hardly shall they that have riches enter into the kingdom of God! | **Sell that thou hast, and give to the poor** Matt. 19:21, Mark 10:21, & Luke 18:22 |
| | | |
| | Mark 10:24a And the disciples were astonished at his words. | |
| Matt. 19:24 And again I say unto you, It is easier for a camel to go through the eye of a needle, than for a rich man to enter into the kingdom of God | Mark 10:24b But Jesus answereth again, and saith unto them, Children, how hard is it for them that trust in riches to enter into the kingdom of God! Mark 10:25 It is easier for a camel to go through the eye of a needle, than for a rich man to enter into the kingdom of God. | |
| Matt. 19:25 When his disciples heard it, they were exceedingly amazed, saying, Who then can be saved? Matt. 19:26 But Jesus beheld them, and said unto them, With men this is impossible; but with God all things are possible. | Mark 10:26 And they were astonished out of measure, saying among themselves, Who then can be saved? Mark 10:27 And Jesus looking upon them saith, With men it is impossible, but not with God: for with God all things are possible. | |
| Time Lock - Time Lock | Time Lock - Time Lock | |

| ministry year | Key Scriptures & Footnotes | Luke | John |
|---|---|---|---|
| | | | |
| | 10:10 And **in the house** his disciples asked him again of the same matter. | | |
| | Little children brought. | Time Lock - Time Lock | |
| | 19:13...there **brought unto him** little children,...his disciples **rebuked** those that brought them.<br><br>19:15 And he laid his hands on them, and **departed** thence. | Luke 18:15 And they brought unto him also infants, that he would touch them: but when his disciples saw it, they rebuked them.<br>Luke 18:16 But Jesus called them unto him, and said, Suffer little children to come unto me, and forbid them not: for of such is the kingdom of God.<br>Luke 18:17 Verily I say unto you, Whosoever shall not receive the kingdom of God as a little child shall in no wise enter therein. | 11:54 |
| | Sell and give to the poor | Time Lock - Time Lock | |
| | 10:17 And when he was gone forth into the way,...Good Master, what shall I do that I may inherit eternal life?<br><br><br><br><br><br><br>19:21...sell whatsoever thou hast, and give to the poor,.... | Luke 18:18 And a certain ruler asked him, saying, Good Master, what shall I do to inherit eternal life?<br>Luke 18:19 And Jesus said unto him, Why callest thou me good? none is good, save one, that is, God.<br>Luke 18:20 Thou knowest the commandments, Do not commit adultery, Do not kill, Do not steal, Do not bear false witness, Honour thy father and thy mother.<br>Luke 18:21 And he said, All these have I kept from my youth up.<br>Luke 18:22 Now when Jesus heard these things, he said unto him, Yet lackest thou one thing: sell all that thou hast, and distribute unto the poor, and thou shalt have treasure in heaven: and come, follow me.<br>Luke 18:23 And when he heard this, he was very sorrowful: for he was very rich.<br>Luke 18:24 And when Jesus saw that he was very sorrowful, he said, How hardly shall they that have riches enter into the kingdom of God! | |
| | | Luke 18:25 For it is easier for a camel to go through a needle's eye, than for a rich man to enter into the kingdom of God. | 11:54 |
| | | | |
| | | | |
| | | Luke 18:26 And they that heard it said, Who then can be saved?<br>Luke 18:27 And he said, The things which are impossible with men are possible with God. | |
| | We have left all. | Time Lock - Time Lock | |

| Matthew | Mark | Important Events |
|---|---|---|
| Matt. 19:27   Then answered Peter and said unto him, Behold, we have forsaken all, and followed thee; what shall we have therefore?<br>Matt. 19:28   And Jesus said unto them, Verily I say unto you, That ye which have followed me, in the regeneration when the Son of man shall sit in the throne of his glory, ye also shall sit upon twelve thrones, judging the twelve tribes of Israel. | Mark 10:28   Then Peter began to say unto him, Lo, we have left all, and have followed thee.<br>Mark 10:29a   And Jesus answered and said, Verily I say unto you, | |
| Matt. 19:29   And every one that hath forsaken houses, or brethren, or sisters, or father, or mother, or wife, or children, or lands, for my name's sake, shall receive an hundredfold, and shall inherit everlasting life. | Mark 10:29b   There is no man that hath left house, or brethren, or sisters, or father, or mother, or wife, or children, or lands, for my sake, and the gospel's,<br>Mark 10:30   But he shall receive an hundredfold now in this time, houses, and brethren, and sisters, and mothers, and children, and lands, with persecutions; and in the world to come eternal life. | **But he shall receive an hundredfold now**<br>Matt. 19:29, Mark 10:30, & Luke 18:30 |
| Matt. 19:30   But many that are first shall be last; and the last shall be first. | Mark 10:31   But many that are first shall be last; and the last first. | |
| Matt. 20:1   For the kingdom of heaven is like unto a man that is an householder, which went out early in the morning to hire labourers into his vineyard.<br>Matt. 20:2   And when he had agreed with the labourers for a penny a day, he sent them into his vineyard.<br>Matt. 20:3   And he went out about the third hour, and saw others standing idle in the marketplace,<br>Matt. 20:4   And said unto them; Go ye also into the vineyard, and whatsoever is right I will give you. And they went their way.<br>Matt. 20:5   Again he went out about the sixth and ninth hour, and did likewise.<br>Matt. 20:6   And about the eleventh hour he went out, and found others standing idle, and saith unto them, Why stand ye here all the day idle?<br>Matt. 20:7   They say unto him, Because no man hath hired us. He saith unto them, Go ye also into the vineyard; and whatsoever is right, that shall ye receive.<br>Matt. 20:8   So when even was come, the lord of the vineyard saith unto his steward, Call the labourers, and give them their hire, beginning from the last unto the first.<br>Matt. 20:9   And when they came that were hired about the eleventh hour, they received every man a penny.<br>Matt. 20:10   But when the first came, they supposed that they should have received more; and they likewise received every man a penny.<br>Matt. 20:11   And when they had received it, they murmured against the goodman of the house,<br>Matt. 20:12   Saying, These last have wrought but one hour, and thou hast made them equal unto us, which have borne the burden and heat of the day.<br>Matt. 20:13   But he answered one of them, and said, Friend, I do thee no wrong: didst not thou agree with me for a penny?<br>Matt. 20:14   Take that thine is, and go thy way: I will give unto this last, even as unto thee.<br>Matt. 20:15   Is it not lawful for me to do what I will with mine own? Is thine eye evil, because I am good?<br>Matt. 20:16   So the last shall be first, and the first last: for many be called, but few chosen. | | |

| ministry year | Key Scriptures & Footnotes | Luke | John |
|---|---|---|---|
| | 19:27 Then answered Peter and said unto him, Behold, we have forsaken all,.... | Luke 18:28  Then Peter said, Lo, we have left all, and followed thee.<br>Luke 18:29a   And he said unto them, Verily I say unto you, | 11:54 |
| | 10:30 But he shall receive an hundredfold now in this time,.... | Luke 18:29b  There is no man that hath left house, or parents, or brethren, or wife, or children, for the kingdom of God's sake,<br>Luke 18:30  Who shall not receive manifold more in this present time, and in the world to come life everlasting. | |
| | 19:30 But many that are first shall be last; and the last shall be first. [114] | | |
| | 20:16 So the last shall be first, and the first last: [115] for many be called, but few chosen. [116] | | 11:54 |

---

[114] Matthew 19:30 But **many** that are **first** shall be **last**; and the last shall be first. (*Jesus made a similar statement twice more on this last trip to Jerusalem. See Luke 13:30  And, behold, there are* last *which shall be* first, *and there are* **first** *which shall be* **last**. *Also see Matthew 20:16  So the* last *shall be* first, *and the* **first last**.... )

[115] Matthew 20:16  So the last shall be first, and the **first last**.... (*See Matthew 19:30  But many that are* **first** *shall be* **last**; *and the* last *shall be* first. *Next see Mark 10:31  But many that are* **first** *shall be* **last**; *and the* last first.... *Finally see Luke 13:30  And, behold, there are* last *which shall be* first, *and there are* **first** *which shall be* **last**. )

[116] Matthew 20:16  ...for many be called, but few chosen. (*Jesus repeats this in Matthew 22:14 saying,* 'For many are called, but few are chosen.")

| Matthew | Mark | Important Events |
|---|---|---|
| Time Lock - Time Lock | Time Lock - Time Lock | |
| Matt. 20:17   And Jesus going up to Jerusalem took the twelve disciples apart in the way, and said unto them,<br>Matt. 20:18   Behold, we go up to Jerusalem; and the Son of man shall be betrayed unto the chief priests and unto the scribes, and they shall condemn him to death,<br>Matt. 20:19   And shall deliver him to the Gentiles to mock, and to scourge, and to crucify him: and the third day he shall rise again. | Mark 10:32   And they were in the way going up to Jerusalem; and Jesus went before them: and they were amazed; and as they followed, they were afraid. And he took again the twelve, and began to tell them what things should happen unto him,<br>Mark 10:33   Saying, Behold, we go up to Jerusalem; and the Son of man shall be delivered unto the chief priests, and unto the scribes; and they shall condemn him to death, and shall deliver him to the Gentiles:<br>Mark 10:34   And they shall mock him, and shall scourge him, and shall spit upon him, and shall kill him: and the third day he shall rise again. | **Behold, we go up to Jerusalem**<br>Matt. 20:18, Mark 10:33, & Luke 18:31<br><br>Map 102 |
| Matt. 20:20a   Then came to him the mother of Zebedee's children with her sons, worshipping him, | Mark 10:35a   And James and John, the sons of Zebedee, come unto him, | |
| | Mark 10:35b   saying, Master, we would that thou shouldest do for us whatsoever we shall desire. | |
| Matt. 20:20b   and desiring a certain thing of him.<br>Matt. 20:21   And he said unto her, What wilt thou? She saith unto him, Grant that these my two sons may sit, the one on thy right hand, and the other on the left, in thy kingdom. | | |
| | Mark 10:36   And he said unto them, What would ye that I should do for you?<br>Mark 10:37   They said unto him, Grant unto us that we may sit, one on thy right hand, and the other on thy left hand, in thy glory. | |
| Matt. 20:22 But Jesus answered and said, Ye know not what ye ask. Are ye able to drink of the cup that I shall drink of, and to be baptized with the baptism that I am baptized with? They say unto him, We are able.<br>Matt. 20:23   And he saith unto them, Ye shall drink indeed of my cup, and be baptized with the baptism that I am baptized with: but to sit on my right hand, and on my left, is not mine to give, but it shall be given to them for whom it is prepared of my Father.<br>Matt. 20:24   And when the ten heard it, they were moved with indignation against the two brethren.<br>Matt. 20:25 But Jesus called them unto him, and said, Ye know that the princes of the Gentiles exercise dominion over them, and they that are great exercise authority upon them.<br>Matt. 20:26   But it shall not be so among you: but whosoever will be great among you, let him be your minister;<br>Matt. 20:27   And whosoever will be chief among you, let him be your servant:<br>Matt. 20:28   Even as the Son of man came not to be ministered unto, but to minister, and to give his life a ransom for many. | Mark 10:38   But Jesus said unto them, Ye know not what ye ask: can ye drink of the cup that I drink of? and be baptized with the baptism that I am baptized with?<br>Mark 10:39   And they said unto him, We can. And Jesus said unto them, Ye shall indeed drink of the cup that I drink of; and with the baptism that I am baptized withal shall ye be baptized:<br>Mark 10:40   But to sit on my right hand and on my left hand is not mine to give; but it shall be given to them for whom it is prepared.<br>Mark 10:41   And when the ten heard it, they began to be much displeased with James and John.<br>Mark 10:42 But Jesus called them to him, and saith unto them, Ye know that they which are accounted to rule over the Gentiles exercise lordship over them; and their great ones exercise authority upon them.<br>Mark 10:43   But so shall it not be among you: but whosoever will be great among you, shall be your minister:<br>Mark 10:44   And whosoever of you will be the chiefest, shall be servant of all.<br>Mark 10:45   For even the Son of man came not to be ministered unto, but to minister, and to give his life a ransom for many. | |
| Time Clue - Time Clue | Time Clue - Time Clue | |
| | | **1st of four blind men healed at Jericho**<br>Luke 18:35<br><br>Map 103 |

| ministry year | Key Scriptures & Footnotes | Luke | John |
|---|---|---|---|
| | Son...will be delivered... | Time Lock - Time Lock | |
| | 10:32 ... they were afraid[117].... <br> 20:17 And Jesus going up to Jerusalem took the twelve disciples apart...and said unto them, <br> 20:18 **Behold, we go up to Jerusalem; and the Son of man shall be betrayed**.... <br> 20:19...and the **third day** he shall rise again. | Luke 18:31 Then he took unto him the twelve, and said unto them, Behold, we go up to Jerusalem, and all things that are written by the prophets concerning the Son of man shall be accomplished. <br> Luke 18:32 For he shall be delivered unto the Gentiles, and shall be mocked, and spitefully entreated, and spitted on: <br> Luke 18:33 And they shall scourge him, and put him to death: and the third day he shall rise again. <br> Luke 18:34 And they understood none of these things: and this saying was hid from them, neither knew they the things which were spoken. | 11:54 |
| | 20:21 ...She saith unto him, Grant that these my two sons may sit...**in thy kingdom**. | | |
| | 10:37 They[118] said unto him, Grant unto us that we may sit...**in thy glory**. | | 11:54 |
| | 20:26 But it shall not be so among you: but whosoever will be great among you, let him be your minister; <br> 20:27 And whosoever will be chief among you, let him be your servant: | | |
| | Come nigh unto Jericho. | Time Clue - Time Clue | |
| | 18:35 And it came to pass, that as he was **come nigh unto Jericho, a certain** blind man sat by the way side begging: | Luke 18:35 And it came to pass, that as he was come nigh unto Jericho, a certain blind man sat by the way side begging: <br> Luke 18:36 And hearing the multitude pass by, he asked what it meant. <br> Luke 18:37 And they told him, that Jesus of Nazareth passeth by. <br> Luke 18:38 And he cried, saying, Jesus, thou son of | 11:54 |

[117] Mark 10:32 And they were in the way **going up to Jerusalem**; and Jesus went before them: and they were amazed; and as they followed, **they were afraid**. (*Why were the disciples afraid? Twice during the previous feast of dedication **in Jerusalem** the Jews had taken up stones to stone Jesus. These events are recorded in John 8:59 and in John 10:31. Later, after Jesus called Lazarus forth from the grave in John 11:43, the chief priests and Pharisees **in Jerusalem** "took counsel together for to put him to death.")*

[118] Mark 10:37 **They** said unto him.... (*James and John said, "Master, we would that thou shouldest do for us whatsoever we shall desire." Both James and John and their mother "desired a certain thing" of Jesus. Jesus showed respect for their mother by asking her first, "What wilt thou?" After her request was known, Jesus turned to James and John and said, "What would ye that I should do for you?" After both of their requests were known, Jesus said, "Ye know not what ye ask.... "*)

| Matthew | Mark | Important Events |
|---------|------|------------------|
| | | |
| | Mark 10:46a   And they came to Jericho: | Map 104 |
| | | **Zacchaeus...today I must abide at thy house.**<br>Luke 19:2<br><br>Map 105 |
| | | **Jesus was nigh to Jerusalem**<br>Luke 19:11 |

| inistry year | Key Scriptures & Footnotes | Luke | John |
| --- | --- | --- | --- |
| | David, have mercy on me. | | |
| 18:39 And they which went before rebuked him, that he should hold his peace: but he cried so much the more, **Thou son of David, have mercy on me.** | Luke 18:39 And they which went before rebuked him, that he should hold his peace: but he cried so much the more, Thou son of David, have mercy on me.<br>Luke 18:40 And Jesus stood, and commanded him to be brought unto him: and when he was come near, he asked him,<br>Luke 18:41 Saying, What wilt thou that I shall do unto thee? And he said, Lord, that I may receive my sight. | | |
| 18:42 And Jesus said unto him, **Receive thy sight: thy faith hath saved thee.** | Luke 18:42 And Jesus said unto him, Receive thy sight: thy faith hath saved thee.<br>Luke 18:43 And immediately he received his sight, and followed him, glorifying God: and all the people, when they saw it, gave praise unto God. | | |
| 19:1 And Jesus **entered and passed through** Jericho.<br>19:2 And, behold, there was a man named **Zacchaeus**,.... | Luke 19:1 And Jesus entered and passed through Jericho.<br>Luke 19:2 And, behold, there was a man named Zacchaeus, which was the chief among the publicans, and he was rich.<br>Luke 19:3 And he sought to see Jesus who he was; and could not for the press, because he was little of stature.<br>Luke 19:4 And he ran before, and climbed up into a sycamore tree to see him: for he was to pass that way.<br>Luke 19:5 And when Jesus came to the place, he looked up, and saw him, and said unto him, Zacchaeus, make haste, and come down; for today I must abide at thy house.<br>Luke 19:6 And he made haste, and came down, and received him joyfully.<br>Luke 19:7 And when they saw it, they all murmured, saying, That he was gone to be guest with a man that is a sinner.<br>Luke 19:8 And Zacchaeus stood, and said unto the Lord; Behold, Lord, the half of my goods I give to the poor; and if I have taken any thing from any man by false accusation, I restore him fourfold.<br>Luke 19:9 And Jesus said unto him, This day is salvation come to this house, forsomuch as he also is a son of Abraham.<br>Luke 19:10 For the Son of man is come to seek and to save that which was lost. | 11:54 |
| 19:11...he added and spake a parable, because he was **nigh to Jerusalem**,.... | Luke 19:11 And as they heard these things, he added and spake a parable, because he was nigh to Jerusalem, and because they thought that the kingdom of God should immediately appear.<br>Luke 19:12 He said therefore, A certain nobleman went into a far country to receive for himself a kingdom, and to return.<br>Luke 19:13 And he called his ten servants, and delivered them ten pounds, and said unto them, Occupy till I come.<br>Luke 19:14 But his citizens hated him, and sent a message after him, saying, We will not have this man to reign over us.<br>Luke 19:15 And it came to pass, that when he was returned, having received the kingdom, then he commanded these servants to be called unto him, to whom he had given the money, that he might know how much every man had gained by trading.<br>Luke 19:16 Then came the first, saying, Lord, thy pound hath gained ten pounds.<br>Luke 19:17 And he said unto him, Well, thou good servant: because thou hast been faithful in a very little, have thou authority over ten cities.<br>Luke 19:18 And the second came, saying, Lord, thy pound hath gained five pounds.<br>Luke 19:19 And he said likewise to him, Be thou also over five cities. | 11:54 |

| Matthew | Mark | Important Events |
|---|---|---|
| | | |
| Time Lock - Time Lock | Time Lock - Time Lock | Time Lock |
| Matt. 20:29   And as they departed from Jericho, a great multitude followed him.<br>Matt. 20:30   And, behold, two blind men sitting by the way side, when they heard that Jesus passed by, cried out, saying, Have mercy on us, O Lord, thou Son of David.<br>Matt. 20:31   And the multitude rebuked them, because they should hold their peace: but they cried the more, saying, Have mercy on us, O Lord, thou Son of David.<br>Matt. 20:32   And Jesus stood still, and called them, and said, What will ye that I shall do unto you?<br>Matt. 20:33   They say unto him, Lord, that our eyes may be opened.<br>Matt. 20:34   So Jesus had compassion on them, and touched their eyes: and immediately their eyes received sight, and they followed him. | Mark 10:46b   and as he went out of Jericho with his disciples and a great number of people, blind Bartimaeus, the son of Timaeus, sat by the highway side begging.<br>Mark 10:47   And when he heard that it was Jesus of Nazareth, he began to cry out, and say, Jesus, thou son of David, have mercy on me.<br>Mark 10:48   And many charged him that he should hold his peace: but he cried the more a great deal, Thou son of David, have mercy on me.<br>Mark 10:49   And Jesus stood still, and commanded him to be called. And they call the blind man, saying unto him, Be of good comfort, rise; he calleth thee.<br>Mark 10:50   And he, casting away his garment, rose, and came to Jesus.<br>Mark 10:51   And Jesus answered and said unto him, What wilt thou that I should do unto thee? The blind man said unto him, Lord, that I might receive my sight.<br>Mark 10:52   And Jesus said unto him, Go thy way; thy faith hath made thee whole. And immediately he received his sight, and followed Jesus in the way. | **2nd, 3rd, & 4th blind men healed at Jericho**<br>Matt. 20:30 & Mark 10:46<br><br>Map 106 |
| Time Lock - Time Lock | Time Lock - Time Lock | Time Lock |
| | | |
| Time Clue - Time Clue | Time Clue - Time Clue | |
| | | **4th Passover was nigh.**<br>John 11:55 |
| | | |
| | | **Bethany, six days before the** |

| Ministry year | Key Scriptures & Footnotes | Luke | John |
|---|---|---|---|
| | | Luke 19:20   And another came, saying, Lord, behold, here is thy pound, which I have kept laid up in a napkin:<br>Luke 19:21   For I feared thee, because thou art an austere man: thou takest up that thou layedst not down, and reapest that thou didst not sow.<br>Luke 19:22   And he saith unto him, Out of thine own mouth will I judge thee, thou wicked servant. Thou knewest that I was an austere man, taking up that I laid not down, and reaping that I did not sow:<br>Luke 19:23   Wherefore then gavest not thou my money into the bank, that at my coming I might have required mine own with usury?<br>Luke 19:24   And he said unto them that stood by, Take from him the pound, and give it to him that hath ten pounds.<br>Luke 19:25   (And they said unto him, Lord, he hath ten pounds.)<br>Luke 19:26   For I say unto you, That unto every one which hath shall be given; and from him that hath not, even that he hath shall be taken away from him.<br>Luke 19:27   But those mine enemies, which would not that I should reign over them, bring hither, and slay them before me. | |

**Departing Jericho.**

| | Key Scriptures & Footnotes | Time Lock - Time Lock | |
|---|---|---|---|
| | 20:29  And as they **departed from** Jericho,....<br>20:30  And, behold, **two blind men**....<br>10:46...and as he **went** out of Jericho...**blind Bartimaeus**, the son of Timaeus, sat by the highway side begging.[119] | Luke 19:28a   And when he had thus spoken, he went before, | 11:54 |

**Ascending to Jerusalem.**

| | Key Scriptures & Footnotes | Time Lock - Time Lock | |
|---|---|---|---|
| | 19:28b ascending up to Jerusalem. | Luke 19:28b   ascending up to Jerusalem. | |

**Passover at hand.**

| | Key Scriptures & Footnotes | Time Clue - Time Clue | Time Clue - Time Clue |
|---|---|---|---|
| | 11:55 And the Jews' passover was nigh at hand:.... | | John 11:55   And the Jews' passover was nigh at hand: and many went out of the country up to Jerusalem before the passover, to purify themselves. |
| | 11:56 Then sought they for Jesus,.... | | John 11:56   Then sought they for Jesus, and spake among themselves, as they stood in the temple, What think ye, that he will not come to the feast?<br>John 11:57   Now both the chief priests and the Pharisees had given a commandment, that, if any man knew where he were, he should show it, that they might take him. |
| | 12:1 Then Jesus **six days** before the | | John 12:1   Then Jesus six days before the passover came to Bethany, where Lazarus was which had |

[119] Mark 10:46b ...blind Bartimaeus.... (*On Jesus' last trip through Jericho, the Gospel writers recorded the healing of four different blind men. As Jesus came nigh unto Jericho, Luke 18:35 tells of Jesus healing a certain blind man. And as they departed from Jericho, Matthew 20:30 tells of Jesus healing two blind men. In addition, as Jesus went out of Jericho, Mark 10:46b tells of Jesus healing blind Bartimaeus.*)

| Matthew | Mark | Important Events |
|---------|------|------------------|
| | | **4th passover** John 12:1 Map 107 |
| | | **Mary anointed the feet of Jesus** John 12:3 |
| | | |
| Time Lock - Time Lock | Time Lock - Time Lock | |
| Matt. 21:1   And when they drew nigh unto Jerusalem, and were come to Bethphage, unto the mount of Olives, then sent Jesus two disciples, Matt. 21:2  Saying unto them, Go into the village over against you, and straightway ye shall find an ass tied, and a colt with her: loose them, and bring them unto me. Matt. 21:3  And if any man say aught unto you, ye shall say, The Lord hath need of them; and straightway he will send them. Matt. 21:4  All this was done, that it might be fulfilled which was spoken by the prophet, saying, Matt. 21:5  Tell ye the daughter of Zion, Behold, thy King cometh unto thee, meek, and sitting upon an ass, and a colt the foal of an ass. | Mark 11:1  And when they came nigh to Jerusalem, unto Bethphage and Bethany, at the mount of Olives, he sendeth forth two of his disciples, Mark 11:2  And saith unto them, Go your way into the village over against you: and as soon as ye be entered into it, ye shall find a colt tied, whereon never man sat; loose him, and bring him. Mark 11:3  And if any man say unto you, Why do ye this? say ye that the Lord hath need of him; and straightway he will send him hither. | **Sunday afternoon, Find a colt tied.** Matt. 21:2, Mark 11:2, Luke 19:30, & John 12:14 Map 108 |
| Matt. 21:6  And the disciples went, and did as Jesus commanded them, Matt. 21:7  And brought the ass, and the colt, and put on them their clothes, and they set him thereon. | Mark 11:4  And they went their way, and found the colt tied by the door without in a place where two ways met; and they loose him. Mark 11:5  And certain of them that stood there said unto them, What do ye, loosing the colt? Mark 11:6  And they said unto them even as Jesus had commanded: and they let them go. | |

| ministry year | Key Scriptures & Footnotes | Luke | John |
|---|---|---|---|
| | passover came to Bethany,....[120] | | been dead, whom he raised from the dead. |
| | 12:2 There they made him a supper;....[121] 12:3 Then took Mary a pound of ointment of spikenard,...and anointed the feet of Jesus....[122] | | John 12:2 There they made him a supper; and Martha served: but Lazarus was one of them that sat at the table with him. John 12:3 Then took Mary a pound of ointment of spikenard, very costly, and anointed the feet of Jesus, and wiped his feet with her hair: and the house was filled with the odour of the ointment. John 12:4 Then saith one of his disciples, Judas Iscariot, Simon's son, which should betray him, John 12:5 Why was not this ointment sold for three hundred pence, and given to the poor? John 12:6 This he said, not that he cared for the poor; but because he was a thief, and had the bag, and bare what was put therein. |
| | 12:7 Then said Jesus, Let her alone: against the day of my burying hath she kept this. | | John 12:7 Then said Jesus, Let her alone: against the day of my burying hath she kept this. John 12:8 For the poor always ye have with you; but me ye have not always. |
| | 12:9 Much people of the Jews therefore knew that he was there: and they came not for Jesus' sake only....[123] 12:10 But the chief priests consulted that they might put Lazarus also to death; | | John 12:9 Much people of the Jews therefore knew that he was there: and they came not for Jesus' sake only, but that they might see Lazarus also, whom he had raised from the dead. John 12:10 But the chief priests consulted that they might put Lazarus also to death; John 12:11 Because that by reason of him many of the Jews went away, and believed on Jesus. |
| | Sent two disciples. | Time Lock - Time Lock | Time Lock - Time Lock |
| | 11:1...unto Bethphage and Bethany, at the mount called the mount of Olives,.... 21:2...find an ass tied, and a colt with her:...bring them unto me. | Luke 19:29 And it came to pass, when he was come nigh to Bethphage and Bethany, at the mount called the mount of Olives, he sent two of his disciples, Luke 19:30 Saying, Go ye into the village over against you; in the which at your entering ye shall find a colt tied, whereon yet never man sat: loose him, and bring him hither. Luke 19:31 And if any man ask you, Why do ye loose him? thus shall ye say unto him, Because the Lord hath need of him. | |
| | | Luke 19:32 And they that were sent went their way, and found even as he had said unto them. Luke 19:33 And as they were loosing the colt, the owners thereof said unto them, Why loose ye the colt? Luke 19:34 And they said, The Lord hath need of him. | |

---

[20] John 12:1 Then Jesus six days before **the passover** came to Bethany,.... (*This was Friday afternoon. At sunset was the beginning of the Sabbath, the 9th day of the month.* **The LORD's Passover** *was on the fourteenth of the month and the seven day* **feast of unleavened bread**, *which is also called* **the Passover** *in Luke 22:1, started on the 15th of the month. The fixed dates of* **The LORD's Passover** *and* **feast of unleavened bread** *are found in Exodus 12:6-20, Leviticus 23:5-6, and Numbers 28:16-25.*)

[21] John 12:2 There they made him a supper.... (*They would not have* made him a supper *until after the Sabbath was completed. So, the supper would have occurred Saturday at sundown, which was the beginning of the tenth day of the month. See The Calendar of Passover in the section following the maps.*)

[22] John 12:3 Then took Mary a pound of ointment of spikenard.... (*This was early in of the* **tenth day** *of the month. Mary was the first to choose "a lamb" for the Passover. Exodus 12:3 says, "Speak ye unto all the congregation of Israel, saying, In the* **tenth day** *of this month they shall take to them* **every man a lamb**, *according to the house of their fathers, a lamb for an house:." This was Jesus' second anointing by a woman. See Luke 7:37 for the first anointing and Matthew 26:7 & Mark 14:3 for the third anointing.*)

[23] John 12:9 Much people of the Jews therefore knew that he was there: and they came not for Jesus' sake only, but that they might see Lazarus also, whom he had raised from the dead. (*This happened Saturday after sunset, which was the beginning of the tenth day of the month. People who had seen Jesus in the synagogue during the Sabbath would have had time to bring their out-of-town friends after the Sabbath was complete. There would have been time for supper before much people came to see Jesus and Lazarus.*)

| Matthew | Mark | Important Events |
|---|---|---|
| | Mark 11:7   And they brought the colt to Jesus, and cast their garments on him; and he sat upon him. | |
| Matt. 21:8   And a very great multitude spread their garments in the way; others cut down branches from the trees, and strawed them in the way.<br>Matt. 21:9   And the multitudes that went before, and that followed, cried, saying, Hosanna to the son of David: Blessed is he that cometh in the name of the Lord; Hosanna in the highest. | Mark 11:8   And many spread their garments in the way: and others cut down branches off the trees, and strawed them in the way.<br>Mark 11:9   And they that went before, and they that followed, cried, saying, Hosanna; Blessed is he that cometh in the name of the Lord:<br>Mark 11:10   Blessed be the kingdom of our father David, that cometh in the name of the Lord: Hosanna in the highest. | |
| Matt. 21:10   And when he was come into Jerusalem, all the city was moved, saying, Who is this?<br>Matt. 21:11   And the multitude said, This is Jesus the prophet of Nazareth of Galilee. | Mark 11:11   And Jesus entered into Jerusalem, and into the temple: and when he had looked round about upon all things, and now the eventide was come, he went out unto Bethany with the twelve. | Map 109<br>Map 110 |
| Time Clue - Time Clue | Time Lock - Time Lock | |
| | Mark 11:12   And on the morrow, when they were come from Bethany, he was hungry:<br>Mark 11:13   And seeing a fig tree afar off having leaves, he came, if haply he might find any thing thereon: and when he came to it, he found nothing but leaves; for the time of figs was not yet.<br>Mark 11:14   And Jesus answered and said unto it, No man eat fruit of thee hereafter for ever. And his disciples heard it. | **Monday, N o man eat fruit of thee hereafter for ever.**<br>Mark 11:14<br>Map 111 |
| Time Lock - Time Lock | Time Lock - Time Lock | |
| Matt. 21:12   And Jesus went into the temple of God, | Mark 11:15   And they come to Jerusalem: and Jesus | |

| ministry year | Key Scriptures & Footnotes | Luke | John |
|---|---|---|---|
| | | Luke 19:35 And they brought him to Jesus: and they cast their garments upon the colt, and they set Jesus thereon. | |
| | 12:12 On the next day....[124]<br><br>12:13 Took branches of palm trees,....<br>21:9...cried, saying, Hosanna to the son of David: Blessed is he that cometh in the name of the Lord;[125]....<br>12:15 Fear not, daughter of Zion: behold, thy King cometh, sitting on an ass's colt.<br>19:40...I tell you that, if these should hold their peace, the stones would immediately cry out. | Luke 19:36 And as he went, they spread their clothes in the way.<br>Luke 19:37 And when he was come nigh, even now at the descent of the mount of Olives, the whole multitude of the disciples began to rejoice and praise God with a loud voice for all the mighty works that they had seen;<br>Luke 19:38 Saying, Blessed be the King that cometh in the name of the Lord: peace in heaven, and glory in the highest.<br>Luke 19:39 And some of the Pharisees from among the multitude said unto him, Master, rebuke thy disciples.<br>Luke 19:40 And he answered and said unto them, I tell you that, if these should hold their peace, the stones would immediately cry out. | John 12:12 On the next day much people that were come to the feast, when they heard that Jesus was coming to Jerusalem,<br>John 12:13 Took branches of palm trees, and went forth to meet him, and cried, Hosanna: Blessed is the King of Israel that cometh in the name of the Lord.<br>John 12:14 And Jesus, when he had found a young ass, sat thereon; as it is written,<br>John 12:15 Fear not, daughter of Zion: behold, thy King cometh, sitting on an ass's colt.<br>John 12:16 These things understood not his disciples at the first: but when Jesus was glorified, then remembered they that these things were written of him, and that they had done these things unto him.<br>John 12:17 The people therefore that was with him when he called Lazarus out of his grave, and raised him from the dead, bare record.<br>John 12:18 For this cause the people also met him, for that they heard that he had done this miracle.<br>John 12:19 The Pharisees therefore said among themselves, Perceive ye how ye prevail nothing? behold, the world is gone after him. |
| | 19:41...he beheld the city, and wept over it,[126] | Luke 19:41 And when he was come near, he beheld the city, and wept over it,<br>Luke 19:42 Saying, If thou hadst known, even thou, at least in this thy day, the things which belong unto thy peace! but now they are hid from thine eyes.<br>Luke 19:43 For the days shall come upon thee, that thine enemies shall cast a trench about thee, and compass thee round, and keep thee in on every side,<br>Luke 19:44 And shall lay thee even with the ground, and thy children within thee; and they shall not leave in thee one stone upon another; because thou knewest not the time of thy visitation. | |
| | 11:11 And Jesus entered...into the temple: and when he had looked round...and now the eventide was come,[127] he went out unto Bethany with the twelve. | | |
| | Monday morning. | Time Clue - Time Clue | |
| | 11:12 And on the morrow....[128]<br>11:13 And seeing a fig tree afar off....[129] | | |
| | Jesus cast them out. | Time Lock - Time Lock | |
| | 11:15 And they **come** | Luke 19:45 And he went into the temple, and began | |

[24] John 12:12 On **the next day**... (This was *Sunday. It was still the tenth day of the month. On the tenth day of the month the Passover lamb was chosen according to Exodus 12:3.*)

[25] Matthew 21:9 And the multitudes that went before, and that followed, cried, saying, Hosanna to the son of David: **Blessed is he that cometh in the name of the Lord**; Hosanna in the highest. (*This is the fulfillment of Jesus' prophesy in Luke 13:35 behold,...Ye shall not see me, until the time come when ye shall say,* **Blessed is he that cometh in the name of the Lord**.)

[26] Luke 19:41 And when he was come near, he beheld the city, and wept over it, (*This is not the same prophecy as Luke 13:34 when Jesus said, "O Jerusalem, Jerusalem, which killest the prophets, and stonest them...." or Matthew 23:37 where He said, "O Jerusalem, Jerusalem, thou that killest the prophets, and stonest them....")*

[27] Mark 11:11 And Jesus entered into Jerusalem, and into the temple: and when he had looked round about upon all things, and now the eventide was come, he went out unto Bethany with the twelve. (*Jesus probably entered into Jerusalem in the afternoon. It is recorded that after He looked round about upon all things it was* **eventide**.)

[28] Mark 11:12 And on the morrow...: (This was *Monday, the eleventh day of the month.*)

[29] Mark 11:13 And seeing a fig tree afar off having leaves, he came.... (*This is the first fig tree that Jesus cursed. It is located between Bethany and Jerusalem. See Matthew 21:19a for the second fig tree.*)

| Matthew | Mark | Important Events |
|---|---|---|
| and cast out all them that sold and bought in the temple, and overthrew the tables of the moneychangers, and the seats of them that sold doves, | went into the temple, and began to cast out them that sold and bought in the temple, and overthrew the tables of the moneychangers, and the seats of them that sold doves;<br>Mark 11:16　And would not suffer that any man should carry any vessel through the temple. | |
| Matt. 21:13　And said unto them, It is written, My house shall be called the house of prayer; but ye have made it a den of thieves. | Mark 11:17　And he taught, saying unto them, Is it not written, My house shall be called of all nations the house of prayer? but ye have made it a den of thieves. | **Monday, M y house shall be called the house of prayer**<br>Matt. 21:13, Mark 11:17, & Luke 19:46<br>Map 112 |
| Matt. 21:14　And the blind and the lame came to him in the temple; and he healed them. | | |
| Matt. 21:15　And when the chief priests and scribes saw the wonderful things that he did, and the children crying in the temple, and saying, Hosanna to the son of David; they were sore displeased,<br>Matt. 21:16　And said unto him, Hearest thou what these say? And Jesus saith unto them, Yea; have ye never read, Out of the mouth of babes and sucklings thou hast perfected praise? | | |
| | Mark 11:18　And the scribes and chief priests heard it, and sought how they might destroy him: for they feared him, because all the people was astonished at his doctrine. | |
| Time Lock - Time Lock | Time Lock - Time Lock | |
| Matt. 21:17　And he left them, and went out of the city into Bethany: and he lodged there. | Mark 11:19　And when even was come, he went out of the city. | Map 113 |
| Time Lock - Time Lock | Time Lock - Time Lock | |
| Matt. 21:18a　Now in the morning | Mark 11:20　And in the morning, as they passed by, they saw the fig tree dried up from the roots. | **Tuesday, 1st fig tree dried up**<br>Mark 11:20<br>Map 114 |
| | Mark 11:21　And Peter calling to remembrance saith unto him, Master, behold, the fig tree which thou cursedst is withered away.<br>Mark 11:22　And Jesus answering saith unto them, Have faith in God.<br>Mark 11:23　For verily I say unto you, That whosoever shall say unto this mountain, Be thou removed, and be thou cast into the sea; and shall not doubt in his heart, but shall believe that those things which he saith shall come to pass; he shall have | |

| ministry year | Key Scriptures & Footnotes | Luke | John |
|---|---|---|---|
| | **to Jerusalem**: and Jesus went into the temple, and began to cast out them that sold and bought in the temple,[130] | to cast out them that sold therein, and them that bought; | |
| | 21:13...It is written, My house shall be called the house of prayer;.... | Luke 19:46  Saying unto them, It is written, My house is the house of prayer: but ye have made it a den of thieves. | 12:19 |
| | 21:14  And the blind and the lame came to him in the temple; and **he healed them**. | | |
| | | | |
| | | | |
| | 19:47 And **he taught daily in the temple**.....[131] | Luke 19:47    And he taught daily in the temple. But the chief priests and the scribes and the chief of the people sought to destroy him,<br>Luke 19:48  And could not find what they might do: for all the people were very attentive to hear him. | 12:19 |
| | Monday evening. | Time Clue - Time Clue | |
| | 21:17  And he left them, and went out of the city into Bethany; and he lodged there.[132] | | |
| | Tuesday morning. | Time Clue - Time Clue | |
| | 11:20 ...they saw the fig tree **dried up from the roots**. | | |
| | | | 12:19 |
| | 11:22 And Jesus answering saith unto them, Have faith in God.<br>11:23...That whosoever shall **say unto this mountain**,[133] | | |

---

[130] Mark 11:15 ...Jesus went into the temple, and began to cast out them that sold and bought in the temple...; (*This is the second cleansing" of the temple by Jesus. The first time Jesus "cleansed" the temple is found in John 2:15. At that time Jesus* made a scourge of small cords *and* drove them all out of the temple.)

[131] Luke 19:47  And he taught daily in the temple.... (*He taught Monday, Tuesday, and possibly Wednesday. See Luke 21:37* And in the day time he was teaching in the temple; and at night he went out, and abode in the mount that is called the mount of Olives.)

[132] Matthew 21:17 ...and he lodged there. (*This was Monday night which was the start of the 12th day of the month.*)

[133] Mark 11:23  For verily I say unto you, That whosoever shall **say unto this mountain**, Be thou removed.... (*Jesus taught His disciples "say unto this mountain" three separate times. First, at the feast of the dedication in Matthew 17:20* And Jesus said unto them, Because of your unbelief: for verily I say unto you, If ye have faith as a grain of mustard seed, ye shall **say unto this mountain**, Remove hence to yonder place; and it shall remove; and nothing shall be impossible unto you. *Second, on this Tuesday morning recorded here in Mark 11:23, outside of the city of Jerusalem. Third, less than one hour later inside of the city of Jerusalem in Matthew 21:21-22* Jesus answered and said unto them, Verily I say unto you, If ye have faith, and doubt not, ye shall

| Matthew | Mark | Important Events |
|---------|------|------------------|
|  | whatsoever he saith.<br>Mark 11:24 Therefore I say unto you, What things soever ye desire, when ye pray, believe that ye receive them, and ye shall have them.<br>Mark 11:25 And when ye stand praying, forgive, if ye have aught against any: that your Father also which is in heaven may forgive you your trespasses.<br>Mark 11:26 But if ye do not forgive, neither will your Father which is in heaven forgive your trespasses. |  |
| Time Lock - Time Lock | Time Lock - Time Lock |  |
| Matt. 21:18b    as he returned into the city, he hungered.<br>Matt. 21:19a  And when he saw a fig tree in the way, he came to it, and found nothing thereon, but leaves only, and said unto it, Let no fruit grow on thee henceforward for ever. | Mark 11:27a   And they come again to Jerusalem: | **Tuesday, Let no fruit grow on thee henceforward for ever.**<br>Matt. 21:19a<br><br>Map 115 |
| Matt. 21:19b    And presently the fig tree withered away. |  | **2nd fig tree instantly withered away**<br>Matt. 21:19b |
| Matt. 21:20    And when the disciples saw it, they marvelled, saying, How soon is the fig tree withered away!<br>Matt. 21:21    Jesus answered and said unto them, Verily I say unto you, If ye have faith, and doubt not, ye shall not only do this which is done to the fig tree, but also if ye shall say unto this mountain, Be thou removed, and be thou cast into the sea; it shall be done.<br>Matt. 21:22  And all things, whatsoever ye shall ask in prayer, believing, ye shall receive. |  |  |
| Time Lock - Time Lock | Time Lock - Time Lock |  |
| Matt. 21:23  And when he was come into the temple, the chief priests and the elders of the people came unto him as he was teaching, and said, By what authority doest thou these things? and who gave thee this authority?<br>Matt. 21:24  And Jesus answered and said unto them, I also will ask you one thing, which if ye tell me, I in like wise will tell you by what authority I do these things.<br>Matt. 21:25   The baptism of John, whence was it? from heaven, or of men? And they reasoned with themselves, saying, If we shall say, From heaven; he will say unto us, Why did ye not then believe him?<br>Matt. 21:26  But if we shall say, Of men; we fear the people; for all hold John as a prophet.<br>Matt. 21:27  And they answered Jesus, and said, We cannot tell. And he said unto them, Neither tell I you by what authority I do these things. | Mark 11:27b    and as he was walking in the temple, there come to him the chief priests, and the scribes, and the elders,<br>Mark 11:28    And say unto him, By what authority doest thou these things? and who gave thee this authority to do these things?<br>Mark 11:29  And Jesus answered and said unto them, I will also ask of you one question, and answer me, and I will tell you by what authority I do these things.<br>Mark 11:30    The baptism of John, was it from heaven, or of men? answer me.<br>Mark 11:31    And they reasoned with themselves, saying, If we shall say, From heaven; he will say, Why then did ye not believe him?<br>Mark 11:32   But if we shall say, Of men; they feared the people: for all men counted John, that he was a prophet indeed.<br>Mark 11:33  And they answered and said unto Jesus, We cannot tell. And Jesus answering saith unto them, Neither do I tell you by what authority I do these things. |  |
| Matt. 21:28  But what think ye? A certain man had two sons; and he came to the first, and said, Son, go work today in my vineyard. |  |  |

| nistry year | Key Scriptures & Footnotes | Luke | John |
|---|---|---|---|
| | Be thou removed, and be thou cast into the sea; and shall not doubt in his heart, but shall believe that those things which he saith shall come to pass; he shall have whatsoever he saith. | | |
| | Enter Jerusalem. | | |
| | 11:27a And they **come again to Jerusalem:** 21:18b as he returned **into the city**, he hungered. 21:19a And when he saw a fig tree in the way....[134] | | 12:19 |
| | Matt. 21:19b And **presently**[135] the fig tree withered away. | | |
| | 21:20 And when the disciples saw it, **they marvelled**, saying, How **soon**[136] is the fig tree withered away! 21:21 Jesus answered and said unto them, Verily I say unto you, If ye have faith, and doubt not,....[137] | | |
| | By what authority? | Time Lock - Time Lock | |
| | 11:28...By what authority doest thou these things?.... | Luke 20:1 And it came to pass, that on one of those days, as he taught the people in the temple, and preached the gospel, the chief priests and the scribes came upon him with the elders, Luke 20:2 And spake unto him, saying, Tell us, by what authority doest thou these things? or who is he that gave thee this authority? Luke 20:3 And he answered and said unto them, I will also ask you one thing; and answer me: Luke 20:4 The baptism of John, was it from heaven, or of men? Luke 20:5 And they reasoned with themselves, saying, If we shall say, From heaven; he will say, Why then believed ye him not? Luke 20:6 But and if we say, Of men; all the people will stone us: for they be persuaded that John was a prophet. Luke 20:7 And they answered, that they could not tell whence it was. Luke 20:8 And Jesus said unto them, Neither tell I you by what authority I do these things. | 12:19 |
| | | | |

ot only do this which is done to the fig tree, but also if ye shall **say unto this mountain**, Be thou removed, and be thou cast into the ea; it shall be done.)

[34] Matthew 21:19a And when he saw a fig tree in the way.... (*From Matthew 21:18b we know this second fig tree is in the city of erusalem. See Mark 11:13 for the first fig tree Jesus cursed.*)

[35] Matthew 21:19b And **presently**.... (*Some translations say* **immediately** *or* **instantly**. *This is Tuesday morning.*)

[36] Matthew 21:20 ...they marvelled, saying, How **soon** is the fig tree withered away! (*Some translations say* **immediately** *or* **nstantly**.)

[37] Matthew 21:21 Jesus answered and said unto them, Verily I say unto you, If ye have faith, and doubt not, ye shall not only do his which is done to the fig tree, but also if ye shall say unto this mountain, Be thou removed, and be thou cast into the sea; it shall e done. (*Since the second fig tree died instantly, Jesus implied that a mountain could also be removed instantly.*)

| Matthew | Mark | Important Events |
|---|---|---|
| Matt. 21:29   He answered and said, I will not: but afterward he repented, and went.<br>Matt. 21:30   And he came to the second, and said likewise. And he answered and said, I go, sir: and went not.<br>Matt. 21:31   Whether of them twain did the will of his father? They say unto him, The first. Jesus saith unto them, Verily I say unto you, That the publicans and the harlots go into the kingdom of God before you.<br>Matt. 21:32   For John came unto you in the way of righteousness, and ye believed him not: but the publicans and the harlots believed him: and ye, when ye had seen it, repented not afterward, that ye might believe him. | | |
| Time Lock - Time Lock | Time Lock - Time Lock | |
| Matt. 21:33   Hear another parable: There was a certain householder, which planted a vineyard, and hedged it round about, and digged a winepress in it, and built a tower, and let it out to husbandmen, and went into a far country:<br>Matt. 21:34   And when the time of the fruit drew near, he sent his servants to the husbandmen, that they might receive the fruits of it.<br>Matt. 21:35   And the husbandmen took his servants, and beat one, and killed another, and stoned another.<br>Matt. 21:36   Again, he sent other servants more than the first: and they did unto them likewise.<br>Matt. 21:37   But last of all he sent unto them his son, saying, They will reverence my son.<br>Matt. 21:38   But when the husbandmen saw the son, they said among themselves, This is the heir; come, let us kill him, and let us seize on his inheritance.<br>Matt. 21:39   And they caught him, and cast him out of the vineyard, and slew him.<br>Matt. 21:40   When the lord therefore of the vineyard cometh, what will he do unto those husbandmen?<br>Matt. 21:41   They say unto him, He will miserably destroy those wicked men, and will let out his vineyard unto other husbandmen, which shall render him the fruits in their seasons.<br>Matt. 21:42   Jesus saith unto them, Did ye never read in the scriptures, The stone which the builders rejected, the same is become the head of the corner: this is the Lord's doing, and it is marvellous in our eyes?<br>Matt. 21:43   Therefore say I unto you, The kingdom of God shall be taken from you, and given to a nation bringing forth the fruits thereof.<br>Matt. 21:44   And whosoever shall fall on this stone shall be broken: but on whomsoever it shall fall, it will grind him to powder. | Mark 12:1   And he began to speak unto them by parables. A certain man planted a vineyard, and set an hedge about it, and digged a place for the winevat, and built a tower, and let it out to husbandmen, and went into a far country.<br>Mark 12:2   And at the season he sent to the husbandmen a servant, that he might receive from the husbandmen of the fruit of the vineyard.<br>Mark 12:3   And they caught him, and beat him, and sent him away empty.<br>Mark 12:4   And again he sent unto them another servant; and at him they cast stones, and wounded him in the head, and sent him away shamefully handled.<br>Mark 12:5   And again he sent another; and him they killed, and many others; beating some, and killing some.<br>Mark 12:6   Having yet therefore one son, his wellbeloved, he sent him also last unto them, saying, They will reverence my son.<br>Mark 12:7   But those husbandmen said among themselves, This is the heir; come, let us kill him, and the inheritance shall be ours.<br>Mark 12:8   And they took him, and killed him, and cast him out of the vineyard.<br>Mark 12:9   What shall therefore the lord of the vineyard do? he will come and destroy the husbandmen, and will give the vineyard unto others.<br>Mark 12:10   And have ye not read this scripture; The stone which the builders rejected is become the head of the corner:<br>Mark 12:11   This was the Lord's doing, and it is marvellous in our eyes? | **A certain man planted a vineyard**<br>Matt. 21:33, Mark 12:1, & Luke 20:9 |
| Matt. 21:45   And when the chief priests and Pharisees had heard his parables, they perceived that he spake of them.<br>Matt. 21:46   But when they sought to lay hands on him, they feared the multitude, because they took him for a prophet. | Mark 12:12  And they sought to lay hold on him, but feared the people: for they knew that he had spoken the parable against them: and they left him, and went their way. | |
| Matt. 22:1   And Jesus answered and spake unto them again by parables, and said,<br>Matt. 22:2   The kingdom of heaven is like unto a certain king, which made a marriage for his son,<br>Matt. 22:3   And sent forth his servants to call them that were bidden to the wedding: and they would not come.<br>Matt. 22:4   Again, he sent forth other servants, saying, Tell them which are bidden, Behold, I have prepared my dinner: my oxen and my fatlings are killed, and all things are ready: come unto the marriage.<br>Matt. 22:5 But they made light of it, and went their | | |

| Ministry year | Key Scriptures & Footnotes | Luke | John |
|---|---|---|---|
| | 21:32 For John came...and ye, when ye had seen it, repented not afterward, that ye might believe him. | | |
| | Man planted a vineyard. | Time Lock - Time Lock | |
| | 12:1...A certain man planted a vineyard,.... | Luke 20:9  Then began he to speak to the people this parable; A certain man planted a vineyard, and let it forth to husbandmen, and went into a far country for a long time.<br>Luke 20:10  And at the season he sent a servant to the husbandmen, that they should give him of the fruit of the vineyard: but the husbandmen beat him, and sent him away empty.<br>Luke 20:11  And again he sent another servant: and they beat him also, and entreated him shamefully, and sent him away empty.<br>Luke 20:12  And again he sent a third: and they wounded him also, and cast him out.<br>Luke 20:13  Then said the lord of the vineyard, What shall I do? I will send my beloved son: it may be they will reverence him when they see him.<br>Luke 20:14  But when the husbandmen saw him, they reasoned among themselves, saying, This is the heir: come, let us kill him, that the inheritance may be ours.<br>Luke 20:15  So they cast him out of the vineyard, and killed him. What therefore shall the lord of the vineyard do unto them?<br>Luke 20:16  He shall come and destroy these husbandmen, and shall give the vineyard to others. And when they heard it, they said, God forbid.<br>Luke 20:17  And he beheld them, and said, What is this then that is written, The stone which the builders rejected, the same is become the head of the corner?<br>Luke 20:18  Whosoever shall fall upon that stone shall be broken; but on whomsoever it shall fall, it will grind him to powder. | 12:19 |
| | 21:42...The stone which the builders rejected, the same is become the head of the corner:... | | |
| | 12:12 And they sought to lay hold on him,.... | Luke 20:19  And the chief priests and the scribes the same hour sought to lay hands on him; and they feared the people: for they perceived that he had spoken this parable against them. | |
| | 22:1...Jesus answered and spake unto them again by parables, and said, | | 12:19 |

---

[38] Matthew 22:14  For many are called, but few are chosen. (*See Matthew 20:16* ...for many be called, but few chosen.)

| Matthew | Mark | Important Events |
|---|---|---|
| ways, one to his farm, another to his merchandise:<br>Matt. 22:6   And the remnant took his servants, and entreated them spitefully, and slew them.<br>Matt. 22:7  But when the king heard thereof, he was wroth: and he sent forth his armies, and destroyed those murderers, and burned up their city.<br>Matt. 22:8    Then saith he to his servants, The wedding is ready, but they which were bidden were not worthy.<br>Matt. 22:9   Go ye therefore into the highways, and as many as ye shall find, bid to the marriage.<br>Matt. 22:10    So those servants went out into the highways, and gathered together all as many as they found, both bad and good: and the wedding was furnished with guests.<br>Matt. 22:11   And when the king came in to see the guests, he saw there a man which had not on a wedding garment:<br>Matt. 22:12    And he saith unto him, Friend, how camest thou in hither not having a wedding garment? And he was speechless.<br>Matt. 22:13  Then said the king to the servants, Bind him hand and foot, and take him away, and cast him into outer darkness; there shall be weeping and gnashing of teeth.<br>Matt. 22:14    For many are called, but few are chosen. | | |
| Time Clue - Time Clue | Time Clue - Time Clue | |
| | | |

22:14 For many are called, but few are chosen. [138]

| Time Clue - Time Clue | Time Clue - See footnote for John 12:34 |
|---|---|

12:20 And there were certain Greeks among them that came up to worship **at the feast**:

12:23...**The hour is come,** that the Son of man should be glorified.

12:28 Father, glorify thy name. Then came there **a voice from heaven, saying, I have both glorified it, and will glorify it again.** [139]
12:30...This voice came... for your sakes.
12:31 **Now is the judgment of this world**: now shall the prince of this world be cast out.
12:32 And I, if I be lifted up from the earth, will draw all men unto me.
12:34 The people answered him,...how sayest thou, The Son

John 12:20 And there were certain Greeks among them that came up to worship at the feast:
John 12:21 The same came therefore to Philip, which was of Bethsaida of Galilee, and desired him, saying, Sir, we would see Jesus.
John 12:22 Philip cometh and telleth Andrew: and again Andrew and Philip tell Jesus.
John 12:23 And Jesus answered them, saying, The hour is come, that the Son of man should be glorified.
John 12:24 Verily, verily, I say unto you, Except a corn of wheat fall into the ground and die, it abideth alone: but if it die, it bringeth forth much fruit.
John 12:25 He that loveth his life shall lose it; and he that hateth his life in this world shall keep it unto life eternal.
John 12:26 If any man serve me, let him follow me; and where I am, there shall also my servant be: if any man serve me, him will my Father honour.
John 12:27 Now is my soul troubled; and what shall I say? Father, save me from this hour: but for this cause came I unto this hour.
John 12:28 Father, glorify thy name. Then came there a voice from heaven, saying, I have both glorified it, and will glorify it again.
John 12:29 The people therefore, that stood by, and heard it, said that it thundered: others said, An angel spake to him.
John 12:30 Jesus answered and said, This voice came not because of me, but for your sakes.
John 12:31 Now is the judgment of this world: now shall the prince of this world be cast out.
John 12:32 And I, if I be lifted up from the earth, will draw all men unto me.
John 12:33 This he said, signifying what death he should die.
John 12:34 The people answered him, We have heard out of the law that Christ abideth for ever: and how sayest thou, The Son of man must be lifted up? who is this Son of man?
John 12:35 Then Jesus said unto them, Yet a little while is the light with you. Walk while ye have the

---

[39] John 12:28 ...saying, **I have both glorified it, and will glorify it again.** (*This was Tuesday. The lamb of God had been inspected by the Father and the Father would be glorified by the sacrifice and the resurrection.*)

| Matthew | Mark | Important Events |
|---|---|---|
| | | |
| *Time Lock - Time Lock* | *Time Lock - Time Lock* | |
| Matt. 22:15 Then went the Pharisees, and took counsel how they might entangle him in his talk.<br>Matt. 22:16 And they sent out unto him their disciples with the Herodians, saying, Master, we know that thou art true, and teachest the way of God in truth, neither carest thou for any man: for thou regardest not the person of men.<br>Matt. 22:17 Tell us therefore, What thinkest thou? Is it lawful to give tribute unto Caesar, or not?<br>Matt. 22:18 But Jesus perceived their wickedness, and said, Why tempt ye me, ye hypocrites?<br>Matt. 22:19 Show me the tribute money. And they brought unto him a penny.<br>Matt. 22:20 And he saith unto them, Whose is this image and superscription?<br>Matt. 22:21a They say unto him, Caesar's. | Mark 12:13 And they send unto him certain of the Pharisees and of the Herodians, to catch him in his words.<br>Mark 12:14 And when they were come, they say unto him, Master, we know that thou art true, and carest for no man: for thou regardest not the person of men, but teachest the way of God in truth: Is it lawful to give tribute to Caesar, or not?<br>Mark 12:15 Shall we give, or shall we not give? But he, knowing their hypocrisy, said unto them, Why tempt ye me? bring me a penny, that I may see it.<br>Mark 12:16 And they brought it. And he saith unto them, Whose is this image and superscription? And they said unto him, Caesar's. | **Whose is this image and superscription?** Matt. 22:20, Mark 12:16, & Luke 20:24 |
| *Time Lock - Time Lock* | *Time Lock - Time Lock* | |
| Matt. 22:21b Then saith he unto them, Render therefore unto Caesar the things which are Caesar's; and unto God the things that are God's.<br>Matt. 22:22 When they had heard these words, they marvelled, and left him, and went their way. | Mark 12:17 And Jesus answering said unto them, Render to Caesar the things that are Caesar's, and to God the things that are God's. And they marvelled at him. | |
| Matt. 22:23 The same day came to him the Sadducees, which say that there is no resurrection, and asked him,<br>Matt. 22:24 Saying, Master, Moses said, If a man die, having no children, his brother shall marry his wife, and raise up seed unto his brother.<br>Matt. 22:25 Now there were with us seven brethren: and the first, when he had married a wife, deceased, and having no issue, left his wife unto his brother:<br>Matt. 22:26 Likewise the second also, and the third, unto the seventh.<br>Matt. 22:27 And last of all the woman died also.<br>Matt. 22:28 Therefore in the resurrection whose wife shall she be of the seven? for they all had her.<br>Matt. 22:29 Jesus answered and said unto them, Ye do err, not knowing the scriptures, nor the power of God.<br>Matt. 22:30 For in the resurrection they neither marry, nor are given in marriage, but are as the angels of God in heaven.<br>Matt. 22:31 But as touching the resurrection of the dead, have ye not read that which was spoken unto you by God, saying,<br>Matt. 22:32 I am the God of Abraham, and the God of Isaac, and the God of Jacob? God is not the God of the dead, but of the living.<br>Matt. 22:33 And when the multitude heard this, they were astonished at his doctrine.<br>Matt. 22:34 But when the Pharisees had heard that he had put the Sadducees to silence, they were gathered together. | Mark 12:18 Then come unto him the Sadducees, which say there is no resurrection; and they asked him, saying,<br>Mark 12:19 Master, Moses wrote unto us, If a man's brother die, and leave his wife behind him, and leave no children, that his brother should take his wife, and raise up seed unto his brother.<br>Mark 12:20 Now there were seven brethren: and the first took a wife, and dying left no seed.<br>Mark 12:21 And the second took her, and died, neither left he any seed: and the third likewise.<br>Mark 12:22 And the seven had her, and left no seed: last of all the woman died also.<br>Mark 12:23 In the resurrection therefore, when they shall rise, whose wife shall she be of them? for the seven had her to wife.<br>Mark 12:24 And Jesus answering said unto them, Do ye not therefore err, because ye know not the scriptures, neither the power of God?<br>Mark 12:25 For when they shall rise from the dead, they neither marry, nor are given in marriage; but are as the angels which are in heaven.<br>Mark 12:26 And as touching the dead, that they rise: have ye not read in the book of Moses, how in the bush God spake unto him, saying, I am the God of Abraham, and the God of Isaac, and the God of Jacob?<br>Mark 12:27 He is not the God of the dead, but the God of the living: ye therefore do greatly err. | |
| Matt. 22:35 Then one of them, which was a lawyer, asked him a question, tempting him, and saying,<br>Matt. 22:36 Master, which is the great commandment in the law? | Mark 12:28 And one of the scribes came, and having heard them reasoning together, and perceiving that he had answered them well, asked him, Which is the first commandment of all? | |

| ministry year | Key Scriptures & Footnotes | Luke | John |
|---|---|---|---|
| | of man must be lifted up?...? [140]<br>12:35 Then Jesus said unto them, **Yet a little while is the light with you.....** | | light, lest darkness come upon you: for he that walketh in darkness knoweth not whither he goeth.<br>John 12:36a While ye have light, believe in the light, that ye may be the children of light. |
| | Pharisees & Herodians. | *Time Lock - Time Lock* | |
| | 12:13 And they send unto him certain of the Pharisees and of the Herodians, to catch him in his words. | Luke 20:20 And they watched him, and sent forth spies, which should feign themselves just men, that they might take hold of his words, that so they might deliver him unto the power and authority of the governor.<br>Luke 20:21 And they asked him, saying, Master, we know that thou sayest and teachest rightly, neither acceptest thou the person of any, but teachest the way of God truly:<br>Luke 20:22 Is it lawful for us to give tribute unto Caesar, or no?<br>Luke 20:23 But he perceived their craftiness, and said unto them, Why tempt ye me?<br>Luke 20:24 Show me a penny. Whose image and superscription hath it? They answered and said, Caesar's. | 12: 36a |
| | Render to Caesar. | *Time Lock - Time Lock* | |
| | 12:17...Render to Caesar the things that are Caesar's, and to God the things that are God's. | Luke 20:25 And he said unto them, Render therefore unto Caesar the things which be Caesar's, and unto God the things which be God's.<br>Luke 20:26 And they could not take hold of his words before the people: and they marvelled at his answer, and held their peace. | |
| | 22:23 The same day came to him the Sadducees,....<br><br><br><br><br><br><br><br><br><br><br><br>22:30 For in the **resurrection....**<br>12:25 For when **they shall rise from the dead,....** | Luke 20:27 Then came to him certain of the Sadducees, which deny that there is any resurrection; and they asked him,<br>Luke 20:28 Saying, Master, Moses wrote unto us, If any man's brother die, having a wife, and he die without children, that his brother should take his wife, and raise up seed unto his brother.<br>Luke 20:29 There were therefore seven brethren: and the first took a wife, and died without children.<br>Luke 20:30 And the second took her to wife, and he died childless.<br>Luke 20:31 And the third took her; and in like manner the seven also: and they left no children, and died.<br>Luke 20:32 Last of all the woman died also.<br>Luke 20:33 Therefore in the resurrection whose wife of them is she? for seven had her to wife.<br>Luke 20:34 And Jesus answering said unto them, The children of this world marry, and are given in marriage:<br>Luke 20:35 But they which shall be accounted worthy to obtain that world, and the resurrection from the dead, neither marry, nor are given in marriage:<br>Luke 20:36 Neither can they die any more: for they are equal unto the angels; and are the children of God, being the children of the resurrection.<br>Luke 20:37 Now that the dead are raised, even Moses showed at the bush, when he calleth the Lord the God of Abraham, and the God of Isaac, and the God of Jacob.<br>Luke 20:38 For he is not a God of the dead, but of the living: for all live unto him. | 12: 36a |
| | 12:28 And one of the scribes came, and ... asked him, Which is the **first** | | 12: 36a |

---

[140] John 12:34 The people answered him,...how sayest thou, **The Son of man must be lifted up? who is this Son of man?** (*These questions had to be asked before Matthew 22:46, Mark 12:34, and Luke 20:40 when* "no man after that durst ask him **any question**.")

| Matthew | Mark | Important Events |
|---|---|---|
| Matt. 22:37  Jesus said unto him, Thou shalt love the Lord thy God with all thy heart, and with all thy soul, and with all thy mind.<br>Matt. 22:38  This is the first and great commandment.<br>Matt. 22:39  And the second is like unto it, Thou shalt love thy neighbour as thyself.<br>Matt. 22:40  On these two commandments hang all the law and the prophets. | Mark 12:29  And Jesus answered him, The first of all the commandments is, Hear, O Israel; The Lord our God is one Lord:<br>Mark 12:30  And thou shalt love the Lord thy God with all thy heart, and with all thy soul, and with all thy mind, and with all thy strength: this is the first commandment.<br>Mark 12:31  And the second is like, namely this, Thou shalt love thy neighbour as thyself. There is none other commandment greater than these. | |
| | Mark 12:32  And the scribe said unto him, Well, Master, thou hast said the truth: for there is one God; and there is none other but he:<br>Mark 12:33  And to love him with all the heart, and with all the understanding, and with all the soul, and with all the strength, and to love his neighbour as himself, is more than all whole burnt offerings and sacrifices.<br>Mark 12:34b  And when Jesus saw that he answered discreetly, he said unto him, Thou art not far from the kingdom of God. | |
| | Time Lock - Time Lock | |
| | Mark 12:34b  And no man after that durst ask him any question. | **Tuesday, And no man after that durst ask him any question.**<br>Mark 12:34, Luke 20:39, & Matt. 22:46 |
| Time Lock - Time Lock | Time Lock - Time Lock | |
| Matt. 22:41  While the Pharisees were gathered together, Jesus asked them,<br>Matt. 22:42  Saying, What think ye of Christ? whose son is he? They say unto him, The son of David. | | |
| | Mark 12:35  And Jesus answered and said, while he taught in the temple, How say the scribes that Christ is the son of David? | |
| Matt. 22:43  He saith unto them, How then doth David in spirit call him Lord, saying,<br>Matt. 22:44  The LORD said unto my Lord, Sit thou on my right hand, till I make thine enemies thy footstool?<br>Matt. 22:45  If David then call him Lord, how is he his son?<br>Matt. 22:46  And no man was able to answer him a word, neither durst any man from that day forth ask him any more questions. | Mark 12:36  For David himself said by the Holy Ghost, The LORD said to my Lord, Sit thou on my right hand, till I make thine enemies thy footstool.<br>Mark 12:37  David therefore himself calleth him Lord; and whence is he then his son? And the common people heard him gladly. | |
| Matt. 23:1  Then spake Jesus to the multitude, and to his disciples,<br>Matt. 23:2  Saying, The scribes and the Pharisees sit in Moses' seat:<br>Matt. 23:3  All therefore whatsoever they bid you observe, that observe and do; but do not ye after their works: for they say, and do not.<br>Matt. 23:4  For they bind heavy burdens and grievous to be borne, and lay them on men's shoulders; but they themselves will not move them with one of their fingers.<br>Matt. 23:5  But all their works they do for to be seen of men: they make broad their phylacteries, and enlarge the borders of their garments,<br>Matt. 23:6  And love the uppermost rooms at feasts, and the chief seats in the synagogues, | | |

| Key Scriptures & Footnotes | Luke | John |
|---|---|---|
| **commandment** of all?[141]<br>12:30 And thou shalt love the Lord thy God with all thy heart, and with all thy soul, and with all thy mind, and with all thy strength: this is the first commandment. | | |
| | | |
| No man asked question.<br>12:34b... And **no man after that durst ask him any question**[142] | Time Lock - Time Lock<br>Luke 20:39 Then certain of the scribes answering said, Master, thou hast well said.<br>Luke 20:40 And after that they durst not ask him any question at all. | |
| LORD said unto my Lord<br>22:41 While the Pharisees were gathered together,.... | Time Lock - Time Lock | |
| | Luke 20:41 And he said unto them, How say they that Christ is David's son? | |
| 20:44 **David therefore calleth him Lord, how is he then his son?** | Luke 20:42 And David himself saith in the book of Psalms, The LORD said unto my Lord, Sit thou on my right hand,<br>Luke 20:43 Till I make thine enemies thy footstool.<br>Luke 20:44 David therefore calleth him Lord, how is he then his son? | 12: 36a |
| 23:1 Then spake Jesus to the multitude, and to his disciples,<br>23:2 Saying, The scribes and the Pharisees sit in Moses' seat: | | |

---

[141] Mark 12:28 And one of the scribes came, and...asked him, **Which is the first commandment of all?** (*The answer to a different question is the same. See Luke 10:35b* And, behold, a certain lawyer stood up, and tempted him, saying, **Master, what shall I do to inherit eternal life?**)

[142] Mark 12:34 ...And no man after that durst ask him any question. (*This was Tuesday. The Lamb of God had been chosen on the 10th day of the month and was inspected on the 11th and 12th days of the month. The Lamb was found spotless and, therefore, ready for sacrifice.*)

| Matthew | Mark | Important Events |
|---------|------|------------------|
| Matt. 23:7   And greetings in the markets, and to be called of men, Rabbi, Rabbi.<br>Matt. 23:8   But be not ye called Rabbi: for one is your Master, even Christ; and all ye are brethren.<br>Matt. 23:9   And call no man your father upon the earth: for one is your Father, which is in heaven.<br>Matt. 23:10   Neither be ye called masters: for one is your Master, even Christ.<br>Matt. 23:11   But he that is greatest among you shall be your servant.<br>Matt. 23:12   And whosoever shall exalt himself shall be abased; and he that shall humble himself shall be exalted.<br>Matt. 23:13   But woe unto you, scribes and Pharisees, hypocrites! for ye shut up the kingdom of heaven against men: for ye neither go in yourselves, neither suffer ye them that are entering to go in. | | |
| Matt. 23:14   Woe unto you, scribes and Pharisees, hypocrites! for ye devour widows' houses, and for a pretence make long prayer: therefore ye shall receive the greater damnation. | | |
| Matt. 23:15   Woe unto you, scribes and Pharisees, hypocrites! for ye compass sea and land to make one proselyte, and when he is made, ye make him twofold more the child of hell than yourselves.<br>Matt. 23:16   Woe unto you, ye blind guides, which say, Whosoever shall swear by the temple, it is nothing; but whosoever shall swear by the gold of the temple, he is a debtor!<br>Matt. 23:17   Ye fools and blind: for whether is greater, the gold, or the temple that sanctifieth the gold?<br>Matt. 23:18   And, Whosoever shall swear by the altar, it is nothing; but whosoever sweareth by the gift that is upon it, he is guilty.<br>Matt. 23:19   Ye fools and blind: for whether is greater, the gift, or the altar that sanctifieth the gift?<br>Matt. 23:20   Whoso therefore shall swear by the altar, sweareth by it, and by all things thereon.<br>Matt. 23:21   And whoso shall swear by the temple, sweareth by it, and by him that dwelleth therein.<br>Matt. 23:22   And he that shall swear by heaven, sweareth by the throne of God, and by him that sitteth thereon.<br>Matt. 23:23   Woe unto you, scribes and Pharisees, hypocrites! for ye pay tithe of mint and anise and cummin, and have omitted the weightier matters of the law, judgment, mercy, and faith: these ought ye to have done, and not to leave the other undone.<br>Matt. 23:24   Ye blind guides, which strain at a gnat, and swallow a camel.<br>Matt. 23:25   Woe unto you, scribes and Pharisees, hypocrites! for ye make clean the outside of the cup and of the platter, but within they are full of extortion and excess.<br>Matt. 23:26   Thou blind Pharisee, cleanse first that which is within the cup and platter, that the outside of them may be clean also.<br>Matt. 23:27   Woe unto you, scribes and Pharisees, hypocrites! for ye are like unto whited sepulchres, which indeed appear beautiful outward, but are within full of dead men's bones, and of all uncleanness.<br>Matt. 23:28   Even so ye also outwardly appear righteous unto men, but within ye are full of hypocrisy and iniquity.<br>Matt. 23:29   Woe unto you, scribes and Pharisees, hypocrites! because ye build the tombs of the prophets, and garnish the sepulchres of the righteous,<br>Matt. 23:30   And say, If we had been in the days of our fathers, we would not have been partakers with them in the blood of the prophets.<br>Matt. 23:31   Wherefore ye be witnesses unto | | |

| inistry year | Key Scriptures & Footnotes | Luke | John |
|---|---|---|---|
| | 23:14 Woe unto you, scribes and Pharisees, hypocrites!.... | 20:44 | 12: 36a |
| | 23:15 Woe unto you,.... | 20:44 | 12: 36a |
| | 23:23 Woe unto you, scribes and Pharisees, hypocrites! for ye pay tithe of mint and anise and cummin, and have omitted the weightier matters of the law, judgment, mercy, and faith: these ought ye to have done, and not to leave the other undone. | | |
| | 23:31 Wherefore | | |

| Matthew | Mark | Important Events |
|---|---|---|
| yourselves, that ye are the children of them which killed the prophets.<br>Matt. 23:32    Fill ye up then the measure of your fathers.<br>Matt. 23:33    Ye serpents, ye generation of vipers, how can ye escape the damnation of hell?<br>Matt. 23:34    Wherefore, behold, I send unto you prophets, and wise men, and scribes: and some of them ye shall kill and crucify; and some of them shall ye scourge in your synagogues, and persecute them from city to city:<br>Matt. 23:35    That upon you may come all the righteous blood shed upon the earth, from the blood of righteous Abel unto the blood of Zacharias son of Barachias, whom ye slew between the temple and the altar.<br>Matt. 23:36    Verily I say unto you, All these things shall come upon this generation. | | |
| Matt. 23:37  O Jerusalem, Jerusalem, thou that killest the prophets, and stonest them which are sent unto thee, how often would I have gathered thy children together, even as a hen gathereth her chickens under her wings, and ye would not!<br>Matt. 23:38    Behold, your house is left unto you desolate.<br>Matt. 23:39  For I say unto you, Ye shall not see me henceforth, till ye shall say, Blessed is he that cometh in the name of the Lord. | | |
| Time Clue - Time Clue | Time Clue - Time Clue | |
| | Mark 12:38   And he said unto them in his doctrine, Beware of the scribes, which love to go in long clothing, and love salutations in the marketplaces,<br>Mark 12:39   And the chief seats in the synagogues, and the uppermost rooms at feasts:<br>Mark 12:40   Which devour widows' houses, and for a pretence make long prayers: these shall receive greater damnation. | |
| | Mark 12:41   And Jesus sat over against the treasury, and beheld how the people cast money into the treasury: and many that were rich cast in much.<br>Mark 12:42   And there came a certain poor widow, and she threw in two mites, which make a farthing.<br>Mark 12:43    And he called unto him his disciples, and saith unto them, Verily I say unto you, That this poor widow hath cast more in, than all they which have cast into the treasury:<br>Mark 12:44    For all they did cast in of their abundance; but she of her want did cast in all that she had, even all her living. | |
| Time Lock - Time Lock | Time Lock - Time Lock | |
| Matt. 24:1a  And Jesus went out, and departed from the temple: | Mark 13:1a   And as he went out of the temple, | **Jesus departed & hid himself from them.**<br>Matt. 24:1a, Mark 13:1a, & John 12:36b<br>Map 116 |
| | | |

| ministry year | Key Scriptures & Footnotes | Luke | John |
|---|---|---|---|
| | ye...are the children of them which killed the prophets. | | |
| | 23:36  Verily I say unto you, All these things shall come upon this generation. | | |
| | 23:37  O Jerusalem, Jerusalem, thou that killest the prophets,....[143] 23:39  For I say unto you, Ye shall not see me henceforth, till ye shall say, Blessed is he that cometh in the name of the Lord.[144] | 20:44 | 12: 36a |
| | Beware of the scribes. | Time Clue - Time Clue | |
| | 12:38...Beware of the scribes,.... | Luke 20:45   Then in the audience of all the people he said unto his disciples, Luke 20:46   Beware of the scribes, which desire to walk in long robes, and love greetings in the markets, and the highest seats in the synagogues, and the chief rooms at feasts; Luke 20:47   Which devour widows' houses, and for a show make long prayers: the same shall receive greater damnation. | 12:36a |
| | 12:43   And he called unto him his disciples, and saith unto them, Verily I say unto you, That this poor widow hath cast more in, than all they which have cast into the treasury: | Luke 21:1   And he looked up, and saw the rich men casting their gifts into the treasury. Luke 21:2   And he saw also a certain poor widow casting in thither two mites. Luke 21:3   And he said, Of a truth I say unto you, that this poor widow hath cast in more than they all: Luke 21:4   For all these have of their abundance cast in unto the offerings of God: but she of her penury hath cast in all the living that she had. | |
| | Jesus hid Himself. | | Time Lock - Time Lock |
| | 12:36b  These things spake Jesus, and departed, and did hide himself from **them.** 13:1a  And as he went out of the temple,.... | 21:4 | John 12:36b   These things spake Jesus, and departed, and did hide himself from them. |
| | 12:37  But though he had done so many miracles before **them,** yet **they** believed not on him: | | John 12:37    But though he had done so many miracles before them, yet they believed not on him: John 12:38   That the saying of Esaias the prophet might be fulfilled, which he spake, Lord, who hath believed our report? and to whom hath the arm of the |

[143] Matthew 23:37   O Jerusalem, Jerusalem, thou that killest the prophets, and stonest them.... (*See Luke 13:34* O Jerusalem, erusalem, which killest the prophets, and stonest them.... *Also see Luke 19:41* And when he was come near, he beheld the city, nd wept over it,.)
[144] Matthew 23:39   For I say unto you, Ye shall not see me henceforth, till ye shall say, Blessed is he that cometh in the name of he Lord. (*Luke 13:34 was fulfilled by Matthew 21:9 when, on "Palm Sunday," the people said,* "Blessed is he that cometh in the ame of the Lord." *The people of Jerusalem will not fulfill Matthew 23:39, and therefore will not see Jesus until they again say,* Blessed is he that cometh in the name of the Lord.")

| Matthew | Mark | Important Events |
|---|---|---|
| Matt. 24:1b   and his disciples came to him for to show him the buildings of the temple. Matt. 24:2  And Jesus said unto them, See ye not all these things? verily I say unto you, There shall not be left here one stone upon another, that shall not be thrown down. | Mark 13:1b   one of his disciples saith unto him, Master, see what manner of stones and what buildings are here! Mark 13:2  And Jesus answering said unto him, Seest thou these great buildings? there shall be not left one stone upon another, that shall not be thrown down. | |
| Time Lock - Time Lock | Time Lock - Time Lock | |
| Matt. 24:3a  And as he sat upon the mount of Olives, the disciples came unto him privately, saying, | Mark 13:3  And as he sat upon the mount of Olives over against the temple, Peter and James and John and Andrew asked him privately, | |
| Matt. 24:3b  Tell us, when shall these things be? and what shall be the sign of thy coming, and of the end of the world? | Mark 13:4  Tell us, when shall these things be? and what shall be the sign when all these things shall be fulfilled? | **When shall these things be?** Matt. 24:3, Mark 13:4, & Luke 21:7 Map 117 |
| Matt. 24:4  And Jesus answered and said unto them, Take heed that no man deceive you. Matt. 24:5  For many shall come in my name, saying, I am Christ; and shall deceive many. Matt. 24:6  And ye shall hear of wars and rumours of wars: see that ye be not troubled: for all these things must come to pass, but the end is not yet. Matt. 24:7  For nation shall rise against nation, and kingdom against kingdom: and there shall be famines, and pestilences, and earthquakes, in divers places. Matt. 24:8  All these are the beginning of sorrows. | Mark 13:5  And Jesus answering them began to say, Take heed lest any man deceive you: Mark 13:6  For many shall come in my name, saying, I am Christ; and shall deceive many. Mark 13:7  And when ye shall hear of wars and rumours of wars, be ye not troubled: for such things must needs be; but the end shall not be yet. Mark 13:8  For nation shall rise against nation, and kingdom against kingdom: and there shall be earthquakes in divers places, and there shall be famines and troubles: these are the beginnings of sorrows. | |
| Matt. 24:9a  Then shall they deliver you up to be afflicted, and shall kill you: | Mark 13:9a  But take heed to yourselves: for they shall deliver you up to councils; and in the synagogues ye shall be beaten: | |
| | Mark 13:9b   and ye shall be brought before rulers and kings | |
| Matt. 24:9b  and ye shall be hated of all nations | | |
| Matt. 24:9c  for my name's sake. | Mark 13:9c  for my sake, | |
| | Mark 13:9d  for a testimony against them. | |
| | Mark 13:10  And the gospel must first be published among all nations. | |
| | Mark 13:11   But when they shall lead you, and deliver you up, take no thought beforehand what ye shall speak, neither do ye premeditate: but whatsoever shall be given you in that hour, that speak ye: for it is not ye that speak, but the Holy Ghost. | |
| Matt. 24:10  And then shall many be offended, and shall betray one another, and shall hate one another. | Mark 13:12  Now the brother shall betray the brother to death, and the father the son; and children shall rise up against their parents, and shall cause them to | |

| ministry year | Key Scriptures & Footnotes | Luke | John |
|---|---|---|---|
| | | | Lord been revealed? John 12:39   Therefore they could not believe, because that Esaias said again, John 12:40   He hath blinded their eyes, and hardened their heart; that they should not see with their eyes, nor understand with their heart, and be converted, and I should heal them. John 12:41   These things said Esaias, when he saw his glory, and spake of him. John 12:42   Nevertheless among the chief rulers also many believed on him; but because of the Pharisees they did not confess him, lest they should be put out of the synagogue: John 12:43   For they loved the praise of men more than the praise of God. |
| | 12:42  Nevertheless among the chief rulers also **many** believed on him;.... | | |
| | | Luke 21:5  And as some spake of the temple, how it was adorned with goodly stones and gifts, he said, Luke 21:6  As for these things which ye behold, the days will come, in the which there shall not be left one stone upon another, that shall not be thrown down. | |
| | End time prophesy | Time Lock - Time Lock | |
| | 13:3 And as he sat upon the mount of Olives over against the temple,....[145] | Luke 21:7a  And they asked him, saying, | |
| | 13:4 Tell us, when shall these things be?.... | Luke 21:7b  Master, but when shall these things be? and what sign will there be when these things shall come to pass? | |
| | | Luke 21:8   And he said, Take heed that ye be not deceived: for many shall come in my name, saying, I am Christ; and the time draweth near: go ye not therefore after them. Luke 21:9   But when ye shall hear of wars and commotions, be not terrified: for these things must first come to pass; but the end is not by and by. Luke 21:10  Then said he unto them, Nation shall rise against nation, and kingdom against kingdom: Luke 21:11  And great earthquakes shall be in divers places, and famines, and pestilences; and fearful sights and great signs shall there be from heaven. | |
| | | Luke 21:12a But before all these, they shall lay their hands on you, and persecute you, delivering you up to the synagogues, and into prisons, | |
| | | Luke 21:12b  being brought before kings and rulers | |
| | | Luke 21:12c  for my name's sake. | |
| | | Luke 21:13  And it shall turn to you for a testimony. | |
| | | Luke 21:14  Settle it therefore in your hearts, not to meditate before what ye shall answer: | |
| | | Luke 21:15  For I will give you a mouth and wisdom, which all your adversaries shall not be able to gainsay nor resist. | |
| | | Luke 21:16   And ye shall be betrayed both by parents, and brethren, and kinsfolks, and friends; and some of you shall they cause to be put to death. | |

[45] Mark 13:3   And as he sat upon the mount of Olives over against the temple.... (*We know this was night time because it is recorded in Luke 21:37   And in the day time he was teaching in the temple; and at night he went out, and abode in the mount that is called the mount of Olives. Therefore, this was Tuesday night, after the start of the 13th day of the month.*)

| Matthew | Mark | Important Events |
|---|---|---|
| | be put to death. | |
| | Mark 13:13a  And ye shall be hated of all men for my name's sake: | |
| Matt. 24:11  And many false prophets shall rise, and shall deceive many.<br>Matt. 24:12  And because iniquity shall abound, the love of many shall wax cold. | | |
| Matt. 24:13  But he that shall endure unto the end, the same shall be saved. | Mark 13:13b  but he that shall endure unto the end, the same shall be saved. | |
| Matt. 24:14  And this gospel of the kingdom shall be preached in all the world for a witness unto all nations; and then shall the end come. | | |
| Matt. 24:15  When ye therefore shall see the abomination of desolation, spoken of by Daniel the prophet, stand in the holy place, (whoso readeth, let him understand:) | Mark 13:14a  But when ye shall see the abomination of desolation, spoken of by Daniel the prophet, standing where it ought not, (let him that readeth understand,) | |
| Matt. 24:16  Then let them which be in Judaea flee into the mountains: | Mark 13:14b  then let them that be in Judaea flee to the mountains: | |
| Matt. 24:17  Let him which is on the housetop not come down to take any thing out of his house:<br>Matt. 24:18  Neither let him which is in the field return back to take his clothes.<br>Matt. 24:19  And woe unto them that are with child, and to them that give suck in those days!<br>Matt. 24:20  But pray ye that your flight be not in the winter, neither on the sabbath day: | Mark 13:15  And let him that is on the housetop not go down into the house, neither enter therein, to take any thing out of his house:<br>Mark 13:16  And let him that is in the field not turn back again for to take up his garment.<br>Mark 13:17  But woe to them that are with child, and to them that give suck in those days!<br>Mark 13:18  And pray ye that your flight be not in the winter. | |
| Time Lock - Time Lock | Time Lock - Time Lock | |
| Matt. 24:21  For then shall be great tribulation, such as was not since the beginning of the world to this time, no, nor ever shall be.<br>Matt. 24:22  And except those days should be shortened, there should no flesh be saved: but for the elect's sake those days shall be shortened.<br>Matt. 24:23  Then if any man shall say unto you, Lo, here is Christ, or there; believe it not.<br>Matt. 24:24  For there shall arise false Christs, and false prophets, and shall show great signs and wonders; insomuch that, if it were possible, they shall deceive the very elect. | Mark 13:19  For in those days shall be affliction, such as was not from the beginning of the creation which God created unto this time, neither shall be.<br>Mark 13:20  And except that the Lord had shortened those days, no flesh should be saved: but for the elect's sake, whom he hath chosen, he hath shortened the days.<br>Mark 13:21  And then if any man shall say to you, Lo, here is Christ; or, lo, he is there; believe him not:<br>Mark 13:22  For false Christs and false prophets shall rise, and shall show signs and wonders, to seduce, if it were possible, even the elect. | |
| Matt. 24:25  Behold, I have told you before.<br>Matt. 24:26  Wherefore if they shall say unto you, Behold, he is in the desert; go not forth: behold, he is in the secret chambers; believe it not.<br>Matt. 24:27  For as the lightning cometh out of the east, and shineth even unto the west; so shall also the coming of the Son of man be.<br>Matt. 24:28  For wheresoever the carcase is, there will the eagles be gathered together. | Mark 13:23  But take ye heed: behold, I have foretold you all things. | |
| Matt. 24:29  Immediately after the tribulation of those days shall the sun be darkened, and the moon shall not give her light, and the stars shall fall from heaven, and the powers of the heavens shall be shaken:<br>Matt. 24:30  And then shall appear the sign of the Son of man in heaven: and then shall all the tribes of the earth mourn, and they shall see the Son of man coming in the clouds of heaven with power and great glory. | Mark 13:24  But in those days, after that tribulation, the sun shall be darkened, and the moon shall not give her light,<br>Mark 13:25  And the stars of heaven shall fall, and the powers that are in heaven shall be shaken.<br>Mark 13:26  And then shall they see the Son of man coming in the clouds with great power and glory. | |

| | | | |
|---|---|---|---|
| | | Luke 21:17  And ye shall be hated of all men for my name's sake.<br>Luke 21:18  But there shall not an hair of your head perish.<br>Luke 21:19  In your patience possess ye your souls. | |
| | | | |
| | | | |
| | | | |
| | | | |
| | | Luke 21:20    And when ye shall see Jerusalem compassed with armies, then know that the desolation thereof is nigh. | |
| | | Luke 21:21a  Then let them which are in Judaea flee to the mountains; | 12:43 |
| | | Luke 21:21b  and let them which are in the midst of it depart out; and let not them that are in the countries enter thereinto.<br>Luke 21:22  For these be the days of vengeance, that all things which are written may be fulfilled.<br>Luke 21:23  But woe unto them that are with child, and to them that give suck, in those days! for there shall be great distress in the land, and wrath upon this people. | |
| | | Luke 21:24    And they shall fall by the edge of the sword, and shall be led away captive into all nations: and Jerusalem shall be trodden down of the Gentiles, until the times of the Gentiles be fulfilled. | |
| Except days be shortened | | Time Clue - Time Clue | |
| | 24:22  And except those days should be shortened, there should no flesh be saved: but for the elect's sake those days shall be shortened. | | 12:43 |
| | | | |
| | 24:29 Immediately after the tribulation of those days....<br><br>13:26 And then shall they see the Son of man coming in the clouds with great power and glory. | Luke 21:25  And there shall be signs in the sun, and in the moon, and in the stars; and upon the earth distress of nations, with perplexity; the sea and the waves roaring;<br>Luke 21:26  Men's hearts failing them for fear, and for looking after those things which are coming on the earth: for the powers of heaven shall be shaken.<br>Luke 21:27  And then shall they see the Son of man coming in a cloud with power and great glory. | |
| | | Luke 21:28  And when these things begin to come to pass, then look up, and lift up your heads; for your | |

| Matthew | Mark | Important Events |
|---|---|---|
| Matt. 24:31 And he shall send his angels with a great sound of a trumpet, and they shall gather together his elect from the four winds, from one end of heaven to the other. | Mark 13:27 And then shall he send his angels, and shall gather together his elect from the four winds, from the uttermost part of the earth to the uttermost part of heaven. | |
| Time Lock - Time Lock | Time Lock - Time Lock | |
| Matt. 24:32 Now learn a parable of the fig tree; When his branch is yet tender, and putteth forth leaves, ye know that summer is nigh: Matt. 24:33 So likewise ye, when ye shall see all these things, know that it is near, even at the doors. Matt. 24:34 Verily I say unto you, This generation shall not pass, till all these things be fulfilled. Matt. 24:35 Heaven and earth shall pass away, but my words shall not pass away. Matt. 24:36 But of that day and hour knoweth no man, no, not the angels of heaven, but my Father only. | Mark 13:28 Now learn a parable of the fig tree; When her branch is yet tender, and putteth forth leaves, ye know that summer is near: Mark 13:29 So ye in like manner, when ye shall see these things come to pass, know that it is nigh, even at the doors. Mark 13:30 Verily I say unto you, that this generation shall not pass, till all these things be done. Mark 13:31 Heaven and earth shall pass away: but my words shall not pass away. Mark 13:32 But of that day and that hour knoweth no man, no, not the angels which are in heaven, neither the Son, but the Father. | **Parable of the fig tree** Matt. 24:32, Mark 13:28, & Luke 21:29 |
| Matt. 24:37 But as the days of Noe were, so shall also the coming of the Son of man be. Matt. 24:38 For as in the days that were before the flood they were eating and drinking, marrying and giving in marriage, until the day that Noe entered into the ark, Matt. 24:39 And knew not until the flood came, and took them all away; so shall also the coming of the Son of man be. Matt. 24:40 Then shall two be in the field; the one shall be taken, and the other left. Matt. 24:41 Two women shall be grinding at the mill; the one shall be taken, and the other left. | | |
| Matt. 24:42 Watch therefore: for ye know not what hour your Lord doth come. Matt. 24:43 But know this, that if the goodman of the house had known in what watch the thief would come, he would have watched, and would not have suffered his house to be broken up. Matt. 24:44 Therefore be ye also ready: for in such an hour as ye think not the Son of man cometh. | Mark 13:33 Take ye heed, watch and pray: for ye know not when the time is. Mark 13:34 For the Son of man is as a man taking a far journey, who left his house, and gave authority to his servants, and to every man his work, and commanded the porter to watch. Mark 13:35 Watch ye therefore: for ye know not when the master of the house cometh, at even, or at midnight, or at the cockcrowing, or in the morning: Mark 13:36 Lest coming suddenly he find you sleeping. Mark 13:37 And what I say unto you I say unto all, Watch. | |
| Matt. 24:45 Who then is a faithful and wise servant, whom his lord hath made ruler over his household, to give them meat in due season? Matt. 24:46 Blessed is that servant, whom his lord when he cometh shall find so doing. Matt. 24:47 Verily I say unto you, That he shall make him ruler over all his goods. Matt. 24:48 But and if that evil servant shall say in his heart, My lord delayeth his coming; Matt. 24:49 And shall begin to smite his fellowservants, and to eat and drink with the drunken; Matt. 24:50 The lord of that servant shall come in a day when he looketh not for him, and in an hour that he is not aware of, Matt. 24:51 And shall cut him asunder, and appoint him his portion with the hypocrites: there shall be weeping and gnashing of teeth. | | |

| ministry year | Key Scriptures & Footnotes | Luke | John |
|---|---|---|---|
| | | redemption draweth nigh. | |
| | | | |
| Parable of fig tree | | Time Lock - Time Lock | |
| | 24:32 Now learn a parable of the fig tree;.... | Luke 21:29  And he spake to them a parable; Behold the fig tree, and all the trees;<br>Luke 21:30  When they now shoot forth, ye see and know of your own selves that summer is now nigh at hand.<br>Luke 21:31  So likewise ye, when ye see these things come to pass, know ye that the kingdom of God is nigh at hand.<br>Luke 21:32  Verily I say unto you, This generation shall not pass away, till all be fulfilled.<br>Luke 21:33  Heaven and earth shall pass away: but my words shall not pass away. | 12:43 |
| | | Luke 21:34  And take heed to yourselves, lest at any time your hearts be overcharged with surfeiting, and drunkenness, and cares of this life, and so that day come upon you unawares.<br>Luke 21:35  For as a snare shall it come on all them that dwell on the face of the whole earth.<br>Luke 21:36  Watch ye therefore, and pray always, that ye may be accounted worthy to escape all these things that shall come to pass, and to stand before the Son of man. | |
| | | | |
| | | | 12:43 |
| | | | |

| Matthew | Mark | Important Events |
|---|---|---|
| Matt. 25:1 Then shall the kingdom of heaven be likened unto ten virgins, which took their lamps, and went forth to meet the bridegroom. <br> Matt. 25:2 And five of them were wise, and five were foolish. <br> Matt. 25:3 They that were foolish took their lamps, and took no oil with them: <br> Matt. 25:4 But the wise took oil in their vessels with their lamps. <br> Matt. 25:5 While the bridegroom tarried, they all slumbered and slept. <br> Matt. 25:6 And at midnight there was a cry made, Behold, the bridegroom cometh; go ye out to meet him. <br> Matt. 25:7 Then all those virgins arose, and trimmed their lamps. <br> Matt. 25:8 And the foolish said unto the wise, Give us of your oil; for our lamps are gone out. <br> Matt. 25:9 But the wise answered, saying, Not so; lest there be not enough for us and you: but go ye rather to them that sell, and buy for yourselves. <br> Matt. 25:10 And while they went to buy, the bridegroom came; and they that were ready went in with him to the marriage: and the door was shut. <br> Matt. 25:11 Afterward came also the other virgins, saying, Lord, Lord, open to us. <br> Matt. 25:12 But he answered and said, Verily I say unto you, I know you not. <br> Matt. 25:13 Watch therefore, for ye know neither the day nor the hour wherein the Son of man cometh. | | **The ten virgins** <br> Matt. 25:1 |
| Matt. 25:14 For the kingdom of heaven is as a man travelling into a far country, who called his own servants, and delivered unto them his goods. <br> Matt. 25:15 And unto one he gave five talents, to another two, and to another one; to every man according to his several ability; and straightway took his journey. <br> Matt. 25:16 Then he that had received the five talents went and traded with the same, and made them other five talents. <br> Matt. 25:17 And likewise he that had received two, he also gained other two. <br> Matt. 25:18 But he that had received one went and digged in the earth, and hid his lord's money. <br> Matt. 25:19 After a long time the lord of those servants cometh, and reckoneth with them. <br> Matt. 25:20 And so he that had received five talents came and brought other five talents, saying, Lord, thou deliveredst unto me five talents: behold, I have gained beside them five talents more. <br> Matt. 25:21 His lord said unto him, Well done, thou good and faithful servant: thou hast been faithful over a few things, I will make thee ruler over many things: enter thou into the joy of thy lord. <br> Matt. 25:22 He also that had received two talents came and said, Lord, thou deliveredst unto me two talents: behold, I have gained two other talents beside them. <br> Matt. 25:23 His lord said unto him, Well done, good and faithful servant; thou hast been faithful over a few things, I will make thee ruler over many things: enter thou into the joy of thy lord. <br> Matt. 25:24 Then he which had received the one talent came and said, Lord, I knew thee that thou art an hard man, reaping where thou hast not sown, and gathering where thou hast not strawed: <br> Matt. 25:25 And I was afraid, and went and hid thy talent in the earth: lo, there thou hast that is thine. <br> Matt. 25:26 His lord answered and said unto him, Thou wicked and slothful servant, thou knewest that I reap where I sowed not, and gather where I have not strawed: <br> Matt. 25:27 Thou oughtest therefore to have put my | 13:37 | |

| Ministry year | Key Scriptures & Footnotes | Luke | John |
|---|---|---|---|
| | 25:1 Then shall the kingdom of heaven be likened unto ten virgins,.... | 21:36 | 12:43 |
| | 25:15 And unto one he gave five talents, to another two,.... | 21:36 | 12:43 |
| | 25::23 His lord said unto him, Well done, good and faithful servant;... | | |

| Matthew | Mark | Important Events |
|---|---|---|
| money to the exchangers, and then at my coming I should have received mine own with usury.<br>Matt. 25:28  Take therefore the talent from him, and give it unto him which hath ten talents.<br>Matt. 25:29  For unto every one that hath shall be given, and he shall have abundance: but from him that hath not shall be taken away even that which he hath.<br>Matt. 25:30  And cast ye the unprofitable servant into outer darkness: there shall be weeping and gnashing of teeth. | | |
| Matt. 25:31  When the Son of man shall come in his glory, and all the holy angels with him, then shall he sit upon the throne of his glory:<br>Matt. 25:32  And before him shall be gathered all nations: and he shall separate them one from another, as a shepherd divideth his sheep from the goats:<br>Matt. 25:33  And he shall set the sheep on his right hand, but the goats on the left.<br>Matt. 25:34  Then shall the King say unto them on his right hand, Come, ye blessed of my Father, inherit the kingdom prepared for you from the foundation of the world:<br>Matt. 25:35  For I was an hungred, and ye gave me meat: I was thirsty, and ye gave me drink: I was a stranger, and ye took me in:<br>Matt. 25:36  Naked, and ye clothed me: I was sick, and ye visited me: I was in prison, and ye came unto me.<br>Matt. 25:37  Then shall the righteous answer him, saying, Lord, when saw we thee an hungred, and fed thee? or thirsty, and gave thee drink?<br>Matt. 25:38  When saw we thee a stranger, and took thee in? or naked, and clothed thee?<br>Matt. 25:39  Or when saw we thee sick, or in prison, and came unto thee?<br>Matt. 25:40  And the King shall answer and say unto them, Verily I say unto you, Inasmuch as ye have done it unto one of the least of these my brethren, ye have done it unto me.<br>Matt. 25:41  Then shall he say also unto them on the left hand, Depart from me, ye cursed, into everlasting fire, prepared for the devil and his angels:<br>Matt. 25:42  For I was an hungred, and ye gave me no meat; I was thirsty, and ye gave me no drink:<br>Matt. 25:43  I was a stranger, and ye took me not in: naked, and ye clothed me not: sick, and in prison, and ye visited me not.<br>Matt. 25:44  Then shall they also answer him, saying, Lord, when saw we thee an hungred, or athirst, or a stranger, or naked, or sick, or in prison, and did not minister unto thee?<br>Matt. 25:45  Then shall he answer them, saying, Verily I say unto you, Inasmuch as ye did it not to one of the least of these, ye did it not to me.<br>Matt. 25:46  And these shall go away into everlasting punishment: but the righteous into life eternal. | 13:37 | **He shall separate His sheep from the goats**<br>Matt. 25:32 |

| ministry year | Key Scriptures & Footnotes | Luke | John |
|---|---|---|---|
| | 25:31 When the Son of man shall come in his glory,.... <br> 25:32...and he shall separate them one from another, as a shepherd divideth his sheep from the goats:.... | 21:36 | 12:43 |
| | 25:46 And these shall go away into everlasting punishment: but the righteous into life eternal. | | |
| | 12:44 Jesus cried and said,[146] He that believeth on me, believeth not on me, but on him that sent me. <br> 12:46 **I am come a light into the world, that whosoever believeth on me should not abide in darkness.** | | John 12:44 Jesus cried and said, He that believeth on me, believeth not on me, but on him that sent me. <br> John 12:45 And he that seeth me seeth him that sent me. <br> John 12:46 I am come a light into the world, that whosoever believeth on me should not abide in darkness. <br> John 12:47 And if any man hear my words, and believe not, I judge him not: for I came not to judge the world, but to save the world. <br> John 12:48 He that rejecteth me, and receiveth not my words, hath one that judgeth him: the word that I |

---

[146] John 12:44 Jesus cried and said.... (*This happened on Tuesday night. On Tuesday afternoon,* John 12:36b, These things spake Jesus, and departed, and did hide himself from them. *Tuesday night, John and the disciples were with Jesus. However, on Wednesday John went with Peter and was not with Jesus. See Luke 22:8.*)

| Matthew | Mark | Important Events |
|---|---|---|
| | | |
| | | |
| Matt. 26:1   And it came to pass, when Jesus had finished all these sayings, he said unto his disciples, Matt. 26:2  Ye know that after two days is the feast of the passover, and the Son of man is betrayed to be crucified. | Mark 14:1a   After two days was the feast of the passover, and of unleavened bread: | **The feast of unleavened _bread_ drew nigh** Matt. 26:1, Mark 14:1a, & Luke 22:1 |
| Matt. 26:3      Then assembled together the chief priests, and the scribes, and the elders of the people, unto the palace of the high priest, who was called Caiaphas, Matt. 26:4  And consulted that they might take Jesus by subtlety, and kill him. Matt. 26:5   But they said, Not on the feast day, lest there be an uproar among the people. | Mark 14:1b   and the chief priests and the scribes sought how they might take him by craft, and put him to death. Mark 14:2  But they said, Not on the feast day, lest there be an uproar of the people. | |
| Matt. 26:6  Now when Jesus was in Bethany, in the house of Simon the leper, Matt. 26:7  There came unto him a woman having an alabaster box of very precious ointment, and poured it on his head, as he sat at meat. Matt. 26:8  But when his disciples saw it, they had indignation, saying, To what purpose is this waste? Matt. 26:9  For this ointment might have been sold for much, and given to the poor. Matt. 26:10  When Jesus understood it, he said unto them, Why trouble ye the woman? for she hath wrought a good work upon me. Matt. 26:11  For ye have the poor always with you; but me ye have not always. Matt. 26:12  For in that she hath poured this ointment on my body, she did it for my burial. Matt. 26:13  Verily I say unto you, Wheresoever this gospel shall be preached in the whole world, there shall also this, that this woman hath done, be told for a memorial of her. | Mark 14:3   And being in Bethany  in the house of Simon the leper, as he sat at meat, there came a woman having an alabaster box of ointment of spikenard very precious; and she brake the box, and poured it on his head. Mark 14:4       And there were some that had indignation within themselves, and said, Why was this waste of the ointment made? Mark 14:5  For it might have been sold for more than three hundred pence, and have been given to the poor. And they murmured against her. Mark 14:6      And Jesus said, Let her alone; why trouble ye her? she hath wrought a good work on me. Mark 14:7  For ye have the poor with you always, and whensoever ye will ye may do them good: but me ye have not always. Mark 14:8  She hath done what she could: she is come aforehand to anoint my body to the burying. Mark 14:9  Verily I say unto you, Wheresoever this gospel shall be preached throughout the whole world, this also that she hath done shall be spoken of for a memorial of her. | **The alabaster box of very precious ointment was poured on Jesus head** Matt. 26:7 & Mark 14:3 Map 118 |
| Time Lock - Time Lock | Time Lock - Time Lock | Time Lock |
| Matt. 26:14   Then one of the twelve, called Judas | Mark 14:10   And Judas Iscariot, one of the twelve, | **Judas  Iscariot** |

| | Key Scriptures & Footnotes | Luke | John |
|---|---|---|---|
| | 12:48 He that rejecteth me, and receiveth not my words, hath one that judgeth him: the word that I have spoken, the same shall judge him **in the last day**. | | have spoken, the same shall judge him in the last day. John 12:49 For I have not spoken of myself; but the Father which sent me, he gave me a commandment, what I should say, and what I should speak. John 12:50 And I know that his commandment is life everlasting: whatsoever I speak therefore, even as the Father said unto me, so I speak. |
| | 21:37 And in the day time he was teaching in the temple;....[147] | Luke 21:37 And in the day time he was teaching in the temple; and at night he went out, and abode in the mount that is called the mount of Olives. Luke 21:38 And all the people came early in the morning to him in the temple, for to hear him. | |
| | 14:1a After two days was *the feast of* the **passover, and of unleavened** *bread*:[148] 26:2 Ye know that after two days is the **feast of the passover,**[149] and the Son of man is betrayed to be crucified. | Luke 22:1 Now the feast of unleavened *bread* drew nigh, which is called the Passover. | |
| | | Luke 22:2 And the chief priests and scribes sought how they might kill him; for they feared the people | 12:50 |
| | 14:2 But they said, **Not on the feast day,**[150] lest there be an uproar of the people. | | |
| | 14:3 And being in Bethany in the house of Simon the leper, as he sat at meat, there came a woman having an alabaster box of ointment of spikenard...and poured it on his head.[151] 26:12 For in that she hath poured this ointment on my body, she did it for my burial.[152] | | |
| | Judas and chief priests. | Time Lock - Time Lock | |
| | 14:10 And Judas | Luke 22:3 Then entered Satan into Judas surnamed | 12:50 |

[147] Luke 21:37 And in the day time he was teaching in the temple; and at night he went out.... (*See Luke 19:47* And he taught daily in the temple. But the chief priests and the scribes and the chief of the people sought to destroy him,.)

[148] Mark 14:1a After two days was *the feast of* the passover, and of unleavened bread:.... (*Therefore, it was Tuesday, after sunset, because Thursday at sunset was the start of the week long feast of Unleavened Bread. The Passover of the LORD was on the 14th day of the month. It lasted from the 13th, Wednesday, at sunset to the 14th, Thursday, at sunset. The feast of Unleavened Bread started on the 15th day of the month, the day following the 24 hour long Passover of the LORD, according to the law found in Numbers 28:16 and 17. The "feast of Unleavened Bread" or "the feast of the Passover" lasted one week.*)

[149] Matthew 26:2 Ye know that after two days is the feast of the passover, and the Son of man is betrayed to be crucified. (*The "feast of the Passover" is only two days away.* **The Passover of the LORD** *or* **the LORD's Passover**, *is only one day away.*)

[150] Mark 14:2 But they said, Not on **the feast day**.... (**The feast day,** the 15th, *was a* **holy convocation**, *a* **Sabbath**. *It was the first day of the week long* **feast of Unleavened Bread. The feast day** *lasted from the 14th, Thursday, at sunset, to the 15th, Friday, at sunset.*)

[151] Mark 14:3 And being in Bethany in the house of Simon the leper, as he sat at meat, there came a woman having an alabaster box of ointment of spikenard very precious.... (*See John 12:3 for the first time that Jesus was anointed on this trip to Jerusalem.*)

[152] Matthew 26:12 ...she did it for my burial. (*See John 12:7* Then said Jesus, Let her alone: against the day of my burying hath she kept this.)

| Matthew | Mark | Important Events |
|---|---|---|
| Iscariot, went unto the chief priests, <br> Matt. 26:15 And said unto them, What will ye give me, and I will deliver him unto you? And they covenanted with him for thirty pieces of silver. <br> Matt. 26:16 And from that time he sought opportunity to betray him. | went unto the chief priests, to betray him unto them. <br> Mark 14:11 And when they heard it, they were glad, and promised to give him money. And he sought how he might conveniently betray him. | **went to betray Jesus** <br> Matt. 26:16, Mark 14:10, & Luke 22:4 |
| Time Lock - Time Lock | Time Lock - Time Lock | |
| Matt. 26:17 Now the first *day* of the *feast of* unleavened bread the disciples came to Jesus, saying unto him, Where wilt thou that we prepare for thee to eat the passover? | Mark 14:12 And the first day of unleavened bread, when they killed the passover, his disciples said unto him, Where wilt thou that we go and prepare that thou mayest eat the passover? | |
| Matt. 26:18 And he said, Go into the city to such a man, and say unto him, The Master saith, My time is at hand; I will keep the passover at thy house with my disciples. <br> Matt. 26:19 And the disciples did as Jesus had appointed them; and they made ready the passover. | Mark 14:13 And he sendeth forth two of his disciples, and saith unto them, Go ye into the city, and there shall meet you a man bearing a pitcher of water: follow him. <br> Mark 14:14 And wheresoever he shall go in, say ye to the goodman of the house, The Master saith, Where is the guestchamber, where I shall eat the passover with my disciples? <br> Mark 14:15 And he will show you a large upper room furnished and prepared: there make ready for us. <br> Mark 14:16 And his disciples went forth, and came into the city, and found as he had said unto them: and they made ready the passover. | |
| Matt. 26:20 Now when the even was come, he sat down with the twelve. | Mark 14:17 And in the evening he cometh with the twelve. | Map 119 |
| | | |

| Ministry year | Key Scriptures & Footnotes | Luke | John |
|---|---|---|---|
| | Iscariot, one of the twelve, went unto the chief priests, to betray him unto them. | Iscariot, being of the number of the twelve. Luke 22:4   And he went his way, and communed with the chief priests and captains, how he might betray him unto them. Luke 22:5   And they were glad, and covenanted to give him money. Luke 22:6   And he promised, and sought opportunity to betray him unto them in the absence of the multitude. | |
| | First day of unleavened | Time Lock - Time Lock | |
| | 26:17 Now the first *day of the feast of* unleavened bread.... [153] 14:12  And the first day of unleavened bread, when they killed the passover,.... | Luke 22:7   Then came the day of unleavened bread, when the passover must be killed. | |
| | 22:8  And he **sent Peter and John**,....[154] 26:18  And he said, Go into the city to such a man, and say unto him, The Master saith, My time is at hand; I will keep the passover at thy house with my disciples. 14:15  And he will show you a large upper room furnished **and prepared**:.... | Luke 22:8   And he sent Peter and John, saying, Go and prepare us the passover, that we may eat. Luke 22:9   And they said unto him, Where wilt thou that we prepare? Luke 22:10   And he said unto them, Behold, when ye are entered into the city, there shall a man meet you, bearing a pitcher of water; follow him into the house where he entereth in. Luke 22:11   And ye shall say unto the goodman of the house, The Master saith unto thee, Where is the guestchamber, where I shall eat the passover with my disciples? Luke 22:12   And he shall show you a large upper room furnished: there make ready. Luke 22:13   And they went, and found as he had said unto them: and they made ready the passover. | 12:50 |
| | 26:20 **Now when the even was come**,[155] he sat down with the twelve. | Luke 22:14   And when the hour was come, he sat down, and the twelve apostles with him. | |
| | 22:15... With desire I have desired to eat this passover with you before I suffer:[156] 22:16  For I say unto you, **I will not any more eat** thereof, until it be fulfilled in the kingdom of God. 22:17  And he took the cup and gave thanks, and said, Take | Luke 22:15   And he said unto them, With desire I have desired to eat this passover with you before I suffer: Luke 22:16   For I say unto you, I will not any more eat thereof, until it be fulfilled in the kingdom of God. Luke 22:17   And he took the cup, and gave thanks, and said, Take this, and divide it among yourselves: Luke 22:18   For I say unto you, I will not drink of the fruit of the vine, until the kingdom of God shall come. | |

[3] Matthew 26:17   Now the **first *day* of the *feast of* unleavened bread** the disciples came to Jesus.... (*The words "day" and "feast of" were added by the translators.  The original Greek says "and on the **first unleavened** came the disciples to Jesus...."  This was not the 15th of the month and thus was not the first day of the seven day* feast of Unleavened Bread.  *This was Wednesday the 13th.  That evening after sunset would be the start of the 14th day of the month.  They were to eat unleavened bread with the passover [lamb] at the beginning of the 14th day according to Exodus 12:6 and 12:8.  By the beginning of the 15th day they were to have all leaven out of the house according to Exodus 12:19.  On the 14th of the month they would eat the Passover [lamb] to celebrate the night in Egypt when the LORD passed over the homes which had blood on their lintel and on the door posts.  The LORD did not allow the destroyer to come into those homes.  This event is found in Exodus 12:23.*)

[4] Luke 22:8   And he sent Peter and John.... (See *Luke 22:7   Then came the day of unleavened bread, when the passover must be killed.  This was Wednesday.  Jesus sent Peter and John to the city to prepare the Passover.  Jesus may not have seen John for the rest of the day.  If John was not with Jesus until that evening, then all of John chapter 12 happened before this* day of unleavened bread, *Wednesday, when Jesus sent Peter and John to Jerusalem to prepare the Passover.*)

[5] Matthew 26:20   Now when the even was come.... (This was *Wednesday evening, start of the 14th day of the month.  Numbers 3:16   And the fourteenth day of the first month is the **passover of the LORD**.  Exodus 12:6   And ye shall keep it [the lamb]* **up until the fourteenth day** *of the same month: and the whole assembly of the congregation of Israel shall kill it in the evening.  This was one day before* **the Passover** *which is also called* **the Feast of Unleavened Bread**.)

[6] Luke 22:15   And he said unto them, With desire I have desired to eat this passover with you before I suffer:  (*There were two "suppers" that night.  This passover, found in Luke 22:15, is the* supper *mentioned in John 13:2.  This is not "Communion" also called "The Lord's Supper" or "The Last Supper" found in Matthew 21:26, Mark 14:22, and Luke 22:19.*)

| Matthew | Mark | Important Events |
|---|---|---|
| | | **And supper being ended**<br>John 13:2 |
| | | **Jesus began to wash the disciples' feet**<br>John 13:5 |
| Matt. 26:21  And as they did eat, he said, <sup>Verily I say</sup> unto you, that one of you shall betray me.<br>Matt. 26:22   And they were exceeding sorrowful, and began every one of them to say unto him, Lord, is it I? | Mark 14:18  And as they sat and did eat, Jesus said, Verily I say unto you, One of you which eateth with me shall betray me.<br>Mark 14:19  And they began to be sorrowful, and to say unto him one by one, Is it I? and another said, Is it | **One of you shall betray me.**   Matt. 26:21, Mark |

| --- | --- | --- | --- |
| | this, and divide it among yourselves:[157]<br>22:18 For I say unto you, **I will not drink** of the fruit of the vine, until the kingdom of God shall come. | | |
| | 13:1 **Now before the feast of the passover,....**[158] | | John 13:1 Now before the feast of the passover, when Jesus knew that his hour was come that he should depart out of this world unto the Father, having loved his own which were in the world, he loved them unto the end. |
| | 13:2 **And supper being ended,** the devil having now put **into the heart** of Judas Iscariot, Simon's son, to betray him; | | John 13:2 And supper being ended, the devil having now put into the heart of Judas Iscariot, Simon's son, to betray him;<br>John 13:3 Jesus knowing that the Father had given all things into his hands, and that he was come from God, and went to God;<br>John 13:4 He riseth from supper, and laid aside his garments; and took a towel, and girded himself. |
| | 13:5 After that he poureth water into a basin, and began to **wash** the disciples' feet, | 22:18 | John 13:5 After that he poureth water into a basin, and began to wash the disciples' feet, and to wipe them with the towel wherewith he was girded.<br>John 13:6 Then cometh he to Simon Peter: and Peter saith unto him, Lord, dost thou wash my feet?<br>John 13:7 Jesus answered and said unto him, What I do thou knowest not now; but thou shalt know hereafter.<br>John 13:8 Peter saith unto him, Thou shalt never wash my feet. Jesus answered him, If I wash thee not, thou hast no part with me.<br>John 13:9 Simon Peter saith unto him, Lord, not my feet only, but also my hands and my head. |
| | 13:10 Jesus saith to him,...and ye are clean, but not all.<br>13:11 For he knew who should betray him; therefore said he, Ye are not all clean. | | John 13:10 Jesus saith to him, He that is washed needeth not save to wash his feet, but is clean every whit: and ye are clean, but not all.<br>John 13:11 For he knew who should betray him; therefore said he, Ye are not all clean.<br>John 13:12 So after he had washed their feet, and had taken his garments, and was set down again, he said unto them, Know ye what I have done to you?<br>John 13:13 Ye call me Master and Lord: and ye say well; for so I am.<br>John 13:14 If I then, your Lord and Master, have washed your feet; ye also ought to wash one another's feet.<br>John 13:15 For I have given you an example, that ye should do as I have done to you.<br>John 13:16 Verily, verily, I say unto you, The servant is not greater than his lord; neither he that is sent greater than he that sent him.<br>John 13:17 If ye know these things, happy are ye if ye do them. |
| | 13:18 I speak not of you all: I know whom I have chosen: but that the scripture may be fulfilled, He that eateth bread with me hath lifted up his heel against me. | | John 13:18 I speak not of you all: I know whom I have chosen: but that the scripture may be fulfilled, He that eateth bread with me hath lifted up his heel against me.<br>John 13:19 Now I tell you before it come, that, when it is come to pass, ye may believe that I am he.<br>John 13:20 Verily, verily, I say unto you, He that receiveth whomsoever I send receiveth me; and he that receiveth me receiveth him that sent me. |
| | 13:21...Jesus...testified, and said, Verily, verily, I say unto you, that one of you shall betray me. | 22:18 | John 13:21 When Jesus had thus said, he was troubled in spirit, and testified, and said, Verily, verily, I say unto you, that one of you shall betray me.<br>John 13:22 Then the disciples looked one on another, doubting of whom he spake. |

[7] Luke 22:17 And he took the cup, and gave thanks, and said, Take this, and divide it among yourselves: (*This is not the cup of he new testament" found three verses later. See Luke 22:20* Likewise also the cup after supper, saying, This cup is the new stament in my blood, which is shed for you.)

[8] John 13:1 Now before the **feast of the passover,....** (*The* **feast of the Passover** *was also called* **the Passover** *or the* **feast of nleavened Bread**. *It started on Thursday at sunset, the start of the 15th day of the month, and lasted one week.*)

| Matthew | Mark | Important Events |
|---|---|---|
| | I? | 14:18, & John 13:21 |
| Matt. 26:23  And he answered and said, He that dippeth his hand with me in the dish, the same shall betray me.<br>Matt. 26:24  The Son of man goeth as it is written of him: but woe unto that man by whom the Son of man is betrayed! it had been good for that man if he had not been born.<br>Matt. 26:25  Then Judas, which betrayed him, answered and said, Master, is it I? He said unto him, Thou hast said. | Mark 14:20  And he answered and said unto them, It is one of the twelve, that dippeth with me in the dish.<br>Mark 14:21  The Son of man indeed goeth, as it is written of him: but woe to that man by whom the Son of man is betrayed! good were it for that man if he had never been born. | |
| Matt. 26:26  And as they were eating, Jesus took bread, and blessed it, and brake it, and gave it to the disciples, and said, Take, eat; this is my body. | Mark 14:22  And as they did eat, Jesus took bread, and blessed, and brake it, and gave to them, and said, Take, eat: this is my body. | **The "Lord's Supper"**<br>Matt. 26:26, Mark 14:22, & Luke 22:19 |
| Matt. 26:27  And he took the cup, and gave thanks, and gave it to them, saying, Drink ye all of it;<br>Matt. 26:28  For this is my blood of the new testament, which is shed for many for the remission of sins.<br>Matt. 26:29  But I say unto you, I will not drink henceforth of this fruit of the vine, until that day when I drink it new with you in my Father's kingdom. | Mark 14:23  And he took the cup, and when he had given thanks, he gave it to them: and they all drank of it.<br>Mark 14:24  And he said unto them, This is my blood of the new testament, which is shed for many.<br>Mark 14:25  Verily I say unto you, I will drink no more of the fruit of the vine, until that day that I drink it new in the kingdom of God. | |
| | | **Behold, the hand of him that betrayeth me....**<br>Luke 22:21 |
| | | |
| | | **Judas went immediately out: and it was night.**<br>John 13:30 |
| | | |
| 26:29 | 14:25 | |

| Ministry year | Key Scriptures & Footnotes | Luke | John |
|---|---|---|---|
| | 26:23 And he answered and said, He that dippeth his hand with me in the dish, the same shall betray me. 14:20 And he ... said unto them, It is one of the twelve, that dippeth with me in the dish.159 | | |
| | 26:26 ...Jesus took bread, and blessed it, and brake it, and gave it to the disciples, and said, Take, eat; this is my body. | Luke 22:19 And he took bread, and gave thanks, and brake it, and gave unto them, saying, This is my body which is given for you: this do in remembrance of me. | |
| | 22:20 Likewise also the cup **after** supper,160 saying, **This cup** is the new testament in my blood, which is shed for you. | Luke 22:20 Likewise also the cup after supper, saying, This cup is the new testament in my blood, which is shed for you. | |
| | 22:21 **But, behold, the hand** of him that betrayeth me is with me on the table. | Luke 22:21 But, behold, the hand of him that betrayeth me is with me on the table. Luke 22:22 And truly the Son of man goeth, as it was determined: but woe unto that man by whom he is betrayed! | |
| | 22:23 And they began to inquire161...which of them it was.... | Luke 22:23 And they began to inquire among themselves, which of them it was that should do this thing. | |
| | 13:26...He it is, to whom I shall give a sop, when I have dipped it....he gave it to Judas Iscariot,.... 13:27 And after the sop **Satan entered into him**....That thou doest, do quickly. 13:30 He then having received the sop **went immediately out**: and it was night. | | John 13:23 Now there was leaning on Jesus' bosom one of his disciples, whom Jesus loved. John 13:24 Simon Peter therefore beckoned to him, that he should ask who it should be of whom he spake. John 13:25 He then lying on Jesus' breast saith unto him, Lord, who is it? John 13:26 Jesus answered, He it is, to whom I shall give a sop, when I have dipped it. And when he had dipped the sop, he gave it to Judas Iscariot, the son of Simon. John 13:27 And after the sop Satan entered into him. Then said Jesus unto him, That thou doest, do quickly. John 13:28 Now no man at the table knew for what intent he spake this unto him. John 13:29 For some of them thought, because Judas had the bag, that Jesus had said unto him, Buy those things that we have need of against the feast; or, that he should give something to the poor. John 13:30 He then having received the sop went immediately out: and it was night. |
| | 13:31 Therefore, when he was gone out, Jesus said, Now is the Son of man glorified,.... | | John 13:31 Therefore, when he was gone out, Jesus said, Now is the Son of man glorified, and God is glorified in him. John 13:32 If God be glorified in him, God shall also glorify him in himself, and shall straightway glorify him. |
| | 22:24...was also a strife among them.... | Luke 22:24 And there was also a strife among them, which of them should be accounted the greatest. | |
| | | Luke 22:25 And he said unto them, The kings of the Gentiles exercise lordship over them; and they that | |

159 Mark 14:20 And he answered and said unto them, It is one of **the twelve**, that dippeth with me in the dish. (*This implies that there were more than the twelve disciples eating this meal with Jesus.*)

160 Luke 22:20 Likewise also the cup after **supper**.... (*This* **supper** *translates as meaning "after having supped."*)

161 Luke 22:23 And they began to inquire.... (*Earlier that evening Jesus spoke of betrayal in John 13:21-22 and the disciples looked at one another. This time they began to inquire among themselves.*)

| Matthew | Mark | Important Events |
|---------|------|------------------|
| | | |
| | | |
| | | **1st time that Jesus said, The cock shall not crow, till thou hast denied me thrice.** John 13:38 |
| 26:29 | 14:25 | **2nd time that Jesus said,** before the cock crow, thou shalt thrice deny me. Luke 22:34 |
| 26:29 | 14:25 | |

| | | Luke | John |
|---|---|---|---|
| | | exercise authority upon them are called benefactors.<br>Luke 22:26 But ye shall not be so: but he that is greatest among you, let him be as the younger; and he that is chief, as he that doth serve.<br>Luke 22:27 For whether is greater, he that sitteth at meat, or he that serveth? is not he that sitteth at meat? but I am among you as he that serveth.<br>Luke 22:28 Ye are they which have continued with me in my temptations.<br>Luke 22:29 And I appoint unto you a kingdom, as my Father hath appointed unto me;<br>Luke 22:30 That ye may eat and drink at my table in my kingdom, and sit on thrones judging the twelve tribes of Israel. | |
| | | | John 13:33 Little children, yet a little while I am with you. Ye shall seek me: and as I said unto the Jews, Whither I go, ye cannot come; so now I say to you.<br>John 13:34 A new commandment I give unto you, That ye love one another; as I have loved you, that ye also love one another.<br>John 13:35 By this shall all men know that ye are my disciples, if ye have love one to another. |
| Simon Peter said. | | | Time Clue - Time Clue |
| 13:37 Peter said...I **will lay down my life** for thy sake.<br>13:38 Jesus answered him, Wilt thou lay down thy life for my sake? Verily, verily, I say unto thee, The cock shall not crow, till thou hast **denied me thrice.**[162] | | | John 13:36 Simon Peter said unto him, Lord, whither goest thou? Jesus answered him, Whither I go, thou canst not follow me now; but thou shalt follow me afterwards.<br>John 13:37 Peter said unto him, Lord, why cannot I follow thee now? I will lay down my life for thy sake.<br>John 13:38 Jesus answered him, Wilt thou lay down thy life for my sake? Verily, verily, I say unto thee, The cock shall not crow, till thou hast denied me thrice. |
| Simon, Simon | Time Clue - Time Clue | | Time Clue - Time Clue |
| 22:31...Simon, behold, Satan hath desired to have you,....<br>22:33 And he said unto him, Lord, I am ready to go with thee, both **into prison, and to death.**<br>22:34...the cock shall not crow **this day**, before that thou shalt **thrice deny that thou knowest me.**[163] | Luke 22:31 And the Lord said, Simon, Simon, behold, Satan hath desired to have you, that he may sift you as wheat:<br>Luke 22:32 But I have prayed for thee, that thy faith fail not: and when thou art converted, strengthen thy brethren.<br>Luke 22:33 And he said unto him, Lord, I am ready to go with thee, both into prison, and to death.<br>Luke 22:34 And he said, I tell thee, Peter, the cock shall not crow this day, before that thou shalt thrice deny that thou knowest me. | |
| 14:2 In my Father's house are many mansions:.... | | | John 14:1 Let not your heart be troubled: ye believe in God, believe also in me.<br>John 14:2 In my Father's house are many mansions: if it were not so, I would have told you. I go to prepare a place for you.<br>John 14:3 And if I go and prepare a place for you, I will come again, and receive you unto myself; that where I am, there ye may be also.<br>John 14:4 And whither I go ye know, and the way ye know.<br>John 14:5 Thomas saith unto him, Lord, we know not whither thou goest; and how can we know the way?<br>John 14:6 Jesus saith unto him, I am the way, the truth, and the life: no man cometh unto the Father, but by me.<br>John 14:7 If ye had known me, ye should have known my Father also: and from henceforth ye know |

---

[162] John 13:38 Jesus answered him, Wilt thou lay down thy life for my sake? Verily, verily, I say unto thee, The cock shall not crow, **till thou hast denied me thrice.** (*This is the first of three identical prophecies to Peter. See Luke 22:34 for the second prophecy and Matthew 26:34 & Mark 14:30 for the third prophecy.*)

[163] Luke 22:34 And he said, I tell thee, Peter, the cock shall not crow this day, before that **thou shalt thrice deny** that thou knowest me. (*This is the second identical prophecy to Peter. See John 13:38 for the first and Matthew 26:34 & Mark 14:30 for the third prophecy.*)

| Matthew | Mark | Important Events |
|---------|------|------------------|
|         |      |                  |

**14:16** And I will pray the Father, and he shall give you another Comforter, that he may abide with you for ever;

**14:26** But the Comforter, which is the Holy Ghost, whom the Father will send in my name, he shall teach you all things, and bring all things to your remembrance, whatsoever I have said unto you.

him, and have seen him.

John 14:8   Philip saith unto him, Lord, show us the Father, and it sufficeth us.

John 14:9   Jesus saith unto him, Have I been so long time with you, and yet hast thou not known me, Philip? he that hath seen me hath seen the Father; and how sayest thou then, Show us the Father?

John 14:10   Believest thou not that I am in the Father, and the Father in me? the words that I speak unto you I speak not of myself: but the Father that dwelleth in me, he doeth the works.

John 14:11   Believe me that I am in the Father, and the Father in me: or else believe me for the very works' sake.

John 14:12   Verily, verily, I say unto you, He that believeth on me, the works that I do shall he do also; and greater works than these shall he do; because I go unto my Father.

John 14:13   And whatsoever ye shall ask in my name, that will I do, that the Father may be glorified in the Son.

John 14:14   If ye shall ask any thing in my name, I will do it.

John 14:15   If ye love me, keep my commandments.

John 14:16   And I will pray the Father, and he shall give you another Comforter, that he may abide with you for ever;

John 14:17   Even the Spirit of truth; whom the world cannot receive, because it seeth him not, neither knoweth him: but ye know him; for he dwelleth with you, and shall be in you.

John 14:18   I will not leave you comfortless: I will come to you.

John 14:19   Yet a little while, and the world seeth me no more; but ye see me: because I live, ye shall live also.

John 14:20   At that day ye shall know that I am in my Father, and ye in me, and I in you.

John 14:21   He that hath my commandments, and keepeth them, he it is that loveth me: and he that loveth me shall be loved of my Father, and I will love him, and will manifest myself to him.

John 14:22   Judas saith unto him, not Iscariot, Lord, how is it that thou wilt manifest thyself unto us, and not unto the world?

John 14:23   Jesus answered and said unto him, If a man love me, he will keep my words: and my Father will love him, and we will come unto him, and make our abode with him.

John 14:24   He that loveth me not keepeth not my sayings: and the word which ye hear is not mine, but the Father's which sent me.

John 14:25   These things have I spoken unto you, being yet present with you.

John 14:26   But the Comforter, which is the Holy Ghost, whom the Father will send in my name, he shall teach you all things, and bring all things to your remembrance, whatsoever I have said unto you.

John 14:27   Peace I leave with you, my peace I give unto you: not as the world giveth, give I unto you. Let not your heart be troubled, neither let it be afraid.

John 14:28   Ye have heard how I said unto you, I go away, and come again unto you. If ye loved me, ye would rejoice, because I said, I go unto the Father: for my Father is greater than I.

John 14:29   And now I have told you before it come to pass, that, when it is come to pass, ye might believe.

John 14:30   Hereafter I will not talk much with you: for the prince of this world cometh, and hath nothing in me.

John 14:31a   But that the world may know that I love the Father; and as the Father gave me commandment,

| Matthew | Mark | Important Events |
|---|---|---|
| | | |
| Time Lock - Time Lock | Time Lock - Time Lock | Time Lock |
| Matt. 26:30  And when they had sung an hymn, they went out into the mount of Olives. | Mark 14:26  And when they had sung an hymn, they went out into the mount of Olives. | Map 120 |
| | | |

| | | | even so I do. |
|---|---|---|---|
| 22:36..But now, he that hath a purse, let him take it,.... | Luke 22:35 And he said unto them, When I sent you without purse, and scrip, and shoes, lacked ye any thing? And they said, Nothing.<br>Luke 22:36 Then said he unto them, But now, he that hath a purse, let him take it, and likewise his scrip: and he that hath no sword, let him sell his garment, and buy one.<br>Luke 22:37 For I say unto you, that this that is written must yet be accomplished in me, And he was reckoned among the transgressors: for the things concerning me have an end.<br>Luke 22:38 And they said, Lord, behold, here are two swords. And he said unto them, It is enough. | | |
| 14:31b Arise,.... | | | John 14:31b Arise, let us go hence. |
| **Sung and went out** | **Time Lock - Time Lock** | | **Time Lock - Time Lock** |
| 26:30 And when they had sung an hymn, they went out into the mount of Olives.[164] | Luke 22:39 And he came out, and went, as he was wont, to the mount of Olives; and his disciples also followed him. | | |
| 15:6 If a man abide not in me, he is cast forth as a branch, and is withered; and men gather them, and cast them into the fire, and they are burned. | | | John 15:1 I am the true vine, and my Father is the husbandman.<br>John 15:2 Every branch in me that beareth not fruit he taketh away: and every branch that beareth fruit, he purgeth it, that it may bring forth more fruit.<br>John 15:3 Now ye are clean through the word which I have spoken unto you.<br>John 15:4 Abide in me, and I in you. As the branch cannot bear fruit of itself, except it abide in the vine; no more can ye, except ye abide in me.<br>John 15:5 I am the vine, ye are the branches: He that abideth in me, and I in him, the same bringeth forth much fruit: for without me ye can do nothing.<br>John 15:6 If a man abide not in me, he is cast forth as a branch, and is withered; and men gather them, and cast them into the fire, and they are burned.<br>John 15:7 If ye abide in me, and my words abide in you, ye shall ask what ye will, and it shall be done unto you.<br>John 15:8 Herein is my Father glorified, that ye bear much fruit; so shall ye be my disciples.<br>John 15:9 As the Father hath loved me, so have I loved you: continue ye in my love.<br>John 15:10 If ye keep my commandments, ye shall abide in my love; even as I have kept my Father's commandments, and abide in his love.<br>John 15:11 These things have I spoken unto you, that my joy might remain in you, and that your joy might be full.<br>John 15:12 This is my commandment, That ye love one another, as I have loved you.<br>John 15:13 Greater love hath no man than this, that a man lay down his life for his friends.<br>John 15:14 Ye are my friends, if ye do whatsoever I command you.<br>John 15:15 Henceforth I call you not servants; for the servant knoweth not what his lord doeth: but I have called you friends; for all things that I have heard of my Father I have made known unto you.<br>John 15:16 Ye have not chosen me, but I have chosen you, and ordained you, that ye should go and bring forth fruit, and that your fruit should remain: that whatsoever ye shall ask of the Father in my name, he may give it you.<br>John 15:17 These things I command you, that ye love one another.<br>John 15:18 If the world hate you, ye know that it hated me before it hated you.<br>John 15:19 If ye were of the world, the world would |

[4] Matthew 26:30 And when they had sung an hymn, they went out into the mount of Olives. (*All of John chapters 15, 16, and 17 happened on the way to the mount of Olives.*)

| Matthew | Mark | Important Events |
|---|---|---|
|  |  |  |
| 26:30 | 14:26 |  |

| | | Luke | John |
|---|---|---|---|
| | | | love his own: but because ye are not of the world, but I have chosen you out of the world, therefore the world hateth you.<br>John 15:20  Remember the word that I said unto you, The servant is not greater than his lord. If they have persecuted me, they will also persecute you; if they have kept my saying, they will keep yours also.<br>John 15:21  But all these things will they do unto you for my name's sake, because they know not him that sent me.<br>John 15:22  If I had not come and spoken unto them, they had not had sin: but now they have no cloak for their sin.<br>John 15:23  He that hateth me hateth my Father also.<br>John 15:24  If I had not done among them the works which none other man did, they had not had sin: but now have they both seen and hated both me and my Father.<br>John 15:25  But this cometh to pass, that the word might be fulfilled that is written in their law, They hated me without a cause.<br>John 15:26  But when the Comforter is come, whom I will send unto you from the Father, even the Spirit of truth, which proceedeth from the Father, he shall testify of me:<br>John 15:27  And ye also shall bear witness, because ye have been with me from the beginning. |
| 16:1 These things have I spoken unto you, that ye should not be offended. | 22:39 | | John 16:1  These things have I spoken unto you, that ye should not be offended.<br>John 16:2  They shall put you out of the synagogues: yea, the time cometh, that whosoever killeth you will think that he doeth God service.<br>John 16:3  And these things will they do unto you, because they have not known the Father, nor me.<br>John 16:4  But these things have I told you, that when the time shall come, ye may remember that I told you of them. And these things I said not unto you at the beginning, because I was with you.<br>John 16:5  But now I go my way to him that sent me; and none of you asketh me, Whither goest thou?<br>John 16:6  But because I have said these things unto you, sorrow hath filled your heart.<br>John 16:7  Nevertheless I tell you the truth; It is expedient for you that I go away: for if I go not away, the Comforter will not come unto you; but if I depart, I will send him unto you.<br>John 16:8  And when he is come, he will reprove the world of sin, and of righteousness, and of judgment:<br>John 16:9  Of sin, because they believe not on me;<br>John 16:10  Of righteousness, because I go to my Father, and ye see me no more;<br>John 16:11  Of judgment, because the prince of this world is judged.<br>John 16:12  I have yet many things to say unto you, but ye cannot bear them now. |
| 16:13 Howbeit when he, the Spirit of truth, is come, he will guide you into all truth:.... | | | John 16:13  Howbeit when he, the Spirit of truth, is come, he will guide you into all truth: for he shall not speak of himself; but whatsoever he shall hear, that shall he speak: and he will show you things to come.<br>John 16:14  He shall glorify me: for he shall receive of mine, and shall show it unto you.<br>John 16:15  All things that the Father hath are mine: therefore said I, that he shall take of mine, and shall show it unto you.<br>John 16:16  A little while, and ye shall not see me: and again, a little while, and ye shall see me, because I go to the Father.<br>John 16:17  Then said some of his disciples among themselves, What is this that he saith unto us, A little while, and ye shall not see me: and again, a little while, and ye shall see me: and, Because I go to the Father?<br>John 16:18  They said therefore, What is this that he |

| Matthew | Mark | Important Events |
|---------|------|------------------|
| | | |
| 26:30 | 14:26 | Map 121 |
| | | |

| | | | saith, A little while? we cannot tell what he saith. |
|---|---|---|---|
| | | | John 16:19 Now Jesus knew that they were desirous to ask him, and said unto them, Do ye inquire among yourselves of that I said, A little while, and ye shall not see me: and again, a little while, and ye shall see me? |
| | | | John 16:20 Verily, verily, I say unto you, That ye shall weep and lament, but the world shall rejoice: and ye shall be sorrowful, but your sorrow shall be turned into joy. |
| | | | John 16:21 A woman when she is in travail hath sorrow, because her hour is come: but as soon as she is delivered of the child, she remembereth no more the anguish, for joy that a man is born into the world. |
| | | | John 16:22 And ye now therefore have sorrow: but I will see you again, and your heart shall rejoice, and your joy no man taketh from you. |
| | | | John 16:23 And in that day ye shall ask me nothing. Verily, verily, I say unto you, Whatsoever ye shall ask the Father in my name, he will give it you. |
| | | | John 16:24 Hitherto have ye asked nothing in my name: ask, and ye shall receive, that your joy may be full. |
| | | | John 16:25 These things have I spoken unto you in proverbs: but the time cometh, when I shall no more speak unto you in proverbs, but I shall show you plainly of the Father. |
| | | | John 16:26 At that day ye shall ask in my name: and I say not unto you, that I will pray the Father for you: |
| | | | John 16:27 For the Father himself loveth you, because ye have loved me, and have believed that I came out from God. |
| | | | John 16:28 I came forth from the Father, and am come into the world: again, I leave the world, and go to the Father. |
| | | | John 16:29 His disciples said unto him, Lo, now speakest thou plainly, and speakest no proverb. |
| | | | John 16:30 Now are we sure that thou knowest all things, and needest not that any man should ask thee: by this we believe that thou camest forth from God. |
| | | | John 16:31 Jesus answered them, Do ye now believe? |
| 16:32 Behold, the hour cometh, yea, is now come, that ye shall be scattered, every man to his own, and shall leave me alone: | | | John 16:32 Behold, the hour cometh, yea, is now come, that ye shall be scattered, every man to his own, and shall leave me alone: and yet I am not alone, because the Father is with me. |
| | | | John 16:33 These things I have spoken unto you, that in me ye might have peace. In the world ye shall have tribulation: but be of good cheer; I have overcome the world. |
| 17:1...Jesus...lifted up his eyes to heaven, and said, Father, the hour is come; glorify thy Son, that thy Son also may glorify thee:[165] | 22:39 | | John 17:1 These words spake Jesus, and lifted up his eyes to heaven, and said, Father, the hour is come; glorify thy Son, that thy Son also may glorify thee: |
| | | | John 17:2 As thou hast given him power over all flesh, that he should give eternal life to as many as thou hast given him. |
| | | | John 17:3 And this is life eternal, that they might know thee the only true God, and Jesus Christ, whom thou hast sent. |
| | | | John 17:4 I have glorified thee on the earth: I have finished the work which thou gavest me to do. |
| | | | John 17:5 And now, O Father, glorify thou me with thine own self with the glory which I had with thee before the world was. |
| | | | John 17:6 I have manifested thy name unto the men which thou gavest me out of the world: thine they were, and thou gavest them me; and they have kept thy word. |
| | | | John 17:7 Now they have known that all things whatsoever thou hast given me are of thee. |
| | | | John 17:8 For I have given unto them the words |

[165] John 17:1 These words spake Jesus, and lifted up his eyes to heaven.... (*This was outside on the way to Mount of Olives.*)

| Matthew | Mark | Important Events |
|---|---|---|
| | | |
| Matt. 26:31 Then saith Jesus unto them, All ye shall be offended because of me this night: for it is written, I will smite the shepherd, and the sheep of the flock shall be scattered abroad.<br>Matt. 26:32 But after I am risen again, I will go before you into Galilee. | Mark 14:27 And Jesus saith unto them, All ye shall be offended because of me this night: for it is written, I will smite the shepherd, and the sheep shall be scattered.<br>Mark 14:28 But after that I am risen, I will go before you into Galilee. | |
| *Time Lock - Time Lock* | *Time Lock - Time Lock* | |
| Matt. 26:33 Peter answered and said unto him, Though all men shall be offended because of thee, yet will I never be offended.<br>Matt. 26:34 Jesus said unto him, Verily I say unto thee, That this night, before the cock crow, thou shalt deny me thrice. | Mark 14:29 But Peter said unto him, Although all shall be offended, yet will not I.<br>Mark 14:30 And Jesus saith unto him, Verily I say unto thee, That this day, even in this night, before the cock crow twice, thou shalt deny me<br>Mark 14:31 But he spake the more vehemently, If I | **3rd time that Jesus said, Before the cock crow. thou shalt deny me** |

| nistry year | Key Scriptures & Footnotes | Luke | John |
|---|---|---|---|
| | | | which thou gavest me; and they have received them, and have known surely that I came out from thee, and they have believed that thou didst send me.<br>John 17:9 I pray for them: I pray not for the world, but for them which thou hast given me; for they are thine.<br>John 17:10 And all mine are thine, and thine are mine; and I am glorified in them.<br>John 17:11 And now I am no more in the world, but these are in the world, and I come to thee. Holy Father, keep through thine own name those whom thou hast given me, that they may be one, as we are.<br>John 17:12 While I was with them in the world, I kept them in thy name: those that thou gavest me I have kept, and none of them is lost, but the son of perdition; that the scripture might be fulfilled.<br>John 17:13 And now come I to thee; and these things I speak in the world, that they might have my joy fulfilled in themselves.<br>John 17:14 I have given them thy word; and the world hath hated them, because they are not of the world, even as I am not of the world.<br>John 17:15 I pray not that thou shouldest take them out of the world, but that thou shouldest keep them from the evil.<br>John 17:16 They are not of the world, even as I am not of the world.<br>John 17:17 Sanctify them through thy truth: thy word is truth.<br>John 17:18 As thou hast sent me into the world, even so have I also sent them into the world.<br>John 17:19 And for their sakes I sanctify myself, that they also might be sanctified through the truth.<br>John 17:20 Neither pray I for these alone, but for them also which shall believe on me through their word;<br>John 17:21 That they all may be one; as thou, Father, art in me, and I in thee, that they also may be one in us: that the world may believe that thou hast sent me.<br>John 17:22 And the glory which thou gavest me I have given them; that they may be one, even as we are one:<br>John 17:23 I in them, and thou in me, that they may be made perfect in one; and that the world may know that thou hast sent me, and hast loved them, as thou hast loved me.<br>John 17:24 Father, I will that they also, whom thou hast given me, be with me where I am; that they may behold my glory, which thou hast given me: for thou lovedst me before the foundation of the world.<br>John 17:25 O righteous Father, the world hath not known thee: but I have known thee, and these have known that thou hast sent me.<br>John 17:26 And I have declared unto them thy name, and will declare it: that the love wherewith thou hast loved me may be in them, and I in them. |
| | 14:27...**All ye shall be offended** because of me this night:....<br>26:32 But after I am risen again, I will go before you into Galilee. | 22:39 | |
| | I will not be offended | | |
| | 14:29 But Peter said... Although all shall be offended, **yet will not I.**<br>14:30...before the cock crow **twice**, thou | | |

| Matthew | Mark | Important Events |
|---|---|---|
| Matt. 26:35 Peter said unto him, Though I should die with thee, yet will I not deny thee. Likewise also said all the disciples. | should die with thee, I will not deny thee in any wise. Likewise also said they all. | **thrice.** Matt. 26:34 & Mark 14:30 |
| Time Lock - Time Lock | Time Lock - Time Lock | |
| Matt. 26:36 Then cometh Jesus with them unto a place called Gethsemane, and saith unto the disciples, Sit ye here, while I go and pray yonder. | Mark 14:32 And they came to a place which was named Gethsemane: and he saith to his disciples, Sit ye here, while I shall pray. | **Jesus enters the garden named Gethsemane** Matt. 26:36, Mark 14:32, Luke 22:40, & John 18:1b  Map 122 |
| Time Lock - Time Lock - Time Lock - Time Lock | Time Lock - Time Lock - Time Lock - Time Lock | |
| Matt. 26:37 And he took with him Peter and the two sons of Zebedee, and began to be sorrowful and very heavy. Matt. 26:38 Then saith he unto them, My soul is exceeding sorrowful, even unto death: tarry ye here, and watch with me. Matt. 26:39 And he went a little farther, and fell on his face, and prayed, saying, O my Father, if it be possible, let this cup pass from me: nevertheless not as I will, but as thou wilt. | Mark 14:33 And he taketh with him Peter and James and John, and began to be sore amazed, and to be very heavy; Mark 14:34 And saith unto them, My soul is exceeding sorrowful unto death: tarry ye here, and watch. Mark 14:35 And he went forward a little, and fell on the ground, and prayed that, if it were possible, the hour might pass from him. Mark 14:36 And he said, Abba, Father, all things are possible unto thee; take away this cup from me: nevertheless not what I will, but what thou wilt. | **1st time Jesus asked to let this cup pass** Matt. 26:39, Mark 14:35, & Luke 22:41 |
| Matt. 26:40 And he cometh unto the disciples, and findeth them asleep, and saith unto Peter, What, could ye not watch with me one hour? Matt. 26:41 Watch and pray, that ye enter not into temptation: the spirit indeed is willing, but the flesh is weak. | Mark 14:37 And he cometh, and findeth them sleeping, and saith unto Peter, Simon, sleepest thou? couldest not thou watch one hour? Mark 14:38 Watch ye and pray, lest ye enter into temptation. The spirit truly is ready, but the flesh is weak. | |
| Matt. 26:42 He went away again the second time, and prayed, saying, O my Father, if this cup may not pass away from me, except I drink it, thy will be done. Matt. 26:43 And he came and found them asleep again: for their eyes were heavy. | Mark 14:39 And again he went away, and prayed, and spake the same words. Mark 14:40 And when he returned, he found them asleep again, (for their eyes were heavy,) neither wist they what to answer him. | **2nd time Jesus asked to let this cup pass** Matt. 26:42 & Mark 14:39 |
| Matt. 26:44 And he left them, and went away again, and prayed the third time, saying the same words. | | **3rd time Jesus asked to let this cup pass** Matt. 26:44 |
| Matt. 26:45a Then cometh he to his disciples, and saith unto them, Sleep on now, and take your rest: | Mark 14:41a And he cometh the third time, and saith unto them, Sleep on now, and take your rest: | |
| Time Lock - Time Lock | Time Lock - Time Lock | |

| nistry year | Key Scriptures & Footnotes | Luke | John |
|---|---|---|---|
| | shalt deny me thrice.[166] | | |
| | 18:1a When Jesus had spoken...he went forth... over the brook Cedron, | | John 18:1a When Jesus had spoken these words, he went forth with his disciples over the brook Cedron, |
| | Enter the garden. | Time Lock - Time Lock | Time Lock - Time Lock |
| | 26:36 Then cometh Jesus with them unto a place called Gethsemane,.... 22:40...Pray that ye enter not into temptation. | Luke 22:40 And when he was at the place, he said unto them, Pray that ye enter not into temptation. | John 18:1b where was a garden, into the which he entered, and his disciples. |
| | Taketh Peter, James, John | Time Lock - Time Lock | |
| | 22:42 Saying, Father, ...nevertheless not my will, but thine, be done. | Luke 22:41 And he was withdrawn from them about a stone's cast, and kneeled down, and prayed, Luke 22:42 Saying, Father, if thou be willing, remove this cup from me: nevertheless not my will, but thine, be done. | |
| | 22:44...sweat was as it were great drops of blood... | Luke 22:43 And there appeared an angel unto him from heaven, strengthening him. Luke 22:44 And being in an agony he prayed more earnestly: and his sweat was as it were great drops of blood falling down to the ground. | |
| | 14:37 And he cometh, and findeth them sleeping,....[167] 14:38 Watch ye and pray, lest ye enter into temptation. | Luke 22:45 And when he rose up from prayer, and was come to his disciples, he found them sleeping for sorrow, Luke 22:46 And said unto them, Why sleep ye? rise and pray, lest ye enter into temptation. | |
| | 26:42 He went away again the **second** time, and **prayed**, saying, O my Father,... thy will be done. 26:43 And he came....[168] | | |
| | 26:44 And he left them,...**prayed** the **third** time, saying the **same words**. | | |
| | 14:41 And he cometh the **third time**,....[169] | | |
| | | | John 18:2 And Judas also, which betrayed him, knew the place: for Jesus ofttimes resorted thither with his disciples. John 18:3 Judas then, having received a band of men and officers from the chief priests and Pharisees, cometh thither with lanterns and torches and weapons. |
| | | | Time Lock - Time Lock |

[6] Mark 14:30 And Jesus saith unto him, Verily I say unto thee...**thou shalt deny me**. & Matthew 26:34 Jesus said unto him, Verily I say unto thee...**thou shalt deny me thrice**. (*This is the third time that Jesus prophesied this to Peter. See John 13:38 for e first prophecy and Luke 22:34 for the second prophecy.*)
[7] Mark 14:37 And he cometh, and findeth them sleeping.... (*This was the first of three times that Jesus comes and finds them sleep.*)
[8] Matthew 26:43 And he came and found them asleep again.... (*This is the second time Jesus finds the disciples asleep.*)
[9] Mark 14:41 And he cometh the third time.... (*This is the third and final time that Jesus finds them sleeping.*)

| Matthew | Mark | Important Events |
|---|---|---|
| Matt. 26:45b behold, the hour is at hand, and the Son of man is betrayed into the hands of sinners. Matt. 26:46 Rise, let us be going: behold, he is at hand that doth betray me . | Mark 14:41b it is enough, the hour is come; behold, the Son of man is betrayed into the hands of sinners. Mark 14:42 Rise up, let us go; lo, he that betrayeth me is at hand . | |
| Time Lock - Time Lock | Time Lock - Time Lock | |
| Matt. 26:47 And while he yet spake, lo, Judas, one of the twelve, came, and with him a great multitude with swords and staves, from the chief priests and elders of the people. | Mark 14:43 And immediately, while he yet spake, cometh Judas, one of the twelve, and with him a great multitude with swords and staves, from the chief priests and the scribes and the elders. | |
| Matt. 26:48 Now he that betrayed him gave them a sign, saying, Whomsoever I shall kiss, that same is he: hold him fast. | Mark 14:44 And he that betrayed him had given them a token, saying, Whomsoever I shall kiss, that same is he; take him, and lead him away safely. | |
| Matt. 26:49 And forthwith he came to Jesus, and said, Hail, master; and kissed him. Matt. 26:50a And Jesus said unto him, Friend, wherefore art thou come? | Mark 14:45 And as soon as he was come, he goeth straightway to him, and saith, Master, master; and kissed him. | |
| Matt. 26:50b Then came they, and laid hands on Jesus, and took him. | Mark 14:46 And they laid their hands on him, and took him. | |
| Time Lock - Time Lock | Time Lock - Time Lock | |
| Matt. 26:51 And, behold, one of them which were with Jesus stretched out his hand, and drew his sword, and struck a servant of the high priest's, and smote off his ear. | Mark 14:47 And one of them that stood by drew a sword, and smote a servant of the high priest, and cut off his ear. | **Peter cut off the ear of the high priest's servant** Matt. 26:51, Mark 14:47, Luke 22:50, & John 18:10 |
| Matt. 26:52 Then said Jesus unto him, Put up again thy sword into his place: for all they that take the sword shall perish with the sword. Matt. 26:53 Thinkest thou that I cannot now pray to my Father, and he shall presently give me more than twelve legions of angels? Matt. 26:54 But how then shall the scriptures be fulfilled, that thus it must be? | | |
| Time Lock - Time Lock | Time Lock - Time Lock | |
| Matt. 26:55 In that same hour said Jesus to the multitudes, Are ye come out as against a thief with swords and staves for to take me? I sat daily with you teaching in the temple, and ye laid no hold on me. Matt. 26:56a But all this was done, that the scriptures of the prophets might be fulfilled. | Mark 14:48 And Jesus answered and said unto them, Are ye come out, as against a thief, with swords and with staves to take me? Mark 14:49 I was daily with you in the temple teaching, and ye took me not: but the scriptures must be fulfilled. | |
| Matt. 26:56b Then all the disciples forsook him, and fled. | Mark 14:50 And they all forsook him, and fled. | |
| | Mark 14:51 And there followed him a certain young man, having a linen cloth cast about his naked body; | |

| ministry year | Key Scriptures & Footnotes | Luke | John |
|---|---|---|---|
| | | | |
| | While he yet spake. | Time Lock - Time Lock | |
| | 14:43...while he yet spake, cometh Judas,.... | Luke 22:47a    And while he yet spake, behold a multitude, | |
| | | | |
| | 22:48  But Jesus said unto him, Judas, betrayest thou the Son of man with a kiss? | Luke 22:47b and he that was called Judas, one of the twelve, went before them, and drew near unto Jesus to kiss him.<br>Luke 22:48  But Jesus said unto him, Judas, betrayest thou the Son of man with a kiss? | |
| | | | John 18:4    Jesus therefore, knowing all things that should come upon him, went forth, and said unto them, Whom seek ye?<br>John 18:5    They answered him, Jesus of Nazareth. Jesus saith unto them, I am he. And Judas also, which betrayed him, stood with them.<br>John 18:6  As soon then as he had said unto them, I am he, they went backward, and fell to the ground.<br>John 18:7    Then asked he them again, Whom seek ye? And they said, Jesus of Nazareth.<br>John 18:8    Jesus answered, I have told you that I am he: if therefore ye seek me, let these go their way:<br>John 18:9    That the saying might be fulfilled, which he spake, Of them which thou gavest me have I lost none. |
| | | Luke 22:49   When they which were about him saw what would follow, they said unto him, Lord, shall we smite with the sword? | |
| | Peter cut off an ear | Time Lock - Time Lock | Time Lock - Time Lock |
| | 18:10  Then Simon Peter having a sword drew it, and smote the high priest's servant, and cut off his right ear. | Luke 22:50    And one of them smote the servant of the high priest, and cut off his right ear. | John 18:10  Then Simon Peter having a sword drew it, and smote the high priest's servant, and cut off his right ear. The servant's name was Malchus. |
| | 22:51 And Jesus... touched his ear, and healed him. | Luke 22:51   And Jesus answered and said, Suffer ye thus far. And he touched his ear, and healed him. | |
| | 18:11  Then said Jesus unto Peter, Put up thy sword.... | | John 18:11    Then said Jesus unto Peter, Put up thy sword into the sheath: the cup which my Father hath given me, shall I not drink it? |
| | Jesus answered. | Time Lock - Time Lock | |
| | 14:48  And Jesus answered...Are ye come out, as against a thief, with swords and with staves to take me? | Luke 22:52    Then Jesus said unto the chief priests, and captains of the temple, and the elders, which were come to him, Be ye come out, as against a thief, with swords and staves?<br>Luke 22:53    When I was daily with you in the temple, ye stretched forth no hands against me: but this is your hour, and the power of darkness. | |
| | 14:50  And they all forsook him, and fled. | | |
| | 14:51  And there followed him a | | |

| | | and the young men laid hold on him:<br>Mark 14:52 And he left the linen cloth, and fled from them naked. | |

| Matthew About Jesus | Matthew About Peter | Mark About Jesus | Mark About Peter | |
|---|---|---|---|---|
| Matt. 26:57a And they that had laid hold on Jesus led him away | | Mark 14:53a And they led Jesus away | | **Jesus taken to Annas' house**<br>John 18:13<br><br>Map 123 |
| | | | | |
| | Matt. 26:58a But Peter followed him afar off. | | Mark 14:54a And Peter followed him afar off, | |
| | Matt. 26:58b unto the high priest's palace, | | Mark 14:54b even into the palace of the high priest: | |
| | | | | |
| | Matt. 26:58c and went in, and sat with the servants, to see the end. | | Mark 14:54c and he sat with the servants, and warmed himself at the fire. | |
| | Time Lock - Time Lock | | Time Lock - Time Lock | |
| 26:57a | | 14:53a | | **1st time Peter was <u>identified</u> to others - 1st part of Peter's 1st denial of Jesus**<br>Luke 22:57 |
| | | | | **1st time Peter was <u>questioned</u> - 2nd part of Peter's 1st denial of Jesus**<br>John 18:17 |
| | Matt. 26:69 Now Peter sat without in the palace: | | Mark 14:66 And as Peter was beneath in the | **1st time Peter was <u>accused</u> to** |

| | | Luke | John |
|---|---|---|---|
| **certain young man,....**[170] | | | |
| **See footnote**[171] | | Luke | John |
| | Luke 22:54a  Then took they him, | | John 18:12    Then the band and the captain and officers of the Jews took Jesus, and bound him, <br> John 18:13  And led him away to Annas first; for he was father-in-law to Caiaphas, which was the high priest that same year. <br> John 18:14    Now Caiaphas was he, which gave counsel to the Jews, that it was expedient that one man should die for the people. |
| 22:54b...and brought him into the high priest's house.[172] | Luke 22:54b  and led him, and brought him into the high priest's house. | | |
| 22:54c  And Peter followed afar off. | Luke 22:54c  And Peter followed afar off . | | John 18:15a  And Simon Peter followed Jesus, and so did another disciple: |
| 18:15b  that disciple was known....[173] | | | John 18:15b    that disciple was known unto the high priest, and went in with Jesus into the palace of the high priest. |
| 18:16  But Peter **stood** at the door without...and brought **in** Peter. | | | John 18:16  But Peter stood at the door without. Then went out that other disciple, which was known unto the high priest, and spake unto her that kept the door, and brought in Peter. |
| | Luke 22:55  And when they had kindled a fire in the midst of the hall, and were set down together, Peter sat down among them. | | |
| Peter's **first** denial[174] | Time Lock - Time Lock | | Time Lock - Time Lock |
| 22:56...and said, **This man was also with him**. <br> 22:57  And he denied him (Jesus), saying, Woman, **I know him(Jesus) not**. | Luke 22:56  But a certain maid beheld him as he sat by the fire, and earnestly looked upon him, and said, This man was also with him. <br> Luke 22:57    And he denied him, saying, Woman, I know him not. | | |
| 18:17  Then saith the damsel that kept the door unto Peter, **Art not thou also one of this man's disciples? He saith, I am not.** | | | John 18:17  Then saith the damsel that kept the door unto Peter, Art not thou also one of this man's disciples? He saith, I am not. <br> John 18:18    And the servants and officers stood there, who had made a fire of coals; for it was cold: and they warmed themselves: and Peter stood with them, and warmed himself. |
| 26:69  Now Peter sat without in the palace: | | | |

[170] Mark 14:51    And there followed him a certain young man.... (Many believe that this is *Mark, the author of the Gospel of Mark*.)

[171] Matthew and Mark *are "Split" into Jesus and Peter columns.* (*In this section the four Gospel stories are placed in time sequence using the theory that Peter's first, second, and third denials in each Gospel account are relative in time to the first, second, and third denials in the other Gospel accounts. To allow this comparison, Matthew and Mark's columns are each split which makes their two columns into four columns. Matthew and Mark remain sequential through this section as they report the accounts of Jesus and Peter. However, Matthew and Mark both tell about Jesus being led to Caiaphas' house and then go back and report that Peter sat with the servants. Peter first sat with the servants when Jesus was at Annas' palace before Jesus was taken to Caiaphas. Matthew and Mark then jump forward and tell everything that happened to Jesus at Caiaphas' house. Once more Matthew and Mark go back and note Peter's three denials of Jesus. The first denial was at Annas' palace while the second and third denials took place after Jesus was sent to Caiaphas. The individual accounts about Jesus and the individual accounts about Peter are sequential in relation to themselves. It is clear when individually reading Matthew and Mark that they "jump" back and forth in time to record the events of this night. Luke and John remain totally sequential throughout this time period.*)

[172] Luke 22:54b  and brought him into the high priest's house. (*This was Annas' house. Annas was father-in-law to Caiaphas and was the former high priest. Annas was still referred to as the high priest.*)

[173] John 18:15b  **that disciple** was known unto the high priest.... ("That disciple" *was John, the writer of the Gospel of John*.)

[174] Luke 22:57    And he denied him, saying, Woman, I know him not. (*Peter will deny Jesus "three times three." See the section called* Solutions to Gospel Mysteries. *It is interesting to note that E. W. Bullinger, J. M. Chaney, and A. G. Secrett believe that Peter denied Jesus six times.*)

| Matthew | | Mark | | Important Events |
|---------|--|------|--|------------------|
| | and a damsel came unto him, saying, Thou also wast with Jesus of Galilee. Matt. 26:70 But he denied before them all, saying, I know not what thou sayest. | | palace, there cometh one of the maids of the high priest: Mark 14:67 And when she saw Peter warming himself, she looked upon him, and said, And thou also wast with Jesus of Nazareth. Mark 14:68a But he denied, saying, I know not, neither understand I what thou sayest. | **his face - 3rd part of Peter's 1st denial of Jesus** Matt. 26:69-70 & Mark 14:67-68a |
| | | | Mark 14:68b And he went out into the porch; and the cock crew. | |
| | | | | |
| Time Clue - Time Clue | | Time Clue - Time Clue | | |
| | | | | **Now Annas sent Jesus bound unto Caiaphas** John 18:24 Map 124 |
| | Time Lock - Time Lock | | Time Lock - Time Lock | |
| 26:57a | Matt. 26:71 And when he was gone out into the porch, another maid saw him, and said unto them that were there, This fellow was also with Jesus of Nazareth. Matt. 26:72 And again he denied with an oath, I do not know the man. | 14:53a | Mark 14:69 And a maid saw him again, and began to say to them that stood by, This is one of them. Mark 14:70a And he denied it again. | **2nd time Peter was _identified_ to others - 1st part of Peter's 2nd denial of Jesus** Matt. 26:71-72 & Mark 14:69-70a |
| | | | | **2nd time Peter was _questioned_ - 2nd part of Peter's 2nd denial of Jesus** John 18:25 |
| | | | | **2nd time Peter was _accused_ to his face - 3rd part of Peter's 2nd denial of Jesus** |

| | Key Scriptures & Footnotes | Luke | John |
| --- | --- | --- | --- |
| | and a damsel came unto him, saying, **Thou also wast with Jesus of Galilee.** 26:70 But he denied before them all, saying, **I know not what thou sayest** | | |
| | Mark 14:68b And he went out into the porch; **and the cock crew.**[175] | | |
| | | | John 18:19 The high priest then asked Jesus of his disciples, and of his doctrine. John 18:20 Jesus answered him, I spake openly to the world; I ever taught in the synagogue, and in the temple, whither the Jews always resort; and in secret have I said nothing. John 18:21 Why askest thou me? ask them which heard me, what I have said unto them: behold, they know what I said. John 18:22 And when he had thus spoken, one of the officers which stood by struck Jesus with the palm of his hand, saying, Answerest thou the high priest so? John 18:23 Jesus answered him, If I have spoken evil, bear witness of the evil: but if well, why smitest thou me? |
| | *Sent Jesus unto Caiaphas* | | *Time Clue - Time Clue* |
| | 18:24 Now Annas had sent him bound unto Caiaphas the high priest. | | John 18:24 Now Annas had sent him bound unto Caiaphas the high priest. |
| | *Peter's **second** denial* | *Time Lock - Time Lock* | *Time Lock - Time Lock* |
| | 26:71 ...**another maid**[176] saw him.... 14:69 And a **maid saw him again**, and began to say to them that stood by, **This is one of them.** 26:72 And again he denied with an oath, **I do not know the man.** | | |
| | 18:25 ... They said therefore unto him, **Art not thou also one of his disciples?** He denied it, and said, **I am not.** | | John 18:25 And Simon Peter stood and warmed himself. They said therefore unto him, Art not thou also one of his disciples? He denied it, and said, I am not. |
| | 22:58 And after a little while another saw him, and said, **Thou art also of them.** And Peter said, **Man, I am not.** | Luke 22:58 And after a little while another saw him, and said, Thou art also of them. And Peter said, Man, I am not. | |

---

[175] Mark 14:68b And he went out into the porch; and the cock crew. (*Peter had denied Jesus three times in rapid succession. ↄme argue that this was just "one" denial. Peter will have more opportunities to deny Jesus.*)
[176] Matthew 26:71 And when he was gone out into the porch, **another** maid saw him.... & Mark 14:69 And a maid **saw him ↄain**.... (*These are probably two different maids who there identifying Peter to others at about the same time.*)

| Matthew | | Mark | | Important Events |
|---|---|---|---|---|
| | | | | Luke 22:58 |
| | Time Lock - Time Lock | | Time Lock - Time Lock | |
| | Matt. 26:73a And after a while | | Mark 14:70b And a little after, | |
| | | | | **3rd time Peter was <u>identified</u> to others - 1st part of Peter's 3rd denial of Jesus**<br>Luke 22:59-60a |
| | | | | **3rd time Peter was <u>questioned</u> - 2nd part of Peter's 3rd denial of Jesus**<br>John 18:26-27 |
| | Matt. 26:73b came unto him they that stood by, and said to Peter, Surely thou also art one of them; for thy speech betrayeth thee.<br>Matt. 26:74a Then began he to curse and to swear, saying, I know not the man. | | Mark 14:70c they that stood by said again to Peter, Surely thou art one of them: for thou art a Galilaean, and thy speech agreeth thereto.<br>Mark 14:71 But he began to curse and to swear, saying, I know not this man of whom ye speak. | **3rd time Peter was <u>accused</u> to his face - 3rd part of Peter's 3rd denial of Jesus**<br>Matt. 26:73-74a & Mark 14:70b-71 |
| | Time Lock - Time Lock | | Time Lock - Time Lock | |
| 26:57a | Matt. 26:74b And immediately the cock crew. | 14:53a | Mark 14:72a And the second time the cock crew. | **Immediately the cock crew**<br>Matt. 26:74b, Mark 14:72a, Luke 22:60b, & John 18:27b |
| | Time Lock - Time Lock | | Time Lock - Time Lock | |
| | | | | |
| | Time Lock - Time Lock | | Time Lock - Time Lock | |
| | Matt. 26:75 And Peter remembered the word of Jesus, which said unto him, Before the cock crow, thou shalt deny me thrice. And he went out, and wept bitterly. | | Mark 14:72b And Peter called to mind the word that Jesus said unto him, Before the cock crow twice, thou shalt deny me thrice. And when he thought thereon, he wept. | |
| | | | | |
| Matt. 26:57b to Caiaphas the high priest, where the scribes and the elders were assembled. | | Mark 14:53b to the high priest: and with him were assembled all the chief priests and the elders and the scribes. | | **To Caiaphas they were all assembled**<br>Matt. 26:57b, Mark 14:53b, & Luke |

| | Key Scriptures & Footnotes | Luke | John |
|---|---|---|---|
| | Peter's **third** denial | Time Lock - Time Lock | Time Lock - Time Lock |
| | | Luke 22:59a   And about the space of one hour after | |
| | 22:59 ...**about the space of one hour** after another confidently affirmed, saying, **Of a truth this fellow also was with him**... 22:60a   And Peter said, **Man, I know not what thou sayest.** | Luke 22:59b   another confidently affirmed, saying, Of a truth this fellow also was with him: for he is a Galilaean. Luke 22:60a   And Peter said, Man, I know not what thou sayest. | |
| | 18:26  One of the servants ... saith, **Did not I see thee in the garden with him?** 18:27a  Peter then **denied again:** | | John 18:26   One of the servants of the high priest, being his kinsman whose ear Peter cut off, saith, Did not I see thee in the garden with him? John 18:27a   Peter then denied again: |
| | 14:70b ...**Surely thou art one of them: for thou art a Galilaean, and thy speech agreeth thereto.** 14:71  But he began to curse and to swear, saying, **I know not this man of whom ye speak.** | | |
| | The cock crew | Time Lock - Time Lock | Time Lock - Time Lock |
| | 26:74b  And immediately the cock crew. 14:72a  And the second time the cock crew.[177] | Luke 22:60b   And immediately, while he yet spake, the cock crew. | John 18:27b   and immediately the cock crew. |
| | The Lord turned | Time Lock - Time Lock | Time Lock - Time Lock |
| | 22:61a  **And the Lord turned, and looked upon Peter**. | Luke 22:61a  And the Lord turned, and looked upon Peter. | |
| | Peter remembered | Time Lock - Time Lock | Time Lock - Time Lock |
| | | Luke 22:61b And Peter remembered the word of the Lord, how he had said unto him, Before the cock crow, thou shalt deny me thrice. Luke 22:62   And Peter went out, and wept bitterly. | |
| | 22:64  And when they had blindfolded him, they **struck** him on the face, and asked him, saying, Prophesy, who is it that smote thee? | Luke 22:63    And the men that held Jesus mocked him, and smote him. Luke 22:64    And when they had blindfolded him, they struck him on the face, and asked him, saying, Prophesy, who is it that smote thee? Luke 22:65    And many other things blasphemously spake they against him. | |
| | 22:66a And **as soon** as it was **day** | Luke 22:66a  And as soon as it was day | |
| | | Luke 22:66b  the elders of the people and the chief priests and the scribes came together, and led him to their council | 18:27b |

[7] Mark 14:72a  And the second time the cock crew. (*Mark heard Jesus say, in Mark 14:30, that the cock would crow twice. Then Mark, who was standing outside of the palace gate, heard the cock crow twice.  Is it possible that the others heard the cock crow only once?  This is an unsolved mystery.*)

| Matthew | | Mark | | Important Events |
|---|---|---|---|---|
| | | | | 22:66b |
| | | | | Map 125 |
| Matt. 26:59    Now the chief priests, and elders, and all the council, sought false witness against Jesus, to put him to death; Matt. 26:60    But found none: yea, though many false witnesses came, yet found they none. At the last came two false witnesses, Matt. 26:61    And said, This fellow said, I am able to destroy the temple of God, and to build it in three days. | | Mark 14:55    And the chief priests and all the council sought for witness against Jesus to put him to death; and found none. Mark 14:56    For many bare false witness against him, but their witness agreed not together. Mark 14:57    And there arose certain, and bare false witness against him, saying , Mark 14:58    We heard him say, I will destroy this temple that is made with hands, and within three days I will build another made without hands. Mark 14:59    But neither so did their witness agree together | | **The chief priests, and elders, and all the council, sought false witness** Matt. 26:59 & Mark 14:55 |
| Matt. 26:62  And the high priest arose, and said unto him,    Answerest   thou nothing? what is it which these   witness   against thee? Matt. 26:63a    But Jesus held his peace. | 26:75 | Mark 14:60  And the high priest stood up in the midst, and asked Jesus, saying, Answerest thou nothing ? what is it which these   witness   against thee? Mark 14:61a  But he held his peace, and answered nothing. | 14:72b | |
| | | | | |
| Matt. 26:63b    And the high priest answered and said unto him, I adjure thee by the living God, that thou tell us whether thou be the Christ, the Son of God. Matt. 26:64a  Jesus saith unto him, Thou hast said: | | | | |
| | | Mark 14:61b    Again the high priest asked him, and said unto him, Art thou the Christ, the Son of the Blessed? Mark 14:62a    And Jesus said, I am: | | |
| Matt. 26:64b nevertheless I say unto you, Hereafter shall ye see the Son of man sitting on the right hand of power,   and coming in the clouds of heaven. | 26:75 | Mark 14:62b        and ye shall see the Son of man sitting on the right hand of power, and coming in the clouds of heaven. | 14:72b | |
| Matt. 26:65    Then the high priest   rent   his clothes, saying, He hath spoken blasphemy; what further need have we of | | Mark 14:63    Then the high priest   rent   his clothes, and saith, What need   we   any   further witnesses? | | |

| nistry / year | Key Scriptures & Footnotes | Luke | John |
|---|---|---|---|
| | | | |
| | 26:62  And the high priest arose, and said unto him, Answerest thou nothing?.... | | 18:27b |
| | Luke 22:69 Hereafter shall the Son of man sit on the right hand of the power of God. | Luke 22:66c saying, Luke 22:67 Art thou the Christ? tell us. And he said unto them, If I tell you, ye will not believe: Luke 22:68 And if I also ask you, ye will not answer me, nor let me go. Luke 22:69 Hereafter shall the Son of man sit on the right hand of the power of God. Luke 22:70 Then said they all, Art thou then the Son of God? And he said unto them, Ye say that I am. | |
| | Matt. 26:63b  And the high priest answered.... | | |
| | Mark 14:61b  **Again** the high priest asked him,... Mark 14:62a  And Jesus said, I am: | | |
| | 14:62b  **and ye shall see** the Son of man sitting on the right hand of power, and **coming in the clouds of heaven**. | | |
| | | Luke 22:71    And they said, What need we any further witness? for we ourselves have heard of his own mouth. | |

| Matthew | Mark | Important Events |
|---|---|---|
| witnesses? behold, now ye have heard his blasphemy. Matt. 26:66 What think ye? They answered and said, He is guilty of death. | Mark 14:64 Ye have heard the blasphemy: what think ye? And they all condemned him to be guilty of death. | |
| Matt. 26:67 Then did they spit in his face, and buffeted him; and others smote him with the palms of their hands, Matt. 26:68 Saying, Prophesy unto us, thou Christ, Who is he that smote thee? | Mark 14:65 And some began to spit on him, and to cover his face, and to buffet him, and to say unto him, Prophesy: and the servants did strike him with the palms of their hands. | |
| <center>Time Lock - Time Lock</center> | <center>Time Lock - Time Lock</center> | |
| Matt. 27:1 When the morning was come, all the chief priests and elders of the people took counsel against Jesus to put him to death: Matt. 27:2 And when they had bound him, they led him away, and delivered him to Pontius Pilate the governor. | Mark 15:1 And straightway in the morning the chief priests held a consultation with the elders and scribes and the whole council, and bound Jesus, and carried him away, and delivered him to Pilate. | **Delivered Jesus to Pontius Pilate** Matt. 27:2, Mark 15:1, Luke 23:1, & John 18:28 Map 126 |
| Matt. 27:3 Then Judas, which had betrayed him, when he saw that he was condemned, repented himself, and brought again the thirty pieces of silver to the chief priests and elders, Matt. 27:4 Saying, I have sinned in that I have betrayed the innocent blood. And they said, What is that to us? see thou to that. Matt. 27:5 And he cast down the pieces of silver in the temple, and departed, and went and hanged himself. | | |
| Matt. 27:6 And the chief priests took the silver pieces, and said, It is not lawful for to put them into the treasury, because it is the price of blood. Matt. 27:7 And they took counsel, and bought with them the potter's field, to bury strangers in. Matt. 27:8 Wherefore that field was called, The field of blood, unto this day. Matt. 27:9 Then was fulfilled that which was spoken by Jeremy the prophet, saying, And they took the thirty pieces of silver, the price of him that was valued, whom they of the children of Israel did value; Matt. 27:10 And gave them for the potter's field, as the Lord appointed me. | | |
| | | |
| | | |
| <center>Time Lock - Time Lock</center> | <center>Time Lock - Time Lock</center> | |
| Matt. 27:11a And Jesus stood before the governor: | Mark 15:2a And Pilate asked him, Art thou the King | **Art thou the** |

| | | **Luke** | **John** |
|---|---|---|---|
| | | | |
| | | | |
| **In the morning** | | Time Lock - Time Lock | Time Lock - Time Lock |
| 27:1 When the morning[178] was come,...took counsel against Jesus.... 23:1...and led him unto Pilate. 18:28...**but that they might eat the passover.**[179] | Luke 23:1 And the whole multitude of them arose, and led him unto Pilate. | | John 18:28 Then led they Jesus from Caiaphas unto the hall of judgment: and it was early; and they themselves went not into the judgment hall, lest they should be defiled; but that they might eat the passover. |
| 27:3 Then Judas, which had betrayed him, when he saw that he was condemned, repented himself,.... | | | |
| 27:8 Wherefore that field was called, The field of blood, unto this day. | | | |
| 18:29 Pilate...said, What accusation...? 18:30 They answered and said unto him, If he were not a **malefactor**,.... | | | John 18:29 Pilate then went out unto them, and said, What accusation bring ye against this man? John 18:30 They answered and said unto him, If he were not a malefactor, we would not have delivered him up unto thee. John 18:31 Then said Pilate unto them, Take ye him, and judge him according to your law. The Jews therefore said unto him, It is not lawful for us to put any man to death: John 18:32 That the saying of Jesus might be fulfilled, which he spake, signifying what death he should die. |
| 23:2 And they began to accuse him, saying,...this fellow...**saying that he himself is Christ** a King. | Luke 23:2 And they began to accuse him, saying, We found this fellow perverting the nation, and forbidding to give tribute to Caesar, saying that he himself is Christ a King. | | |
| **Art thou the king?** | | Time Lock - Time Lock | Time Lock - Time Lock |
| 18:33 Then Pilate | Luke 23:3a And Pilate asked him, saying, Art thou | | John 18:33 Then Pilate entered into the judgment |

[8] Matthew 27:1 When the morning was come.... (*This was early Thursday morning.*)

[9] John 18:28 ...and they themselves went not into the judgment hall, lest they should be defiled; but that they might eat the passover. (*The words,* **eat the passover** *are referring to the week long* **feast of Passover** *that started that same Thursday at sunset.*)

| Matthew | Mark | Important Events |
|---|---|---|
| and the governor asked him, saying, Art thou the King of the Jews? | of the Jews? | **King of the Jews?**<br>Matt. 27:11a, Mark 15:2a, Luke 23:3a, & John 18:33 |
| | | |
| Matt. 27:11b  And Jesus said unto him, Thou sayest. | Mark 15:2b  And he answering said unto him, , Thou sayest it. | **And Jesus said unto him, Thou sayest.**<br>Matt. 27:11b, Mark 15:2b, Luke 23:3b, & John 18:37 |
| | | |
| Matt. 27:12  And when he was accused of the chief priests and elders, he answered nothing. | Mark 15:3  And the chief priests accused him of many things: but he answered nothing. | |
| Matt. 27:13  Then said Pilate unto him, Hearest thou not how many things they witness against thee? | | |
| | Mark 15:4  And Pilate asked him again, saying, Answerest thou nothing? behold how many things they witness against thee. | |
| Matt. 27:14  And he answered him to never a word; insomuch that the governor marvelled greatly. | Mark 15:5  But Jesus yet answered nothing; so that Pilate marvelled. | |
| | | |
| | | |
| | | Map 127<br>Map 128 |
| | | **3rd time that Pilate found no** |

| nistry<br>year | Key Scriptures<br>& Footnotes | Luke | John |
|---|---|---|---|
| | entered into the judgment hall again, and called Jesus, and said unto him, **Art thou the King of the Jews?** | the King of the Jews? | hall again, and called Jesus, and said unto him, Art thou the King of the Jews? |
| | 18:37a Pilate therefore said unto him, Art thou a king then?[180] | | John 18:34   Jesus answered him, Sayest thou this thing of thyself, or did others tell it thee of me?<br>John 18:35   Pilate answered, Am I a Jew? Thine own nation and the chief priests have delivered thee unto me: what hast thou done?<br>John 18:36   Jesus answered, My kingdom is not of this world: if my kingdom were of this world, then would my servants fight, that I should not be delivered to the Jews: but now is my kingdom not from hence.<br>John 18:37a   Pilate therefore said unto him, Art thou a king then? |
| | 15:2b...And he answering said unto him, **Thou sayest** it. | Luke 23:3b   And he answered him and said, Thou sayest it. | John 18:37b   Jesus answered, Thou sayest that I am a king. To this end was I born, and for this cause came I into the world, that I should bear witness unto the truth. Every one that is of the truth heareth my voice. |
| | 18:38 ...I find in him **no fault at all.** | | John 18:38   Pilate saith unto him, What is truth? And when he had said this, he went out again unto the Jews, and saith unto them, I find in him no fault at all. |
| | 15:3   And the chief priests accused him of many things: but he answered nothing. | | |
| | 15:4   And Pilate asked him **again,**.... | | |
| | 27:14   And he answered him to never a word;... | | |
| | 23:4 ...I find **no fault** in this man. | Luke 23:4   Then said Pilate to the chief priests and to the people, I find no fault in this man. | |
| | 23:5...**they were the more fierce,**.... | Luke 23:5   And they were the more fierce, saying, He stirreth up the people, teaching throughout all Jewry, beginning from Galilee to this place. | |
| | 23:7...he sent him to Herod,.... | Luke 23:6   When Pilate heard of Galilee, he asked whether the man were a Galilaean.<br>Luke 23:7   And as soon as he knew that he belonged unto Herod's jurisdiction, he sent him to Herod, who himself also was at Jerusalem at that time.<br>Luke 23:8   And when Herod saw Jesus, he was exceeding glad: for he was desirous to see him of a long season, because he had heard many things of him; and he hoped to have seen some miracle done by him.<br>Luke 23:9   Then he questioned with him in many words; but he answered him nothing. | |
| | 23:10   And the chief priests and scribes stood and **vehemently accused him.** | Luke 23:10   And the chief priests and scribes stood and vehemently accused him.<br>Luke 23:11   And Herod with his men of war set him at nought, and mocked him, and arrayed him in a gorgeous robe, and sent him again to Pilate.<br>Luke 23:12   And the same day Pilate and Herod were made friends together: for before they were at enmity between themselves. | |
| | 23:14...I, having | Luke 23:13   And Pilate, when he had called together the chief priests and the rulers and the people,<br>Luke 23:14   Said unto them, Ye have brought this | |

John 18:37   Pilate therefore said unto him, Art thou a king then? (*Pilate asked a very similar question in John 18:33* ...Art thou
e King of the Jews?)

| Matthew | Mark | Important Events |
|---|---|---|
| | | |
| Matt. 27:15  Now at that feast the governor was wont to release unto the people a prisoner, whom they would.<br>Matt. 27:16  And they had then a notable prisoner, called Barabbas.<br>Matt. 27:17  Therefore when they were gathered together, Pilate said unto them, Whom will ye that I release unto you? Barabbas, or Jesus which is called Christ?<br>Matt. 27:18  For he knew that for envy they had delivered him. | Mark 15:6  Now at that feast he released unto them one prisoner, whomsoever they desired.<br>Mark 15:7  And there was one named Barabbas, which lay bound with them that had made insurrection with him, who had committed murder in the insurrection.<br>Mark 15:8  And the multitude crying aloud began to desire him to do as he had ever done unto them.<br>Mark 15:9  But Pilate answered them, saying, Will ye that I release unto you the King of the Jews?<br>Mark 15:10  For he knew that the chief priests had delivered him for envy. | |
| Matt. 27:19  When he was set down on the judgment seat, his wife sent unto him, saying, Have thou nothing to do with that just man: for I have suffered many things this day in a dream because of him. | | |
| Matt. 27:20  But the chief priests and elders persuaded the multitude that they should ask Barabbas, and destroy Jesus.<br>Matt. 27:21  The governor answered and said unto them, Whether of the twain will ye that I release unto you? They said, Barabbas. | Mark 15:11  But the chief priests moved the people, that he should rather release Barabbas unto them. | |
| Matt. 27:22  Pilate saith unto them, What shall I do then with Jesus which is called Christ? They all say unto him, Let him be crucified. | Mark 15:12  And Pilate answered and said again unto them, What will ye then that I shall do unto him whom ye call the King of the Jews?<br>Mark 15:13  And they cried out again, Crucify him. | |
| Matt. 27:23a  And the governor said, Why, what evil hath he done? | Mark 15:14a  Then Pilate said unto them, Why, what evil hath he done? | |
| Matt. 27:23b  But they cried out the more, saying, Let him be crucified.<br>Matt. 27:24  When Pilate saw that he could prevail nothing, but that rather a tumult was made, he took water, and washed his hands before the multitude, saying, I am innocent of the blood of this just person: see ye to it.<br>Matt. 27:25  Then answered all the people, and said, His blood be on us, and on our children. | Mark 15:14b  And they cried out the more exceedingly, Crucify him. | |
| Time Lock - Time Lock | Time Lock - Time Lock | |
| Matt. 27:26  Then released he Barabbas unto them: and when he had scourged Jesus, he delivered him to be crucified.<br>Matt. 27:27  Then the soldiers of the governor took Jesus into the common hall, and gathered unto him the whole band of soldiers.<br>Matt. 27:28  And they stripped him, and put on him a scarlet robe.<br>Matt. 27:29  And when they had plaited a crown of thorns, they put it upon his head, and a reed in his right hand: and they bowed the knee before him, and mocked him, saying, Hail, King of the Jews!<br>Matt. 27:30  And they spit upon him, and took the reed, and smote him on the head. | Mark 15:15  And so Pilate, willing to content the people, released Barabbas unto them, and delivered Jesus, when he had scourged him, to be crucified.<br>Mark 15:16  And the soldiers led him away into the hall, called Praetorium; and they call together the whole band.<br>Mark 15:17  And they clothed him with purple, and plaited a crown of thorns, and put it about his head,<br>Mark 15:18  And began to salute him, Hail, King of the Jews!<br>Mark 15:19  And they smote him on the head with a reed, and did spit upon him, and bowing their knees worshipped him. | **Pilate scourged Jesus and delivered Him to be crucified**<br>Matt. 27:26, Mark 15:15, Luke 23:25, & John 19:1 |
| | | **5th time .** |

| --- | --- | --- | --- |
| examined him before you, have found **no fault** in this man.... | man unto me, as one that perverteth the people: and, behold, I, having examined him before you, have found no fault in this man touching those things whereof ye accuse him: Luke 23:15 No, nor yet Herod: for I sent you to him; and, lo, nothing worthy of death is done unto him. | |
| 23:16 **I will** therefore chastise him, and **release** him. | Luke 23:16 I will therefore chastise him, and release him. Luke 23:17 (For of necessity he must release one unto them at the feast.) | John 18:39 But ye have a custom, that I should release unto you one at the passover: will ye therefore that I release unto you the King of the Jews? |
| 23:18 And they cried out all at once, saying, Away with this man,.... | Luke 23:18 And they cried out all at once, saying, Away with this man, and release unto us Barabbas: Luke 23:19 (Who for a certain sedition made in the city, and for murder, was cast into prison.) | |
| | | John 18:40 Then cried they all again, saying, Not this man, but Barabbas. Now Barabbas was a robber. |
| 15:12 And **Pilate answered and said again**, 15:13 And they cried out **again**, Crucify him. | Luke 23:20 Pilate therefore, willing to release Jesus, spake again to them. Luke 23:21 But they cried, saying, Crucify him, crucify him. | |
| 23:22 And he said unto them the **third** time,...I have found **no cause**.... | Luke 23:22 And he said unto them the third time, Why, what evil hath he done? I have found no cause of death in him: I will therefore chastise him, and let him go. | |
| 23:23 And they were instant with loud voices, requiring that he might be crucified. | Luke 23:23 And they were instant with loud voices, requiring that he might be crucified. And the voices of them and of the chief priests prevailed. | |
| 27:25...His blood be on us,.... | | |
| Pilate delivered Jesus. | Time Lock - Time Lock | Time Lock - Time Lock |
| 15:17 And they clothed him with purple, and plaited a crown of thorns, and put it about his head,.... | Luke 23:24 And Pilate gave sentence that it should be as they required. Luke 23:25 And he released unto them him that for sedition and murder was cast into prison, whom they had desired; but he delivered Jesus to their will. | John 19:1 Then Pilate therefore took Jesus, and scourged him. John 19:2 And the soldiers plaited a crown of thorns, and put it on his head, and they put on him a purple robe, John 19:3 And said, Hail, King of the Jews! and they smote him with their hands. |
| 19:4 ...know that I find **no fault** in him. | | John 19:4 Pilate therefore went forth again, and saith unto them, Behold, I bring him forth to you, that ye may know that I find no fault in him. John 19:5 Then came Jesus forth, wearing the crown of thorns, and the purple robe. And Pilate saith unto them, Behold the man! |
| 19:6...Pilate saith unto | | John 19:6 When the chief priests therefore and |

| Matthew | Mark | Important Events |
|---|---|---|
| | | **Pilate saith. "I find no fault in him."** John 19:6 |
| Time Lock - Time Lock | Time Lock - Time Lock | |
| Matt. 27:31  And after that they had mocked him, they took the robe off from him, and put his own raiment on him, and led him away to crucify him. | Mark 15:20  And when they had mocked him, they took off the purple from him, and put his own clothes on him, and led him out to crucify him. | |
| Time Lock - Time Lock | Time Lock - Time Lock | |
| Matt. 27:32  And as they came out, they found a man of Cyrene, Simon by name: him they compelled to bear his cross. | Mark 15:21  And they compel one Simon a Cyrenian, who passed by, coming out of the country, the father of Alexander and Rufus, to bear his cross. | **Simon, a Cyrenian, bear His cross** Matt. 27:32, Mark 15:21, & Luke 23:26 |
| Time Lock - Time Lock | Time Lock - Time Lock | |
| Matt. 27:33  And when they were come unto a place called Golgotha, that is to say, a place of a skull, | Mark 15:22  And they bring him unto the place Golgotha, which is, being interpreted, The place of a skull. | **Jesus came to Golgotha,** |

| ministry year | Key Scriptures & Footnotes | Luke | John |
|---|---|---|---|
| | them, Take ye him, and crucify him: for I find **no fault** in him.<br>19:7...because he made himself the Son of God. | | officers saw him, they cried out, saying, Crucify him, crucify him. Pilate saith unto them, Take ye him, and crucify him: for I find no fault in him.<br>John 19:7  The Jews answered him, We have a law, and by our law he ought to die, because he made himself the Son of God.<br>John 19:8  When Pilate therefore heard that saying, he was the more afraid;<br>John 19:9  And went again into the judgment hall, and saith unto Jesus, Whence art thou? But Jesus gave him no answer.<br>John 19:10  Then saith Pilate unto him, Speakest thou not unto me? knowest thou not that I have power to crucify thee, and have power to release thee?<br>John 19:11  Jesus answered, Thou couldest have no power at all against me, except it were given thee from above: therefore he that delivered me unto thee hath the greater sin. |
| | 19:12  And from thenceforth **Pilate sought to release him:**.... | | John 19:12  And from thenceforth Pilate sought to release him: but the Jews cried out, saying, If thou let this man go, thou art not Caesar's friend: whosoever maketh himself a king speaketh against Caesar.<br>John 19:13  When Pilate therefore heard that saying, he brought Jesus forth, and sat down in the judgment seat in a place that is called the Pavement, but in the Hebrew, Gabbatha. |
| | 19:14  And it **was the preparation of the passover**[181], and **about the sixth hour:**[182] and he saith unto the Jews, Behold your King! | | John 19:14  And it was the preparation of the passover, and about the sixth hour: and he saith unto the Jews, Behold your King!<br>John 19:15  But they cried out, Away with him, away with him, crucify him. Pilate saith unto them, Shall I crucify your King? The chief priests answered, We have no king but Caesar. |
| | They led him away | | Time Lock - Time Lock |
| | | | John 19:16  Then delivered he him therefore unto them to be crucified. And they took Jesus, and led him away. |
| | Simon the Cyrenian | Time Lock - Time Lock | |
| | | Luke 23:26  And as they led him away, they laid hold upon one Simon, a Cyrenian, coming out of the country, and on him they laid the cross, that he might bear it after Jesus. | John 19:17a  And he bearing his cross went forth |
| | | Luke 23:27  And there followed him a great company of people, and of women, which also bewailed and lamented him.<br>Luke 23:28  But Jesus turning unto them said, Daughters of Jerusalem, weep not for me, but weep for yourselves, and for your children.<br>Luke 23:29  For, behold, the days are coming, in the which they shall say, Blessed are the barren, and the wombs that never bare, and the paps which never gave suck.<br>Luke 23:30  Then shall they begin to say to the mountains, Fall on us; and to the hills, Cover us.<br>Luke 23:31  For if they do these things in a green tree, what shall be done in the dry?<br>Luke 23:32  And there were also two other, malefactors, led with him to be put to death. | |
| | The place of the skull | Time Lock - Time Lock | Time Lock - Time Lock |
| | 19:17b  into a place called the place of a skull, which is called | Luke 23:33a  And when they were come to the place, which is called Calvary, | John 19:17b  into a place called the place of a skull, which is called in the Hebrew Golgotha:<br>John 19:18  Where they crucified him, and two other |

---

[181] John 19:14  And it was **the preparation** of the passover.... (**The passover** *was* **the feast of Passover** *which was also called* **the feast of Unleavened**. *The* feast of Unleavened *was a seven day feast that started at sunset of the 14th day. This was the same as the beginning of the 15th day of the month. So, this year* the feast of Unleavened *started that Thursday evening at sunset. The hours before sunset on Thursday were used to prepare for* the feast of Unleavened *or* the feast of Passover. *That is why Thursday was called* **the preparation**.)

[182] John 19:14  ...about the **sixth hour**.... (*See Solutions to Gospel Mysteries to discover some keys to why* **John's sixth hour**, *9:00 AM, was the same as* **Mark's third hour**, *9:00 AM, as mentioned in Mark 15:25.*)

| Matthew | Mark | Important Events |
|---|---|---|
| | | **Calvary**<br>Matt. 27:33, Mark 15:22, Luke 23:33, & John 19:17b<br><br>Map 129 |
| Matt. 27:34 They gave him vinegar to drink mingled with gall: and when he had tasted thereof, he would not drink. | Mark 15:23 And they gave him to drink wine mingled with myrrh: but he received it not. | |
| Time Lock - Time Lock | Time Lock - Time Lock | |
| Matt. 27:35 And they crucified him, and parted his garments, casting lots: that it might be fulfilled which was spoken by the prophet, They parted my garments among them, and upon my vesture did they cast lots. | Mark 15:24 And when they had crucified him, they parted his garments, casting lots upon them, what every man should take. | |
| Matt. 27:36 And sitting down they watched him there;<br>Matt. 27:37 And set up over his head his accusation written, THIS IS JESUS THE KING OF THE JEWS. | Mark 15:25 And it was the third hour, and they crucified him.<br>Mark 15:26 And the superscription of his accusation was written over, THE KING OF THE JEWS. | |
| Matt. 27:38 Then were there two thieves crucified with him, one on the right hand, and another on the left.<br>Matt. 27:39 And they that passed by reviled him, wagging their heads,<br>Matt. 27:40 And saying, Thou that destroyest the temple, and buildest it in three days, save thyself. If thou be the Son of God, come down from the cross.<br>Matt. 27:41 Likewise also the chief priests mocking him, with the scribes and elders, said,<br>Matt. 27:42 He saved others; himself he cannot save. If he be the King of Israel, let him now come down from the cross, and we will believe him.<br>Matt. 27:43 He trusted in God; let him deliver him now, if he will have him: for he said, I am the Son of God.<br>Matt. 27:44 The thieves also, which were crucified with him, cast the same in his teeth. | Mark 15:27 And with him they crucify two thieves; the one on his right hand, and the other on his left.<br>Mark 15:28 And the scripture was fulfilled, which saith, And he was numbered with the transgressors.<br>Mark 15:29 And they that passed by railed on him, wagging their heads, and saying, Ah, thou that destroyest the temple, and buildest it in three days,<br>Mark 15:30 Save thyself, and come down from the cross.<br>Mark 15:31 Likewise also the chief priests mocking said among themselves with the scribes, He saved others; himself he cannot save.<br>Mark 15:32 Let Christ the King of Israel descend now from the cross, that we may see and believe. And they that were crucified with him reviled him. | |
| | | |
| | | |

| nistry / year | Key Scriptures & Footnotes | Luke | John |
|---|---|---|---|
| | in the Hebrew Golgotha: | | with him, on either side one, and Jesus in the midst. |
| | | | John 19:19  And Pilate wrote a title, and put it on the cross. And the writing was, JESUS OF NAZARETH THE KING OF THE JEWS. John 19:20  This title then read many of the Jews: for the place where Jesus was crucified was nigh to the city: and it was written in Hebrew, and Greek, and Latin. John 19:21  Then said the chief priests of the Jews to Pilate, Write not, The King of the Jews; but that he said, I am King of the Jews. John 19:22  Pilate answered, What I have written I have written. |
| | 27:34  They gave him vinegar to drink mingled with gall:.... | | |
| | They crucified Jesus | Time Lock - Time Lock | Time Lock - Time Lock |
| | 23:34  Then said Jesus, Father, forgive them; for they know not what they do. | Luke 23:33b  there they crucified him, and the malefactors, one on the right hand, and the other on the left. Luke 23:34  Then said Jesus, Father, forgive them; for they know not what they do. And they parted his raiment, and cast lots. | John 19:23  Then the soldiers, when they had crucified Jesus, took his garments, and made four parts, to every soldier a part; and also his coat: now the coat was without seam, woven from the top throughout. John 19:24  They said therefore among themselves, Let us not rend it, but cast lots for it, whose it shall be: that the scripture might be fulfilled, which saith, They parted my raiment among them, and for my vesture they did cast lots. These things therefore the soldiers did. |
| | 15:25  And it was the **third hour**,[183] and they crucified him. | Luke 23:35  And the people stood beholding. And the rulers also with them derided him, saying, He saved others; let him save himself, if he be Christ, the chosen of God. Luke 23:36  And the soldiers also mocked him, coming to him, and offering him vinegar, Luke 23:37  And saying, If thou be the king of the Jews, save thyself. Luke 23:38  And a superscription also was written over him in letters of Greek, and Latin, and Hebrew, THIS IS THE KING OF THE JEWS. | |
| | 15:27  And with him they crucify two thieves;.... | | |
| | 27:44  The thieves also, which were crucified with him, **cast the same** in his teeth. | | |
| | 23:39...If thou be Christ, save thyself and us. | Luke 23:39  And one of the malefactors which were hanged railed on him, saying, If thou be Christ, save thyself and us. | |
| | 23:40  But the other answering rebuked him, saying,.... | Luke 23:40  But the other answering rebuked him, saying, Dost not thou fear God, seeing thou art in the same condemnation? Luke 23:41  And we indeed justly; for we receive | |

[183] Mark 15:25  And it was the **third hour**, and they crucified him. (*The sun rose at about 6:00 AM and set at about 6:00 PM. So, according to Roman time, the **third hour** was 9 AM, the sixth hour was Noon, and the ninth hour was 3:00 PM.*)

| Matthew | Mark | Important Events |
|---|---|---|
| Matt. 27:45 Now from the sixth hour there was darkness over all the land unto the ninth hour. | Mark 15:33 And when the sixth hour was come, there was darkness over the whole land until the ninth hour. | |
| Matt. 27:46 And about the ninth hour Jesus cried with a loud voice, saying, Eli, Eli, lama sabachthani? that is to say, My God, my God, why hast thou forsaken me? <br> Matt. 27:47 Some of them that stood there, when they heard that, said, This man calleth for Elias. | Mark 15:34 And at the ninth hour Jesus cried with a loud voice, saying, Eloi, Eloi, lama sabachthani? which is, being interpreted, My God, my God, why hast thou forsaken me? <br> Mark 15:35 And some of them that stood by, when they heard it, said, Behold, he calleth Elias. | |
| Matt. 27:48 And straightway one of them ran, and took a sponge, and filled it with vinegar, and put it on a reed, and gave him to drink. <br> Matt. 27:49 The rest said, Let be, let us see whether Elias will come to save him. | Mark 15:36 And one ran and filled a sponge full of vinegar, and put it on a reed, and gave him to drink, saying, Let alone; let us see whether Elias will come to take him down. | |
| Time Lock - Time Lock | Time Lock - Time Lock | |
| Matt. 27:50 Jesus, when he had cried again with a loud voice, yielded up the ghost. <br> Matt. 27:51 And, behold, the veil of the temple was rent in twain from the top to the bottom; and the earth did quake, and the rocks rent; <br> Matt. 27:52 And the graves were opened; and many bodies of the saints which slept arose, <br> Matt. 27:53 And came out of the graves after his resurrection, and went into the holy city, and appeared unto many. | Mark 15:37 And Jesus cried with a loud voice, and gave up the ghost. <br> Mark 15:38 And the veil of the temple was rent in twain from the top to the bottom. | **Jesus gave up the ghost** <br> Matt. 27:50, Mark 15:37, Luke 23:45, & John 19:30 <br> Map 130 |
| Matt. 27:54 Now when the centurion, and they that were with him, watching Jesus, saw the earthquake, and those things that were done, they feared greatly, saying, Truly this was the Son of God. | Mark 15:39 And when the centurion, which stood over against him, saw that he so cried out, and gave up the ghost, he said, Truly this man was the Son of God. | |

| | Key Scriptures & Footnotes | Luke | John |
|---|---|---|---|
| | 23:43 And Jesus said unto him,...Today shalt thou be with me in paradise. | the due reward of our deeds: but this man hath done nothing amiss. Luke 23:42 And he said unto Jesus, Lord, remember me when thou comest into thy kingdom. Luke 23:43 And Jesus said unto him, Verily I say unto thee, Today shalt thou be with me in paradise. | |
| | 27:45 Now from the sixth hour **there was darkness** over all the land unto the ninth hour. | Luke 23:44 And it was about the sixth hour, and there was a darkness over all the earth until the ninth hour. | |
| | 19:26...he saith unto his mother, Woman, behold thy son! John 19:27 Then saith he to the disciple, Behold thy mother! And **from that hour** that disciple took her unto his own home. | | John 19:25 Now there stood by the cross of Jesus his mother, and his mother's sister, Mary the wife of Cleophas, and Mary Magdalene. John 19:26 When Jesus therefore saw his mother, and the disciple standing by, whom he loved, he saith unto his mother, Woman, behold thy son! John 19:27 Then saith he to the disciple, Behold thy mother! And from that hour that disciple took her unto his own home. |
| | 27:46...Eli, Eli, lama sabachthani? that is to say, My God, my God, why hast thou forsaken me? | | |
| | 19:28 After this, Jesus...saith, I thirst. | | John 19:28 After this, Jesus knowing that all things were now accomplished, that the scripture might be fulfilled, saith, I thirst. |
| | 15:36 And one ran and filled a sponge full of vinegar,.... | | John 19:29 Now there was set a vessel full of vinegar: and they filled a sponge with vinegar, and put it upon hyssop, and put it to his mouth. |
| | 19:30...he said, It is finished:.... | | John 19:30a When Jesus therefore had received the vinegar, he said, It is finished: |
| | Jesus gave up the ghost | Time Lock - Time Lock | Time Lock - Time Lock |
| | 23:45 And **the sun was darkened**, and the veil of the temple was rent in the midst. 23:46 And when Jesus had cried with a **loud voice**, he said, Father, into thy hands I commend my spirit:.... | Luke 23:45 And the sun was darkened, and the veil of the temple was rent in the midst. Luke 23:46 And when Jesus had cried with a loud voice, he said, Father, into thy hands I commend my spirit: and having said thus, he gave up the ghost. | John 19:30b and he bowed his head, and gave up the ghost. |
| | 15:39...Truly this man was the Son of God. | Luke 23:47 Now when the centurion saw what was done, he glorified God, saying, Certainly this was a righteous man. | |
| | 19:31 The Jews therefore, because it was the preparation, that the bodies should not remain upon the cross on the sabbath day, (for that sabbath day[184] was an high day,).... 19:34 But one of the soldiers with a spear pierced his side, and forthwith came there out blood and water. | | John 19:31 The Jews therefore, because it was the preparation, that the bodies should not remain upon the cross on the sabbath day, (for that sabbath day was an high day,) besought Pilate that their legs might be broken, and that they might be taken away. John 19:32 Then came the soldiers, and brake the legs of the first, and of the other which was crucified with him. John 19:33 But when they came to Jesus, and saw that he was dead already, they brake not his legs: John 19:34 But one of the soldiers with a spear pierced his side, and forthwith came there out blood and water. John 19:35 And he that saw it bare record, and his record is true: and he knoweth that he saith true, that |

John 19:31 The Jews therefore, because it was the preparation, that the bodies should not remain upon the cross on the bbath day, (for **that sabbath day** was an high day,).... (*That* **sabbath day** *started at sunset. Sunset was the start of the 15th day of  month and was the start of the seven day* feast of Unleavened. *See Numbers 28:18* In the first day shall be **an holy nvocation**; ye shall do no manner of work therein:. *Also, see Sabbath days in Leviticus 23:7-8 and 23:32-39 where* **an holy nvocation** *is called a Sabbath.*)

| Matthew | Mark | Important Events |
|---|---|---|
| Matt. 27:55   And many women were there beholding afar off, which followed Jesus from Galilee, ministering unto him: <br> Matt. 27:56   Among which was Mary Magdalene, and Mary the mother of James and Joses, and the mother of Zebedee's children. | Mark 15:40   There were also women looking on afar off: among whom was Mary Magdalene, and Mary the mother of James the less and of Joses, and Salome; <br> Mark 15:41   (Who also, when he was in Galilee, followed him, and ministered unto him;) and many other women which came up with him unto Jerusalem | |
| Matt. 27:57   When the even was come, there came a rich man of Arimathaea, named Joseph, who also himself was Jesus' disciple: <br> Matt. 27:58   He went to Pilate, and begged the body of Jesus. Then Pilate commanded the body to be delivered. <br> Matt. 27:59   And when Joseph had taken the body, he wrapped it in a clean linen cloth, <br> Matt. 27:60   And laid it in his own new tomb, which he had hewn out in the rock: and he rolled a great stone to the door of the sepulchre, and departed. <br> Matt. 27:61   And there was Mary Magdalene, and the other Mary, sitting over against the sepulchre. | Mark 15:42   And now when the even was come, because it was the preparation, that is, the day before the sabbath, <br> Mark 15:43   Joseph of Arimathaea, an honourable counsellor, which also waited for the kingdom of God, came, and went in boldly unto Pilate, and craved the body of Jesus. <br> Mark 15:44   And Pilate marvelled if he were already dead: and calling unto him the centurion, he asked him whether he had been any while dead. <br> Mark 15:45   And when he knew it of the centurion, he gave the body to Joseph. <br> Mark 15:46   And he bought fine linen, and took him down, and wrapped him in the linen, and laid him in a sepulchre which was hewn out of a rock, and rolled a stone unto the door of the sepulchre. <br> Mark 15:47   And Mary Magdalene and Mary the mother of Joses beheld where he was laid. | Map 131 |
| Matt. 27:62   Now the next day, that followed the day of the preparation, the chief priests and Pharisees came together unto Pilate, <br> Matt. 27:63   Saying, Sir, we remember that that deceiver said, while he was yet alive, After three days I will rise again. <br> Matt. 27:64   Command therefore that the sepulchre be made sure until the third day, lest his disciples come by night, and steal him away, and say unto the people, He is risen from the dead: so the last error shall be worse than the first. <br> Matt. 27:65   Pilate said unto them, Ye have a watch: go your way, make it as sure as ye can. <br> Matt. 27:66   So they went, and made the sepulchre sure, sealing the stone, and setting a watch. | | |
| Time Lock - Time Lock | Time Lock - Time Lock | |
| Matt. 28:1   In the end of the sabbath, as it began to dawn toward the first day of the week, came Mary Magdalene and the other Mary to see the sepulchre. | Mark 16:1   And when the sabbath was past, Mary Magdalene, and Mary the mother of James, and Salome, had bought sweet spices, that they might come and anoint him. | **They came unto the sepulchre** <br> Matt. 28:1, Mark 16:1, Luke 24:1, & |

| Key Scriptures & Footnotes | Luke | John |
|---|---|---|
| 19:35 And **he that saw it bare record**, and his record is true:.... | | ye might believe.<br>John 19:36 For these things were done, that the scripture should be fulfilled, A bone of him shall not be broken.<br>John 19:37 And again another scripture saith, They shall look on him whom they pierced. |
| | Luke 23:48 And all the people that came together to that sight, beholding the things which were done, smote their breasts, and returned.<br>Luke 23:49 And all his acquaintance, and the women that followed him from Galilee, stood afar off, beholding these things. | |
| 15:42 And now when the even was come, because it was **the preparation**, that is, the day before the **sabbath**,<br><br><br><br><br><br><br>19:42 There laid they Jesus therefore because of the Jews' preparation day[185]; for the sepulchre was nigh at hand. | Luke 23:50 And, behold, there was a man named Joseph, a counsellor; and he was a good man, and a just:<br>Luke 23:51 (The same had not consented to the counsel and deed of them;) he was of Arimathaea, a city of the Jews: who also himself waited for the kingdom of God.<br>Luke 23:52 This man went unto Pilate, and begged the body of Jesus.<br>Luke 23:53 And he took it down, and wrapped it in linen, and laid it in a sepulchre that was hewn in stone, wherein never man before was laid.<br>Luke 23:54 And that day was the preparation, and the sabbath drew on.<br>Luke 23:55 And the women also, which came with him from Galilee, followed after, and beheld the sepulchre, and how his body was laid. | John 19:38 And after this Joseph of Arimathaea, being a disciple of Jesus, but secretly for fear of the Jews, besought Pilate that he might take away the body of Jesus: and Pilate gave him leave. He came therefore, and took the body of Jesus.<br>John 19:39 And there came also Nicodemus, which at the first came to Jesus by night, and brought a mixture of myrrh and aloes, about an hundred pound weight.<br>John 19:40 Then took they the body of Jesus, and wound it in linen clothes with the spices, as the manner of the Jews is to bury.<br>John 19:41 Now in the place where he was crucified there was a garden; and in the garden a new sepulchre, wherein was never man yet laid.<br>John 19:42 There laid they Jesus therefore because of the Jews' preparation day; for the sepulchre was nigh at hand. |
| 23:56 And they returned,[186] and prepared spices and ointments: and rested the sabbath day.... | Luke 23:56 And they returned, and prepared spices and ointments: and rested the sabbath day according to the commandment. | |
| 27:62 Now the next day, that followed the day of the preparation,....[187]<br>27:63...After three days I will rise again.<br><br><br><br><br>27:65 Pilate said unto them, Ye have a watch: go your way, make it as sure as ye can. | | |
| First day of the week | Time Lock - Time Lock | Time Lock - Time Lock |
| 20:1a...cometh Mary Magdalene... when it was yet dark,[188]....<br>16:2 And very early | Luke 24:1 Now upon the first day of the week, very early in the morning, they came unto the sepulchre, bringing the spices which they had prepared, and certain others with them. | John 20:1a The first day of the week cometh Mary Magdalene early, when it was yet dark, unto the sepulchre, |

[5] John 19:42 There laid they Jesus therefore because of the Jews' preparation day.... (*Thursday evening at sunset was the start* *of the 15th day of the month and also the start of the seven day feast of Unleavened. See Numbers 28:18 In the first day an holy* *onvocation: ye shall do no manner of work therein:*.)

[6] Luke 23:56 And they returned, and prepared spices and ointments: and rested the sabbath *day*.... (*They returned on Thursday* *efore sunset to prepare spices. Friday, which was* **an holy convocation**, *and Saturday, which was the seventh day of the week,* *ere both "Sabbath days." The word* **"day"** *is not present in the Greek. They then rested the two days of the Sabbath, in* *cordance to the commandment*.)

[7] Matthew 27:62 Now the next day, that followed the day of the preparation.... (*This was Friday, a day of* **an holy convocation**. *o work should be done on that day. In Leviticus 23 these* holy convocations *are also called* Sabbaths.)

[8] John 20:1a ...cometh Mary Magdalene early, when it was yet dark, unto the sepulchre, (*Green's* _Literal Translation of the Bible_ *ys*, "...Mary Magdalene came early to the tomb, **darkness yet being on it.**" *John knows it was Mary Magdalene because she ran* *rectly to John and gave him an eye witness account in John 20:2. The women walked to the tomb from as far away as Bethany.*)

| Matthew | Mark | Important Events |
|---|---|---|
| | Mark 16:2   And very early in the morning the first day of the week, they came unto the sepulchre at the rising of the sun.<br>Mark 16:3   And they said among themselves, Who shall roll us away the stone from the door of the sepulchre? | John 20:1a |
| Matt. 28:2   And, behold, there was a great earthquake: for the angel of the Lord descended from heaven, and came and rolled back the stone from the door, and sat upon it.<br>Matt. 28:3   His countenance was like lightning, and his raiment white as snow:<br>Matt. 28:4   And for fear of him the keepers did shake, and became as dead men. | | |
| | Mark 16:4   And when they looked, they saw that the stone was rolled away: for it was very great. | |
| Matt. 28:5   And the angel answered and said unto the women, Fear not ye: for I know that ye seek Jesus, which was crucified.<br>Matt. 28:6   He is not here: for he is risen, as he said. Come, see the place where the Lord lay. | | |
| | | **Mary Magdalene runneth**<br>John 20:2a |
| | Mark 16:5   And entering into the sepulchre, they saw a young man sitting on the right side, clothed in a long white garment; and they were affrighted.<br>Mark 16:6   And he saith unto them, Be not affrighted: Ye seek Jesus of Nazareth, which was crucified: he is risen; he is not here: behold the place where they laid him. | |
| Matt. 28:7   And go quickly, and tell his disciples that he is risen from the dead; and, behold, he goeth before you into Galilee; there shall ye see him: lo, I have told you. | Mark 16:7   But go your way, tell his disciples and Peter that he goeth before you into Galilee: there shall ye see him, as he said unto you. | |
| | | |
| | | |
| Matt. 28:8a   And they departed quickly from the sepulchre with fear and great joy; | Mark 16:8a   And they went out quickly, and fled from the sepulchre; for they trembled and were amazed: | |
| | Mark 16:8b neither said they any thing to any man; for they were afraid. | |

| | Key Scriptures & Footnotes | Luke | John |
|---|---|---|---|
| | in the morning the first day of the week,[189] they came unto the sepulchre at the rising of the sun. | | |
| | 28:2 And, behold, there was a great earthquake:.... <br> 28:4 And **for fear of him the keepers did shake, and became as dead men.** | | |
| | 24:2 And they found the stone rolled away from the sepulchre. | Luke 24:2 And they found the stone rolled away from the sepulchre. | John 20:1b and seeth the stone taken away from the sepulchre. |
| | John 20:2a Then she runneth, | | John 20:2a Then she runneth, |
| | 16:5 **And entering into the sepulchre,** they saw a young man sitting on the right side,.... | Luke 24:3 And they entered in, and found not the body of the Lord Jesus. | |
| | 24:4 **And it came to pass,** as they were much perplexed thereabout, **behold,**[190] two men stood by them in shining garments: 24:6 He is not here, but is risen:.... <br><br> Luke 24:8 **And they remembered his words,** | Luke 24:4 And it came to pass, as they were much perplexed thereabout, behold, two men stood by them in shining garments: <br> Luke 24:5 And as they were afraid, and bowed down their faces to the earth, they said unto them, Why seek ye the living among the dead? <br> Luke 24:6 He is not here, but is risen: remember how he spake unto you when he was yet in Galilee, <br> Luke 24:7 Saying, The Son of man must be delivered into the hands of sinful men, and be crucified, and the third day rise again. <br> Luke 24:8 And they remembered his words, | |
| | 20:2b and cometh to Simon Peter, and to the other disciple,[191].... | | John 20:2b and cometh to Simon Peter, and to the other disciple, whom Jesus loved, and saith unto them, They have taken away the Lord out of the sepulchre, and we know not where they have laid him. |
| | 16:8b ...**neither said they any thing to any man;**[192] .... | | |

---

[9] Mark 16:2 And very early in the morning the first day of the week, **they came unto the sepulchre at the rising of the sun**. *This was Sunday morning.*)

[0] Luke 24:4 And **it came to pass**, as **they were much perplexed** thereabout, **behold, two** men stood by them in shining garments: *The women did not run from the sepulchre after seeing the* "young man sitting on the right side, clothed in a long white garment" *of [M]ark 16:5. The women waited because* **they were much perplexed**. *Luke's words* **it came to pass** *and* **behold** *indicate a passage [of] time. Now* "two men stood by them in shining garments." *These two angels were also sent by God to comfort and instruct the [w]omen.*)

[1] John 20:2b and cometh to Simon Peter, and to the other disciple, whom Jesus loved.... (*Mary Magdalene ran to Peter and John. [Th]ey may have been spending their nights in the area of the mount of Olives. The week before they had spent their nights there with [Je]sus.*)

| Matthew | Mark | Important Events |
|---|---|---|
| Matt. 28:8b  and did run to bring his disciples word. | | |
| | | **1st time Peter went to see the sepulchre**<br>John 20:3 |
| | Mark 16:9   Now when Jesus was risen early the first day of the week, he appeared  first  to  Mary Magdalene, out of whom he had cast seven devils. | **Jesus appeared first to Mary Magdalene**<br>Mark 16:9 & John 20:16<br><br>Map 132 |
| Time Clue - Time Clue  - - John 20:17 & Matt. 28:9 | | Map 133 |
| Matt. 28:9   And as they went to tell his disciples, behold, Jesus met them, saying,  All hail. And they came and held him by the feet, and worshipped him.<br>Matt. 28:10   Then said Jesus unto them, Be not afraid: go tell my brethren that they go into Galilee, and there shall they see me. | | Map 134 |
| Matt. 28:11   Now when they were going, behold, some of the watch came into the city, and showed unto the chief priests all the things that were done.<br>Matt. 28:12   And when they were assembled with the elders, and had taken counsel, they gave large money unto the soldiers,<br>Matt. 28:13   Saying, Say ye, His disciples came by night, and stole him away while we slept.<br>Matt. 28:14   And if this come to the governor's ears, we will persuade him, and secure you.<br>Matt. 28:15   So they took the money, and did as they | | |

| Key Scriptures & Footnotes | Luke | John |
|---|---|---|
| 20:3  Peter therefore went forth, and that other disciple, and came to the sepulchre. | | John 20:3  Peter therefore went forth, and that other disciple, and came to the sepulchre.<br>John 20:4  So they ran both together: and the other disciple did outrun Peter, and came first to the sepulchre.<br>John 20:5  And he stooping down, and looking in, saw the linen clothes lying; yet went he not in.<br>John 20:6  Then cometh Simon Peter following him, and went into the sepulchre, and seeth the linen clothes lie, |
| 20:8  Then went in also that other disciple,[193] which came first to the sepulchre, and **he saw, and believed**.<br>John 20:10  Then **the disciples went away** again unto their own home. | | John 20:7  And the napkin, that was about his head, not lying with the linen clothes, but wrapped together in a place by itself.<br>John 20:8  Then went in also that other disciple, which came first to the sepulchre, and he saw, and believed.<br>John 20:9  For as yet they knew not the scripture, that he must rise again from the dead.<br>John 20:10  Then the disciples went away again unto their own home. |
| 20:11  **But Mary stood without** at the sepulchre weeping:.... | | John 20:11  But Mary stood without at the sepulchre weeping: and as she wept, she stooped down, and looked into the sepulchre,<br>John 20:12  And seeth two angels in white sitting, the one at the head, and the other at the feet, where the body of Jesus had lain.<br>John 20:13  And they say unto her, Woman, why weepest thou? She saith unto them, Because they have taken away my Lord, and I know not where they have laid him. |
| 16:9  Now when Jesus was risen early the first day of the week, **he appeared first to Mary Magdalene**,....<br>20:15  Jesus saith unto her, Woman, why weepest thou? whom seekest thou?...<br>20:17  Jesus saith unto her, **Touch me not**; for I am not yet ascended to my Father, and your Father;.... | 24:8 | John 20:14  And when she had thus said, she turned herself back, and saw Jesus standing, and knew not that it was Jesus.<br>John 20:15  Jesus saith unto her, Woman, why weepest thou? whom seekest thou? She, supposing him to be the gardener, saith unto him, Sir, if thou have borne him hence, tell me where thou hast laid him, and I will take him away.<br>John 20:16  Jesus saith unto her, Mary. She turned herself, and saith unto him, Rabboni; which is to say, Master.<br>John 20:17  Jesus saith unto her, Touch me not; for I am not yet ascended to my Father: but go to my brethren, and say unto them, I ascend unto my Father, and your Father; and to my God, and your God. |
| Time Clue [194] | | Time Clue - Time Clue  - - John 20:17 & Matt. 28:9 |
| 28:9...behold, Jesus met them, saying, All hail. **And they came and held him by the feet**,.... | | |
| 28:11  **Now when they were going**, behold, some of the watch came into the city, and showed unto the chief priests all the things that were done. | | |

[2] Mark 16:8b  neither said they any thing to any man; for they were afraid. (*The women did not stop to talk to strangers. They aded directly to the disciples.*)
[3] John 20:8  Then went in also that other disciple.... (This was *John*.)
[4] John 20:17  Jesus saith unto her, **Touch me not; for I am not yet ascended** to my Father, but go to my brethren, and say unto em, **I ascend** unto my Father....(*After John 20:17 Jesus ascended to his Father and then returned. So, by Matthew 28:9 the other omen could hold Jesus by the feet.*)

| Matthew | Mark | Important Events |
|---|---|---|
| were taught: and this saying is commonly reported among the Jews until this day. | | |
| Time Lock - Time Lock | Time Lock - Time Lock | Time Lock |
| | Mark 16:10   And she went and told them that had been with him, as they mourned and wept.<br>Mark 16:11   And they, when they had heard that he was alive, and had been seen of her, believed not. | |
| | | **2nd time arose Peter and ran unto the sepulchre**<br>Luke 24:12 |
| 28:15 | Mark 16:12   After that he appeared in another form unto two of them, as they walked, and went into the country. | Map 135 |

| | Mary Magdalene came | Time Lock - Time Lock | Time Lock - Time Lock |
|---|---|---|---|
| | 20:18 Mary Magdalene came and told the disciples.... 24:9 And returned from the sepulchre, and told all these things... | Luke 24:9 And returned from the sepulchre, and told all these things unto the eleven, and to all the rest. Luke 24:10 It was Mary Magdalene, and Joanna, and Mary the mother of James, and other women that were with them, which told these things unto the apostles. | John 20:18 Mary Magdalene came and told the disciples that she had seen the Lord, and that he had spoken these things unto her. |
| | 24:11...and they believed them not. 24:12 Then arose Peter,[195] and ran unto the sepulchre;.... and departed, wondering in himself.... | Luke 24:11 And their words seemed to them as idle tales, and they believed them not. Luke 24:12 Then arose Peter, and ran unto the sepulchre; and stooping down, he beheld the linen clothes laid by themselves, and departed, wondering in himself at that which was come to pass. | |
| | 16:12 After that he appeared **in another form** unto two of them, as they walked, and went into the country. 24:13 to a village called Emmaus,.... 24:15...Jesus himself drew near,.... | Luke 24:13 And, behold, two of them went that same day to a village called Emmaus, which was from Jerusalem about threescore furlongs. Luke 24:14 And they talked together of all these things which had happened. Luke 24:15 And it came to pass, that, while they communed together and reasoned, Jesus himself drew near, and went with them. Luke 24:16 But their eyes were holden that they should not know him. Luke 24:17 And he said unto them, What manner of communications are these that ye have one to another, as ye walk, and are sad? | |
| | 24:18...Cleopas, answering said unto him, Art thou only a stranger in Jerusalem,...? | Luke 24:18 And the one of them, whose name was Cleopas, answering said unto him, Art thou only a stranger in Jerusalem, and hast not known the things which are come to pass there in these days? Luke 24:19 And he said unto them, What things? And they said unto him, Concerning Jesus of Nazareth, which was a prophet mighty in deed and word before God and all the people: Luke 24:20 And how the chief priests and our rulers delivered him to be condemned to death, and have crucified him. Luke 24:21 But we trusted that it had been he which should have redeemed Israel: and beside all this, today is the third day since these things were done. Luke 24:22 Yea, and certain women also of our company made us astonished, which were early at the sepulchre; Luke 24:23 And when they found not his body, they came, saying, that they had also seen a vision of angels, which said that he was alive. Luke 24:24 And certain of them which were with us went to the sepulchre, and found it even so as the women had said: but him they saw not. Luke 24:25 Then he said unto them, O fools, and slow of heart to believe all that the prophets have spoken: Luke 24:26 Ought not Christ to have suffered these things, and to enter into his glory? Luke 24:27 And beginning at Moses and all the prophets, he expounded unto them in all the scriptures the things concerning himself. Luke 24:28 And they drew nigh unto the village, whither they went: and he made as though he would have gone further. Luke 24:29 But they constrained him, saying, Abide with us: for it is toward evening, and the day is far spent. And he went in to tarry with them. Luke 24:30 And it came to pass, as he sat at meat with them, he took bread, and blessed it, and brake, | |

[5] Luke 24:12 Then arose Peter, and ran unto the sepulchre;.... (*This is the second time that Peter ran to the sepulchre that day. ee John 20:3 for the first time.*)

| Matthew | Mark | Important Events |
|---|---|---|
| | | |
| | | |
| 28:15 | Mark 16:13 And they went and told it unto the residue: neither believed they them. | |
| | | Map 136 |
| | | **1st time that Jesus stood in the midst of the disciples** Luke 24:36 & John 20:19  Map 137 |
| | | **2nd time Jesus came to the disciples** John 20:26  Map 138 |

| ministry year | Key Scriptures & Footnotes | Luke | John |
|---|---|---|---|
| | | and gave to them.<br>Luke 24:31    And their eyes were opened, and they knew him; and he vanished out of their sight.<br>Luke 24:32    And they said one to another, Did not our heart burn within us, while he talked with us by the way, and while he opened to us the scriptures? | |
| | | Luke 24:33a  And they rose up the same hour, and returned to Jerusalem, | |
| | 16:13  And they went and told it unto the residue: **neither believed they them**. | | |
| | | Luke 24:33b  and found the eleven gathered together, and them that were with them,<br>Luke 24:34    Saying, The Lord is risen indeed, and hath appeared to Simon.<br>Luke 24:35    And they told what things were done in the way, and how he was known of them in breaking of bread. | |
| | 20:19  Then the same day at evening, being the first day of the week, when the doors were shut...<br>came Jesus and stood in the midst, and saith unto them, Peace be unto you.<br><br>20:22...he breathed on them, and saith unto them, Receive ye the Holy Ghost: | Luke 24:36    And as they thus spake, Jesus himself stood in the midst of them, and saith unto them, Peace be unto you.<br>Luke 24:37    But they were terrified and affrighted, and supposed that they had seen a spirit.<br>Luke 24:38    And he said unto them, Why are ye troubled? and why do thoughts arise in your hearts?<br>Luke 24:39  Behold my hands and my feet, that it is I myself: handle me, and see; for a spirit hath not flesh and bones, as ye see me have.<br>Luke 24:40    And when he had thus spoken, he showed them his hands and his feet.<br>Luke 24:41    And while they yet believed not for joy, and wondered, he said unto them, Have ye here any meat?<br>Luke 24:42    And they gave him a piece of a broiled fish, and of an honeycomb.<br>Luke 24:43    And he took it, and did eat before them.<br>Luke 24:44    And he said unto them, These are the words which I spake unto you, while I was yet with you, that all things must be fulfilled, which were written in the law of Moses, and in the prophets, and in the psalms, concerning me.<br>Luke 24:45    Then opened he their understanding, that they might understand the scriptures,<br>Luke 24:46    And said unto them, Thus it is written, and thus it behooved Christ to suffer, and to rise from the dead the third day:<br>Luke 24:47    And that repentance and remission of sins should be preached in his name among all nations, beginning at Jerusalem.<br>Luke 24:48  And ye are witnesses of these things.<br>Luke 24:49  And, behold, I send the promise of my Father upon you: but tarry ye in the city of Jerusalem, until ye be endued with power from on high. | John 20:19    Then the same day at evening, being the first day of the week, when the doors were shut where the disciples were assembled for fear of the Jews, came Jesus and stood in the midst, and saith unto them, Peace be unto you.<br>John 20:20    And when he had so said, he showed unto them his hands and his side. Then were the disciples glad, when they saw the Lord.<br>John 20:21    Then said Jesus to them again, Peace be unto you: as my Father hath sent me, even so send I you.<br>John 20:22    And when he had said this, he breathed on them, and saith unto them, Receive ye the Holy Ghost:<br>John 20:23    Whosoever sins ye remit, they are remitted unto them; and whosesoever sins ye retain, they are retained. |
| | 20:26  And after eight days again his disciples were within, and Thomas with them: then came Jesus, the doors being shut.... | | John 20:24    But Thomas, one of the twelve, called Didymus, was not with them when Jesus came.<br>John 20:25    The other disciples therefore said unto him, We have seen the Lord. But he said unto them, Except I shall see in his hands the print of the nails, and put my finger into the print of the nails, and thrust my hand into his side, I will not believe.<br>John 20:26    And after eight days again his disciples were within, and Thomas with them: then came Jesus, the doors being shut, and stood in the midst, and said, Peace be unto you.<br>John 20:27    Then saith he to Thomas, Reach hither thy finger, and behold my hands; and reach hither thy hand, and thrust it into my side: and be not faithless, but believing.<br>John 20:28    And Thomas answered and said unto him, My Lord and my God.<br>John 20:29    Jesus saith unto him, Thomas, because |

| Matthew | Mark | Important Events |
|---|---|---|
| | | |
| 28:15 | 16:13 | **3rd time Jesus came to the disciples** John 21:4 & 21:14 Map 139 |

| | Key Scriptures & Footnotes | Luke | John |
|---|---|---|---|
| | | | thou hast seen me, thou hast believed: blessed are they that have not seen, and yet have believed. |
| | 20:30 And many other signs truly did Jesus in the presence of his disciples, which are not written in this book: | | John 20:30 And many other signs truly did Jesus in the presence of his disciples, which are not written in this book: |
| | | | John 20:31 But these are written, that ye might believe that Jesus is the Christ, the Son of God; and that believing ye might have life through his name. |
| | 21:1 After things Jesus showed himself again to the disciples at the sea of Tiberias;.... | 24:49 | John 21:1 After these things Jesus showed himself again to the disciples at the sea of Tiberias; and on this wise showed he himself. |
| | | | John 21:2 There were together Simon Peter, and Thomas called Didymus, and Nathanael of Cana in Galilee, and the sons of Zebedee, and two other of his disciples. |
| | | | John 21:3 Simon Peter saith unto them, I go a-fishing. They say unto him, We also go with thee. They went forth, and entered into a ship immediately; and that night they caught nothing. |
| | | | John 21:4 But when the morning was now come, Jesus stood on the shore: but the disciples knew not that it was Jesus. |
| | | | John 21:5 Then Jesus saith unto them, Children, have ye any meat? They answered him, No. |
| | | | John 21:6 And he said unto them, Cast the net on the right side of the ship, and ye shall find. They cast therefore, and now they were not able to draw it for the multitude of fishes. |
| | | | John 21:7 Therefore that disciple whom Jesus loved saith unto Peter, It is the Lord. Now when Simon Peter heard that it was the Lord, he girt his fisher's coat unto him, (for he was naked,) and did cast himself into the sea. |
| | | | John 21:8 And the other disciples came in a little ship; (for they were not far from land, but as it were two hundred cubits,) dragging the net with fishes. |
| | | | John 21:9 As soon then as they were come to land, they saw a fire of coals there, and fish laid thereon, and bread. |
| | | | John 21:10 Jesus saith unto them, Bring of the fish which ye have now caught. |
| | | | John 21:11 Simon Peter went up, and drew the net to land full of great fishes, an hundred and fifty and three: and for all there were so many, yet was not the net broken. |
| | | | John 21:12 Jesus saith unto them, Come and dine. And none of the disciples durst ask him, Who art thou? knowing that it was the Lord. |
| | | | John 21:13 Jesus then cometh, and taketh bread, and giveth them, and fish likewise. |
| | 21:14 This is now the third time that Jesus showed himself to his disciples, after that he was risen from the dead. | | John 21:14 This is now the third time that Jesus showed himself to his disciples, after that he was risen from the dead. |
| | | | John 21:15 So when they had dined, Jesus saith to Simon Peter, Simon, son of Jonas, lovest thou me more than these? He saith unto him, Yea, Lord; thou knowest that I love thee. He saith unto him, Feed my lambs. |
| | | | John 21:16 He saith to him again the second time, Simon, son of Jonas, lovest thou me? He saith unto him, Yea, Lord; thou knowest that I love thee. He saith unto him, Feed my sheep. |
| | | | John 21:17 He saith unto him the third time, Simon, son of Jonas, lovest thou me? Peter was grieved because he said unto him the third time, Lovest thou me? And he said unto him, Lord, thou knowest all things; thou knowest that I love thee. Jesus saith unto him, Feed my sheep. |
| | | | John 21:18 Verily, verily, I say unto thee, When thou wast young, thou girdedst thyself, and walkedst whither thou wouldest: but when thou shalt be old, thou shalt stretch forth thy hands, and another shall gird thee, and carry thee whither thou wouldest not. |

| Matthew | Mark | Important Events |
|---|---|---|
| | | |
| Matt. 28:16   Then the eleven disciples went away into Galilee, into a mountain where Jesus had appointed them.<br>Matt. 28:17       And when they saw him, they worshipped him: but some doubted. | | **4th time Jesus came to the disciples**<br>Matt. 28:16<br><br>Map 140 |
| Matt. 28:18   And Jesus came and spake unto them, saying, All power is given unto me in heaven and in earth.<br>Matt. 28:19   Go ye therefore, and teach all nations, baptizing them in the name of the Father, and of the Son, and of the Holy Ghost:<br>Matt. 28:20       Teaching them to observe all things whatsoever I have commanded you: and, lo, I am with you always, even unto the end of the world. Amen. | | |
| | Mark 16:14   Afterward he appeared unto the eleven as they sat at meat, and upbraided them with their unbelief and hardness of heart, because they believed not them which had seen him after he was risen.<br>Mark 16:15   And he said unto them, Go ye into all the world, and preach the gospel to every creature.<br>Mark 16:16   He that believeth and is baptized shall be saved; but he that believeth not shall be damned.<br>Mark 16:17   And these signs shall follow them that believe; In my name shall they cast out devils; they shall speak with new tongues;<br>Mark 16:18   They shall take up serpents; and if they drink any deadly thing, it shall not hurt them; they shall lay hands on the sick, and they shall recover. | **5th time Jesus came to the disciples**<br>Mark 16:14<br><br>Map 141 |
| | | Map 142 |
| | | |
| | | |
| | Mark 16:19   So then after the Lord had spoken unto them, he was received up into heaven, and sat on the right hand of God. | Map 143 |
| | | |
| | | |

| Key Scriptures & Footnotes | Luke | John |
|---|---|---|
| | | John 21:19  This spake he, signifying by what death he should glorify God. And when he had spoken this, he saith unto him, Follow me.<br>John 21:20    Then Peter, turning about, seeth the disciple whom Jesus loved following; which also leaned on his breast at supper, and said, Lord, which is he that betrayeth thee?<br>John 21:21   Peter seeing him saith to Jesus, Lord, and what shall this man do?<br>John 21:22  Jesus saith unto him, If I will that he tarry till I come, what is that to thee? follow thou me.<br>John 21:23   Then went this saying abroad among the brethren, that that disciple should not die: yet Jesus said not unto him, He shall not die; but, If I will that he tarry till I come, what is that to thee? |
| 28:16  Then the eleven disciples went away into Galilee, into a mountain....<br>28:17...they saw him...but some doubted. | 24:49 | |
| 28:18  And Jesus came and spake....<br>28:19 Go ye therefore, and teach all nations, baptizing them in the name of the Father, and of the Son, and of the Holy Ghost:<br>28:20 Teaching them to observe all.... | | |
| 16:15  And he said unto them, Go ye into all the world, and preach the gospel to every creature. | | |
| 24:50a  And he led them out as far as to Bethany,<br><br>See footnote[196] | Luke 24:50a    And he led them out as far as to Bethany, | |
| | Luke 24:50b  and he lifted up his hands, and blessed them. | |
| 16:19...he was received[197] up into heaven, and sat on the right hand of God. | Luke 24:51    And it came to pass, while he blessed them, he was parted from them, and carried up into heaven. | |
| 24:52  And they worshipped him, and returned to Jerusalem.... | Luke 24:52  And they worshipped him, and returned to Jerusalem with great joy:<br>Luke 24:53    And were continually in the temple, praising and blessing God. Amen. | |
| 21:24  This is the **disciple which testifieth**[198] of these | | John 21:24    This is the disciple which testifieth of these things, and wrote these things: and we know that his testimony is true. |

Acts 1:4-8 (*This is where Acts 1:4-8 fits in the time sequence of the Gospels.*)
Acts 1:9-10 (*This is where Acts 1:9-10 fits in the time sequence of the Gospels.*)
John 21:24   This is the disciple which **testifieth** of these things, and wrote these things: and we know that **his testimony is true.**
e John 19:35  And he **that saw it** bare record, and his **record is true**: and he knoweth that **he saith true,** that ye might believe.
n wrote a testimony of those events in which he actually took part or of which he had first hand information.*)

| Matthew | Mark | Important Events |
|---------|------|------------------|
| | | |
| | Mark 16:20    And they went forth, and preached every where, the Lord working with them, and confirming the word with signs following. Amen. | |

| | | | |
|---|---|---|---|
| | things: and we know that his testimony is true.<br>21:25 And there are also many other things which Jesus did,... | | John 21:25 And there are also many other things which Jesus did, the which, if they should be written every one, I suppose that even the world itself could not contain the books that should be written. Amen. |
| | 16:20 And they went forth, and preached every where.... | | |

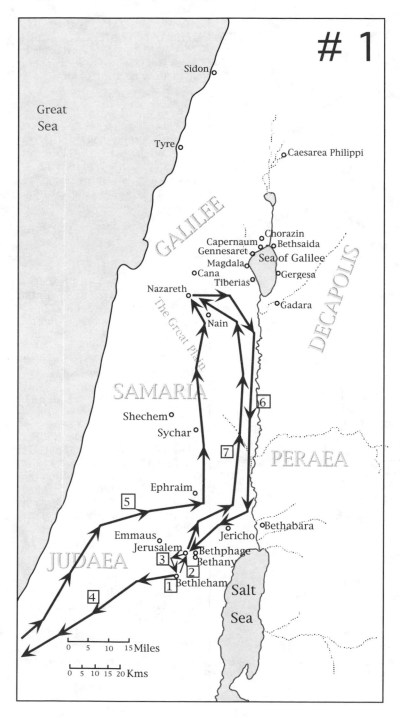

# 1

Great
Sea

Sidon o

Tyre o

o Caesarea Philippi

GALILEE

Chorazin
Capernaum   o Bethsaida
Gennesaret o   Sea of Galilee
Magdala o
Cana o      o Gergesa
Tiberias

Nazareth o

o Gadara

DECAPOLIS

Nain o

SAMARIA

Shechem o

Sychar o

PERAEA

Ephraim o

5

Emmaus o        Jericho
Jerusalem     o Bethabara
3       Bethphage
2       Bethany

4       1   Bethleham

Salt

Sea

JUDAEA

0   5   10   15 Miles

0   5  10 15  20 Kms

Map 1    JESUS BORN IN
BETHLEHEM Matt. 1:25a &
Luke 2:7  And she brought forth
her firstborn son,
                    PAGE 5

Map 2   BETHLEHEM TO
JERUSALEM -- Luke 2:22 ...
they brought him to Jerusalem,

                    PAGE 5

Map 3    JERUSALEM TO
BETHLEHEM -- Matt. 2:8 &
2:9   And he sent them to
Bethlehem, ... till it came and
stood over where the young child
was.
                    PAGE 7

Map 4   BETHLEHEM TO
EGYPT -- Matt. 2:14  When he
arose, he took the young child
and his mother by night, and
departed into Egypt:
                    PAGE 7

Map 5        EGYPT TO
NAZARETH -- Matt. 2:23 &
Luke 2:39b they returned into
Galilee, to their own city
Nazareth.
                    PAGE 7

Map 6    NAZARETH TO
JERUSALEM -- Luke 2:42
And when he was twelve years
old, they went up to Jerusalem

                    PAGE 7

Map 7    JERUSALEM TO
NAZARETH -- Luke 2:51  And
he went down with them, and
came to Nazareth, ...
                    PAGE 7

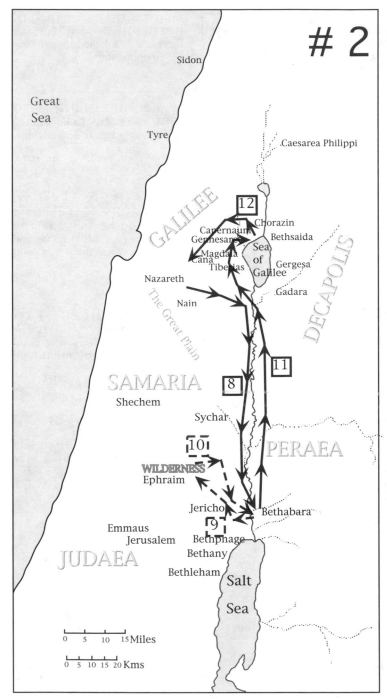

Map 8 FROM GALILEE TO JORDAN -- Mark 1:9, Luke 3:21, & Matt. 3:13 Then cometh Jesus from Galilee to Jordan unto John, to be baptized of him.

PAGE 9

Map 9 FROM JORDAN INTO THE WILDERNESS FOR 40 DAYS -- Matt. 4:1, Mark 1:12, & Luke 4:1 And Jesus being full of the Holy Ghost returned from Jordan, and was led by the Spirit into the wilderness,

PAGE 10

Map 10 WILDERNESS TO JORDAN TO LISTEN TO JOHN THE BAPTIST FOR THREE DAYS -- John 1:26 ... but there standeth one among you, ..., John 1:29 The next day John seeth Jesus coming ..., & John 1:35 & 36 Again the next day... Behold the Lamb of God!

PAGE 11

Map 11 JORDAN TO GALILEE -- TO AREA OF BETHSAIDA? -- Luke 4:14a & John 1:43a The day following Jesus would go forth into Galilee, John 1:43b & 1:44 and findeth Philip... Now Philip was of Bethsaida, ...

PAGE 12

Map 12 TO CANA OF GALILEE -- John 2:1 And the third day there was a marriage in Cana of Galilee; ...

PAGE 13

Number of lines = year of Jesus' Ministry ↓

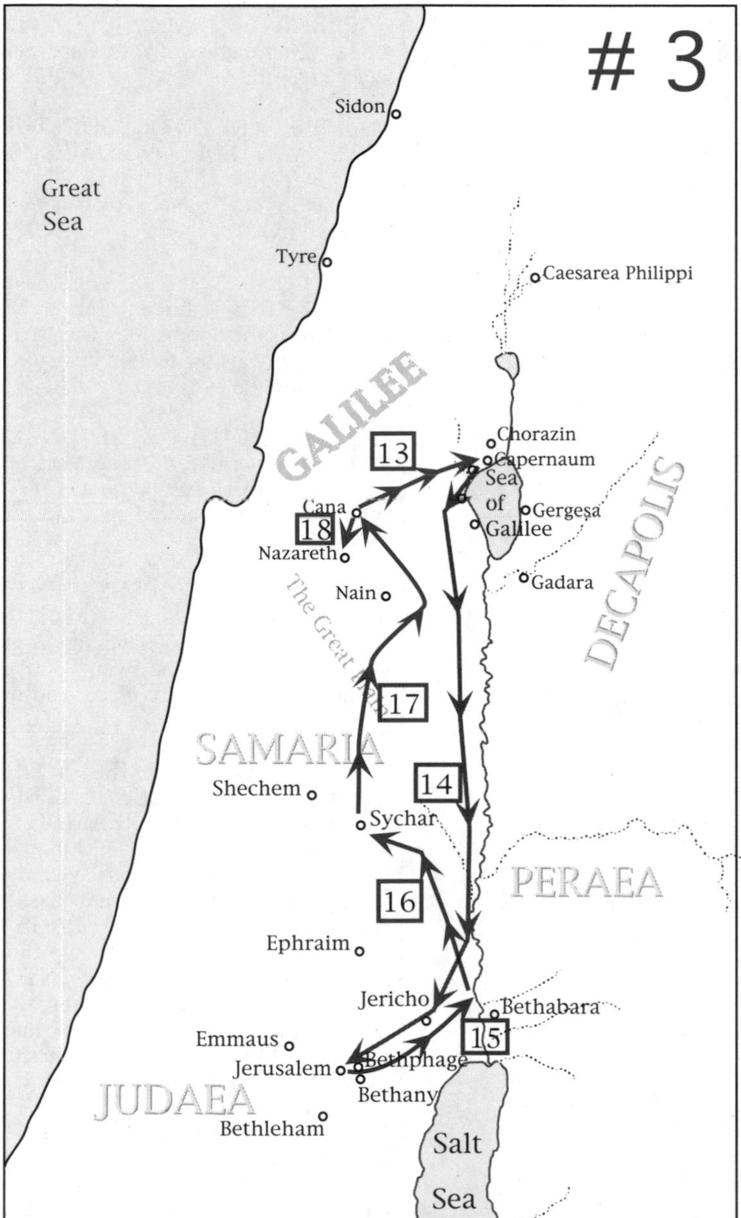

# 3

Great
Sea

Sidon

Tyre

Caesarea Philippi

GALILEE

13

Chorazin
Capernaum
Sea
of
Galilee

Cana

18

Gergesa

Nazareth

Gadara

DECAPOLIS

Nain

The Great

17

SAMARIA

Shechem

14

Sychar

16

PERAEA

Ephraim

Jericho

Bethabara

Emmaus

Bethphage

15

Jerusalem

Bethany

JUDAEA

Bethany

Bethleham

Salt

Sea

0　5　10　15 Miles

0　5　10　15　20 Kms

Map 13　CANA TO CAPERNAUM -- John 2:12 After this he went down to Capernaum,

PAGE 13

Map 14　CAPERNAUM TO JERUSALEM FOR 1ST PASSOVER -- John 2:13　And the Jews' passover was at hand

PAGE 13

Map 15　JERUSALEM TO JORDAN RIVER -- John 3:22 After these things came Jesus and his disciples into the land of Judaea; and there he tarried with them, and baptized.

PAGE 14

Map 16　JORDAN RIVER TO SYCHAR -- John 4:5　Then cometh he to a city of Samaria, which is called Sychar,

PAGE 15

Map 17　SYCHAR TO GALILEE TO CANA -- John 4:43　Now after two days he departed thence, and went into Galilee. John 4:46　So Jesus came again to Cana of Galilee.

PAGE 17

Map 18　JESUS TO NAZARETH -- Luke 4:16 And he came to Nazareth,

PAGE 17

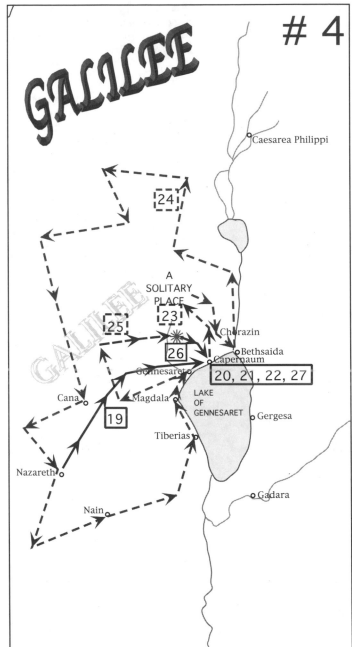

**Map 19     NAZARETH TO CAPERNAUM**    Matt. 4:13 & Luke 4:31a   And came down to Capernaum, a city of Galilee,          PAGE 18

**Map 20    THEY FORSOOK THEIR NETS AND FOLLOWED JESUS --** Matt. 4:20 & Mark 1:18          And straightway they forsook their nets, and followed him.          PAGE 18

**Map 21          CAPERNAUM SYNAGOGUE --** Luke 4:31b & Mark 1:21   And they went into Capernaum; and straightway on the sabbath day he entered into the synagogue,   PAGE 19

**Map 22    HOUSE OF SIMON AND ANDREW --** Luke 4:38 & Mark 1:29 ..., when they were come out of the synagogue, they entered into the house of Simon and Andrew, ...   PAGE 19

**Map 23   1ST TIME JESUS WENT TO A SOLITARY PLACE --** Mark 1:35 And in the morning, rising up a great while before day, he went out, and departed into a solitary place, and there prayed.          PAGE 19

**Map 24    1ST TIME JESUS WENT ABOUT ALL GALILEE TEACHING, PREACHING, AND HEALING --** Matt. 4:23, Mark 1:39, & Luke 4:44 And he preached in their synagogues throughout all Galilee, and cast out devils.          PAGE 19

**Map 25    HE WENT UP INTO A MOUNTAIN --** Matt. 5:1   And seeing the multitudes, he went up into a mountain Matt. 5:2   And he opened his mouth, and taught them,     PAGE 19

**Map 26        AT THE LAKE OF GENNESARET --** Luke 5:1 & 5:5   And it came to pass, ... by the lake of Gennesaret,...   he sat down, and taught the people out of the ship.     PAGE 24

**Map 27   THEY FORSOOK ALL, AND FOLLOWED HIM. --** Luke 5:11   And when they had brought their ships to land, they forsook all, and followed him.
PAGE 25

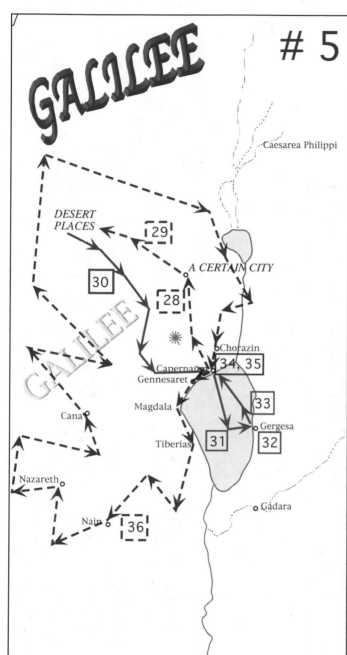

**Map 28  A CERTAIN CITY A LEPER HEALED** -- Matt. 8:1, Mark 1:40, & Luke 5:12    ...a man full of leprosy...besought him, saying, Lord, if thou wilt, thou canst make me clean. And he put forth his hand, and touched him, saying, I will: be thou clean.
PAGE 25

**Map 29  IN DESERT PLACES THEY CAME TO HIM** -- Mark 1:45   Jesus could no more openly enter into the city, but was without in desert places:
PAGE 25

**Map 30    ENTERED INTO CAPERNAUM A CENTURION** -- Matt. 8:5  And when Jesus was entered into Capernaum, there came unto him a centurion, beseeching him,   PAGE 25

**Map 31   JESUS CALMED THE 1ST STORM AT SEA** -- Matt. 8:24   And, behold, there arose a great tempest in the sea,   PAGE 26

**Map 32   JESUS SET TWO MEN FREE OF DEVILS IN THE GERGESENES** -- Matt. 8:28 ... there he met two possessed with devils, coming out of the tombs, ...   PAGE 26

**Map 33    GERGESENES TO CAPERNAUM BY SHIP** -- Matt. 9:1 And he entered into a ship, and passed over, and came into his own city.
PAGE 27

**Map 34 IN CAPERNAUM** -- Matt. 9:9, Mark 2:14, & Luke 5:27 ... and saw a publican, named Levi, sitting at the receipt of custom: and he said unto him, Follow me.   PAGE 27

**Map 35   A CERTAIN RULER AND THE 1ST WOMAN WITH AN ISSUE OF BLOOD TWELVE YEARS** -- Matt. 9:18  A certain ruler, and worshipped him, saying, My daughter is even now dead   PAGE 28

**Map 36   2ND TIME JESUS WENT ABOUT ALL THE CITIES AND VILLAGES** -- Matt. 9:35  Jesus went about all the cities and villages, teaching ...and preaching the gospel of the kingdom, and healing   PAGE 29

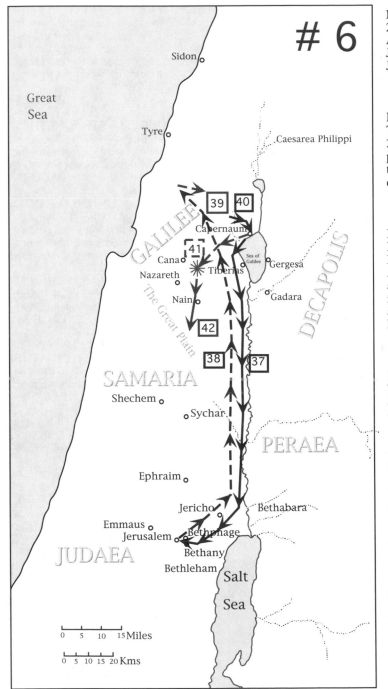

Map 37  TO JERUSALEM FOR 2ND PASSOVER -- John 5:1 After this there was a feast of the Jews; and Jesus went up to Jerusalem.

PAGE 29

Map 38  1ST TRIP THROUGH THE CORN FIELDS -- Mark 2:23 & Luke 6:1 And it came to pass on the second sabbath after the first, that he went through the corn fields;

PAGE 31

Map 39  JESUS HEALS 1ST MAN WITH A WITHERED HAND -- Mark 3:1 & Luke 6:6 And it came to pass also on another sabbath, that he entered into the synagogue and taught: and there was a man whose right hand was withered.

PAGE 31

Map 40  JESUS WITHDREW TO THE SEA -- Mark 3:7 But Jesus withdrew himself with his disciples to the sea

PAGE 31

Map 41  JESUS WENT INTO A MOUNTAIN AND CHOSE TWELVE -- Mark 3:13 And he goeth up into a mountain & Luke 6:13 And when it was day, he called unto him his disciples: and of them he chose twelve

PAGE 32

Map 42  JESUS STOOD IN THE PLAIN -- Luke 6:17 And he came down with them, and stood in the plain

PAGE 32

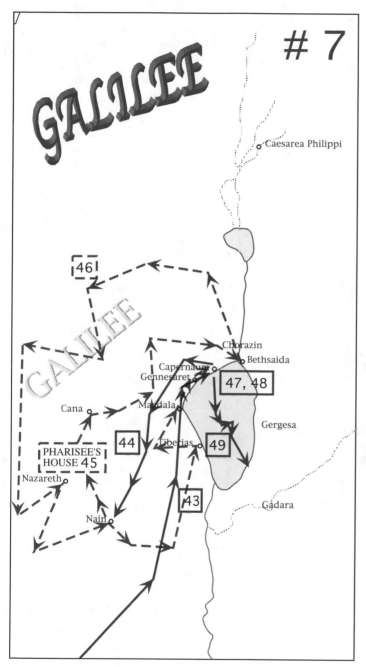

Map 43  JESUS ENTERED CAPERNAUM AND A CERTAIN CENTURION'S SERVANT... -- Luke 7:1 ... he entered into Capernaum. Luke 7:2   And a certain centurion's servant, ...

PAGE 34

Map 44   JESUS WENT TO NAIN -- Luke 7:11   And it came to pass the day after, that he went into a city called Nain ... Luke 7:15   And he that was dead sat up, ...

PAGE 35

Map 45   JESUS WENT TO THE PHARISEE'S HOUSE AND WAS ANOINTED-- Luke 7:37   And, behold, a woman in the city, which was a sinner, when she knew that Jesus sat at meat in the Pharisee's house, brought an alabaster box of ointment, ...

PAGE 36

Map 46   3RD TIME JESUS WENT THROUGH EVERY CITY AND VILLAGE OF GALILEE -- Luke 8:1 And it came to pass afterward, that he went throughout every city and village, preaching ...

PAGE 37

Map 47   JESUS TAUGHT BY THE SEA SIDE -- Mark 4:1   And he began again to teach by the sea side:

PAGE 37

Map 48   2ND TIME JESUS' MOTHER CAME -- Luke 8:19 Then came to him his mother and his brethren, and could not come at him for the press.

PAGE 38

Map 49   JESUS CALMED THE 2ND STORM AT SEA -- Mark 4:35 & Luke 8:22 Let us go over unto the other side of the lake. Mark 4:37 And there arose a great storm of wind, and the waves beat into the ship

PAGE 38

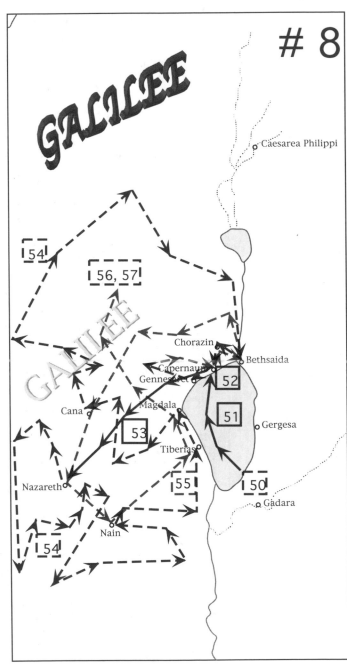

**Map 50   JESUS SET A MAN FREE OF DEVILS IN THE COUNTRY OF GADARENES** -- Mark 5:1 & Luke 8:26 And they arrived at the country of the Gadarenes, which is over against Galilee. Luke 8:33   Then went the devils out of the man, and entered into the swine....
PAGE 39

**Map 51   JESUS WENT BY SHIP TO THE OTHER SIDE OF THE SEA** -- Luke 8:40 & Mark 5:21   And when Jesus was passed over again by ship unto the other side....          PAGE 40

**Map 52   IN CAPERNAUM JESUS RAISED JAIRUS' DAUGHTER FROM THE DEAD** -- Matt. 9:18, Mark 5:22, & Luke 8:41   And, behold, there came a man named Jairus, and he was a ruler of the synagogue...:          PAGE 40

**Map 53   JESUS' 2ND MINISTRY TRIP TO NAZARETH** -- Mark 6:1   And he went out from thence, and came into his own country; and his disciples follow him.
PAGE 41

**Map 54   JESUS WENT ABOUT  THE VILLAGES OF GALILEE** -- Mark 6:6b And Jesus went about the villages, teaching          PAGE 41

**Map 55   JESUS DEPARTED TO TEACH AND TO PREACH IN THE APOSTLES' CITIES** -- Mark 6:12, Luke 9:6 & Matt. 11:1  And it came to pass, when Jesus had made an end of commanding his twelve disciples, he departed thence to teach and to preach in their cities.          PAGE 43

**Map 56   JESUS' 2ND TRIP THROUGH THE CORN IN GALILEE**-- Matt. 12:1 At that time Jesus went on the sabbath day through the corn;          PAGE 44

**Map 57   JESUS HEALED 2ND MAN WITH WITHERED HAND** -- Matt. 12:9 And when he was departed thence, he went into their synagogue: & Matt. 12:10 And, behold, there was a man which had his hand withered.          PAGE 45

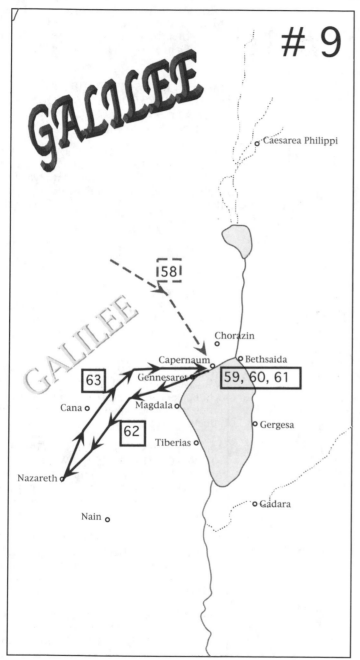

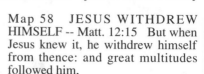

Map 58   JESUS WITHDREW HIMSELF -- Matt. 12:15  But when Jesus knew it, he withdrew himself from thence: and great multitudes followed him,

PAGE 45

Map 59   3RD TIME JESUS' MOTHER AND HIS BRETHREN STOOD WITHOUT -- Matt. 12:46 While he yet talked to the people, behold, his mother and his brethren stood without, desiring to speak with him.

PAGE 47

Map 60   JESUS SAT BY THE SEA -- Matt. 13:1   The same day went Jesus out of the house, and sat by the sea side.

PAGE 47

Map 61   JESUS WENT INTO A SHIP TO TEACH THE MULTITUDE -- Matt. 13:2   And great multitudes were gathered together unto him, so that he went into a ship, and sat; ...

PAGE 47

MAP 62  3RD MINISTRY TRIP TO NAZARETH -- Matt. 13:54 And when he was come into his own country, he taught them in their synagogue,

PAGE 49

Map 63   JESUS RETURNED TO CAPERNAUM(?) BEFORE JOHN THE BAPTIST'S DEATH. -- Matt 14:12   And his disciples came and took up the body, and buried it, and went and told Jesus.

PAGE 49

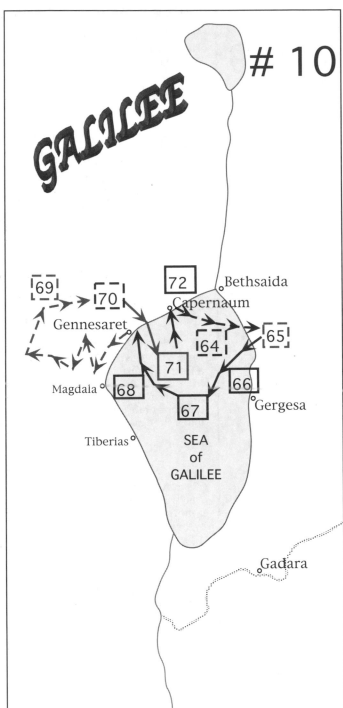

Map 64   JESUS HEARD OF JOHN'S DEATH AND DEPARTED BY SHIP -- Matt. 14:13a, Mark 6:32, Luke 9:10,& John 6:1   After these things Jesus went over the sea of Galilee, which is the sea of Tiberias.                                                                PAGE 50

Map 65   JESUS SENT THE 5000 AWAY AND DEPARTED INTO A MOUNTAIN TO PRAY -- Matt. 14:23 & Mark 6:46   he departed into a mountain to pray. PAGE 51

Map 66   1ST NIGHT THAT JESUS WALKS ON THE WATER -- Mark 6:48 & Matt. 14:25   And in the fourth watch of the night Jesus went unto them, walking on the sea.                                                PAGE 51

Map 67   AND THE WIND CEASED Mark 6:51 & Matt. 14:32   And when they were come into the ship, the wind ceased.                                                       PAGE 51

Map 68   THEY CAME INTO THE LAND OF GENNESARET -- Mark 6:53 & Matt. 14:34   And when they were gone over, they came into the land of Gennesaret.                                                  PAGE 51

Map 69   JESUS ENTERED INTO VILLAGES AND CITIES Mark 6:56   And whithersoever he entered, into villages, or cities, or country, they laid the sick in the streets                                               PAGE 52

Map 70   JESUS LEAVES WITHOUT SENDING THE PEOPLE AWAY -- John 6:15   When Jesus therefore perceived that they would come and take him by force, to make him a king, he departed again into a mountain himself alone.        PAGE 52

Map 71   2ND NIGHT THAT JESUS WALKS ON THE WATER -- John 6:19 So when they had rowed about five and twenty or thirty furlongs, they see Jesus walking on the sea, ...        PAGE 52

Map 72   IMMEDIATELY THE SHIP WAS AT CAPERNAUM -- John 6:21 Then they willingly received him into the ship: and immediately the ship was at the land whither they went. John 6:59   These things said he in the synagogue, as he taught in Capernaum.        PAGE 52

Number of lines = year of Jesus' Ministry ↓

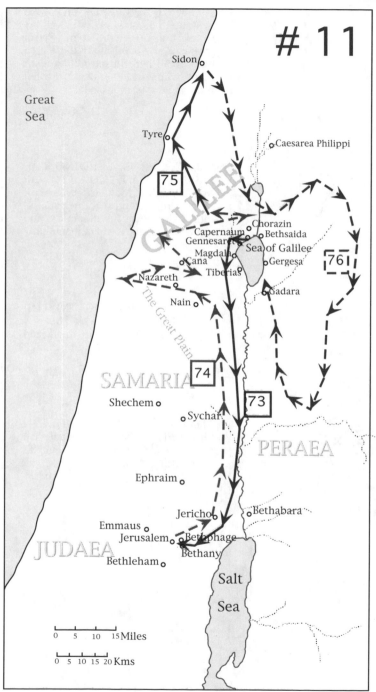

**Map 73  3RD PASSOVER, JESUS WENT FROM CAPERNAUM TO JERUSALEM--** John 6:4 And the passover, a feast of the Jews, was nigh ... John 7:1 After these things ... (That were done in chapter 6 of John.)

PAGE 54

**MAP 74  JESUS WALKED FROM JERUSALEM TO GALILEE --** John 7:1 After these things Jesus walked in Galilee: for he would not walk in the Jewry, because theJews sought to kill him.

PAGE 55

**MAP 75   GALILEE TO TYRE AND SIDON --** Matt. 15:21 & Mark 7:24  And from thence he arose, and went into the borders of Tyre and Sidon

PAGE 56

**MAP 76     TYRE AND SIDON    THROUGH DECAPOLIS UNTO THE SEA OF GALILEE --.** Matt. 15:29 & Mark 7:31   And again, departing from the coasts of Tyre and Sidon, he came unto the sea of Galilee, through the midst of the coasts of Decapolis.

PAGE 56

Number of lines = year of Jesus' Ministry ↓

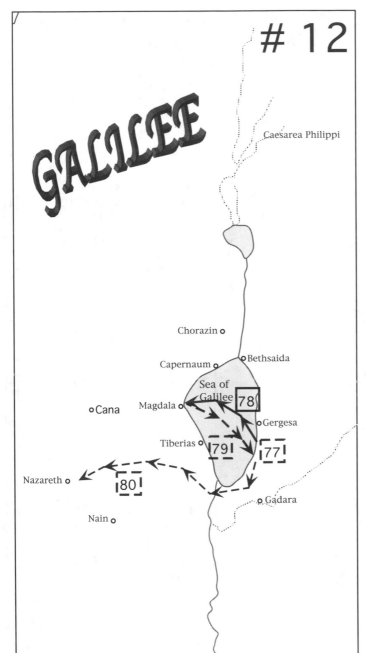

# 12

GALILEE

Caesarea Philippi

Chorazin o

Capernaum o          o Bethsaida

Sea of
Galilee          78

o Cana          Magdala o

o Gergesa

Tiberias o          79          77

Nazareth o          80

Nain o          o Gadara

Map 77   JESUS FEEDS THE 4000 -- Matt. 15:33 & Mark 8:4   And his disciples answered him, From whence can a man satisfy these men with bread here in the wilderness? Mark 8:9a   And they that had eaten were about four thousand:

PAGE 56

Map 78   FROM FEEDING THE 4000 TO THE COASTS OF MAGDALA -- Matt. 15:39 & Mark 8:10   And straightway he entered into a ship with his disciples, and came into the parts of Dalmanutha.

PAGE 57

Map 79   DEPARTED TO THE OTHER SIDE -- Matt. 16:4b & Mark 8:13   And he left them, and entering into the ship again departed to the other side.

PAGE 57

Map 80  JESUS ABODE STILL IN GALILEE -- John 7:9   When he had said these words unto them, he abode still in Galilee.

PAGE 58

Number of lines = year of Jesus' Ministry ↓

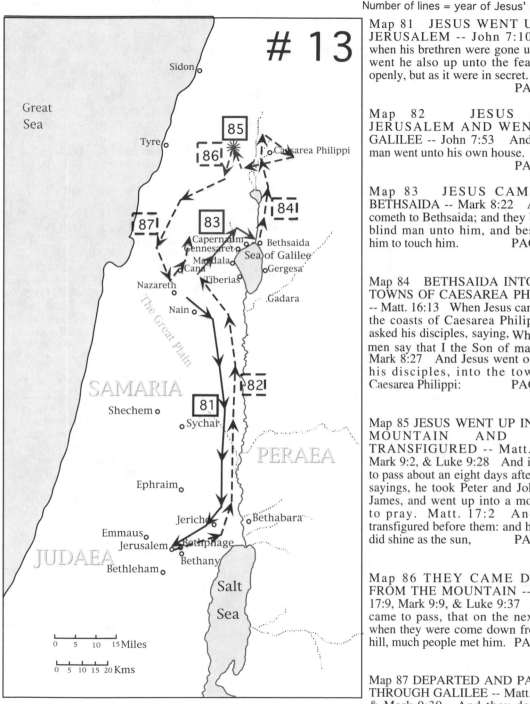

# 13

Great
Sea

Sidon

Tyre

Caesarea Philippi

85

86

87

83

84

Capernaum
Gennesaret
Magdala
Cana
Nazareth
Bethsaida
Sea of Galilee
Gergesa
Tiberias

Nain

Gadara

SAMARIA

Shechem

82

81

Sychar

PERAEA

Ephraim

Jericho

Bethabara

Emmaus

Jerusalem

Bethphage

JUDAEA

Bethany

Bethleham

Salt

Sea

The Great Plain

0   5   10   15 Miles

0   5   10  15  20 Kms

**Map 81   JESUS WENT UP TO JERUSALEM** -- John 7:10   But when his brethren were gone up, then went he also up unto the feast, not openly, but as it were in secret.
                              PAGE 58

**Map  82      JESUS  LEFT JERUSALEM  AND  WENT  TO GALILEE** -- John 7:53   And every man went unto his own house.
                              PAGE 59

**Map 83    JESUS  CAME  TO BETHSAIDA** -- Mark 8:22   And he cometh to Bethsaida; and they bring a blind man unto him, and besought him to touch him.         PAGE  59

**Map 84   BETHSAIDA INTO THE TOWNS OF CAESAREA PHILIPPI** -- Matt. 16:13   When Jesus came into the coasts of Caesarea Philippi, he asked his disciples, saying, Whom do men say that I the Son of man am? Mark 8:27   And Jesus went out, and his disciples, into the towns of Caesarea Philippi:         PAGE 60

**Map 85 JESUS WENT UP INTO A MOUNTAIN    AND    WAS TRANSFIGURED** -- Matt. 17:1, Mark 9:2, & Luke 9:28   And it came to pass about an eight days after these sayings, he took Peter and John and James, and went up into a mountain to pray.   Matt. 17:2   And was transfigured before them: and his face did shine as the sun,         PAGE 61

**Map 86 THEY CAME DOWN FROM THE MOUNTAIN** -- Matt. 17:9, Mark 9:9, & Luke 9:37   And it came to pass, that on the next day, when they were come down from the hill, much people met him.  PAGE 61

**Map 87 DEPARTED AND PASSED THROUGH GALILEE** -- Matt. 17:22 & Mark 9:30   And they departed thence, and passed through Galilee
                              PAGE 62

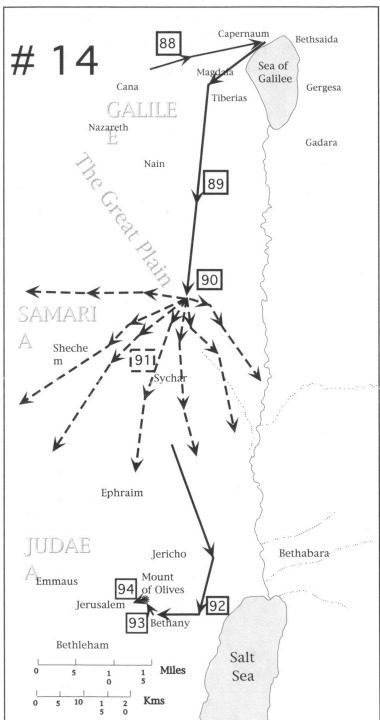

# 14

Capernaum
Bethsaida
88
Magdala
Sea of Galilee
Cana
Tiberias
Gergesa
GALILEE
Nazareth
Gadara
Nain
89
The Great Plain
90
SAMARIA
Shechem
91
Sychar
Ephraim
JUDAEA
Jericho
Bethabara
Emmaus
Mount of Olives
94
Jerusalem
92
93 Bethany
Bethleham
Salt Sea
0 5 1 0 1 5 Miles
0 5 10 1 5 2 0 Kms

Map 88 AND CAME TO CAPERNAUM -- Mark 9:33a & Matt. 17:24 And when they were come to Capernaum, they that received tribute money came to Peter, PAGE 62

Map 89 JESUS SET HIS FACE TOWARD JERUSALEM -- Luke 9:51 And it came to pass,when the time was come that he should bereceived up, he stedfastly set his face to go to Jerusalem. PAGE 65

Map 90 JESUS SENT MESSENGERS INTO A VILLAGE OF THE SAMARITANS Mark 10:1a & Matt. 19:1a And it came to pass, that when Jesus had finished these sayings, he departed from Galilee,... Luke 9:52 And sent messengers before his face: and they went, and entered into a village of the Samaritans, to make ready for him. PAGE 65

MAP 91 SEVENTY BEFORE HIS FACE INTO EVERY CITY AND PLACE -- Luke 10:1 After these things the Lord appointed other seventy also, and sent them two and two before his face into every city and place, whither he himself would come. PAGE 65

Map 92 TO MARTHA & MARY'S HOUSE IN BETHANY -- Luke 10:38 Now it came to pass, as they went, that he entered into a certain village: and a certain woman named Martha received him into her house. PAGE 67

MAP 93 BETHANY TO THE MOUNT OF OLIVES -- John 8:1 Jesus went unto the mount of Olives. PAGE 73

Map 94 JERUSALEM THE FEAST OF THE DEDICATION John 10:22 And it was at Jerusalem the feast of the dedication, PAGE 78

Number of lines = year of Jesus' Ministry ↓

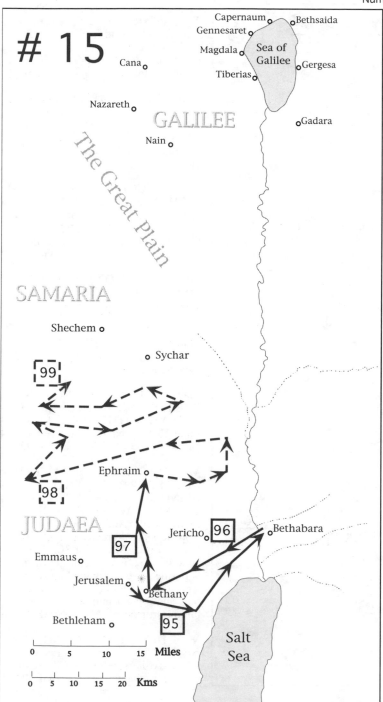

# # 15

**Map 95  JERUSALEM TO BEYOND JORDAN** -- John 10:40  And went away again beyond Jordan into the place where John at first baptized; and there he abode.

PAGE 78

**Map 96  JESUS CAME TO BETHANY TO CALL LAZARUS FORTH** -- John 11:17  Then when Jesus came, he found that he had lain in the grave four days already.

PAGE 79

**Map 97  JESUS WENT TO A CITY CALLED EPHRAIM** -- John 11:54  Jesus therefore walked no more openly among the Jews; but went thence unto a country near to the wilderness, into a city called Ephraim,

PAGE 80

**MAP 98  HE WENT THROUGH THE CITIES AND VILLAGES, TEACHING** Luke 13:22  And he went through the cities and villages, teaching, and journeying toward Jerusalem.

PAGE 81

**MAP 99  JESUS TAUGHT IN HEROD'S TERRITORY** -- Luke 13:31  The same day there came certain of the Pharisees, saying unto him, Get thee out, and depart hence: for Herod will kill thee.

PAGE 81

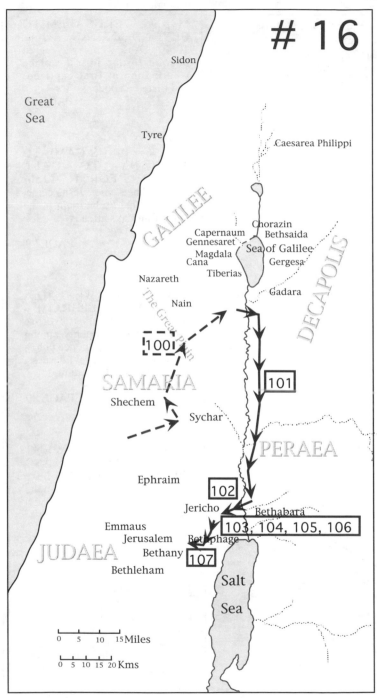

# 16

Great
Sea

Sidon

Tyre

Caesarea Philippi

GALILEE

Chorazin
Capernaum    Bethsaida
Gennesaret
Magdala    Sea of Galilee
Cana              Gergesa
Nazareth    Tiberias

DECAPOLIS

Nain                    Gadara

100

SAMARIA

101

Shechem

Sychar

PERAEA

Ephraim

102

Jericho        Bethabara

Emmaus              103, 104, 105, 106
Jerusalem    Bethphage
Bethany
107

Bethleham

Salt

Sea

0    5    10   15 Miles

0   5  10  15 20 Kms

Map 100   JESUS TRAVILED UP
TO SAMARIA AND GALILEE --
Luke 17:11   And it came to pass,
as he went to Jerusalem, that he
passed through the midst of Sama
ria and Galilee.          PAGE 86

Map 101   CAME INTO THE
COASTS OF JUDAEA BEYOND
JORDAN -- Matt. 19:1b & Mark
10:1b ... and cometh into the coasts
of Judaea by the farther side of Jor
dan:              PAGE 89

Map 102  GOING UP TO
JERUSALEM Luke 18:31, Matt.
20:17   And Jesus going up to
Jerusalem...& Mark 10:32   And
they were in the way going up to
Jerusalem;          PAGE 91

Map 103   1ST OF FOUR BLIND
MEN HEALED AT JERICHO --
1st of four blind men healed at Jer
icho ...          PAGE 91

Map 104   AND THEY CAME TO
JERICHO -- Mark 10:46a   And
they came to Jericho:     PAGE 92

Map 105   JESUS ENTERED AND
PASSED THROUGH JERICHO
AND ATE WITH ZACCHAEUS --
Luke 19:1   And Jesus entered and
passed through Jericho.  PAGE 92

Map 106   THEY DEPARTED
FROM JERICHO AND TWO
BLIND MEN ANB BLIND BAR-
TIMAEUS WERE HEALED --
Matt. 20:29   And as they departed
from Jericho, a great multitude fol
lowed him. Matt. 20:30   And,
behold, two blind men sitting by the
way side ... Mark 10:46b   and as he
went out of Jericho with his disciples and a great number of people,
blind Bartimaeus,        PAGE 93

Map 107   JESUS CAME TO
BETHANY -- John 12:1   Then
Jesus six days before the passover
came to Bethany,        PAGE 94

Number of lines = year of Jesus' Ministry

# Jerusalem # 17

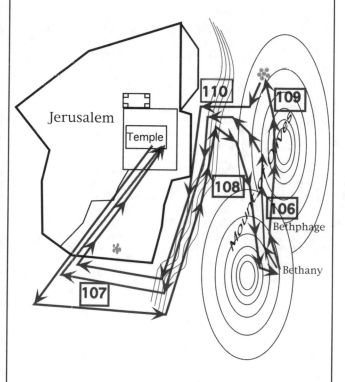

MAP 108 CAME TO THE MOUNT OF OLIVES SUNDAY AFTERNOON -- Mark 11:1, Luke 19:29, & Matt. 21:1 And when they drew nigh unto Jerusalem, and were come to Bethphage, unto the mount of Olives,

PAGE 94

Map 109 JESUS ENTERED INTO JERUSALEM -- Mark 11:11a And Jesus entered into Jerusalem, and into the temple: ...

PAGE 95

Map 110 JESUS WENT OUT UNTO BETHANY -- Mark 11:11b ... now the eventide was come, he went out unto Bethany with the twelve.

PAGE 95

Map 111 COME FROM BETHANY TO 1ST FIG TREE ON MONDAY MORNING -- Mark 11:12 And on the morrow, when they were come from Bethany, he was hungry: Mark 11:13 And seeing a fig tree afar off ...

PAGE 95

Map 112 HE WENT INTO THE TEMPLE -- Matt. 21:12, Mark 11:15 & Luke 19:45 And he went into the temple, and began to cast out them that sold therein,

PAGE 96

# Jerusalem   # 18

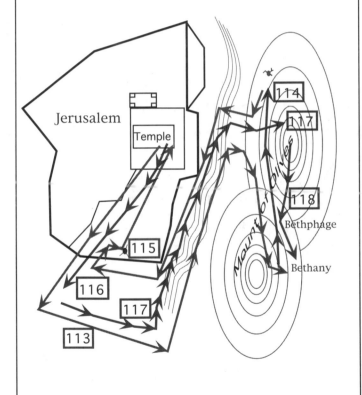

**MAP 113   JESUS WENT OUT OF THE CITY INTO BETHANY** Mark 11:19 & Matt. 21:17 And he left them, and went out of the city into Bethany;

PAGE 96

**MAP 114   JESUS CAME FROM BETHANY TO THE DRIED UP FIG TREE ON TUESDAY MORNING** Matt. 21:18a & Mark 11:20  And in the morning, as they passed by, they saw the fig tree dried up ...

PAGE 96

**Map 115   TUESDAY MORNING THEY   CAME   AGAIN   TO JERUSALEM WHEN HE SAW A 2ND FIG TREE ... HE THEN ENTERED THE TEMPLE** -- Mark 11:27a & Matt. 21:18b   as he returned into the city, he hungered. Matt. 21:19a   And when he saw a fig tree in the way, ... . Matt. 21:23 And when he was come into the temple,...

PAGE 97

**Map 116   JESUS WENT OUT, AND DEPARTED FROM THE TEMPLE** Matt. 24:1a, Mark 13:1a, & John 12:36b These things spake Jesus, and departed, and did hide himself from them.

PAGE 103

**Map 117   HE SAT UPON THE MOUNT OF OLIVES** -- Matt. 24:3 & Mark 13:3   And as he sat upon the mount of Olives over against the temple,

PAGE 104

**Map 118   BEING IN BETHANY A WOMAN ANOINTED JESUS' HEAD** -- Matt. 26:6 & Mark 14:3   And being in Bethany in the house of Simon the leper, as he sat at meat, there came a woman having an alabaster box of ointment of spikenard very precious;

PAGE 109

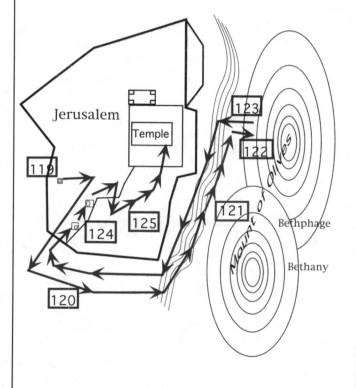

# Jerusalem # 19

Jerusalem

Temple

119

124

125

123

122

121

Bethphage

Bethany

Mount of Olives

120

**Map 119   IN JERUSALEM FOR THE PASSOVER MEAL** -- Matt. 26:20, Mark 14:17, & Luke 22:14 And when the hour was come, he sat down, and the twelve apostles with him.

PAGE 110

**Map 120   THEY LEFT FOR THE MOUNT OF OLIVES** -- Mark 14:26 & Matt. 26:30    And when they had sung an hymn, they went out into the mount of Olives.

PAGE 115

**Map 121   JESUS ON THE HILL ON THE WAY DOWN TO THE GARDEN** -- John 17:1    These words spake Jesus, and lifted up his eyes to heaven, and said ...

PAGE 117

**Map 122   JESUS ENTERS THE GARDEN NAMED GETHSEMANE** -- Mark 14:32, Luke 22:40, John 18:1b, & Matt. 26:36    Then cometh Jesus with them unto a place called Gethsemane,

PAGE 119

**MAP 123   JESUS TAKEN TO ANNAS' HOUSE** -- John 18:13 And led him away to Annas first ...

PAGE 121

**MAP 124   JESUS SENT BOUND UNTO CAIAPHAS** -- Matt. 26:57b, Mark 14:53b & John 18:24b    unto Caiaphas the high priest.

PAGE 122

**Map 125   THEY LED JESUS TO THEIR COUNCIL** -- Luke 22:66 ... the elders of the people and the chief priests and the scribes came together, and led him to their council ...

PAGE 124

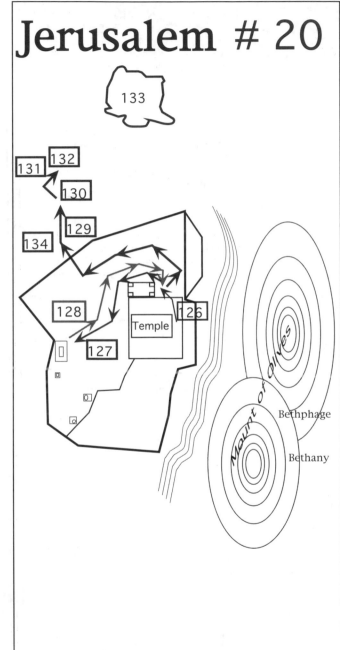

# Jerusalem # 20

133

131  132
130
129
134

128
Temple    126
127

Mount of Olives

Bethphage

Bethany

Map 126   THEY LED JESUS TO PILATE -
- Matt. 27:1, Mark 15:1, John 18:28, & Luke
23:1    And the whole multitude of them
arose, and led him unto Pilate.    PAGE 125

Map 127    PILATE SENT JESUS TO
HEROD -- Luke 23:7   ... he sent him to
Herod, who himself also was at Jerusalem at
that time.    PAGE 126

Map 128   HEROD SENT JESUS BACK TO
PILATE -- Luke 23:11 And Herod with his
men of war set him at nought, and mocked
him, and arrayed him in a gorgeous robe, and
sent him again to Pilate.    PAGE 126

Map 129   JESUS CAME TO GOLGOTHA,
CALVARY -- Matt. 27:33, Mark 15:22,
Luke 23:33, & John 19:17   And he bearing
his cross went forth into a place called the
place of a skull, which is called in the
Hebrew Golgotha: John 19:18   Where they
crucified him, and two other with him ...
PAGE 129

Map 130    JESUS GAVE UP THE GHOST
Matt. 27:50, Mark 15:37, Luke 23:45, &
John 19:30 When Jesus therefore had
received the vinegar, he said, It is finished:
and he bowed his head, and gave up the
ghost.    PAGE 130

MAP 131    THEY LAID THE BODY OF
JESUS IN A NEW TOMB -- Matt. 27:60,
Mark 15:46, Luke 23:53 & John 19:41  Now
in the place where he was crucified there was
a garden; and in the garden a new sepulchre,
wherein was never man yet laid. John 19:42
There laid they Jesus ...    PAGE 131

MAP 132    JESUS APPEARED FIRST TO
MARY MAGDALENE -- Mark 16:9 & John
20:16 Jesus saith unto her, Mary. She turned
herself, and saith unto him, Rabboni; which
is to say, Master. John 20:17   Jesus saith
unto her, Touch me not; for I am not yet
ascended to my Father ...    PAGE 133

MAP 133    JESUS ASCENDED TO HIS
FATHER AND THEN RETURNED
PAGE 133

MAP 134    JESUS APPEARED TO THE
OTHER WOMEN AND LET THEM
TOUCH HIM. -- Matt. 28:9   And as they
went to tell his disciples, behold, Jesus met
them, saying, All hail. And they came and
held him by the feet,,    PAGE 133

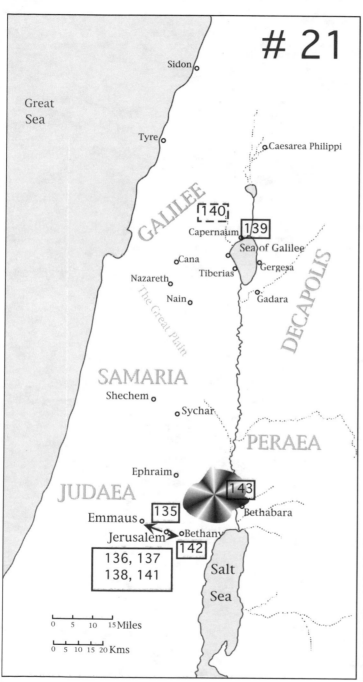

# 21

Great Sea

Sidon

Tyre

Caesarea Philippi

GALILEE

140

Capernaum  139

Cana

Sea of Galilee

Tiberias    Gergesa

Nazareth

Nain    Gadara

DECAPOLIS

The Great Plain

SAMARIA

Shechem

Sychar

PERAEA

Ephraim

JUDAEA    143

135    Bethabara

Emmaus

Jerusalem    Bethany

136, 137    142

138, 141    Salt

Sea

0  5  10  15 Miles

0  5  10  15  20 Kms

MAP 135  JESUS WALKED AND TALKED TO TWO MEN ON THE ROAD TO EMMAUS -- Luke 24:15 ... Jesus himself drew near, and went with them.          PAGE 134

Map 136   JESUS APPEARED TO SIMON PETER (THIS COULD HAVE HAPPENED BEFORE EMMAUS)-- Luke 24:34   Saying, The Lord is risen indeed, and hath appeared to Simon.
          PAGE 135

Map 137   JESUS HIMSELF STOOD IN THE MIDST OF THEM -- John 20:19 & Luke 24:36   And as they thus spake, Jesus himself stood in the midst of them, and saith unto them, Peace be unto you.          PAGE 135

Map138   JESUS CAME TO THE ELEVEN IN JERUSALEM -- John 20:26   And after eight days again his disciples were within, and Thomas with them: then came Jesus, the doors being shut, and stood in the midst ..PAGE 135

Map 139   JESUS CAME TO THE ELEVEN AT THE SEA OF TIBERIAS -- John 21:1   After these things Jesus showed himself again to the disciples at the sea of Tiberias;          PAGE 136

Map 140   JESUS CAME TO THE ELEVEN AT A MOUNTAIN -- Matt. 28:16   Then the eleven disciples went away into Galilee, into a mountain where Jesus had appointed them.  Matt. 28:17   And when they saw him, they worshipped him ...          PAGE 137

MAP 141   JESUS APPEARED TO THE ELEVEN AS THEY SAT AT MEAT -- Mark 16:14   Afterward he appeared unto the eleven as they sat at meat,          PAGE 137

MAP 142   JESUS LED THEM OUT AS FAR AS TO BETHANY Luke 24:50a  And he led them out as far as to Bethany,          PAGE 137

MAP 143   JESUS WAS CARRIED UP INTO HEAVEN -- Mark 16:19 & Luke 24:51   And it came to pass, while he blessed them, he was parted from them, and carried up into heaven.  PAGE 137

This two page calendar shows the last month of Jesus ministry.  The calendar demonstrates the accuracy of Jesus' prophesy that He would be **three days and three nights** in the heart of the earth.

> Matthew 12:40    For as Jonas was **three days and three nights** in the whale's belly; so shall the **Son of man be three days and three nights** in the heart of the earth.

Jesus was raised from the dead early the first day of the week, Sunday morning, after being in the heart of the earth **three nights**.

> Matthew 28:1    In the end of the sabbath, **as it began to dawn** toward **the first day of the week**, came Mary Magdalene and the other Mary to see the sepulchre.

Those nights had to be Saturday night, Friday night, and Thursday night.  Jesus was **three days** in the heart of the earth.  Those days had to be Saturday, Friday, and Thursday.  In fact, Jesus was three days, three evenings, three nights, and three mornings in the heart of the earth.

| | | | | |
|---|---|---|---|---|
| 1 | Thursday **day** | Thursday evening | Thursday **night** | Friday morning |
| 2 | Friday **day** | Friday evening | Friday **night** | Saturday morning |
| 3 | Saturday **day** | Saturday evening | Saturday **night** | Sunday morning |

**So, Jesus "gave up the ghost" and went into the heart of the earth on Thursday afternoon at about the ninth hour** (the hour of time between 2:00 PM and 3:00 PM).

Scriptures from the New and Old Testaments are needed to understand and study the calendar.  So, following the calendar are *Scriptures Used in Preparing The Calendar of Passover* .  At the end of that section there are three scripture quotations from Jesus saying that He would give that generation "the sign of the prophet Jonas."  Next, there are nine more scriptures that prophesy that Jesus would be raised from the dead on the third day.  Finally, there are five scriptures proclaiming that Jesus was raised from the dead on the third day.

# The Sequential Gospels©

| | Sunset | Midnight | Sunrise | Noon | Sunset | Midnight | Sunrise | Noon | Sunset | Midnight | Sunrise | Noon | Sunset |

**20th Century Week** - Note:
New day begins at midnight

| | – Sunday – | – Monday – | – Tuesday – |

**Jewish Week** - Note:
New day starts at Sunset

Genesis 1:5b  And the evening and the morning were the first day.

| | – 1st Day – | | | | – 2nd Day – | | | | – 3rd Day – | | | |
| Evening | Night | Morning | Day | Evening | Night | Morning | Day | Evening | Night | Morning | Day |

## The First Month in the Jewish Calendar

Exodus 12:2a  This month shall be unto you the **beginning of months**: it shall be the **first month** of the year to you.

## Month of Abib

Exodus 13:3-4   And Moses said unto the people, Remember this day, in which ye came out from Egypt, out of the house of bondage; for by strength of hand the LORD brought you out from this place: there shall no leavened bread be eaten.   This day came ye out in the **month Abib**.

## *Side Note

Holy convocations of the **feast of tabernacles** are called Sabbaths.

Leviticus 23:34-35  ...The fifteenth day of this seventh month shall be the **feast of tabernacles** for seven days unto the LORD. On the **first day** shall be an **holy convocation**: ye shall do no servile work therein.

Leviticus 23:39  Also in the fifteenth day of the seventh month, when ye have gathered in the fruit of the land, ye shall keep a feast unto the LORD seven days: on the **first day** shall be a **sabbath**, and on the eighth day shall be a **sabbath**.

So, there is good reason to believe that the two holy convocations of the **feast of Passover** were also called Sabbaths.

| 3 | 4 | 5 |

| 10  *4 days before Passover* | 11  *3 days before Passover* | 12  *2 days before Passover* |

**10** — *4 days before Passover*

Lambs Selected
and
Lambs Inspected

Exodus 12:3 ...In the tenth day of this month they shall take to them every man a lamb, according to the house of their fathers, a lamb for an house:

John 12:3
Then took Mary ... ointment ... and anointed the feet of Jesus....

Matthew 21:9
And the multitudes... cried, saying, Hosanna to the son of David: Blessed is he that cometh in the name of the Lord;

**11** — *3 days before Passover*

Lambs Inspected

Exodus 12:5  Your lamb shall be **without blemish**, a male of the first year: ye shall take it out from the sheep, or from the goats:

Luke 19:47
And he taught daily in the temple....

**12** — *2 days before Passover*

Lambs Inspected

Mark 12:34
And when Jesus saw that he answered discreetly, he said unto him, Thou art not far from the kingdom of God. **And no man after that durst ask him any question.**

| 17  *3rd day of feast of Passover* | 18  *4th day of feast of Passover* | 19  *5th day of feast of Passover* |

Jesus in the grave
the heart of the earth.

*Evening 3*   *Night 3*   *Morning 3*

# HE IS RISEN...

| 24 | 25 | 26 |

| Sunset | Midnight | Sunrise | Noon | Sunset | Midnight | Sunrise | Noon | Sunset | Midnight | Sunrise | Noon | Sunset | Midnight | Sunrise | Noon | Sunset |
|---|---|---|---|---|---|---|---|---|---|---|---|---|---|---|---|---|

| – Wednesday – | – Thursday – | – Friday – | – Saturday – |
|---|---|---|---|

| – 4th Day – | | | | – 5th Day – | | | | – 6th Day – | | | | – SABBATH – | | | |
|---|---|---|---|---|---|---|---|---|---|---|---|---|---|---|---|
| Evening | Night | Morning | Day | Evening | Night | Morning | Day | Evening | Night | Morning | Day | Evening | Night | Morning | Day |

|  |  |  |  | **1** | **2** – SABBATH – |
|---|---|---|---|---|---|

**6** | **7** | **8** | **9** – SABBATH –

**8**
John 12:1 Then Jesus six days before the Passover came to Bethany,
*6 days before Passover*

**9 – SABBATH –**
Exodus 20:10  But **the seventh day** is the **sabbath of the LORD** thy God: in it **thou shalt not do any work....**
*5 days before Passover*

**13**

Matthew 26:2 Ye know that after **two days** is the **feast of the passover**, and the son of man is betrayed to be crucified.

Matthew 26:12  For in that she hath poured this ointment on my body, she did it for my burial.

*1 day before Passover*
## Lambs Killed
Mark 14:12 & 16 And the **first day of unleavened bread**, when they **killed the passover**...and ...made ready **the passover**.

Exodus 12:6 And ye shall keep it **up until the fourteenth day**...and the whole assembly...**shall kill it in the evening**.

**14** Passover of the Lord
## Crucifixion
John 19:14  It was **the day of preparation** of **the passover week**.... (NIV)

Mark 15:42 And now when the even was come, because **it was the preparation,** that is, the **day before the sabbath,** at even.

Luke 22:15 And he said unto them, With desire I have desired to eat this **passover** with you before I suffer:

Matthew 26:28 For this is my blood of the new testament, which is shed for many for the remission of sins.

**15** – SABBATH –
*1st day of feast of Passover*

Numbers 28:17-18 And the fifteenth of this month is the feast: seven days shall unleavened bread be eaten.  In the **first day** an **holy convocation: ye shall do nor of work therein:**

John 19:3 ...(for **that sabbath day** was an high day,)....

*See **Side Note** to left of calendar.

Exodus 12:18  In the first month on the 14th day of the month **at even** ye shall eat unleavened bread until the 21st day of the month at even.

**16** – SABBATH –
*2nd day of feast of Passover*

Exodus 20:8-10  Remember the **sabbath day**, to keep it holy.  Six days shalt thou labour, and do all thy work: But **the seventh day** is the **sabbath of the LORD** thy God: in it **thou shalt not do any work....**

Matthew 12:40
For as Jonas...so shall the son of man be **three days** and **three nights** in

## Jesus in the grave

| Day 1 | Evening 1 | Night 1 | Morning 1 | Day 2 | Evening 2 | Night 2 | Morning 2 | Day 3 |
|---|---|---|---|---|---|---|---|---|

**20**
*6th day of feast of Passover*

**21** – SABBATH –
*7th day of feast of Passover*
Numbers 28:25  And on the **seventh day** ye shall have an **holy convocation**; ye shall do no servile work.
*See **Side Note** to left of calendar.

**22**

**23** – SABBATH –

# JESUS IS ALIVE...

**27** | **28**

# Index

### Introduction to The Calendar of Passover

*The Calendar of Passover* is a one month calendar which includes the first "Palm Sunday" and the first "Easter." The calendar lays out details which help clarify the relationships between Old Testament prophecies and Jesus' fulfillment of these prophecies.

Some of the words and phrases used to describe this month are identical but mean different things depending on their context. Also, different words and phrases are often used to describe the same thing. The calendar gives a visual reference that is particularly helpful in understanding the many different names given to the days associated with Passover. The **first day of unleavened bread,** the **13th** day of Abib, is the day when **the Passover** [lamb] was killed (Mark 14:12). This is the day that Jesus sent Peter and John to prepare **the Passover**. At sunset, the beginning of the **14th** day of Abib, Jesus and His disciples ate **the Passover.** This meal began the 24 hours known as **the Passover of the Lord**, **the LORD's Passover**, or **the preparation.** Since the Jewish "day" was a 24 hour period beginning at sunset, the sunset following **the Passover of the Lord** began the seven day **feast of unleavened bread**, **the feast of Passover**, or simply **the Passover**. The first and the last days of the seven day **feast of unleavened bread** were **holy convocations** or **Sabbaths.** These **Sabbaths** were always on the **15th** and the **21st** days of Abib, and are different from the **seventh day of rest**, also called the **Sabbath of rest** or simply **the Sabbath**.

*The Sequential Gospels* allows a fresh look at the events of Jesus' crucifixion and resurrection. The time period of **three days and three nights** is one of the known fixed prophecies concerning the week of Jesus' crucifixion and resurrection.

> Matthew 12:40   For as Jonas was **three days and three nights** in the whale's belly; so shall the **Son of man be three days and three nights** in the heart of the earth.

On the day that Jesus was crucified, at about the ninth hour (the hour of time between 2:00 PM and 3:00 PM), Jesus cried, 'Eli, Eli, lama sabachani? that is to say, My God, my God, why hast thou forsaken me?" (Matthew 27:46). Soon after that, Jesus yielded up the ghost and His spirit and soul went 'in the heart of the earth." Jesus' body was placed in the sepulchre before sunset. Mary Magdalene arrived at the sepulchre as it began to dawn on the first day of the week, **Sunday morning**.

> Matthew 28:1   In the end of the sabbath, **as it began to dawn** toward **the first day of the week**, came Mary Magdalene and the other Mary to see the sepulchre.

This was early **Sunday morning**, just after sunrise. The period of time from the ninth hour of Thursday to Sunday morning gives the three days and nights necessary to fulfill prophecy.

### Summary of the Last Week

Frequent reference to *The Sequential Gospels* and the two page *Calendar of Passover* will explain some of the time relationships described in this summary. *Solutions to Gospel Mysteries* numbers 16 through 24 detail some of the events which occurred on the 10th day through the 17th day of this month.

On Friday, Jesus and His disciples walked from Jericho up toward Jerusalem.

> Luke 19:28   And when he had thus spoken, he went before, ascending up to Jerusalem.

Then Jesus came to Bethany.

> John 12:1 Then Jesus six days before **the passover** came to Bethany, where Lazarus was which had been dead, whom he raised from the dead.

This was Friday afternoon near sunset, "six days before **the passover**." **The Passover** of the Lord is always celebrated on the 14th day of the first month (Numbers 28:16). **The feast of Passover** starts on the 15th day of the first month and lasts one week (Numbers 28:17). Jesus came to Bethany on the afternoon of the 8th day of the month. Sunset marked the beginning of the 9th day of the month. That year the 9th day of the month was a weekly seventh day of rest or a **Sabbath**. A Sabbath is observed on the seventh day of each week (Exodus 20:8-11). It is also called the **Sabbath of rest** (Exodus 31:15). Jesus kept the **Sabbath of rest** according to the Law. He attended synagogue on that **Sabbath**. A **Sabbath of rest** starts Friday at sunset and ends Saturday at sunset. Saturday at sunset was the beginning of the 10th day of the month. "There [in Bethany] they made him a supper; and Martha served:...Then took Mary a pound of ointment of spikenard, very costly, and anointed the feet of Jesus..."(John 12:2 & 3). Many of the Jews came to see Jesus and Lazarus when the Sabbath was ended (John 12:9).

By the Law, in the 10th day of the first month, the [Passover] **lamb** was chosen (Exodus 12:3). The time of day to chose their lamb is not specified in the Law. This year the morning and the afternoon of the 10th day of the first month was a Sunday. That afternoon, Jesus rode into Jerusalem on a colt, the foal of an ass. The people chose their "Passover lamb" when they cried, "... Hosanna to the son of David: Blessed is he that cometh in the name of the Lord; Hosanna in the highest." (Matthew 21:9)

The Law required that the (Passover) **lamb** should not only be chosen but also should be separated **and** inspected before it was used as **the Passover** (Mark 14:12). Jesus, our "Passover lamb," was chosen by the people on Sunday. He was separated and inspected by the scribes and the Pharisees on Monday and Tuesday. By Tuesday afternoon the inspection was complete.

> Mark 12:34 And when Jesus saw that he answered discreetly, he said unto him, "Thou art not far from the kingdom of God." **And no man after that durst ask Him any question**.

Tuesday at sunset was the beginning of the 13th day of the month. Jesus was anointed at the house of Simon the leper (Matthew 26:6-13 & Mark 14:3-9).

> Mark 14:8 She hath done what she could: she is come aforehand to anoint my body to the burying.

Wednesday was the **first day** of **unleavened bread**. This is the day "when they killed **the Passover**" (Mark 14:12). On Wednesday morning the disciples said to Jesus, "Where wilt thou that we go and prepare that thou mayest eat **the passover**?" (Mark 14:12). Jesus sent Peter and John to Jerusalem to prepare **the Passover** (Luke 22:8). After sunset, which was the beginning of the fourteenth day of the month, they ate the Passover (Exodus 12:6). The evening started at sunset an lasted until it got dark.

> Exodus 12:6 And ye shall keep it **up until the fourteenth day** of the same month: and the whole assembly of the congregation of Israel shall kill it in the evening.

> Luke 22:15 & 17 And he said unto them, With desire I have desired to eat this **passover** with you before I suffer: And he took the cup, and gave thanks, and said, Take this, and divide it among yourselves:

> John 13:1-5   Now before **the feast of the  passover**...And  supper being
> ended...Jesus...riseth  up  from supper...and began  to  wash  the disciples
> feet....

**The feast of the passover**, in John 13:1, is the week  long feast which always starts on the 15th of the month.  After washing the disciples' feet, Jesus took bread and a second cup and gave them to the disciples.

> Luke 22:19 & 20   And he took bread, and gave thanks, and brake it,  and
> gave unto them, saying, This is my body which is  given for you: this
> do in remembrance of me.  Likewise also the cup after supper, saying,
> This cup is the new testament in my blood, which is shed for you.

Then, Jesus and the disciples went to a garden called Gethsemane.  Jesus prayed to His Father three different times.

> Matthew 26:39   And he went a little farther, and fell on his face, and prayed,
> saying, O my Father, if it be possible, let this cup pass from me:
> nevertheless not as I will, but as thou wilt.

That night Jesus was taken prisoner to the high priest's house (Luke 22:54).   He was brought before Pilate in the morning.  It was still the 14th day of the month.   Jesus was crucified at the third hour, between 8:00 AM and 9:00 AM, on this Thursday morning (Mark 15:25).   At about the ninth hour, between 2:00 PM and 3:00 PM, Jesus died.  Immediately He descended into hell (Acts 2:31); however, He did not stay there long.  Jesus had promised the thief on the cross, "...Verily I say unto thee, **Today** shalt thou be with me in paradise" (Luke 23:43).   So,  that day, Jesus finished His work in hell and went to paradise.  Both hell and paradise were in the heart of the earth.

Before this  day ended the disciples took Jesus' body off of the cross and put it into the tomb.

> Mark 15:42-43 And now when the even  was  come,  because it  was  the
> preparation, that is, the day before the sabbath,   Joseph of Arimathaea,
> an honourable counsellor, which also waited for the kingdom of God,
> came, and went in boldly unto Pilate, and craved the body of Jesus.

> Luke 23:53  And he took it down, and wrapped it in linen, and laid it in a
> sepulchre that was hewn in stone, wherein never man before was laid.

This Thursday, the 14th day of the month, was a busy day.  While some crucified Jesus, the others prepared for the week long feast of unleavened bread.  This "...was **the preparation**, that is, the day before **the sabbath**..." (Mark 15:42).   The feast always began with **a  holy convocation**, **a Sabbath**, on which no work could be done (see *Holy Convocations and Sabbath* scriptures in the *Scripture Used...* section following this summary).

In the year that Jesus died, the **feast of unleavened  bread** began Thursday at sundown.   This was the beginning of the 15th day of the month.  As always, the first day of the feast was **a holy convocation**, **a Sabbath**.  This year the first day of the feast ended Friday at sundown.  Then the second day of the feast began.  The second day of the feast was a normal weekly **seventh day of rest** or a **Sabbath**. So, this **feast of unleavened bread** began with two Sabbath days in a row.[1]

As always, the first day of the week started on Saturday night at sunset. The next morning was Sunday morning, the morning that Jesus arose from the dead. The women arrived at the sepulcher early Sunday morning, at dawn. At that time there was still darkness over the face of the tomb (John 20:1[2]) because it is located in the south-west face of a large hill[3]. (So, at sunrise the tomb is in the shadow of this hill.) On the south face of this hill is Golgotha, the place of the skull, where they crucified Jesus (Mark 15:22). Sunday morning the women were at the tomb when the angel of the Lord rolled away the stone from the door and then spoke to them.

> Matthew 28:2-6 And, behold, there was a great earthquake: for the angel of the Lord descended from heaven, and came and rolled back the stone from the door, and sat upon it. His countenance was like lightning, and his raiment white as snow: And for fear of him the keepers did shake, and became as dead men. And the angel answered and said unto the women, Fear not ye: for I know that ye seek Jesus, which was crucified. He is not here: for he is risen, as he said. Come, see the place where the Lord lay.

> Mark 16:4 And when they looked, they saw that the stone was rolled away: for it was very great.

At sunrise the night had ended and the morning had begun. At that moment Jesus fulfilled the prophecies that He had spoken. Thus, He arose. This is why the angel could say, "He is not here: for he is risen, as he said."

Jesus first showed Himself to Mary Magdalene.

---

[1] Two Sabbath days in a row is not unusual since, in the first month, this occurs four times in every seven years. The 15th and the 21st days are both holy convocations or Sabbaths and either the **15th** or the **21st** will immediately precede or come after a seventh day of rest four times in every seven years. Two Sabbath days in a row happen more frequently in the seventh month because there are four "extra" holy convocations or Sabbaths in that month:

#1--Leviticus 23:24 In the seventh month, in the **first** day of the month shall, ye have a sabbath, a memorial of blowing of trumpets, an holy convocation.

#2--Leviticus 23:27 Also on the tenth day of this month there shall be a **day of atonement**: it shall be a an holy convocation unto you....

#3--Leviticus 23:34-35 ...on the fifteenth day of this seventh month shall be the **feast of tabernacles** for seven days unto the LORD. On the **first** day shall be an holy convocation....

#4--Leviticus 23:36 ...on the **eighth** day shall be an holy convocation....

[2] John 20:1 ...Mary Magdalene came early to the tomb, darkness yet being on it. (Green's *Literal Translation of the Bible*)

[3] "Gordon's Calvary" is just north of Jerusalem and is outside of the old city walls. The "face of the skull" is clearly seen in the south side of this hill. The "skull" is formed by several large cave like openings in the side of the hill. There are many tombs cut into south west side of this hill. One of the tombs at the base of the hill is inside of a large garden. Many think that Joseph of Arimathaea placed Jesus' body in this tomb.

John 20:16   Jesus saith unto her, Mary. She turned herself, and saith unto him, Rabboni; which is to say, Master.

Jesus did not allow her to touch Him.

John 20:17   Jesus saith unto her, Touch me not; for I am not yet ascended to my Father: but go to my brethren, and say unto them, I ascend unto my Father, and your Father; and to my God, and your God.

Jesus then ascended to His Father. A short time later, while the other women were still on their way to tell the disciples what they had seen and heard, Jesus appeared to them. Since He had already ascended to His Father, Jesus allowed them touch Him.

Matthew 28:9   And as they went to tell his disciples, behold, Jesus met them, saying, All hail. And they came and held him by the feet, and worshipped him.

That same day Jesus appeared to two of His disciples as they walked to Emmaus.

Luke 24:13-16   And, behold, two of them went that same day to a village called Emmaus, which was from Jerusalem about threescore furlongs. And they talked together of all these things which had happened.   And it came to pass, that, while they communed together and reasoned, Jesus himself drew near, and went with them.   But their eyes were holden that they should not know him.

Jesus also appeared that day unto Simon Peter.

Luke 24:34   ...The Lord is risen indeed, and hath appeared to Simon.

Then, Jesus appeared to the disciples when the doors were shut.

John 20:19   Then the same day at evening, being the first day of the week, when the doors were shut where the disciples were assembled for fear of the Jews, came Jesus and stood in the midst, and saith unto them, Peace be unto you.

Jesus had prophesied that He would be in the heart of the earth three days and three nights.

Matthew 12:40   For as Jonas was **three days and three nights** in the whale's belly; so shall the **Son of man be three days and three nights** in the heart of the earth.

The order in which Jesus prophesied the words "**three days and three nights**" is important. Jesus was in the heart of the earth for a part of Thursday day, all of Thursday evening, Thursday night, Friday morning, Friday day, Friday evening, Friday night, Saturday morning, Saturday day, Saturday evening, Saturday night, and a very short time Sunday morning. Note that Jesus was in the heart of the earth **three days**, three evenings, **three nights**, and three mornings. Jesus fulfilled His prophecies concerning His resurrection from the dead.

## Scriptures Used in Preparing The Calendar of Passover

Scriptures from both the Old and New Testaments are needed to understand *The Calendar of Passover*. The Old Testament Scriptures are the basis for all Passover ceremonies. We know that throughout His ministry, Jesus celebrated the **Passover of the LORD** and the **feast of unleavened bread** according to the Law found in these Old Testament Scriptures. The New Testament Scriptures trace Jesus' activity during this last Passover time.

### The Jewish day starts at sunset.

1 -- The Jewish day starts in the evening at sunset.

The evening and the morning were called a **day**. God also called the light "**Day**" and the darkness "**Night**."

> Genesis 1:5   And God called the light **Day**, and the darkness he called **Night**. And the <u>evening and the morning were the first **day**</u>. 8 And God called the firmament Heaven. And the <u>evening and the morning were the second **day**</u>. 13 And the <u>evening and the morning were the third **day**</u>. 19 And the <u>evening and the morning were the fourth **day**</u>. 23 And the <u>evening and the morning were the fifth **day**</u>. 31 And God saw every thing that he had made, and, behold, it was very good. And the <u>evening and the morning were the sixth **day**</u>.

### Jesus is our Passover Lamb.

2 -- Take **a lamb** on the 10th day of the month.

> Exodus 12:2-3   This month shall be unto you the beginning of months: it shall be the first month of the year to you.   Speak ye unto all the congregation of Israel, saying, In the **tenth day** of this month they shall take to them **every man a lamb**, according to the house of their fathers, **a lamb** for an house:

3 -- Jesus was chosen on the **10th** day of the month, "Palm Sunday."

This is the same day God said that **the lamb** was to be chosen.

> Matthew 21:9   And the multitudes that went before, and that followed, cried, saying, **Hosanna** to the son of David: Blessed is he that cometh in the name of the Lord; **Hosanna in the highest**.

> Exodus 12:3   Speak ye unto all the congregation of Israel, saying, In the **tenth day** of this month they shall take to them every man **a lamb**, according to the house of their fathers, a lamb for an house:

Mary started the choosing process Saturday night at the beginning of the 10th day of the month.

> John 12:3 & 7   Then took Mary a pound of ointment of spikenard, very costly, and anointed the feet of Jesus, and wiped his feet with her hair: and the house was filled with the odour of the ointment.   Then said Jesus, Let her alone: against the day of my burying hath she kept this.

### *Keep the passover lamb up until the 14th day.*

4 -- Keep **the passover** (lamb) until the beginning of the **14th** day (sunset of the 13th day).

On the first Passover in Egypt they waited until evening, at sunset, to kill the lamb.

> Exodus 12:6-7   And ye shall keep it **up until the fourteenth day** of the same month: and the whole assembly of the congregation of Israel shall kill it in the evening.   And they shall take of the blood, and strike it on the two side posts and on the upper door post of the houses, wherein they shall eat it.   And they shall eat the flesh in that night, roast with fire, and unleavened bread; and with bitter herbs they shall eat it.

Kill **the passover** (lamb) at sunset of the 13th day, the beginning of the **14th** day.

> Exodus 12:21   Then Moses called for all the elders of Israel, and said unto them, Draw out and take you **a lamb** according to your families, and kill **the passover**.

5 -- The **first day of unleavened bread** is the 13th day of the first month.

Mark 14:12 shows that in Jesus' time the priests did not wait until sundown to kill the passover lambs that were needed for the people.  Thus, the killing of **the passover** (lamb) started in the afternoon of the 13th day of the month, just before the beginning of the 14th day.  The 13th day is not **the preparation** or **the feast**.  The 13th day is the **first day of unleavened bread**, the day before **the preparation**.

> Mark 14:12     And the **first day of unleavened bread**, **when they killed the passover**, his disciples said unto him, Where wilt thou that we go and prepare that thou mayest eat the passover?

### *The LORD's passover and the preparation are both the 14th day of the first month.*

6 -- Keep **the LORD's passover** as a memorial feast forever.

Keep it **a feast**.

> Exodus 12:6   And ye shall keep it **up until the fourteenth day** of the same month: and the whole assembly of the congregation of Israel shall kill it in the evening.
>
> Exodus 12:11 & 14   And thus shall ye eat it; with your loins girded, your shoes on your feet, and your staff in your hand; and ye shall eat it in haste: it is **the LORD's passover**....And this **day** shall be unto you for a **memorial**; and ye shall **keep it a feast** to the LORD throughout your generations; ye shall keep it **a feast** by an ordinance **for ever**.
>
> John 19:14 And it was **the preparation of the passover**, and about the sixth hour: and he saith unto the Jews, Behold your King!

7 -- The **14th** day of the month is **the LORD's passover** or **the passover of the LORD**.

*The Amplified Bible* clarifies Leviticus 23:5 in the *King James Version* by saying, "On the fourteenth day of the first month **between evenings** is the **Lord's passover**." This would be the 13th day at sundown to the 14th day at sundown.

> Exodus 12:11   And thus shall ye eat it; with your loins girded, your shoes on your feet, and your staff in your hand; and ye shall eat it in haste: it is **the LORD's passover**.
>
> Leviticus 23:5-6   **In** the **fourteenth day** of the first month **at even** is **the LORD's passover**.   And on the **fifteenth day** of the same month is **the feast of unleavened bread** unto the LORD: **seven days** ye must eat unleavened bread.
>
> Num. 9:2-3   Let the children of Israel also keep **the passover** at his appointed season.   **In the fourteenth day** of this month, at even, ye shall keep it in his appointed season: according to all the rites of it, and according to all the ceremonies thereof, shall ye keep it.
>
> Numbers 28:16   And in the **fourteenth day** of the first month is **the passover of the LORD**.

8 -- The 14th day of the month was **the preparation.**

The 15th day of the month the children of Israel could do no work because the 15th day was a **holy convocation**, a **Sabbath**.   **The day of preparation** was used to remove all of the leaven from the house and prepare for the first day of the week long **feast of unleavened bread,** also called **the feast of the passover**.   The 15th day started at sunset of the 14th day.

> John 19:14 And it was **the preparation of the passover**, and about the sixth hour: and he saith unto the Jews, Behold your King!
>
> In the New International Version of the Bible, this 14th day of the month is called, "the **day of Preparation of Passover Week**."
>
> John 19:14   It was **the day of Preparation of Passover Week**, about the sixth hour. "Here is your king," Pilate said to the Jews. (New International Version)
>
> Mark 15:42-43   And now when the even was come, because it was **the preparation**, that is, **the day before the Sabbath**, Joseph of Arimathaea, an honourable counsellor, which also waited for the kingdom of God, came, and went in boldly unto Pilate, and craved the body of Jesus.

9 -- **That feast**, when the governor released a prisoner, was **the feast** or **the passover**.

We learn about these variations when we review what the different Gospel writers reported on Thursday morning.

> Matthew 27:15   Now **at that feast** the governor was wont to release unto the people a prisoner, whom they would
>
> Mark 15:6   Now **at that feast** he released unto them one prisoner, whomsoever they desired.

> Luke 23:16-7    I will therefore chastise him, and release him.    (For of necessity he must release one unto them **at the feast**.)
>
> John 18:39    But ye have a custom, that I should release unto you one **at the passover**: will ye therefore that I release unto you the King of the Jews?

### The passover is the 15th day through the 21st day.

10 -- The **passover** lasts one week.

The **passover** is also called **the feast of unleavened bread**

> Exodus. 12:15    **Seven days** shall ye eat unleavened bread; even the first day ye shall put away leaven out of your houses: for whosoever eateth leavened bread from the first day until the seventh day, that soul shall be cut off from Israel.

The **feast of unleavened bread,** or **the feast,** starts on the "fourteenth day of the month at even," that is the beginning of the **fifteenth** day of the first month.  It lasts "until the 21st day at even," that is the start of the 22nd day.

> Exodus 12:18-20    In the first month, **on** the **fourteenth day of the month at even**, ye shall eat unleavened bread, **until** the **one and twentieth day** of the month **at even**.    **Seven days** shall there be no leaven found in your houses: for whosoever eateth that which is leavened, even that soul shall be cut off from the congregation of Israel, whether he be a stranger, or born in the land.    Ye shall eat nothing leavened; in all your habitations shall ye eat unleavened bread.
>
> Leviticus 23:6    And on the **fifteenth day** of the same month is the **feast of unleavened bread** unto the LORD: **seven days** ye must eat unleavened bread.
>
> Numbers 28:17    And in the **fifteenth day** of this month is **the feast**: **seven days** shall unleavened bread be eaten.

11 -- The feast of unleavened bread has five other names.

> Leviticus 23:6    And on the **fifteenth day** of the same month is the **feast of unleavened bread** unto the LORD: **seven days** ye must eat unleavened bread.

It is also called "the feast," " the feast of the passover," "the feast of passover, and of unleavened bread," "the feast of unleavened *bread*," or simply "the passover."  On the week that Jesus was crucified, two days before the feast of unleavened bread was Tuesday evening at sunset.  Matthew reports Jesus' Tuesday evening comment about " the feast of the passover."  On this same Tuesday evening Mark and Luke also give an update about the Passover.

> Numbers 28:17    And in the **fifteenth day** of this month is **the feast**: **seven days** shall unleavened bread be eaten.
>
> Matthew 26:2    Ye know that after **two days** is **the feast of the passover**, and the Son of man is betrayed to be crucified.
>
> Mark 14:1a    **After two days** was **the feast of the passover, and of unleavened bread**:

Luke 22:1    Now **the feast of unleavened** *bread* drew nigh, which is called **the Passover**.

### *Holy Convocations are Sabbaths.*

12 -- Mark and John called Friday the 15th a **Sabbath day**.

Mark and John both called the day following the crucifixion a **Sabbath**.

Mark 15:42    And now when the even was come, because it was the preparation, that is, the day before the **sabbath**,

John 19:31    The Jews therefore, because it was the preparation, that the bodies should not remain upon the cross on the **sabbath day**, (for that **sabbath day** was an high day,) besought Pilate that their legs might be broken, and that they might be taken away.

13 -- The seventh day of each week is called an holy convocation.

It is  also called the **Sabbath of the Lord, Sabbath of rest,** or **the Sabbath day**.

Exodus 20:8-11    Remember the **sabbath day**, to keep it holy.  Six days shalt thou labour, and do all thy work:  But **the seventh day** is the **sabbath of the LORD** thy God: in it thou shalt not do any work, thou, nor thy son, nor thy daughter, thy manservant, nor thy maidservant, nor thy cattle, nor thy stranger that is within thy gates:  For in six days the LORD made heaven and earth, the sea, and all that in them is, and rested **the seventh day**: wherefore the LORD blessed the **sabbath day**, and hallowed it.

Exodus 31:15    Six days may work be done; but in the seventh is the **sabbath of rest**, holy to the LORD: whosoever doeth any work in the sabbath day, he shall surely be put to death.

Leviticus 23:3   Six days shall work be done: but the **seventh day** is the **sabbath of rest**, **an holy convocation**; ye shall do **no work** therein: **it is the sabbath of the LORD** in all your dwellings.

14 -- The **first** and the **seventh** days of the **feast of unleavened bread** are **holy convocations**.

In the month that Jesus was crucified these occurred on Friday the 15th day of the first month and Thursday the 21st day of the first month.  These are the seven days following the one day long **LORD's passover**.

Exodus 12:16-17    And in the **first** day there shall be an **holy convocation**, and in the **seventh** day there shall be an **holy convocation** to you; no manner of work shall be done in them, save that which every man must eat, that only may be done of you.  And ye shall observe the **feast of unleavened bread**; for in this selfsame day have I brought your armies out of the land of Egypt: therefore shall ye observe this day in your generations by an ordinance for ever.

Leviticus 23:2-8    Speak unto the children of Israel, and say unto them,
Concerning **the feasts of the LORD**, which ye shall proclaim to
be **holy convocations**, even these are my feasts.    Six days shall
work be done: but the **seventh day** is the **sabbath of rest**, **an**
**holy convocation**; ye shall do **no work** therein: **it is the**
**sabbath of the LORD** in all your dwellings.    These are the **feasts**
**of the LORD**, even **holy convocations**, which ye shall proclaim
in their seasons.    In the **fourteenth day** of the first month **at even**[4]
**is the LORD's passover**.    And on the **fifteenth day of the**
**same month is the feast of unleavened bread** unto the LORD:
seven days ye must eat unleavened bread.    In the **first day** ye shall
have an **holy convocation**: ye shall do **no** servile **work** therein.
But ye shall offer an offering made by fire unto the LORD seven days:
in the **seventh day** is an **holy convocation**: ye shall do **no** servile
**work** therein.

Numbers 28:18    In the **first day** shall be an **holy convocation**; ye shall
do **no** manner of servile **work** therein:

Numbers 28:25    And on the **seventh day** ye shall have an **holy**
**convocation**; ye shall do **no** servile **work**.

15 -- There is more than one Sabbath in some weeks.

Leviticus 16:29-31, 23:24, and 23:27-39 show that some weeks contain **more than one**
**Sabbath**.   These scriptures show there are four "extra" Sabbaths in the seventh month; the day
long memorial of blowing of trumpets, the day of atonement, and the week long feast of
tabernacles.    Some of these Sabbaths are also called **holy convocations.**   Since **holy**
**convocations** are called **Sabbaths** in the seventh month, it is logical that **holy**
**convocations** are also called **Sabbaths** in the first month.    There are two "extra" **holy**
**convocations** in the first month; one at the beginning and one at the end of the week long **feast**
**of unleavened bread**.   Note that some of these "extra" Sabbaths or holy convocations could fall
on the same day as a regular seventh day of the week Sabbath of rest.   (* Particularly note
Leviticus 16:31, 23:24, 23:27, 23:32, and 23:39.)

Leviticus 16:29-31    And this shall be a statute for ever unto you: that in the
**seventh month**, on the **tenth day** of the month, ye shall afflict
your souls, and do **no work** at all, whether it be one of your own
country, or a stranger that sojourneth among you:   For on that day shall
the priest make an atonement for you, to cleanse you, that ye may be
clean from all your sins before the LORD.   * It shall be a **sabbath of**
**rest** unto you, and ye shall afflict your souls, by a statute for ever.

---

[4] Leviticus 23:5    In the **fourteenth day** of the first month **at even is the LORD's**
**Passover**.   (*The Amplified Bible* says, "On the fourteenth day of the first month **between**
**evenings** is the **Lord's passover**."   This would be the 13th day at sundown to the 14th day at
sundown.)

Leviticus 23:6-8  And on the fifteenth day of the same month is the **feast of unleavened bread** unto the LORD: seven days ye must eat unleavened bread.    In the **first day** ye shall have an **holy convocation**: ye shall do no servile work therein.    But ye shall offer an offering made by fire unto the LORD seven days: in the **seventh day** is an **holy convocation**: ye shall do no servile work therein.

Leviticus 23:24  * Speak unto the children of Israel, saying, In the **seventh month**, in the **first day** of the month, shall ye have **a sabbath**, a memorial of blowing of trumpets, an **holy convocation**.

Leviticus 23:27-31  * Also on the **tenth day** of this **seventh month** there shall be a **day of atonement**: it shall be an **holy convocation** unto you; and ye shall afflict your souls, and offer an offering made by fire unto the LORD.   And ye shall do **no work** in that same day: for it is a **day of atonement**, to make an atonement for you before the LORD your God.  For whatsoever soul it be that shall not be afflicted in that same day, he shall be cut off from among his people.  And whatsoever soul it be that doeth any work in that same day, the same soul will I destroy from among his people.   Ye shall do **no manner of work**: it shall be a statute for ever throughout your generations in all your dwellings.

Leviticus 23:32-38  * It shall be unto you **a sabbath of rest**, and ye shall afflict your souls: in the ninth day of the month **at even**, from even unto even[5], shall ye celebrate **your sabbath**.   And the LORD spake unto Moses, saying,  Speak unto the children of Israel, saying, The **fifteenth day** of this seventh month shall be the **feast of tabernacles** for seven days unto the LORD.   On the **first day** shall be an **holy convocation**: ye shall do **no** servile **work** therein.  Seven days ye shall offer an offering made by fire unto the LORD: on the **eighth day** shall be an **holy convocation** unto you; and ye shall offer an offering made by fire unto the LORD: it is a solemn assembly; and ye shall do **no** servile **work** therein.  **These are the feasts of the LORD**, which ye shall proclaim to be **holy convocations**, to offer an offering made by fire unto the LORD, a burnt offering, and a meat offering, a sacrifice, and drink offerings, every thing upon his day:  **Beside the sabbaths** of the LORD, and beside your gifts, and beside all your vows, and beside all your freewill offerings, which ye give unto the LORD.

Leviticus 23:39  * Also in the **fifteenth day** of the **seventh month**, when ye have gathered in the fruit of the land, ye shall keep a **feast unto the LORD** seven days: on the **first day** shall be **a sabbath**, and on the **eighth day** shall be **a sabbath**.

---

[5] This would be from the end of the 9th day to the end of the 10th day.

16 -- **Sacred assemblies** (or **holy convocations**) are **Sabbaths**.

The New International Version of the Bible uses similar language to show **sacred assemblies** (or **holy convocations**) were also called **Sabbaths**.

> Leviticus 23:27 & 32    The **tenth day** of this **seventh month** is the **Day of Atonement**. Hold a **sacred assembly** and deny yourselves, and present an offering made to the LORD by fire....It is a **sabbath of rest** for you, and you must deny yourselves. From the evening of the ninth day of the month until the following evening you are to observe your **sabbath**. (New International Version)

> Leviticus 23:37-38    These are the **LORD's appointed feasts**, which you are to proclaim as **sacred assemblies** for bringing offerings made to the LORD by fire -the burnt offerings and grain offerings, sacrifices and drink offerings required for each day.  These offerings are in addition to those for **the LORD's Sabbaths** and in addition to your gifts and whatever you have vowed and all the freewill offerings you give to the LORD. (New International Version)

17 -- The word **Sabbath** is also used in the Old Testament in reference to years.

This use of the word Sabbath is not seen in the Gospels.

> Leviticus 25:2-8  Speak unto the children of Israel, and say unto them, When ye come into the land which I give you, then shall the land keep a **sabbath** unto the LORD.  Six years thou shalt sow thy field, and six years thou shalt prune thy vineyard, and gather in the fruit thereof;  But in the **seventh year** shall be a **sabbath of rest** unto the land, a **sabbath for the LORD**: thou shalt neither sow thy field, nor prune thy vineyard.  That which groweth of its own accord of thy harvest thou shalt not reap, neither gather the grapes of thy vine undressed: for it is a year of rest unto the land.  And the sabbath of the land shall be meat for you; for thee, and for thy servant, and for thy maid, and for thy hired servant, and for thy stranger that sojourneth with thee,  And for thy cattle, and for the beast that are in thy land, shall all the increase thereof be meat.  And thou shalt number **seven sabbaths** of years unto thee, seven times seven years; and the space of the **seven sabbaths** of years shall be unto thee forty and nine years.

## Jesus was three days and nights in the heart of the earth.

**(Thursday day and night, Friday day and night, and Saturday day and night)**
18 -- **Jesus prophesied that the Son of man be three days and three nights in the heart of the earth**.

Jesus called this the **sign of the prophet Jonas.**  Jonah was in the belly of a fish three days and three nights.

1 -- Now the LORD had prepared a great fish to swallow up Jonah. And Jonah was in the belly of the fish **three days** and **three nights**.

2--Matthew 12:39-40   But he answered and said unto them, An evil and adulterous generation seeketh after a sign; and there shall no sign be given to it, but the **sign of the prophet Jonas**:  For as Jonas was three days and three nights in the whale's belly; **so shall the Son of man be** **three days** and **three nights** in the heart of the **earth**.

3--Matthew 16:4   A wicked and adulterous generation seeketh after a sign; and there shall no sign be given unto it, but the **sign of the prophet Jonas**. And he left them, and departed.

4--Luke 11:29  And when the people were gathered thick together, he began to say, This is an evil generation: they seek a sign; and there shall no sign be given it, but the **sign of Jonas the prophet**.

19 -- Nine scriptures prophesy that **Jesus would rise** from the dead **the third day**.

1--John 2:19  Jesus answered and said unto them, Destroy this temple, and in **three days** I will raise it up.

2--Matthew 16:21    From that time forth began Jesus to show unto his disciples, how that he must go unto Jerusalem, and suffer many things of the elders and chief priests and scribes, and be killed, and be raised again the **third day**.

3--Matthew 17:23  And they shall kill him, and the **third day** he shall be raised again. And they were exceeding sorry.

4--Matthew 20:19   And shall deliver him to the Gentiles to mock, and to scourge, and to crucify him: and the **third day** he shall rise again.

5--Matthew 27:63   Saying, Sir, we remember that that deceiver said, while he was yet alive, After **three days** I will rise again.

6-- Mark 9:31  For he taught his disciples, and said unto them, The Son of man is delivered into the hands of men, and they shall kill him; and after that he is killed, he shall rise the **third day**.

7-- Mark 10:34  And they shall mock him, and shall scourge him, and shall spit upon him, and shall kill him: and the **third day** he shall rise again.

8--Luke 9:22   Saying, The Son of man must suffer many things, and be rejected of the elders and chief priests and scribes, and be slain, and be raised the **third day**.

9--Luke 18:33  And they shall scourge him, and put him to death: and the **third day** he shall rise again.

20 -- Five scriptures proclaim that **Jesus was raised** from the dead **the third day**.

1--Luke 24:6-7  He is not here, but is risen: remember how he spake unto you when he was yet in Galilee,   Saying, The Son of man must be delivered into the hands of sinful men, and be crucified, and the **third day** rise again.

2--Luke 24:21-23   But we trusted that it had been he which should have redeemed Israel: and beside all this, today is the **third day** since these things were done.   Yea, and certain women also of our company made us astonished, which were early at the sepulchre; And when they found not his body, they came, saying, that they had also seen a vision of angels, which said that he was alive.

3--Luke 24:46   And said unto them, Thus it is written, and thus it behooved Christ to suffer, and to rise from the dead the **third day**:

4--Acts 10:40   Him God raised up the **third day**, and showed him openly;

5--1 Corinthians 15:4   And that he was buried, and that he rose again the **third day** according to the scriptures: unto thee forty and nine years.

21 -- Many heard that Jesus would be raised up on the third day.

Matthew 27:39-40   And they that passed by reviled him, wagging their heads,   And saying, Thou that destroyest the temple, and buildest it in **three days**, save thyself. If thou be the Son of God, come down from the cross.

Mark 15:29-30   And they that passed by railed on him, wagging their heads, and saying, Ah, thou that destroyest the temple, and buildest it in **three days**,   Save thyself, and come down from the cross.

22 -- The chief priests and Pharisees heard that Jesus would be raised up on the third day.

Matthew 27: 62-64   Now the next day, that followed the day of the preparation, the chief priests and Pharisees came together unto Pilate, Saying, Sir, we remember that that deceiver said, while he was yet alive, After **three days** I will rise again.   Command therefore that the sepulchre be made sure until the **third day**, lest his disciples come by night, and steal him away, and say unto the people, He is risen from the dead: so the last error shall be worse than the first.

23 -- Soldiers were paid to lie about the third day resurrection of Jesus.

Matthew 28:11-15 Now when they were going, behold, some of the watch came into the city, and showed unto the chief priests all the things that were done.   And when they were assembled with the elders, and had taken counsel, **they gave large money unto the soldiers**, Saying, Say ye, His disciples came by night, and stole him away while we slept.   And if this come to the governor's ears, we will persuade him, and secure you.   So they took the money, and did as they were taught: and this saying is commonly reported among the Jews until this day.

# Solutions to Gospel Mysteries

Jesus never changes. Many clear examples of this are demonstrated in the Gospels when Jesus uses the same words to handle similar circumstances. The slight variations in Jesus' response to different situations show a new aspect of Jesus and His teaching. Jesus always shows more of Himself to those that seek His face.

"Gospel Parallels" and "Gospel Harmonies" do not look at the text of the Gospels sequentially. However, without looking sequentially, many interrelationships are missed and many mysterious "discrepancies" are encountered. While these truly appear to be discrepancies, how could they be present in a text written by authors who were inspired by God? Investigation of *The Sequential Gospels* will show that no discrepancies are present. In the macro view, the writers all wrote sequentially. There is no reason to assume that they did not write sequentially on the micro level.

Reference to the text and footnotes of *The Sequential Gospels* will be necessary to understand the interrelationships and time elements involved in the following *Solutions to Gospel Mysteries*. The solutions to some of these *Gospel Mysteries* have long been known by Bible scholars and other believers in the Word of God.

## Index to Mysteries and Solutions

# *Mysteries and Solutions*

## 1 -- Wise men and Egypt contained in Luke 2:39!

All the events of Matthew 2:1-23 occurred in the middle of verse thirty-nine of the second chapter of Luke. If Luke is the only source used to follow Jesus' travels, it appears that Jesus and His family went directly from His "presentation to the Lord" in Jerusalem, Luke 2:22, to Nazareth, Luke 2:39b.

> Luke 2:22　And when the days of her purification according to the law of
> Moses were accomplished, they brought him to Jerusalem, to present
> him to the Lord;

> Luke 2:39a　And when they had performed all things according to the law of
> the Lord,

> Luke 2:39b　they returned into Galilee, to their own city Nazareth.

However, after His "presentation to the Lord" in Jerusalem, Jesus and His family returned to Bethlehem. In Matthew 2:1-23 Jesus and His family were in Bethlehem when the wise men came to worship the child Jesus and give their gifts to Him. Then, being warned by an angel, Joseph and his family arose and fled by night to Egypt. After Herod's death, the angel of the Lord told Joseph to go "into the land of Israel," Matthew 2:20. This is when Matthew 2:23 says,"And he came and dwelt in a city called Nazareth: that it might be fulfilled which was spoken by the prophets, He shall be called a Nazarene." So, although Luke 2:39a and Luke 2:39b are sequential in themselves, they are separated by a long span of time.

## 2 -- The Four Temptations of Jesus.

Time sequencing on the micro level shows that Satan tempted Jesus two times with the "same" temptation. Matthew, Mark, and Luke record that Jesus was led up of the Spirit into the wilderness, fasted forty days and forty nights, and was forty days tempted of the devil.

> Matthew 4:1-2    Then was Jesus **led up of the Spirit into the wilderness** to be tempted of the devil.    And when he had **fasted forty days and forty nights**, he was afterward an hungered.

> Mark 1:12-13a   And immediately the Spirit driveth him into the wilderness. And he was there in the wilderness forty days, tempted of Satan; and was with the wild beasts;

> Luke 4:1-2 And Jesus being full of the Holy Ghost returned from Jordan, and was led by the Spirit into the wilderness,    **Being forty days tempted of the devil**. And in those days he did eat nothing: and when they were ended, he afterward hungered.

Only Matthew and Luke record any of the specific temptations in the wilderness. Matthew records temptations #1, #3, and #4 while Luke records temptations #1, #2, and #3. Only temptations #1 and #3 are identical. This means that there were four separate temptations. To understand the true testing that Jesus faced, the sequence of all four temptations is important.

◊    Temptation #1 --- Matthew and Luke both tell us that after the forty days in the wilderness, Jesus was hungry.  At that point, Jesus was tempted by the devil to change stones into bread.

> Matthew 4:3-4    And when the tempter came to him, he said, If thou be the Son of God, command that these stones be made bread.  But he answered and said, It is written, Man shall not live by bread alone, but by every word that proceedeth out of the mouth of God.

> Luke 4:3-4   And the devil said unto him, If thou be the Son of God, command this stone that it be made bread.   And Jesus answered him, saying, It is written, That man shall not live by bread alone, but by every word of God.

◊    Temptation #2 --- Preserving the sequence of the Gospels, only Luke tells us the **first** time that Satan tempted Jesus with the power and the glory of the kingdoms of the world.

> Luke 4:5-8    And the devil, taking him up into an high mountain, showed unto him **all the kingdoms of the world** in a moment of time. And the devil said unto him, All this **power** will I give thee, and **the glory of them**: for that is delivered unto me; and to whomsoever I will I give it.    If thou therefore wilt worship me, all shall be thine.    And Jesus answered and said unto him, **Get thee behind me**, Satan: for it is written, Thou shalt worship the Lord thy God, and him only shalt thou serve.

◊    Temptation #3 --- Matthew and Luke both describe the temptation "on a pinnacle of the temple."

> Matthew 4:5-7    Then the devil taketh him up into the holy city, and setteth him **on a pinnacle of the temple**,    And saith unto him, If thou be

the Son of God, cast thyself down: for it is written, He shall give his angels charge concerning thee: and in their hands they shall bear thee up, lest at any time thou dash thy foot against a stone.　Jesus said unto him, It is written again, Thou shalt not tempt the Lord thy God.

> Luke 4:9-12　And he brought him to Jerusalem, and set him **on a pinnacle of the temple**, and said unto him, If thou be the Son of God, cast thyself down from hence:　For it is written, He shall give his angels charge over thee, to keep thee:　And in their hands they shall bear thee up, lest at any time thou dash thy foot against a stone.　And Jesus answering said unto him, It is said, Thou shalt not tempt the Lord thy God.

◊　Temptation #4 --- Preserving the sequence of the Gospels, only Matthew tells us that Satan **again** tempted Jesus with all the kingdoms of the world and their glory.　Here Satan directs Jesus to "fall down and worship."

> Matthew 4:8-10　**Again**, the devil taketh him up into an exceeding high mountain, and showeth him **all the kingdoms of the world**, and **the glory of them**;　And saith unto him, All these things will I give thee, if thou wilt **fall down** and worship me.　Then saith Jesus unto him, **Get thee hence**, Satan: for it is written, Thou shalt worship the Lord thy God, and him only shalt thou serve.

Now compare Jesus' responses to Temptations #2 and #4. In Temptation #2, the first time Satan offered Jesus the kingdoms of the world, Jesus said, "Get thee behind me, Satan:...."　In Temptation #4, the second time Satan offered Jesus the kingdoms of the world, Jesus said, "Get thee hence, Satan,...."　The underlined words are different Greek words in the "Received Text." (The "Received Text" is used for the King James Version of the Bible.) So the difference in the wording between Matthew and Luke in the King James Version is not just a translation difference. There is even more difference in the Greek "Alexandrian" textbase (used for the New International Version of the Bible). In Temptation #2, the "Alexandrian" textbase completely omits the phrase "Get thee behind me, Satan:...."　In both Temptations #2 and #4 Jesus quoted the same scripture from Deuteronomy.

> Deuteronomy 6:13　Thou shalt fear the LORD thy God, and serve him, and shalt swear by his name.

Jesus said, "...it is written, Thou shalt worship the Lord thy God, and him only shalt thou serve."

Jesus used the Word of God four times to overcome these four temptations of Satan.　When the same temptation came more than once, Jesus quoted the same Word of God.　He is our example.

## 3 -- Simon, James, and John abandon Jesus.　Andrew remains faithful.

Simon, James, and John forsook their nets for only a short time.　Weeks later they were willing to forsake all.

◊　Followed Jesus #1 --- Simon and Andrew **left** or **forsook their nets**.  James, and John **left the ship and their father**.

> Matthew 4:18-22　　And Jesus, walking by the sea of Galilee, saw two brethren, **Simon called Peter**, and **Andrew** his brother, casting a net into the sea: for they were fishers.　And he saith unto them, Follow me, and I will make you fishers of men.　And they straightway **left their nets**, and followed him.　And going on from thence, he saw other two brethren, James the son of Zebedee, and John his brother, in a ship with Zebedee their father, mending their nets; and he called them.　And they immediately **left the ship and their father**, and followed him.

> Mark 1:16-20　Now as he walked by the sea of Galilee, he saw Simon and Andrew his brother casting a net into the sea: for they were fishers.　And Jesus said unto them, Come ye after me, and I will make you to become fishers of men.　And straightway they **forsook their nets**, and followed him.　And when he had gone a little farther thence, he saw James the son of Zebedee, and John his brother, who also were in the ship mending their nets.　And straightway he called them: and they **left their father** Zebedee in the ship with the hired servants, and went after him.

By time sequence we discover that although  Simon, James, and John immediately forsook their nets to follow Jesus, they did not follow Him for a long time. Jesus taught in Capernaum. Simon was there when Jesus healed Simon's wife's mother (Mark 1:31 and Luke 4:39).  Jesus then healed many that were sick (Mark 1:32-35 and Luke 4:40-42).  After this, Simon Peter and they that were with him followed Jesus to the place were He was praying (Mark 1:36-37).

> Mark 1:38　And he said unto them, Let us go into the next towns, that I may preach there also: for therefore came I forth.

Jesus then left Capernaum to preach throughout "all Galilee" (Matthew 4:23-8:1, Mark 1:39, and Luke 4:44).  However, Simon, James, and John remained in Capernaum and returned to their nets.

> Matthew 4:23　　And Jesus went **about all Galilee**, teaching in their synagogues, and preaching the gospel of the kingdom, and healing all manner of sickness and all manner of disease among the people.

> Mark 1:39　　And he **preached in their synagogues** throughout **all Galilee**, and cast out devils.

> Luke 4:44　And he preached in the **synagogues of Galilee**.

When Jesus returned to Capernaum He found Simon (Luke 5:5) and also James and John (Luke 5:10) washing their nets (Luke 5:2).  They apparently did not go with Jesus as He "preached in their synagogues throughout all Galilee." Jesus preached from Simon Peter's ship (Luke 5:3). Then Jesus said, "Launch out into the deep, and let down your nets for a draught." Simon Peter answered, "**we** have **toiled all the night**, and have taken nothing" (Luke 5:5). After they let down the net, "they inclosed a great multitude of fishes" (Luke 5:6).

> Luke 5:1-10　And it came to pass, that, as the people pressed upon him to hear the word of God, he stood by the lake of Gennesaret,　And saw two ships standing by the lake: but **the fishermen** were gone out of them,

and **were washing their nets**. And he entered into one of the ships, which was Simon's, and prayed him that he would thrust out a little from the land. And he sat down, and taught the people out of the ship. Now when he had left speaking, he said unto Simon, Launch out into the deep, and let down your nets for a draught. And **Simon** answering said unto him, Master, **we** have **toiled all the night**, and have taken nothing: nevertheless at thy word I will let down the net. And when they had this done, **they inclosed a great multitude of fishes**: and their net brake. And they **beckoned unto their partners**, which were in the other ship, that they should come and help them. And they came, and filled both the ships, so that they began to sink. When Simon Peter saw it, he fell down at Jesus' knees, saying, Depart from me; for I am a sinful man, O Lord. For he was astonished, and all that were with him, at the draught of the fishes which they had taken: And so was **also James**, and **John**, the sons of Zebedee, which were **partners with Simon**. And Jesus said unto Simon, Fear not; from henceforth thou shalt catch men.

◊ Followed Jesus #2 --- When the ships were brought to shore, they **forsook all** and followed Jesus.

> Luke 5:11 And when **they** had brought their ships to land, **they** forsook **all**, and followed him.

They did not go back to their nets until after the resurrection of Jesus from the dead. It is possible that Andrew stayed with Jesus for the entire Galilee campaign since Andrew was not specifically mentioned in Luke 5:1-11.

## 4 -- One healing was not enough for Simon Peter's wife's mother.

Jesus healed Simon's wife's mother two different times.

◊ Healing #1 --- The first time the disciples asked Jesus to help her.

> Mark 1:30-31 But Simon's wife's mother lay sick of a fever, and **anon they tell him** of her. And he came and took her by the hand, and lifted her up; and immediately the fever left her, and she ministered unto them.

> Luke 4:38-39 And he arose out of the synagogue, and entered into Simon's house. And Simon's wife's mother was taken with a great fever; and **they besought him** for her. And he stood over her, and rebuked the fever; and it left her: and immediately she arose and ministered unto them.

◊ Healing #2 --- Many weeks later, after He preached in the synagogues throughout Galilee, Jesus healed her again. This time the others did not need to ask Jesus to heal her. He went to her when He saw her need.

> Matthew 8:14-15 And when Jesus was come into Peter's house, **he saw** his wife's mother laid, and sick of a fever. And he touched her hand, and the fever left her: and she arose, and ministered unto them.

These two different healings show different aspects of Jesus as a healer. The first time other people asked Jesus to help her and He went to her and healed her. The second time, Jesus had a personal relationship with Simon's wife's mother. When Jesus saw that she was sick, He went directly to her and healed her.

## 5 -- The centurion had enough faith for two healings.

Jesus healed two different people in a certain centurion's household.[1]

◊ Healing #1 --- In Capernaum, a centurion arrived in person to ask Jesus for help.

> Matthew 8:5-6   And when Jesus was entered into, **there came unto him  a centurion**, beseeching him,    And saying, Lord, my servant lieth at home sick of the palsy, grievously tormented.

◊ Healing #2 --- Much later, (after the first storm at sea, the second ministry Passover, and the ordaining of the twelve), a certain centurion sent the Jewish elders to Jesus for help.

> Luke 7:1-3   Now when he had ended all his sayings in the audience of the people, he entered into Capernaum.   And a certain centurion's servant, who was dear unto him, was sick, and ready to die.   And when he heard of Jesus, **he sent unto him** the elders of the Jews, beseeching him that he would come and heal his servant.

Both times Jesus "marvelled" and said to them that followed, "...I have not found so great faith, no, not in Israel."

◊ Healing #1 ---

> Matthew 8:7-13   And Jesus saith unto him, I will come and heal him.    The centurion answered and said, Lord, I am not worthy that thou shouldest come under my roof: but **speak the word only**, and my servant shall be healed.   For I am a man under authority, having soldiers under me: and I say to this man, <u>Go, and he goeth; and to another, Come, and he cometh; and to my servant, Do this, and he doeth it</u>.   When Jesus heard it, he marvelled, and said to them that followed, Verily **I say unto you, I have not found so great faith, no, not in Israel**.   And I say unto you, That many shall come from the east and west, and shall sit down with Abraham, and Isaac, and Jacob, in the kingdom of heaven. But the children of the kingdom shall be cast out into outer darkness: there shall be weeping and gnashing of teeth.   And Jesus said unto the centurion, Go thy way; and as thou hast believed, so be it done unto thee. And his servant was healed in the selfsame hour.

◊ Healing #2 ---

> Luke 7:6-10 Then Jesus went with them. And when he was now not far from the house, the centurion sent friends to him, saying unto him, Lord, trouble not thyself: for I am not worthy that thou shouldest enter under my roof:  Wherefore neither thought I myself worthy to come unto thee: but **say in a word**, and my servant shall be healed.   For I also am a

---

[1] Some scholars believe that there were two different centurions who lived in Capernaum and asked Jesus for help.  It is certain that there were two different people healed.

man set under authority, having under me soldiers, and I say unto one, <u>Go, and he goeth; and to another, Come, and he cometh; and to my servant, Do this, and he doeth it</u>. When Jesus heard these things, he **marvelled at him**, and turned him about, and said unto the people that followed him, **I say unto you, I have not found so great faith, no, not in Israel**. And they that were sent, returning to the house, found the servant whole that had been sick.

By not going to Jesus personally, the centurion showed more faith for the second healing than it took for the first healing. So, Jesus could again say, "**I have not found so great faith, no, not in Israel**."

## 6 -- Two storms at sea. Little faith changed to no faith.

Jesus calmed two different storms at sea. During each storm the disciples awoke Him in the back of the ship. During the first storm the disciples used **little faith**. During the second storm the disciples used **no faith**. Jesus did not change. Both times He used His faith to calm the storm.

◊ Storm #1 --- The first storm at sea is only found in Matthew. There is no mention of any other ships on the sea. The storm rose up and the disciples showed **little faith** when they said, "**Lord, save us**: we perish."

> Matthew 8:24-27 And, behold, there arose a great tempest in the sea, insomuch that the ship was covered with the waves: but he was asleep. And his disciples came to him, and awoke him, saying, **Lord, save us**: we perish. And he saith unto them, Why are ye fearful, O ye of **little faith**? **Then he arose**, and rebuked the winds and the sea; and there was a great calm. But the men **marvelled**, saying, **What manner of man is this**, that even the winds and the sea obey him!

◊ Storm #2 --- Months later, (after a feast in Jerusalem, the first trip through the corn field, and choosing the twelve), there was a second storm at sea. Many little ships were following them. During this storm the disciples called Jesus "master" but then used **no faith** when they said, "**Master, carest thou not that we perish?**" Jesus calmed the storm **before** He talked to the disciples. By doing this, Jesus gave immediate aid to all of the "other little ships." He then asked the disciples to consider why they had **no faith**.

> Mark 4:36-41 And when they had sent away the multitude, they took him even as he was in the ship. And there were also with him **other little ships**. And there arose a great storm of wind, and the waves beat into the ship, so that it was now full. And he was in the hinder part of the ship, asleep on a pillow: and they awake him, and say unto him, **Master, carest thou not that we perish**? And he arose, and rebuked the wind, and said unto the sea, Peace, be still. And the wind ceased, and there was a great calm. And he said unto them, Why are ye so fearful? how is it that ye have **no faith**? And they **feared exceedingly**, and said one to another, **What manner of man is this**, that even the wind and the sea obey him?

Luke 8:23-25a  But as they sailed he fell asleep: and there came down a storm of wind on the lake; and they were filled with water, and were in jeopardy. And they came to him, and awoke him, saying, **Master, master, we perish**. Then he arose, and rebuked the wind and the raging of the water: and they ceased, and there was a calm.   And he said unto them, **Where is your faith**? And they being **afraid wondered**, saying one to another, **What manner of man is this!** for he commandeth even the winds and water, and they obey him.

The disciples **again** marvelled and said, "**What manner of man is this!**"

## 7 -- Jesus cast devils into swine two different times.

◊  Exorcism #1 --- This exorcism happened after the first storm at sea.  Jesus landed in the **Gergesenes** and was met by **two possessed** with devils.  This exorcism is recorded only in Matthew.

Matthew 8:28-32  And when he was come to the other side into the country of the Gergesenes, there met him **two possessed** with devils, coming out of the tombs, exceeding fierce, so that no man might pass by that way. And, behold, they cried out, saying, What have we to do with thee, Jesus, thou Son of God? art thou come hither to torment us before the time? And there was a good way off from them an herd of many swine feeding. So the devils **besought him**, saying, If thou cast us out, **suffer us to go away into the herd of swine**.   And he said unto them, **Go**. And when they were come out, they went into the herd of swine:    and, behold, the whole herd of swine **ran violently down a steep place** into the sea, and perished in the waters.

◊  Exorcism #2 --- By time sequence we know that this second exorcism in the **Gadarenes** happened many months after the exorcism in the Gergesenes.  Immediately following the calming of the second storm at sea, Jesus landed in the country of the Gadarenes.  He was met by **a certain man** who was possessed with devils.  These devils also asked to **enter into** a herd of swine.  This event is found in Mark and Luke.

Mark 5:1-2 & 5:11-13    And they came over unto the other side of the sea, into the country of the Gadarenes.    And when he was come out of the ship, immediately there met him out of the tombs **a man** with an unclean spirit...Now there was there nigh unto the mountains a great herd of swine feeding.   And all the devils **besought him**, saying, **Send us into the swine**, that we may **enter into** them.   And forthwith Jesus gave them leave. And the unclean spirits went out, and entered into the swine: and the herd **ran violently down a steep place** into the sea, (they were about two thousand;) and **were choked** in the sea.

Luke 8:27 & 8:30-33  And when he went forth to land, there met him out of the city **a certain man**, which had devils long time, and ware no clothes, neither abode in any house, but in the tombs...And Jesus asked him, saying, What is thy name? And he said, **Legion**: because many devils were entered into him.   And they besought him that he would not command them to go out into the deep.    And there was there an herd of many swine feeding on the mountain: and they **besought him** that he would suffer them to **enter into** them.  And he suffered them.    Then went the devils out of the man, and entered into the swine: and **the herd ran violently down a steep place** into the lake, and **were choked**.

In Exorcism #1 and Exorcism #2 the swine acted the same way to the presence of devils. They "**ran violently down a steep place into the sea**" and perished.

## 8 -- The women with an issue of blood twelve years.

Two different women with an issue of blood were healed when they touched Jesus' garment. The two healings were separated in time by the second Passover, the ordaining of the twelve, and a second storm at sea.

◊    Account of a certain ruler's daughter -- After calling Matthew, Jesus sat at meat in Matthew's house (Matthew 9:10, Mark 2:15, & Luke 5:29).    Then came a certain ruler.  He said, "My daughter **is even now dead**...."  Jesus arose, and followed him.

> Matthew 9:18-19   While he spake these things unto them, behold, there came a certain ruler, and worshipped him, saying, My daughter **is even now dead**: but come and lay thy hand upon her, and she shall live.    And Jesus arose, and followed him, and so did his disciples.

◊    Account of Jairus' daughter -- The events surrounding Jairus' daughter are different from the events found in Matthew 9:18-26.  Jairus came to Jesus at the sea side and said, "My little daughter **lieth at the point of death**: I pray thee, come and lay thy hands on her, that she may be healed; and she shall live."

> Mark 5:21-24   And when Jesus was passed over again by ship unto the other side, much people gathered unto him: and he was **nigh unto the sea**. And, behold, there cometh one of the rulers of the synagogue, Jairus by name; and when he saw him, he fell at his feet,    And besought him greatly, saying, My little daughter **lieth at the point of death**: I pray thee, come and lay thy hands on her, that she may be healed; and she shall live.    And Jesus went with him; and much people followed him, and thronged him.

> Luke 8:41-42   And, behold, there came a man named Jairus, and he was a ruler of the synagogue: and he fell down at Jesus' feet, and besought him that he would come into his house:   For he had one only daughter, about twelve years of age, and she lay a dying. But as he went the people thronged him.

◊    Account of a certain ruler -- In Matthew's account, a woman, who was diseased with an issue of blood twelve years, came behind him, and touched the hem of his garment.    There was no crowd of people.

> Matthew 9:20-21   And, behold, a woman, which was diseased with an issue of blood twelve years, came behind him, and touched the hem of his garment:   For she said within herself, If I may but touch his garment, I shall be whole.

◊ Account of Jairus' daughter -- By time sequence, the woman found in Mark 5:25 and Luke 8:43 is not the woman found in Matthew 9:20.

> Mark 5:25-27 And a certain woman, which had an issue of blood twelve years, And had suffered many things of many physicians, and had spent all that she had, and was nothing bettered, but rather grew worse, When she had heard of Jesus, came in the press behind, and touched his garment.

> Luke 8:43-44 And a woman having an issue of blood twelve years, which had spent all her living upon physicians, neither could be healed of any, Came behind him, and touched the border of his garment: and immediately her issue of blood stanched

◊ Accounts similar -- Both women had been sick for twelve years. They were both healed when they touched Jesus' garment. As usual, Jesus said the same thing to both women.

> First woman -- Matthew 9:22 But Jesus turned him about, and when he saw her, he said, Daughter, be of good comfort; thy faith hath made thee whole. And the woman was made whole from that hour.

> Second woman -- Mark 5:34 And he said unto her, Daughter, thy faith hath made thee whole; go in peace, and be whole of thy plague.

> Second woman -- Luke 8:48 And he said unto her, Daughter, be of good comfort: thy faith hath made thee whole; go in peace.

◊ Account of Jairus' daughter -- In the Jairus account, it was then reported that Jairus' daughter had died.

> Mark 5:35 While he yet spake, there came from the ruler of the synagogue's house certain which said, Thy daughter is dead: why troublest thou the Master any further?

> Luke 8:49 While he yet spake, there cometh one from the ruler of the synagogue's house, saying to him, Thy daughter is dead; trouble not the Master.

◊ Accounts similar -- From this point, the events between the two stories are very similar. Jesus raised both daughters from the dead.

> A certain ruler's daughter -- Matthew 9:25 But when the people were put forth, he went in, and took her by the hand, and the maid arose.

> Jairus' daughter -- Mark 5:41 And he took the damsel by the hand, and said unto her, Talitha cumi; which is, being interpreted, Damsel, I say unto thee, arise.

> Jairus' daughter -- Luke 8:54 And he put them all out, and took her by the hand, and called, saying, Maid, arise.

## 9 -- The "ears of corn" were probably barley <u>and</u> wheat.

Jesus' disciples "plucked the ears of corn" on two different Sabbath[2] days. Corn as we know it, comes from North America and was not grown in Europe until the 1500's. Therefore, the "corn" must have been some kind of grain. The seasonal calendar reveals which kind of grain would be in season.

◊ Picking #1 --- Just after His second ministry Passover, Jesus and His disciples were walking through "the corn fields on the sabbath day." Jesus' disciples began to pluck the "ears of corn." This was the season of the barley harvest.

> Mark 2:23-24   And it came to pass, that he went through the corn fields on the sabbath day; and his disciples began, as they went, to pluck the **ears of corn**.   And the Pharisees said unto him, Behold, why do they on the sabbath day that which is not lawful?

> Luke 6:1-2   And it came to pass on the second sabbath after the first, that he went through the corn fields; and his disciples plucked the **ears of corn**, and did eat, rubbing them in their hands.   And certain of the Pharisees said unto them, Why do ye that which is not lawful to do on the sabbath days?

The Pharisees simply ask "why" Jesus' disciples did "on the sabbath day that which is not lawful." Jesus answered with the story of David and the showbread.

> Mark 2:25-28   And he said unto them, Have ye never read what David did, when he had need, and was an hungered, he, and they that were with him?   How he went into the house of God in the days of Abiathar the high priest, and did eat the showbread, which is not lawful to eat but for the priests, and gave also to them which were with him?   And he said unto them, The sabbath was made for man, and not man for the sabbath: Therefore the Son of man is Lord also of the sabbath.

> Luke 6:3-5   And Jesus answering them said, Have ye not read so much as this, what David did, when himself was an hungered, and they which were with him.   How he went into the house of God, and did take and eat the showbread, and gave also to them that were with him; which it is not lawful to eat but for the priests alone?   And he said unto them, That the Son of man is Lord also of the sabbath.

◊ Picking #2 --- Months later, (after Jesus ordained the twelve, preached the sermon on the plain, healed the centurion's servant in Luke 7:2, was anointed in a Pharisees' house, went through every city and village preaching, raised Jairus' daughter from the dead, again went about all of the cities and villages teaching, and sent forth the twelve two by two), the disciples again plucked the "ears of corn." This time it was during the season of the wheat harvest.

> Matthew 12:1   At that time Jesus went on the sabbath day through the corn; and his disciples were an hungered, and began to pluck the **ears of corn**, and to eat.

---

[2] Sabbath  (Today the word "Sabbath" is generally capitalized but it is not capitalized in the King James Version of the Bible.)

The Pharisees again went to Jesus. This time they flatly condemned the disciples for breaking the law.

> Matthew 12:2    But when the Pharisees saw it, they said unto him, Behold, thy disciples do that which is not lawful to do upon the sabbath day.

Jesus did not change. He again defended His disciples using the story of David and the showbread. Jesus then added a teaching about the priests in the temple. Finally, He addressed the condemning attitude of these Pharisees by saying, "But if ye had known what this meaneth, **I will have mercy, and not sacrifice**, ye would not have condemned the guiltless." Perhaps these are the same Pharisees to whom Jesus said, "But go ye and learn what that meaneth, **I will have mercy, and not sacrifice**:" (Matthew 9:13a).

> Matthew 12:3-8    But he said unto them, Have ye not read what David did, when he was an hungered, and they that were with him; How he entered into the house of God, and did eat the showbread, which was not lawful for him to eat, neither for them which were with him, but only for the priests? Or have ye not read in the law, how that on the sabbath days the priests in the temple profane the sabbath, and are blameless? But I say unto you, That in this place is one greater than the temple. But if ye had known what this meaneth, **I will have mercy, and not sacrifice**, ye would not have condemned the guiltless. For the Son of man is Lord even of the sabbath day.

## 10 -- The two withered hands.

Jesus healed two different men with withered hands.

◊   Healed Hand #1 --- The scribes and Pharisees "watched" Jesus to see whether He would heal on the Sabbath day. Jesus knew their thoughts. He said to them, "Is it lawful to do good on the sabbath days, or to do evil? to save life, or to kill?"

> Mark 3:1-5    And he entered again into the synagogue; and there was a man there which had **a withered hand**. And they **watched** him, whether he would heal him on the sabbath day; that they might accuse him. And he saith unto the man which had the withered hand, Stand forth. And he saith unto them, **Is it lawful to do good on the sabbath days, or to do evil? to save life, or to kill?** But they held their peace. And when he had looked round about on them with anger, being grieved for the hardness of their hearts, he saith unto the man, Stretch forth thine hand. And he stretched it out: and his hand was **restored whole as the other**.

> Luke 6:6-10    And it came to pass also on another sabbath, that he entered into the synagogue and taught: and there was a man whose **right hand** was **withered**. And the scribes and Pharisees **watched** him, whether he would heal on the sabbath day; that they might find an accusation against him. But **he knew their thoughts**, and said to the man which had the withered hand, Rise up, and stand forth in the midst. And he arose and stood forth. Then said Jesus unto them, **I will ask you one thing; Is it lawful on the sabbath days to do good, or to do evil?**

**to save life, or to destroy it?** And looking round about upon them all, he said unto the man, Stretch forth thy hand. And he did so: and his hand was **restored whole as the other**.

◊    Healed Hand #2 --- Months later, (after Jesus ordained the twelve, preached the sermon on the plain, healed the centurion's servant in Luke 7:2, was anointed in a Pharisees house, went through every city and village preaching, raised Jairus' daughter from the dead, again went about all of the cities and villages teaching, and sent forth the twelve two by two), the scribes and Pharisees expected Jesus to heal on the Sabbath. So they were first to ask the question, "Is it lawful to heal on the sabbath days?" (This is similar to the question that Jesus had asked the scribes and Pharisees in Mark 3:4.) After Jesus answered their question, He healed "a man which had his hand withered." Like Healed Hand #1, this man's hand was "**restored whole**, like **as the other**."

>    Matthew 12:9-13    And when he was departed thence, he went into their synagogue: And, behold, there was a man which had his hand withered. And **they asked him**, saying, Is it lawful to heal on the sabbath days? that they might accuse him. And he said unto them, What man shall there be among you, that shall have one sheep, and if it fall into a pit on the sabbath day, will he not lay hold on it, and lift it out? How much then is a man better than a sheep? Wherefore it is lawful to do well on the sabbath days. Then saith he to the man, Stretch forth thine hand. And he stretched it forth; and it was **restored whole**, like **as the other**.

## 11 -- Jesus' mother and brethren called for Jesus three times.

Jesus' mother and brethren tried to call Jesus out of three different meetings during His second year of preaching.

◊    Call #1 --- This call followed soon after Jesus ordained the twelve.

>    Mark 3:31-32    There came then his brethren and his mother, and, standing without, sent unto him, **calling him**. And the multitude sat about him, and they said unto him, Behold, thy mother and thy brethren without **seek for thee**.

Jesus responded, "Who is my mother, or my brethren?"

>    Mark 3:33-5    And he answered them, saying, Who is my mother, or my brethren? And he looked round about on them which sat about him, and said, Behold my mother and my brethren! For **whosoever shall do the will of God**, the same is my brother, and my sister, and mother.

◊    Call #2 --- By sequential alignment of the Gospel text, Call #1 was followed by Jesus raising a widow woman's son from the dead and preaching in "every city and village" (this included Nazareth). After this time, Jesus' brethren and mother tried to call Him out of another meeting.

>    Luke 8:19-20    Then came to him his mother and his brethren, and could not come at him for the press. And it was told him by certain which said, Thy mother and thy brethren stand without, **desiring to see thee**.

Jesus responded, "My mother and my brethren are...."

Luke 8:21  And he answered and said unto them, My mother and my brethren are **these which hear the word of God, and do it**.

◊  Call #3 --- After Call #2 Jesus calmed the second storm at sea, went on His second ministry trip to Nazareth, and sent forth the twelve.  Then, Jesus had a meeting with "certain of the scribes and of the Pharisees."  His mother and his brethren stood without for the third time.

Matthew 12:38 & 46-47    Then **certain of the scribes and of the Pharisees** answered, saying, Master, we would see a sign from thee. ... While he yet talked to the people, behold, his mother and his brethren stood without, **desiring to speak** with him.   Then one said unto him, Behold, thy mother and thy brethren stand without, **desiring to speak** with thee.

For the third time Jesus used the word "**do**" to help define His mother and brethren.

Matthew 12:48-50  But he answered and said unto him that told him, **Who is my mother? and who are my brethren?**    And he stretched forth his hand toward his disciples, and said, Behold my mother and my brethren!   For **whosoever shall do the will of my Father** which is in heaven, the same is my brother, and sister, and mother.

Soon after this third call, Jesus took His third special ministry trip to Nazareth.  It is interesting to note that Jesus went to Nazareth soon after Call #1, Call #2, and Call #3.  In this way, Jesus honored His mother by visiting her in Nazareth each time that she showed a special need.

## 12 -- Jesus went on three special ministry trips to Nazareth.

Jesus took three specific trips to Nazareth.  We know that he also ministered in Nazareth when He went about all of the cities and villages of Galilee.  It is possible that Jesus also went to Nazareth each year to help prepare for the feast of tabernacles with His family.

◊  Ministry Trip #1 --- John left Jesus in Cana and traveled with the nobleman to Capernam (John 4:46-54).  Jesus traveled from Cana to Nazareth.  This was during Jesus' first full year of ministry.  Jesus read from the prophet Esaias, Isaiah 61:1 & 2a.

Luke 4:16-19  And he came to Nazareth, where he had been brought up: and, as his custom was, he went into the synagogue on the sabbath day, and stood up for to read.  And there was delivered unto him the book of the prophet Esaias. And when he had opened the book, he found the place where it was written,   The Spirit of the Lord is upon me, because he hath anointed me to preach the gospel to the poor; he hath sent me to heal the brokenhearted, to preach deliverance to the captives, and recovering of sight to the blind, to set at liberty them that are bruised, To preach the acceptable year of the Lord.

There is no report that Jesus healed anyone on this trip.  In fact, some wanted to kill Him.

Luke 4:29-30  And rose up, and thrust him out of the city, and led him unto the brow of the hill whereon their city was built, **that they might cast him down headlong**.   But he passing through the midst of them went his way.

◊   Ministry Trip #2--- Both Trips #2 and #3 were during Jesus' second full year of ministry. By this time there were some who reached out in faith to receive their healing.

> Mark 6:1 & 5   And he went out from thence, and came into his own country; and his disciples follow him. ... And he could there do no mighty work, save that he laid his hands upon **a few sick folk, and healed them**.

◊   Ministry Trip #3 --- This trip shows that the Word of God that Jesus preached on His previous trips to Nazareth was starting to grow. Some people were able to receive a "mighty work" from Jesus, although others were still unable to receive "because of their unbelief."

> Matthew 13:54 & 58    And when he was come into his own country, he taught them in their synagogue, insomuch that they were astonished, and said, Whence hath this man this wisdom, and **these mighty works**? ... And he **did not many mighty works** there because of their unbelief.

## 13 -- Jesus walked on the sea twice.

Jesus walked on the sea to help the disciples two different times. These walks were probably more than a week apart.

◊   Walk on Sea #1 --- Jesus had just fed the 5000. Jesus told the disciples to get into the ship and to go "to the other side before unto Bethsaida." [3]   Then He personally "sent the multitudes away" and "went up into a mountain apart to pray."

> Matthew 14:22-23   And straightway Jesus constrained his disciples to get into a ship, and to go before him unto the other side, while he sent the multitudes away.   And when **he had sent the multitudes away**, he went up into a mountain apart to pray: and when the evening was come, **he was there alone**.

> Mark 6:45-46   And straightway he constrained his disciples to get into the ship, and to go to the other side before unto Bethsaida, while he sent away the people.   And when he had sent them away, he departed into a mountain to pray.

Jesus then saw the disciples "toiling in rowing." He went to them (Matthew 14:25) but they had to "cry out" or he "would have passed them by" (Mark 6:48). Jesus said, "Be of good cheer; it is I; be not afraid."

> Matthew 14:25-29   And in the fourth watch of the night **Jesus went** unto them, walking on the sea.   And when the disciples saw **him walking on the sea**, they were troubled, saying, It is a spirit; and they **cried**

---

[3] Mark 6:45   And straightway he constrained his disciples to...go...unto Bethsaida, while he sent away the people. (*The disciples were sent to Bethsaida. It is possible that they were returning from Bethsaida when Jesus saw them* "toiling in rowing" *in Mark 6:48. In Mark 6:51, Jesus* "went up unto them into the ship; and the wind ceased:..." *Then, in Mark 6:53,* "...they came into the land of Gennesaret....")

out for fear.    But straightway Jesus spake unto them, saying, Be of good cheer; **it is I; be not afraid**.    And Peter answered him and said, Lord, if it be thou, bid me come unto thee on the water.    And he said, Come. And when Peter was come down out of the ship, he walked on the water, to go to Jesus.

Mark 6:48-50    And he saw them toiling in rowing; for the wind was contrary unto them: and about the fourth watch of the night he cometh unto them, **walking upon the sea**, and **would have passed by them**.    But when they saw **him walking upon the sea**, they supposed it had been a spirit, and **cried out**:    For they all saw him, and were troubled. And immediately he talked with them, and saith unto them, Be of good cheer: **it is I; be not afraid.**

The "wind ceased" when Jesus and Peter entered the ship (Matthew 14:32).    They then **came to the land of Gennesaret**. Jesus healed their sick.    He visited their villages and cities, "and as many as touched him were made whole."

Mark 6:53, 56    And when they had passed over, they came into the land of Gennesaret, and drew to the shore....And whithersoever **he entered**, into **villages**, or **cities**, or **country**, they laid the sick in the streets, and besought him that they might touch if it were but the border of his garment: and **as many as touched him were made whole**.

Matthew 14:36    And besought him that they might only touch the hem of his garment: and **as many as touched were made perfectly whole**.

◊    Walk on Sea #2 --- Now look back to the last verse of the feeding of the 5000 in John.

John 6:13    Therefore they gathered them together, and filled twelve baskets with the fragments of the five barley loaves, which remained over and above unto them that had eaten.

Immediately after this, "Jesus constrained his disciples to get into a ship, and to go before him unto the other side, while he sent the multitudes away" (Matthew 14:22).    John went with the disciples when they went before Jesus "unto the other side" (Matthew 14:22).    John only wrote about those things that he saw (John 19:35).    So, he did not write about what happened to the crowd of 5000 men when Jesus "**had sent the multitudes away**."

However in John 6:14-15 there is a group of men that Jesus perceived would "would come and take him by force."    This is not the same group that Jesus calmly sent home after feeding the 5000.    This group of men saw the events of Matthew 14:24-36 and Mark 6:47-56.    They saw that everyone that touched the hem of Jesus' garment was made whole.    This was a miracle. When Jesus perceived that "**those men**" would come and take him by force, He departed "**again**" into a mountain alone.    John was there when Jesus departed.

John 6:14-15    Then **those men**, when they had seen the miracle that Jesus did, said, This is of a truth that prophet that should come into the world. When Jesus therefore perceived that they **would come and take him by force**, to make him a king, he departed **again** into a mountain himself alone.

When evening came, the disciples again departed by ship.    This time they went toward Capernaum.    For the second time, they needed help.    This time Jesus went directly to the disciples, "walking on the sea." Jesus again said, "It is I; be not afraid." When He entered the ship, "**immediately** the ship was at the land whither they went."

> John 6:16-21  And when even was now come, his disciples went down unto the sea,  And entered into a ship, and went over the sea toward Capernaum.  And it was now dark, and Jesus was not come to them. And the sea arose by reason of a great wind that blew.  So when they had rowed about five and twenty or thirty furlongs, they see **Jesus walking on the sea**, and drawing nigh unto the ship: and they were afraid.  But **he saith** unto them, **It is I; be not afraid**.  Then they willingly received him into the ship: and **immediately  the ship  was at the land whither they went.**

## 14 -- Jesus began and ended His ministry by teaching the *"Lord's Prayer."*

Jesus taught the *"Lord's Prayer"* two different times.

◊    Teaching #1 --- Jesus was preaching to the multitudes in Galilee at the beginning of His ministry.  It was soon after His first ministry Passover.  The *"Lord's Prayer"* is a small part of *"The Sermon on the Mount"* found in the 4th, 5th, and 6th chapters of Matthew.

> Matthew 6:9-13  After this manner therefore pray ye: Our Father which art in heaven, Hallowed be thy name.   Thy kingdom come. Thy will be done in earth, as it is in heaven.   Give us this day our daily bread.   And forgive us our debts, as we forgive our debtors.   And lead us not into temptation, but deliver us from evil: For thine is the kingdom, and the power, and the glory, for ever. Amen

◊    Teaching #2 --- It was more than two and one half years later when the disciples in Judea asked Jesus how to pray.  They were near Bethany and it was the time of the Feast of Dedication.

> Luke 11:1-4  And it came to pass, that, as he was praying in a certain place, when he ceased, one of his disciples said unto him, Lord, teach us to pray, as John also taught his disciples.   And he said unto them, When ye pray, say, Our Father which art in heaven, Hallowed be thy name. Thy kingdom come. Thy will be done, as in heaven, so in earth.   Give us day by day our daily bread.   And forgive us our sins; for we also forgive every one that is indebted to us. And lead us not into temptation; but deliver us from evil.

## 15 -- But seek ye first the kingdom of God.... - year after year.

◊    Teaching #1 --- Jesus taught this truth in the spring time soon after His first ministry Passover.  It is part of "The Sermon on the Mount" found in the 4th, 5th, and 6th chapters of Matthew.

> Matthew 6:33  But seek ye first the kingdom of God, and his righteousness; and all these things shall be added unto you.

◊    Teaching #2 --- Jesus again taught this truth in the third year of His ministry, during the time of the Feast of Dedication. It was winter (John 10:22). Jesus was speaking to an "innumerable multitude" (Luke 12:1).

> Luke 12:31   But rather seek ye the kingdom of God; and all these things shall be added unto you.

## 16 -- Four blind men healed near Jericho.

Jesus healed **a certain blind man** on His way into Jericho. Jesus entered and passed through Jericho (Luke 19:1). Jesus abode at Zacchaeus' house (Luke 19:2-27). He may have stayed with Zacchaeus for more than one day. While departing from Jericho, Jesus healed **two blind men** and **blind Bartimaeus**. Each time these blind men called Jesus the **Son of David**. (It would have been easy for the **certain blind man** to tell **the two blind men** and **blind Bartimaeus** what to say to Jesus so that they could also be healed.) Each time Jesus responded by standing still, calling them, and asking them, "What will ye that I shall do unto you?"

◊    Blind Man #1 --- As Jesus came near to Jericho, **a certain blind man** was healed when Jesus said, "**Receive thy sight: thy faith hath saved thee.**"

> Luke 18:35, 38-39, 40-43   And it came to pass, that as he was come nigh unto Jericho, **a certain blind man** sat by the way side begging:....And he cried, saying, Jesus, **thou son of David, have mercy on me**. And they which went before rebuked him, that he should hold his peace: but he cried so much the more, **Thou son of David, have mercy on me**....And Jesus stood, and commanded him to be brought unto him: and when he was come near, he asked him, Saying, What wilt thou that I shall do unto thee? And he said, Lord, that I may receive my sight. And Jesus said unto him, **Receive thy sight: thy faith hath saved thee**. And immediately he received his sight, **and followed him**, glorifying God: and all the people, when they saw it, gave praise unto God.

◊    Blind Men #2 and #3 --- While departing from Jericho, **two blind men** were healed when Jesus had compassion on them and **touched their eyes**.

> Matthew 20:29-34    And as they departed from Jericho, a great multitude followed him. And, behold, **two blind men** sitting by the way side, when they heard that Jesus passed by, cried out, saying, Have mercy on us, O Lord, **thou Son of David**. And the multitude rebuked them, because they should hold their peace: but they cried the more, saying, **Have mercy on us**, O Lord, thou Son of David. And Jesus stood still, and called them, and said, What will ye that I shall do unto you? They say unto him, Lord, that our eyes may be opened. So **Jesus had compassion** on them, and **touched their eyes**: and immediately their eyes received sight, and they followed him.

◊　Blind Man #4 --- While departing from Jericho, Jesus also healed **blind Bartimaeus** when He said, "Go thy way; **thy faith hath made thee whole.**"

> Mark 10:46b-52　and as he went out of Jericho with his disciples and a great number of people, **blind Bartimaeus**, the son of Timaeus, sat by the highway side begging.　And when he heard that it was Jesus of Nazareth, he began to cry out, and say, Jesus, **thou son of David, have mercy on me**.　And many charged him that he should hold his peace: but he cried the more a great deal, **Thou son of David, have mercy on me**.　And Jesus stood still, and commanded him to be called. And they call the blind man, saying unto him, Be of good comfort, rise; he calleth thee.　And he, casting away his garment, rose, and came to Jesus. And Jesus answered and said unto him, What wilt thou that I should do unto thee? The blind man said unto him, Lord, that I might receive my sight.　And Jesus said unto him, Go thy way; **thy faith hath made thee whole.** And immediately he received his sight, and followed Jesus in the way.

## 17 -- The money changers did not learn.

Jesus drove the changers of money out of the temple on **two** occasions three years apart.

◊　Cleansing of the Temple #1 --- The first cleansing was during Jesus' first ministry Passover. Jesus said, "Take these things hence; make not my Father's house an **house of merchandise**."

> John 2:15-17　And when he had **made a scourge** of small cords, he drove them all out of the temple, and the **sheep**, and the **oxen**; and poured out the changers' money, and overthrew the tables;　And said unto them that sold doves, Take these things hence; **make not** my Father's house an **house of merchandise**.　And his disciples remembered that it was written, The zeal of thine house hath eaten me up.

◊　Cleansing of the Temple #2 --- The second cleansing was the Monday before Jesus' fourth and last ministry Passover.　Jesus did not use a scourge this time.　Perhaps there were no oxen or sheep present.　However, this time He said that they had made the house of prayer "**a den of thieves**."

> Matthew 21:12-13　And Jesus went into the temple of God, and cast out all them that sold and bought in the temple, and overthrew the tables of the moneychangers, and the seats of them that sold doves, And said unto them, It is written, My house shall be called the house of prayer; but **ye have made it a den of thieves**.

> Mark 11:15-17　And they come to Jerusalem: and Jesus went into the temple, and began to cast out them that sold and bought in the temple, and overthrew the tables of the moneychangers, and the seats of them that sold doves;　And would not suffer that any man should carry any vessel through the temple.　And he taught, saying unto them, Is it not written, My house shall be called of all nations the house of prayer? but ye have **made it a den of thieves**.

Luke 19:45-46   And he went into the temple, and began to cast out them that sold therein, and them that bought; Saying unto them, It is written, My house is the house of prayer: but ye have **made it a den of thieves**.

## 18 -- You can have what you say, instantly.   The accounts of the two fig trees.

Jesus cursed two different fig trees on the Monday and Tuesday before His last Passover of the LORD.   While both fig trees dried up, the second one dried up instantly.

◊    Fig Tree #1 --- On Monday Jesus saw the first fig tree **afar off** as He came from Bethany, before He entered the city of Jerusalem.

Mark 11:12-15   And on the morrow, when they were come **from Bethany**, he was hungry:   And seeing **a fig tree afar off** having leaves, he came, if haply he might find any thing thereon: and when he came to it, he found nothing but leaves; for the time of figs was not yet.   And Jesus answered and said unto it, **No man eat fruit of thee hereafter for ever.** And his disciples heard it.   **And they come to Jerusalem**: and Jesus went into the temple, and began to cast out them that sold and bought in the temple, and overthrew the tables of the moneychangers, and the seats of them that sold doves;

The next day they saw "the fig tree dried up from the roots." This was outside of Jerusalem.

Mark 11:20-27a   And in the morning, as they passed by, they saw **the fig tree dried up from the roots**. And Peter calling to remembrance saith unto him, Master, behold, the fig tree which thou cursedst is withered away.   And Jesus answering saith unto them, Have faith in God. For verily I say unto you, That whosoever shall say unto this mountain, Be thou removed, and be thou cast into the sea; and shall not doubt in his heart, but shall believe that those things which he saith shall come to pass; he shall have whatsoever he saith. Therefore I say unto you, What things soever ye desire, when ye pray, believe that ye receive them, and ye shall have them.   And when ye stand praying, forgive, if ye have aught against any: that your Father also which is in heaven may forgive you your trespasses.   But if ye do not forgive, neither will your Father which is in heaven forgive your trespasses. **And they come again to Jerusalem**:

◊    Fig Tree #2 --- By sequential timing we know that Matthew 21:12-17 occurred on Monday and Matthew 21:18-22 occurred on Tuesday morning.   On Tuesday morning, after they entered Jerusalem, Jesus spoke to the second fig tree **in the way**.   This fig tree died up **presently**.[4]   Jesus taught again on prayer, faith, doubt, and the power of our words. He did not repeat His teaching on forgiveness.

Matthew 21:18-22   Now in the morning as he returned into **the city**, he hungered.   And when he saw **a fig tree in the way**, he came to it, and

---

[4] Matthew 21:19 ...And **presently....** (Also translated **immediately** or **instantly**.)

found nothing thereon, but leaves only, and said unto it, **Let no fruit grow on thee henceforward for ever.** And **presently** the fig tree withered away. And when the disciples saw it, they marvelled, saying, **How soon** is the fig tree withered away! Jesus answered and said unto them, Verily I say unto you, If ye have faith, and doubt not, ye shall not only do this which is done to the fig tree, but also if ye shall say unto this mountain, Be thou removed, and be thou cast into the sea; it shall be done. And all things, whatsoever ye shall ask in prayer, believing, ye shall receive.

## 19 -- Jesus' three prophecies over Jerusalem.

Two of these three prophecies have already come to pass.

◊    Prophecy #1 --- After raising Lazarus from the dead, Jesus departed to Ephraim.   He then taught, journeying toward Jerusalem.

> Luke 13:22    And he went through the cities and villages, teaching, and journeying toward Jerusalem.

On this trip toward Jerusalem, Jesus prophesied over Jerusalem.

> Luke 13:34-35    O Jerusalem, Jerusalem, which killest the prophets, and stonest them that are sent unto thee; how often would I have gathered thy children together, as a hen doth gather her brood under her wings, and ye would not!  Behold, your house is left unto you desolate: and verily I say unto you, Ye shall not see me, until the time come when ye shall say, **Blessed is he that cometh in the name of the Lord**.

Prophecy #1 was fulfilled on "Palm Sunday." This important fulfillment of prophecy is found in all four gospels.

> Matthew 21:9  And the multitudes that went before, and that followed, cried, saying, Hosanna to the son of David: **Blessed is he that cometh in the name of the Lord**; Hosanna in the highest.

> Mark 11:9  And they that went before, and they that followed, cried, saying, Hosanna; **Blessed is he that cometh in the name of the Lord**:

> Luke 19:38    Saying, **Blessed be the King that cometh in the name of the Lord**: peace in heaven, and glory in the highest.

> John 12:13    Took branches of palm trees, and went forth to meet him, and cried, Hosanna: **Blessed is the King of Israel that cometh in the name of the Lord**.

◊    Prophecy #2 --- On the same Sunday that Prophecy #1 was fulfilled, *"Palm Sunday,"* Jesus wept over Jerusalem and then prophesied to it.

> Luke 19:41-44    And when he was come near, he beheld the city, and wept over it,  Saying, If thou hadst known, even thou, at least in this thy day, the things which belong unto thy peace! but now they are hid from thine eyes.   For the days shall come upon thee, that thine enemies shall cast a trench about thee, and compass thee round, and keep thee in on every side,  And shall lay thee even with the ground, and thy children within

thee; and they shall not leave in thee one stone upon another; because thou knewest not the time of thy visitation.

Prophecy #2 was fulfilled when the Roman army completely destroyed Jerusalem in 70 AD.

◊   Prophecy #3 -- On Tuesday afternoon, two days after *"Palm Sunday,"* Jesus prophesied to Jerusalem again. This prophecy is almost identical to Luke 13:34-35. The major difference is the time of fulfillment.

> Matthew 23:37-39   O Jerusalem, Jerusalem, thou that killest the prophets, and stonest them which are sent unto thee, how often would I have gathered thy children together, even as a hen gathereth her chickens under her wings, and ye would not!  Behold, your house is left unto you desolate.  For I say unto you, Ye shall not see me henceforth, till ye shall say, **Blessed is he that cometh in the name of the Lord**.

This prophecy has not been fulfilled.  It will not be fulfilled until Jesus returns to Jerusalem.

## 20 -- Jesus was anointed three times.

Jesus was anointed with ointment three different times.  Each time someone was offended. Each time Jesus gave an explanation.

◊   Anointing #1 --- Jesus was at Simon the Pharisee's house.  In the middle of Jesus' second year of ministry, **a sinner** anointed Jesus' feet with ointment.

> Luke 7:36-38   And one of the Pharisees desired him that he would eat with him. And he went into the **Pharisee's house**, and sat down to meat. And, behold, a woman in the city, which was **a sinner**, when she knew that Jesus sat at meat in the Pharisee's house, brought an alabaster box of ointment,  And stood at his feet behind him weeping, and began to wash his feet with tears, and did wipe them with the hairs of her head, and kissed his **feet**, and **anointed them** with the ointment.

◊   Anointing #2 --- About one and a half years later, Jesus was anointed in Bethany by Lazarus' sister Mary.  Jesus arrived in Bethany on Friday afternoon.  The Sabbath started at sunset. When the Sabbath ended, Martha served Jesus and a large company of disciples "supper." This was the beginning of the tenth day of the first month, the day that the lamb was chosen for the LORD's Passover (Exodus 12:3-21).  After supper Mary anointed Jesus' feet.

> John 12:2-3   There they made him a **supper**; and Martha **served**: but Lazarus was one of them that sat at the table with him.   Then took **Mary** a pound of ointment of spikenard, very costly, and anointed the **feet** of Jesus, and wiped his feet with her hair: and the house was filled with the odour of the ointment.

◊   Anointing #3 --- Three nights later, two days before the feast of the Passover, Jesus was anointed again. They were **in the house of Simon the leper**.  **A woman having an alabaster box** anointed Jesus **on his head**.

> Matthew 26:6-7   Now when Jesus was in Bethany, **in the house of Simon the leper**,   There came unto him **a woman having an alabaster box** of very precious ointment, and poured it **on his head**, as he sat at meat.

> Mark 14:3    And being in Bethany **in the house of Simon the leper**, as he sat at meat, there came **a woman having an alabaster box** of ointment of spikenard very precious; and she brake the box, and poured it **on his head**.

At each anointing, someone became offended.

◊    Reaction to Anointing #1 -- The host of the meal, Simon the Pharisee, was offended.

> Luke 7:39    Now when the Pharisee which had bidden him saw it, he spake within himself, saying, This man, if he were a prophet, would have known who and what manner of woman this is that toucheth him: for she is a sinner.

◊    Reaction to Anointing #2 -- Judas Iscariot was offended.

> John 12:4-5    Then saith one of his disciples, Judas Iscariot, Simon's son, which should betray him,    Why was not this ointment sold for three hundred pence, and given to the poor?

◊    Reaction to Anointing #3 -- Many disciples were offended.

> Matthew 26:8-9    But when his disciples saw it, they had indignation, saying, To what purpose is this waste?    For this ointment might have been sold for much, and given to the poor.

> Mark 14:4-5    And there were some that had indignation within themselves, and said, Why was this waste of the ointment made?    For it might have been sold for more than three hundred pence, and have been given to the poor. And they murmured against her.

Each time Jesus explained to those around Him why they should not be offended.  Each time Jesus defended the one who anointed Him.

◊    Explanation #1 --- Jesus told Simon the Pharisee about a certain creditor which had two debtors.  The debtor who will love most is the one who was forgiven most.  Jesus ended the teaching by speaking to the woman, "Thy sins are forgiven."

> Luke 7:47-48    Wherefore I say unto thee, Her sins, which are many, are forgiven; for she loved much: but to whom little is forgiven, the same loveth little.  And he said unto her, Thy sins are forgiven.

◊    Explanation #2 --- Jesus spoke directly to Judas Iscariot.

> John 12:7-8    Then said Jesus, Let her alone: **against the day of my burying hath she kept this**.    For the poor always ye have with you; but me ye have not always.

◊    Explanation #3 --- Jesus spoke to His disciples of the woman's good work and His burial.

> Matthew 26:10-13    When Jesus understood it, he said unto them, Why trouble ye the woman? for **she hath wrought a good work upon me**.  For ye have the poor always with you; but me ye have not always.  For in that she hath poured this ointment on my body, **she did it for my burial**.    Verily I say unto you, Wheresoever this gospel shall be preached in the whole world, there shall also this, that this woman hath done, be told for a memorial of her.

> Mark 14:6-9    And Jesus said, Let her alone; why trouble ye her? **she hath wrought a good work on me**.    For ye have the poor with you

always, and whensoever ye will ye may do them good: but me ye have not always.  She hath done what she could: **she is come aforehand to anoint my body to the burying**.  Verily I say unto you, Wheresoever this gospel shall be preached throughout the whole world, this also that she hath done shall be spoken of for a memorial of her.

## 21 -- The time of "the Passover" is not always "the Passover."

"The Passover"[5] has multiple meanings.  The words "**the Passover**" may refer to a meal, a week long feast, a single day, or a lamb.  The context of the situation is essential in determining which **Passover** is which.

**The Passover** may be referring to a lamb (Exodus 12:3 & 21).  **The Passover** (lamb) was partaken of at the beginning of the 14th day of the first month.  **The Passover** (lamb) was killed at sunset of the 13th day, the beginning of the 14th day.  "And ye shall keep it **up until the fourteenth day** of the same month..." (Exodus 12:6).

> Exodus 12:3   Speak ye unto all the congregation of Israel, saying, In the **tenth day** of this month they shall take to them **every man a lamb**, according to the house of their fathers, **a lamb** for an house:

> Exodus 12:6   And ye shall keep it **up until the fourteenth day** of the same month: and the whole assembly of the congregation of Israel shall **kill it** in the evening.

> Exodus 12:11   And thus shall ye **eat it**; with your loins girded, your shoes on your feet, and your staff in your hand; and ye shall eat it in haste: it is **the LORD's passover**.

> Exodus 12:21   Then Moses called for all the elders of Israel, and said unto them, Draw out and take you **a lamb** according to your families, and **kill the passover**.

On Wednesday morning of the 13th day of the first month, the disciples asked Jesus a question concerning **the Passover** (lamb) and **the LORD's Passover** (See Exodus 12:21 and 12:11).

> Mark 14:12   And the first day of unleavened bread, when they **killed the passover**, his disciples said unto him, Where wilt thou that we go and prepare that thou mayest eat **the passover**?

**The Passover** is also **the feast of unleavened bread** which can be called **the feast, the feast of the passover**, or "**the feast of the passover, and of unleavened bread**."  On the week that Jesus was crucified, Tuesday after sunset was two days before the beginning of the week long **feast of unleavened bread**.  Matthew reports Jesus' Tuesday night comment about **the feast of the passover**.  On this same Tuesday night Mark and Luke also give an update about **the Passover**.

---

[5] **The Passover** (Today the word "Passover" is generally capitalized but it is usually not capitalized in the King James Version of the Bible.  Luke 22:1 is an exception to this, "Now the feast of unleavened *bread* drew nigh, which is called the Passover.")

> Matthew 26:2    Ye know that after **two days** is **the feast of the passover**, and the Son of man is betrayed to be crucified.

> Mark 14:1a   **After two days** was the **feast of the passover, and of unleavened bread**:

> Luke 22:1   Now **the feast of unleavened** *bread* drew nigh, which is called **the Passover**.

> Numbers 28:17   And in the **fifteenth day** of this month is **the feast**: seven days shall unleavened bread be eaten.

The section of this book called *The Calendar of Passover* contains many more "Passover scriptures." These scriptures detail many different ways that the word Passover is used.

## 22 -- Jesus prophesied three times that Peter would deny Him.

In the same night that Jesus was betrayed, the beginning of the 14th day of the month, Peter gave **four** testimonies of loyalty to Jesus.

◊   Testimony #1 --- "... I will lay down my life for thy sake" (John 13:37).

◊   Testimony #2 --- "... I am ready to go with thee, both into prison, and to death " (Luke 22:33).

◊   Testimony #3 --- "Though all men shall be offended because of thee, yet will I never be offended" (Matthew 26:33).

◊   Testimony #4 --- "Though I should die with thee, yet will I not deny thee" (Matthew 26:35) and "If I should die with thee, I will not deny thee in any wise..." (Mark 14:31).

Jesus' answer to Peter's first **three** testimonies of loyalty all contained the same prophecy. (There is a difference in this portion of Matthew's report and Mark's report. This difference is an unsolved mystery . See *Solutions to Gospel Mysteries* - Peter denied Jesus three times three.)

◊   Answer to Peter's Testimony #1 --- "... The cock shall not crow, till
     **thou hast denied me thrice** " (John 13:38).

◊   Answer to Peter's Testimony #2 --- "... the cock shall not crow this day, before
     that **thou shalt thrice deny** that thou knowest **me** " (Luke 22:34).

◊   Answers to Peter's Testimony #3 --- "... before the cock crow,
     **thou shalt deny me thrice** " (Matthew 26:34) and
                                        "...before the cock crow **twice**,
     **thou shalt deny me** " (Mark 14:30).

◊   Prophecy #1 --- The first and second prophecies to Peter occurred in the upper room after Judas had gone out (John 13:30).

> John 13:36-38   Simon Peter said unto him, Lord, whither goest thou? Jesus answered him, Whither I go, thou canst not follow me now; but thou shalt follow me afterwards.   Peter said unto him, Lord, why cannot I follow thee now? **I will lay down my life for thy sake.**   Jesus answered him, Wilt thou lay down thy life for my sake? Verily, verily, I say unto thee, **The cock shall not crow, till thou hast denied me thrice.**

◊　　Prophecy #2 --- Jesus' first prophecy is immediately followed by His second.

> Luke 22:31-34  And the Lord said, Simon, Simon, behold, Satan hath desired to have you, that he may sift you as wheat:  But I have prayed for thee, that thy faith fail not: and when thou art converted, strengthen thy brethren.  And he said unto him, Lord, **I am ready to go with thee, both into prison, and to death**.  And he said, I tell thee, Peter, **the cock shall not crow this day, before that thou shalt thrice deny that thou knowest me**.

◊　　Prophecy #3 --- Jesus' third prophecy to Peter occurred after they left the upper room headed for the garden.  Just prior to entering the garden Jesus warned that all men would be offended at Him.  Peter argued with Jesus, giving his third testimony of loyalty.  Jesus again answered Peter with a prophecy.  This prophecy is found in both Matthew and Mark.

> Matthew 26:33-34  Peter answered and said unto him, Though all men shall be offended because of thee, yet will I never be offended.  Jesus said unto him, Verily I say unto thee, That this night, **before the cock crow, thou shalt deny me thrice**.

> Mark 14:29-30  But Peter said unto him, Although all shall be offended, yet will not I.  And Jesus saith unto him, Verily I say unto thee, That this day, even in this night, **before the cock crow twice, thou shalt deny me**.

Peter continued to argue with Jesus, giving his fourth testimony of loyalty.

> Matthew 26:35  Peter said unto him, **Though I should die with thee, yet will I not deny thee**. Likewise also said all the disciples.

> Mark 14:31 But he spake the more vehemently, **If I should die with thee, I will not deny thee in any wise**. Likewise also said they all.

## 23 -- Peter denied Jesus three times three.

Three different times in one night, Peter was **identified** to others, directly **questioned**, and then **accused** to his face.  Each time the identification, questioning, and accusations happened in rapid succession.  Each time Peter denied the identification, gave a false answer to the question, and lied when he was accused.[6]

### The First Denials

◊　　Identification #1 ---

> Luke 22:56  But a certain maid beheld him as he sat by the fire, and earnestly looked upon him, and said, **This man was also with him.**

◊　　Denial to Identification #1 ---

---

[6] It is interesting to note that E. W. Bullinger, J. M. Chaney, and A. G. Secrett believe that Peter denied Jesus six times.  See Appendix #4 for the titles of their books.

Luke 22:57    And he denied him (Jesus), saying, **Woman, I know him not.**

◊    Question #1 and Denial to Question #1 ---

John 18:17    Then saith the damsel that kept the door unto Peter, **Art not thou also one of this man's disciples?** He saith, **I am not.**

◊    Accusation #1 ---

Matthew 26:69    Now Peter sat without in the palace: and a damsel came unto him, saying, **Thou also wast with Jesus of Galilee.**

Mark 14:66-67    And as Peter was beneath in the palace, there cometh one of the maids of the high priest:  And when she saw Peter warming himself, she looked upon him, and said, **And thou also wast with Jesus of Nazareth.**

◊    Denial to Accusation #1 ---

Matthew 26:70    But he denied before them all, saying, **I know not what thou sayest.**

Mark 14:68a    But he denied, saying, **I know not, neither understand I what thou sayest.**

As seen above, Peter denied, lied, and lied for the "first" time.

It could be argued that the denials to this first **identification**, this first **question**, and this first **accusation** only counted as **"one denial."**  However, after this first set of denials, Mark (and probably Peter) heard a cock crow.

Mark 14:68b    And he went out into the porch; **and the cock crew**.

After Anus sent Jesus bound to Caiaphas, Peter was **identified** to others, directly **questioned**, and then **accused** to his face for the second time.

## The Second Denials

◊    Identification #2 ---

Matthew 26:71    And when he was gone out into the porch, another maid saw him, and said unto them that were there, **This fellow was also with Jesus of Nazareth.**

Mark 14:69    And a maid saw him again, and began to say to them that stood by, **This is one of them.**

◊    Denial to Identification #2 ---

Matthew 26:72    And again he denied with an oath, **I do not know the man.**

Mark 14:70a    And he **denied it again.**

◊    Question #2 and Denial to Question #2 ---

John 18:25    And Simon Peter stood and warmed himself. They said therefore unto him, **Art not thou also one of his disciples?** He denied it, and said, **I am not.**

◊    Accusation #2 and Denial to Accusation #2 ---

Luke 22:58    And after a little while another saw him, and said, **Thou art also of them.** And Peter said, **Man, I am not.**

As seen above, Peter denied, denied, and lied for the "second" time.

About one hour later, Luke 22:59, Peter was **identified** to others, directly **questioned**, and then **accused** to his face for the third time.

## The Third Denials

◊    Identification #3 ---

Luke 22:59b    another confidently affirmed, saying, **Of a truth this fellow also was with him: for he is a Galilaean.**

◊    Denial to Identification #3 ---

Luke 22:60a    And Peter said, **Man, I know not what thou sayest.**

◊    Question #3

John 18:26    One of the servants of the high priest, being his kinsman whose ear Peter cut off, saith, **Did not I see thee in the garden with him?**

◊    Denial to Question #3

John 18:27a    Peter then **denied again**:

◊    Accusation #3 ---

Matthew 26:73    And after a while came unto him they that stood by, and said to Peter, **Surely thou also art one of them; for thy speech betrayeth thee.**

Mark 14:70b    And a little after, they that stood by said again to Peter, **Surely thou art one of them: for thou art a Galilaean, and thy speech agreeth thereto.**

◊    Denial to Accusation #3 ---

Matthew 26:74a    Then began he to curse and to swear, saying, **I know not the man.**

Mark 14:71    But he began to curse and to swear, saying, **I know** not this man of whom ye speak.

As seen above, Peter denied, lied, and lied for a "third" time. Immediately the cock crew.[7]

Matthew 26:74b    And immediately the cock crew.

Mark 14:72a    And the second time the cock crew.

Luke 22:60b    And immediately, while he yet spake, the cock crew.[8]

---

[7] Mark says that this is the second time the cock crew. It is possible that Mark was the only Gospel writer to hear the first time that the cock crew, over an hour earlier. In Mark 14:30 we read, "And Jesus saith unto him, Verily I say unto thee, That this day, even in this night, before the cock crow twice, thou shalt deny me." However, in Matthew 26:34 we read, "Jesus said unto him, Verily I say unto thee, That this night, before the cock crow, thou shalt deny me thrice." This difference is an unsolved mystery.

John 18:27b   and immediately the cock crew.

At this point, Jesus looked at Peter.

> Luke 22:61a  And the Lord turned, and looked upon Peter.

Peter remembered the word of Jesus and he went out, and wept bitterly.

> Matthew 26:75    And Peter remembered the word of Jesus, which said unto him, Before the cock crow, thou shalt deny me thrice. And he went out, and wept bitterly.

> Mark 14:72b    And Peter called to mind the word that Jesus said unto him, Before the cock crow twice, thou shalt deny me thrice. And when he thought thereon, he wept.

> Luke 22:61b-62 And Peter remembered the word of the Lord, how he had said unto him, Before the cock crow, thou shalt deny me thrice.   And Peter went out, and wept bitterly.

## 24 -- The third hour of Mark equals the sixth hour of John.

**Mark** said that "it was the **third** hour" when they crucified Jesus.  **John** said that it was "about the **sixth** hour" when Pilate delivered Jesus to be crucified.   Yet, Mark and John did not disagree.

> Mark 15:25   And it was the **third** hour, and they crucified him.

> John 19:14-16   And **it was the preparation of the passover**, and about the **sixth** hour: and he saith unto the Jews, Behold your King!   But they cried out, Away with him, away with him, crucify him. Pilate saith unto them, Shall I crucify your King? The chief priests answered, We have no king but Caesar.    Then delivered he him therefore unto them to be crucified. And they took Jesus, and led him away.

There were by definition twelve hours in a Roman day from sunrise to sunset.   Jesus agreed with this when He said, "Are there not **twelve hours in the day**?"

> John 11:9-10   Jesus answered, Are there not twelve hours in the day? If any man walk in the day, he stumbleth not, because he seeth the light of this world.   But if a man walk in the night, he stumbleth, because there is no light in him. If any man walk in the day, he stumbleth not, because he seeth the light of this world.

Sunrise of the crucifixion day was very close to 6:00 AM.   The normal time for sunset on crucifixion day was about 6:00 PM.   This means that for an normal day was twelve modern hours long.   6:00 AM to 7:00 AM would be called the Roman **first** hour and 8:00 AM to 9:00 AM would be called the Roman **third** hour.   11:00 AM to 12:00 noon or mid-day would be called the **sixth** hour and 2:00 AM to 3:00 PM would be called the **ninth** hour.   So Mark's **third** hour would have been the hour from 8:00 AM to 9:00 AM.

---

[8] Luke 22:60b    And **immediately, while he yet spake**, the cock crew.   (Matt. 26:74b, Luke 22:60b, and John 18:27b all say **immediately**. Since all three accounts are true, Peter did not stop talking while he was denying three separate accusations, all at virtually the same time.)

However, this was not a normal day! There was **darkness over all the land** from the **sixth** hour to the **ninth** hour.

> Matthew 27:45  Now from the **sixth** hour there was **darkness** over all the land unto the **ninth** hour.

> Mark 15:33  And when the **sixth** hour was come, there was **darkness** over the whole land until the **ninth** hour.

> Luke 23:44  And it was about the **sixth** hour, and there was a **darkness** over all the earth until the **ninth** hour.

If John considered that **darkness over all the earth** was by Roman definition "the end of the day," then on the day Jesus was crucified John would call the normal **sixth** hour the **twelfth** hour. The "day" would be only be six modern hours long. Each "Roman hour" would equal 30 modern minutes. Then the **first** "hour" would be 6:00 AM to 6:30 AM, the **sixth** "hour" would be 8:30 AM to 9:00 AM, and the **twelfth** "hour" would be from 11:30 AM to 12:00 noon.

In summary, there were only six modern hours of daylight on the day of Jesus' crucifixion, 6:00 AM to 12:00 noon. "Mid-day" was at 9:00 AM. Mid-day, by the Roman definition, occures at the sixth and seventh hours. John acknowledged this in his account of Jesus' crucifixion. "And **it was the preparation of the passover**, and about the **sixth** hour...Then delivered he him therefore unto them to be crucified..." (John 19:14 & 16). Mark recorded his time as a normal twelve hour day that ended at 6:00 PM. "And it was the **third** hour, and they crucified him" (Mark 15:25). "And when the **sixth** hour was come, there was **darkness** over the whole land until the **ninth** hour" (Mark 15:33). Mark's **third** hour would have been 8:00 AM to 9:00 AM. John's **sixth** "hour" would be about 8:30 AM to 9:00 AM. So, they delivered Jesus to be crucified about 8:30 AM to 9:00 AM.

There are many articles in the literature that use different logic and reasoning to explain the differences in Mark and John's time frames. One thing is certain. Mark and John were not incorrect in their thinking or writing.

## 25 -- Were there four angels or six angels at the tomb?

Time sequence helps us understand what happened at the tomb on Resurrection morning. Mary Magdalene, Mary the mother of James, Salome, and certain others came to the sepulchre.

> Matthew 28:1  In the end of the sabbath, as it began to dawn toward the first day of the week, came **Mary Magdalene** and the **other Mary** to see the sepulchre.

> Mark 16:1  And when the sabbath was past, **Mary Magdalene**, and **Mary the mother of James, and Salome**, had bought sweet spices, that they might come and anoint him.

> Luke 24:1  Now upon the first day of the week, very early in the morning, **they** came unto the sepulchre, bringing the spices which they had prepared, and **certain others** with them.

> John 20:1a  The first day of the week cometh **Mary Magdalene** early, when it was yet dark, unto the sepulchre....

◊ Angel #1 --- The angel of the Lord (Angel #1) descended from heaven, and came and rolled back the stone from the door, and sat upon it.

> Matthew 28:2-4   And, behold, there was a great earthquake: for **the angel of the Lord** descended from heaven, and came and rolled back the stone from the door, and sat upon it.   His countenance was like lightning, and his raiment white as snow:   And for fear of him the keepers did shake, and became as dead men.

When the women looked, the stone was already rolled away.

> Mark 16:4   And when they looked, they saw that the stone was rolled away: for it was very great.

> John 20:1b ... and seeth the stone taken away from the sepulchre.

**The women** mentioned in Matthew 28:5 included **Mary Magdalene** and the other **Mary** (Matthew 28:1).  They heard what the angel of the Lord had to say.

> Matthew 28:5-6   And the angel answered and said unto **the women**, Fear not ye: for I know that ye seek Jesus, which was crucified.   He is not here: for he is risen, as he said. Come, see the place where the Lord lay.

But Mary Magdalene did not stay.  She left the other women and ran to get Peter and John.

> John 20:2   Then **she runneth**, and cometh to Simon Peter, and to the other disciple, whom Jesus loved, and saith unto them, They have taken away the Lord out of the sepulchre, and we know not where they have laid him.

◊ Angel #2 --- All of the women, except Mary Magdalene, entered into the sepulchre.  They saw **a young man** (Angel #2).

> Mark 16:5-6    And entering into the sepulchre, they saw **a young man** sitting on the right side, clothed in a long white garment; and they were affrighted.   And he saith unto them, Be not affrighted: Ye seek Jesus of Nazareth, which was crucified: he is risen; he is not here: behold the place where they laid him.

This second angel left their presence and "they were much perplexed."

◊ Angels #3 and #4 --- We do not know the length of time that the women stood in the tomb.  The word **behold** indicates a passage of time.  Then **two men** (Angels #3 and #4) appeared to comfort and direct them.

> Luke 24:4-5    And **it came to pass**, as they were much perplexed thereabout, **behold**, **two men** stood by them in shining garments:   And as they were afraid, and bowed down their faces to the earth, they said unto them, Why seek ye the living among the dead?

The women did not understand what had happened to Jesus until these angels quoted Jesus.  Then, "they remembered His words."

> Luke 24:6-8   He is not here, but is risen: remember how he spake unto you when he was yet in Galilee,   Saying, The Son of man must be delivered into the hands of sinful men, and be crucified, and the third day rise again.   And they **remembered his words**,

The women left the tomb as instructed.

◊    Angels #5 and #6 or Angels #3 and #4? --- Mary returned to the sepulchre with Peter and John. She stayed after Peter and John went home. Then Mary "looked into the sepulchre" and saw **two angels**. These may have been the same two angels that the other women saw in Luke 24:4-5 (Angels #3 and #4) or two new angels (Angels #5 and #6).

> John 20:11-13  But Mary stood without at the sepulchre weeping: and as she wept, she stooped down, and looked into the sepulchre,  And seeth **two angels** in white sitting, the one at the head, and the other at the feet, where the body of Jesus had lain.  And they say unto her, Woman, why weepest thou? She saith unto them, Because they have taken away my Lord, and I know not where they have laid him.

Mary had now seen three angels but she still did not understand that Jesus had risen.

> John 20:14-17  And when she had thus said, she turned herself back, and saw Jesus standing, and knew not that it was Jesus.  Jesus saith unto her, Woman, why weepest thou? whom seekest thou? She, supposing him to be the gardener, saith unto him, Sir, if thou have borne him hence, tell me where thou hast laid him, and I will take him away.  Jesus saith unto her, Mary. She turned herself, and saith unto him, Rabboni; which is to say, Master.  Jesus saith unto her, Touch me not; for I am not yet ascended to my Father: but go to my brethren, and say unto them, I ascend unto my Father, and your Father; and to my God, and your God.

## 26 -- Peter's two trips to check the empty tomb.

Peter ran to the sepulcher two different times on Resurrection morning.

◊    Trip #1 --- Mary Magdalene heard the first angel say, "Be not affrighted: Ye seek Jesus of Nazareth, which was crucified: he is risen; he is not here: behold the place where they laid him" (Mark 16:6). But Mary Magdalene did not understand what the angel said to her.  She ran to Peter and John (John 20:2a). She told them, "They have taken away the Lord out of the sepulchre, and we know not where they have laid him" (John 20:2b). Both Peter and John "went into the sepulchre." John "saw, and believed" (John 20:8), even though "they knew not the scripture, that he must rise again from the dead" (John 20:9).

> John 20:3-10  Peter therefore went forth, and that other disciple, and came to the sepulchre.  So they ran both together: and the other disciple did outrun Peter, and came first to the sepulchre.  And he stooping down, and looking in, saw the linen clothes lying; yet went he not in.  Then cometh Simon Peter following him, and **went into the sepulchre**, and seeth the linen clothes lie,  And the napkin, that was about his head, not lying with the linen clothes, but wrapped together in a place by itself.  Then **went in also** that other disciple, which came first to the sepulchre, and he **saw, and believed**.  For as yet **they knew not the scripture**, that he must rise again from the dead.  Then the disciples went away again unto their own home.

◊ Trip #2 --- All of the women saw Jesus alive that morning (Mark 16:9, John 20:14, and Matthew 28:9-10). They came and told the disciples. The disciples did not believe them. However, Peter took a second look at the sepulcher.

> Luke 24:10-12 It was Mary Magdalene, and Joanna, and Mary the mother of James, and other women that were with them, which told these things unto the apostles. And their words seemed to them as idle tales, and they believed them not. **Then arose Peter, and ran unto the sepulchre**; and stooping down, he beheld the linen clothes laid by themselves, and departed, wondering in himself at that which was come to pass.

Jesus honored Simon Peter's second trip to the sepulchre since later that day, Jesus "appeared to Simon."

> Luke 24:33-34 And they rose up the same hour, and returned to Jerusalem, and found the eleven gathered together, and them that were with them, Saying, The Lord is risen indeed, and hath **appeared to Simon**.

↓   of lines = year of Jesus' ministry

↓↓↓

| Pericopes | Matt. | Mark | Luke | John | Pg# |
|---|---|---|---|---|---|
| The beginning | | | | 1:1-4 | 1 |
| The beginning of the gospel | 1:1 | 1:1 | 1:1-4 | 1:5 | 1 |
| Priest named Zacharias | | | 1:5-23 | | 1 |
| Elisabeth conceived | | | 1:24-25 | | 2 |
| Gabriel sent to Mary | | | 1:26-56 | | 2 |
| Elisabeth brought forth a son | | | 1:57-79 | | 3 |
| John grew | | | 1:80 | | 4 |
| Joseph's lineage | 1:2-17 | | | | 4 |
| A angel speaks to Joseph | 1:18-24 | | | | 4 |
| Decree from Caesar Augustus | | | 2:1-6 | | 5 |
| Jesus born to Mary | 1:25a | | 2:7-20 | | 5 |
| The circumcising of Jesus | 1:25b | | 2:21 | | 5 |
| They presented Jesus to the Lord | | | 2:22-39a | | 5 |
| Wise men from the east came to Bethlehem | 2:1-12 | | | | 6 |
| Joseph, Mary, And Jesus flee into Egypt | 2:13-14 | | | | 7 |
| Herod slew all the children in Bethlehem | 2:16-18 | | | | 7 |
| Joseph, Mary, and Jesus return to Nazareth | 2:19-23 | | 2:39b-40 | | 7 |
| Jesus twelve years old | | | 2:41-52 | | 7 |
| John the Baptist preaching in the wilderness | 3:1-10 | 1:2-6 | 3:1-15 | 1:6-14 | 8 |
| John prophesies that Jesus, "shall baptize you with the Holy Ghost, and with fire." | 3:11-12 | 1:7-8 | 3:16-20 | | 9 |
| Jesus baptized by John | 3:13-17 | 1:9-11 | 3:21-22 | | 9 |
| Mary and Jesus' lineage | | | 3:23-38 | | 9 |
| Jesus led up of the Spirit into the wilderness and temped | 4:1-11 | 1:12-13b | 4:1-13 | | 10 |
| John bare witness of him,.... | | | | 1:15-25 | 11 |
| 1st day Jesus among them | | | | 1:26-28 | 11 |
| 2nd day Jesus among them, Behold the Lamb of God | | | | 1:29-34 | 12 |
| 3rd day, Jesus among them, Behold the Lamb of God | | | | 1:36-42 | 12 |
| Jesus returned in the power of the Spirit into Galilee | | | 4:14a | 1:43a | 12 |
| Jesus found Philip and met Nathanael | | | | 1:43b-51 | 12 |
| Marriage in Cana of Galilee | | | | 2:1-11 | 13 |
| Jesus went down to Capernaum | | | | 2:12 | 13 |
| Jesus went to 1st ministry Passover and cleansed the temple | | | | 2:13-22 | 13 |
| In the feast day, Jesus did miracles. | | | | 2:23-25 | 14 |
| A Pharisee named Nicodemus | | | | 3:1-21 | 14 |
| Jesus and his disciples baptized many in the land of Judaea | | | | 3:22-4:3a | 14 |
| John put in prison | | 1:14a | | | 15 |
| Jesus departed to Galilee | 4:12. | | | 4:3b | 15 |
| Jesus speaks to a woman of Samaria at Jacob's well | | | | 4:5-42 | 15 |
| Jesus went into Galilee | | 1:14b | | 4:43-45 | 17 |
| Jesus came again into Cana and healed a nobleman's son in Capernaum | | | | 4:46-54 | 17 |
| Fame of Jesus went through all the region | | | 4:14b-15 | | 17 |
| Jesus' 1st ministry trip to Nazareth | | | 4:16-30 | | 17 |
| Jesus came to Capernaum and preached repent | 4:13-17 | 1:14c-15 | 4:31a | | 18 |
| They forsook their nets, and followed him. | 4:18-22 | 1:16-20 | | | 18 |
| In Capernaum, on the Sabbath, Jesus healed a man with an unclean spirit | | 1:21-28 | 4:33-37 | | 18 |
| 1st time Jesus healed Simon's wife's mother | | 1:29-31 | 4:38-39 | | 19 |
| Jesus healed many that were sick and then departed to pray | | 1:32-38 | 4:40-43 | | 19 |
| 1st time Jesus went about all Galilee, preaching | 4:23-25 | 1:39 | 4:44 | | 19 |
| Jesus preached on a mountain , "Blessed are the poor in spirit" | 5:1-8:1 | | | | 19 |
| Jesus taught from Simon's ship | | | 5:3-10a | | 24 |
| They forsook all, and followed him. | | | 5:10b-11 | | 25 |
| There came a leper to him saying, "if thou wilt, thou canst make me clean." | 8:2-4 | 1:40-45 | 5:12-15 | | 25 |
| Jesus "withdrew himself into the wilderness, and prayed." | | | 5:16 | | 25 |
| 1st time a centurion came to Jesus | 8:5-13 | | | | 25 |
| 2nd time Jesus healed Peter's wife's mother | 8:14-15 | | | | 26 |
| Jesus healed all that were sick | 8:15-17 | | | | 26 |

↓  of lines = year of Jesus' ministry

↓↓↓

| Pericopes | Matt. | Mark | Luke | John | Pg# |
|---|---|---|---|---|---|
| Jesus gave commandment to depart unto the other side | 8:18 | | | | 26 |
| Let the dead bury the dead | 8:19-22 | | | | 26 |
| 1st great tempest in the sea, and there was a great calm. | 8:24-27 | | | | 26 |
| Gergesenes there met him two possessed with devils. | 8:28-34 | | | | 26 |
| And again he entered into Capernaum | 9:1 | 2:1 | | | 27 |
| One sick of the palsy & they uncovered the roof | 9:2-8 | 2:2-12 | 5:17-26 | | 27 |
| And he went forth again by the sea side | | 2:13 | | | 27 |
| Jesus said to Matthew, "Follow Me" | 9:9 | 2:14 | 5:27-28 | | 27 |
| Jesus taught in Matthew's house. | 9:10-13 | 2:15-17 | 5:29-32 | | 27 |
| Why do the disciples of John fast often? | 9:14-17 | 2:18-22 | 5:33-39 | | 27 |
| A certain ruler and the 1st woman with an issue of blood twelve years | 9:18-26 | | | | 27 |
| two blind men were healed | 9:27-31 | | | | 27 |
| The dumb spake | 9:32-34 | | | | 27 |
| 1st time Jesus went about all the cities and villages, teaching in their synagogues | 9:35-38 | | | | 29 |
| 2nd ministry Passover and healing of a man at the pool of Bethesda | | | 5:1-15 | | 29 |
| The Jews sought to slay Jesus but Jesus answered them and taught. | | | 5:16-47 | | 30 |
| 1st trip through the corn field | | 2:23-28 | 6:1-5 | | 31 |
| 1st man healed of a withered hand. | | 3:1-6 | 6:6-11 | | 31 |
| Jesus taught by the sea | | 3:7-12 | | | 31 |
| Jesus went out into a mountain to pray | | 3:13a | 6:12 | | 32 |
| Jesus ordained the twelve | | 3:14-19 | 6:13-16 | | 32 |
| Jesus stood in the plain and taught, "Blessed be the poor...." | | | 6:17-49 | | 32 |
| Jesus taught the multitude, "How can Satan cast out Satan?" | | 3:20-30 | | | 33 |
| 1st time Jesus' mother tried to call Him out of a meeting | | 3:31-35 | | | 34 |
| In Capernaum, the 2nd time a centurion had someone sick and ready to die at his house | | | 7:1-10 | | 34 |
| In Nain, Jesus raised the widow's son from the dead | | | 7:11-17 | | 35 |
| 1st time John the Baptist sent two of his disciples to ask Jesus questions | | | 7:20-28 | | 35 |
| The publicans, justified God | | | 7:29-35 | | 35 |
| Jesus' feet anointed with alabaster box of ointment | | | 7:36-50 | | 36 |
| Jesus went throughout every city and village, preaching | | | 8:1-3 | | 36 |
| 2nd time Jesus entered into a ship to teach | | 4:1 | | | 37 |
| Parable of the sower | | 4:2-9 | 8:4-8 | | 37 |
| Jesus explained the mystery of the kingdom | | 4:10-13 | 8:9-10 | | 37 |
| Parable of the sower | | 4:14-20 | 8:11-15 | | 37 |
| Candle set on a candlestick | | 4:21-25 | 8:16-18 | | 38 |
| Parable of the blade, ear, and full corn | | 4:26-29 | | | 38 |
| 2nd time Jesus' mother and brothers came calling for Him | | | 8:19-21 | | 38 |
| Parable of the grain of mustard seed | | 4:30-34 | | | 38 |
| 2nd storm of wind on the lake | | 4:35-41 | 8:22-24 | | 38 |
| Jesus set the man of the Gadarenes free | | 5:1-20 | 8:26-39 | | 39 |
| Jesus was passed over again by ship | | 5:21 | 8:40 | | 40 |
| Jairus' daughter & the 2nd woman, with an issue of blood | · | 5:22-43 | 8:41-56 | | 40 |
| 2nd ministry trip to Nazareth | | 6:1-6a | | | 40 |
| Jesus went round about the villages, teaching | | 6:6b | | | 41 |
| Jesus called the twelve, sent forth by two and two | 10:1-42 | 6:7-11 | 9:1-5 | | 41 |
| Jesus departed to preach in their cities. | 11:1 | 6:12-13 | 9:6 | | 43 |
| 2nd time John sent two of his disciples to Jesus | 11:2-30 | | | | 43 |
| 2nd trip through the corn field | 12:1-8 | | | | 44 |
| 2nd man healed of a withered hand | 12:9-14 | | | | 45 |
| Multitudes followed him, and he healed them all | 12:15-21 | | | | 45 |
| Jesus healed one possessed with a devil, blind, and dumb | 12:22-37 | | | | 45 |
| We would see a sign from thee | 12:38-45 | | | | 46 |
| 3rd time Jesus' mother tried to call Him out of a meeting | 12:46-50 | | | | 46 |
| Parable of the sower, taught at sea side | 13:1-30 | | | | 47 |
| Parables of mustard seed, leaven, and tares | 13:31-52 | | | | 48 |
| 3rd ministry trip to Nazareth | 13:53-58 | | | | 49 |
| King Herod heard of Jesus and the killing of John | 14:1-12 | 6:14-29 | 9:7-9 | | 49 |
| Jesus heard of John's death and departed by ship | 14:13-14 | 6:30-34 | 9:10-11 | 6:1-3 | 50 |

↓  of lines = year of Jesus' ministry

↓↓↓

| Pericopes | Matt. | Mark | Luke | John | Pg# |
|---|---|---|---|---|---|
| 3rd Passover was nigh | | | | 6:4 | 50 |
| Jesus feeds the 5000 | 14:15-22 | 6:35-45 | 9:12-17 | 6:5-13 | 50 |
| Jesus sent the 5000 away | 14:23a | 6:46a | | | 51 |
| 1st night that Jesus walks on the water | 14:23b-33 | 6:46b-52 | | | 51 |
| In Gennesaret, whoever touched the hem of His Garment was healed | 14:34-36 | 6:53-56 | | | 51 |
| Jesus departed again into a mountain | | | | 6:14-18 | 52 |
| 2nd night that Jesus walks on the water | | | | 6:19-20 | 52 |
| Immediately the ship was at Capernaum | | | | 6:21-59 | 52 |
| His disciples, when they had heard this, said, This is an hard saying; who can hear it? | | | | 6:60-71 | 54 |
| (Time of the 3rd passover) | | | | (6:4&7:1) | 54 |
| Then came Pharisees which were of Jerusalem | 15:1-14 | 7:1-16 | | | 54 |
| Whatsoever thing from without entereth into the man, it cannot defile him | 15:15-20 | 7:17-23 | | | 55 |
| Jesus walked in Galilee | | | | 7:1 | 55 |
| Jesus heals the daughter of a woman of Canaan | 15:21-28 | 7:24-30 | | | 56 |
| Departing Tyre and Sidon, He came unto the sea of Galilee | 15:29-31 | 7:31-37 | | | 56 |
| Jesus feeds the 4000 | 15:32-38 | 8:1-9a | | | 56 |
| Jesus sent away the 4000 and came into the parts of Dalmanutha | 15:39-4a | 8:9b-12 | | | 57 |
| Take heed and beware of the leaven of the Pharisees | 16:4b-12 | 8:13-21 | | | 57 |
| Now the Jews' feast of tabernacles was at hand. | | | 7:2-36 | | 57 |
| If any man thirst, let him come unto me, and drink. | | | 7:37-53 | | 59 |
| Jesus came to Bethsaida | | 8:22-26 | | | 59 |
| Trip to the towns of Caesarea Philippi | 16:13-28 | 8:27-9:1 | 9:18-27 | | 60 |
| Jesus was transfigured | 17:1-13 | 9:2-13 | 9:28-37a | | 60 |
| Jesus healed the lunatic son | 17:14-21 | 9:14-29 | 9:37b-42 | | 61 |
| They abode in Galilee | 17:22-23 | 9:30-32 | 9:43-45 | | 62 |
| Reasoning among them, which of them should be greatest | | | 9-46-48 | | 62 |
| They that received tribute money in Capernaum | 17:24-27 | 9:33a | | | 62 |
| If any man desire to be first, the same shall be last of all, and servant of all. | 18:1-4 | 9:33b-36 | | | 62 |
| Whoso shall receive one such little child in my name receiveth me | 18:5-11 | 9:37 | | | 63 |
| One of them be gone astray, doth he not leave the ninety and nine | 18:12-20 | | | | 63 |
| Forgive seventy times seven | 18:21-22 | | | | 63 |
| One servant owed him ten thousand talents | 18:23-35 | | | | 64 |
| We saw one casting out devils in thy name | | 9:38-50 | 9:49-50 | | 64 |
| Jesus departed from Galilee and sent messengers before his face | 19:1a | 10:1a | 9:51-62 | | 65 |
| The Lord appointed other seventy | | | 10:1-24 | | 65 |
| The story of the "good Samaritan" | | | 10:25-37 | | 66 |
| Mary hath chosen that good part | | | 10:38-42 | | 67 |
| When ye pray, say, Our Father which art in heaven | | | 11:1-13 | | 67 |
| Jesus was accused of casting out devils through Beelzebub | | | 11:14-28 | | 68 |
| No sign be given it, but the sign of Jonas the prophet | | | 11:29-36 | | 69 |
| Laying wait for him, and seeking to catch something out of his mouth, that they might accuse him | | | 11:37-54 | | 69 |
| But unto him that blasphemeth against the Holy Ghost it shall not be forgiven | | | 12:1-15 | | 70 |
| Thou fool, this night thy soul shall be required of thee | | | 12:16-30 | | 70 |
| But rather seek ye the kingdom of God | | | 12:31-48 | | 71 |
| I am come to send fire on the earth | | | 12:49-13:9 | | 72 |
| Woman was taken in adultery | | | | 8:1-11 | 73 |
| Jesus taught in the temple | | | | 8:12-57 | 73 |
| 1st time in Jerusalem they took up stones to cast at Jesus | | | | 8:58-59 | 75 |
| Jesus made clay of the spittle, and he anointed the eyes of the blind man | | | | 9:1-38 | 75 |
| For judgment I am come into this world | | | | 9:39-10:21 | 77 |
| And it was at Jerusalem the feast of the dedication, and it was winter. | | | | 10:22-30 | 78 |
| 2nd time they took up stones to cast at Jesus | | | | 10:31-38 | 78 |
| Jesus went away again beyond Jordan | | | | 10:39-42 | 78 |

↓ of lines = year of Jesus' ministry

↓↓↓

| Pericopes | Matt. | Mark | Luke | John | Pg# |
|---|---|---|---|---|---|
| Now a certain man was sick, named Lazarus....Lazarus, come forth | | | | 11:1-53 | 78 |
| Jesus went into a city called Ephraim | | | | 11:54 | 80 |
| Jesus healed a woman who had a spirit of infirmity eighteen years | | | 13-:10-17 | | 80 |
| The kingdom of God like... a grain of mustard... leaven | | | 13:18-21 | | 81 |
| And he went through the cities and villages, teaching, and journeying toward Jerusalem. | | | 13:22-35 | | 81 |
| Jesus healed a man with dropsy on the Sabbath and taught | | | 14:1-15 | | 82 |
| A certain man made a great supper, and bade many | | | 14:16-35 | | 82 |
| What man of you, having an hundred sheep, if he lose one of them... | | | 15:1-10 | | 83 |
| A certain man had two sons | | | 15:11-32 | | 83 |
| Give an account of thy stewardship | | | 16:1-18 | | 85 |
| A certain rich man and a certain beggar named Lazarus | | | 16:1917:10 | | 85 |
| Ten lepers cleansed | | | 17:11-19 | | 86 |
| The kingdom of God cometh not with observation | | | 17:20-18:8 | | 87 |
| Two men went up into the temple to pray; the one a Pharisee, and the other a publican. | | | 18:9-14 | | 88 |
| Coasts of Judaea beyond Jordan | 19:1b-2 | 10:1b | | | 88 |
| Jesus taught on divorce | 19:3-12 | 10:2-12 | | | 88 |
| Suffer the little children to come unto me | 19:13-15 | 10:13-16 | 18:15-17 | | 89 |
| Sell that thou hast, and give to the poor | 19:1626 | 10:17-27 | 18:18-27 | | 89 |
| We have left all, and have followed thee | 19:27-30 | 10:28-31 | 18:28-30 | | 90 |
| And when he had agreed with the labourers for a penny a day | 20:1-16 | | | | 90 |
| Behold, we go up to Jerusalem | 20:17-19 | 10:32-34 | 18:31-33 | | 91 |
| Ye know not what ye ask. Are ye able to drink of the cup...? | 20:20-28 | 10:35-45 | | | 91 |
| 1st of four blind men healed at Jericho | | | 18:35-43 | | 92 |
| Zacchaeus...today I must abide at thy house. | | | 19:1-27 | | 92 |
| Jesus went out and 2nd, 3rd, & 4th blind men healed at Jericho | 20:29-34 | 10:46b-52 | 19:28 | | 93 |
| Bethany, six days before the 4th passover | | | | 11:55-12:1 | 93 |
| Mary anointed the feet of Jesus | | | | 12:2-11 | 94 |
| Sunday afternoon, Find a colt tied. | 21:1-11 | 11:1-11 | 19:29-44 | 12:12-19 | 94 |
| Monday, No man eat fruit of thee hereafter for ever. | | 11:12-14 | | | 95 |
| Monday, My house shall be called the house of prayer | 21:12-13 | 11:15-17 | 19:45-46 | | 96 |
| The blind were healed and the chief priests sought how they might destroy Him | 21:16 | 11:18 | 19:47 | | 96 |
| Jesus went out to Bethany | 21:17 | 11:19 | | | 96 |
| Tuesday, 1st fig tree dried up and 2nd fig tree instantly withered away | 21:18a-22 | 11:20-27a | | | 96 |
| Jesus taught in the temple | 21:23-32 | 11:27b-33 | 20:1-8 | | 97 |
| A certain man planted a vineyard | 21:33-46 | 12:1-12 | 20:9-19 | | 98 |
| A certain king, which made a marriage for his son | 22:1-14 | | | | 98 |
| And there were certain Greeks...Then came there a voice from heaven | | | | 12:20-36a | 99 |
| Whose is this image and superscription? | 22:15-22 | 12:13-17 | 20:26 | | 100 |
| Jesus taught and after that no man durst ask him any question. | 22:23-40 | 12:18-34 | 20:27-40 | | 100 |
| What think ye of Christ? whose son is he? | 22:41-46 | 12:35-37 | 20:41-44 | | 101 |
| Woe unto you, scribes and Pharisees | 23:1-36 | | | | 101 |
| O Jerusalem, Jerusalem | 23:37-39 | | | | 103 |
| Beware of the scribes -- and a certain poor widow | | 12:38-44 | 20:45-21:4 | | 103 |
| Jesus departed from the temple and hid himself from them. | 24:1-2 | 13:1-2 | 21:5-6 | 12:36b-43b | 103 |
| Jesus taught end time prophecy | 24:3-51 | 13:3-37 | 21:7-36 | | 104 |
| The ten virgins and five, two, and one talents | 25:1-46 | | | | 107 |
| Jesus cried and said, He that believeth on me, believeth not on me, but on him that sent me | | | | 12:44-50 | 108 |
| And in the day time he was teaching in the temple | | | 21:37-38 | | 109 |
| After two days was the feast of the passover | 26:1-2 | 14:1a | 22:1 | | 109 |
| The chief priests and the scribes consulted how they might kill Jesus | 26:3-5 | 14:1b-2 | 22:2 | | 109 |
| The alabaster box of very precious ointment was poured on Jesus | 26:6-13 | 14:3-9 | | | 109 |

↓  of lines = year of Jesus' ministry

↓↓↓

| Pericopes | Matt. | Mark | Luke | John | Pg# |
|---|---|---|---|---|---|
| head | | | | | |
| Judas Iscariot  went to betray Jesus | 26:14-16 | 14:10-11 | 22:3-6 | | 110 |
| The first day of unleavened bread | 26:17 | 14:12 | 22:7 | | 110 |
| There shall a man meet you, bearing a pitcher of water | 26:18-19 | 14:13-16 | 22:8-13 | | 110 |
| Now when the even was come, he sat down with the twelve. | 26:20 | 14:17 | 22:14-18 | | 110 |
| And supper being ended... Jesus began to wash the disciples' feet | | | | 13:1-20 | 111 |
| One of you shall betray me... Take, eat: this is my body. | 26:21-29 | 14:18-25 | 22:19-23 | 13:21-32 | 112 |
| Jesus prophesied two times that The cock shall not crow, till thou hast denied me thrice. | | | 22:24-34 | 13:33-38 | 113 |
| Jesus taught | | | | 14:1-31a | 113 |
| Arise, let us go hence | 26:30 | 14:26 | 22:35-39 | 14:31b | 115 |
| Jesus taught | | | | 15:1-17:26 | 115 |
| 3rd time that Jesus said, before the cock crow, thou shalt deny me thrice | 26:31-35 | 14:27-31 | | | 118 |
| Jesus enters the garden named Gethsemane | 26:36 | 14:32 | 22:40 | 18:1b | 119 |
| Three times Jesus asked to let this cup pass | 26:37-44 | 14:33-40 | 22:41-46 | | 119 |
| Jesus betrayed | 26:45-56a | 41-49 | 47-53 | 18:2-11 | 119 |
| And they all forsook him, and fled | 26:56b | 14:50-52 | | | 120 |
| Jesus taken to Annas' house | 26:57a | 14:53a | 22:54 | 18:12-14 | 121 |
| Peter followed and 1st time Peter denies Jesus | 26:58&69-70 | 14:54&66-68a | 22:54b-57 | 18:15-18 | 121 |
| The high priest then asked Jesus of his disciples, and of his doctrine. | | | | 18:19-23 | 121 |
| Now Annas had sent him bound unto Caiaphas the high priest | | | | 18:24 | 122 |
| 2nd and third times Peter denies Jesus | 26:71-75 | 14:68b-72 | 22:58-62 | 18:25-27 | 122 |
| The chief priests, and elders, and all the council, sought false witness | 26:57b&59-68 | 14:53b&55-65 | 22:63-71 | | 123 |
| Delivered Jesus to Pontius Pilate | 27:1-2 | 15:1 | 23:1 | 18:28 | 125 |
| Then Judas went and hanged himself | 27:3-10 | | | | 125 |
| Jesus before Pilate | 27:11-14 | 15:2-5 | 23:2-5 | 18:29-38 | 125 |
| Jesus sent to Herod | | | 23:6-15 | | 126 |
| Pilate was willing to release Jesus but eventually delivered Jesus crucified | 27:15-31 | 15:6-20 | 23:16-25 | 18:39-19:16 | 127 |
| Simon, a Cyrenian, bear His cross to Golgotha | 27:32-33 | 15:21-22 | 23:26-33a | 19:17-22 | 128 |
| They crucified Jesus | 27:34-37 | 15:23-26 | 23:33b-38 | 19:23-24 | 129 |
| Two thieves were crucified with him | 27:38-44 | 15:27-32 | | | 129 |
| Lord, remember me when thou comest into thy kingdom | | | 23:39-43 | | 129 |
| Sixth hour, and there was a darkness over all the earth until the ninth hour | 27:45 | 15:33 | 23:44 | | 130 |
| Woman, behold thy son! | | | | 19:25-27 | 130 |
| Eloi, Eloi, lama sabachthani? | 27:46-47 | 15:34-35 | | | 130 |
| I thirst | | | | 19:28 | 130 |
| One ran and filled a sponge | 27:48-49 | 15:36 | | 19:29 | 130 |
| It is finished | | | | 19:30a | 130 |
| Father, into thy hands I commend my spirit: and he gave up the ghost | 27:50-54 | 15:37-39 | 23:45-47 | 19:30b | 130 |
| But one of the soldiers with a spear pierced his side, and forthwith came there out blood and water | | | | 19:31-37 | 130 |
| Joseph of Arimathaea went in boldly unto Pilate, and craved the body of Jesus | 27:55-61 | 15:40-47 | 23:48-56 | 19:38-42 | 131 |
| The chief priests and Pharisees came together unto Pilate | 27:62-66 | | | | 131 |
| They came unto the sepulchre... and the angel said, He is risen | 28:1-6 | 16:1-4 | 24:1-2 | 20:1 | 131 |
| Mary Magdalene runneth | | | | 20:2a | 132 |
| They entered into the sepulchre | 28:7 | 16:5-7 | 24:3-8 | | 132 |
| Mary Magdalene came to John and Peter | | | | 20:2b | 132 |
| The women left the sepulchre | 28:8 | 16:8 | | | 132 |
| 1st time Peter went to see the sepulchre | | | | 20:3-10 | 133 |
| Jesus appeared first to Mary Magdalene | | 16:9 | | 20:11-17 | 133 |
| Jesus met the other women | 28:9-15 | | | | 133 |
| The disciples did not believe that Jesus was alive | | 16:10-11 | 24:9-10 | 20:18 | 134 |
| 2nd time  arose Peter and ran unto the sepulchre | | | 24:11-12 | | 134 |
| Jesus met two disciples as they went to Emmaus | | 16:12-13 | 24:13-33a | | 134 |

↓ of lines = year of Jesus' ministry

↓↓↓

| Pericopes | Matt. | Mark | Luke | John | Pg# |
|---|---|---|---|---|---|
| The eleven believed saying, The Lord is risen indeed | | | 24:33b-35 | | 135 |
| 1st time that Jesus stood in the midst of the disciples | | | 24:36-49 | 20:19-23 | 135 |
| 2nd time Jesus came to the disciples | | | | 20:24-31 | 135 |
| 3rd time Jesus came to the disciples | | | | 21:1-23 | 136 |
| 4th time Jesus came to the disciples | 28:16-20. | | | | 137 |
| 5th time Jesus came to the disciples | | 16:14-18 | | | 137 |
| And Jesus led them out as far as to Bethany and was carried up into heaven | | 16:19 | 24:50-51 | | 137 |
| They worshipped Jesus and they went forth and preached | | 16:20 | 24:52-53 | 21:24-25 | 137 |

# *The Companion Bible*

This pericope index was prepared by copying and combining three different appendicies from *The Companion Bible*[1].

In appendix 94 on page 134 of *The Companion Bible*  Ethelbert W. Bullinger wrote, "While modern critics are occupied with the problem as to the origin of the Four Gospels, and with their so-called 'discrepancies,' we believe that Matthew, Mark, Luke, and John got their respective Gospels where Luke got his, viz. anothen= 'from above' (Luke 1. 3, see note there); and that the 'discrepancies', so called, are the creation of the Commentators and Harmonists themselves. The latter particularly; for when they see two *similar* events, they immediately assume they are *identical;* and when they read 'similar' discourses of our Lord, they at once assume that they are discordant accounts of the same, instead of seeing that they are *repetitions*, made at different times, under different circumstances, with different antecedents and consequence, which necessitate  the employment of words and expressions so as to accord with the several occasions. These differences thus become proofs of accuracy and perfection.

"The Bible claims to be the Word of God, coming from Himself as His revelation to man. If these claims be not true, then the Bible cannot be even 'a good book.' In this respect 'the living Word' is like the written Word; for, if the claims of the Lord Jesus to be God were not true, He could not be even 'a good man.' As to those claims, man can believe them, or leave them In the former case, he goes to the Word of God, and is overwhelmed with evidences of its truth; in the latter case, he abandons Divine revelation for man's imagination."

---

[1] Bullinger, Ethelbert W. 1911. The Companion Bible. London: Humphrey Milford Oxford University Press.

# APPENDIX 97 THE UNITY OF THE FOUR GOSPELS

|  | Matthew | Mark | Luke | John |
|---|---|---|---|---|
|  |  |  |  | 1:1-5 |
|  |  |  |  | 1:6-14 |
|  |  |  | 1:1--2:7 |  |
| PRE-MINISTERIAL | 1:1-25 |  |  |  |
|  | 2:1 |  |  |  |
|  |  |  | 2:8-20 |  |
|  |  |  | 2:21 |  |
|  |  |  | 2:22-39a |  |
|  | 2:2-23 |  | 2: 40 |  |
|  |  |  | 2:41-52 |  |
| THE FORERUNNER | 3:1-12 | 1:2-8 | 3:1-20 | 1:15-28 |
| THE BAPTISM | 3:13-17 | 1:9-11 | 3:21-22 | 1:29-34 |
|  |  |  | 3:23-38 |  |
| THE TEMPTATION | 4:1-2 | 1:12,13 | 4:1-2 |  |
|  |  |  | 4:3-13 |  |
|  | 4:3-11a |  |  |  |
|  | 4: 11b | 1: -13 |  |  |
|  |  |  |  | 1:35-51 |
| THE MINISTRY (FIRST PERIOD) | 4:12-17 | 1:14,15 |  |  |
|  |  |  | 4:14,15 |  |
|  |  |  | 4:16-32 |  |
|  | 4:18-22 | 1:16-20 |  |  |
|  |  |  |  | 2:1--4:54 |
|  | 4:23-7:29 |  |  |  |
| THE MINISTRY (SECOND PERIOD) | 8:1 |  |  |  |
|  |  | 1:21- |  |  |
|  | 8:2-13 |  |  |  |
|  |  | 1:-21-28 | 4:33-37 |  |
|  | 8:14-17 | 1:29-34 | 4:38-41 |  |
|  |  | 1:35-39 | 4:42-44 |  |
|  |  |  | 5:1-11 |  |
|  |  | 1:40-45 | 5:12-16 |  |
|  | 8:18-9:1 |  |  |  |
|  | 9-2-26 | 2:1-12 | 5:17-26 |  |
|  |  | (2:13-22 not included in outline) | (5:27-39 not included in outline) |  |
|  | 9:27--11:30 |  |  | 5:1-47 ("after this") |
|  | 12:1-21 ("at that time") | 2:23-3:6 | 6:1-11 |  |
|  |  | 3:7-21 |  |  |
|  |  |  | 6:12--8:18 |  |
|  | 12:22-45 | 3:22-30 |  |  |
|  | 12:46-50 | 3:31-35 | 8:19-21 |  |
|  | 13:1-52 | 4:1-34 |  |  |
|  |  | 4:35--5:20 | 8:22-39 |  |
|  |  | 5:21-43 | 8:40-56 |  |
|  |  | 6:1-6 |  |  |
|  |  | 6:7-13 | 9:1-6 |  |
|  | 14:1-14 | 6:14-29 | 9:7-9 | 6:1,2 |

Blocks that are in substantial agreement with *The Sequential Gospels* are outlined with double lines.

| | | | |
|---|---|---|---|
| ("at that time") | | | |
| 14:15-22 | 6:30-46 | 9:10-17 | 6:3-15 |
| 14:23-46 | | | 6:16-21 |
| | | | 6:22-71 |
| 15:1--16:12 | 7:1--8:21 | | |
| | 8:22-26 | | |
| 16:13-20 | 8:27-30 | 9:18-21 | |
| 16:21--18:9 | 8:31--9:50 | 9:22-50 | |
| 18:10-35 | | | |
| 19:1a | 10:1a | 9:51-56 | 7:1-10 |
| 19:1b-2 | 10: 1b | 9:57-62 | |
| | | 10:1-42 | |
| | | | 7:11-13 |
| | | | 7:14--10:21 |
| | | 11:1-28 | |
| 19:3-12 | 10:2-12 | 11:29--13:22 | |
| | | | 10:22-42 |
| | | 13:23-30 | |
| | | 13:31-35 | |
| | | 14:1-24 | |
| | | 14:25-35 | |
| | | 15:1--18:14 | |
| | | | 11:1-16 ("then") |
| | | | 11:17-54 ("after that") |
| 19:13-20 | 10:13-34 | 18:15-34 | |
| 20:20-28 | 10:35-45 | | |
| | | 18:35-43 | |
| | 10:46-52 | | |
| 20:29-34 | | | |
| | | 19:1-28 | |

THE MINISTRY (THIRD PERIOD)

# APPENDIX 156   SIX DAYS BEFORE THE PASSOVER

### (Thursday sunset to Friday sunset.)

| | | | |
|---|---|---|---|
| The Lord approaches Jerusalem from Jerico | | 19:1-10 | |
| He passes our Thursday night at the house of Zacchaeus (Luke 19:5) and delivers the Parable of the Pounds | | 19:11-27 | |
| He proceeds toward Jerusalem | | 19:28 | |
| He sends two disciples for an ass and a colt | 21:1-7 | | |
| And makes his first entry from Bethphage (not Bethany) (Ap. 153) | 21:8-9 | | |
| He is unexpected, and they ask, "Who is this?" | 21:10-11 | | |
| He cleanses the temple | 21:12-16 | | |
| He returns to Bethany | 21:17 | | 12:1 |

Blocks that are in substantial agreement with *The Sequential Gospels* are outlined with double lines.

# Pericope Index   *The Companion Bible*
## By   Ethelbert W. Bullinger

## THE FIFTH DAY BEFORE THE PASSOVER, THE 10th DAY OF NISAN
### (Our Friday sunset to Saturday sunset.)

| | Matthew | Mark | Luke | John |
|---|---|---|---|---|
| The Lord passes the Sabbath at Bethany: and after sunset (on our Saturday), the first of three suppers was made, probably at the house of Lazarus, in Bethany (Ap. 157) | | | | 12:2 |
| At this supper the first of two anointings took place (Ap. 158) | | | | 12:3-11 |

## THE FORTH DAY BEFORE PASSOVER, THE 11th DAY OF NISAN.   Our
### Saturday sunset to Sunday sunset), the Gentile "Palm Sunday".

| | Matthew | Mark | Luke | John |
|---|---|---|---|---|
| The second, or triumphal entry into Jerusalem. He sends two disciples (*katenanti*) for a colt (one animal). see Ap. 153 | | 11:1-7 | 19:20-35 | 12:12a |
| The Lord starts from Bethany (not Bethphage) and is met by multitudes from Jerusalem (Ap. 153) | | 11:8-10 | 19:36-40 | 12:12b-19 |
| He weeps over the city | | | 19:41-44 | |
| He enters the Temple, looks around | | 11:11a | | |
| And returns to Bethany | | 11:11b | | |

## THE THIRD DAY BEFORE THE PASSOVER, THE 12th DAY OF NISAN
### (Our Sunday sunset to Monday sunset).

| | Matthew | Mark | Luke | John |
|---|---|---|---|---|
| In the morning (our Monday a.m.) the Lord returns to Jerusalem | 21:18 | 11:12 | | |
| The Fig-tree cursed | 21:19-22 | 11:13-14 | | |
| The Temple. Further cleansing | | 11:15-17 | 19:45-46 | |
| In the Temple. further teaching "Certain Greeks" | | | 19:47a | 12:20-50 |
| Opposition of Rulers | | 11:18 | 19:47b-48 | |
| He goes out of the city (probably to Bethany; see Luke 21: 37-38 below) | | 11:19 | | |

## THE SECOND DAY BEFORE THE PASSOVER, THE 13th DAY OF NISAN.
### (Our Monday sunset to Tuesday sunset.)

| | Matthew | Mark | Luke | John |
|---|---|---|---|---|
| In the morning (our Tuesday a.m.) on the way to Jerusalem, the question of the disciples about the Fig Tree | | 11:20-26 | | |
| In Jerusalem again: and in the Temple | 21:23-27 | 11:27-33 | 20:1-8 | |
| In Jerusalem teaching in Parables: and questions | 21:28-23:39 | 12:1-44 | 20:9-21:4 | |
| The first great prophecy, in the Temple (Ap. 155.) | | | 21:5-36 | |
| (Parenthetical statement as to the Lord's custom during this last week) | | | 21:37-38 | |
| The second great prophecy, on the Mount of Olives | 24:1-51 | 13:1-37 | | |
| The second great prophecy, continued (see Ap. 155) | 25:1-46 | | | |
| "After two days is the Passover" | 26:1-5 | 14:1-2 | | |
| HE RETURNS TO BETHANY, and is present at the second supper in the house of Simon the leper. The second Anointing. See Ap. 157 and 158 | 26:6-13 | 14:3-9 | | |

**Blocks that are in substantial agreement with *The Sequential Gospels* are outlined with double lines.**

## -THE DAY BEFORE THE PASSOVER --THE 14th DAY OF NISAN- "THE PREPARATION DAY"--THE DAY OF THE CRUCIFIXION.

(Our Tuesday sunset to Wednesday sunset.)

| | | | | |
|---|---|---|---|---|
| The plot of Judas Iscariot to betray the Lord 1 26:14-l6 | 26:14-16 | 14:10-11 | 2\1-6 | |
| The "preparation" for the last supper 1 | 26:17-19 | 14:12-16 | 22:7²-13 | |
| "The even was come" (our Tuesday after sunset) when the plot for the betrayal was ripe for execution | 26:20 | 14:17 | | |
| The last supper, commencing with the washing of the feet | | | | 13:1-20 |
| The announcement of the betrayal, &c... | 26:21-25 | 14:18-21 | | 13:21-30 |
| The supper eaten, the" New Covenant" made (Jer. 31:3l). The lamb abolished, bread and wine substituted.. | 26:26-29 | 14:22-25 | 22:14-23 | |
| The first prophecy of Peter's denials (Ap. 160) | | | | 13:31-38 |
| The strife; who should be the greatest, &c.. | | | 22:24-30 | |
| The second prophecy of Peter's denials (Ap. 160) | | | 22:31-34 | |
| The final appeal to His first commission (Luke 9:3) | | | 22:35-38 | |
| The last discourse to the eleven, followed by His prayer | | | | 14:1-17:26 |
| They go to Gethsemane | 26:30-35 | 14:26-29 | 22:39 | 18:1 |
| The third prophecy of Peter's denials (Ap. 160) | | 14:30-31 | | |
| The agony in the garden | 26:36-46 | 14:32-42 | 22:40-46 | |
| The apprehension of the Lord (Ap. 165) | 26:47-56 | 14:43-50 | 22:47-54a | 18:2-11 |
| The escape of Lazarus (see notes on Mark 14:51-52) | | 14:51-52 | | |
| The trials: continued throughout our Tuesday night | 26:57-27:31a | 14:53-15:19 | 22:54b-23:25 | 18:12-19:13 |
| About the sixth hour (our Tuesday midnight) Pilate said "Behold your King" | | | | 19:14-15 |
| Led away to be crucified | 27:31b-34 | 15:20-23 | 23:26-31 | 19:16-17 |
| And "led with Him "two" malefactors" (kakourgoi) Ap. 164) | | | 23:32-33 | 19:18 |
| Discussion with Pilate about the Inscriptions (Ap. 163) | | | | 19:19-22 |
| The dividing of the garments | 27:35-37 | 15:24 | 23:34 | 19:23-24 |
| "It was the third hour, and they crucified Him" (our 9 a m. Wednesday) | | 15:25-26 | | |
| "Then were there two robbers" (lestai) crucified with Him " (Ap. 164) | 27:38 | 15:27-28 | | |
| The revilings of the rulers, both "robbers", and one "malefactor" | 27:39-44 | 15:29-32 | 23:35-43 | |
| The Lord's mother and John.. | | | | 19:25-27 |
| "The sixth hour" (our Wednesday noon) and the darkness (Ap. 165) . | 27:45-49 | 15:33 | 23:44-45 | |
| "The ninth hour" (our Wednesday 3 p.m.) and the expiring cry (Ap. 165) | 27:50 | 15:34-37 | 23:46 | 19:28-30 |
| Subsequent events | 27:51-56 | 15:38-41 | 23:47-49 | 19:31-37 |
| Buried in haste before sunset (our Wednesday about 6 p.m.), before the "high day" (the first day of the Feast began), our Wednesday sunset | 27:57-66 | 15:24-47 | 23:50-56 | 19:38-42 |

---

² The words in Mark 14:12 and Luke 22:7 refer to "the first day of unleavened bread", which was the 14th day of Nisan, and therefore " the preparation day". That is why the Lord goes on to tell the two disciples to go and make preparation for the Passover.

**Blocks that are in substantial agreement with *The Sequential Gospels* are outlined with double lines.**

## *** 166 THE SEQUENCE OF EVENTS FOLLOWING THE LORD'S RESURRECTION.

**The order of these events in the Four Gospels is partly independent and partly supplementary, taking up the narrative at different points of time. They may be set out as follows:**

| | | | | |
|---|---|---|---|---|
| The observation of the women where and how the body was laid | 27:61 | 15:47 | 23:55 | |
| The preparation of the spices by the women from Galilee on the eve of the High Sabbath | | | 23:56a | |
| Their rest according to the Commandment(Lev. 3. 7). See Ap. 156 | | | 23:56b | |
| The visit of the women at the close of the *weekly* Sabbath, on "the first day of the week" | 28:1 | 16:1-2 | 24:1 | 20:1a |
| "Who shall roll away the stone?" | | 16:3 | | |
| The stone already rolled away | 28:2-4 | | | |
| They find the stone rolled away | | 16:4-5 | 24:2 | 20:1b |
| Address of the angel to the women | 28:5-7 | 16:6-7 | 24:3-7 | |
| Departure of the women | 28:8 | 16:8 | 24:8-9 | |
| They meet with the Lord | 28:9-10 | | | |
| And tell His disciples, and Peter | | 16:9-11 | 24:10-11 | 20:2 (*oun*) |
| The report of the watch | 28:11-15 | | | |
| The visit of Peter and John | | | 24:12 | 20:3-10 (*oun*) |
| Mary's visit to the sepulchre | | | | 20:11-18 |
| The appearing to the two going to Emmaus | | 16:12 (*meta tauta*) | 24:13-32 | |
| Their return to the eleven | | 16:13 | 24:33-35 | |
| The first appearance of the Lord to the eleven | | | 24:36-44 | 20:19-23 |
| The FIRST COMMISSION | | | 24:45-49 | |
| The second appearance to the eleven (and Thomas) | | 16:14 (*husteron*) | | 20:24-29 |
| The SECOND COMMISSION.. | | 16:15-18 | | |
| [Parenthetic al statement by the Evangelist] | | | | 20:30-31 |
| Departure of the eleven into Galilee | 28:16-18 | | | |
| The THIRD COMMISSION | 28:19-20 | | | |
| The appearance to the seven in Galilee | | | | 21:1-23 (*meta tauta*) |
| The Ascension and after | | 16:19-20 | 24:50-53 | |
| [Closing statement of the Evangelist] | | | | 21:24-25 |

| | | | | |
|---|---|---|---|---|
| * | Appendix | 97, | pages | 140 &141 | The Companion Bible |
| ** | Appendix | 156, | pages | 180 &181 | The Companion Bible |
| *** | Appendix | 166, | page | 189 | The Companion Bible |

---

**Blocks that are in substantial agreement with *The Sequential Gospels* are outlined with double lines.**

# A Combined Analysis of the Four Gospels

This pericope index was prepared by reading through the entire text of *A Combined Analysis of the Four Gospels* and making this pericope table from the layout of the text.   This table was then compared to *The Sequential Gospels* text layout.   Places where there is agreement are outlined with a double line.   On page 14 of *A Combined Analysis of the Four Gospels*[1] A. G. Secrett wrote, "**This book is not a 'harmony of the Gospels.'   No Liberties are taken with the text.   No clause, sentence or passage is transposed.   Every word of each Gospel is set down in exact sequence in which it was placed by the evangelist.**"

| | | | | |
|---|---|---|---|---|
| | | | | 1:1-14 |
| | | | 1:1-4 | |
| | | | 1:5-23 | |
| | | | 1:24-25 | |
| | | | 1:26-56 | |
| | | | 1:57-79 | |
| | | | 1:80 | |
| | 1:2-17 | | | |
| | 1:2-17 | | | |
| | 1:18-25 | | | |
| | | | 2:1-7 | |
| | | | 2:8-20 | |
| | | | 2:21 | |
| | | | 2:22-39 | |
| **PERIOD # 1** | 2:1-12 | | | |
| | 2:13-14 | | | |
| | 2:16-18 | | | |
| **PREPARATORY** | 2:19-23 | | 2: 40-50 | |
| | | | 2:51-52 | |
| | | | 3:1-2 | |
| | 3:1-6 | 1:1-5 | 3:3-6 | |
| | 3:1-10 | | 3:1-15 | |
| | 3:11-12 | 1:6-8 | 3:116-17 | |
| | | | 3:18 | |
| | | | | 1:16-18 |
| | | | 3:19-20 | |
| | 3:13-15 | | | |
| | 3:16-17 | 1:9-11 | 3:21-22 | |
| | | | 3:23-38 | |
| | 4:1-2 | 1:12-13a | 4:1-2 | |
| | | | 4:3-13 | |
| | 4:3-11a | | | |
| | 4:11b | 1:13b | | |
| | | | | 1:19-28 |
| | | | | 1:29-31 |

[1] Secrett, A. G. 1927. *A Combined Analysis of the Four Gospels.* London: Chas. J. Thynne & Jarvis LTD

Blocks that are in substantial agreement with *The Sequential Gospels* are outlined with double lines.

| | | | | |
|---|---|---|---|---|
| | | | | 1:32-34 |
| | | | | 1:35-51 |
| | | | | 2:1-11 |
| PERIOD # 2 | | | | 2:12 |
| | | | | 2:13-22 |
| THE | | | | 2:23-25 |
| PROCLAMATION | | | | 3:1-12 |
| OF | | | | 3:13-21 |
| THE | | | | 3:22-36 |
| KINGDOM | 4:12. | 1:14a | 4:14a | 4:1-3 |
| OF | | | | 4:5-42 |
| GOD | | 1:14b-15 | 4:14b-15 | 4:43-45 |
| | | | | 4:46-54 |
| | | | 4:16-29 | |
| PERIOD # 3 | 4:13-17 | | 4:30-32 | |
| | 4-18-22 | 1:16-20 | | |
| | 4:23-24 | | | |
| THE | 4:23-7:29 | | | |
| | 8:1-4 | | | |
| PRESENTATION | | 1:21-22a | | |
| | 8-5-13 | | | |
| OF | | 1-21b-22 | | |
| | | 1:23-28 | 4:33-37 | |
| THE | 8:14-15 | 1:29-31 | 4:38-39 | |
| | 8:16-17 | 1:32-34 | 4:40-41 | |
| KING | | 1:35-38 | 4:42a | |
| | | | 4:42b-43 | |
| | | 1:39 | 4:44 | |
| | | | 5:1-11 | |
| | | 1:40-45a | 5:12-15 | |
| | | | 5:16 | |
| | | 1:45b | | |
| | 8:18 | | | |
| | 8:19-22 | | | |
| | 8:23-27 | | | |
| | 8:28-33 | | | |
| | 8:34 | | | |
| | 9:1 | 2:1a | | |
| | | 2:1b-2 | 5:17 | |
| | 9:2-8 | 2:3-12 | 5:18-26 | |
| | | 2:13 | | |
| | 9:9-13 | 2:14-17 | 5:27-32 | |
| | 9:14-17 | 2:18-22 | 5:33-39 | |
| | 9:18-26 | | | |
| | 9:27-31 | | | |
| | 9:32-34 | | | |
| | 9:35-10:42 | | | |
| | 11:1 | | | |
| | 11:2-6 | | | |
| | 11:7-19 | | | |
| | 11:20-24 | | | |
| | 11:25-30 | | | |
| | | | | 5:1-9 |
| | | | | 5:9-18 |
| | | | | 5:19-38 |

Blocks that are in substantial agreement with *The Sequential Gospels* are outlined with double lines.

| | | | |
|---|---|---|---|
| | | | 5:39-47 |
| 12:1-8 | 2:23-28 | 6:1-5 | |
| 12:9-14 | 3:1-6 | 6:6-11 | |
| 12:15-21 | 3:7-12 | | |
| 12:22-23 | | | |
| | 3:13-19 | 6:12-16 | |
| | | 6:17-49 | |
| | | 7:1-10 | |
| | | 7:11-16 | |
| | | 7:17-28 | |
| | | 7:20-28 | |
| | | 7:29-35 | |
| | | 7:36-50 | |
| | | 8:1-3 | |
| | | 8:4-15 | |
| | | 8:16-18 | |
| | 3:19-21 | | |
| 12:24-37 | 3:22-30 | | |
| 12:38-45 | | | |
| 12:46-50 | 3:31-35 | 8:19-21 | |
| 13:1-2 | 4:1 | | |
| 13:3-9 | 4:2-9 | | |
| 13:10-23 | 4:10-20 | | |
| | 4:21-25 | | |
| | 4:26-29 | | |
| 13:24-30 | | | |
| 13:31-32 | 4:30-32 | | |
| | 4:33-34 | | |
| 13:33 | | | |
| 13:43-35 | | | |
| 13:36-43 | | | |
| 13:44 | | | |
| 13:45-46 | | | |
| 13:47-50 | | | |
| 13:51-52 | | | |
| 13:53 | 4:35-41 | 8:22-25 | |
| | 5:1-17 | 8:26-37 | |
| | 5:18-20 | 8_37-39 | |
| | 5:21-34 | 8:40-48 | |
| | 5:25-43 | 8:49-56 | |
| 13:54-58 | 6:1-6 | | |
| | 6:7-13 | 9:1-6 | |
| 14:1-3 | 6:14-16 | 9:7-9 | |
| 14:5-11 | 6:17-28 | | |
| 14:12 | 6:29 | | |
| 14:13-14 | 6:30-34 | 9:10-11 | 6:1-3 |
| | | | 6:4 |
| | | | 6:5-7 |
| 14:15 | 6:35-36 | 9:12 | 6:8-13 |
| 14:16 | 6:37a | 9:13a | |
| | 6:37b-38 | | |
| 14:17 | 6:38 | 9:13b-14 | |
| 14:18-21 | 6:39-44 | 9:14-17 | 6:10-14 |
| 14:22-23 | 6:45-47 | | 6:15-17a |

Blocks that are in substantial agreement with *The Sequential Gospels* are outlined with double lines.

| | Matthew | Mark | Luke | John |
|---|---|---|---|---|
| | 14:24-34 | 6:48-53 | | 6:17b-21 |
| | 14:35-36 | 6:54-56 | 9:22-25 | |
| | | | | 6:26-59 |
| | | | | 6:60-66 |
| | | | | 6:67-71 |
| | 15:1-9 | 7:1-7 | | |
| | | 7:8-13 | | |
| | 15:10-11 | 7:14-16 | | |
| | 15:12-14 | | | |
| | 15:15-20 | 7:17-23 | | |
| | 15:21-28 | 7:24-30 | | |
| | 15:29a | 7:31 | | |
| | | 7:32-37 | | |
| | 15:29b-31 | | | |
| | 15:32-38 | 8:1-9 | | |
| | 15:39-16:4 | 8:10-13 | | |
| | 16:5-12 | 8:14-21 | | |
| | | 8:22-26 | | |
| | | 8:27a | | |
| | 16:13-16 | 8:27b-29 | 9:18-20 | |
| | 16:17-19 | | | |
| | 16:20 | 8:30 | 9:21 | |
| | 16:21 | 8:31 | 9:22 | |
| **PERIOD # 4** | 16:22-23 | 9:32-33 | | |
| | 16:24-27 | 8:34-38 | 9:23-26 | |
| | 16:28-17:8 | 9:1-8 | 9:27-36a | |
| | 17:9-13 | 9:9-13 | 9:36b | |
| | 17:14-17 | 9:14-19 | 9:37-43 | |
| | | 9:20-24 | | |
| **THE** | 17:18 | 9:25-27 | 9:42 | |
| | 17:19-21 | 9:28-29 | | |
| **REJECTION** | 17:22-23a | 9:30-31 | 9:43-44 | |
| | 17:23b | 9:32 | 9:45 | |
| | | 9:33 | | |
| **AND** | 17:24-27 | | | |
| | | | 9:46 | |
| **MURDER** | 18:1 | | | |
| | | 9:33 | | |
| **OF** | 18:2-5 | 9:35-37 | 9:47-48 | |
| | | 9:38-40 | 9:49-50 | |
| **THE** | | 9:41 | | |
| | 18:6-9 | 9:42-48 | | |
| **KING** | | 9:49-50 | | |
| | 18:10-14 | | | |
| | 18:15-20 | | | |
| | 18:21-35 | | | |
| | | | | 7:2-9 |
| | 19:1a | 10:1a | 9:51 | 7:10 |
| | | | 9:52-56 | |
| | | | 9:56-62 | |
| | | | | 7:11-36 |
| | | | | 7:37-39 |
| | | | | 7:40-53 |
| | | | | 8:1-11 |

Blocks that are in substantial agreement with *The Sequential Gospels* are outlined with double lines.

| | | | |
|---|---|---|---|
| | | | 8:12-20 |
| | | | 8:21-30 |
| | | | 8:31-59 |
| | | | 9:1-41 |
| | | | 10:1-18 |
| | | | 10:19-21 |
| | | 10:1-11 | |
| | | 10:12-16 | |
| | | | 10:22-39 |
| | | 10:17-24 | |
| | | 10:25-37 | |
| | | 10:38-42 | |
| 19:1-2 | 10:1 | | 10:40-42 |
| | | 11:1-13 | |
| | | 11:14-26 | |
| | | 11:27-28 | |
| | | 11:29-32 | |
| | | 11:33-36 | |
| | | 11:37-44 | |
| | | 11:45-52 | |
| | | 11:53-54 | |
| | | 12:1-12 | |
| | | 12:13-21 | |
| | | 12:22-40 | |
| | | 12:41-53 | |
| | | 12:54-59 | |
| | | 13:1-9 | |
| | | 13:10-16 | |
| | | 13:17-21 | |
| | | 13-:22 | |
| | | 13:23-30 | |
| | | 13:31-33 | |
| | | 14:1-24 | |
| | | 14:25-35 | |
| | | 15:1-32 | |
| | | 16:1-13 | |
| | | 16:14-31 | |
| | | 17:1-10 | |
| | | 17:11-19 | |
| | | 17:20-37 | |
| | | 18:1-8 | |
| 19:3-9 | 10:2-9 | | |
| 19:10-12 | 10:10-12 | | |
| | | 18:9-14 | |
| | | | 11:1-16 |
| 19:13-15 | 10:13-16 | 18:15-17 | |
| 19:16-26 | 10:17-27 | 18:18-27 | |
| 19:27-29 | 10:28-31 | 18:28-30 | |
| 19:30 | | | |
| 20:1-16 | | | |
| | | | 11:17-37 |
| | | | 11:38-44 |
| | | | 11:45-53 |
| | | | 11:54 |

Blocks that are in substantial agreement with *The Sequential Gospels* are outlined with double lines.

| | | | |
|---|---|---|---|
| | | | 11:55-57 |
| 20: 17-19 | 10:32-34 | 18:31-33 | |
| 20:20-23 | 10:35-40 | | |
| 20:24-28 | 10:41-45 | | |
| | | 18:35-43 | |
| | 10:46a | | |
| | | 19:1-7 | |
| | | 19:8-10 | |
| | | 19:11-27 | |
| | | 19:28 | |
| | 10:46b-52a | | |
| | 10:52b | | |
| 20:29-34 | | | |
| 21:1-9 | | | |
| 21:10-16 | | | |
| 21:17 | | | 12:1 |
| | | | 12:2-8 |
| | | | 12:9-11 |
| | | | 12:12-13 |
| | 11:1-6 | 19:29-34 | |
| | 11:7-10 | 19:35-38 | 12:14-15 |
| | | 19:39-40 | |
| | | | 12:16-19 |
| | | 19:41-44 | |
| | 11:11 | | |
| 21:18-19 | 11:12-14 | | |
| | 11:15-17 | 19:45-46a | |
| | 11:18 | 19:46b-48 | |
| | | | 12:20-36 |
| | | | 12:37-43 |
| | | | 12:44-50 |
| | 11:19 | | |
| | 11:20 | | |
| 21:20-22 | 11:21-26 | | |
| 21:23-27 | 11:27-33 | 20:1-8 | |
| 21:28-32 | | | |
| 21:33-44 | 12:1-11 | 20:9-18 | |
| 21:45-46 | 12:12 | 20:19 | |
| 22:1-14 | | | |
| 22:15 | | | |
| | | 20:20 | |
| 22:16-22 | 12:13-17 | 20:26 | |
| 22:23-32 | 12:18-27 | 20:27-38 | |
| 22:33 | | | |
| 22:34-40 | 12:28-31 | | |
| | | 20:39 | |
| | 12:32-34a | | |
| | 12: 34b | 20:40 | |
| 22:41-45 | 12:35-37a | 20:41-44 | |
| 22:46 | | | |
| | 12:37b | | |
| | 12:38-40 | 20:45-47 | |
| 23:1-12 | | | |
| 23:13-35 | | | |

Blocks that are in substantial agreement with *The Sequential Gospels* are outlined with double lines.

| | | | |
|---|---|---|---|
| 23:36-39 | | | |
| | 12:41-44 | 21:1-4 | |
| 24:1-2 | 13:1-2 | 21:5-6 | |
| | | 21:7 | |
| | | 21:8 | |
| | | 21:9-11 | |
| | | 21:12-19 | |
| | | 21:20-24 | |
| | | 21:25-28 | |
| 24:3 | 13:3-4 | | |
| 24:4-6 | 13:5-7 | | |
| 24:7-14 | 13:8-13 | | |
| 24:15-22 | 13:14-20 | | |
| 24:23-28 | 13:21-23 | | |
| 24:29-31 | 13:24-27 | | |
| 24:32-34 | 13:28-30 | 21:29-32 | |
| 24:35 | 13:31 | 21:33 | |
| 24:36 | 13:32 | | |
| | 13:33-37 | | |
| | | 21:34-36 | |
| 24:37-44 | | | |
| 24:45-51 | | | |
| 25:1-13 | | | |
| 25:14-30 | | | |
| 25:31-46 | | | |
| | | 21:37-38 | |
| 26:1-2 | | | |
| 26:3-5 | 14:1-2 | | |
| 26:6-13 | 14:3-9 | | |
| | | 22:1-2 | |
| 26:14-15 | 14:10-11 | 22:3-5 | |
| 26:16 | 14:11 | 22:6 | |
| 26:17-19 | 14:12-16 | 22:7-13 | |
| | | | 13:1 |
| 26:20 | 14:17 | 22:14 | |
| | | 22:15-18 | |
| | | | 13:2-20 |
| 26:21-22 | 14:18-19 | | 13:21-22 |
| 26:23-24 | 14:20-21 | | |
| 26:25 | | | |
| 26:26-28 | 14:22-24 | 22:19-20 | |
| 26:29 | 14:25 | | |
| | | 22:21-23 | |
| | | | 13:23-30 |
| | | | 13:31-35 |
| | | | 13:36-38 |
| | | 22:24-30 | |
| | | 22:31-34 | |
| | | 22:35-38 | |
| | | | 14:1-31 |
| | | | 15:1-16:33 |
| | | | 17:1-26 |

Blocks that are in substantial agreement with *The Sequential Gospels* are outlined with double lines.

| | | | |
|---|---|---|---|
| 26:30 | 14:26 | 22:39 | 18:1a |
| 26:31-35 | 14:27-31 | | |
| 26:36-41 | 14:32-38 | 22:40-46 | 18:1b |
| 26:42-43 | 14:39-40 | | |
| 26:44 | | | |
| 26:45-46 | 14:41-42 | | |
| 26:47 | 14:43 | 22:47a | 18:2-3 |
| | | | 18:4-9 |
| 26:48 | 14:44 | | |
| 26:49 | 14:45 | 22:47b-48 | |
| 26:50 | | | |
| | | 22:49 | |
| 26:50 | 14:46 | | |
| 26:51 | 14:47 | 22:50 | 18:10 |
| | | 22:51 | |
| 26:52-54 | | | 18:11 |
| 26:55-56a | 14:48-49 | 22:52-53 | |
| 26:56b | 14:50 | | |
| | 14:51-52 | | |
| 26:57-58 | 14:53-54 | 22:54a | 18:12-15 |
| 26:58a | | | 18:15-17 |
| 26:58b | | 22:54b | |
| | | | 18:18 |
| | | | 18:19-24 |
| 26:58 | 14:54 | 22:55 | |
| 26:59-66 | 14:55-64 | | |
| 26:67-68 | 14:65 | | |
| 26:69-70 | 14:66-68a | 22:56-57 | |
| | | | 18:25-26 |
| | 14:68b | | 18:27 |
| 26:71-72 | 14:69-70 | | |
| | | 22:58 | |
| 26:73-74a | 14:70-71 | 22:59-60a | |
| 26:74b-75 | 14:72 | 22:60b-62 | |
| | | 22:63-65 | |
| 27:1 | 15:1a | 22:66a | |
| | | 22:66b-71 | |
| 27:2 | 15:1b | 23:1 | 18:28 |
| 27:3-10 | | | |
| 27:11a | | | 18:29-32 |
| | | | 18:33-38a |
| 27:11b | 15:2 | 23:3 | |
| | | 23:4 | 18:38b |
| 27:12-14 | 15:3-5 | | |
| | | 23:5-7 | |
| | | 23:8-12 | |
| | | 23:13-17 | |
| 27:15-18 | 15:6-7 | | |
| | 15:8 | | |
| | 15:9-10 | | 18:39 |
| | 15:11 | | |
| | | 23:18-19 | 19:40 |

Blocks that are in substantial agreement with *The Sequential Gospels* are outlined with double lines.

| | | | |
|---|---|---|---|
| 27:19-21 | | | |
| 27:22 | 15:12-13 | 23:20-21 | |
| 27:23 | 15:14 | 23:22-23 | |
| 27:24-25 | | | |
| 27:26 | 15:15 | 23:24-25 | 19:1 |
| 27:27-30 | 15:16-19 | | 19:2-3 |
| | | | 19:4-6a |
| | | | 19:6b-16a |
| 27:31 | 15:20 | | 19:16b |
| 27:-32 | 15:-21 | 23:26 | |
| | | 23:27-31 | |
| 27:33-40 | 15:22-30 | 23:32-38 | 19:17-24 |
| 27:41-44 | 15-31-32 | | |
| | | | 19:25-27 |
| | | 23:39-43 | |
| 27:45 | 15:33 | 23:44-45a | |
| 27:46-47 | 15:34-35 | | |
| | | | 19:28 |
| 27:48-49 | 15:36 | | 19:29 |
| 27:50-53 | 15:37-38 | 23:45b-46 | 19:30 |
| 27:54-56 | 15:39-41 | 23:47-49 | |
| | | | 19:31-37 |
| 27:57-60 | 15:42-45 | 23:50-54 | 19:38-40 |
| | 15:46 | | 19:41-42 |
| 27:61 | 15:47 | 23:55-56a | |
| | | 23:56b | |
| 27:62-66 | | | |
| | | | 20:1-10 |
| 28:1 | 16:1-3 | 24:1 | |
| 28:2-4 | ? | | |
| 28:4b-5 | ? | 24:2-3 | |
| 28:5-7 | 16:6-7 | | |
| | 16:8 | | |
| | | | 20:11-13 |
| | 16:9 | | 20:14-17 |
| | 16:10-11 | | 20:18 |
| | | 24:4-7 | |
| 28:8 | | 24:8-9 | |
| 28:9-10 | | | |
| 28:11-15 | | | |
| | | 24:9-12 | |
| | 16:12 | 24:13-32 | |
| | | 24:33-34 | |
| | 16: 13 | 24:35 | |
| | | 24:36 | 20:19 |
| | | 24:37-39 | |
| | | 24:40 | 20:20a |
| | | | 20:20b |
| | | 24:41-48 | |
| | | | 20:21-23 |
| | | | 20:24-25 |
| | 16:14 a | | 20:26 |
| | 16:14 b | | |

PERIOD # 5

THE

PATH

OF

LIFE

Blocks that are in substantial agreement with *The Sequential Gospels* are outlined with double lines.

| | | | | |
|---|---|---|---|---|
| | | | | 20:27-29 |
| | | 16:15-18 | | |
| | | | | 20:30-31 |
| | 28:16a | | | |
| | | | | 21:1-14 |
| | | | | 21:15-23 |
| | | | | 21:24-25 |
| | 28:16b-20 | | | |
| | | | 24:50a | |
| | | | | ACTS 1: 4-8 |
| | | | 24:50b | |
| | | 16:19 | 24: 51 | ACTS 1:9 |
| | | | | ACTS 10-11 |
| | | | 24:52 | ACTS 1:12 |
| | | | | ACTS 1:13-14 |
| | | | 24: 53 | |
| | | 16:20 | | |

# Comparison of Seven "Gospel Harmony" Books
## Two Books Written Sequentially

Two books, *The Companion Bible*[1] written by Ethelbert W. Bullinger in 1911 and *A Combined Analysis of the Four Gospels*[2] written by A. G. Secrett in 1927, use the same sequential viewpoint as *The Sequential Gospels*. While the authors of these two books do not always agree on which Gospel accounts are identical, they do agree that each Gospel writer recorded the life of Jesus using true event sequence as a fundamental base.

◊ Ethelbert W. Bullinger's *The Companion Bible,* contains 197 appendices. Three of these appendices outline in pericope form a Gospel event sequence. In this Gospel event sequence, Bullinger kept all scriptures in their original sequential order. Bullinger's work therefore has many major sections that agree with *The Sequential Gospels*. Bullinger's areas of agreement are marked with double line boxes in Appendix #2.

◊ A. G. Secrett's *A Combined Analysis of the Four Gospels* has every verse of the four Gospels in sequential order. There are many sections of this book that closely agree with *The Sequential Gospels*. A. G. Secrett's book was published with no blank spaces on any page. Therefore, some pages have four columns containing portions of all four Gospels while other pages may be filled with the writings of only one Gospel writer. The major areas of similarity with *The Sequential Gospels* are shown in Appendix #3.

Areas of disagreement between different sequentially arranged books can easily be compared. In the following paragraphs, a set of pericopes from *The Companion Bible, A Combined Analysis of the Four Gospels,* and *The Sequential Gospels* are evaluated. This pericope review investigates a single event sequence. It demonstrates some of the beauties of examining the Gospels as four separate but interrelated sequential accounts of Jesus' life. This review demonstrates that even when there is an area of disagreement, the authors can still come back together in agreement.

## Bullinger & Secrett's Event Sequence

Ethelbert W. Bullinger and A. G. Secrett believe that the three different Gospel accounts of the healing of Simon Peter's wife's mother are all a single event. These accounts are found in Matthew 8:14-15, Mark 1:30-31, and Luke 4:38-39. If Bullinger and Secrett are correct, then there are two different lepers that believed that Jesus **could** heal them but they did not know if Jesus **would** heal them. The first leper account is found in Matthew 8:2-4 before the healing of Simon Peter's wife's mother in Matthew 8:14-15. The second leper account is found in Mark 1:40-44 & Luke 5:12-14 after the healing of Simon Peter's wife's mother in Mark 1:30-31 & Luke 4:38-39.

---

[1] Bullinger, Ethelbert W. 1911. *The Companion Bible.* London: Humphrey Milford Oxford University Press.

[2] Secrett, A. G. 1927. *A Combined Analysis of the Four Gospels.* London: Chas. J. Thynne & Jarvis LTD.

## The Ashtons' Event Sequence

Without changing the original order of the scriptures, it is possible that the three leper accounts are a single event. If this is true, then by simple time sequencing Simon Peter's wife's mother was healed two times by Jesus.

### First Mother-in-law Healing

The first mother-in-law healing is found in Mark 1:30-31 & Luke 4:38-39.

> Mark 1:30-31   But Simon's wife's mother lay sick of a fever, and anon **they tell him of her**. And he came and took her by the hand, and lifted her up; and immediately the fever left her, and she ministered unto them.
>
> Luke 4:38-39 ...**they besought him for her**. And he stood over her, and rebuked the fever; and it left her...."

### The Leper Healed

Then the leper is healed in Matthew 8:2-4, Mark 1:40-44, & Luke 5:12-14.
In all three leper accounts the leper said,

> (Matthew = Mark = Luke)  "...**if thou wilt, thou canst make me clean.**"

In all three leper accounts, Jesus said,

> (Matthew = Mark = Luke)  "...**I will; be thou clean....**"

Then Jesus said,

> (Matthew = Mark = Luke)  "...**See thou tell no man; but g o thy way, show thyself to the priest,**
>
> (Matthew) <u>and</u> **offer** <u>the gift that</u>
>
> (Mark) **offer** <u>for thy cleansing those things which</u>
>
> (Luke) **offer** <u>for thy cleansing, according as</u>
>
> (Matthew = Mark = Luke)  **Moses commanded, for a testimony unto them.**"

The quotations in the three leper accounts are **word** for **word** identical except for the small differences in syntax of the <u>underlined portions</u> shown above. If these three leper accounts are a single event, then Peter's mother-in-law was healed twice.

### Second Mother-in-Law Healing

The second mother-in-law healing is found in Matthew 8:14-15.

> Matthew 8:14-15  And when Jesus was come into Peter's house, **he saw** his wife's mother laid, and sick of a fever. And he touched her hand, and the fever left her: and she arose, and ministered unto them.

The differences in the actions of Jesus in the first and second mother-in-law events also implies two different events. In the first event "**they tell him of her**" or "**they besought him for her**." However, in the second event Jesus "**saw** his [Peter's] wife's mother" and went over and "touched her hand." Jesus did not have to be asked to heal her the second time.

Even with these different event sequences, *The Sequential Gospels, The Companion Bible,* and *A Combined Analysis of the Four Gospels* are only "out of phase" with each other for a short period of time.  They then "lock back together" when one sick of the palsy was let down through the tiling and Jesus healed him (Matthew 9:2-8, Mark 2:2-12 and Luke 5:17-26).

# Five Books Not Written Sequentially

The following five books are representative of many "Gospel Harmony" or "Gospel Parallel" books.  They all change the order of chapters and verses so that different Gospel accounts can be compared.  While many informative attributes are present in these books, the sequencing of the pericopes of will be emphasized here.  At the end of this section is a note about Papias.

◊  In John Franklin Carter's *A Layman's Harmony of the Gospels*[3], all four Gospels are included.  Similar stories found in different Gospels are treated as the same story even though the names of places, numbers of people, and other details are different.  An example of this is found on page 136, the story of "Healing the Gergesens (Gadarens) demoniac (or demoniacs),...." Chapters and verses of Matthew, Mark, Luke, and John are not kept in their original numerical order.

◊  In the preface of *The Life Of Christ In Stereo*[4], Johnson M. Chaney wrote, "One of the purposes of this book is to display the fact that the four Gospels agree together in all their details and reveal the guiding hand of an unseen Author.  In many circles today, scholarly and otherwise, it is commonly held that, 'the life of Jesus cannot be reconstructed in biographical form;...the comforting  figure of the Sunday School color cards is gone.'  These folk contend that the four Gospels can no longer be regarded as history because, 'in detail and many important points, the Gospels do not agree.'  On the contrary, this minute combination displays the fact that they agree so completely and minutely that they fit together into a single coherent story, without the additions or omission of a single detail."
While Johnson M. Chaney states that "the four Gospels agree together in all their details," he does not use the same sequential viewpoint as *The Sequential Gospels*.  This delightful book is written as one continuous, flowing narrative.  However, chapters and verses of Matthew, Mark, Luke, and John are not always kept in their original order.  This leads to some confusion as to the order of events in the life of Christ.  Also, parts of chapters and verses of Matthew, Mark, Luke, and John are not included because of the narrative style.  This makes it more difficult to compare Chaney's event sequences with other books.

◊  Tatian's *Diatessaron*[5] was written in the second century AD.  It combines all four Gospels into one account. Tatian changes the order of many chapters and verses and does not include every verse found in Matthew, Mark, Luke, and John.

---

[3] Carter, John Franklin. 1961. *A Layman's Harmony of the Gospels*. Nashville: Tennessee: Broadman Press.
[4] Chaney, Johnson M. 1969. *The Life Of Christ In Stereo. The Four Gospels Combined As One*. Portland Oregon: Western Baptist Seminary Press.
[5] McFall, Leslie . 1994. Tatian's Diatessaron: Mischievous or Misleading? *Westminster Theological Journal* 56:87-114.

*References to Other Works*

◊   In B. H. Throckmorton Jr's *Gospel Parallels: A Synopsis of the First Three Gospels*[6], Matthew, Mark, Luke, and some Noncanonical books are arranged in a parallel form. The index is done in sequential order for Matthew, Mark, and Luke but similar stories are duplicated throughout the index. Consequently, stories are duplicated in the main manuscript. For example: there is a duplication of the story about "Jairus' Daughter and a Woman's Faith." This story duplication is found on pages 38 and 74. Thus, the reader does not know if "The Stilling Of The Storm" found on page 71 came before or after the account of "Jairus' Daughter and a Woman's Faith."

◊   In E. S. Young's *The Life of Christ - A Harmony Of The Four Gospels*[7], all four Gospels are placed in columns in "chronological order." Similar stories are placed side by side. The original chapter order of each Gospel has been changed numerous times to allow for the lining up of "the same events." The chapter order of Matthew was changed 5 times, Mark 2 times, Luke 6 times, and John 2 times. Two of the chapters in John were not included in this work.

⇒   A Note About Papias - Papias is one of the least reliable authorities on the scriptures available to us because of the impossibility to directly quote Papias. We have only "fragmentary quotations" of Papias' writings found in other books (Ferguson, Everett, Encyclopedia of Early Christianity, Garland Publishing, Inc., New York & London 1990, 686). One man who quoted Papias was Eusebius (ca. 260- ca. 339). The Encyclopedia of Early Christianity says, "The earliest attestation of Mark as the evangelist is found in Eusebius (H.E. 3.39.15), who cites Papias (ca 125-130), who in turn refers to the testimony of John the elder. Papias's claim is that Mark was the 'interpreter' of Peter during his stay in Rome and wrote from memory the materials that Peter used in preaching, thus materials already adapted to an audience. Later variations on this tradition (e.g., Origen in Eusebius, H.E. 6.25.5) give Peter a more direct role, along with Mark, in the composition of the Gospel" (ibid., 571-572). Another record cites Papias saying that Mark "faithfully recording the preaching of Peter but [the recording was] not set out in good order" (ibid., 686).

      Some people believe that Papias' work proves that the Gospel of Mark is not written in sequential order. However, none of these "quotations" from Papias suggest that the Gospel of Mark is not written in sequential order.

---

[6] Throckmorton, B. H., Jr., ed. 1979. *Gospel Parallels: A Synopsis of the First Three Gospels*. Nashville/New York: Thomas Nelson Inc.

[7] Young, E. S. 1902. *The Life of Christ - A Harmony Of The Four Gospels*. Canton, Ohio: The Bible Student Co.

# The Ashtons

Romney was a student in the school of Electrical Engineering at Purdue University for one and one half years before transferring to Purdue's Department of Biology. Three years later he graduated from Purdue University with a bachelor's degree in science. Following four more years of study, he graduated from Indiana University Medical School with a doctor of medicine degree in March of 1971. Four years and three licensing and board examinations later, he completed his work at the University of Missouri as a board certified diagnostic radiologist. Then, Romney was in the private practice of diagnostic radiology for nineteen years. During these years he was continuously on the staffs of both Memorial Hospital of South Bend, Indiana and Elkhart General Hospital of Elkhart, Indiana. He was chairman of the Department of Radiology at Elkhart General Hospital for more than five years. He was Chief of Staff of Elkhart General Hospital for the year 1992. In the summer of 1994, Romney felt compelled by God to quit his practice of radiology and devote his entire time to preaching and teaching the Word of God. He has been an international director of LeSEA Global *Feed The Hungry* for the last twelve years. During that time *Feed The Hungry* has distributed over 54 million pounds of food and relief supplies (worth over $100,000,000) to 54 countries.

Ruth Ann graduated from Purdue University with a bachelor's degree in science and spent two years at the University of Illinois earning a masters degree of education in curriculum development. After her marriage to Romney, she taught 8th grade Science for one year and worked in a medical research laboratory for two years. Her first book, *God's Presence Through Music* was published in 1993. On seven separate occasions Ruth Ann has been a guest lecturer at Notre Dame University for a class called *Protestant Praise and Worship*. In April of 1999, she was invited to Oral Roberts University to teach a seminar on *Tabernacle Worship*. Just prior to this, she published a praise and worship CD which demonstrates the concept of *Tabernacle Worship* found in her book. All of the original songs for the CD were written and performed by Ruth Ann and three of her friends.

Romney and Ruth Ann are the parents of two daughters, Heather and Dawn, and one son, Nathan. Heather is doing her Family Practice Residency nearby in South Bend. Her husband, Greg, teaches high school mathematics. They have a baby boy named Brendan Gregory Macklem. Nathan graduated from Purdue University with a Bachelor of Science in Biology. Then, after attending and graduating from Bible School in Sweden, he returned to the United States to start a audio and video tape Christian ministry called Imaginative Art Ministries. Nathan's wife, Lydia, is from Sweden. She is a full time student in the School of Music at Oral Roberts University. Dawn, a full time student in the School of Music at Indiana University, has taken a one year leave from Indiana University to attend Bible School in Sweden.

Both Romney and Ruth Ann are licensed members of the clergy and have taught semester long courses at World Harvest Bible School, now called Indiana Christian University. They have been on missionary trips to the Philippines, Hong Kong, South Korea, Scotland, and the Czech Republic. Their education, work experience, and family have uniquely prepared them to do pioneer work in the study of the scriptures.

Romney and Ruth Ann have written, produced, and aired 165 "special English" programs called *This Is Good News*. These 30 minute programs have been aired on short wave radio to Europe, South America, and Asia. In addition they have written, produced, and aired 234 English/Mandarin programs called *Word of Life*. These were transmitted to China by short wave radio. A major feature of the short wave broadcasts was a series called *Show Me Jesus*. In the *Show Me Jesus* series, extra time and effort was taken to be certain that listeners would not be confused about the sequence of events in Jesus' life. This seemed especially important for listeners who did not have access to a Bible. *The Sequential Gospels* was born out of the *Show Me Jesus* series.

God is opening up to this generation hidden truths in His Word. These hidden truths are being revealed at an increasing rate since Israel became a nation in 1948. God said, "But thou, O Daniel, shut up the words, and seal the book, even to the time of the end: many shall run to and fro, and knowledge shall be increased" (Daniel 12:4). The time of the end is here. Daniel 12:4 is being fulfilled. The Holy Ghost has broken the seal and opened the Word of God to those who "turn to the Lord" (2 Corinthians 3:16).

## The Blood Bond Connection:
## Firstar's Bond

### by Nathan Ashton

This is the first set of a series of audio tape allegories. Hear 6 hours of adventure patterned after the life of Abraham. Voyage with Firstar as he follows God, the I AM. Jesus, the SON, leads Firstar through every encounter with men and angels.

The episodes are titled:
1: Introductions - Faith, what else is important?
2: New Company - What does it cost to follow the Almighty?
3: Trust - The price for failure is death.
4: In the Beginning - Pride leads to rebellion in the heavenlies.
5: The Clan - Evil must stop God's man or suffer the consequences.
6: RiverVale - The LORD is rich and richly rewards those who follow Him.
7: The Tenth - Who has robbed God?
8: Union - The Blood Bond will redeem the world and cause the Son's death.
9: SelfPower - How can a tiny demon bring great destruction?
10: Mercy - The SON always looks for a way to act in Mercy.
11: My Only Son - The child of promise must lie upon the altar.
12: Passing the Bond - I AM is not the God of the dead, but of the living.

Each episode ends with a practical application of the scripture used. This series is suitable for families of all ages, Home and Church Bible studies, and Home School study. Pamphlet materials can be obtained from Imaginative Art Ministries for teaching the study of allegory. The cost of the audio series is $27 and can be ordered from:

*Imaginative Art Ministries, Inc.*
PO Box 1532
Elkhart, IN  46515-1532

# God's Presence Through Music
## by Ruth Ann Ashton

This book teaches Tabernacle Worship. You do not need to be a singer or musician to enjoy this book. Come with us on a simple journey into the presence of our Heavenly Father through music. Learn to order the songs you enjoy to walk deeper into thanksgiving, praise, repentance, and loving worship. Come out refreshed and more able to serve our Lord Jesus Christ.

This book provides simple help to those who lead praise and worship in churches and Home Bible studies.

It brings creativity to home worship. Praise not only prepares our hearts to hear from God but it also destroys the works of Satan. The cost of this book is $12 All proceeds automatically go to *FEED THE HUNGRY*, the emergency relief center of *LeSea Ministries.*     It can be obtained by writing to: LeSea Publishing Co.

PO Box 12

South Bend, IN 46624.

# You're Always There
## by Ruth Ann Ashton, Lydia Ashton, and Paul and Carma Whitehead.

This product illustrates the principles of tabernacle worship found in the Bible and explained in Ruth Ann Ashton's book, *God's Presence Through Music.* There are eight original songs to lead you through the Gate of testimony, the Court of praise, and into the loving presence of our Heavenly Father. It is one of the few Pentecostal recordings available.

The cost is $17.75 for CD and $12. 50 for tape.     *Imaginative Art Ministries, Inc.*

To order, write to:     PO Box 1532

Elkhart, IN 46515-1532